11/03

KITCHEN REDOS

REVAMPS
REMODELS
AND REPLACEMENTS

JAN WEIMER

KITCHEN REDOS REVAMPS REMODELS and REPLACEMENTS

WITHOUT
MURDER, SUICIDE, OR DIVORCE

William Morrow and Company, Inc.
New York

Photograph credits, constituting the continuation of the copyright page, appear on
page 382.

Library of Congress Cataloging-in-Publication Data
Weimer, Jan.
    Kitchen redos, revamps, remodels, and replacements:
without murder, suicide, or divorce / Jan
Weimer.
      p. cm.
    Includes index.
    ISBN 0-688-08589-X
    1. Kitchens—Remodeling. I. Title.
TH4816.3.K58W45 1997
643'.3—dc20   96-33408
                                                      CIP

Printed in the United States of America

First Edition

1 2 3 4 5 6 7 8 9 10

BOOK DESIGN BY JOEL AVIROM

DESIGN ASSISTANTS: JASON SNYDER AND MEGHAN DAY HEALEY

To my husband, Sandy Weimer, who made this book possible,
and in loving memory of my grandmother, Fannie Schwartz,
and my father, Albert S. Friedman

ACKNOWLEDGMENTS

I am indebted to the many people in the kitchen design and remodeling business who patiently aided me in my quest for knowledge and answered my questions while gently suggesting that there were no right answers. Among the people who have contributed to my education are:

Abbaka: Frank Paone. **American Standard:** Nora Munroe. **Bay Cities Kitchens and Appliances:** Will Farasat. **Belwith-Keeler:** John J. Longfellow. **Berberian Kitchens:** Paul Barton, Raffie Berberian. **Blanco:** James S. Tomafsky. **California Kitchens:** Bob Selinger. **Dacor:** Susan Bentley. **Elkay:** Helen Josephson. **Eurowest Title:** Kathleen Fought. **Fisher:** Ray Fisher. **Franke:** Rick Brinton, Alicia Cannell. **Fry Communications:** Reed and Melody Fry. **Gaskins Creative Communications, Inc.:** Paula and Stanley Gaskins. **Gemini:** Patty Hourlland. **Gene Schick Company:** Richard C. Kerner. **Glitsa:** Brett Wheeler. **Green & Roberts:** Susan M. Fink. **Hansa:** Michael Isaacs. **Hardwood Floors & Design Center:** Karen Christmas. **Hoffman, York & Compton:** Nancy B. Deptolla. **Kitchen Design Studio:** Michael Caroff. **Kroin:** Jennifer Guli. **Lightwave:** Benny Levi. **Merit Kitchens:** Roger Moras. **Moen:** Bill Doyle. **Porcher:** Tom Kahler, Lawrence Taylor. **Rohl:** Sylvia Maloney, Louis M. Rohl. **S. E. Rykoff:** Rick Brown, Howard A. Novak. **Scotsman:** Horace Grant. **SI Sepco:** Jack Abel. **Southern California Edison:** Jacqueline L. Rains, Sheri F. Tucker. **Southern California Gas Company:** Fil Albano. **Sues, Young & Brown:** Jim Converse. **Syndesis:** David Hertz. **Thacker & Frank:** Jan C. MacLatchie. **VAH Marketing:** Bob Bergstrom. **Vance:** Sophie A. Melko. **Viking:** John R. Helms, Jr. **Wolf:** Ron Binder, Joseph Guerrero, Stan Waldman, Brad Gilbertson.

I am grateful as well for the information imparted by the many inspiring lecturers and writers in the kitchen design field with a special nod to Morton M. Block, Ellen Cheever, Leslie B. Hart, James Keough, Jim G. Krengel, Florence Perchuk, and Eliot Sefrin, who have taught me about quality in good kitchen design and the importance of looking at the overall picture as each decision is made.

I have also had the wise counsel of designers Collette Friedman and Matt Wolf, architect Brian Alfred Murphy, contractors Ron Couch and Brad Pearson, and cabinetmaker Scott Vaughan. I will forever be grateful to contractor Michael E. Murphy, who finally got us cooking again, and to carpenter Kent Sachs, whose even temperament was healing as well as helpful. And then there are Sam Anker and Jonathan L. Rosenbloom, the lawyers who created the contracts in this book, which are equitable to homeowner and contractor/designer alike. Drawing on years of experience in construction law, while putting aside automatic historic responses and prejudices, they gave this subject a fresh new look, resulting in a designer and contractor contract that allows both sides to win.

I am extremely appreciative of the many companies that have loaned photographs of their products for inclusion in this book, of Bess Petlak, who shepherded them in, and of photographer Tim Street-Porter, who not only chronicled my kitchen magnificently for *Food & Wine* magazine but magnanimously presented me with the pictures. Special kudos to photographer Mike Fink, who recorded my kitchen remodeling from demolition derby day to the final touches with his keen well-focused eye, while adding a voice of reason and serenity to the hysteria and chaos swirling around his camera lens.

For presenting me with challenging writing assignments on this ever-fascinating subject, I offer my heartfelt thanks to *Metropolitan Home* magazine's Editor in Chief Donna Warner and Articles Director Michael Lassell, and to *Food & Wine* magazine's editorial lineup, including Denise Martin, Malachy Duffy, Eric A. Berthold, Tina Ujlaki, and Jane Sigal and former editors Carole Lalli, Mary Simons, and Donna Sapolin.

To my mother, Cyrille Friedman, who spent her get-out-of-the-cold-Midwest winters filing kitchen catalogs for me in California, and to the rest of my family and friends who have supported me throughout this almost never-ending project, I can only say that I am blessed by your friendship and I love you.

In this listing I have saved the best acknowledgments for last: my agent, Susan Lescher, and my editor at William Morrow, Ann Bramson, who not only provided the foundation building blocks for this project but who never gave up on it even when it looked as if it would not have a roof over its head. Everyone at William Morrow has generously worked to shape this book, and I feel truly fortunate to have had the careful, considered input of super-editors Gail Kinn and Chris Benton, assistant editor Jennifer Kaye, project editor Ann Cahn, production manager Karen Lumley, and art director Richard Oriolo. Designer Joel Avirom and his staff, Meghan Day Healey and Jason Snyder, have done wonders in weaving innocuous product shots into a beautiful book that pulsates with the emotional and spiritual magic of a kitchen.

Finally, an ambivalent thanks to architect Gary Gilbar, who knew not what he unleashed as he casually observed, "When you finish remodeling your kitchen, you will have so much information you could write a book."

ACKNOWLEDGMENTS *vi*

PROLOGUE *xi*

PRODUCING A KITCHEN REMODEL: An Overview

1 ▪ SETTING THE STAGE

Working Up to a Redo 3

Planning Strategically: Research and Mulling Time 5

2 ▪ CHOOSING THE PLAYERS

Rounding Up a Remodeling Team 32

Writing Contracts for Success 43

3 ▪ SCRIPTING THE PROCESS FROM CONCEPT TO CONSTRUCTION

Designing Dreamworks That Cook 54

Reviewing the Nitty-Gritty of a Layout 69

Tearing It Down and Building It Up 106

BACKDROP

4 ▪ UP AGAINST THE WALL

Cabinets 131

Cabinet Helpers 159

Hardware 167

5 ▪ SURFACE SCENERY AND COSTUME

Cover-ups 173

Meet the Materials 176

Putting Them to Work 188

6 ▪ DRAMATIC LIGHTING

Illuminating Choices 199

Windows: A Natural Act 211

CONTENTS

BASIC PROPS, TOOLS, AND APPLIANCES

7 ▪ COOKERS

Cooktops, Ovens, and Ranges 225

Microwave Ovens 249

Ventilation 255

8 ▪ CHILLERS

Refrigerators and Freezers 263

Wine Coolers 275

Icemakers 276

9 ▪ WATERWORKS

Sinks 278

Faucets 288

Water Treatment Systems: Still Water Problems Run Deep 294

Dishwashers 298

10 ▪ TAKING OUT THE TRASH

Garbage Disposers 306

Trash Compactors 307

Trash Holes 309

Waste and Recycling Bins 309

CASTING CALL

11 ▪ SHOPPING AND INFORMATION SOURCES 313

12 ▪ KITCHENS BY THE NUMBERS 360

13 ▪ REMODELING CONTRACTS 367

Contractor's Contract 368

Designer's Contract 373

SELECTED BIBLIOGRAPHY 376

INDEX 383

PROLOGUE

"It's beautiful," the saleswoman said, describing the serpentine grid on the $1,600 cooktop. "It is beautiful," I concurred. "But surely there must be some advantage to having this configuration over standard individual burners. The intensity of the flame? The speed at which the grid fires up and cools down? The uniformity of the heat conduction?"

"It's beautiful," she said.

Sixteen hundred dollars for a cooktop, and the saleswoman at Los Angeles's premier upscale kitchen store could not tell me what was special about it? I was glad this cooktop was beautiful, but I intended to use it, not just gaze at it. I cared about its function—and also about its cost.

This book began that day. A professional recipe developer and food consultant to restaurants and industry, I was seeking responsive heavy-duty equipment for the upcoming remodel of my home kitchen. Yet the information I needed to make decisions was not available.

Once I started asking questions, I couldn't stop. As a former chef and caterer, I knew how to lay out a kitchen and organize it efficiently. Now I wanted to understand what made a particular appliance or material the *best* deputy for the job.

It's been ten years since I began asking, "Which stove? What kind of countertop? Wood or tile flooring?" Ventilation, windows, and lighting—neglected elements that quietly control our comfort level by regulating temperature along with emissions of smoke and steam—have attracted my scrutiny as well as the latest hot sexy new appliances.

During this process I have learned that there are no correct answers, only what is right for each individual. To find out what is right for you, it is first neces-

sary to learn which features provide value and high performance in an item. Never out of date, this timeless information can be generalized from one model to another, one year's latest entry to the next.

Since my investigations began, for example, dual-fuel ranges have been introduced. Though these combo stoves are an innovation, not so their individual components. If you know about burner grates, cooktop configurations, and fuel sources, you can easily choose among the offerings after deciding whether this is the right piece of equipment for you.

Given the speed and frequency brands and models go out of production, the knowledge of what is important becomes imperative in picking a replacement. Too often consumers arrive at a store, serial number of a coveted appliance in hand, only to find that the numbers have changed or it is no longer being made, that the company has gone out of business. When armed with an understanding of how things function, you can easily settle on a substitute. Over 60 percent of the sources I'd identified as excellent went out of production during the brief editing period for this book. An informed buyer will not find these changes a problem.

Forged by the varying lifestyles of its occupants, each kitchen is unique. Yet the formula for its creation is universal: *A great kitchen brings family and friends together and fosters the preparation of healthful sustenance in a safe, pleasing, ecologically responsible manner.* To help you create this special space, "Primary Principles of Good Kitchen Design" is presented on page 102.

Adapting these guidelines can be as simple as giving the kitchen a new coat of paint or changing doors on a cabinet to ripping it—and the warren of adjacent rooms—down to the studs. How to attack either scenario—and everything in between—is the subject of this book.

This information is meant for people who will work with an architect or designer or take charge of the job themselves. It is geared to those with hours to devote to this cause and to the impatient who want it all now. Targeted are homeowners who will hire a general contractor, act as the general contractor, or roll up their sleeves and start swinging a hammer. Pacing is for a job that proceeds piecemeal in phases according to a master plan or haphazardly in response to whim; for a project completed in one fell swoop or over years as funds and time amass. At the other end of the spectrum, it is there for the already proud owners of a fantasy kitchen when their freezer fizzles and a replacement is needed *now.*

This book is directed at apartment dwellers with a bar-size refrigerator and pip squeak budget as well as at dreamers laying down $80,000 for La Broche system with stoves, grills, pizza hearths, warming ovens, and rotisseries. And for renters who want to take it with them when they move, there are many portable innovations to brighten life in their kitchens.

A plea to manufacturers of kitchen equipment and materials: This book is my request to leave bells and whistles for a symphony orchestra. To make harmonious kitchen music with banging pots and whirring whisks, we need solid, sturdy equipment sized appropriately for the task, priced so we mortals can afford them, and cleanable by working folks bereft of dallying time. I'm speaking about *quality, practicality, and good common sense:* about a broiler rack that pulls out serenely with a tray underneath to prevent meat juices from sloshing all over the floor, about a countertop finish that can withstand hot pots. The eloquence of well-designed tools is their ability to make our work a mite easier and more enjoyable. My greatest finds have been small gadget friends; the pop-up drain plug that keeps hands out of scummy water, the disposer button that fits on a sink ledge when no wall is nearby.

VALUE

■

Most kitchens look magnificent when they're spanking new. Five years—or five months—later, they are all beaten up—not because they weren't cared for properly but because the materials used were too shoddy to stand up to the travails demanded of them. People frequently choose a fragile product because of aesthetics or ignorance of its properties, a problem education ameliorates. Other times, though, they do so because it costs less money. They have a specific budget; a certain amount they can spend and no more.

Before making any purchase, I urge you to deter- mine the actual total price by factoring in longevity and replacement costs. When an item turns out to be more expensive over the long haul than another item bearing a higher price tag initially, you're better off going for the more durable piece.

If the up-front money is more than you have at the time, either do the kitchen in stages, buy fewer accoutrements, change patterns to a mottled *no-show* look, declare your kitchen country style and outfit it with distressed materials, or celebrate our industrial revolution with recycled factory parts.

I have structured this book so you can find both facts on a particular product you are considering and information on actual work to be performed. At the same time, the overall organization has been conceived to correspond to the *process* of remodeling: the order in which you will encounter a situation and the points at which you must make a decision. Designed to provide the specific information needed to make the best choice at an optimal point, it identifies and focuses priorities, even at the risk of repetition. You will probably want to go back and forth among the process of remodeling, the merchandise employed, and the means of procuring it.

Regardless of kitchen subject, the number of details to absorb is staggering. Did you remember the remote skywindow opener when planning electric circuits? Have you confirmed that those lights will fit under the cabinets? With one decision based on another, it is almost impossible to keep everything in mind; to recall all the interconnections among elements. For this reason, I present pertinent information at the exact point you must deal with it.

To provide an overview, the first three chapters of the book introduce the remodeling process chronologically, enumerating the order for tackling tasks. A summary, "Countdown to a Remodel," is there to review throughout your project, both to alert you to what comes next and to ensure you've done your homework and are ready for it. At this early point in the book, you might not understand expectations completely, but they are listed here so you can antici-pate them. The same philosophy underlies the placement of "Money-Saving Tips," whose frequent perusal should help hold costs down as you make choices. The hard hat's approach to becoming hardheaded, the construction chapter guides your appraisals as overseer, bill payer, and cook of the realm.

The following sections delve into single subjects by category. Chapters 4 through 6 are devoted to cabinetry, surfaces, windows, and lighting, the major purchases that dictate the form and ambience of the room. The next grouping of chapters (7 through 10) includes kitchen equipment and appliances. Presented with the background stats to make an informed choice, each and every item has its paragraph in the sun. Though most of us will be more than content with a basic repertoire, I have included the extravagant items to complete my exploration of glorious possibilities.

After getting acquainted with what's available for the home kitchen, you'll find Chapter 11—on shopping. A laundry list, it has been drawn up for your use on purchasing expeditions. (It is not intended for reading unless you like boring repetitive text.) As cautioned previously, don't be disheartened if the exact model mentioned is not in the store by the time you go to look for it.

Finally, you will find "Kitchens by the Numbers," a chart of recommended sizes and allotments. Use it as a quick reference while laying out the kitchen and to double- check that you've provided adequate space.

HEAVEN-SENT REMODELING

■

Underlying all the material I present is my desire that this pursuit proceed effortlessly for you. Remodeling a kitchen can be hell. With many positive experiences standing as exceptions to contradict me, this undertaking often assumes the aura of a fraternity hazing or the nightmarish on-call schedule of a med-ical intern. Before a wonderful kitchen can be yours, it seems there are burning hoops to jump through, atavistic initiation rites to survive.

As Suzanne X. observes, "I never realized it was possible to get as angry as I did. I would have shot my contractor, my designer, and the company that manufactured my stove, but I hear the food isn't too good in jail. And the social life isn't great either," she adds. Will W. calls the thieving cabinetmaker who defrauded him "slipperier than a snake's snot." 'Tain't always pretty.

When one architect I interviewed inquired if I had a place to live during my teardown, I replied, "I'm checking myself into a mental hospital." "Good," he said. "This process can be disruptive."

Disruptive, yes. That's to be expected in a dust storm. But not a debilitating horror film. There is not one justifiable reason for it. Victims of a broken remodel often recommend lining up a lawyer and psychiatrist before getting started. "You'll need them," I'm constantly told. Although this is all too frequently true, *I believe hassles are avoidable if you do your homework, stay on top of the job, and sever relationships as soon as you see they aren't working.* With a little vigilance, the process can proceed without heartbreak. As architecture critic Ada Louise Huxtable observed, "A building is as good as its client."

To guarantee smooth sailing for you—and the people you're working with—I've had one remodeling contract drawn up to use with your contractor (page 368); another for your architect or designer (page 373). Written by the law firm of Anker & Hymes in Encino, California, they were created to avoid the crossroads where so many jobs go astray— the point where a potentially satisfying endeavor hits the brick wall of breakdown. It is my great hope that suggestions in this book will enable you to meet the challenges of modifying a kitchen head-on. Problems will arise, but they become creative opportunities when faced cooperatively. When you are done, you should have a beautiful new cooktop—whatever the cost—and one that functions well, too.

*"On days when warmth is the most important need
of the human heart, the kitchen is the place
you can find it. . . . "*

—E. B. White

PRODUCING A KITCHEN REMODEL:

AN OVERVIEW

1

SETTING THE STAGE

WORKING UP TO A REDO

■

Often it's the little things: the kids playing dodgem carrots between the stove and refrigerator while you're trying to cook dinner, the empty pop cans towering toward Pisa in the corner when the stuffed crisper cracks (that extra head of lettuce didn't fit after all). A kitchen's inadequacies gnaw gradually; sometimes consciously, sometimes not. One day you find yourself kicking the cabinets. The vague irritation has become a raging obsession: It's time to remodel.

That's one scenario. For me, it was hate at first sight. The beautiful old Mediterranean house I fell in love with in Los Angeles possessed the ugliest kitchen I'd ever seen. Its looks—as my mother taught me—weren't everything. Cooking in it proved even worse than I had anticipated.

Composed of crooked grayish toothlike tiles, the countertop was a dentist's nightmare: impossible to brush. The vintage ceramic cooktop burned the bottom out of all my pots, and the refrigerator was so small I had to pack its contents in coolers every time I entertained.

I had bought this house planning to tackle the kitchen immediately. When my stove died three years later, I still hadn't dealt with it. A friend lent me a small countertop convection oven to use temporarily. "Since we're planning to remodel, it's not worth it to buy new appliances," I reminded my frustrated husband, who became increasingly hungry for food not baked in a fourteen-inch cavity. Five years post-stove-mortem, we finally began our remodeling project.

I had always been the shoemaker's child; the professional cook without a decent laboratory. No matter where I lived, my kitchen always fell somewhere in the lower depths of the inadequate continuum.

Winner of "Worst Kitchen Ever" was the *private* bath without running water where I hooked up a stove while inhabiting a hotel-cum-brothel in Gondar, Ethiopia. Fifty cents a day bought a room fitted with a bare bulb, a steel-framed camp cot, and a window from which I watched men come and go while witnessing the slaughter of the tough old goat that I later attempted to cook for dinner.

A cubbyhole in a Paris garret wasn't much better. Boasting a lone burner, the *cuisine* was so small that guests lined up outside to hold the pots containing our evolving meal while, one at a time, I performed the ablutions of stirring and mixing that each required.

Probably the best kitchen I had prior to this remodel was in San Francisco. But even there I spent six months cooking indoors on my Coleman stove (until a spattering duck almost burned down the house) while I waited for the new range I'd ordered to arrive.

From this multitude of strange spaces I learned that you can cook in any surroundings and on any kind of equipment. Fancy appliances do not make a better cook. No matter how primitive, makeshift, or minute a kitchen, you can prepare food in it to share with family and friends.

This psychological aspect—the emotional nurturing that comes from dining with loved ones—has made the kitchen a part of my very soul. This hallowed room is where I relax and putter around; the center where guests gravitate even when I pretend to be grown up and try shooing them into the living room. When I don't cook a simple meal at least even an omelet or bowl of soup, my natural rhythm is shattered. There is no harmony. Something is skewed; off balance; awry.

With a gorgeous newly remodeled state-of-the-art kitchen, I no longer have to make *do*. Certainly it is more fun to cook in this sphere than over the Bunsen burners on my camp stove. But it is only when I'm preparing food with family and friends that the communion and sense of well-being my kitchen provides are complete.

When I fantasized about a new kitchen, I yearned primarily for a room where people could congregate; for a kitchen that fostered love and intimacy. Ever articulate, my husband summarized our objective as "to create harmony and aesthetics around a core of practicality." Stating what the kitchen meant to us and how it fit into our lifestyle was the first step of our remodeling process, as it should be for you.

The kitchen is the most personal and idiosyncratic space in a home, reflecting the collective quirks and consciousness of its occupants. These days, when a refrigerator can cost $5,000, the kitchen's role has gone way beyond meal preparation. We are no longer speaking just about *need*.

In a survey, R. H. Bruskin Market Research Associates describes the kitchen as a communications center, listing the primary activities in this room as talking on the phone, taking care of correspondence, watching TV, playing games, entertaining guests, and arguing with family members. Cooking? Not a mention of it.

What you want for your kitchen is sure to differ from what I wanted, if only slightly. Perhaps you seek an open "command center" or "after-five" kitchen/family room where you can stand watch as children gather to do homework or hobbies or just to hang out. You may, like Professor Margaret Visser, view the kitchen as a socialization center for instilling manners, values, and sound nutritional practices. Or you may identify with an Ann Landers reader who is going to replace the kitchen in her new home with vending machines.

One friend just wants to say "ahhhhh" as she runs through her beautiful kitchen on the way out to dinner. She doesn't care if it functions. This "power kitchen," as *Saveur* editor-in-chief Dorothy Kalins once called it, "is overequipped and underused and so refined that almost all connection with food has been bred out of it."

Regardless of what type of kitchen you select, you must first clearly define your needs and wishes—your goals for the outcome of the remodel—to be assured of fulfilling your dream. Figuring out what constitutes your ideal kitchen takes a great deal of time and effort, mandating an ample planning period. In a new home, a "getting to know you" phase clarifies how the kitchen works—and doesn't work—as it flows into other rooms. Some nasty surprises may be unveiled as this relationship develops. To have a realistic economic picture and understanding of the job's complexities, you're best discovering termites and other *friends* before engaging assistance.

It takes extensive research to ferret out information you need to make choices, even if you've lived in your home for some years. A considerable mulling stretch is necessary for needs and desires to gel on the unconscious level. As architect Michael McDonough says, "The benefits of the thought process come back to you over time. You can synthesize solutions only by accepting problems and living with the ideas." The eight years it took me were, admittedly, rather excessive (more likely insane). But allowing a year or more for contemplation is not unreasonable.

If you plan to hire an architect, a designer, and/or a contractor to work with you on the remodeling project (Chapter 2), it will be helpful to have a clear idea of what you want before seeking aid. Studying the market reveals how to evaluate workmanship, what to expect in fees and procedures, and when you should scream "halt." When you choose to ignore a recommendation, it will be for sound reasons. If not, you may find yourself under the thumb of one snooty designer I know who shrugs, "I don't really care what things cost. I just design."

I assumed that people hire an expert to help them narrow down options, but this rarely turns out to be the case. Many professional designers neither know nor care about function, particularly in regard to what is right for you. Following their advice can leave you holding a pretty useless tool bag. As the teacher of a kitchen design class I took callously explained, "We're not there to educate the client; we're there to sell."

Once you hire someone, the meter starts running, and you are expected to make millions of infinitesimal decisions in rapid-fire succession.

Drowning in minutiae, the planning process overwhelms and exhausts, even if you have done your homework. Making just the major decisions can be a frustrating task. By the time you get to details such as drawer pulls or light switches, you don't care anymore. But you care later on, when you're working in shadows and can't open cabinets with greasy hands.

Even more alarming is the statistic reported at a contractors' seminar in Anaheim, California: "Ninety-eight percent of all purchases made are decided by the contractor," said Walter Stoeppelwerth, president of HomeTech. "Standardize the products you use," he advised. "You'll get better prices, routinize installation, and estimate your jobs more accurately."

Contractors who follow Mr. Stoeppelwerth's recommendations will find their work easier and more remunerative, but the kitchens they build are less likely to be tailored to their customers' needs. Tales are told of some plain dumb luck exceptions, *but if you don't educate yourself before beginning the remodeling process, chances are excellent that your new kitchen will cost more than it should and be right for the person constructing it, not for you.* Once the process is under way, you won't have time to make rational well-considered decisions.

PLANNING STRATEGICALLY

■

Research and Mulling Time

PREPARE A BUDGET AND ARRANGE FINANCES

Not many of us have the $500,000 Barbara and George budgeted to overhaul the White House kitchen. Some brakes usually need to be applied even if funds are ample. And no one wants to dribble money away; to spend more than necessary; to overbuild. All jobs—big or small—have an irritating propensity for skyrocketing out of control. Unchecked, even the wealthy find themselves in deep

doo-doo. And, yes, I do mean to alarm you. I can't stress enough how tightly you have to stay on top of the money.

Once the wheels of remodeling start turning in your mind, the very first step is to prepare a budget. By determining precisely how much money exists for a remodel, you can use funds wisely, designating them for objects with "most desired" status. Declaring an inviolable ceiling also heads off fantasy tangents likely to crash in frustration and disappointment.

In 1994 consumers spent an average of $17,600 for a remodel; the same year the gorgeous kitchens they ogled in magazines bore price tags *starting* at $50,000. People could knock off ideas from these kitchens, but all too often the photographs just raised desires and expectations that couldn't be met. Reality can be awfully cruel, but it's less painful when faced early on.

To determine how much money you can spend on a kitchen remodel, look at current income, savings, and expenses, as well as at future obligations and the higher taxes and insurance costs levied on an improved property. If you deem it vital to borrow money, you must possess the collateral and wherewithal to qualify for a loan as well as to pay it back. You don't want to invest time and money in pre-remodeling efforts and then have your request denied. You may be able to cover payments now, but not in several years, when college tuitions loom. Conversely, more money may be accessible later on, suggesting that a remodel may be attacked prudently in phases.

The good news is that remodeling costs and some purchases can be added to a property's original purchase price, lowering the capital gains tax on its eventual sale. Income tax deductions may also accrue from interest rates on borrowed money for mortgages. (Save every receipt, even those from jaunts to the hardware store.) A rebate is offered increasingly from some utility companies on improvements friendly to the environment. Before planning how to spend these anticipated refunds, check with your accountant, for many are taxable.

Resale Value

In addition to looking at what you can afford for a kitchen remodel, you might consider whether it is worth spending money this way. Musings along these lines usually bring people to discussions about resale value.

All kinds of statistics exist to prove that all—or most—of the money spent on a kitchen remodel is returned when the home is sold. Yet Los Angeles Realtor Fred Sands comes closest to the mark, recognizing that "remodels are for the purpose of improving your lifestyle while you are there."

With the market fluctuating widely, there is no guarantee what your house will be worth at the moment you put it up for sale. The sooner it goes on the block after a remodel, the more likely you'll realize a return on your investment, yet it rarely makes sense to redo a property you won't live in for at least several years afterward.

To maximize an investment, follow basic commonsense guidelines even if you envision yourself ensconced for a lifetime:

> **Don't spend more than 10 percent of your home's current value.**
>
> **Don't overremodel your house to be the most expensive in the neighborhood.**
>
> **Don't expect a return on money spent fixing pipes and plumbing you can't see.**
>
> **Don't expect someone to pay for your weird taste. Limit selections to timeless conservative classics.**
>
> **Don't forget that a new trash receptacle and a cosmetic coat of paint can completely transform a kitchen.**

Financing a Remodel

Moving to the subject of financing a remodel, I'd like to repeat the last statement: *Don't forget that a new trash receptacle and a cosmetic coat of paint can completely transform a kitchen.* A simple face-lift can mask many a kitchen wrinkle, providing comfort to homeowners with limited budgets and a more salable interior to those wanting to move on.

It may be better not to burden yourself with debt than to have a fancy kitchen you can ill afford. If you can pay for a remodel out of pocket or cover its costs with an inheritance or sale of stocks or property, all well and good. If you have to borrow money, this will be an expensive proposition. Depending on the type of loan, it can double or triple the cost of a remodel.

To obtain a loan can take many months, enrolling your project in the molasses school of remodeling. Before doing so, poll your accountant and tax adviser for their assessment. Regardless of the advice they give, *don't sign on the dotted line until you shop around.* And before you do so, have a lawyer give a look-see to be sure you haven't signed away your property or birthright.

The best loan, according to one personable builder, is a G.I. (Generous In-law) benefit. If this is not forthcoming, there are other people to hit up as long as it is not the dealer from whom you are purchasing cabinets, appliances, or materials. *And, at all costs, avoid financing the job through your contractor.*

First of all, you will probably pay more for this indiscretion than you would if you went directly to the third party who is lending these folks the money to lend you. Relieved to get the money, you may then feel pressured to close a deal before adequately shopping for better people, better products, or better terms.

Comparing the terrible loss of control and one-down position of feeling beholden, borrowing money from someone you've hired is even worse than borrowing from your parents. Indebting your-self to a dealer or contractor eliminates the separation of church and state, the protective system of checks and balances. If workmanship is below par or problems arise during construction, you will be bereft of the leverage and negotiating power that owing money brings. And you will have to pay it back, regardless of how poorly the job is done. As an article in the *Los Angeles Times* cautioned its readers after the 1994 earthquake, "be wary of any contractor who insists on specifying who you select as a lender—you could become the victim of a kickback scheme that will increase your costs."

Keep your guard up even if you borrow from a neutral loan company. Standard practice dictates that the officer make payments to the contractor or designer. Don't allow it. Though many institutions insist on approving professionals before they authorize a loan, their jurisdiction does not extend to monitoring their work. Uninformed about what is happening on the job, the company may pay out money inappropriately. *To control the amount and moment of fund dispersal, you must be its recipient.*

SECURING A LOAN

Doug Diana, vice president of sales and marketing at Atlantic Financial Corporation, urges borrowers to obtain the proper credit application form from the lender and then make sure that it is completed in full and backed up by copies of personal financial statements and recent tax returns. Let the financial institution know what the money is for—how, specifically, it will be used—and don't leave out any piece of the puzzle, he advises, for blanks invite a rejection. To hasten absolution, explain any previous credit problems at the onset of the loan interview.

Before applying for a loan, do some reality testing. Research how much money is typically allotted to someone with your equity and financial profile and determine if this will be enough to cover your job. If a loan is worth pursuing, present a budget along with your application. You may also be asked to submit a layout and bid. Catch-22: It will be hard to get this done without having the money already in hand.

After a personal loan, the quickest, easiest way to get a small loan is to borrow on your credit card. No muss, no fuss. But interest will be high, and it's not deductible. You can also borrow on your savings account, certificates of deposit, whole life insurance policy, or retirement plan such as a 401K. If applicable, you can apply for a loan through a credit union, the Veterans Administration, or the Federal Housing Administration.

Many banks, savings and loan associations, and financial lending institutions specialize in home improvement or construction loans that list your home as collateral. A new type of mortgage allows consumers to borrow against the projected future market value of their remodeled residence. A bank's interest rates are lower than those of a financial corporation. If you do use the latter institution, check its reliability and credit rating with Dun & Bradstreet.

What constitutes an optimum loan varies with the market. When interest rates are high, a second mortgage is the better deal because it must be paid back quickly. When they are low, refinancing is more economic. An *equity line of credit* may also be extended. Providing money as you need it rather than in a single lump sum, it puts payments in place for extra costs that pop up unexpectedly.

In comparing loan prices, look at interest rates and determine whether they are tax deductible and of a fixed or variable nature. With the latter type, note when the rate can change, what will precipitate it, and the cap or maximum amount beyond which it cannot rise. You will want to know the length of the loan, the amount due each month, pre- and late-payment penalties, and the points (interest) charged for its structuring. Check fees levied for an attorney, appraisal, loan application, title search, credit check, survey, discount points, and closing papers. You may want to review the numbers with an accountant or attorney.

Fees are generally inversely related to interest rates. Lower fees are the better deal for a short-term loan; lower interest rates are advantageous over a longer haul. Unless you can sock away the money, avoid the balloon payment loan that requires the complete principal to be paid at once. *To save fees on a new home that requires remodeling, apply for both home and remodeling loans simultaneously.*

GET ORGANIZED

With "Be Prepared" the motto of all successful remodels, it's helpful to organize a filing system as soon as financial computations affirm the remodel is a *go*. Once the process starts, you'll be deluged with a mountain of catalogs, spec sheets, forms, notes, and samples steep enough to rate an advanced hiker's badge.

Attempting to ride this onslaught's crest, many people organize the papers in binders, but it is faster to throw them into well-labeled files and boxes. The more categories (files) established, the easier to retrieve that snippet with the important phone number when you need it.

Struggling continually under an avalanche of paper, I realized how to organize files only after my remodel was complete. At the risk of being judged obsessed, I share this list in the hope that it will be helpful:

- Pictures of kitchens you like with intriguing details marked

- Interview notes and bids

- Contracts, permits, change orders

- Daily diary

- Photographic record from predemolition through completion

- Invoices and lien releases

- Work schedules

- Supplier and *subcontractor* (licensed specialized worker) lists with names, addresses, phone numbers, licenses, and insurance information

- Layouts from rough sketches to final design

- Catalogs and installation information on all equipment and materials being considered

- Purchasing forms and records of all materials ordered

- Cleaning and maintenance information

- Warranties, authorized service dealers and phone numbers, repair records and receipts

DETERMINE THE EXTENT
OF THE REMODEL
Reorganization, Refurbishment, Replacement, Gut Job, or Steamroll?

Budget in hand and filing system in place, it's time to start gathering information and making preliminary reality-based decisions. If the remodel is to take place in a home you are just purchasing, ponder the extent of disorder you can cope with before entering escrow. The type of person who prefers living in someone else's idea of *great* to spending time and energy remodeling will not be happy facing a massive makeover. When you do consummate a real estate deal, obtain original blueprints, any still-existing warranties, and names of all contractors and subcontractors who have worked on the premises.

Define the scope of your project: Do you need only a new dishwasher or desire to tear down the kitchen and the rest of the house along with it? (This decision often hinges more on the state of your checkbook than on the room.)

On occasion, what seems like an untenable mess can be transformed with a minor reorganization. Ronnie Burak claimed that nothing in her new kitchen worked right, but after switching the interiors of several drawers she found the only things missing were shelves for cookbooks. Sequestering a bookcase behind the dining table, we instantly *remodeled* her *despised* space.

If a kitchen's layout works well, there is no need to rip everything out. Outmoded appliances can be modernized with a new panel or replaced if no longer functional. Cabinets can be refurbished in their entirety or their doors traded out and up. In many cases, only minor adjustments are necessary for a new child, elderly parent, or physically challenged family member. The point comes, however, when it may be better to get down to the studs: when new items vary significantly in size from ones they are replacing, or when changing one component, such as a floor, interferes with cabinets or appliances.

As stated, when finances are meager, a gut job can be done in stages. Since labor costs remain unvarying, you get more for your money by renovating one small area at a time with the materials you want than by completely transforming it with lesser-quality products.

A gut job may involve changing the structure: moving walls, doors, and windows; incorporating other rooms or pushing out the current kitchen beyond the exterior frame or what is called the *envelope* of the house. With these major changes, you may still be able to recycle equipment from a previous kitchen. Just allow enough space to replace it down the road without having to further modify the structure. If budget permits, don't salvage sinks or other still-serviceable items that will look out of place in a shiny new arena.

Jobs have a life of their own. "Curiouser and curiouser," they get bigger like Alice, creating their own Wonderland. To predict this black magic, a building inspector in some municipalities will assess plumbing, electric, and heating to diagnose problems lying in wait. To poke about the innards, you may also hire someone from the American Society of Home Inspectors, Inc.

We're playing dominoes here, where, almost inevitably, additional costs pile up. To counteract this trend, homeowners must never utter the three most dangerous words in the remodeling lexicon— "might as well," as in "We're doing the kitchen, so we *might as well* do the bathroom."

APPRAISE YOUR CURRENT KITCHEN
Likes, Dislikes, and Storage Needs

After deciding the extent of your remodel, analyze what you want to change and why. For a new kitchen to play the role it's assigned, the faults of the old one must be understood. Is it too small? Lacking a separate dining area? Short on working or storage space? Is the layout awkward? Do you run a marathon circling the island for a spoon? Are your appliances sputtering on their last legs? Rickety dinosaur wimps in this New Stainless Age of High Function? Or are we talking aesthetics, ambience, and atmosphere? Is your kitchen dark, cold, and cavelike, unpleasant to be in? A place people avoid because it makes them feel bad? Is it—pardon the expression—ugly?

Survey your kitchen formally and then write down every single thing that irks you about it and why. We're talking both major and minor irritations here. After finishing the preliminary list, keep it in the kitchen to jot down the unconscious mutterings about things you didn't even know you hated that surface while you work. You will be amazed at what you learn from several weeks of kitchen consciousness raising.

Once you complete this analysis, establish priorities (in descending order) of what you would like to change, distinguishing between *wants* and *needs*. As one savvy organizer suggests, list just the problems, such as "counters are too high for kneading bread," without trying to reach a solution (e.g., install a pullout table). With many possible directions to take, you don't want to close off options at this early juncture.

While you're compiling this book of lists, dedicate a second category to everything you like about your current kitchen (there must be something). In the heady flush of starting anew, it's very easy to throw the baby out with the bathwater, to eliminate the things that really worked along with those that didn't. Alice Medrich was so excited to have a new kitchen that she didn't realize her designer had traded the drawers she found so convenient for cumbersome cabinet doors with pullout shelves.

Have everyone who uses the kitchen in any capacity—children, too—draw up each of these two lists independently and then try to reconcile differences. And what would the family pet say about access to his bed or food?

During this initial survey, start a third list of everything you store in the kitchen. Note special requirements of large or odd-shaped items, distinguish equipment to be left out from that to be secured behind closed doors, and begin the wrenching process of elimination.

What better opportunity to discard Aunt Millie's wedding present lying dormant in its box or those space-hog gadgets whose *raison d'être* was forgotten long ago? If you haven't used something during the last two years, it's probably time to throw it out. Paring a kitchen down to essentials frees space for more satisfying pursuits.

EDUCATE YOURSELF

Talk is cheap information, so discuss the project with friends who have undergone this process and survived. But don't stop there. Start a dialogue with everyone you meet: the florist and the fishmonger, the masseuse and the hairdresser, and, if you live in California, the clairvoyant, the seismographer, and the personal trainer. Ask chefs and caterers what they think constitutes a good kitchen and check with the line cooks and household maids who actually use (and clean) them. Evaluate kitchens installed in local cooking schools and query owners and guest instructors about what it is like to cook in them.

Helpful information comes from unexpected sources. Find out what people like and don't like and pay attention to details when visiting other home and restaurant kitchens. Snoop in corners, open drawers, and, wherever possible, cook in these places to see how their layout flows and equipment works.

I planned on having stacked wall ovens; then one day I tested this arrangement. Pulling a rack out of the upper oven, I burned my chin and then found myself too short to reach inside. Better luck came from copying Karen Berk, who keeps measuring spoons close by in a basket on the shelf above the stove.

Ideas lurk in public facilities as well. I hadn't known you could install a volume control to regulate kitchen speakers until I serendipitously observed a maître d' lowering the sound in a restaurant dining room.

Other voyeuristic opportunities exist in charity-sponsored kitchen tours or state-of-the-art showcase houses. Tour model homes and analyze the tricks decorators have played to enlarge a kitchen. Browse in home, kitchen, and appliance centers and in wholesale showrooms that present the latest products long before they hit retail stores.

Many marts have special visitor days when they are open to the public, but as long as you are not buying you can generally walk into any showroom.

The Los Angeles and New York design centers are, for example, easily cracked without a membership card.

A great deal of information can also be gleaned by attending home, builder, and kitchen shows. Many are open just to the trade, but a friendly salesperson at an appliance center may be willing to get you an admission ticket. Solicit an invitation to a wholesale distributor's warehouse by calling and expressing interest in his line.

Check magazine stands in supermarkets for biannual and quarterly books devoted solely to kitchens. Do library time skimming remodeling tomes and magazines featuring exemplary kitchens and equipment information, such as *Better Homes and Gardens, Consumer Reports, Country Living, Elle Décor, Food & Wine, Bon Appétit, House & Garden, Home, House Beautiful, Metropolitan Home, Old House Journal,* and *Sunset.* City magazines and other local publications are helpful, too, particularly as sources for products to purchase and professionals to hire. You might also order the kitchen design books from Kasmar Publications.

Most library reference departments have *Thomas' Regional Industrial Buying Guides* and *Sweet's Catalog,* compilations of manufacturers' brochures. Ask friends who are builders, contractors, or architects if you can look through their personal collection. If you are interested in a certain period, review books about that era. A local college or university with a design program will have relevant materials in its library, including trade and technical magazines. Armed with the straight scoop, you will be able to recognize a salesperson's hype. As you peruse, keep both eyes open for work you like and people to interview.

To compare characteristics between products, read a publication's advertisements as well as its editorial copy. Books offer bibliographies for additional research while the back section of most shelter magazines lists mail-order brochures, information sources, and opportunities for purchasing items wholesale.

Contact your state contractor boards, consumer associations, and national trade associations to see what consumer materials they offer gratis. In California, for example, the Contractors State License Board sends out an excellent booklet entitled *What You Should Know Before You Hire a Contractor.* Writing to the Consumer Information Center brings a *Consumer Resource Handbook.* Call appliance and cabinet companies (most have an 800 number) to request their brochures. Obtain restaurant and bar equipment catalogs through local food service purveyors (check your business pages).

Become an ardent follower of *Crate & Barrel, Gardener's Eden, Hammacher Schlemmer, Hold Everything, Pottery Barn, Renovator's, Self, Williams-Sonoma,* and *Chef's Catalog,* for they present good ideas as well as specific products. Always be on the lookout for unusual sources. Shelley Smith found stunning lights to hang over an island in a Sears farm directory. I discovered a wrought-iron cookbook stand in a Pottery Barn ad that I prefer to holders designed specifically for this purpose. Whatever you look at, be sensitive to the colors, textures, and materials that appeal to you.

Contemplating doing anything unusual? This is the time to obtain information on mechanical, plumbing, electric, energy, and zoning construction codes to see if your ideas are feasible. You'll want information on permits early on as well, for you may be required to obtain a construction permit before a loan request will be granted. Speed up the inevitable by consulting with an asbestos expert or acquiring a soil or environmental impact report at this stage. Finally, get a copy of your state's lien laws and learn when and how each document must be served from a preliminary notice to a lawsuit. And while you're at it, light a few joss sticks.

IDENTIFY QUALITY

"The bitterness of poor quality lasts longer than the sweetness of low price."

—*Remodeling* magazine

Educating yourself involves more than learning the dimensions of a product or construction procedure, for ultimate satisfaction depends on *quality*—the workmanship, design, and detail that imbue a special aura and sensibility.

Special is not always readily apparent. Once recognized, it may be difficult to verbalize. Yet persisting in the identification of these intangibles is imperative. Arriving at this knowledge is no elitist's exercise in navel contemplation but the key to getting the kitchen you want.

"What the hell is Quality? What *is* it?" demands Robert M. Pirsig in *Zen and the Art of Motorcycle Maintenance*. "Quality isn't something you lay on top of subjects and objects like tinsel on a Christmas tree. Real quality must be the source of the subjects and objects, the cone from which the tree must start."

To discover the cone—the core value—involves careful, deliberate scrutiny and comparison. You must begin to study and contrast each item—the way a handle is affixed, tile edges lined up. Why does one job look magnificent, another shoddy and sloppy? Where is the seamless union between fine form and superior functioning?

Once you learn what constitutes *the best*, you'll have the power to determine when it is appropriate. "The best" is not something you always need or can afford. Why would you put a solid gold faucet in a rental apartment? In some cases, a lesser-priced item does a better job. Do two potatoes bake more efficiently in a forty-eight-inch commercial oven or a fifteen-inch countertop model? Establish priorities so you spend money purposefully, cutting corners where consequences aren't functional. For an example, look to Julia Child, who hangs her costly hand-forged copper pots on a simple utilitarian pegboard.

Remember, too, that *price and quality are not automatically related*. A lower price does not always imply lower quality. The contractor with the lower bid may well outperform the one who came in at a higher number.

One of the *highest-quality* conveniences in my kitchen is the thirty-dollar cutting board that interlocks with a debris basket in my sink. Well designed for multifunctioning, one side has a flat surface for chopping, the other a routed juice-catching channel that transforms it into a meat serving tray.

So where does this leave you, the consumer trying to get the best value and highest quality for the least money?

Once you've learned to recognize quality/value, use these parameters to make your decisions and selections. Articulate these needs as well when you hire people to perform your job. Communicate the level of workmanship you can accept, illustrating expectations with pictures and real-life examples.

We all believe we know what quality is and what people mean when they say they "want" or "can deliver" a "quality" job; that they are operating on the same wavelength. Yet nowhere in the annals of kitchen remodeling is there greater evidence of communication breakdown, of the severing of the relationship between remodeler and remodelee, than over differing perceptions of quality. Don't assume that a contractor will automatically miter a molding on a cabinet door or finish its interior to match the exterior. If this constitutes quality for you, learn to express this definition; don't presume it.

EVALUATE UTILITY CAPABILITIES

Before making precise design and purchasing choices, you must appraise current utility capabilities. Improving electric, gas, plumbing, and heating systems can be an expensive undertaking. By obtaining a rough forecast of these costs, you know how much is left in the budget to spend elsewhere—the type of equipment you can buy.

Electricity

Electricity flows into the home *service panel* through an overhead (*service drop*) or underground (*service lateral*) conductor. The amount of *power* allotted to the panel is expressed in watts. *Wattage* is determined by multiplying *amperage*, the rate or volume of the electricity's flow, by *voltage*, its pressure. Divided among a number of *branch circuits*, this *electric current* (power) is conducted through wires from the box to outlets and switches for a specific group of lights and/or appliances.

Providing the maximum capacity at each outlet,

a modern electric system consists of 20-amp circuits with *three-wire* service to both 120- and 240-volt appliances. In an apartment—where someone else pays the bills—you may be limited to a *two-wire* 120-volt system. Running a heavy lineup of electric appliances in a big kitchen can easily up an amperage total to the 150-to-200 range.

A new or recently remodeled home will probably have enough electricity to service any appliance you are considering, whereas one untouched for twenty years or so will be due for alteration. Hosting more appliances today than it did several decades ago, a kitchen's electrical appetite has grown apace. Even if appliance numbers remain the same, changes in code may require the system's modernization.

Not to be ignored, strong hints that you're already underpowered include fuses blowing, circuit breakers tripping, and lights blinking on and off during an appliance's operation: the refrigerator surges, and down go the lights.

Appliances may overheat or underheat and start giving shocks. An electric upgrade—a larger service panel or additional circuits—is usually indicated with systems employing 120 volts, old-fashioned knob-and-tube wiring, and systems employing a fuse box instead of circuit breakers.

You can determine the adequacy of your current electric service by assessing its total power, the sufficiency of its amperage, and the feasibility of adding circuits, but it will be much easier to have an electrician perform the following tasks.

For the analysis, look at all the circuits feeding your current kitchen appliances and lights, whether or not they are in the same room. If other rooms are being remodeled as well, include their circuits in the evaluation.

To check each circuit, turn it off, label the appliances and lights it feeds, and write down the maximum wattage devoured by each item. (This is stamped on a metal plate affixed to the appliance and light fixture housing.) When only amps are given, multiply these by the circuit's volts to figure wattage.

Once you know the wattage consumed, check the number stamped on the service panel to see if it and its individual circuits can handle additional current without exceeding their maximum. If room remains, you will probably not have to change your service panel. When its location is awkward, check out possible new sites with your electric company.

As part of the electric power examination, consider your home's foundation. If the kitchen will be built on an existing slab, you will be pretty much stuck with the electric system you have. Buried in concrete, electric wires will most likely be too expensive to jackhammer out.

When the kitchen is built on a wood joist system with flooring and subflooring you intend to keep, an electrician can determine the efficacy of moving wiring by poking around the crawl space. If an island with a sink or stove figures in your fantasies, have him check out this possibility, too, for there's no point in designing one that can't be serviced.

Gas

A lucky cook will have a gas line in the current kitchen. In its absence, investigate the cost and complication of bringing one in, for a cooktop fueled by gas is much more responsive and efficient (page 228) than one plugging along on electricity.

Derived from the ground, *natural gas* is piped into the home from the gas company. Its consumption is measured on a *meter*. Gas can be diverted to the kitchen most readily when a line is already present in the home or running through your property or street. In these cases, an investigation centers on the cost of extending this service and the destruction and consequential repair involved in doing so.

In rural areas not serviced by a utility company, gas is available in liquid form (*liquid petroleum gas* or *LPG*). Composed of *butane, propane,* or a mixture of the two compounds, it is shipped in tanks or bottles that must be stored on your property. Less convenient to use in these forms, it is still worth the hassle when you have no access to natural gas—as long as someone can deliver it.

Plumbing

Pipes carry water to the house from a well or municipal system while gravity removes waste and gases from the premises in a drain/waste/vent ensemble that runs through the walls and a primary- or secondary-branch *vertical stack*. Moving downhill, at a slope of one-quarter inch for every horizontal foot, waste moves to a drain and then to a city sewer system, cesspool, or septic tank on your property.

If you are not hooked up to a sewer system, inquire if this is possible. If not, compute the size of septic tank you'll need when additional water-guzzling equipment is attached. For input and help with calculations, confer with the public health department or department of building and safety.

Water pressure adequacy is another area to evaluate. Water flows into the home at a pressure of twenty to eighty pounds *per square inch (psi)*, with thirty to sixty most typical. Actual pressure at the faucet is affected by the route's directness, its distance from the service line and water heater, the condition of the pipes, the number of fixtures serviced, and whether they're operated simultaneously. If pressure is not strong enough, one or all of these areas will have to be ameliorated.

Pipes must be looked at as well for corrosion and lead content, and the water supply must be tested (page 295). If your water contains more than .015 milligram of lead per liter, pipes and fixtures will have to be evaluated to discover their contribution to the problem.

Clanging pipes, or *water hammer*, derive from a sink valve switching off the water supply too hastily and signal the need for a *coiled air changer* to be attached to supply lines.

The cost and likelihood of moving plumbing depend somewhat on crawl space configuration. A slab foundation is as hostile to plumbing changes as it is to electric ones. New plumbing lines may mean new holes in the roof and the expense of flashing. Other changes? The vertical vent stack may need to be repositioned with a skylight or new windows; an old-fashioned S-style drain trap replaced with a new P or O shape. And we're not reciting the alphabet.

Heating

In anticipation of a remodel, have a licensed HVAC (heating/ventilation/air-conditioning) contractor evaluate the current heating and cooling system in the house, and do a *heat-loss analysis*. Stepping up insulation may be all that is needed. If you're planning an addition, determine whether the heating system can be extended or moved and a second furnace deployed in the event the first is more than forty feet away from the new room. In some cases, a heat pump or separate *zoned* radiant-heat system may prove more practical.

Evaluate the existing furnace's capacity to heat and cool any additional space. Does it meet current energy standards of 78 percent efficiency? Is it modifiable, or must it be replaced? If cooling is not currently possible, do you want this capability added?

The majority of new American homes are heated by forced air or gravity. With judicious planning, adding ducts and registers will be a breeze. On the other hand, an ancient hydronic (steam or hot water) system, distributed through pipes to radiators, convectors, or fan-coil units, may present enough challenges for you to contemplate its replacement. Radiators balk at being disassembled and pipes lay claim to walls you want to break through. Learn which can be altered, which must be left intact. Once again, a slab foundation complicates the modification of any system.

Solar heat is another option to review. A *passive* system harnesses heat directly from the sun; an *active* one turns to collectors and pumps for heat distribution. One final question: Do you want an *electronic air cleaner* added to the system?

KITCHENSPEAK: UTILITIES

ELECTRICITY

Amperage: Rate or volume of electricity flow. A twenty-amp circuit handles up to two thousand watts of power.

Branch Circuits: The wires that carry the electric current or power from the service panel where it enters a building throughout the premises to outlets and switches that control a specific group of lights and/or appliances. See also Service Panel.

Central Disconnect Switch: An emergency switch that turns off all the electricity flowing into a building.

Circuit Breaker: See Fuse.

Electrostrip: A sheath containing electricity that allows a plug to be installed at any place along its length. It is designed for mounting out of sight under a cabinet. See also Surface Runways.

Fuse: A safety device located in the service panel that blows when the electrical system is overloaded. Fuses are gradually being phased out in favor of circuit breakers. Though less sensitive to a problem than a fuse, these are readily switched back on when blown, whereas a fuse must be replaced.

Ground-Fault Circuit Interrupter: This protector is installed within six inches of the sink to interrupt the electric current when a leak occurs and prevent shocks.

Grounding: An appliance must be grounded with a polarized plug (one wider prong) connected to a three-hole receptacle or a two-hole receptacle with a grounding adapter. If a malfunction occurs, electricity will be discharged harmlessly into the ground.

Junction Box: A metal box enclosing wires that have been spliced together.

Service Drop: Overhead conductors that are strung between utility poles to bring electricity into a building.

Service Lateral: Underground conductors that bring in electricity from a service main located nearby.

Service Panel: A box or cabinet where electricity enters a building. From here it is distributed to the branch circuit wires that conduct it throughout the premises. In many kitchen remodels, the service panel must be increased to handle specified lighting and appliances. Any new box should offer twenty-amp circuits with space for additional circuits to be added in the future.

Smart House: A modern concept of integrating the operation of all electrically controlled tasks on a single programmable electronic keypad or bus.

Surface Runways: Electric strips with built-in equidistant plug outlets to be mounted out of sight under a cabinet. See also Electrostrips.

Surge Arrestor: A protective device installed at the main service panel to prevent a fire when voltage or electric current increases suddenly.

Switch Box: An enclosure that houses wires that have been run from the service panel to a switch.

Voltage: Pressure of electricity flow.

Watts: The amount of power a service panel has for distribution. Watts are determined by multiplying amperage by voltage.

GAS

Btus: These are British thermal units, with one unit equal to the amount of heat necessary to increase the temperature of one pound of water by one degree Fahrenheit. The higher the number of Btus, the greater the power and heat the system delivers.

Liquid Petroleum Gas (LPG): A liquid form of butane or propane gas—or a mixture of the two compounds—that is shipped, stored, and utilized in tanks or bottles.

Meter: An instrument installed on a building to measure the gas consumption on the premises.

Natural Gas: A source of power derived from the ground that is piped into a building by the gas company.

Quick-Disconnect: A flexible coupling to use between the gas line and an appliance you want to be able to move easily. It should be employed in tandem with a restrainer that prevents the appliance from tipping over or moving unexpectedly.

Shutoff Valve: **Each gas line must have its own shutoff valve whose location is usually decreed by code. Automatic shutoff valves are available for earthquake country.**

PLUMBING

Air Gap: **A vacuum breaker that prevents contaminated water from backing up into a dishwasher when the drain is clogged.**

Septic Tank: **A waste collection container that is stored underground on properties not hooked up to a municipal sewer system. Its capacity must be taken into account when determining the type of appliances to purchase.**

Vertical Stack: **A drain/vent ensemble of pipes that runs through the walls to remove wastes and gases from the premises. At a slope of one-quarter inch per horizontal foot, it does its work with the aid of gravity.**

Water Hammer: **The clanging noises pipes make when a sink valve switches off the water supply too quickly. This condition is usually ameliorated by attaching a coiled air changer to water supply lines.**

Water Pressure: **Measured per square inch (psi), water typically flows into the home at a psi of twenty to eighty pounds with thirty to sixty most common. The actual pressure at the tap may vary from that at the entrance, affected by the route's directness, condition of the pipes, distance from the service line and water heater, total number of fixtures serviced, and whether they're used simultaneously.**

HEATING

Forced Air or Gravity Heating System: **The primary method of residential heating used today, which operates by moving warmed air through ducts with the aid of a fan.**

Hydronic Heating System: **A method of heating found in older buildings where steam or hot water is distributed through pipes to radiators, convectors, or fan-coil units.**

Radiant Heating System: **This system is fed by hot water pipes or electric cables and regulated by a heat sensor. Installed in the subfloor, it gives great comfort to the barefoot-inclined.**

Solar Heating System: **An energy-efficient system that uses the sun's warmth to heat the home. In a passive system the heat is harnessed directly from the sun; in an active one it is gathered and distributed by a group of collectors and pumps.**

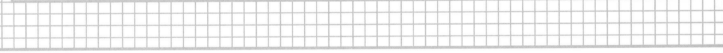

SELECT APPLIANCES AND MATERIALS

Once the limitations of heating, plumbing, gas, and electric systems are known quantities, you can begin winnowing your selection of new appliances and materials. As explained, you must possess a pretty clear notion of what you want before beginning the design process. Determining a backup or second choice is important, too, in case the first pick isn't available. For the broadest selection, look at items with the fewest alternatives first: Choose among limited cabinet finishes before settling on a floor covering that offers more numerous possibilities.

Your equipment's performance ability will determine the ease and efficiency of your movements in the kitchen, so let these choices drive the design process. With appliances identified in advance, the layout can be planned around them. Otherwise you'll be sorely limited to items that fit an allotted space.

After making selections at this preremodeling point, remain open to informed suggestion. A product may emerge that is more appropriate, more exciting, or just plain superior. Something new may be introduced to the market. Or you may find a better deal.

To kick off your search, get a copy of local building codes so you don't find yourself smitten by an item prohibited in your area. California energy legislation, for example, outlaws the installation of a professional cooktop or range in a residence. If you want one, you must apply for a *variance* from the building department. This permit is *usually* granted, but it can take months, for a great deal of red tape separates you from its acquisition. Obtain it before starting design work, for clearances will be based on its prescriptions.

To learn how to compare and procure equipment, cabinetry, lighting, and materials, follow suggestions under "Educate Yourself" (page 10), read the pertinent chapters, and observe the guidelines in Chapter 11 entitled "Shopping and Information Sources."

Start your search at the most upscale store around. Checking it out probably won't yield any deals, but you'll see the highest-quality merchandise available to use as a benchmark. When the price is right on something you're sure you want, buy it. Just don't go as far as Adrienne Martin, who stored her new stove so long in the garage that the warranty expired before it was uncrated.

With little existing data on how to identify the best sources, you'll have to ferret out the facts on which to base a solid decision. Other than providing beautiful pictures, the glossy brochures bombarding us shed little meaningful light on their subject. With all due respect to the exception, most salespeople know nothing about the merchandise they sell off the floor or offer in their catalogs. When they are aware of their existence, they usually don't have a clue about features or fabrication. Calling a company's customer service department is an exercise in eye rolling: Most of the time you think you've dialed the wrong number. Speaking to a technical assistant or engineer can sometimes be helpful once you figure out how to get to that person. If this sounds like an entreaty for firms to educate their personnel, you're reading it correctly.

Complicating the shopping process is the explosion of possibilities. What used to be a toss-up between just a couple of models has seemingly stretched into infinity. To deal with this *blitzkrieg*, many people are harkening back to the fifties bedroom-set approach and buying a single line of appliances. This tactic permits all purchasing and service to be done through the same dealer (chalk up a plus) and eliminates the design challenge of lining up trims and toe kicks (chalk up plus two).

Different appliances are, however, rarely created equal by the same company. Driven by a desire to capture more of the market, many lines have expanded by hanging their name on products produced by someone else, often an inferior someone. Better to view myriad choices in the same manner writer Alan Davidson regards the profusion of fish: "as life enriching."

To cut a swath through the competing stimuli, some companies have coordinated the colors of their wares for easy mixing and matching with other labels. The program, begun by Kohler and involving varying participants, bears investigation if only for its assistance in reaching a verdict.

While struggling to identify what you want, build confidence on the fact that there are no right answers, only what is best for you. Keep asking. The more people you speak to, the better chance you have of getting it and of learning what questions to ask.

Upon hearing she could bring a gas line into her home, Ruthie Schwartz bought a gas cooktop and tore out her moribund stove. Several thousand dollars, many weeks, and several contractors who threw up their hands later, the new cooker was finally at rest. Next time this consumer will ask not only *if* gas can be brought in but also *how* it gets to the kitchen, *what* will be torn up along the way, and *how much* it will cost.

When soliciting and comparing opinions, always remain wary of your source. One store may service designers; another plumbers. Find out what someone's bias is based on and evaluate it accordingly. What is positive for one person may be construed as negative by another.

Salespeople and designers excel at knocking whatever their competition has recommended.

Often they receive kickbacks or free trips for pushing a particular brand. A kitchen featured in a magazine may be showcasing an advertiser's wares, not breaking noteworthy news. A friend's vote for "stove of the month" may be driven by price, not by what is *best*.

Don't be snookered by repetitive mention of the same names. You may just be picking up a trend or hearing what is advertised the most. Before being sucked in, go through the motions of using the item in your head. The company touting the merits of its sink's attached drainboard for carving a turkey fails to mention that stainless isn't a cutting surface and that the bird's juices will run down the drain.

Food writer Craig Claiborne's kitchen includes a restaurant-size Garland range, an electric wall oven, a microwave, a Tandoor Indian oven, a gas-fired Chinese pork oven, and a commercial grill. Yet in an interview with the *Detroit Free Press*, he claims he would have only "the best standard four-burner gas range I could get" were it not for his professional demands.

Deep pockets are increasingly filled with European products. As handsome as these imports are, they have many drawbacks for our domestic market. Coming from afar, they take longer to arrive than local profferings. So do their parts when they break down. Unfamiliar with their instructions, installers inevitably put them in wrong, and service is less readily available. Most were developed for a populace that shops daily, is limited in energy sources, and is ensconced in a small kitchen. Decrease the migraines and buy an American knockoff that emulates the best of European design. Still Euro-stuck? Go for a model that has been widely sold, serviced, or retooled for sale in the United States.

Another trendy temptress in this Garden of Eatin' is the restaurant line or restaurant-style equipment with a professional look. For all commercial equipment's sturdy steadfastness, it's missing those accessories and convenience aids that we spoiled home folks have come to depend on.

Vying for attention are built-in appliances that offer alternative design more than functional superiority. If you build them in, you'll still have to get them out to fix, and you won't be able to take them with you to another location. For all these drawbacks, you'll also have the dubious privilege of paying more money.

Making decisions is a monstrous task no matter how carefully you have educated yourself. Stores undermine firm choices by assaulting you with other possibilities. When you're caught up in this debilitating process, towel racks you couldn't care less about loom as life-and-death determinants. You make one commitment, and others rush out to await your judgment. You choose a stove, and its finish commands attention. And do you want that griddle or grill? Would that extra cold-water spigot be more helpful at the sink or on the refrigerator door? You're happy, and your spouse is miserable, a discrepancy often resolved by having one person in charge of inside matters, the other outside.

Gary Bishop from Showcase Kitchens has observed many customers "reaching the never-never land of totally losing their minds until, paralyzed, they can't make any decision." He sent one distraught woman to a shrink, but this physician couldn't deal with it either. "You'll have to go elsewhere," he told her. "I'm redoing my own house this year."

Hem and haw all you want during your shop-and-you-will-drop-athons, but try not to vacillate and drag things out. You can go back and forth until you're crazed and still not reach a choice. As Laura Chenel—one remodeler who's been there—says, "You have to make a decision eventually; you might just as well make it sooner as later on."

COMPARE COSTS

To avoid a protracted search, it's helpful to start out knowing the cost of appliances and materials. This way you can narrow your choice to items you can afford or figure a way to copy what you want. Marlene Sorosky coveted white porcelain drawer knobs with painted flowers until she found out their price. Undaunted, her designer made sure she got them. After painting twenty-seven-and-a-half-cent wooden

KITCHEN APPLIANCE SHOPPING LIST

	YES	NO	QUANTITY		YES	NO	QUANTITY
Range	☐	☐		Separate Hose	☐	☐	
Radiant Oven	☐	☐		Instant Hot Water	☐	☐	
Convection Oven	☐	☐		Instant Cold Water	☐	☐	
Wood-burning Range	☐	☐		Air Gap	☐	☐	
Wood-burning Oven	☐	☐		Pot Filler	☐	☐	
Cooktop	☐	☐		Disposer Button	☐	☐	
Griddle	☐	☐		Disposer	☐	☐	
Grill	☐	☐		Dishwasher	☐	☐	
Wok	☐	☐		Trash Compactor	☐	☐	
Deep Fryer	☐	☐		Water Filter	☐	☐	
Microwave Oven	☐	☐		Built-in Toaster	☐	☐	
Warming Drawer	☐	☐		Built-in Can Opener	☐	☐	
Warming Light	☐	☐		Computer	☐	☐	
Warming Shelf	☐	☐		Telephone	☐	☐	
Hood	☐	☐		Intercom	☐	☐	
Refrigerator	☐	☐		Security	☐	☐	
Freezer	☐	☐		Television	☐	☐	
Wine Cooler	☐	☐		Stereo System	☐	☐	
Icemaker	☐	☐		Speakers	☐	☐	
Beer Tap	☐	☐		Remote Stereo Button	☐	☐	
Single Sink	☐	☐		Radio	☐	☐	
Double Sink	☐	☐		Heating	☐	☐	
Triple Sink	☐	☐		Air-conditioning	☐	☐	
Faucet	☐	☐					

knobs shiny white, he sent them to a manicurist renowned for decorating nails with flowers.

When $20,000 or less is allocated for a kitchen remodel, you are, of necessity, limited to appliances and materials in the lower and middle ranges of the chart on page 20. That does not mean that everything you choose must lie in this bracket. Go ahead and splurge on a high-end ticket; just balance other picks with it. Or wait to buy new equipment until you've amassed sufficient funds.

Above $20,000, there is more leeway, but cautious decisions still need to be made according to budget, the permanence of your situation, and the importance of the item for high kitchen functioning.

Familiarizing yourself with price is a great theory that doesn't work as well as it needs to in practice, for cost is the best-kept secret in the remodeling industry. Charges are so cleverly concealed we often don't know how much something costs even when we've paid for it. Unlike most business transactions, where the question "How much does this cost?" is followed by an actual answer, remodeling fees are shrouded in mystery.

In many instances, people don't learn that something is not affordable until after it has been delivered and billed. Prices and discounts vary so much from store to store and state to state that it doesn't even help to learn what someone else paid. Misleading us further, the stated figure rarely corresponds to ultimate cost.

Ceramic tile, for example, is one of the lowest-priced surface materials—if you use large simple squares. Start hacking those tiles into small facets for an intricate mosaic, and the fee soars beyond the most expensive top-of-the-line granite. There are hidden costs, too, that aren't readily apparent on a price tag. It's not enough to spring for the markup on a refrigerator that delivers ice and water to the door. You also have to come up with a couple of hundred dollars extra for the water line.

Despite the difficulty, it is imperative to get a sense of cost as early in the project as possible. If you find you can't afford Corian after designing the kitchen around it—or, worse, building it—you'll have to start anew, watching design fees skyrocket in the tumult.

With these factors in mind, this chart is intended as a rough guide for considering material and equipment options even when the exact price is ephemeral. Actual costs will depend on brand, accessories, and custom adjustments. Items whose prices fluctuate appear in multiple categories.

WHAT THE KITCHEN DOLLAR BUYS

CABINETS

It is often estimated that cabinet costs consume one third of a budget.

LOW RANGE

- Stock
- Laminate finish in limited colors and some wood stains
- Oak or maple hardwood
- Fixed shelves
- Simple flat panel or square raised panel door
- Visible hinges

MIDDLE RANGE

- Semicustom; some nonstandard sizes
- Wider selection of woods, including hickory and cherry
- Premium laminates, foils, or painted, stained, or pickled finishes
- Simple flat, recessed, or raised panel door
- Plain glass panel door
- Some storage options such as pullouts
- Matching panels for appliance doors
- Semivisible hinges

HIGH RANGE

- Custom, with imported European boxes most expensive of all
- Exotic veneers and hardwoods; high-gloss laminates
- Curved doors
- Glass doors with mullions
- Invisible hinges
- Architectural moldings and trims
- Lacquer, polyester, and white enamel finishes
- Custom glazes
- Built-in storage accessories such as pantries, roll-out shelves, and appliance garages
- Self-closing drawers; full-extension or overextension glides

COUNTERTOPS

LOW RANGE

- Laminate

MIDDLE RANGE

- Ceramic tile
- Solid surface
- Wood
- Color-through laminate
- Stainless steel
- Soapstone
- Decorative edge treatment

HIGH RANGE

- Marble
- Granite
- Ceramic tile
- Hand-painted tile
- Solid surface with inlays
- Stainless steel
- Stone
- Decorative edge treatment

FLOORING

LOW RANGE

- Vinyl

MIDDLE RANGE

- Hardwood
- Ceramic tile
- Cork
- Linoleum

HIGH RANGE

- Stone
- Ceramic tile
- Inlaid wood

LIGHTING

LOW RANGE

- Incandescent (with highest lumens and wattage)
- Contractor-grade incandescent bulbs
- Economic-grade recessed can light fixture

MIDDLE RANGE

- Architect-grade incandescent bulbs
- Delayed-start fluorescent
- Plug-in fluorescent

HIGH RANGE

- Extended-life incandescent bulbs
- Rapid-start fluorescent
- Screw-in fluorescent
- Fluorescent with dimming ballast
- Halogen (electronic transformer and combined fixture and transformer most expensive)

WINDOWS AND SKYLIGHTS

LOW RANGE

- Plastic bubble skylights
- Sliders
- Single-glazed
- Vinyl frames (not recommended in extreme cold)

MIDDLE RANGE

- Double-glazed
- Snap-in grills
- Round or odd-shaped windows
- Casements

HIGH RANGE

- Custom sizes
- Divided panes
- Double- and triple-glazed
- Low E and other climatic protection

COOKTOPS

LOW RANGE

- Four-burner low-wattage electric coils or low-Btu gas (not recommended)

MIDDLE RANGE

- Higher-heat units
- Five or six burners
- Ceramic glass smooth tops
- Halogen
- Induction
- Interchangeable modules

HIGH RANGE

- Halogen
- Induction
- European imports
- Commercial or commercial style

OVENS

LOW RANGE

- Single oven
- Continuous-clean
- Mechanical dials
- White, almond, or black

MIDDLE RANGE

- Double oven
- Self-clean
- True convection
- Spiffy glass castings
- Microwave-radiant combos
- Electronic controls

HIGH RANGE

- True convection
- Stainless steel and anodized colors
- Sleek designer casings
- Combo oven that switches from radiant to convection heat
- Electronic controls

MICROWAVE OVENS

LOW RANGE

- 1.0-cubic-foot capacity
- Mechanical controls
- Two-power (not recommended)

MIDDLE RANGE

- 1.1- to 1.5-cubic-foot capacity
- Multiple power levels
- Electronic controls
- Temperature probe
- Programmable

HIGH RANGE

- Sensors
- Larger
- Microwave convection combo oven

VENTILATION

LOW RANGE

- Not recommended

MIDDLE RANGE

- Overhead ventilation hoods providing 600 cubic feet per minute
- Downdraft (not recommended)

HIGH RANGE

- Custom
- Remoted motors

REFRIGERATION

LOW RANGE

- Small with top-mounted freezer
- Single door for refrigerator and freezer (not recommended)
- White or almond

MIDDLE RANGE

- 20-cubic-foot refrigerator with top-mounted freezer
- Some bottom-mount freezers
- Self-defrosting
- Automatic icemaker
- Delineated storage compartments
- Optional textured black finish

HIGH RANGE

- Built-in
- Side-by-side
- Commercial or commercial style
- Undercounter units with drawers
- Stainless interior
- Ice and water on the door
- Custom panels
- Electronic controls

SINKS

LOW RANGE

- Stainless 20- and 22-gauge (not recommended)
- Enamel on steel (not recommended)
- White or pastel enamel on cast iron
- Shallow seven-inch-deep sinks
- Simple rectangular shapes

MIDDLE RANGE

- Stainless 18-gauge
- Enamel on cast iron in many colors
- Quartz composite
- Contoured shapes
- Offset drains

HIGH RANGE

- Stainless 18-gauge with modern lines, 10-inch-deep bowls
- Solid surface
- Integrated drainboard
- Integrated countertop
- Triple basins

FAUCETS

In this category, highest prices are more indicative of limited production, fancy handles, and expensive finishes than of better quality or function. Some premier lines provide excellent inexpensive faucets by substituting acrylic for metal in decorative, nonessential parts.

LOW RANGE

- Plastic valves (not recommended)
- Extruded brass interior (not recommended)
- Chrome
- Single lever or spout and two handles
- Some black, white, and almond finishes

MIDDLE RANGE

- Die-cast brass interior
- Ceramic disk valves
- More colored finishes or metal and color combos
- Integrated pullout spray spouts
- Pullout sprays
- Wrist-blade handles
- Brass

HIGH RANGE

- Side-mounted single lever
- Large gooseneck spout and specialty handles
- Wall mount
- Limited-production European imports
- More colors, including red, mixed colors, mixed metals, gold, or semiprecious-stone finishes
- Antiscald valves
- Handles from precious gems

DISHWASHERS

LOW RANGE

- Single wash arm (not recommended)
- Two cycles (not recommended)
- Porcelain enamel on steel (not recommended)
- Minimal insulation

MIDDLE RANGE

- Mechanical controls
- Plastic-coated steel interior
- Sound-deadening insulation
- Built-in water heater
- Several wash levels
- Two to four cycles
- Filtering system

HIGH RANGE

- Electronic programmable controls
- Stainless interior
- Silencing insulation
- Adjustable flexible racking
- Triple filtration
- Three or four wash levels
- Multiple cycles

DISPOSERS

LOW RANGE

- 1/3 horsepower (not recommended)

MIDDLE RANGE

- 1/2 horsepower (not recommended)
- Stainless parts
- Some antijamming devices

HIGH RANGE

- 3/4 or 1 horsepower
- Fully insulated
- Antijamming devices

MONEY-SAVING TIPS

Saving money is a matter of approaching decisions practically, independent of the going price. Though many of the principles espoused here will be more readily understood once the entire book is perused, meeting them early on enhances their applicability.

GENERAL PRINCIPLES

- Contain the remodel to what you can pay for out of pocket, rather than carrying the extra expense of a loan that can double a remodel's price.

- An addition costs more than remodeling a preexisting space. Consider what rooms are available to redo for a kitchen before deciding to add on.

- Incorporate principles of Universal Design for a multigenerational kitchen, anticipating special needs that are likely to arise as your family ages.

- Salvage what you can from the original kitchen such as cabinets or flooring. Old floors can, for example, be repaired, or their age and state of disrepair venerated as a virtue.

- Save money where it makes sense. Don't trim costs by installing expensive imported tiles in a thinset mastic bonding that leaves them vulnerable to cracking.

- If your heart is set on an expensive material, use it as a focal point and mix with a supporting cast that doesn't break the bank. Rather than purchasing all cabinet doors with an expensive veneer, reserve them for wall cabinets and choose another material for base cabinets.

- Establish priorities for expenditures, placing a quality cooktop and ventilation at the top of the list.

- Avoid playing custom dominoes (purchasing items tailored for you). Ordering a custom work table suited to my height, I found myself unwittingly committed to custom chairs.

- Purchase standard equipment or materials that don't require difficult, unusual installation. Point of reference: odd-shaped windows.

- Choose standard finishes, looking to color for an inexpensive individual flourish.

- Save yourself a lot of grief: Don't fall in love with something expensive.

PRUNING

- Scale down the scope of the job (e.g., eliminate a skylight).

- Don't build a soffit that can add another $7,000 to $8,000 to a job.

- Let the budget dictate how far you can stray from *essential* to *desired* items; from stripped down basics to fancy frills.

WORK

- Before having the job bid, hire a contractor or an inspector to investigate walls, subfloors, wiring, and pipes. Look for the existence of termites, lead, and radon. This additional outlay will be less than the padding a contractor adds to protect himself from unknown nightmares.

- Perform some of the purchasing or construction tasks yourself.

- Act as a general contractor in all or part of the process.

- Do not issue change orders unless an unexpected problem is encountered for which there is no other solution.

PURCHASING

- Comparison-shop.

- Look for stores, warehouses, or mail-order sources that sell discounted, discontinued, rejected, or slightly damaged wares.

- Purchase used goods wherever possible. Shop for secondhand doors, windows, or hardware at salvage stores or flea markets. The iron door hardware that cost $150 new ran $40 at a wrecking yard, I found; and the quality of the used piece was far superior.

- Check distributor outlets or contractor suppliers.

- To learn an item's price parameters, follow ads for several months before purchasing. A bonus may also surface along the way. Refrigerator suppliers, for example, often throw in an automatic icemaker as an incentive.

- Invest in quality items that last longer, amortizing a higher purchase price over the long haul.

- Buy items that are less costly to operate.

- When estimating purchase price, look for hidden costs. A thousand-pound professional stove demands a reinforced floor.

CONSTRUCTION

- When sinking a new foundation for the kitchen, build it on a slab if soil conditions allow, rather than on a more expensive wood floor joist system.

- Regardless of the foundation type, leave plumbing and electricity as they are. Change out appliances *in situ* rather than moving them around the room. Costs rack up adding new circuits, wiring, or a higher-voltage line. The "nothing" Joan Soloman's architect said it cost to move a sink billed out at $1,000 when the new placement proved impractical and the fixture was returned to its original location.

- As long as appliances aren't moved more than a few feet, the gas line can be lengthened with flexible tubing instead of being replaced.

- It is more expensive to install a sink or cooktop in an island than along a wall, for its pipes and wires must be moved.

- Electrical work costs less in a teardown, where wires are moved while walls are open. In a retrofit, money can be saved by installing wires in surface-mounted conduit. Though this is ugly, it may be acceptable in a pantry, behind a baseboard, or in another area where it won't show.

- Place new electric outlets as close to existing live connections as possible so that a new power source is not necessary.

- A plumbing retrofit is less costly if the floor can be opened up.

- Wherever possible, do not move walls, doors, or windows. Along with the costs of moving and replacing these members, you'll accrue fees for new stoops and sills, plus an upcharge for matching cement to the original.

- Exterior and load-bearing interior walls are more expensive to move or replace than nonstructural walls.

- Place heating vents on the floor or near a window, where gravity will help heat rise naturally.

CABINETS

- Instead of replacing cabinets, refinish, repaint, or change out their doors.

- Shipped flat, knockdown or ready-to-assemble (RTA) cabinets have lower delivery fees than premade boxes.

- Cabinetry designed for commercial distribution is often less expensive than that designed for residences.

- Learn dimensions of standard stock cabinets so they can be accommodated in the layout.

- Reserve purchases of custom cabinetry to pieces with unusual shapes or sizes that aren't available in a stock or semicustom line.

- Use stock and semicustom cabinetry in new and creative ways.

- When custom cabinetry is employed, have it built locally rather than shipped in from afar, saving transportation costs. Exceptions to this advice depend on where you live. In California, cabinets shipped in from Colorado can easily cost less than those made next door.

- For a contoured look, use rectangular cabinets with fillers rather than the more expensive angled box.

- Everything else being equal, framed cabinetry is 15 to 20 percent cheaper than frameless because its installation is simpler. The clean look frameless cabinetry provides can be obtained by using full-overlay doors on standard framed boxes.

- Paint-grade or plastic laminate cabinets are much less expensive than those fabricated from hardwood.

- Reduce the number of cabinets by using larger boxes, but resist making them so large that the door sags and is heavy to operate. Saving on doors and hardware, the least expensive type of cabinet per amount of storage area is a walk-in pantry or floor-to-ceiling utility cabinet.

- Use open shelves to eliminate the cost of doors.

- Simple, flat standard door styles cost considerably less than elaborate or unusual ones.

- Flush doors inset into a frame with a one-eighth-inch *reveal* (gap) are labor-intensive to produce and thus expensive.

- Drawers are less expensive than doors plus shelves.

- Adjustable shelves cost more than fixed.

- Build shallow cabinets that don't require expensive interior storage fittings to make contents accessible.

- Wherever possible, use hinges with a smaller degree of opening.

- Visible and semivisible hinges are often less expensive than concealed hinges.

- Use glides with three-quarter or seven-eighths extension rather than full extension for drawers containing long tools that won't be difficult to see or remove from these partially opened positions.

- Utilize metal glides, not epoxy.

- Small-profile glides for drawer sides are less expensive than both concealed-undermount glides and wider glides for drawer sides.

- Purchase unfinished cabinets and finish them yourself.

- Choose a standard paint finish, not an expensive polyester.

- A stained wood finish is less expensive than a multistep painted procedure.

- Install cabinets directly against an unpainted dry wall surface that will be hidden.

STORAGE

- A pantry inset for a cabinet is more expensive than individual fittings such as pullout shelves and less economical in its use of space.

HARDWARE

- Do not contemplate brass rails or other finishing touches that can really increase the tab.

COUNTERTOP

- For a soft rounded look in the kitchen, use a curved countertop instead of more costly contoured cabinets.

- Avoid intricate patterns in tile or solid surface countertops. For visual impact, choose a dramatic color or bold pattern.

- Avoid a specific pattern that must be matched. Labor costs are higher, and it is wasteful of material.

- Eliminate mitered corners from butcher block. Have one board extend all the way to the corner of a counter, then butt the second board perpendicular to it.

- Review costs of edge treatments. Use a simple self-edge rather than a more costly beveled or double-beveled edge.

- Laminate is the least costly countertop material. Use several colors of laminate on a beveled edge for the effect of solid surface at a lower price.

TILE

- Use trim pieces to compose an original design.

- Use larger tiles rather than small ones, which cost less proportionately and are cheaper to install.

- For a mosaic pattern, use a large tile with a faux mosaic design instead of individual facets.

SOLID SURFACE

- Combine a solid surface material with a less costly laminate from the same company that has been designed to precisely match its color.

- Use Cornice Moldings and Trim, a prefabricated Du Pont Corian trim and coved backsplash, from TFI Corporation.

GRANITE

- Choose a matte finish to save polishing costs.

GLASS BLOCK

- Purchase premounted blocks in a grid panel instead of installing them one by one.

FLOORING

- Vinyl flooring is least expensive.

- As long as subflooring is in good condition and the floor won't be too high, choose a new floor that can be laid over an existing one.

- Flooring made from a *common* grade of wood will have more blemishes but will be equal in quality and lower in price than that from *select* or *clear* grades.

WINDOWS

- Design windows from prefabricated pieces available ready-made, rather than from custom measures.

- Avoid ellipses and other shapes that cost more to install.

- Size windows and skylights so they fit between existing joists.

- The least expensive skylight is a plastic bubble dome. Inoperable skylights are less expensive than those that open.

APPLIANCES

- Buy an appliance that is not distributed through dealers, for this network of intermediaries drives up the cost.

- Purchase white appliances, which are timeless and least costly.

- Freestanding appliances are less expensive than built-ins, and they can be made to look fitted with trim kits and construction tricks.

- Purchase appliances with mechanical controls instead of electronic ones.

- Accept the gas company's generous offer to install your gas appliances for free.

- Build a cabinet on the side of a refrigerator at the end of a run instead of fitting this area with an expensive useless side panel.

RANGE

- Choose a stove that does not require your electrical panel to be augmented or rewired.

VENTILATION

- Don't cut corners on ventilation (or stoves). Get the best quality you can afford.

- Line up all items that require ventilation such as a stove and grill under a single hood.

- Limit a hood's lip to three inches. Another inch adds a hundred dollars without significantly affecting design.

SINKS

- Installation costs increase when sinks are under-mounted or seamed to the countertop outside of the factory for an integral appearance.

FAUCETS

- Pullout sprays are less expensive as individual units than as part of a faucet.

SCHEDULE THE REMODEL

After you've invested time in gathering information, the poignant moment arrives when you must commit yourself to the job, to hiring professionals and making yourself available to move a remodel along. How much time you need to set aside depends on the extent and complexity of your job, the flexibility and time frame of the people you hire, and the degree of detail and perfection you seek.

There is no good occasion for a remodel, just periods that are less bad than others. Unless your family thrives on stress, planning it to coincide with the arrival of a new baby, a job change, or a child's move into junior high is probably not such a good idea. If you don't like surprises—bad ones—this is not a happening to host while you're on vacation either. Nor is tying its completion to an important event.

Barbara Sims Bell's house was supposed to be

finished for her wedding. It was, one year later than the first round of invitations had stated. When it finally took place, the vows included "through a remodel" in addition to "in sickness and health." (If you are already married, be sure the relationship is a stable one.)

Some scheduling scenarios are simple. If you can't identify an interval to devote any time to this project, you just have to table it until you can. Timing is not an issue either for the kind of person who is able blithely to hire someone to "do it" and then disappear until it is done. Most of us, however, fare better being at least somewhat involved. The challenge: how to find sufficient hours to undertake a remodel within the context of a busy life.

First explore the possibility of taking a vacation from your life—an extended one. Though it is fun to imagine life without working, shopping, cleaning, paying bills, and caring for children, it's rare to be able to check out. After this fantasy has dissipated in a poof of reality, assess how many hours you have during the day and in the evening—weekdays and weekends—to dedicate to a remodel and extend the time you allow for completing each phase of the process accordingly.

Working people—with or without children in tow—will require several months at least to conduct interviews and identify a designer and contractor they feel they can work with. And it can take a lot longer, as anyone who has ever hunted for Mr. or Ms. Right knows. If you spend six or seven hours a week minimum, several more months will pass while the kitchen is designed, bids collected, and the construction contract signed. This is a lowball time estimate, which depends on getting the design right during the first few passes and on having equipment and materials pretty well picked. If choices must still be made, the speed of their selection will depend on whether you settle on standard sizes and prefabricated (noncustom) products, purchase most things from the same place, and are good at making snappy decisions.

Speed is very closely connected to personality. The compulsive (me) who insists on researching the entire market and obsessing over every decision will take a lot longer than someone (you, hopefully) who is satisfied with finding something satisfactory and then quickly moving on to the next decision that must be tackled. When estimating your time frame, build in any characteristic ambivalence or make a determined decision to keep it in check.

After hiring a busy contractor, you will have to wait several months for this person to be free and several months after that for cabinets, appliances, and materials to arrive before demolition day. In other words, all these severals add up to at least a nine-month remodeling gestation period.

Nine months may seem like an awfully long time to be babying a kitchen before a hammer is even raised, but that's what it will take for you to nominally maintain your normal routine while pursuing this endeavor. If you don't have the patience to spend all this time, and you can't change your personality, you might also simplify the extent of the job or do it in phases. Think about that cosmetic coat of paint.

When to start construction depends on the extent of the work and an estimate of its duration. When scheduling, you'll want to consider the weather. Not surprisingly, contractors are most often free in January and February, but you won't want them then if you have to take your roof off. Warm months are also kinder to the building materials themselves, for lumber can warp and rot in cold and moisture. And are you going to need that kitchen for the holidays?

Once plans are well detailed and materials onsite, the most complex gut job shouldn't take more than five months to complete—a bit longer if you're living in it—and that's being exceedingly generous. If walls aren't moved or structural changes undertaken, one to two and one-half months should be ample.

Unfortunately, the realization of a job doesn't always correspond to its predicted pacing. At three years, my remodel took just one year less than the construction of the Hoover Dam, one of our country's seven civil engineering wonders. Sydelle Sonkin had a quicker fix. Her job was completed before she realized it had started. "I found this company, they came, and ten days later I was cooking," she says.

Any contractor who tells you it will take more time should be reminded that cookbook author Nathalie Dupree's complete gut job and makeover was finished in three weeks. (And she was furious because it ran seven days longer than promised!) Contractor conventional wisdom states: "What can be built in a day can be remodeled in three—for twice the cost."

C O U N T D O W N   T O   A   R E M O D E L

A summary of steps involved from the conception of a remodel to its execution, this listing has a dual purpose: to give you an overview of the complete process and to alert you to the order in which tasks must be attacked. Knowing what a situation involves allows you to prepare for it financially and emotionally, to locate necessary materials, and to schedule each endeavor so it wreaks the least havoc in your life. Many of the "To Dos" in the following pages will appear unclear or even ambiguous at this stage, but the list is here for you to continually turn to as a reference and a reminder as you reach each stage of the remodeling process.

Going back to the future, every aspect of a remodel is intertwined with what precedes and follows, sending you careening down paths you never planned to tread. Each decision closes down options, leaving you with inevitable choices. By pursuing an orderly attack, you are less likely to make expensive irrevocable pronouncements.

Remodeling a kitchen, like making a dress, builds on each step. Once the fabric is cut, it can't be made bigger or turned into a suit. When a thirty-inch cavity is left for a refrigerator, it's too late to covet that thirty-six-inch box. On occasion, order is arbitrary, and sometimes multiple threads can be followed simultaneously. But the closer you adhere to the pattern's progression, the less chance of error or disappointment.

SETTING THE STAGE

- Formulate a psychological kitchen lifestyle profile of what this room means to you: when you spend time there, with whom, and what type of food you prepare.

- Determine a maximum budget and a source for financing the project. Begin arrangements for a loan if one is to be secured.

- Once the project looks like a go economically, begin collecting photographs of kitchens you like.

- Organize a file system for papers and brochures and a box to house sample materials.

- List what you like and dislike about your current kitchen, and describe your fantasy dream kitchen.

- List *everything* that must be stored in the kitchen, noting dimensions of oversized or unusually shaped items. Discard all unused items.

- Prepare a diary (daily log) for the remodeling. Start keeping it as soon as you begin gathering information.

- Have your water supply tested if its taste or aroma is unpleasant or contamination is suspected.

- Hire professionals to evaluate electric, gas, heating, and plumbing systems. Look at the foundation as well. If it is a slab, change will be difficult unless you can afford great sums to jackhammer original wires out.

  Check each electric circuit to see how much current it can handle or whether the service panel must be changed.

  If you are thinking of locating a sink or cooktop on an island, check the feasibility of this placement.

  When the service panel's location must be altered, investigate new sites with your electric company.

  If no gas line is hooked up, see if one can be brought in.

  If you are not hooked up to a sewer system, inquire if this is possible. If not, compute the size of septic tank you'll need when additional water-guzzling equipment is attached.

Evaluate water pressure adequacy.

Look at pipes for corrosion and lead content.

Have a licensed HVAC contractor do a heat-loss analysis.

Determine whether the capacity of the existing furnace is adequate for heating and cooling any additional space.

Decide whether you want to change a hydronic system to gravity or forced air or add a radiant system for the kitchen zone.

Review the option of solar heating.

Decide whether you want to add an electronic air cleaner to the system.

- If flooring and subflooring are not to be replaced, evaluate their condition and how they will affect cabinet and appliance installation.

- Begin educating yourself about the equipment, appliances, and materials available for the kitchen.

- Request full-line catalogs for appliances and cabinets.

- Learn to identify quality in the items you will be purchasing and in construction jobs.

- Request a copy of local building and energy codes to learn what equipment is restricted in your area. Apply for any necessary variances.

- Pick a first and second choice for every appliance you will be replacing.

- Select surface material type (first and second choices) for floors, countertops, backsplashes, walls, and ceilings.

CHOOSING THE PLAYERS

- Contact the contractor's board for state guidelines.

- Determine what, if any, work you will do yourself.

- Compile a list of appropriate professionals to help with your remodel. Determine if you prefer a one-stop-shop team approach or an independent designer and contractor. In the latter case, seek the designer first and then the contractor to ensure they can work together.

- Interview possible candidates.

- Check references and visit kitchens built by the people you are considering.

- Evaluate three cabinet installations of the line or shop used by the finalists on your list.

- Perform a final document verification and credit check of the people you are considering hiring.

- Engage a designer and/or general contractor to participate in your job from its inception to execution.

- Draw up an all-inclusive contract that can easily be broken if tenets aren't met.

SCRIPTING THE PROCESS FROM CONCEPT TO CONSTRUCTION

DESIGN WORK

- Confirm your budget with the designer.

- Finalize the extent of the remodel.

- Determine who is to manufacture the cabinets, and choose a cabinet door style.

- Bring in consultants as necessary for soil, engineering, landscaping, energy, asbestos, lighting, heating, ventilation, and air-conditioning.

- Choose the size, type, and shape of premade windows you want to use before locking in a design.

- Decide on a method of weather control for the skylight at the same time you delineate its type and configuration and a means for hiding its ugly tracks and hardware.

- Prioritize your appliance list.

- Choose the sink, faucet, water filtration system, and all sink accessories simultaneously.

- If you want instant cold water, decide among an ice-and-chilled-water dispenser on the refrigerator door, an automatic icemaker (freestanding or freezer mount), and a chilled-water tap on the sink.

- Have schematic drawings or rough sketches prepared.

- Assess the efficacy of the floor plan .

- Set a design schedule once you sign off on a floor plan.

- Move to the design development phase.

- Make final equipment, finish, and color selections.

- Before designing cabinets:

    Choose a cooktop and ovens or stove.

    Finalize ventilation plans, leaving space for ducting. Have a ventilation expert confirm the adequacy of ventilation and ducting.

    Choose flooring.

    Orchestrate the heating and air-conditioning system and its placement.

    Know clearances, installation demands, and plumbing, electric, and gas requirements of all appliances, where lines will run, the extent of cords, and how far plugs protrude.

    Finalize the countertop material. Confirm that your chosen faucet will work with any material more than three quarters of an inch thick. When countertops are to be made from solid surface, check the designer's rendering with an approved fabricator of this material to see it can be made as drawn.

    Choose hardware.

- Design the cabinets. Inform the designer about any unusual-sized storage items or wall coverings that will necessitate a change in their dimensions. Allow a month for a sample of a properly finished cabinet door to be made.

- Plan the storage of all kitchen items in the place where they will be used first. In this manner of organization, a pot for cooking rice is stored at the sink, not the stove, unless a water source is hooked up there.

- Determine the color of the ceiling before choosing light fixtures.

- Choose the location and type of lights first, then their housing.

- Visit a lighting lab to view all surface materials and cabinet finishes you've selected under the lights you specced.

- Decide on paint or wallpaper before specifying light switch plate covers.

UTILITIES

- Delineate lighting, electric, gas, and heating systems on the plan.

- Specify ducts, lines, and outlet points, determining how far they will project from the wall and whether extra storage space is required for their connections. Don't place outlets along a plumbing wall that is to remain unless the exact location of the vent pipe is known.

- Run plumbing fixture choices by the plumber and have the plumber, electrician, and HVAC installer confirm that they can do their work according to your plan without interfering with any of its design.

- Have the electrician evaluate the location of receptacle boxes and whether they should be hung vertically or horizontally, where junction boxes will be needed, and if they can be installed flush with the wall. Determine if power can be drawn from preexisting sources.

- Plan lines, connections, and plugs for telephones, speakers, televisions, intercoms, small appliances, and security systems or a Smart House console. Decide whether you want to plumb an island or wire it for electricity or a telephone. Consider a second telephone line for the construction crew.

- Plan undercabinet fittings so task lights, electric plug strips, and pull-down storage units will fit.

- Confirm that appliances and lights you've chosen will not exceed the electric panel's capability.

- Assess the final plan and confirm that its estimated cost is within budget. Revise plans if necessary.

CONSTRUCTION DRAWINGS

- Do elevation drawings.

- Do exterior drawings of the kitchen with views that illustrate the relationship of the room to the site.

- Do perspective drawings.

- Build a model for a more concrete view.

- Draw up a specification schedule for every product and material to be used.

- Submit drawings to the local building department for plan check.

- Put the job out to bid.

CONSTRUCTION

- Obtain a permit from the local building department.
- Review your insurance policies.
- Order cabinets, remeasuring as the job progresses.
- Set up temporary quarters for eating and sleeping.
- Apartment dwellers: Secure permission for worker and material access and removal.
- Contain or remove any hazardous substances.
- Hold a preconstruction meeting.
- Give the contractor a down payment in exchange for a written work schedule.
- Order all materials. Check the quality of everything as it arrives. Begin teardown when cabinets and materials are in place.
- Pack up the old kitchen.
- Protect furniture with tarps and close off doorways with plastic.
- Carefully monitor the construction process:

    Demolition

    Framing

    Mechanicals

    Insulation

    Dry wall

INSTALLATION

- Orchestrate the order of floors and painting.
- Check every installation with a level.
- Ground all appliances and install a surge protector and ground-fault circuit interrupter.
- Attach doorstops immediately after doors are mounted.
- Install the hood before measuring the backsplash.
- Install soffits before cabinets, making sure the refrigerator will fit and be removable for cleaning and repair.
- Install cabinets before measuring and fabricating countertops.
- Finish moldings *on* job.
- Install the backing for any rail systems before the backsplash.
- Make a final punch list of remaining details and tasks to address.
- Secure all lien releases before paying the contractor in full.

2

CHOOSING THE PLAYERS

ROUNDING UP A REMODELING TEAM

■

Your homework is complete; the type of kitchen you want to build defined. Now you must ascertain the kind of help necessary to realize your dreams. In embarking on this quest you make the transition from the preremodeling to the remodeling phase.

Remodeling a kitchen is a two-pronged process: design and construction (implementation of the design). A choice exists at each crossroad: to do it by yourself or to find someone to help you? Who that special someone is and how and where to find that person depend on your budget and the scope of the project.

Should I do it myself?

If you speak to Tanya Correia, who spent only $500 to redo her kitchen with her husband instead of the $20,000 it would have cost to hire a contractor, doing it yourself may seem the only way to go. And indeed it may be *if* you're (1) creative and (2) a skilled do-it-yourselfer with (3) unlimited free time, (4) well-developed biceps, (5) a simple renovation to undertake, and (6) a very tight budget. Even then doing it yourself can be an invitation to a chain saw massacre. Fixing any mistakes you make may cost more than it would have to hire an outside professional at the onset.

A homeowner with an artistic bent can do a simple layout, but it's less likely to have the flair of a designer's rendering, and as a single remodeler you lack the experience to know if something will fly. As a volunteer for general—not hands-on—contractor,

you still have to know the correct manner in which tasks should be done to be able to evaluate tradespeople's work. Regardless of how they do, they'll be less responsive to you than to someone who hires them regularly. And you'll have to build a tight dependable team, an awesome mission impossible that takes pros years to accomplish. The responsible party, you must purchase workers' compensation and personal liability insurance.

An amateur can certainly pitch in with insulation or assume elementary jobs such as painting cabinets, affixing wallpaper, or changing out countertops or appliances. But in an extensive remodel, limit your assignments to demolition and cleanup times—the beginning and end of the process. This way, if you don't finish when promised, you won't disrupt the job schedule and incur a fine.

Before signing up at the nearest lumberyard, give any commitment serious consideration. My husband thought he would save the $500 survey fee by measuring our property himself. In retrospect, this seemingly simple endeavor took so much time, he would have paid someone double the price to have assumed it. And if anyone wants a T square, he has a once-used model available.

REMODELING PROFESSIONALS

For help with the design phase of a kitchen remodel, you can engage the services of an architect, a kitchen designer, a kitchen and bath appliance or cabinet dealer, an interior designer, or a general contractor. Some distinctions can indeed be made among these professional groups, but they are generalizations not always realized.

In addition to a primary designer, you may have to bring in other professionals, among them a lighting designer; a landscape architect; an energy maven; a soil specialist; a hazardous-material chemist; a mechanical, structural, or electrical engineer; and/or a heating and air-conditioning contractor.

Architect

Among basic designers, architects have the most formal education and comprehensive understanding of spatial and structural relationships. Viewing a house as an integral part of its property, they are prepared to change roof lines, extend the *envelope* of the house, demolish supporting walls, raise ceilings, integrate the kitchen with other rooms, and restore it to its original historic period.

Starting from the exterior, an architect can create an exciting dynamic space but may be at a loss in planning what goes where inside. An architect may not know about the latest materials for a kitchen or how to rev it up for a high-octane performance. Jody Kalish's architect didn't even know how to determine the optimum height of a worktable.

Kitchen Designer

For these tasks, a kitchen designer—more specifically, a *certified kitchen designer* (*CKD*)—steps to the fore after fulfilling the professional requirements of the National Kitchen and Bath Association. Balancing the architect's macro view, this group offers the micro perspective. Though its members may be less sophisticated about studs and bearing walls, or even about forging a fabulous space, they should be on target with the latest kitchen gadgets and innova-

tions. Beginning January 1, 1996, all applicants for CKD were also required to take the National Council on Interior Design qualification exam.

Specialists in the ideal placement of every spoon, kitchen designers work either as independent contractors or as staff at an appliance or cabinet dealer. The latter group tends to produce less individualized kitchens, reworking the same few elements with one from column A and one from column B. Independent designers, in contrast, draw from an unlimited range of materials. Free of the obligation to sell a particular product, they work for you. They charge more, for design—not product—is their income base, but they are, accordingly, more willing to redo layouts until clients are pleased. Independent kitchen designers who handle dens, bedrooms, and other heavily used areas in a home may label themselves *residential space planners*.

Dealer

In addition to staff designers, most cabinet dealers have a network of qualified people to handle the different aspects of a remodeling job, making them a solid one-stop shop—that is, if your remodel is limited to the kitchen and/or bath *and* you like the cabinet lines they represent.

A cabinet dealer with neither a design nor support team can usually help conceive a basic floor plan; design, organize, and integrate cabinets into this plan; or refine another person's cabinet design.

By virtue of their volume, home centers, lumberyards, and builders' supply depots are the dealers offering the lowest price. Despite this advantage, they have not enjoyed a stellar reputation in the past. Employees have been disparagingly called "box salesmen" because they know so little about their cabinets and how to integrate them into a working kitchen.

Selling "by the inch, not by the design," their layouts are limited to a computer's regurgitation of a customer's measurements. Delivery and installation are yours to hassle. Nevertheless, things seem to be looking up at these outlets.

A *Kitchen & Bath Business* magazine survey in

February 1994 found 39 percent of home center shoppers happier with results than they had expected to be as compared to 31 percent of boutique dealers' clients. Home centers may well be a very satisfying means of keeping to a restricted budget as long as the design is kept simple and measurements are made correctly. Nevertheless, for a kitchen to be fully viable and responsive to every movement, it needs to be designed by someone knowledgeable about its underpinnings. By design, I'm speaking neither of style nor of the latest hot looks but of function.

Interior Designer

A kitchen designer can also be found among denizens of the interior design community who have added this room to their portfolio. Accessory sleuths, in search of the unusual, they are especially helpful in choosing a color scheme, detailing design elements such as cornices and moldings, and selecting fabric, wallpaper, hardware, and furniture. When it comes to the latest kitchen products, however, they may not be the savviest. With kitchen designers becoming licensed in interior design, their role in this field may diminish over the next few years.

General Contractor

A general contractor with considerable experience in the kitchen market may be able to help with design of a modest job as well as with construction. On a more lavish scale (in states where it is allowed), some large contracting firms provide what is called *design-build,* or a cornucopia of remodeling services from layout through execution.

Once you move from design phase to construction, the type of professional to hire becomes pretty straightforward: The rule of thumb is to hire a general contractor when more than three different trades are used on a job (unless, of course, you elect to assume this role). The contractor hires the subcontractors and organizes, manages, and monitors the flow of their work to ensure it is performed correctly. The rare renaissance artisan with unlimited skills still exists, but be wary. Julie Bloomer was so

impressed with her carpenter she believed his claim to tile layer fame. His cabinets are great, but you can't walk on the floor.

Watch out, too, for the designer who promises it all. Susan Winston's architect signed on to design the kitchen and decorate the home's interior. Though the woman regularly presented bills for the latter task, her heart wasn't in it, and she'd offer but one or two hastily considered suggestions and then insist the subject was closed. Susan didn't get nearly the help she would have received from an interior designer, who would have charged a lower hourly fee.

After reviewing these various options, you should be able to see which professional best suits your needs. You hire an architect if you're moving outside walls, a kitchen designer if function is most important, a dealer when you're interested mainly in cabinetry, an interior designer when you're into color and swatch, and a contractor to design a simple kitchen and build any job.

Right?

Rarely.

A professional title and license have relatively little meaning since requirements vary greatly from one community to another. In many places, they're yours just for filling out a form. Defining the type of professional to hire is not the only issue, however, for budget can throw a ringer.

A CKD can charge $2,500 for the design phase that pays an architect $10,000; a dealer or design-build company nothing. With design a loss leader employed by design-build companies to snare clients, their design fee, if any, rarely runs more than 5 percent of the entire package. For a dealer, the design is a means of obtaining a commitment. A fee is levied for the design only if you don't proceed with its implementation. Otherwise it is applied toward the purchase of cabinetry, appliances, and materials.

Expect to receive what you pay for. Someone who is not subsidized for his time will probably conceive a plan that is less detailed and sophisticated than one drawn by a designer receiving remuneration.

Who lays out the kitchen is just a small part of

the picture. You must also resolve whether you'll be happier working with a variety of people or with a one-stop design-build firm or full-service cabinet studio. Some professionals wear two hats—designer and contractor or designer and proprietor (or brother-in-law of proprietor) of a construction or cabinet firm.

As convenient as it may be to let one company handle your soup-to-nuts job, you'll miss the checks and balances of working with a separate designer and contractor who can catch each other's mistakes and refine the process. If the cabinet dealer (or someone on staff) does not also assume primary responsibility for designing your kitchen, he or any other individual hired to lay out and build the cabinets will be considered a subcontractor on your job.

Appropriate is a word to consider as well when evaluating what's best for you. A small project doesn't require a large company with a huge overhead, just one sizable enough to handle the scope of the work.

One additional worthy—imperative—expenditure is to engage the designer through the end of the project. Too often the designer disappears when the layout is finished, leaving no one to answer the multitude of questions that arise during construction.

If the designer is not available, his drawings will be misinterpreted as he becomes the scapegoat for contractor errors. If you cannot afford to keep an architect or designer through construction, design the kitchen yourself with the contractor's help and hire a designer as a consultant for as many hours as you can cover.

While the designer must necessarily be part of the construction process, it is also increasingly considered smart practice to book the contractor at the inception of the design phase. This approach delivers the advantages of design-build while involving different people in checks and balances. Bidding becomes a bit more complicated (page 000), but issues raised are easily reconciled. By bringing a contractor in at the beginning, you are more likely to get a realizable design without wasting time and money spinning wheels.

Contractors, unlike architects and designers, know whether things are doable and what they really cost. When brought in after plans are completed, they often declare them ghastly expensive and impossible to build. This is a little late to be getting this information. Construction also runs more smoothly when the contractor joins the team at its starting line and develops a sense of ownership in the project.

Within the design community there is a new trend toward collaboration, whether *ad hoc* or formalized. Whoever brings in the job—and this person varies—is then responsible for building a team of specialists. An architect, for example, can outline the kitchen space and then turn the drawings over to a kitchen designer for detailing. Once everything is in place, an interior designer accessorizes the new room.

Individuals who have worked together previously, and welded their egos into a strong single force, can expedite a job. Nevertheless, I think it is advantageous for you, the consumer, to be the one building the team. This takes more time and energy, but it puts you in control, in the pivotal position of receiving objective independent feedback from the people you hire.

When we're talking about a team and specialists, we're talking about a big complex operation played in a six-figure ballpark. Most of us will score just fine with someone to help us design our kitchen and someone to build it. Just be sure to bring these two people together at the onset and keep them at bat until the job is finished.

PROFESSIONAL FEES

Designers and contractors may charge a *flat fee,* an *hourly consultation fee,* a *percentage of job cost,* or *time, materials, and profit* (what is called *cost-plus*). Or they may bill one way for certain aspects of the job; another for others. A contractor may charge an hourly rate for participating in design meetings and a flat fee, time, materials, and profit, or a percentage of job cost for construction. A designer may charge a flat fee for design services and an hourly consultation fee or percentage of job costs for supervising construction.

Some professionals charge for initial visits. Though I understand the need to bill for time and knowledge, I would not consider someone who charges for an introductory meeting. The client and professional should be spending this encounter sizing each other up and ascertaining if they can work together: It may take many *first visits* with a wide variety of people before the homeowner finds a snug fit. Remodeling jobs demand a great deal of give-and-take and a generosity of spirit. A demand for a payment at this stage does not bode well for the relationship.

Flat Fee

A flat fee is easier to determine if tasks are well delineated. If they are unknown or poorly described, you have to work by the hour or on the basis of time, materials, and profit. Surprises emerge even when the scope of the job is understood. Since it is difficult to estimate exactly, people who charge flat fees build in a fat cushion to cover themselves, for they must honor this price. You pay more than is necessary, but cost is a known entity. Less than satisfactory, it is still the safest way to approach a kitchen remodel and the one most frequently adopted.

Time, Materials, and Profit (Cost-Plus)

Time, materials, and profit is the fairest and most honorable assessment method. The consumer pays a bill reflecting the true cost of the job, while the professional is compensated for the actual work done, without worrying about losing money for underbidding or unanticipated problems. There is just one drawback that makes this arrangement inherently risky: For it to work, the professional must have probity.

There are too many horror stories about the costs of home remodels soaring out of control to risk this approach. I personally wouldn't allow it. Even if accounting is meticulous, how do you figure the time it takes to drive to the dump? Markup and basis (wholesale or retail) must be agreed on beforehand, and there is little incentive for saving money, shopping around, or working quickly and efficiently. You know neither the true cost of the job until it is finished nor what the price would have been had someone else done it.

According to Walter Stoeppelwerth, president of HomeTech, a contractor must mark up costs by 50 percent for any job up to $500,000 and 67 percent beyond that to cover expenses and make a profit. If this is what is needed for a contractor to make money, it should be considered a fair price.

A consumer chancing this approach must identify a contractor who works smart, so costs on which this percentage is based are as low as possible. A ceiling must be established on expenses beforehand and *all* original invoices delivered in advance of payment. Every minute charge needs to be recorded and the work-payment schedule tracked closely (page 48).

Percentage of Construction Cost

Some of the same issues that exist with time, materials, and profit are true of percentage of construction cost. This approach encourages even the best-intentioned designer and contractor to spend time and money with abandon, for the more costly the material chosen, the greater their profit. This seems like an excessive penalty to pay for buying a luxurious item you want.

Percentages vary from roughly 10 to 12 percent for a job that runs less than $100,000. Above that the figure usually falls to 8 or 10 percent.

As with time, materials, and profit, markup and ceilings have to be established, original invoices examined, and the work-payment schedule monitored religiously.

All of these payment systems are blind. Their fairness depends on the honesty of the people you work with. If people want to rip you off, they will. You don't know what goes behind your walls, whether you're paying for labor used on other jobs, or if the contractor has persuaded the subs to cut their prices while charging you the original fee. For peace of mind, hire the best people and trust them. But pay very close attention to the financial aspects of your job.

REFERRAL SOURCES

Getting a recommendation is not always easy. Typical are the words of Dae Medman: "I wish we could recommend somebody to you," Dae says, "but we got screwed by everyone. We interviewed lots of people and still ended up with a house abuser who broke all our doors and windows."

Part of the problem is, as alluded to earlier, the difficulty of identifying the type of professional help you need. The nature of the remodeling industry doesn't help. "It is a strange hybrid," says Dewitt Buel, proprietor of the Kitchen Architect in Los Angeles. "It combines the design elements of architecture, the fashion of the clothing industry, construction of carpentry, and salesmanship of the automobile business. Come see my dog Spot, and we'll get you a kitchen."

Difficult does not mean impossible. With some tenacity, you're likely to find a polished professional through a relative, a friend, or a friend of a friend who has had a good experience. (You do not, however, want to hire these relatives, friends, or friends of friends. Roland Gilbert used *friends* who were *architects*. They turned out to be neither.) As Doug Leland defines the bottom line: "Would I rather be screwed by a friend or by someone I don't know?"

The more recently people have worked with the professional they are recommending, the more valid their impressions are likely to be. Economics and situations change. The person who performed fabulously for your friend may end up defrauding you. Money gets tight. The contractor lets his good people go, and you don't get the same job your friend did.

If help doesn't emerge from your personal network, the prehiring research you conducted in local magazines, trade publications, and decorators' showcase houses may bring someone to the fore whose work appeals. Libraries have collections of design-

ers' work to scan. For more specific suggestions, order the *Greenline Guide to Residential Architects, Kitchens by Professional Designers* (Kasmar Publications), or the *Showcase of Kitchen and Baths* (Vitae Publishing).

Watch ads to see if a matchmaker service has hit your city such as Home Services Alliance (Atlanta) or Designers Previews (New York and Los Angeles) to pair consumers with remodelers. See, too, if a kitchen design course is offered through a local extension or university. Its instructor may be available to help or to suggest someone else who could. This teacher's students or associates are good options, too, when your eye is on the budget.

Professionals who are too busy to do your job may be a good lead to other professionals, as are cabinetmakers, appliance dealers, and contractor supply houses. Authors Jane and Michael Stern found their team through "a . . . painter who had done a crackerjack job" on their house. "It seems that good workmen always know other good workmen," they write, "like a secret society that lucky homeowners might have the good fortune to stumble into."

Professional organizations are usually quite cooperative in providing the names of local members. For a list, contact the American Institute of Architects (AIA), National Kitchen & Bath Association (NKBA), American Society of Interior Designers (ASID), Residential Space Planners International (RSPI), National Association of the Remodeling Industry (NARI), National Home Improvement Council (NHIC), and the Remodelers Council of the National Association of Home Builders (NAHB). You might also query people on the city planning board or go on the offensive, driving through neighborhoods where workers are engaged in the business of remodeling. If you don't feel brave enough to ring doorbells, you can at least copy phone numbers from their panel trucks.

THE INTERVIEW PROCESS

Once you have obtained a list of appropriate professionals for your job, conduct a series of interviews to identify the proper people to hire, being sure they can work together. (Within this group, there are likely to be both hes and shes. Rather than making you wade through lists of *he or she*, I've opted for the politically incorrect form when I can't get away with using a plural. Please rest assured that my heart is in the right place, even if my pen is not.)

The interview and follow-up information contained in this section is pertinent regardless of the type of professional you interview and the point in the process you choose to approach them. No one, understandably, has time to invest in dead-end meetings, and you will find yourself pressured to sign a contract at the first encounter. Ignore the squeeze.

After an initial round of interviewing, narrow your choices and then take as much time as necessary to feel comfortable making a final selection. Watching personalities and interactions over time as you pursue preferences, observe follow-through, and ask further questions will be more indicative of what someone will be like to work with than a snap decision based on professional credentials. It never gets better than it is during this courtship period.

Price will, of necessity, be important, but it should be only one of many factors. Someone may operate a successful business, maintain a professional demeanor, and acquire excellent references without speaking your language or sharing your taste. Your friend may love this person. You may not. Find out before making a commitment.

With the goal of the interview process to identify the best person to hire for your remodel, meetings must be held with the person you will be working with. Big firms often send salespeople to pitch the job, introducing its executioner only when the gun goes off. That's not the moment to discover you hate the person you will be confronting daily, half-asleep and stressed out with your teeth unbrushed.

Telltale Signs of a Good Match

Does the person show up on time for an appointment? Return phone calls? Appear organized with paper and pencil? Remember to bring promised materials and complete the bid as scheduled (page 66)? Write a thank-you or follow-up note?

Does the person look and speak as if he is successful? Does he exude confidence and seem to know the business? Does the potential contractor drive a car or truck that can be used to haul materials? (Regardless of the vehicle's condition, you can count on its having frequent breakdowns once the job starts and its owner is expected at the site.)

Is attire appropriate? (Avoid contractors who wear suits and have clean manicured nails.)

Has the person done kitchens with the materials, style, and quality level you like? Has he had experience with your type of job before, or would he be getting in over his head?

How easy is it to communicate with the person? Do you have the same sense of humor? Does the candidate inspire trust? Attempt to find out about you and your lifestyle? Show interest in your perspective of the project? When problems come up, how easy will it be to solve them together? Does the person listen?

The teacher of my kitchen design class stressed listening as the most important trait of a good designer or contractor. Ignoring his own advice, he dismissed the plans I showed him of my kitchen as "stupid." "No one needs a restaurant range or two dishwashers," he said resolutely, never giving me the opportunity to explain I was a professional cook.

Bottom line: Do you like the person?

General Interview Format

Exact questions should be structured in such a way that a comparison among candidates' responses will provide enough information for you to choose the best person for the job. The following subjects should prove useful to explore. To get answers, you may have to make inferences and explore several different avenues of questioning.

- What are the address and telephone number of the person's business?

- Has the person or his company been in business for at least five years?

- Where does the person live? Where does he do most of his work? (The closer the person's home, office, and other jobs are to your venue, the easier to get him there, and the faster your job will move.)

- Is the person familiar with your municipal codes?

- Is the person a prominent member of the community?

- Has the person won any awards? Had his work featured in books or magazines?

- How many kitchens has he done? How much did they cost? What materials and appliances were used in them?

- What is the person's educational background?

- What would the person's dream kitchen be? What would it contain?

- Who is the person's favorite cabinetmaker? What cabinet companies or craftspeople has he worked with before? Has he installed lower-priced stock cabinets? Which ones? Has he done anything creative in the use and combination of their elements? What cabinet door style does he like best? If the person works solely with a particular cabinet line, do you like these cabinets? Does the person feel comfortable working with any cabinets you have in mind?

- Has the person had experience with these special contingencies or needs you have? (If, for example, you are living in a log cabin, the person must deal with the boards' irregularity before hanging cabinets. If you want a brick arch over a cooktop, you need someone experienced with this construction, someone who knows that it needs to be stepped back to leave counter space on each side of the burners.)

- Does the person like your house? Your taste? (Believe it or not, most people will tell you this without a specific query. If not, you can usually tell. Ask directly if you have any doubts. You do not want to work with someone who doesn't like your taste.)

- What does the person do better than or differently from his competitors?

- What kinds of problems has he encountered in his jobs? How has he dealt with them? Has he been sued? How were his suits resolved?

- How does the person deal with any personal traits you may have that could cause a problem? (Are you a perfectionist? Slow to make decisions? Likely to change your mind frequently? Characteristics such as these will surface, so you want to ensure that the person can deal with them.)

- How does the person organize his job schedule? What records does he keep?

- How does the person keep up to date, tracking new materials and technological advances in the industry?

- What trade organizations or other professional groups does the person belong to? Which trade shows does he attend? How recently?

- What professional publications does the person read (*Kitchen & Bath Business, Kitchen & Bath Design News, Wood Digest, Reeves Journal, Remodeling*)?

- What are the person's hobbies? (Chat him up. In Cleveland, it's reportedly impossible to get a contractor to appear during fishing and hunting season.)

- Does the person work by himself? Or is he a member of a partnership or an employee of a large company? Does he have the structure and staff to take on your job? Which of his team members would be involved in your project?

- What other consultants or subcontractors would he call in? How would he interact with these other professionals? Who would be in charge?

- How would the person approach your project? Which steps would he take? In what sequence?

- How busy is the person currently? When could he start your job? How does he view its time frame?

- What other jobs does the person have going simultaneously? How would he go back and forth between them? (How would he ensure that your job remained a top priority?)

- Can the person work within your budget? (This is not the time to give away your hand and reveal how much you are willing to spend. Ferret out the answer to this question by asking the contractor the average price of his jobs, and what he thinks yours will run.)

- How easily does this person discuss money? If he can't, he won't be able to deal with it on the job.

- What kind of fee schedule does the person employ?

- Will the person allow you to use the designer's or contractor's contract (page 367)? (If not, request a copy of the contract he will accept.)

Designer Information to Seek

- Does the person cook? What kind of food does he prepare? (Is it similar to your style of cooking? Though not always the case, someone who operates as you do in a kitchen will be more likely to tailor a more practical space.)

- Does the person ask why you want something, indicating that he will try to plan for your needs?

- Does the person do all the design work himself, or will he be turning it over to a draftsperson? Does he employ a two-tiered system with one charge for the primary worker and different fees for assistants and draftspeople?

- If the designer is an architect, determine his depth of experience with kitchens and whether you will be saddled with the additional cost of hiring a kitchen designer.

- If the person is an independent designer, inquire whether he takes responsibility for getting necessary input from dealers, contractors, or engineers or if he moves the plans only as far as his expertise extends and then turns them over to the client to run with. (A designer who leaves the consumer to oversee the job is considered a consultant. Unless you want to assume this management role, look for someone who takes complete charge.)

- How much time is this person willing to spend educating you about options? How will he do so?

- How many passes will this person make at redoing your plans until you like them? What if you don't like them?

- How will this person be involved in helping you select materials?

- Can the designer jump-start the referral process by recommending neighborhood contractors available for your project?

- What experience has this person had in lighting kitchens? (Request photos of any lighting designs he has done.)

- If the person brings a portfolio of his previous work, assess its quality. Do his rooms look practical? Do you like them? (Request photos if he hasn't brought them.)

Contractor Information to Seek

- Has the contractor received a Certified Remodeler (CR) degree from NARI? (Although not a guarantee of excellence, it indicates the contractor's interest in improving his professional skills and status.)

- Has the contractor received a Certified Graduate Remodeler (CGR) degree from NAHB? (Again, this is not a stamp of approval but an example of professional commitment.)

- Does the contractor do the work himself, supervise it, or turn it over to a team? (The hands-on contractor does not have as high an overhead or payroll to meet.)

- How much time would he spend at your site?

- Where and how does the contractor find his subcontractors? How many subs does he use? Does he depend on one person to be a jack-of-all-trades or hire a specialist for each phase? How long has he worked with them? Are they licensed? Are they independent subcontractors or members of his regular crew who depend on him for their economic support?

- Has he previously installed the appliances you are considering? With more and more products arriving with metric fittings, it is common to encounter equipment not previously serviced and to have problems arise from this lack of experience. Stories making the rounds tell of subs throwing basic parts away and then having to jury-rig the system.

■ If a technical line of questioning doesn't reveal the person who will be the best fit for your job, try a different approach. Find out what radio stations the potential contractor and his subs enjoy. Be sure you like them, for if you're at the job site, you'll be listening too. (You might also want to inquire if the interviewee eats Twinkies. *Remodeling* magazine has connected a report identifying the highest U.S. consumption of Hostess Twinkies in the Midwest and South to the fact that construction economies are healthiest in these regions.)

After you conduct interviews, several designers and contractors usually stand out from the pack as serious candidates. This can be one person or several people, depending on the length of your interview list, the nature of the job, and your mutual affinity. Some people will disqualify themselves, and you will eliminate others. If those who remain don't feel instinctively right, find other people to interview.

Once you make a final cut, thoroughly check references. To do so, speak to previous clients and visit completed jobs as well as work in progress where orderliness, cleanliness, and quality can be observed firsthand.

Though the most meaningful recommendations usually come from people you know, it's important to check with others as well. Tom Philbin, author of *How to Hire a Home Improvement Contractor Without Getting Chiseled*, suggests asking for fifteen to twenty references. This may seem like overkill, but it should be a drop in the bucket for a seasoned pro. Anyone can come up with three names who will vouch for them. Better a large list from which you can choose randomly.

Visit kitchens built by the same subs who will work on your space and that fall within your budget. Notice if they all look the same or whether they were customized to fit their occupants' style. Look carefully at details and workmanship. Are light switches on straight? Do structures look solid and heights line up? Do doors and windows open smoothly? Were cabinets and walls well sanded? Neatly caulked and painted? Are drywall seams and nails popping through?

Ask to see blueprints of previous projects. Are they neat, thorough, and well detailed? Do layouts appear practical for the family they were designed for? Dead giveaways that a designer knows little about kitchens: Wine storage up high or near the stove where heat rises and destroys it, second sinks with little or no counter space on either side, pots hanging above the cooktop where they'll get greasy, or windows placed dangerously behind a cooktop.

Some things you dislike may reflect the homeowners' taste and choice rather than the designer's or contractor's skill, so clarify why they were done that way.

Reference Queries

■ Were the designer's plans biddable and buildable?

■ Did the kitchen look like the homeowner expected and wanted it to?

■ Does the kitchen cook? Does it function well? Is it easy to prepare a meal in this space?

■ What would the homeowners do differently? Why didn't they do it originally?

■ *Did the job come in on time?*

■ *Did the job come in on budget?*

■ What kind of fee schedule was used with this person? How did it work out? (If it feels comfortable, ask the reference to show you his job records. Check how well they were kept.)

■ Were there any unexpected charges?

■ How easy were the designer, the contractor, and their teams to work with?

■ Were there any subs or assistants they weren't happy with?

■ How did they resolve problems? Willingly? Amicably?

■ How was the quality of the work? Attention to details?

■ Did the contractor have to compensate for problems created by their workers or subs such as walls not being plumb?

- Did the workers respect the reference's home and belongings? Were they polite to members of the household?

- Did they leave the work site clean each day?

- Did the last tasks get taken care of immediately, or did they drag on?

- Was the person you're checking on willing to come back after the project was finished and deal with any problems? Did he honor warranties?

- Does the reference know other people who used this designer or contractor other than the names you were given?

- What did the reference like about the person you are checking? What did he dislike? Would he hire this person again?

FINAL SCREENING

Regardless of how glowing the references and positive your instinctual feelings toward a potential designer or contractor, don your best gumshoes and fact-check carefully before hiring. This advice is not the ravings of a paranoid but the reality testing of someone who has paid dearly for her basic trusting nature. If you are lucky to hook up with people who have integrity, this will all seem for naught. But when problems arise, you will be thankful for these documents.

Too many jobs are going astray. Too many seemingly nice responsible professionals are turning out to be jerks and, worse, liars, thieves, and rip-off artists. Confidence isn't built on numbers from the national Institute on Drug Abuse, either, which characterizes construction workers as consuming more drugs and alcohol than hirelings in any other job category.

The recommendations that follow may seem so complicated at first reading that you'll worry about having to quit your job and give up your social life to fulfill them. Don't panic. I'm not talking about much more than a few telephone calls that can be done over whatever period you need to work it into your schedule. That is why I suggested allowing some months for the hiring process.

First, visit the person's stated place of business to confirm it exists.

Ask to see a license if your city and/or state offers one, along with a second piece of identification. Ask for a photocopy of these documents assuring the person that this is your method of record keeping, not an indication of distrust. Confirm whether the contractor is a sole proprietor, a partner in a corporation, or an employee of a large company. Record the names of the company's owners and officers if they differ.

Confirm a contractor's license and date of expiration with the contractor's board. If you work with unlicensed people, you will be held personally liable for accidents and they will not be legally bound to resolve disputes or honor warranties. This can also invalidate your insurance policies. If your contractor splits, you will be ineligible for money from the protection fund licensed contractors contribute to in some states. While you're at it, check to see if your state has this fund.

The National Association of State Contractors maintains a Disciplinary Data Bank in participating states with lists of individuals who have had their licenses revoked. To check, call (602) 953-2210. Also check with the Better Business Bureau, consumer affairs agency, local building department, and trade association to see if any complaints have been lodged.

Ask to see the contractor's insurance policy with the company's tax ID number and amounts of workers' compensation and personal liability that covers you if property is damaged or someone is injured while work is under way. Photocopy these insurance policies, noting both the carrier's and agent's names, addresses, and telephone numbers. Confirm that the same name is used on the policy as on the license.

My contractor went through a wall of one room where he wasn't working and one where he was, destroying the wallpaper in both places. The papers were, of course, no longer being made, so I had to re-cover both rooms. My insurance company covered some of the expense, but I ended up paying a sizable deduction (as well as spending time getting new paper) since I did not have the contractor's insurance information. We may have eventually been able to recover the money, but we had a "no subrogation" clause in our contract, meaning our insurance company could not go after his. You don't want one of these.

Get proof and copies of any bonds the contractor holds.

Run a credit check as well. If you are borrowing money, the lender will conduct the check. If not, the Better Business Bureau may give you access to its Dun & Bradstreet account to research possible complaints.

Get a list of suppliers from the potential contractor and check to see if they are paid regularly and in a timely fashion.

Get a list of subcontractors to be used on the job. Check to see how long they have worked with the contractor, how they view him as an organizer and financial manager, whether they have been paid as agreed, and if there have been any lien problems.

Ask to see samples of records and billings from previous jobs. Are they neat, well detailed, and easy to follow? Pay particular attention to records of cost-plus jobs. They must be kept impeccably in order for assessment to be accurate.

Finally, if the designer or contractor deals with a particular line of cabinets or will be hiring a local shop to build your boxes, see at least three different samples in situ.

So? You've conducted all your interviews, followed up references, and fact-checked credentials. Ad nau-

seam and in depth. Probably—hopefully—one of those people that felt right to hire has panned out. If not, once again start interviewing anew.

The best person for your job is the right person. (I know: Thank you; that helped a lot.) This has less to do with the initials after someone's name than with his particular interests, taste, and experience, mutual emotional compatibility, and your pocketbook. A caveat: I felt such an affinity for my first architect I now buy my clothes where she does. From this relationship I got a nice wardrobe and a layout she forgot to put a refrigerator in. Our friendly architect took me and my $5,000. Having good chemistry with the person you hire is not necessarily the most important attribute.

Once and often burned, I still believe compatibility and common taste are valuable traits, but probably more important is the designer's ability to hear what the client wants. These characteristics are also noteworthy in a contractor; organizing, managing, and juggling skills are imperative.

One of the few ways you can protect yourself is by identifying an ethical person for this endeavor. As the personal ads attest, there is someone for everyone. Finding that special someone, though, is sometimes merely a matter of plain dumb luck or karma. If your karma or aura is out of whack, recourse exists in a fair contract and payment schedule.

WRITING CONTRACTS FOR SUCCESS

■

Two Strikes and You're Out

"In every era," Tracy Kidder writes in *House,* "numbers of people have prepared for the construction of houses as they have prepared for death, by getting their wishes down in writing." Today, a great deal more than wishes needs to be expressed on paper.

With contracts typically drawn up by the designer or contractor, it's not surprising they are

biased against the consumer. Setting out to rectify this disparity, I expect many of these professionals to balk at the following terms that firmly brake ongoing unsavory practices. Reassuring to them, I hope, is the demand that a good contract be equitable for *both* consumer and professional.

The key to the job's structure, *the contract's impor-*

tance cannot be overemphasized. This is not some *pro forma* piece of paper but your guarantor, insurer, and savior; a promise note that a job will go well and any sour relationships immediately be severed. Protect yourself regardless of how good you feel about your designer and contractor. Problems occur even when no ill will is intended. Carley, the respected construction company charged with the renovation of the historic Mission Inn in Riverside, California, declared bankruptcy at $2 million over budget, done in by termites hiding in the walls.

A good contract completely describes the job in writing. Leaving nothing to interpretation, it eliminates potential areas for misunderstanding. It is user-friendly, omitting intimidating legal jargon. Meeting these objectives makes the document quite lengthy, but do not fear its size. Its inclusiveness is your protection.

A Good Contract . . .

- Lists all tasks and responsibilities for both homeowners and professionals.

- Mentions every job cost excluded from the contract as well as what is included. If it doesn't, you may—once you get over the shock—find yourself minus some basics. One writer "made the erroneous assumption that the tile installer who ripped out the baseboards when he demolished the old floor would naturally install new ones." Of all things! Marlene Sorosky was told everything in her remodel was included in the contract, yet each time she asked about missing objects such as doorknobs she was informed they were extra. Since the homeowner has no way of knowing what would naturally be included or excluded, the onus of mentioning exclusions should fall to the designer and contractor.

- Devises an incremental fee schedule that links each small payment to the completion of precise tasks.

- Avoids open-ended, meaningless buzzwords such as *reasonable time, workmanlike,* and *match.* The new cement *matching* our walkway is gray with a pink cast. Our walkway is red.

- Concretely describes the quality you seek.

- Includes a formula for a Las Vegas divorce. Once a relationship flounders, you want to terminate it swiftly and easily, cutting everyone's losses early on. Philip Roy used an AIA contract that assumed the architect to be the good guy; the contractor the bad. When he went to fire his contractor, he found he couldn't dissolve the contract without the architect's approval. She, as evil as the contractor, was long gone when he needed her permission. With all professionals unknown at the start of a job, the consumer must maintain control.

Do not sign a clause that you "have reviewed the contract plans and specifications and understand what you are getting." Most of us don't comprehend the process well enough to understand what we are getting even when we get it.

You should have a separate contract with everyone you work with who is not covered under the contractor's contract. This will be considerably briefer for an appliance or cabinet installer than a contractor or designer, yet it still needs to contain the information listed in this section. *No area should be left to assumption, interpretation, or guesswork.*

Before signing a contract, you may want to have it reviewed by a lawyer specializing in home remodeling and construction. This person can also represent you should a problem arise down the line. For recommendations, contact the bar association in your area.

Many of the following areas may be specified precisely on the final bid or construction documents. When this is the case, these documents can be referred to instead of being spelled out in the contract.

CONTRACTOR'S CONTRACT CONSIDERATIONS

Vital Statistics

- Contractor's name, business address, and business telephone number.

- License number of contractor, his partners or owners of the firm, and anyone else involved in the remodel.

- Insurance company, agent, and policy numbers for workers' compensation and personal liability.

- Bonding company, agent, and filing numbers for any lien, performance or completion bond, or their equivalents held by the contractor (see discussion under Liens, page 49).

- Name, address, telephone number, and designated officer of any funding control office or other company responsible for payments if different from contractee.

- Name, address, and telephone number of contractee. Address and telephone number of venue if different.

Contract Exclusions

A statement should be made stating that the contractor is financially responsible for all costs, materials, and work in the remodel that are not specifically excluded in the contract. Anything that is to be excluded should be stated here. Possible exclusions:

- Costs of transportation, photocopying, long-distance telephone calls, postage, etc.

- Special jobs that the homeowner(s) contracts for separately such as heating and air-conditioning, asbestos or other hazardous waste removal, security, soil or water analysis, landscaping, engineering, earth moving or grading, etc.

- Unforeseen problems such as rot or termites. (Responsibility for these problems needs to be assigned and the procedure for handling them described.)

- Special materials and supplies not covered in the contract. (The plumber hit me up for $185 worth of supplies that had never been mentioned in the contract. Forewarned, we could have negotiated responsibility. If nothing else, I could have purchased these items myself for considerably less money.)

Schedule

Make sure the following are specified:

- The date the contract is signed.

- Effective starting date of the contract.

- The date by which all materials and cabinets will be ordered. The number of days after their arrival that demolition begins and work effectively starts. Once the contractor hooks a job with a signed contract, many moons may elapse before he begins work. ("They get you pregnant, and then they dangle you.") Discourage this behavior by declaring the document null and void if work doesn't begin within five days of the stated date.

- Projected completion date with definition of completion as the removal of all items from the final *punch* (check) list. Define what constitutes completion carefully, for final payment is due on that date.

Communication

In this section you structure a formal process of communication among designer, contractor, and homeowner(s), scheduling frequency of communication by telephone and regular meeting. Also formalize the direction of communication. Do you communicate only through the designer or directly with the contractor (answer "both" here)? Does the contractor contact one or the other homeowner or both to solve a problem or get an okay? One person is quicker; two is safer. Is the designer included in this loop?

Plan for updating the work schedule. Determine who will draw up and maintain the task list and how often it will be reviewed and an assessment made that the job is on track and progressing as scheduled.

Require both the designer and the contractor to wear beepers so communication is fast and direct and problems are handled instantly. No message centers or telephone answering machines. If you are not readily accessible during work hours, carry a beeper, too. Our architect said she would not work with our contractor unless he got a beeper. He got one, but she was never available to speak with him.

Specify that homeowners are to be notified when an inspection is scheduled so you can be there if desired.

Ensure that you will be shown all materials before installation, especially those going in the ground and behind walls that will be closed off from view.

Insist that the contractor introduce each subcontractor to you before the person starts work and that the contractor, subcontractor, and you review work to be done together.

Demand that the contractor, subcontractor, and supplier inform you when they encounter an error in the design, a potential problem with a specified product, or an incorrectly specified product. This must be done before any work begins on the task in question. If you want work to proceed regardless, this must be stated in writing. Omission of this step transfers financial liability to the contractor for fixing any resulting problem.

After her contractor walked off the job, Ruth Friedman tried to get the skylight fixed that was turning her kitchen into a hot box. The company showed her the contractor's invoice with its disclaimer statement, saying it did not recommend the type of glass and would accept no responsibility for it. Neither the contractor nor the installers had discussed this with Ruth.

My architect specced the wrong kind of slate. The subcontractor told the contractor, who put it in anyway. When I confronted the contractor, he said, "I was just doing what the architect told me." The subcontractor said, "I was just doing what the contractor told me."

"I was just doing what I was told" is the mournful mantra of screw-ups on a remodeling job. And when there is no one else to blame, workers develop a serious case of retrograde amnesia.

Mistakenly viewing the contractor as their only referral source, purveyors and subcontractors are loyal to the contractor instead of to the homeowner, an allegiance that often leads to malpractice.

Hopefully, subs will eventually recognize satisfied homeowners as a much better referral source than unscrupulous contractors.

Work Site

How will parts of the house to be remodeled be readied for this work? Furniture moved, dishes packed, etc.? Who is responsible for this? What needs to be accomplished? By when?

How will parts of the home not involved in the remodel be segregated from the work site and protected from filth? How will plants, shrubbery, and the garden be guarded from destruction? Who is responsible for setting up this system and maintaining it?

Who is responsible for removing trash and debris? How will it be done? Who will pay for it?

A Dumpster can be rented through a company that collects its contents each day or after a specified period and may require a permit. A less expensive way to dispose of trash may be to hire a hauling company or a gardener or worker with a truck. Delineate a place for the debris box and pathway to it.

What will cleanup consist of each day? Who will be responsible for it? How will refuse be disposed?

Jeremy Tailor's contract specified that his house had to be "broom clean" when workers departed. Before long, he had to hire a cleaning lady each day so he could continue to live in the house. As plastic came off protected areas, it was not replaced. Even more disconcerting, the paper laid down to protect the floors was attached with tape that removed its finish.

Who is responsible for turning off lights and making the house secure before workers leave each day? How will this be done? When the roof or doors are removed during construction, how will exposed areas be boarded up?

Who is responsible for keeping doors and windows closed during the workday and for monitoring access to the house, discouraging thieves and job-seeking intruders who follow debris boxes?

Who is responsible for securing the work site to prevent injury, particularly to curious neighborhood children? How will this be accomplished?

How are materials to be protected from theft or damage from inclement weather? Who is responsible for replacing materials stolen from the site?

What is the contractor's responsibility for damage to other parts of the house and to the contractee's belongings?

What bathroom facilities will be available for workers? Will they use your facilities or a *porta-toilet*?

Who will pay for a rented unit? We set aside a bathroom for the workers, but many of these individuals, from my horrified firsthand observation, preferred our backyard.

What telephone will they use? How will its access be controlled? Who will pay for it? It will be less expensive to let workers use your line or install an additional one than to turn them loose on a portable. Put all phones under lock and key and give the job foreman responsibility for keeping a user's log. Accounting will improve if any unclaimed calls come out of his pocket. Unmonitored, you can count on a minimum bill of several hundred dollars each month. Most of it will be to a worker's Aunt Madie in Europe, not to a supplier for your job. Initially I shared my line with the workers. But after one too many people interrupted my business calls with the announcement that they wanted to order a pizza, I put in a separate line.

Where will pets be harbored, and who will be responsible for letting them in and out? Ditto children?

Who will sign for UPS and Federal Express? Where will mail be placed when it arrives each day? Agree, too, on where registered lien notices should be sent. Since we were rarely on site when they arrived, we found ourselves continually waiting in line at the post office.

Contractor Obligations

State that the contractor is responsible for hiring all subcontractors and workers on the job: If you have a subcontractor you want to work with, pass the name on to the contractor, but the ultimate choice should be the contractor's.

Securing permits. State cost, location, and name of permit.

Assuming financial responsibility for errors. The script I followed went like this: The architect specified something incorrectly, the contractor unthinkingly built it as specified, and then I paid extra money to have it redone correctly. If the contractor (and architect) knew they would have to pay for mistakes or correct them without charge, one can conclude with 99.9 percent accuracy that there would be fewer errors.

Performing all work to code and in compliance with hazardous waste removal laws or redoing the work at his own expense.

Delineate the contractor's actual responsibilities at the job site. Will he be hands-on or advisory? When and for how long will he be there each day? (If his presence is not stipulated, he will rarely appear.) State who will be responsible for monitoring his work when he is not there.

I was pressured into paying extra for a supervisor to track my job when the contractor wasn't there. Several months into the process, the contractor fired the supervisor, obligating us to pay the contractor the supervisor's fee as well as his own fee (not that he came by any more). Rip-off.

Unless you are doing a huge job, the contractor's fee should cover managerial tasks. If it doesn't, you have to ask why you are paying a contractor. Another scheme is to hire a construction manager to keep tabs on the contractor. I don't know whom you hire to keep track of him, but in the meantime, you have just absolved the contractor of responsibility and taken away his *raison d'être*.

Other Responsibilities

Specify who is responsible for securing product catalogs and installation instructions.

Specify who is responsible for ordering materials. No matter who does the ordering, all materials must be ordered in your name and be paid for by you only after being delivered to the job site. Granite that Julianne Kemper ordered and paid for was delivered to the offices of the subcontractor who had ruined her floors. Not a problem. He kept the granite hostage until receiving the monies for his substandard work.

Specify who is responsible for delivering and installing each material. If you are doing the purchasing, you'll most likely still want the contractor to be responsible for delivery and installation.

Describe what work, if any, you will be responsible for and the date by which it must be accomplished.

Procedures

In this section, specify materials or equipment to be saved from demolition. Also list *every* item to be utilized in the job with its brand name, model, dimensions, weight, grade, quality rating, color, finish, and quantity. This includes all construction materials. One would think that an experienced contractor would know you had to use a washable paint in the kitchen and a halogen spot for an art niche. Don't. Specify what you want. If you don't call for a stainless light switch plate with a dimmer, you'll get a less expensive plastic one. Forget to mention you want casement windows and you'll have a slider slid in on you.

Describe the materials and method of installation to be used for every task. How is granite going to be supported? Tile inlaid?

Detail cabinets according to what has been decided about them up to this point. State the brand name or the name of the cabinetmaker. State the contractor's responsibilities for production, delivery, and installation of cabinets. If the contractor is not responsible for detailing cabinets, state who is. Draw up a separate contract with the cabinet company or cabinetmaker as well (page 156).

Clarify what will be done with unused materials; whether returned, sold to the contractor, or given to you.

Payment Schedule

When a problem arises on a job, it is usually because payments have not been pegged to completed work, and the contractor has gotten ahead of the homeowner. The problem also happens in reverse with the contractor hanging out on a limb, having done too much work without compensation for a client who never intended to pay up.

No matter what type of fee schedule you agree on (page 35), payments should be made in very small increments and in accordance with precise tasks accomplished and specific invoices submitted. Both the chores and the amount of money due at that point must be formalized. Otherwise, you could be the homeowners who paid the entire $250,000 budgeted to gut and remodel their house before realizing that only one-fifth of the work had been done. When a sub queried the contractor on his unethical practices, he said, "These people would have never hired me if I had told them the true cost of their job. This way I collected a weekly payment until they caught on and fired me."

Like purveyors of the world's oldest trade, remodeling professionals want their money up front. With many references suggesting the staggering down payment of 30 to 50 percent, it's not surprising to hear of contractors who ride off into the sunset when they are paid, never to be heard from again.

With no expenses until work actually starts, there is nary a reason for a down payment on a remodeling job. *A contractor who is not solvent enough financially to earn the first payment before receiving it is not stable enough to hire.* Some states specify a down payment ceiling, but none should be necessary.

When the contractor states he needs a 10 percent deposit to order materials, tell him you will pay for each product as he orders it and presents you with a formal bill. When he says 40 percent of the job must be paid the day the project begins, tell him you will pay for each piece of work as it is finished. If you don't pay as promised, he doesn't start the next job. With this arrangement, all players are protected.

The day work starts, a $100 or so payment seems reasonable in exchange for a *work-payment schedule.* This contractor-generated schedule should list each task to be performed and the date by which it is to be completed. Each payment point needs to be described clearly. It is not sufficient to specify the amount due when "framing is finished"; *framing* and *finished* need to be defined.

Each payment should account for no more than a few percentage points of the total job, so you can expect to be making several payments a week. When cabinets or other big-ticket items are at stake, break their payments down into small increments as well. *If you are not happy with a job or material, don't pay for it until you are.*

By linking work to a payment schedule, you track expenditures (even on a time and materials job) so they don't get out of line. This way you won't wake up one morning like the duped homeowners in the sad tale told earlier.

As further protection, the contract should contain a *retention fee* clause stating that 10 to 20 percent of the amount due should be held back from each payment until the job is complete. Whatever is held back should be substantial enough to motivate the contractor to return and rectify a problem.

Make the final payment in two installments: Pay 50 percent after all items have been checked off the final punch list *to satisfaction* and 50 percent thirty days later to cover any problems that emerge in the interim. In addition to these precautions, track bills very carefully so you don't pay for the same thing twice.

With many frustrated remodelers reporting they can't get the contractor back to complete the last few details on the punch list, you might want to establish a *completion date,* after which point no payment will be made. The contractor forfeits the money due, and you hire someone else to complete his work.

The payment schedule should include the point the payment will be presented, to whom it will be submitted, the person responsible for making the payment, time frame for payment, and any late payment penalty fee. State, too, whether payment will be by cash, personal check, or certified check.

The contractor typically submits the bill to the architect or designer, who reviews it, verifying appropriate charges before passing it on to the clients for payment. An excellent safeguard, this strategy is only as good as its players. David Martin apprised his architect of a poorly executed installation, yet she approved the bill without bothering to ascertain firsthand what work had been performed or the quality of its outcome.

Payment Penalties

A *penalty fee* clause should be placed in the contract stating the amount of money the contractor owes the homeowner for every day beyond the specified completion date he has not finished the job. Some people feel this clause encourages sloppy workman-

ship because the contractor will rush to finish by the penalty date. Others are concerned that the contractor will walk off a job he can't complete on time. Regardless, include the clause. You can always renegotiate the date if both parties agree.

You, too, should pay a penalty if the job is held up because you didn't finish work assumed by a promised date.

Balance a penalty with a *reward fee* clause, or additional incentive for finishing early. As part of this scenario, state the hours workers have access to the house. This protects contractors from less-than-scrupulous homeowners who ban entrance when they see a reward coming due.

At $200 a day, George Peters's contractor owed him over $71,000 when he finally walked off the unfinished job one-year-plus beyond his promised completion date. There was no reason for him not to have finished other than his own ineptitude and poor judgment. Although Mr. Peters never collected a cent of the money, the clause's existence acted as a deterrent when the contractor threatened a suit because his last bill wasn't paid.

Liens

A mechanic's or materialman's *lien* is a legal motion a worker or supplier can file against your property if he has not been paid by the contractor. As mind-bogglingly hard as this is to believe, you may have to pay off the lien even if you have already paid the contractor in full for the work in question. You will also have to hire a lawyer. Why this is not double jeopardy, I don't know.

Although lien laws vary across the country, they usually prohibit the owner from refinancing, selling, or transferring ownership of a property while a lien is slapped against it. In Michigan and other states, the government pays off the lien if the contractor is licensed. Don't breathe too easily if a lien is not filed within the required period. Workers and suppliers can sue you regardless.

The greatest safeguard against a lien is to include a *release of lien* clause in the contract stating that the contractor is to be held legally and financially responsible for any liens filed for lack of payment. Protect yourself further by *writing checks directly to these subcontractors and suppliers or jointly to the contractor and the other individual.* This approach may be difficult to negotiate with a fixed-fee contract, but it is a battle worth fighting.

The contractor is legally bound to provide a *preliminary notice of intent to file a lien* from every subcontractor who works on your job so you are aware of who has these rights. Check with these people as work progresses to be sure they are being paid. Make each payment only in exchange for a *partial lien release* (interim payment) and a *final lien release* (final payment). This goes for cabinets and materials as well as for workers. The contractor should be responsible for getting the releases. No exceptions. No release, no money.

When all final releases are in hand, then—and only then—do you make the final payment to the contractor, for this starts the lien clock ticking.

As another option, the contractor can obtain a *payment bond* that guarantees no liens will be filed against the property. A *performance* or *contract bond* is available, too, pledging compensation if the contractor does not finish the job. Some states require one automatically as part of licensure. Bonds, however, are expensive, and you pay for them—either directly or indirectly. And then you have the unrequited frustration of trying to collect on them!

Change Orders

A *change order* is any alteration in the approved construction documents. On occasion, this is a necessity: An inspector may demand it; an unexpected problem can crop up. Even if communication is good, you may not get everything right the first time or know you don't want something until you see it. Nevertheless, make it clear from the onset that you neither expect nor condone change orders.

The result of a last-minute whim or poor planning—remodeling as you go—change orders can destroy a budget. Throwing the process out of whack, they ring up additional costs, delaying the job and revising workers' schedules. Seemingly in cahoots, designers and contractors count on these extra costs-on-the-run to increase their profit from the job. "It's only a few hundred dollars extra," they posture. "What's the big deal?"

"Watch out for the inevitable male-bonding ritual that goes on between male contractors and homeowners during the first 66 percent of the construction process," advises attorney David M. Orbach. "Before you know it, you've put enough insulation in the house to keep Alaska warm and reinforced the structure's foundation to support the Empire State Building. There is no money left for the end of the job, and then the husband is screaming."

When a change order is necessary, it must be described fully and priced in writing with the date payment is due. Before any work begins, the contractees and designer or contractor responsible for performing the work must sign off on the order. In practice, it is ideal to have the change okayed by both designer and contractor as well as by the homeowner, but don't make this contractual in case it's not possible. The change order becomes part of the contract and may necessitate adjustments in the completion date and penalty clause. *The price of the change is added to the job total; any item it's replacing subtracted.*

Warranties

The contractor must turn over to you all warranties that accompany goods and materials he has purchased. In addition, he should offer an unconditional warranty of at least one year against defects in his materials and workmanship. He may also be willing to warranty some things in part or in full for a longer period, but these agreements can be meaningless. The contractor's follow-up work echoes his attitude on the job: A crack contractor returns repeatedly; a sleazy one slithers off.

If your contractor is enrolled in the Home Owners Warranty (HOW) Corporation program, you will be remunerated for faulty workmanship and some defects in materials and structural systems. If he is not a member, you may want to explore this possibility. You, of course, will probably have to assume his premium costs.

Disputes

What kind of person starts thinking about disputes before the job even starts? Someone with a bad attitude? Uh-uh. Someone who believes in getting real. You, I hope. Certainly it's a bummer, but to protect yourself you need to anticipate negative interactions.

Glitches arise on every job no matter how good everyone running it is. When solved congenially, promptly, and resolutely, they aren't a problem. The roofer who hammered nails into my home office ceiling fixed it so quickly there was no time for it even to become an irritation. But not everything is resolved so smoothly.

When a real conflict does surface, you are usually better off paying a little extra money to solve it than getting into a major hassle or litigation. But before throwing a lot of money down the drain in hopes of keeping a job on track, drop the anchor on a relationship that has run aground.

Wherever possible, schedule a meeting and try to hammer out an amicable compromise. When reached, state the problem and its fix in writing and have everyone sign off on it. When no resolution is forthcoming, hire a *mediator* or neutral party to help guide you in finding a mutually satisfying answer. Other than the person's cost, you will have nothing to lose. If the conflict remains, you can seek restitution for claims in small claims courts. Anything larger requires expensive, time-consuming litigation or *arbitration*.

Composed of lawyers and contractors, arbitration boards are sponsored either by the court or by groups such as the American Arbitration Association or Better Business Bureau. Varying in proficiency, they have a reputation for sawing the baby in half. *Nonbinding* arbitration is a waste of time, while *binding* can't be appealed even if a factual error is made. Yet these boards have no muscle to reinforce their findings.

An answer costs less and comes quicker from arbitration than from court, but it is formulated without discovery, interrogatories, and depositions—the tools of the legal trade—and what may have been a sympathetic jury.

If all parties agree, you can decide to go to arbitration at any time, but do not put it in your contract. By including it you waive the option of going to court and the right to file a complaint with the contractor's board. When you choose to engage in arbitration, insist on input in selecting the arbitrators and defining parameters of the hearing.

Documentation-intensive remodeling litigation is very expensive. Be sure the contract states that the losing party will pay all legal fees. Otherwise it can easily cost you $60,000 to win. Request a budget from your attorney in advance and negotiate on how to cut legal costs by doing your own photocopying, research, and paper shuffling.

Despite all these seeming denouements, there is little recourse when a conflict arises. The contractor's board, like an arbitration board, federal court, or bonding or insurance company, rarely does little besides taking your time and money. Once again, protect yourself up front, before problems commence, with a contract that is easily dissolved and a schedule that pegs payments to performance in snail tempo.

To keep things moving, include a clause allowing you to hire someone to continue work if a conflict grinds the job to a halt for more than five days. Otherwise, complicated legal proceedings could leave you with an empty shell for years as the case spins through court dockets.

Cancellation

State laws specify when a contract can be nullified. In California, for example, a homeowner can cancel a contract within three days as long as it was signed at home rather than in a designer or contractor office. When signed in the professional's office, it remains in effect.

As previously mentioned, you should also have the right of annulment if a contractor does not start and continue work within five days of the stated date.

The right to cancel should be given to you if the designer affirms in writing that the room is not being built according to his design and the contractor does not make the necessary corrections within five days.

DESIGNER'S CONTRACT CONSIDERATIONS

This contract should carefully delineate the designer's role and scope of tasks from design through construction. Avoid vague language with no concrete meaning, such as "will assist in obtaining."

Karen Taylor's contract merely stated the architect's obligation "to refine the scheme." Translation: On top of the original, mutually agreed-on fee for what she thought was the entire design process, a fee was levied for construction documents and bidding.

Many issues raised under discussion of the contractor's contract are also relevant for the designer, so pull whatever is appropriate. Conversely, design aspects need to be incorporated into contracts of a one-stop dealer, design-build team, or contractor participating in the design process.

If the designer is not designing and detailing the cabinets, spell out his relationship and responsibility vis-à-vis the cabinet designer. List engineers or other professionals he will consult as well, along with procedures for hiring and handling fees. When he will be employing draftpeople or other assistants, their wages and hours also must be enumerated.

The designer, as the contractor, has no expenses until work actually starts, making any down payment unnecessary.

The first section of a comprehensive designer contract details the entire design process, assigning a fee to the completion of each step.

The first major issue to resolve is *how many different layouts the designer will do until the client is satisfied.* Georgia Brown's contract said "as many as necessary," which is just as it should be. Yet after doing three totally off-base schemes, the architect told Georgia she had used up her design time.

At the conclusion of this first, *schematic drawings* phase, pay only 5 percent of the design fee; 3 percent if the sketch is unacceptable. This way, you can part from a *nonsimpatico* designer without a substantial financial loss.

In keeping with this philosophy, let *design development* represent 25 percent of the job, *construction documents* 50 percent, and the *bidding* process 20 percent.

Pay the fee for schematics, design development , and the bidding process as soon as you and the designer agree these phases are complete, but wait to recompense construction documents until the designer incorporates feedback on the design's efficacy that surfaces during bidding. This is to be expected, particularly from contractors not involved in the design process from the beginning. The contractors called to bid Suzie Berman's plans felt the lighting was insufficient, and, most definitely, it would have been. Since it was the designer's error, he should have redone the lighting drawing—without the extra fee Suzie had to pay.

The designer should also be responsible for redoing a design that bids out at more than 10 percent above budget. There are too many plans lying dormant in the drawer. At $10,000 above budget—$80,000 in one New York high-rise case—they are too expensive to build.

Extra charges are, however, sometimes in order. In a complicated job, you may want a *model* built to help visualize what something will look like. You also need to specify whether *elevations* (a must), *perspective drawings,* and *renderings* (other musts) are included in a design fee and whether the designer will escort drawings through the plan check, an informal review of the construction documents by the department of building and safety.

Hourly fees may also be incurred for the time spent shopping with the designer. What role will he play in regard to choosing materials? Will he bring samples to the home? Take you only to one or two showrooms or go from one to another until all decisions are made?

Most contracts state that the designer has ownership of the drawings. The designer should be able to use them for his portfolio or publication in a magazine with your permission, but you've paid for them: They should be yours. Some dealers and cabinet shops claim entitlement to the drawings on the basis that they charge a retainer, not a project fee. Nonsense.

Include a 10 to 20 percent retention fee clause in the designer's contract as well from the first invoice onward that is not paid until construction is completed.

The second part of the designer's contract should delineate all responsibilities during the construction process. Assured that six visits would be ample during construction, Jason Sloan agreed on a figure based on this assumption and the understanding that additional meetings could be scheduled as necessary for an extra fee. It took more than six visits just to deal with a code problem, resolved ultimately by the contractor once the architect checked out.

During the construction phase the designer's payment schedule, as the contractor's, should be in small increments with fees tied directly to work performed. He must solve any special problems that arise of his making for no extra fee. If the designer is working for an hourly rate during this phase, outline the frequency of payment.

To cover any problems that arise, an architect can purchase an *errors and omissions insurance policy,* but its cost will probably be passed on to you to reckon with.

3

SCRIPTING THE PROCESS FROM CONCEPT TO CONSTRUCTION

DESIGNING DREAMWORKS THAT COOK

■

An Overview

Once you embark on the design process, you've entered the second trimester of the planning period. This activity can easily take three to four months or more. Don't rush it. Even if you have spent a great deal of mulling time before hiring the designer, you need this period to evaluate materials and digest ideas as you live with the new concepts presented to you. You'll probably have other demands on your time as well, such as working, cleaning, cooking, shopping, eating, and child care. Take all the time you need. There's no sense making this process a burden.

Though you've probably begun taking notes during your previous research and interviews, you'll want to keep a daily diary of the actual job as soon as contracts are signed, summarizing every telephone call and meeting. Note follow-up assignments, dates they are to be completed, and the person responsible for their execution. In the land of disputes, the detailed chronicler is king.

The discussion that follows pertains to a complete remodel, yet it is in no way less pertinent to a more circumscribed approach. Just pick and choose according to what's relevant for you. The same principles of good kitchen design are applicable regardless of spatial size of remodel site, be it a home or an apartment, a mountain chalet or a boat.

Most designers divide their layout work into three phases: schematic drawings, design development drawings, and working or construction drawings. At their completion, a bidding sequence is launched. Where one phase ends and another begins varies according to a designer's individual style. Never fear. You will know when that moment arrives, for you will be asked to sign off and pay for it.

Don't sign off on any plan until you are fully comfortable. If even one teeny question remains, resolve it before moving on, despite promises of a solution in the next stage. Once you leave a phase, you are charged for further changes, and you may get too far along to make them. *Questions that aren't* answered when they should be answered tend never to get answered.

Three years postconstruction, I'm still trying to find a home for my husband's commercial popcorn machine. "There is no space for it. Your kitchen is too small," my architect had protested too much. Now, of course, I know the perfect location had it been allocated in the original plan.

First Meeting

For the first meeting, be prepared with the lists of likes, dislikes, desires, dreams, and storage needs you compiled as part of your pre-remodeling homework. Present the pictures of favorite kitchens you gathered, the first cull (with catalogs, if possible) of materials and equipment you're considering, and any

KITCHEN LEGALSPEAK

Arbitration: A method of quickly resolving a dispute by utilizing a special board assembled for this purpose instead of the traditional judicial system. Nonbinding arbitration has no sticking power; binding arbitration cannot be appealed. Neither type can be truly enforced. See also Mediation.

Change Order: Any alteration in the construction documents that occurs during the remodel. This may derive from a change of whim, an inspector's demand, or an unexpected problem. The change must be put in writing, signed by the homeowner and contractor (and designer if specified), and scheduled for a separate payment. Any adjustment to the schedule or the contract that is a result of this change order must be noted as well.

Lien: A mechanic's or materialman's lien is a legal motion that a worker or supplier can file against your property when not paid by the contractor. This can transpire even if you have already paid the contractor in full for the work in question. A property cannot be sold during the period a lien is leveled against it.

    Preliminary Notice of Intent to File a Lien: The contractor is legally bound to provide this form from every subcontractor and supplier who works on your job so you are aware who has the right to file a lien.

    Release of Lien: A clause in a contract that acts as a safeguard for the consumer, stating that the contractor is to be held legally and financially responsible for paying his workers and suppliers.

    Partial Lien Release: A signed document from the supplier or worker indicating receipt of an interim

(partial) payment for his bill. The supplier or worker signs a final lien release upon receipt of the last payment covering all submitted bills.

Mediation: A less formal process than arbitration for trying to resolve a dispute by hiring a neutral party who is mutually agreed on by the contestants to negotiate between them. See also Arbitration.

Payment Bond: A guarantee of payment purchased by the contractor. When this bond is in place, no liens can be filed against your property.

Performance or Contract Bond: A guarantee of job completion purchased by the contractor that ensures the homeowner compensation even if the job is not finished. Some states require this bond automatically as part of licensure.

Retention Fee: A contract clause stating that a certain percentage—usually 10 to 20 percent—of the total amount due the contractor will be held back at each payment point and paid only when the entire job is completed. Since a contractor is more likely to finish a job when owed money, this stands as a bit of a protection for the homeowner.

Work Payment Schedule: A schedule generated by the contractor before construction begins, listing the point at which a specific task is considered complete and an agreed-on fee is due. The homeowner is bound to the tenets of this schedule by the contract.

variances you've received or reports of soil, asbestos, or water problems you've collected. Assemble the *legal description* of your property as found in the owner's title papers, *as-built drawings* of the home or apartment, a *vicinity map*, and a *certified land survey*. Revealing the size of the lot, this pinpoints the building's location on the property, proof that it's within the required legal setback and point of water drainage.

The designer measures areas to be remodeled and equipment to be stored, and examines attics, basements, crawl spaces, and adjacent rooms. If expansion is a consideration, he investigates whether roof lines can be altered and reviews limitations imposed by a historic preservation trust. He traces electric lines, plumbing vents, and heating pipes to see what must be rerouted or brought up to code, identifying load-bearing structures resistant to displacement.

Besides poking around, he conducts a formal interview to learn about your lifestyle, preferred mode of cooking and entertaining, and the ways the room will be utilized by family and friends.

Agreeing on a Budget

The most important point to agree on initially is a strict budget. Though this should have been the first parameter established, its amount is not always easily expressed. For debate purposes, go back to that somewhat arbitrary figure of $20,000 you used to select materials and appliances. If your budget falls below this amount, alert the designer to its precise ceiling *after* subtracting design and construction fees, the state sales tax, and 10 to 15 percent—better 20 percent—for an inevitable override.

Though you can raise a terrific kitchen from the studs in this price category, choices will be limited. Sending a designer down a false budget path will only result in great frustration for both of you.

If you can afford to spend more than $20,000, but aren't eager to do so unnecessarily, your answer becomes somewhat couched and complicated. Tell the designer your maximum amount and he will spend it and then some. Name too low a figure and you may close off splendid options needlessly.

Before disclosing an actual figure, insist on an education. Ask about options and alternatives. How will a $25,000 kitchen vary from one that is $30,000 or $40,000? If the designer balks at responding, you have engaged the wrong person. Call the terminator.

Once you agree with the designer on a maximum job cost, let him know there is no leeway, that you will hold him to redoing the design if bids come in 10 percent or more over this figure. *Refer back to the budget at each phase of the design process* and ascertain—at least informally—if you have strayed from its limits.

EXPRESSING A PERSONAL STYLE

One arena mercifully free of budget constraints is the style of the kitchen. As designer Jarrett Hedborg says, it "is a look, not a price." When expressed successfully, it reflects the unique tastes of its inhabitants. For the designer to incorporate your style, it must be declared before the design process commences. You'll be happy you did so, for a focus narrows the field, simplifying decisions.

Set the Tone

Should the kitchen be formal or informal? Dark or light? Should tools be out for grabs or hidden behind closed doors, providing a peaceful serenity for those with a lot of clutter in their heads? Should the look be streamlined and panther-sleek with interlocking modular units that fit flush, seemingly receding into the woodwork? Or should it feel more like a living room with individual unfitted pieces of furniture? An entirely different approach? How about kitchen as commercial high-tech laboratory, gleaming in stainless steel heft and hulk?

If the room is not being totally redone, must the look help hide flaws? A wall that is not plumb?

Establish a Sensibility

Do you want the kitchen to loosely suggest a traditional, contemporary, or country atmosphere or be further delineated as American country, English country, French country, or country as typified on a street corner in Aix-en-Provence?

Will you research and reproduce a historic period as a purist, authenticating every component down to the last brass tack on the planked floor? Or will you depend on single elements to bespeak bygone times—columns of the neoclassic era or stained glass from the Viennese Secessionist school? You don't need French country doors for a French country look.

Will you search for style in a theme, inspired by a nautical motif, a hobby, or a personal collection, or will you forgo the idea of a set style in favor of the materials you like? Will your kitchen go the way of today's restaurants boasting fusion cuisine: an eclectic mix totaling your experiences?

Whatever style you embrace should be classic and timeless, not something quickly outmoded or so overdone as to become tiresome. *If you get bored easily, express your style in accessories that can be readily changed.*

As important as style is for making a room feel warm and welcoming, it must not impede basic functioning. An unfitted kitchen, for example, with very few cabinets, doesn't provide enough storage for the cook who has bought out Williams-Sonoma.

The kitchen must be harmonious with the rest of the house even if it does not precisely echo the decor of other rooms. And while trying on options, be sure you don't end up with a style that's hard to maintain; a kitchen with multiple moldings to dust.

Once an overall design scheme is identified, a focal point is declared for drama and the room unified by repetition of texture, pattern, and shape. Tying these disparate items together bestows an individual signature on your kitchen while fine detailing gives it a depth and complexity. But "to truly provide pleasure, a kitchen must have . . . heart. Heart transcends style," observes Gale C. Steves, *Home* magazine's editor in chief.

Color It Beautiful

After style comes color, though what we end up with in our kitchens is apparently less dear to us than to somebody else. The Color Association of the United States, an industry group known also as a "color conspiracy," studies trends, politics, the environment, and social situations before decreeing what will be popular several years hence.

Entrenched for the nineties are natural earth tones and blues, greens, reds, and oranges—"ecology" hues of a healthy planet with names like *soleil*, zinnia, toucan, and blue lagoon. Or maybe they're out already. Fashionable colors change so rapidly, they're hard to keep track of.

"Color is power," says Rebecca Ewing, an Atlanta consultant who views it psychologically. Given her interpretations, it is certainly nothing to trifle with. Yellow, probably the most popular color for a kitchen, is apparently a terrible choice. Though it stimulates appetite, it also causes irritability and sets your teeth on edge.

Purple, on the other hand, an appetite depressant, will probably suit a home of dieters. Orange is perky, and red stirs you up. Blue is a slow-down to concentrate on details and the task at hand. Pink makes people want to take care of you, although this may not extend to washing the dishes. And everybody, according to this color maven, likes green and salmon very much.

Brown is considered dull, gray indicative of a state of transition. Black adds a sophisticated sizzle, but it is distancing. White reveals a difficulty in making decisions; a desire for a kitchen to symbolize higher purposes of purity and order.

As a recommended color, white was dismissed long ago. "The day of the laboratory kitchen is past," announces an Iowa State College booklet published in 1929. "The glare of the white walls . . . was tiring to the eyes and monotonous to the soul of the worker." Given the current popularity of white kitchens, one can confidently assume that this message still hasn't been heard.

White, gray, and beige, even black, are neutral background colors to be balanced with brighter accents, alterable in the future when a desire for change draws nigh.

A relatively inexpensive design statement, color conveys a communal spirit and should be used

A DREAM KITCHEN ON ANY BUDGET

- Provides a safe haven in which to work comfortably regardless of your age, size, strength, or ability.
- Facilitates the preparation of healthy, nutritious food.
- Choreographs cooking movements to flow forward without backtracking or interruption.
- Organizes drink preparation and cleanup without interfering in cooking or serving.
- Presents a comely retreat for family and friends.
- Diverts traffic from work areas, avoiding jams and bottlenecks.
- Encourages water and energy conservation.
- Absorbs noise.
- Cleans easily.
- Dismisses odors and pollutants.
- Lights surfaces generously and dramatically.
- Recycles waste efficiently.

- Earmarks an individual storage space for every item.
- Electrifies each piece of equipment at its point of use.
- Controls heating and cooling temperatures appropriately.
- Offers music and entertainment.
- Contains quality, high-functioning appliances:

  A large enough sink to hold a skillet flat.

  Sizable sturdy cooktop burners that go from a gentle simmer to very high heat.

  An oven with an infrared broiler.

  A refrigerator with large produce bins.
- Remains beautiful and durable for many a year.
- Answers "Yes!" to "Will you still love me tomorrow?"

---

freely. By varying tints (add white), shades (add black), or tones (add gray) you can effectively utilize a single color throughout the kitchen. Just don't fall overboard on the dark side, for it can be depressing.

Color has a practical bent, too. Marilyn Ackerman hated her white countertops, witnesses to the soot blown in through her Big Apple windows.

Now that you've heard the pitch, take a color cue from an adjacent room or pick a palette you like.

SCHEMATIC DRAWINGS

Schematic drawings are the exploratory phase of the design, a series of quick rough sketches that offer possible floor plans to vote yea or nay on. This is option time, for comparing alternatives and synchronizing expectations with reality and budget. Before

beginning, basic decisions must be made and limitations identified. If concerns still exist about problem clays, soil conditions, or hazardous wastes, this is the time to bring in a consultant, and perhaps an engineer. Depending on your cabinet source, you may also have to decide on their style and manufacturer.

Once a basic sketch is completed, the designer scribbles possible modifications on tracing paper set over the initial drawing. A quick look-see to determine possible paths, this is not a formal professional rendering measured to scale. It is a waste of your time and money for a designer to detail a scheme before you have finally approved it.

If your want list doesn't fit in this plan, you may have to tear up the sketch and start anew, but expect to hit a brick wall of compromises. It is inevitable here. I abandoned a separate wok for lack of space

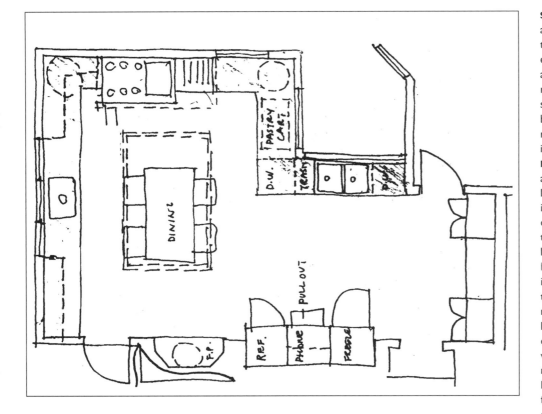

SCHEMATICS Schematic drawings are rough preliminary sketches made in the initial phase of the design process to explore possible placement of cabinetry and equipment and the ultimate configuration of the room. These drawings should be quick and casual until the basic design is determined; there is no reason to spend time and money detailing a layout that won't be used.

FLOOR PLAN Once the rough shape and look of the room has been established with a series of schematic drawings, a formal two dimensional layout is done to scale. Also called a floor plan, this is a view of what the room would look like if it was sliced horizontally in half, and you were standing above looking down on the bottom section after the top half was removed. The cross marks on the plan of my kitchen shown here indicate where upper cabinets exist. Many plans would indicate this with just a series of dashes, no cross marks. To orient yourself in the room, look at the two sets of sinks (A), the fireplace (B), and the table (C) where dashes indicate that there is a drawer below that is not visible from this perspective. Note the evolution of the table's design from Schematics to Floor Plan.

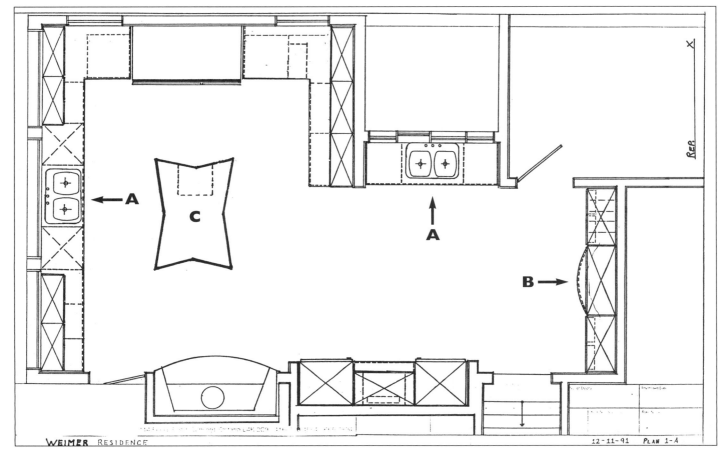

and accepted second best on the stove's position since the most convenient location didn't admit its flue.

When you have trouble picturing a part of the drawing, have the designer get an illustration, bring a sample, or take you to see a real-life example.

An exciting plan should be hatched after one or two meetings and four or five tracing-paper tries. When this doesn't happen, analyze what is going awry and why you and the designer are on different wavelengths. If differences remain irreconcilable, sever the relationship.

Assuming that you are moving merrily along and have decided on the basic layout, this is the moment for the designer to provide a *design schedule.* This document formalizes tasks to be performed in each phase and targets dates for their completion and intervals in between when you can ponder the plan in depth at your leisure. My design languished for six months before I received a countdown, and then the designer wanted all decisions to be made instantly. If I'd had a schedule in advance, the project would have been less stressful.

The ultimate *floor plan* is likely to be a composite of ideas that emerge during this preliminary investigation. A two-dimensional representation, it shows the configuration of the room with the location of doors, windows, cabinets, appliances, and other appurtenances.

DESIGN DEVELOPMENT

Design development is the refinement and detailing of the plan; what architect Brian Allen Murphy calls "hard line" or "up the drawings." This is where the designer starts playing the scales, allotting one-quarter inch (and sometimes one-half inch) to represent each foot of space. This is also the moment of truth. Will things *really* fit?

Before precise measurements are taken and transferred to a plan, final selections must be made for all equipment, finishes, and colors. As you entertain these decisions, keep in mind the overall look you seek. Think about decorative details such as mold-ings and edge treatment as well as repetitive elements unifying your theme. Should Corian be used on hardware, faucets, and a countertop edge, or do you want to brighten the room with copper? *Plot every detail— even where wastebaskets will go—in this phase so each item is assigned an optimal visual and functional spot.*

If a second designer has been engaged for the cabinets, this is his grand entrance. Get him going with your list of storage items and their measurements, noting pieces that are oversized or designated for an appliance garage.

Bring on the consultants: An engineer to review plans for skylights, fireplaces, glass walls, or load-bearing structures. If you want a second opinion about anything, get it now.

Without exception, invite salespeople from several different ventilation companies to make recommendations based on your space and layout. Afterward, check the adequacy of your ventilation choice and installation plan with an HVAC expert who understands air movement and velocity without being distracted by something to sell. Schedule these meetings before cabinets have been designed so ducting paths aren't unwittingly obscured.

When I finally hired a consultant during construction, the instinct that my ventilation was improper proved uncannily right on. The result: I had to rip out two expensive fixtures and redo some plaster and drywall. All the more discouraging, I had eliminated the possibility of ever having sufficient ventilation unless I also removed two expensive windows I had just framed in. My experience was not unique: *Ventilation is universally mishandled.*

Lighting is, too. Visit a lighting lab to view all surface materials and cabinet finishes under lights you've chosen to be sure colors will ring true. Have the consultant confirm whether the number and type of lights specced are appropriate, their layout ideally conceived.

To find a lab, look up wholesale electric supplies in the business pages. Find out, too, whether the electric company in your area offers this service. Or call the American Lighting Association to get the name of a certified lighting professional in your area.

Keep noise pollution in ear as well. Be sure sufficient insulation is being planned for acoustic deafening; vertical structural pieces planted to prevent noise from traveling in a straight line. Take care to muffle sound from adjacent bathrooms or overhead stairs.

Let loudness be a guide when choosing materials: Use acoustic planking for the ceiling and solid-core doors with rubber or plastic gaskets. Wood, vinyl, and, to a lesser extent, laminates are quieter than tile, stainless, or stone. With more surface area, open shelving absorbs more sound than closed cabinets; enameled cast-iron sinks are quieter than stainless. Dishwashers and hoods can be purchased in various decibels, and the motor from a hood or refrigerator compressor remoted on the roof.

When all selections are made, lighting, electric, gas, and heating systems are delineated on the plan and their ducts, lines, and outlet points specified. Plan on lines, connections, and plugs for telephones, speakers, televisions, small appliances, and security systems as well and decide whether you want to plumb an island or wire it for electricity or a telephone. Consider a second line now, too, while its installation is comparatively inexpensive.

It may seem off point to worry about wiring when you're trying to get the layout down, but it cannot be added as efficiently—or at all—later on, and it must correspond to the slope of the ceiling. If not carefully conceived, you may find a plug in the middle of your beautiful tile design. Wait to place heating in the toe kick after cabinets are drawn, and there may be no space for its on-and-off switch. If you spec in a twenty-watt fluorescent tube, you can't decide later on that it should have been forty watts.

Coordination is the key to this phase of the design—the confirmation that one decision will not adversely affect another. Have a plumber, an electrician, and a heating and gas expert confirm that they can route lines without interfering with the design and one another's systems.

Analyzing a Plan

Live with your plan, visualizing what will work for you while analyzing it repeatedly. Set yourself up to

have one of contractor Tom Pelmon's smoothest-running jobs, where "all the mistakes were made on paper, *before* we began construction."

Throughout the process, keep in mind the design advice in a photocopy of a book chapter titled "Motion-Minded" that came my way without attribution:

1. **Build the cabinets to fit the cook.**
2. **Build the shelves to fit the supplies.**
3. **Build the kitchen to fit the family.**

Invite feedback from friends who have remodeled their kitchens or from anyone you can corral to look at your plan. When shopping for cabinets or appliances, show the plan to salespeople and staff designers. Professionals like to criticize each other's work. You won't have to ask for feedback.

Pay close attention to how you are using your current kitchen. Every time you brew a cup of coffee or perform another task, do a mental check that you've planned for these operations to proceed smoothly in the new design. Look for spaces in magazines that are configured similarly to see how they've arranged these operations and compare your plan with those illustrated.

Play with your plan, by photocopying it, cutting it up, and moving the parts around, or purchase a kit with movable cutouts such as Design-Aid, Kitchen Designer Kit, and Design Works. Computer buffs may want to try one of the many available programs geared for kitchen remodeling such as Visio Home's 3.0 Shapeware or Floor-Plan Plus 3D by ComputerEasy International. Or you may want to create your own plan.

Measure the perimeter of the room with a six-foot carpenter's rule that doesn't bend. Transfer these measurements to graph paper, letting each one-quarter-inch grid represent one foot. Add doors and windows, indicating the direction they open. Leave room for sills, trims, and window treatments and indicate existing heating, plumbing, and electric outlets. Make templates of appliances to scale and move them around the plan. To confirm dimensions of any of your equipment, fax your request to

Common Symbols

Architects employ a set of universal symbols in their drawings. Once this code is cracked, you can read any plan. Some of the basic symbols utilized are illustrated here.

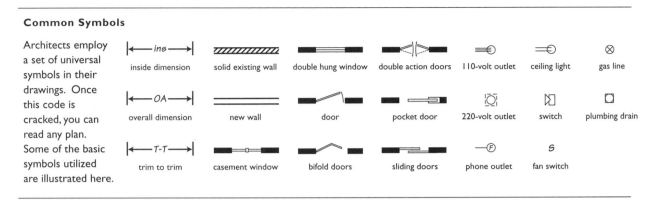

ins	solid existing wall	double hung window	double action doors	110-volt outlet	ceiling light	gas line
inside dimension						
OA	new wall	door	pocket door	220-volt outlet	switch	plumbing drain
overall dimension						
T-T	casement window	bifold doors	sliding doors	phone outlet	fan switch	
trim to trim						

the twenty-four-hour hot line, Dimension Express, (702) 833-3633.

When you're happy with the appliances' arrangement, draw in cabinetry or place cabinet templates to connect them. Add overhead beams and skylights with double-dashed lines. Test casual ideas as the designer does by placing tracing paper over the plan.

A problem getting everything you want to fit into the room? Try changing the walls, moving windows or doors, downsizing appliances or cabinetry, eliminating extras, making minor structural changes, or adding an island or peninsula.

To get a concrete sense of operating in this new kitchen, insert pushpins into the major stations, as author Sam Clark suggests, and then chart movements in preparing a meal by running yarn from pin to pin. Compare possible designs with different-colored yarn.

You can also build a mock-up of the plan. Editor Olivia Buehl mapped out cabinet and appliance placement with masking tape and newspaper. Then, with cornstarch on her feet, she tracked her movements through the motions of preparing a meal, observing how traffic moved around her.

A model of the plan can be constructed to scale on a floor or driveway with cardboard boxes representing cabinets, equipment, and furnishings. Be aware of the direction their doors open. If the design includes an island, pay particular attention to its size and ease of navigating around it.

Elevations

Elevations, a head-on vertical view of each wall and its components, are drawn to scale from floor to ceiling after the plan is firm. Many designers, particularly those working for dealers, balk at supplying them because of the time they take and thus their cost, but they are imperative for visualizing the new space. When there is a significant time lapse between design and actual remodel, they also help recall intended details.

An elevation makes it possible to review storage assignments against lists drawn up during pre-remodeling. Look closely at each section and confirm that room exists to store all items needed to accomplish tasks performed in that zone. Confirm that each item is assigned its own space and is easy to retrieve and put away without interfering with kitchen activities. As author Robin Murrell says, ". . . if it is difficult to get at things, it will be twice as difficult to put them away."

When ample space is unavailable, redesign the cabinets and their interiors, substitute a different type of cabinet or storage aid, or redo the layout of the area.

When reviewing elevations, check that the tops of all windows and doors line up and reassess the space in between the ceiling and the top of wall cabinets. In small kitchens, this is generally taken up with more cabinets, while in larger rooms, it may be left open for displaying collectibles and installing *cove* (hidden) lighting. Plate rails or handsome moldings accent its line while protecting breakables.

Sometimes, as in my kitchen, it is closed with a false front or what is called a *soffit*. Extending twenty-seven inches from the wall, an *Eastern soffit* is large enough to accommodate lights. While this boxed-in area provides a clean, elegant contemporary look

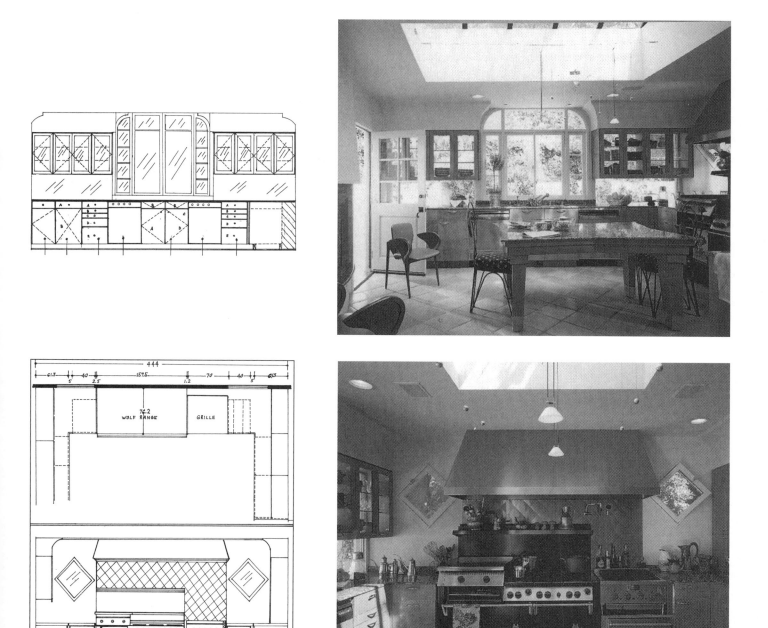

ELEVATIONS An elevation is drawn to scale of each wall with a head-on view of everything placed on it. While a plan indicates the depth and width of each item, an elevation illustrates height and width. Elevations are very important in revealing the relationship between each item in the room, and whether appliances, cabinets, doors, and windows link up horizontally and vertically. These drawings are used as well to assign kitchen tools to a proper storage spot. In the upper elevation of my main sink wall (*top left*), the triangular dashed lines indicate cabinet doors whose hinges are on the side where the lines meet in a single point. The drawing below illustrates how a layout evolves into an elevation, while the photographs of the finished kitchen indicate how the drawings are reproduced during construction.

and even some sculptural definition, it is empty calories, a waste of what could be a more usable storage section, albeit one hard to reach.

If you incorporate a soffit, avoid one designed to be flush with the cabinet. Unless workers are unusually adept, this design is not possible to execute properly, and you are left with an uneven juncture to hide. Either step the soffit back or extend it beyond the cabinets by at least one inch and finish with a molding. In any event, be sure it is sized to accommodate the depth of wall cabinets you want. At only ten inches, Caroline Bream's soffit left her with wall cabinets that were too shallow to hold her dishes.

Perspective drawings, an angled illustration providing a three-dimensional view of the kitchen, and a *rendering* of the finished interior and exterior structure are other important contributions to this phase of the design process. Together they illuminate what the room will actually look like when it is built and its relationship to the site's grading and landscaping. They also provide the opportunity to assess the harmony of new windows with others on the property.

If you, like many people, are unable to imagine the transformation from paper to wood, build a model for a more concrete depiction.

FINAL PLAN REVIEW

To cover all bases before taking the final step, check off the plan presented at the end of design development work to be sure all systems are go.

- Review original want lists to see if desires expressed on it have been satisfied.

- Confirm that the layout is "motion-minded," enabling you to flow from one cooking task to the next with the fewest, simplest, smoothest movements and no to-ing and fro-ing.

- Assess traffic patterns. Can people circulate without bumping into each other? Is there a safe harbor for children?

- Affirm that conversation is feasible during cooking. Can a single cook interact with guests or family members in the kitchen? Multiple cooks work facing each other?

- Compare layout and installation instructions against the "Kitchens by the Numbers" dimensional chart in the appendices to be sure minimum clearances are met for operating effectively. Look at both individual items and their effect on each other. Now—before construction—is the time to learn that chairs have been growing larger and are often too tall to be used at standard tables.

- Check the *exact* measurements of appliances you have selected by going directly to the company's installation manual. Ignore the glossy sales brochures. Numbers are often rounded off in consumer materials so that what you thought was a 24-inch-wide machine may turn out to be $24\frac{1}{8}$ or $23\frac{7}{8}$ when it arrives. Installation instructions and requirements for cutouts, clearances, trim kits, ventilation, and electrical and plumbing hookups are information for you and your designer to obtain in advance before moving to the final layout or working drawings.

- Ascertain whether the sink cabinet and appliances—particularly refrigerators, cooktops, ovens, and dishwashers—can be raised or lowered to suit your height or improve a view without interfering with a countertop.

- Recheck measurements to ensure appliance, equipment, and cabinet doors and drawers can open without hitting each other or interrupting traffic. Check that the degree of door opening is adequate for pulling shelves out of cabinets and refrigerators.

- Assess the floor space that doors occupy when opened and the dimensions they'll need to make their entrance and exit.

- Change the position of any refrigerator, utility cabinet, or wall oven interrupting a countertop expanse.

- Finalize storage placements against the original list, assigning each item its own spot. Where are aprons to be kept?

- Count pullout cutting boards in base cabinets. They should all be removable and grooved so juices don't run off, with stops that lock them into place while in use. Accommodating different heights, these may be at various levels:

  1. Next to a refrigerator or wall oven when no counter exists for a landing space. A board or solid-surface shelf can also be inserted into a drawer below the counter for a sturdier cutting surface.

  2. In a base cabinet that is the same depth as a wall cabinet above it (so you won't have to work with your head against the cabinet).

  3. Over or next to a trash can.

  4. Below an appliance garage mounted on a standard twenty-four-inch-deep countertop.

  Portable cutting boards, set into a countertop or sliding along on top of it, also provide this service. For bread, put in a double-decker board with slats on the top layer and a removable shelf below to catch crumbs. Before settling on a board, try out your knives on it. Some new plastics, in particular, are not good for their edges.

- Define the room's focal point. Do other features repeat and support it? Do they unify the room? Do crown moldings or other decorative components augment or detract from the style you've chosen?

- Evaluate design elements:

  Line: Do lines line up? Is the horizontal toe kick line at the same level throughout the room? Or does it vary wildly on purpose for architectural interest? How about the soffit? Are windows and doors the same height? Do refrigerators and wall ovens line up the way they are supposed to? The cabinets above them? Would the room look less choppy lining up some of its bulkier components?

  Shape: Is there continuity of shape? Is one shape repeated often, lending harmony to the room? Have you employed an unusual shape or a common shape unusually? Is it utilized repetitively?

  Scale: Are both individual items and areas in scale with one another? Tall items balanced with short and vice versa? Major areas with minor ones? Is an element's scale or size appropriate for the scale of the room?

  Contrast: Do elements provide suitable contrast, whether subtle and monochromatic or high in opposing values? Is there enough light and dark and contrast between them?

  Texture: Are different textures well balanced? Harmonious with other design elements? Do they add a depth and organic complexity to the design?

- Comment on the room's attractiveness. Is its appearance consistent with the style of the home and decor of contiguous rooms?

- Imagine the house from the exterior with new windows, a skylight, and a fireplace chimney. Check the view from the interior.

- Will the new space meet its occupants' needs? Will they be happy in it?

- Hire a *feng shui* expert, a Chinese master versed in creating a harmonious environment, to assess your plan.

- Crystal-ball whether this kitchen will be practical five years hence. Will you be able to work safely and comfortably within it as you age? Is the design classic and timeless, or have you succumbed to the latest fads? Will it improve the resale value of your house? Are you overbuilding?

- Ascertain how easy it will be to keep clean.

- Verify that modifications relegated to a later date can be made easily.

- Validate that you got what *you* really wanted. Did you cave in on that commercial stove because the designer insisted it looked too big for the room? Don't.

- Assess costs seriously, for changes made after this point can prove expensive. If a contractor is not participating in the design phase, send the plan to the companies who will bid your job to ascertain if you are within budget. They will not proffer an exact price until a formal bid is requested, but they should be able to ballpark sufficiently for you to determine if the plans are realistic.

CONSTRUCTION DOCUMENTS
OR WORKING DRAWINGS

Construction documents are final drawings, elevations, and renderings of the layout with separate lighting and electrical plans. They are called *blueprints,* though no longer done on blue paper. Permits are drawn and bids and construction based on them. A *finish schedule* (specifications and installation instructions for each product and material to be used in construction) is submitted with the blueprints. When these specs are attached to the drawings, they are called *sheet specs.* Separately, they are known as *book specs.*

Your main task during this phase is to quadruple-check with the designer that every item—down to the last hinge, plate, and switch—has been specified precisely, or you will become the victim of a bait and switch. Anything not delineated will be given a baseline generic allowance, prompting that fun "Oh, that's extra." Once you finally make a choice, count on the price going up, making your job more expensive than anticipated.

The designer often preempts the contractor's application for a permit by submitting finished construction documents to the department of building and safety for what is called a *plan check* or an informal look-see. This way anything the inspector identifies as contrary to local code or an unaccepted practice can be rectified before bidding begins. Eliminating this step can potentially hold up construction and cause a lot of grief down the line. When it is included, the contractor usually sails right through the red tape when he eventually goes to get a permit. My architect shepherded her drawings through plan check along with doughnuts, cappuccino, and a lot of chat that got them cleared in several hours.

One day the layout is actually finished, and it's time to put plans out to bid. Hotelier Bill Wilkinson says, "You change and you change and you change everything for so many months, you think you'll never get it right. Then one day the layout is really done, and you have a final plan. It looks so simple and clean and straightforward, exactly what you want. 'Why couldn't I see this a long time ago?' you ask."

THE BIDDING PROCESS

The designer customarily manages bidding by preparing all forms, photocopying construction documents, and sending them to the three to five contractors identified as potential candidates for your job. Secure comparison bids even if a contractor participated in the design phase and the relationship was a positive one. Though it is usually advantageous to keep the same person throughout construction, competitive bidding should sweeten the package while offering other informed viewpoints.

Bidding rolls differently along the design-build route where numbers are secured before design work starts as a means of comparing different firms and deciding whom to hire. If you aren't happy with the design work of a design-build firm you've hired, have the job rebid when it's time for construction.

Once plans go out to bid, it takes contractors about a month to collect prices from their various subs and tally the figures before sending them back. Be sure they come back with the blueprints. You need multiple copies on the job, and at $30 to $40 a set, they are too expensive and time-consuming to photocopy repeatedly.

Bids are usually good for thirty days, so request them only when you are ready to begin building. If material prices go up, the fee may rise respectively even within this grace period. Before being given plans, a contractor should visit your site and poke around the basement, attic, and crawl space, looking at wiring, vents, and ducts.

In instructions to bidders, include the name of their job you've visited that best reflects the quality level and type of materials you seek. The more concise this description and the better the drawings contractors receive, the more likely each person will bid on the same things; the closer their assessments to the job you want and its actual costs. Encourage these contractors to bid on premium caulks, sealants, boards, and other construction materials, whose superior quality more than compensates for their slightly higher price.

To get a well-considered bid, you want to make the con-

tractor feel you care about quality regardless of budget and that he has a great chance at landing the job.

When anticipating a particular problem to unfold during the course of the remodel, request a bid on its amelioration as well. Otherwise you will be hit up in the middle of the job. "Very old house. Very good, but very bad pipes," said Henry, our plumbing sub, his eyes widening as he mentally added up the extra money he expected to score.

For a job encompassing other rooms in addition to the kitchen, ask for two bids: one for doing the job all at once and one for doing it in phases. Sometimes it is better to pay more, extend the process, and do it in stages than to turn your entire house over to the hordes of invaders who will descend on you, declaring a state of inevitable siege.

In a small company, the contractor does the bidding himself, while larger firms delegate this responsibility. Everyone addresses the bidding process in a different fashion, so ask how figures are arrived at.

Less honorable contractors depend on what Walter Stoeppelwerth calls the *WAG* (wild-assed guess) or *SWAG* (scientific wild-assed guess) approach. At the other extreme, people employ the *stick* or *stick and brick method,* counting every material, task, and labor separately; a time-consuming endeavor. In *unit price,* a variation of stick, materials and tasks are itemized while labor is prefigured. A combination approach is drafted when the unknown is paired with predictable tasks like drywall.

Prices based on *linear feet,* yet another attempt, are virtually meaningless since price depends on what steps are taken in those feet. There is no way to accurately compute the per-foot cost of a job until after it is completed.

A faster approach being promulgated in the industry is *unit cost* or *spreadsheet estimating.* Depending on the use of common products for its practicality and reliability, it is based on the development of an "economy," "deluxe," and "super-deluxe" bid package for standardized jobs. Much like a builder's model whose reproduction lowers costs for all, a uniform design prunes a contractor's expenses.

Using the same materials each time, he elimi-nates the learning curve wasted on handling and installing a large variety of items. Satisfied with the familiar and usual, a consumer who likes the package could find this tack a boon.

Some contractors insist on a *negotiated bid.* Saving time spent on determining costs, the contractor arrives at a price after only a cursory review of the plan and then negotiates it with you. Some design-build firms operate similarly. In this situation, you commit to the company first, stating the amount you can spend. The salesperson then shops for bids to meet your budget.

After speaking to countless people about a negoti-ated bid, I confess to understanding neither how it works nor how it can benefit a consumer. Unless you know what a job should cost, you have no idea if the bid is fair. If you knew the cost of a job, you wouldn't have to get a bid on it. And if the contractor won't par-ticipate in competitive bidding, there is no way you can get the best price or learn what it should be. This is up there in the land of mind bending.

One highly recommended firm informed me that it would review the other bids I received instead of conducting its own bid and then present me with a fixed fee. Excuse me? I was to ask contractors to spend time bidding and then give the job to some-one who based a price on other people's work? I don't think so.

There are advantages to knowing what your job should cost, as difficult and time-consuming as the process of learning how to estimate it will be. By investing this energy, you will be able to gauge if fig-ures are reasonable, enter into a negotiated bid, or track a time and materials job.

To assess what your job should cost, review building permits for similar jobs. When making pur-chases in lumberyards, home centers, and cabinet or appliance dealers, ask salespeople to show you costs of similar kitchens they have done.

Or get really serious and order professional sources such as Means's *Building Construction Cost Data,* HomeTech's *Professional Cost Estimating,* or Craftsmen Book Company's *National Repair & Remodeling Estimator,* which comes with a Windows-based computer program. Prices and labor differ

KITCHENSPEAK: DESIGN

Blueprints: Another name for construction documents that were historically done on blue paper.

Book Specs: A finish schedule presented separately from the drawings.

Construction Documents: The final drawings, elevations, and renderings of the layout on which construction is based. This includes separate lighting and electrical plans and a finish schedule with specifications and installation instructions for each product and material to be used.

Design-Build: An approach to the remodeling process by which the homeowner hires only one firm to provide all design and building services from layout through construction.

Design Development: A formal refinement and detailing of a favored floor plan identified during the schematic drawing phase. Before this can be done, all final selections must be made for equipment, cabinetry, and materials, noting their established sizes and specific installation requirements.

Design Schedule: A document provided by the designer to formalize the tasks to be performed in each phase of the design process with due dates for their completion.

Elevations: A head-on vertical view of each wall with its components and storage assignments drawn to scale from floor to ceiling after the design development plan is completed.

Floor Plan: A two-dimensional representation of the room to be constructed with the location of doors, windows, cabinets, appliances, and other appurtenances delineated.

Negotiated Bid: A type of bidding in which a contractor reaches a mutually agreed-on price with the homeowner by discussion rather than by a review of the plans and determination of construction costs and overhead.

Perspective Drawings: An angled illustration providing a three-dimensional view of a room.

Plan Check: An informal process whereby the designer presents the final construction drawings to the department of building and safety for a preliminary evaluation of code compliance before having potential contractors bid on it.

Rendering: A colored drawing of the interior and exterior plan to better illustrate what the new space will look like.

Schematic Drawings: The first step in the design process, during which the designer makes a series of rough casual sketches of possible floor plans for the client to consider.

Sheet Specs: A finish schedule attached to the drawings.

---

across the country, so obtain corrected figures for your region.

A rough estimate can be made by adding costs of appliances, cabinets, and materials you have selected plus local labor wages and 20 or so percent for overhead and profit—67 percent if the contractor is listening to Walter Stoeppelwerth.

The National Association of Home Builders roughly divides job costs into 29 percent for materials, 37 percent for labor, and 24 percent for overhead and profit. This generalization is only somewhat useful, for these numbers don't reflect complications or unique site conditions. While labor remains static, price of equipment and cabinets can vary enormously according to what you pick.

While preparing bids, contractors ask questions about the plan that you should respond to in writing. Their feedback may also prompt you to make some adjustments. Communicate any changes to each bidder in a letter accompanied by a new drawing that illustrates alterations.

When bids come in, they will most likely differ considerably. Be concerned about one significantly out of line. A substantially higher bid may indicate a contractor with high overhead or little interest in the job. A low bid can signal an unrealistic view or the expectation that price difference will be made up in change orders. The excessively low bidder may cut corners destructively or run out of money before completing the job. Hard-pressed contractors are known to bid low just for a few payments to stay solvent.

Regardless of the bid, ask each contractor what he would do differently if he added or subtracted $2,000 from his bottom line. Whatever the price is, negotiate. When you have only a small job to do, see if the contractor will give you a better price doing it in the off-hours, over a longer period of time, or in exchange for a reference (permission to bring potential customers to your site).

The bid should completely describe all construction materials and their installation method. Review "Tearing It Down and Building It Up" later in this chapter to see what should be included. If you are unsure of what a bid is based on, ask to see samples. Have each task broken down into individual components in case you opt for it to be only partially completed. The contractor's job costs and tools must be included as well, for this bid will eventually form the basis of his contract.

To compare numbers side by side, make a big chart listing tasks and materials down the left; individual contractors along the top. Query the contractors as necessary to clarify what each listing means. What does rough plumbing include? Does demolition come with a Dumpster? How thick is the framing lumber? Does the tile price count delivery, installation, grout, and sealing? What will be used? What type of underlayment will support the floor? How will it be prepared? Will a wood floor be glued or nailed? What grade of wood will it be? How many sandings will it get? What type of paper will be used? What type and how many coats of finish will be applied? If the words *or equivalent* are used, have him state what he would use as an alternative.

To determine your total financial commitment, add charges to the bid for permits, tax, and delivery. Will the new materials and appliances cost more to operate or repair than the ones they are replacing? What will consultant fees run; charges for removing asbestos or changing out a heating system? Do you need extra surveys or soil reports? If not included, compute what you must lay out for tarps, telephone, *porta-toilet,* and debris box.

Figure, too, the tariff for dining out over this period and the price tag on new furniture, cookware, accessories, or decorative finishes necessary to call the job complete. And factor in some money to cover those surprises hiding in the wall. If you are told a job will cost between $20,000 and $30,000, the true cost, cynics say, is their sum.

If bids are too high, explore how to lower them. You may have to substitute one product or technique for another; use drywall instead of that special plaster swathed by a craftsperson. That counter of expensive tiles may be shrunk to one or two accent pieces. The contractor can negotiate with his suppliers and get bids from different subcontractors. Or you may just have to prune.

REVIEWING THE NITTY-GRITTY OF A LAYOUT

■

A kitchen should, as American food doyen James Beard believed, be a combination of function and beauty. What that function is and how beauty is defined are constantly evolving. Reflecting on restaurant kitchens, chef Lydia Shire observes the grill's upstaging of the *bain-marie* in less than a decade. At home, the oven moved farther and farther from the kitchen center during the same period as we roasted and baked less frequently. Now it is moving back. Zapping replaced frying, heralding the microwave. But don't give the deep fryer's space away. It will be reincarnated.

A well-designed kitchen both enhances and reflects the lifestyles of the people who use it. To craft a kitchen fostering this harmony, these individual needs and preferences are married with current trends and basic layout principles. Ultimately, the room, to paraphrase Le Corbusier, becomes a machine for living.

As a first step in creating your kitchen, refer back to the lists assembled during the preremodeling phase (Chapter 1).

QUESTIONS TO RECONSIDER: PRINCIPLES AND PRIORITIES

Observe life in your kitchen. Beginning with breakfast, map the movements of all family members. What is the order in which you do things? How do you flow from cooking to serving to cleaning up to hanging out? Do you shop daily, buying in minute amounts, or hit the market weekly, acquiring a bulk that could service the next national disaster?

Are you a one-pot-per-meal family, or do you empty out the cupboards for even a simple repast? Are you a fresh-foodie, requiring lots of refrigeration, a pantry, and long preparation counters, or a packager, happy with a freezer, microwave, and warming oven? Is your kitchen a backdrop for take-out deli or a Domino's Pizza still life?

Are you a minimalist or hoarder with an old fondue pot still squirreled away? Do you want collectibles on the counter or behind closed doors? Are you a basics cook with a few pans or a one-man United Nations band of ethnic cookery, requiring an international *batterie de cuisine*?

How many cooks do you have? Are they children or caterers, tall or short, right- or left-handed? What is each person's cooking style? Do they cook for two or twenty? Daily or only on Christmas? How does their behavior vary from weekday to weekend; from family meal to a celebration with friends? Do they perch on stools or gather at a table? Are they isolationists or socialists, happiest surrounded by guests? Do they use a buffet or second work area regularly or only on occasion when a desk top might well do double duty; a pull-out or pull-up work area suffice?

Does the baker in the family want his own space? How about the pasta, the pizza, and the candlestick maker? A canner, beer brewer, and kosher homemaker have special requirements, while a winemaker needs a lab for apparatus and, when things don't go as planned, an expanse for fermenting vinegar jars.

Is this to be the mother of all kitchens with a greenhouse, office, bar, mixed-media center, and hangout for play, sewing, and crafts? Does it need a warm, romantic fireplace for snuggling by? Will it host a proofing box, soda fountain, built-in food dryer, or movie popcorn machine?

What other tasks are likely to be performed in this space? Gift wrapping? Flower arranging? How about laundry? Where will the kids put their muddy shoes and their hockey pucks? Where will they do their homework and, more important from their perspective, get their snacks? Is the dog going to be able to get out the door?

Where is the kitchen to be or, as Hamlet pondered, not to be? Will you change its location? Incorporate adjacent spaces such as a pantry, closet, porch, laundry, stairwell, bathroom, mud room, or breakfast nook? Will you relocate these areas? Is there a viable spot for them, or will an odd-shaped space dash your plans? Will you need to move doors for extra room; venture outside exterior walls? How will this affect your lot? What architectural alterations must be made to the property; adjustments to integrate the kitchen with the rest of the house?

Is there a view to celebrate? A southern exposure to dramatize the daylight? Will you be able to keep an eye on children while they play? Do you need a patch nearby for tending an herb and vegetable garden? A place for sorting the harvest with a route to the root cellar? Will you have access to a patio or yard for dining? Do you need a pass-through to the outside or, for that matter, through an interior wall from the kitchen to an eating area or dining room? Must you close off these zones for formal dining?

KITCHEN CONFIGURATIONS

Putting all these questions into a hat and pulling out a functional, beautiful kitchen is a pretty tall order. To do it effectively, most designers start by determining the shape of the cook's room within current confines or a newly created labyrinth.

Do I want an open kitchen?

A very large room—say upward of five hundred to seven hundred square feet—permits a kitchen to assume almost any form or float within its walls. Connected by countertops, this sphere is orbited by secondary work satellites, private sanctums for gazing at the moon, and perhaps a pantry or two. Proceed with caution in executing this canteen-in-the-round, for it is an expensive, complicated undertaking, requiring the expertise of an experienced designer to pull off.

A more commonly built modification, the "open kitchen," a workshop–dining room–tribal gathering suite, is most luxurious when at least four hundred to five hundred square feet are available for it. Nevertheless, its conviviality can be enjoyed in a mere twelve-foot-long one-walled kitchen that faces another room or has a large pass-through to it.

Scaled down in a small self-contained kitchen, the spirit of this concept can be expressed in a couple of easy chairs set in a corner or stools poked under an island.

Regardless of size, a communing kitchen is as welcome in today's casual lifestyle as it was in days of yore, when people gathered in this hub to take a bath.

Even if you prefer to cook (or bathe) without viewers, the flexibility of this arrangement is worth preserving. If you welcome onlookers but once a year, you will be happy not to be isolated. "Food is better, too, because the cook is in the kitchen, the way a chef is in his restaurant," says Julia Child. "No fresh green beans to warm up, losing their texture and color while I am in a dining room." And there's no better way to get help than to seduce onlookers with the heady aromas of their meal being prepared.

These multiplexes can be approached either as a single room or as two distinct zones. Linked together by the same materials, they can be divided temporarily by a sliding door, a screen, or a wall that opens and closes. A tall island or pass-through also helps separate the sections and hide cooking paraphernalia.

Laura Shapiro describes an early precedent in *Perfection Salad* with "sink and oven . . . located in a small adjoining room, so that laundry, baking, and dishwashing—'the most soiling employments'—need not occur . . . within anyone's sight."

If there is no partition, you'll have to dispose of the clutter so you can dine pleasantly in the kitchen after cooking in it. I turn my stove light off and hustle everything into the dishwasher. Julia buries evidence under a tray in her deep sink. The type of ventilation, lighting, heating, and air-conditioning specced assumes ever-greater import in an eat-in kitchen as does the selection of quiet appliances and surfaces.

In both *open* and *closed* kitchens, a *one-row, two-row, U shape, and L shape* are the common configurations. These names hold even when a door or window interrupts the space, impugning efficiency. Given adequate footage, a distance of twelve feet between parallel walls, these kitchens can increase their productivity with an island. U and L kitchens also lend themselves to adopting a peninsula. Though these names and letters may seem like some strange Morse code, they are useful descriptors for analyzing what can be done with your habitat.

One-Row Kitchen

A one-row or one-wall kitchen is a minimalist's fancy. Found most often in an apartment or a room used for other tasks, its presence may be masked by a screen or folding door. With the sink placed between the refrigerator and stove, and a minimum expanse of twelve to sixteen feet, it can prove quite workable for one person. Much smaller than that and you will have to use appliances and cabinets designed specifically for these kitchens from Lilliput.

Two-Row Kitchen

Most natural in a rectangular space, a corridor, galley, or two-row kitchen is composed of two parallel rows or a single row and a long island. Although countertops and storage space are bound to be restricted, this lay-

ONE-ROW KITCHEN

Built in a small space, a one-row kitchen lines up all cabinetry and appliances on a single wall. When part of another room, it can be temporarily closed off with a screen or doors.

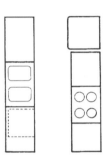

CORRIDOR KITCHEN

Composed of two parallel rows or a single row and a long island, a two-row kitchen is also called a corridor, galley, or pullman kitchen for its resemblance to a train's dining car. This undulating corridor space throws a curve to the more typical straitlaced two-row design.

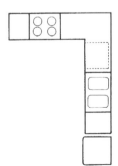

L-SHAPED KITCHEN

When the two parallel walls of a corridor kitchen are turned so they intersect perpendicularly, the kitchen becomes an L-Shape. Additional walls or an island are sometimes added to this practical configuration.

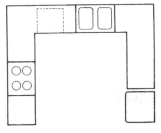

U-SHAPED KITCHEN

This horseshoe-shaped room is a good luck space for working efficiently. With a major appliance installed in each of the three arms, cooks can readily pivot from one to another. To work effectively in this kitchen, its base should measure at least eight feet.

ISLAND

An island, usually a separate freestanding table or cabinet in the center of a work area, is the eye of a kitchen's storm of activity. It can be reserved for dining, and play host to all manner of appliances. Or it can assume a flurry of preparation tasks. This open island functions both as a storage and display shelf.

out is also an efficient atelier for one person. For optimal functioning, place the sink and range on the same side and the refrigerator across the way or the sink and refrigerator on one side and the range on the other. Locate the lone appliance between the other two or across from the sink, where its door can be opened without interference. To open two doors simultaneously across from each other, eight feet must exist between the parallel walls.

With the draw of a train's dining car, this *pullman* kitchen attracts a lot of hungry diners, who get underfoot as they're passing through. Minimize the choo-choo effect by closing off one end of the room for an eating area.

L-Shaped Kitchen

An L-shaped room occupies two perpendicular walls, forming a cozy nook sequestered from disruptive traffic. An island is often added to this configuration in large rooms, further discouraging interlopers while welcoming a bevy of cooks. Here they work facing each other, conversing and collaborating easily as they cook.

An L can be formed with two adjacent walls or by adding a peninsula to one wall. Additional arms can turn it into an E- or F-shaped kitchen. In this octopus alphabet soup, the corners at each junction will have to be planned judiciously for maximal use and multiple door openings.

U-Shaped Kitchen

When space is ample, many kitchen cheerleaders yell, "Give me a U." A three-sided workplace with a separate wall for refrigerator, stove, and sink, this shape embraces its tenants, providing a natural barrier to drop-in traffic. Studies at Purdue University's Motion and Time Study Laboratory found cooks took fewer steps in this horseshoe, substantially cutting food preparation time.

The base of the U, generally housing the sink in its center, should run at least eight feet so the area doesn't feel confining. At the other extreme, in a very large U, appliances must be brought in from the ends of each leg, or they will be much too far apart to be used comfortably.

As in an L, two people can cook here simultaneously, but they will be dancing cheek to cheek with their backs facing each other. Like the L, the U gives you corners to deal with. Adding a peninsula transforms it into a G.

Islands and Peninsulas

An island can constitute an entire kitchen in an open space or, parallel to a wall or second island, it can form a two-row kitchen. Typically it is represented by a freestanding table or cabinet centered in the work site.

An island can be a mere two by two feet, actually more like a worktable, or large enough for a family powwow. Too often, out of control, it becomes a racetrack for the cook workhorse to gallop around. For a long island that's sound, take the Solomonic approach and cut it in half, leaving a space in between for quickly crisscrossing the room.

An island can assume any shape or be adapted from a piece of existing furniture. It can be open on one side; closed on another. Rounding its corners makes it safe to scoot by, while a toe kick protects it from hippopotamus stature. With good legs and an intriguing form, it adds architectural panache. Glass shelves convert it to a display cabinet.

It can be mobilized with casters or, braked or wedded to its spot, it can be plumbed and electrified, eliminating extension cords. If it's wired, avoid protruding plugs or handles that are unpleasant to work against. In all cases, its surface should be well lit. Encircle it with sufficient space for traffic to circulate and doors to open.

Installing a cooktop or sink in an island can shorten distances between appliances, simplifying meal preparation. To be useful and safe, allot a generous amount of counter space on each side of the equipment, place controls behind it or on both sides, and direct it away from cross traffic. Even with these precautions, I must go on record against this placement for a cooktop. It can't be ventilated as effectively in the open and seems like an accident waiting to happen.

An island is a safer harbor for dishwashers,

microwaves, and undercounter refrigerators. It provides an extra countertop for cooking or rolling out pastry, a work space for a second cook, a landing surface for a stove or side-by-side refrigerator, and a snack or dining bar.

As a mealtime haunt it can be casual or formal; for breakfast, dinner, or a party buffet display. Eating and cooking can be separated symbolically by elevating part of the island or building on a second story to shield diners from spatter, presenting a bird's-eye view of the mess. This nook can also be lowered to accept chairs. But, by changing heights, you do lose the flexibility of an expansive unbroken space.

With or without food, family and friends converge on an island, where they can gab without getting in the cook's way. To entertain them, a TV and stereo are often installed in or above this epicenter.

A peninsula, like an island, can divide the working and socializing sections of the kitchen, allowing people to work facing each other. Installing a sink or cooktop in it—same caveat as earlier—offers a view of other work centers while you're occupied at this one.

A cabinet can be hung above a peninsula—with doors in both front and back—providing additional storage space. Just be sure this upper story is stepped back from the base cabinet so you don't bang your head on it. In a small kitchen, a peninsula is more practical than an island. Occupying less space, it also serves as a traffic cop.

Multiple workstations can be created in a kitchen too small for an island or peninsula by sequestering pullout work carts in a corner or closet, attaching lift-up tables to the wall, or installing pullout butcher blocks or cutting boards in a base cabinet.

TRAFFIC PATTERNS

Traffic patterns—where people congregate and how they move in and out of any of these shaped rooms—affect safety and ease of operation in a kitchen. Keep navigation issues foremost in mind as you lay out people movers, establishing clear paths for working and transferring hot food, and a circumscribed area for children to dally.

Locate windows and entrance doors where the opening of one doesn't interfere with the opening of another and out of—not into—the room where someone might be standing with a hot pot. At the kitchen crossroads, make aisles wide enough for several people to pass while appliance and cabinet doors are open.

Lacking the food runners Montezuma had to fetch ice from the mountains, contemporary kitchens beg for direct byways. Create an unobstructed route for harvesting food in the garden, gathering groceries from the garage, and directing dinner to the dining room. Expressways are needed as well for removing refuse and dispensing food to freezers and pantries in other venues. Just don't break up the room with more than three entrances.

WINDOWS/SKYLIGHTS

Once a room's general shape is established, the window of opportunity exists to assign these openings a location before their ideal position is usurped. To bring natural light into a room effectively is not merely a question of plopping a window on a wall but of divining it strategically where it provides the most light during the day, reflecting indirectly off the walls. As long as the right type of window is utilized (page 211), impeccably fit in its opening, and well maintained, it preserves energy and lowers heating bills. It is also a green light on free light.

Window number and dimension are usually calculated to equal 10 percent of a kitchen's floor space or whatever is specified by code. Multiple locations are mandatory for cross-ventilation and light diffusion, preventing glare and sun spots. Window sizes are not standardized, so choose models you want off the shelf and design the wall around them. If you just leave a hole to fill, you'll be stuck with a tab for a custom job.

Take northern exposure out of this picture as an only window and bring it back to TV. Though it provides a soft diffuse light all day, it can be cold in snowy regions. If you do put apertures on a northern wall, sink them low to capture more light.

EASTERN LIGHT WALL
This bank of windows brightens the kitchen, bathing it in morning light.

To sing "Here comes the sun," go south and give at least one major window a southern orientation. Capturing warmth during the winter, the heat can become excessive during summer, but control is possible. Higher in the sky this time of year, the sun can be thwarted with a roof line that extends beyond the window. If the heat can't be focused indirectly under the eaves, harness it with an awning, shade, blind, or resistant glass (page 219).

One clever landscape artist planted deciduous trees outside his window to minimize the glare. Their leaves provided a protective canopy in summer; their bare limbs an entrance for winter sun. Refrain from placing a greenhouse on a southern wall, where the bite of dog days is scorching. A western exposure can be relentlessly hot and glaring in summer as well. Cold in winter, a western window is nevertheless mandatory for catching afternoon rays.

EASTERN LIGHT WALL
This bank of windows brightens the kitchen, bathing it in morning light.

Crossing the room, an eastern window welcomes a bright morning glow.

A skylight's direction depends on the kitchen's location in the home. In cold regions, it may not be worthwhile to have a skylight facing north unless the kitchen is in the interior of the house and this is the only way to light it naturally.

Along with this tack you may want to piggyback on light other rooms receive by opening up the kitchen into adjacent spaces or incorporating glass block into one of its walls.

When outlining the skylight's size and shape (or a high window's), plan its cleaning access as well.

Consider how it will look on the roof and from inside the kitchen and check out the view beforehand from a seated and standing position. After much expense, all Elinor Garner got was her neighbor's utility lines. While you're at it, assign a place for an operable skylight and tall window's telescopic pole.

Though decent exposure is the primary consideration for assigning window placements, the desire to create privacy, capitalize on a scenic view, hide something unsightly, or watch children playing in a yard may take precedence. Windows next to or across from the stove aid in ventilation and provide makeup air while those behind a sink must be coordinated with the venting pipe's run.

Mounting a window flush with a countertop makes it easy to pass things back and forth outside and provides good working light. Raise it three inches to diminish splatter odds. Higher up, at sixty-four inches or so off the floor, light streams in more lavishly than when situated down below.

Window and wall cabinet placement must be juggled so as not to waste space. When placed side by side, leave a gap between them to frame the window, guide light into the room, and cluster curtains on a rod. When devoting walls to cabinets, mount windows in the backsplash.

FILLING IN THE FORM

The kitchen has a shape, and it has windows. Now the challenge is to figure out where to put everything. Although many texts zone the kitchen into individual activity areas—a minicommunity with preparation, mixing, cooking, and maybe an office center—I find it easier to start with the sink, refrigerator, stove, and eating area and then organize activities and supplemental equipment around them. Once these spaces are assigned, the cabinets almost place themselves.

To identify the ideal location for major appliances, imagine food moving throughout your kitchen on an automatic conveyor belt with one area flowing into another. Direction will depend on your handedness. Bring in the groceries and throw them on a table with your keys and the mail. Disperse the items to a refrigerator, freezer, cupboard, drawer, pantry, or even a basement or garage.

Time to consume an ingredient? Retrieve it, wash it, dry it, open it, and chop, mix, beat, or knead it. Will you serve it forth raw or zap it, convection it, griddle it, broil it, poach it, deep-fry it, stir-fry it, or just sauté it over a plain ol' burner? Or will you bake it? To perform any of these tasks, you'll need bowls, pots, pans, and tools. Perhaps you'll need to introduce other ingredients or just water from the tap. You're not done yet. Plate it, transport it to point of consumption, and serve it forth. Along the way or afterward, clean up!

In my ideal work space, fantasized on this conveyor belt journey, the cook transfers food from the refrigerator to a counter where everything is stashed as it is taken in and out. Pushing it along, its next stop is a sink, where it is washed, or counter, where it is prepped along with other ingredients pulled from nearby cupboards and a pantry. After this treatment, it is dispatched to a heatproof counter adjacent to the cooktop or island behind it that serves as the stove's landing space. Next to the cooktop, I'd locate a large serving counter at the ready for plating cooked food and conveying it to the eating area. When finished, all dirty dishes get bused to a counter on the other side of the sink from where food was prepared. The dishwasher is housed here as well.

CONNECTING THE DOTS:
THE KITCHEN TRIANGLE
AND TRAPEZOID

Once the stove, sink, and refrigerator are assigned, a work track drawn between their centers should link them into a triangle, long the classic symbol of good kitchen design.

The triangle's optimum total perimeter has been defined by the National Kitchen & Bath Association as fifteen to twenty-two feet. The organization's guidelines suggest a refrigerator-to-sink arm of five to seven feet, sink-to-range five to six feet, and cooktop-to-refrigerator five to nine feet. If segments are

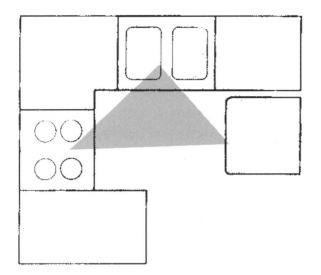

TRIANGLE
The kitchen triangle, long the symbol of good design, is a streamlined work tract formed by an imaginary line that links the centers of the stove, sink, and refrigerator. With more equipment and multiple cooks occupying today's kitchens, the room is evolving geometrically into several separate triangles or one triangle with multiple arms flowing off of it.

closer, the cook is likely to be cramped; countertop space at a premium. Longer than this, and it's trekking time.

Not everyone concurs. "We design kitchen equipment to a two-step rule," says Earl F. McKinney, a principal in Hamill & McKinney Architects and Engineers in Lexington, Kentucky. "Someone who has to take more than two steps to complete a task is wasting time and energy." And this is still one too many steps for homeowner Jeff Zinsmeyer, who wants to do all preparation with one foot firmly planted on the ground. His Boston neighbor, Julia Child, runs as far away as she can from this concept. "I am not one to worry about the scientific relation of how many steps it takes to move from one work place to the other; the more exercise, the better, I think," the grande dame says.

Regardless of whether you prefer to stand pat or sprint for your supper, the triangle is a useful concept to consider in both planning and evaluating a kitchen layout—as long as it is interpreted with an open mind. As kitchens explode with more equipment and more cooks, a new fluidity in movement is mandatory. Pushing out like an amoeba crossed with

an octopus, this room is being reconfigured with new arms and legs.

When multiple cooks use the kitchen, they may share an arm or two of the same triangle and then go off on a separate tangent. Or each person may have his own triangle. Both arrangements are effective as long as the second triangle doesn't cross through the first. When having more than one cook is only an occasional happenstance, you may want to set up a secondary workshop on a temporary basis by making the primary one more flexible and *stretchable*, with, for example, pullout tables and cutting boards.

What each triangle contains depends on the specialties of each cook. Usually the auxiliary area offers an additional sink and maybe a small refrigerator, oven, grill, or cooktop. When there is only one cooktop, place a large counter on each side of it or an island across the way so each individual has a safe haven to work.

When a sink must be shared, an amicable solution is to set two single basins side by side, each with its own faucet.

It is less important whether your kitchen forms a triangle or trapezoid than that it works for you and reflects decisions and compromises you make. The busiest center, the sink's position is primary. Yet it may have to relinquish this position to the stove for ventilation purposes.

The third point on my triangle is warmly occupied by a fireplace and two chairs that displaced the refrigerator down the room apiece. While I have to do a bit of a jig to get supplies, I've gotten used to taking everything out before cooking starts. In thinking about the distance between points, keep in mind that the route should meander by tools most frequently tapped and enjoyed.

ACTIVITY AREAS

Storage

Once the triangle (or trapezoid) is formed, assess each area and what you want to assemble there. In so doing, remember that *everything should have its own space and be stored at the point where you will use it first.* If this is not possible, arrange housing at the last place you will work with it. Gadgets employed in more than one location are best duplicated in a second—and even third—venue or, if two cooks are sharing a space, in the same drawer.

Larger appliances, such as a toaster, microwave, or warming drawer, are equally peripatetic. Either do a body double or decide where they will be handiest.

Time and motion studies have given us excellent information about structuring storage from the ergonomic standpoint of making the work space comfortable to negotiate. In contemplating where to store things, first identify your realm of comfortable access. Cornell University found 79.6 inches the highest comfortable overhead reach for five-foot-three to five-foot-seven individuals; 69 inches over a 25-inch-deep countertop. Forty-eight inches was established as a side-to-side reach and 24 inches the lowest bending point off the floor. Revise these figures according to your height.

Within this comfortable reaching zone, store habitually used items in the front of a cabinet from twenty-four (thirty for the elderly) to fifty-six inches off the floor. Remember as well the conclusion from the 1951 study on oxygen consumed for household tasks: "Reaching up with the arms requires less energy than bending the body."

Other sage storage planning advice from my photocopy on motion-mindedness:

- **Keep items together that are used together.**

- **Store like items together.**

- **Provide clear visibility of all supplies so that everything can be located at a glance.**

- **Arrange items so they are easy to grasp at the point of storage without removing other items first.**

- **Relegate heavy equipment to storage at or near floor level.**

When everything has been assigned a spot, make sure a place had been designated for an apron, candles, a step stool, and those oversized turkey platters, often left out in the cold. As cabinetmaker Peter

De Caprio says of his boxes, "They're not efficient unless you know exactly what's going in them."

Food Preparation

Some kitchens have both a preparation area for peeling, chopping, or otherwise preparing food and a mixing area for blending ingredients into a specific dish. As stated earlier, it seems most efficient to combine these tasks—plus baking and canning—in one large center. Locate this expanse between either the refrigerator and the sink or the sink and the stove. The choice depends on whether the focus is on produce or what you're taking on and off a burner.

Start with the refrigerator, outfitting any cabinet above with half lazy Susans, pullout shelves, or vertical or horizontal tray dividers. Let a microwave reign nearby if children claim it for snacks or if meals are based on frozen foods. Wherever the microwave finally comes to rest, treat it like Nefertiti's tomb and pack bowls, cookware, stirring spoons, and plastic wrap needed for its daily functions around it.

Storage paraphernalia—plastic containers, freezer paper, plastic wrap, aluminum foil, scissors, tape, and marking pens—also need to call this area home. If you use boxes of extra-large restaurant-size wraps, a good way to save money, creative planning is necessary to access these space eaters easily. Keep glasses with a wine and bottle opener at the ready for refrigerated beverages.

At the sink end of the food preparation area, house vegetable brushes, peelers, sieves, colanders, salad dryers, towels (paper and terry), and dry foods in the pasta, rice, beans, and potato families that simmer in water. Prepare for their cooking with some pots plus a colander and cutting board that fit in the sink.

Between the sink and refrigerator (or sink and cooking area), store small electrics in an appliance garage on the counter or a pull-up shelf underneath: blender, mixer, juicer, food processor, coffeemaker, wafflemaker, and machines for bread, ice cream, and pasta. For drying homemade noodles, mount an expandable towel bar in a drawer with a dropped front, a pullout towel rack in a base cabinet, or pull-out dowels on the side of a cabinet at the end of a run.

Hit preparation grounds running with supplies of knives, bowls, whisks, wooden spoons, cooking silver, can openers, potato mashers, measuring cups and spoons, plastic, aluminum and wax paper wraps, and several grooved cutting boards. Spices, condiments, flour, sugar, and other frequently claimed groceries will be up front here (or in an adjacent pantry). Before closing up this area, leave an opening for a chair to sit on while you whistle and work.

Baking

As much as I'd like a separate baking area, I'd have one only if I could outfit it with a second blender, food processor, and mixer. But there is really no need for this; the food preparation area works wonderfully. Molds, tins, and trays can be stored here, or in the vicinity if they aren't part of your regular repertoire. An oven would improve this neighborhood.

Whatever area is used for baking should have a marble- or granite-topped counter. Freestanding, an island or peninsula serves this function beautifully. A pullout cart (with brakes) zooms to the rescue as well, but it may not be able to support a heavy stone top. When no wider than three feet and lowered to six or seven inches below the height of your bent elbow, these surfaces are ideal for rolling pastry and kneading bread. Circling them, you can reach doughs conveniently from all sides.

Major bakers may want to emulate Flo Braker. Fitting a pullout cart with racks for cookie sheets, she created her own restaurant trolley for preparing baked goods. Once formed, they are transferred to a tray underneath and then whisked to one of the extra shelves added to both the refrigerator and freezer for this purpose. From there they pass directly to the oven. Possessed with ideas as good as her cakes, this pastry chef displays her rolling pin collection on the wall and cradles eggs in a groove cut in her countertop to protect them as they come to room temperature.

Looking for a home for a single rolling pin? Emulate another sage who bunkers it in a shelf built under the wall cabinet.

Cooking

The cooking area must be hands off from small hands and have a direct, unobstructed shipping lane to the sink for water transport. This region may be occupied solely by a cooktop (or range) or shared with a griddle, grill, warming drawer, pot filler, and small countertop appliances in the electric fryer, rotisserie, or convection oven categories. Adaptable to other sites, toasters, ovens, and microwaves make themselves at home here as well.

The cooktop can share a counter with the food preparation center as long as it is lengthy enough to accommodate both tasks. A heatproof off-loading space, recommended for every cooktop and oven, is essential next to a grill, electric cooktop, or gas cooktop with an S grate that retains heat even when burners are turned off.

Considerable berthing space is needed on this firing line for cutting boards, pot holders, cake racks, aluminum foil, parchment paper; salt, pepper, oils, and other condiments; pot, pan, and lid paraphernalia; and cooking implements—spatulas, tongs, ladles, wooden spoons, slotted spoons, and whisks.

Pots and pans can be stored above a low or waist-high wall oven, on a hanging rack suspended from the ceiling, or below an independent cooktop whose pipes and depth will dictate their drawer or shelf size. A shelf can be hung above the cooktop as long as it's fireproof and narrow enough not to interfere with the ventilation's draw.

Even with these precautions, it's necessary to stock baking soda, large lids to smother flare-ups, and a fire extinguisher filled with a nontoxic halon gas between the cooking area and exit from the house.

Instead of hunting for those cooling racks as a cake is coming out of the oven, affix a permanent rack to the adjacent wall. You can have a pull-down frame fabricated at a metal shop as Sandra Perry did or a shelf that pulls up on spring-loaded hinges. Just don't install one of those commercial racks on the stove back over your burners, where steam and humidity rise to destroy whatever is cooling.

Serving

Among kitchen activity areas, serving is too often the abandoned orphan. Prepping and cooking claim every inch of counter space, leaving no place for dishing out the food. Best situated between the stove and dining table, this *staging area* (as it is called in restaurantese) requires twelve inches for the pot of food plus another foot for each dinner plate. In smaller rooms, dishes will have to be stacked and served one by one. Factor in an outlet for a hand mixer or an electric knife and storage for cutting boards, serving platters, knives, ladles, tongs, scissors, and paper towels for dabbing plate rims.

Eating

Responding to individual peculiarities, the dimensions and locations of eating areas vary more than any other installation. Some people eschew both major and minor meals in the kitchen because they don't like dining with meal preparation clutter. Others partake of casual snacks at an island aerie in this room and formal meals at a table. Serving and cleanup are easier in this latter scenario, but space may prohibit this choice even when desirable.

Casual or formal, keep the eating area as far away from the stove as possible. Wherever it is, figure out square footage for each boarder and chair—both when stationary and when moved in and out—and *squeeze* space for someone else to get by.

When dining is ensconced in a nook, you may want company from a toaster, microwave, wafflemaker, built-in hot plate, table linens, and breakfast supplies (everyone for himself). Giving a command performance, what better place for a coffee bar with grinder, automatic coffeemaker, espresso machine, and related gimcrackery for brewing caf, decaf, and half-caf creations?

Cleanup

Cleanup, like serving, is a vital center that gets short shrift in the planning phase. If this is not a problem during casual meals, count on it tripping you up during a feast. You can usually finesse one course, but all havoc reigns once dirty dishes start coming back while you're trying to dish out subsequent offerings.

Like Carlos Castaneda, dirty dishes need their own spot, if only a designated counter next to the sink that doesn't interfere with either preparation or cooking. No space? Bring in a rolling cart or folding table for stashing dirty dishes when you entertain.

Cleanup is likely to prove a challenge even in a household with large sinks in two different areas, for logic dictates that major preparation and cleanup transpire in the vicinity where the dishwasher is located. Otherwise you are moving pots, pans, and dishes back and forth.

Two dishwashers come to the rescue in a kitchen generating humongous numbers of dirty dishes. House one on either side of the primary sink unless the second dishwasher is a mini bar model or the household is kosher, separating dishes used for dairy from those handling meat. This way you can start filling the second machine as soon as the first is full. An additional drain may be necessary.

The second sink area can be commandeered for cleaning china, crystal, and other service not destined for the dishwasher. Have a cabinet lying in wait near this sink or in the dining room where they are presented. The closer this sink is to the dining room, the fewer steps must be taken. The primary sink, on the other hand, should be as far away from this elegant room as possible to mute audible cooking and dishwashing noises during a dinner party.

Station everyday dishes, silver, and glassware in a cabinet within easy reach of the dishwasher on a path to the table where you dine. When a peninsula separates eating from working areas, dish cabinets can be placed above with openings on both sides, minimizing steps to set the table and unload the dishwasher.

ACTIVITY AREAS

Both table and island double as eating and working counters.

OVEN PLACEMENT
An oven can be placed outside the main work triangle if it is not used frequently.

BAKING CART
Housed undercounter, Flo Braker's movable pastry cart locks when landed. The sweet treats mixed or rolled on its top are transferred directly to the trays at the bottom, then to the refrigerator or freezer as needed, and ultimately to the oven to bake.

CLEAN-UP AREA
A plate rack is handily placed right next to this clean-up sink and the counter is subtly routed to use for a dish drainer or for food preparation.

MIXING HIDEAWAY
Appliances can be hidden behind cabinet doors and easily pulled out for use.

Above the sink, consider placing an open or closed dish draining cabinet with vertical dividers and a slotted bottom. Limit it to a wall cabinet's depth of twelve inches or less so it doesn't become a head banger.

Besides the sink and dishwasher, the cleanup area includes the garbage can, compost bucket, drainboard, and cleaning supplies (stashed wisely in a child lockout cabinet). Recycling bins and trash compactors are usually placed here, too, if not in the garage or storage room.

When space obliges, house the city's recycling buckets to roll from sink to curb on trash day. To make unloading a cinch, place baskets against an outside wall that opens to the garage or exterior of the house. Or place the bins outside the house or in the garage and a chute in the kitchen for dropping recyclables through to them.

To plan this area, bus dishes mentally from the table, pots from the cooktop, and bowls from the preparation center. Ensure that movements flow from the table to a garbage can to the sink. When you're greeted with multiple sinks, the first stop should be at the smaller basin with the disposer and then on to the second rinsing sink. End this dirty dancing at the dishwasher.

Accumulate dirty dishes on a large counter next to the disposer; drain clean ones in the rinsing sink or over the dishwasher.

SATELLITES

Pantry

For retrieval's sake, store food in wall, base, or utility cabinets where its transformation begins, be it a sink, preparation, baking, or cooking area. Yet, practicality aside, there is something homey and reassuringly old-fashioned about a separate walk-in floor-to-ceiling pantry. Exhibiting the blue-ribbon pickles you've brined, it stashes dry goods and paper supplies along with odd paraphernalia that doesn't fit anyplace else. A pantry can also be designed to warehouse brooms and cleaning supplies.

A pantry's address of distinction lies between the grocery entrance and preparation area. When it's insulated and air-conditioned—or built over an air duct that keeps it at fifty-two to fifty-five degrees—flowers, plants, and soft drinks lie happily in wait here for a party. Potatoes, onions, tomatoes, ripening fruit, cheese, butter, and wine—foods unhappy in a refrigerator—flourish in this larder's fresh cool breezes. Just don't let the big chill come and freeze them.

Like other cabinets and food storage facilities, the walk-in pantry needs to be orchestrated carefully to make it a helpmate. Place shelves close enough together so space is not wasted. Narrow them down so products are only one or two rows deep or fit them with pullout baskets. A horseshoe shape brings easy access with good luck.

Even the best-organized pantry may not be sufficient for bulk provisions. If you're a stockpiler, identify a second storage area off-site for backup.

Bar

Frequent hosts will find it most convivial to set up a bar, even if it is outside the kitchen. Going all the way, stock a grand bar with a separate refrigerator, ice machine, dishwasher, glass washer, glass filler, sink, soda dispenser, and beer tap built into the wall. Garnish with a blender, ice bucket, glasses, cutting board, napkins, towels, coasters, knives, corkscrews, bottle openers, and citrus zesters. While you're at it, gather some wine and liquor, and store it low down in base cabinets, where it won't overheat.

Scaling down to size, assign at least one out-of-the-way counter with a drawer underneath for drinks and their liquid assets: knives, zester, bottle and wine openers, and pullout cutting board. With glasses and ice buckets in a cabinet overhead and wine and liquor bottles below, drinks can be served to a crowd without interfering with dinner preparations.

Broom Closet

Although a broom and dustpan are prerequisites for maintaining a kitchen, the space their closet occupies might be better relegated to finer things (like caviar and Champagne). It also seems more hygienic to banish them to a garage, utility room, or basement stairwell along with a vacuum cleaner and cleaning supplies. Away from view, they can be wall-mounted with hooks or a holder picked up at the hardware store. Wherever they are, provide some means to store paper and plastic bags for recycling. If they ultimately wind up in the kitchen, sweep them into a corner.

Laundry

More and more people seem to be airing their dirty laundry in public with washers and dryers on an external kitchen wall, where they can be vented. Secreted behind closed doors, they suggest a hidden pantry. Some opt for a full-scale operation with a washer, dryer, laundry sink, ironing board, supply cabinet, drip-dry corner, and tilt-down bin for soiled clothes, while others stow a stacked washer and dryer in a closet and pullout ironing board in a drawer. The kitchen table finds new meaning in this washday crowd as a folding center.

Office

Kitchen offices range from a simple message-taking counter to an executive suite replete with a desk, file cabinet, cubbyholes, bookshelves, chalkboard, typewriter, and the latest computer technology. It can be reserved for a cook's private scribblings, shared with children doing homework, or converted to a table-top for a buffet or hobbies.

The telephone can be stationed permanently in the office (as well as on an island or shelf under a countertop), but greater flexibility exists with a portable or wall-hung model with a long cord. If your cooking style is making reservations, this may be the most-used piece of equipment in the kitchen.

Along with its placement, you'll need to decide whether this telephone is an extension or service center to be outfitted with answering machine, telephone book storage, and fax. For a modern communication station, add an intercom or Smart House electric system.

Placing a computer in the kitchen, where it can be destroyed by grease and steam, seems like megabyte suicide. Yet it is a justifiable sacrifice, entertaining children and rallying a family in a common room. Provide for it properly with a surge protector, battery backup, accessible power outlet, software, mouse cage, vibration-free environment, and cables for hiding and tidying wires and plugs. View it ergonomically, assigning the CPU, keyboard, monitor, printer, and paper holder a comfortable working height.

Storing books in a kitchen unleashes the monster of deciding what stays and what goes. The cleverest solutions I've seen were devised by food professionals Lorna Sass, who hides her treasures in decorative columns, and Mitzie Cutler, who marches them around the room on a shelf below the ceiling. A handsome library ladder stands in the corner for their retrieval. Ken Krone keeps a photocopy machine, his "most valued kitchen appliance," in the room for copying recipes that he hangs from a cabinet as cues.

Mixed Media

Hi-fi has become hi-sci-fi as home theaters invade the kitchen and motorized TVs descend from a hiding place in the ceiling or a platform behind closed doors, turning automatically to face their programmed direction. (And I thought I was hip with simple ceiling stereo speakers and a remote volume control in a cabinet for regulating the stereo receiver in my living room!)

TV to earth? How about installing it in a cabinet—either behind or instead of a door—under a wall cabinet or on a flush or pullout shelf? Watch a free-floating TV mounted on swivel wall or ceiling brackets. Alice Medrich is sorry she didn't build the TV on her counter into a cabinet. "Now that the kitchen is so beautiful the little appliances catch your eye when they didn't before," she says.

Wherever it roams, be sure the tube is visible from your line of sight. When closed circuit, it can monitor security or children. Prop a VCR, CD player, and tape deck in the same cabinet along with their spins.

LIBRARY PANTRY
This pantry, which opens like a book, assigns a visible spot to everything stored within. Stacked one item deep, ingredients are both easy to retrieve and put away.

BAR
An undercounter icemaker, small beverage refrigerator, and drink paraphernalia can be stashed outside the main work area in a wet bar that dispenses drinks without interfering with other preparations going on simultaneously in the kitchen. This addition is particularly welcome in kitchens used for entertaining.

BROOM CLOSET
Cleaning supplies, like everything else in the kitchen, should be organized so that each item has its own separate space and is within view. Commercial hanging clips are exceptionally sturdy.

SATELLITES

PLANT LEDGE

This ledge functions like a greenhouse; it houses fresh herbs and other plants between the sink and a window where they add warmth to the kitchen.

KITCHEN OFFICE

A kitchen office can be as simple as this pull-down rack that attaches to the bottom of a wall cabinet, or a separate area fitted with a full-sized desk, filing drawers, and cubbyholes.

Greenhouse

A greenhouse can be a puffery for a few potted plants or a full-fledged ag system in a glass conservatory fitted with electricity for fluorescent tubes or mercury-vapor grow lights. In its most frequent guise, it is secured behind the sink in a bay window or *sun bay*, admitting light through its top as well as its three sides. For ventilation, crank open a roof or side panels.

A faucet's spray hose attachment should take care of watering; an adjacent counter potting, seeding, and transplanting. Store the tools for these tasks in deep drawers with garden and flower-arranging supplies or move these kits with their kaboodles out of the kitchen to a potting shed.

Enamored with the idea of having an indoor garden, many people don't realize how difficult it is to clean a greenhouse situated behind a countertop unless they have arms like a chimpanzee. Before it is a done deal, give good thought to its access. Support the plants' weight with tempered glass or other waterproof shelves and catch dripping water with a removable pan or ledge that slopes down toward the sink.

Pethouse

An animal bed and dishes can be substituted for a base cabinet or carved into an island. One savvy homeowner built a litter box into a base cabinet with a fan to eject its odors outdoors. If the pet is not too large, there may be room for a supply drawer there as well. Along with a house, you may want to encourage your pet's independence with a door or panel it can push to let itself in or out.

While planning storage, make sure you're not one of the many remodelers who end up with a fifty-pound sack of dog food in the middle of their new kitchen and no place to put it. Assign it to a base cabinet with a tilt-out door or pullout bin.

PONDERING PLACEMENTS

Before deciding where in the kitchen you want to put each item, spend time thinking about how you use it, special installation requirements, and its proximity to other tools whose placement you're considering. Although many of these issues have been discussed, more practical assignments can usually be made by focusing on each piece of equipment individually.

Lighting placement is so entwined with the type of fixtures used that it is discussed separately in Chapter 6.

Refrigerator

The center of all kitchen activity—snacks, food preparation, table setting, and cleanup —the refrigerator is most convenient in a central location. Nevertheless, some people prefer it at the very spot where they bring in groceries or in a remote corner where kids can bop in and out unobtrusively for snacks.

If additional cold storage is contemplated—a second bar refrigerator, miniundercounter refrigerator in the kitchen, or freezer in a garage or utility room—review its access and connection with the primary cooler. For all its popularity, the refrigerator requires privacy. It is generally ill advised to place it next to a dishwasher, cooktop, stove, or even microwave. Impaired by heat and steam from these appliances, it expends too much energy doing its job. If no other option exists, separate the area between appliances with fiberglass or foil-faced foam insulation. To protect the refrigerator from heat, keep it out of any area likely to soar above ninety degrees or cool it with a fan or air conditioner.

At the other extreme, don't target its installation for the netherworld below sixty degrees. Frost-free models, in particular, need to come in from the cold. If you live in an extreme climate, ask the manufacturer if the model you are considering can withstand being left to fend for itself in the garage or in an unheated house while you are off sipping hot toddies around a roaring fire in a ski lodge.

Wherever its placement, the refrigerator door should open so it swings away from an adjacent landing counter. This way food can easily be transferred to the counter and sent on its preparation journey. Purchase a refrigerator/freezer that hinges on the proper side or offers reversible hinging, a flexibility provided by units with freezers on the top or bottom but no through-the-door ice dispenser. If you already have a refrigerator, place it where it opens correctly.

Less convenient, a side-by-side refrigerator welcomes a work counter across the way. If this is not feasible, position a counter next to the freezer for goods removed from the refrigerator and, conversely, a counter next to the refrigerator for freezer friends.

Though refrigerators are often installed in a corner or at the end of a cabinet run so as not to break up counter space, a door may have to open more than ninety degrees for crispers to pull out. For this to happen, the unit must be slightly deeper than any cabinet it is placed in. Check on necessary clearances for your unit as well as the amount of space that must be left to operate a lock. Determine, too, how close a refrigerator must be to water lines with an automatic icemaker or on-the-door water dispenser.

Though current fashion dictates that the refrigerator fit flush with a row of cabinets for a streamlined look, you may want to reuse your old refrigerator or pass on the privilege of paying more for a built-in unit. Never fear, the same look can be achieved. The refrigerator can be recessed into a nonstructural wall, framed by a special cabinet, or surrounded by same-depth cabinets above. To permit the refrigerator door to open, cabinets alongside should be slightly shallower.

When determining the necessary depth of this housing (or placement of any unit), build handle depth, plug space, special trim kits, and room for air circulation and heat dissipation into your calculations and see if plugs can be recessed into the wall. Whatever framework you devise, be cautious of burying a freestanding box in a closed space where air necessary for its proper functioning is not available. Make sure, too, that the refrigerator can easily be pulled out to clean its compressor and condenser coils.

Icemaker

For maximum production, a separate icemaker depends on an optimum ambient temperature of seventy degrees and water temperature of fifty degrees. To increase its yield, locate it in the coolest part of the kitchen or in a butler's pantry, away from cooktops, ovens, windows, and skylights.

Wine Cooler

Destroyed by heat and light, wine coolers also relish a cool spot away from cookers, windows, skylights, and bright lights. This is particularly important if the unit has a glass door.

Cooktop

Cooktops conventionally have been placed at countertop level, but smart designers are lowering them to thirty inches or so from the floor, where stirring is easier and a better vantage point exists for peeking into tall pots. While many cooktops and ranges are now trimmed in metal so no crumb space exists between them and adjacent countertops, commercial grills and gas cooktops still have a gap. Fill it with a metal strip that can be pulled out for cleaning or moving the unit.

Cooktop/Range

Center the range in a wall or at least far enough in from the ends, where a fire spreads faster and it is harder to retrieve pots or for more than one person to cook simultaneously. For these reasons, it's also not smart to angle a range across a corner, words to eat in a small one-person kitchen that reaps the benefits of the storage room offered behind this placement. In this case, recess the stove back from the corner so a cook can easily move items to and from the counters flanking it.

When the range grows to professional stature or is on line with a grill, griddle, bank of ovens, and warming drawer, this area becomes a focal point set off nicely in an alcove. Surround a professional range with cabinets that are the same depth or angled back from it.

Grill

Since a separate grill is not generally used continuously or as frequently as a cooktop, it can be specced most anywhere in the kitchen. Sending it out on its own, however, necessitates a second ventilation system.

Oven

Used less frequently than a cooktop, ovens, like a grill, can be placed almost anywhere in the cooking, baking, or eating area. Since they don't require constant monitoring, they can even be built into an island or outback. They can also be angled across a corner as long as they are recessed an inch or two back from it.

When located in the cooking area, ovens can sometimes share a countertop with the cooktop. Otherwise they require a landing space of their own, oriented toward their door opening. Double-stacked ovens can have a pullout board (counter) between them; one with a side hinge can host a counter below.

For the best view of food, least amount of bending, and shortest lift distance, install an oven or pair of ovens side by side with their floors one to three inches below the height of your bent elbow. Coordinate placement, if possible, so controls are at eye level, where they are easy to read and operate. If oven selection is based on an eye-level broiler, make sure you see things this way.

In a double-oven stack, situate the frame between the two ovens at thirty-six inches (standard countertop height) off the floor.

When two ovens are placed side by side at optimal height, countertop space is sacrificed. If you can't afford to forfeit it, stack the ovens or place them below counter. Though you'll get the bends using them in this latter location, it won't be too bad if you don't use the oven frequently. What is *your* best trade-off?

Evaluate door size, amount of floor space it occupies when open, and the reality of approaching it from the front or side. Avoid placing it across from a dishwasher or other wide door. Know, too, the amount of ventilation space prescribed for the model you selected.

Food Warmers

A warming oven can be placed anywhere in the cooking area where space is available except under a counter you will be working at—unless you like having your toes and ankles toasted. Overhead food warmers and warming lights can go under a nearby wall cabinet, while a thermal shelf can be placed on a countertop below or installed directly into the countertop, its controls at the side or remoted. It can also be portable.

Alternatively, warming lights can be hung from the ceiling over a countertop; a thermal shelf on a wall or backsplash and food warmers boxed in by tile or decorative moldings.

Geographically speaking, whatever warming system you use will be in demand between the stove and dining area, and you may want one warmer for the kitchen; another near or in the dining room. The basic guideline is the same as for a cooling rack: not over a stove, where rising vapors destroy whatever food is being warmed.

Microwave

The microwave's residence depends on its job. If its primary function is to defrost meat, reheat leftovers, warm up snacks, or cook vegetables or frozen food, it is the perfect vassal for the refrigerator's fiefdom. For melting butter, chocolate, or jelly for pie glazes, shelter it in baking or food preparation alleys. As an aid at breakfast or a second option for reheating, set up its camp in serving or eating niches. To use as an actual cooker, probably its rarest role, situate it in the cooking lineup.

If the microwave is employed equally at all these stations and only one box is to be purchased, house it in either the cooking or the preparation sanctum so you can perform other activities simultaneously. Otherwise you will have to station an attendant just to minister to its fussings. Priorities change when children are the prime users. In this case, place the microwave where it will be safest and most convenient for them.

Unless you're Michael Jordan, who can do a safe slam-dunk reach overhead, the microwave should be installed on, under, or above a countertop (hung from the bottom of the wall cabinet or a shelf secured to its bottom). Its level, as a wall oven's, should let the cook look down on its contents. Placing the bottom of the appliance three inches below the user's shoulder is considered optimum in general. Make it six inches for the elderly.

Varying in depth, most microwaves extend beyond a standard twelve-inch wall cabinet. To fit flush and look built-in, a microwave needs to be recessed in a wall or combined with cabinets of the same depth. Don't install one permanently; its breakdown-replacement rate is too high.

To prevent overheating and destruction of its *magnetron tube* from heat and humidity, many microwaves are accompanied by trim kits and requirements for air circulation and ventilation. Include the handle here, too, when determining depth and note how the door opens and the degree of clearance necessary. Most microwaves are hinged on the left, but doors drop down in some units designed to be built-in or placed over a regular oven. This can be a problem over a countertop with a bull-nose edge. Let the oven's hinge side determine where its landing space should be.

Probably the most important consideration here is that a microwave be five feet from a television set so its magnetic force doesn't interfere with the picture. Actually, this may be the best location if the microwave is primarily a popcorn popper. At any rate, let the force be with you.

Fireplace

A kitchen fireplace can be a traditional huge masonry wood-burning affair with a mantel surround and Santa-Claus-and-six-reindeers chimney. It emerges also, reduced in scope, as a demure, self-contained unit with a zero-clearance insert fired by gas or wood.

With a *direct-vent* chimney that goes through the wall or roof, a gas zero-clearance unit can be placed almost anyplace in the kitchen and operated by remote control. In contrast, a wood-burning model requires an outside wall, where its more elaborate chimney can be built in accordance with code.

Space permitting, a second hearth can be built on the exterior of the house back to back with the interior box and in partnership with the same chimney. The wood chopper will appreciate an adjacent cavity that opens both outside and in for loading.

When building codes are in alignment with box type, the fireplace generally goes near the dining table. If you plan to cook over the fire pit, or have guests gather in front for hors d'oeuvres while you do dinner, it might be conveniently ensconced in the cooking area instead. In an *open* kitchen, it may cheer as a focal point where the family works or plays after dinner.

Deciding between a gas and a wood fireplace depends in almost all instances on whether you deem it worthwhile to trade the unparalleled primitive glory of a wood fire for gas logs that don't require schlepping, storage, starting, or sweeping out. Have the best of both of these cozy worlds by installing a gas ignition line in a wood fireplace. As soon as the logs catch, you turn the gas off. Unfortunately, a gas sweeper has not yet been invented for these hearths.

A wood-burning box requires open or closed shelves nearby for stashing matches, wood, paper and kindling, metal tongs, poker, brushes, and grills or other cookery tools. With no other convenient place, I house my wood in a pullout plastic recycling bin.

Balanced with the size of the room and competing with other equipment for placement, a fireplace is usually raised in a kitchen so its dancing flames are visible while you are seated. Depending on position, its aperture can be frontal or wrapped around a corner for a double- or triple-sided fireworks display.

Sink

Sink placement is limited by plumbing location, its flexibility, and whether you want to spring for the cost of moving it. Even if the answer to the last question is affirmative, few options exist in high-rise apartments unless ceilings are high enough to raise the floor and hide pipes under a platform. When an island is too distant from a vent pipe, a sink can't be moored in it.

In deference to cooks who continually wash sticky hands and carry heavy pots of pasta water, locate at least one sink on the same wall or across the way from a cooking surface and/or preparation area. Avoid the popular angled corner placement that isolates the sink's operator and prevents an adjacent dishwasher from being conveniently loaded and unloaded.

As sinks become deeper, acquiring more accessories, the cabinet below needs to be delineated carefully to ensure space for the sink cutout, its attachments, and any insertion for a knee or foot pedal. Fighting for a corner: a tilt-down sponge drawer, and host of plugs, fittings, and valves for garbage disposal, instant hot and cold water mechanisms, water treatment system, soap dispensers, pull-out towel bar, trash cans, etc.

To break up a long monotonous run of cabinetry, the sink's cabinet is sometimes made deeper than its adjacent twenty-four-inch neighbors. Plants can be squirreled in its newly acquired space or a dish drainer sequestered behind the basins.

By sidestepping the common practice of centering a sink under a window, you can often gain more storage space for the kitchen. To minimize this deviation, select an asymmetrical sink and a window without a central post. Just beware of moving a sink too close to a corner set at right angles to another countertop: Work space in this setting will be cramped for even one person. If you spend a lot of time with your hands at the bottom of a deep sink, raise it (and its countertop) several inches higher for comfort (or get a shallower sink).

When a double or triple sink is used, their order should correspond to the direction dishes are bused from the table or stove. Right-handed people are often advised to move right to left, but left to right may feel more natural.

Faucet

For true luxury, add a faucet next to your electric mixer with a visible temperature gauge that bread bakers are sure to think hot.

A pot filler is conveniently installed above the cooktop. If your stove has a back, place it to the side of the stove instead. On high, it will operate like a waterfall, spashing all over. Another alternative: a filler with a hose that clips onto a rail around the hood or under the hood.

Dishwasher

The dishwasher is wedded to the sink for the practical transfer of dishes and for plumbing purposes. A separation of much more than two and one-half feet leaves you with leaks to confront.

Challenging this timeless position, many designers are speccing dishwashers anyplace there is water and electricity. The basis of this belief—that dishes no longer have to be prerinsed in new model dishwashers—is erroneous. *Less* rinsing, perhaps. But, depending on what's on them, they still need at least a squirt or two.

Another long-term rule being looked at anew is the height at which the dishwasher is installed. To minimize bending, it is raised several feet off the floor with a drawer making the most of the newly created space below. As a result, the countertop is unusually—perhaps unpleasantly—high.

In addition to being near the sink, a dishwasher—even with its door open—should be within easy reach of a dish cabinet. To make sure you get help unloading into this cabinet, allow plenty of room on both sides for acolytes to stand.

Many texts recommend placing the dishwasher to the left of the sink for a right-handed person and vice versa for a left-handed person. As a rightie, I'm much more comfortable working with it to the right, so practice turning to find your comfort zone.

A convertible dishwasher (portable with built-in capabilities) usually marks its spot between the preparation and dining areas or between the refrigerator and cooktop. Yet it may be more convenient to store it in the dining room or utility area and get it on a roll into the kitchen at cleanup time.

Trash Compactors and Recycling Bins

To collect waste generated throughout the kitchen, bins are usually centered under a sink, at an island, next to a cutting board, and near the exit. Facilitate disposal by gathering scraps into a bowl while you work. Though it seems logical to keep bins for recycling together, there is no reason why they cannot be dispersed to any odd corner or nook or moved outside the kitchen to a passageway, garage, or utility room. The primary assignment is to give bins a home so they don't end up where they are most in the way: in the center of the room with no place to hide.

When a trash compactor is used to lighten the load, place it close to the sink or in the food preparation area between refrigerator and sink—on the side opposite the dishwasher, whose steam can be detrimental. When space is limited, move the trash compactor outside the kitchen to keep recycling bins company.

Disposers

Assign a disposer to each location where a sink resides. When two single sinks and faucets are placed side by side for multiple cooks, install a disposer in each sink.

In addition to housing a disposer in a sink, it may be helpful to adopt the food-service practice of placing one in an island or worktable. If you're not composting, this location will be appreciated when fresh produce is used extensively in a work area some distance from the sink, generating considerable trimmings for disposal.

Locating a switch for a continuous disposer is a puzzle when the sink is in front of a large window without a wall nearby. Rather than positioning it behind a panel that must be opened—or below the sink, where you knock against it—mount a push-button air-activated switch on the sink deck or counter along with the faucet.

Tables and Chairs

One myth to dispel is that a counter and stool take up less room than a table and chairs. In either case, allot the same amount of space per person. When weighing pros and cons, the counter and table also come out equal, offering a surface that does double duty for other activities.

For dining, countertops must extend beyond base cabinets for stool and knee room. They can also be cantilevered out and supported with a leg to form a high table. If stools are placed along one side, curve the counter so people can see whom they are conversing with.

Shrinking to standard table size, a pullout, pull-up, or drop-leaf surface can be attached to a wall or stored in a cabinet. Versatile, a table can also be built into an alcove, the back side of an island, or a bay window. Round and oval tables seat more people proportionately than rectangles. Increasing in height, seating possibilities include benches, banquettes, window seats, chairs, and stools.

WEATHERING HEIGHTS

Equipment location is only one part of the kitchen equation; how easy it is to reach the other. Based on denizens' average heights, standard dimensions have been issued to minimize fabrication costs, maximize resale values, and simplify the designer's job. Yet for a *belle* who departs from this curve in either direction, cooking in the kitchen is not going to be a ball.

"Home construction equipment remains one industry that is stalwartly holding to a belief in the convenience of the supplier over the consumer," writes seer Faith Popcorn. "Why are cabinets and cooking ranges all the same height, when cooks come in all sizes?" she asks. With due cause.

Bearing some cooperation from kitchen appliance manufacturers, the ideal solution, a custom kitchen, is just not possible for most people. Neither is two of everything when pairs in this Noah's Ark differ in height. There is, however, no reason why at least one counter or worktable can't be raised or lowered to suit each user and why pullout cutting boards or butcher blocks can't be installed at different levels throughout the kitchen. Moving a counter up and down on a hydraulic lift is another option.

Shorter people, aka the vertically challenged, can shrink the base cabinet stack to thirty and one-half inches by using one intended for a *vanity*. Lowering wall cabinets to fifteen inches or less above the

APPLIANCE HEIGHT
Install appliances at a height that enables the cook to work comfortably. Shorter people will appreciate having the cooktop installed below the standard 36-inch countertop. When this appliance is shared with a taller person, attach it to a hydraulic lift that adjusts up and down.

counter brings a greater portion of shelves within their reach. Windows can be moved down, too, for easy access or fit with reciprocal hardware operable from any height. Regardless of modifications, shelter a sturdy step stool where it can come effortlessly to the rescue.

Base cabinets can be ordered with a lower toe kick for short people; a higher one for taller folks. Topping them up: an extra-thick or extra-thin butcher block or granite countertop. Tall or short,

choose flexible appliances that go where you tell them such as a separate cooktop, drop-in range, built-in oven or dishwasher.

MAXIMIZING SPACE
Nod to a Tiny Kitchen; Bow to a Big One

The definition of a *small* kitchen is as vague as the number of hours in a recipe stating "leave over-night." Though 150 square feet is usually the demarcation point between small and large, the images of crowding, narrow traffic lanes, difficult working conditions, and lack of storage space conjured up by the word *small* may be more an issue of poor planning than of actual size.

For cooking's sake, a minikitchen can actually be more efficient than a monster whose distances keep you on the run.

Techniques for aggrandizing a small space can—and should—be entertained in a room of any size, for they enhance its organization and practicality. The room appears more gracious and inviting, regardless of whether its proportions have actually been augmented.

Sometimes *small* is incontestably small; maybe microscopic. But even in these circumstances, try to solve spatial problems without downsizing equipment drastically. For state-of-the-art ideas, cruise boat shows and mobile home marathons.

To make a room look larger, push its lines into seemingly infinite vistas: vertical struts that soar to a skylight or vaulted ceiling, diagonal floor and countertop patterns. Horizontals—long unbroken runs of countertops, open shelves, or cabinetry—extend, lengthen, and streamline.

Materials magnify as well. Call on sheers and see-throughs (rattan, glass doors, or walls) and shiny surfaces that reflect light and depth (mirrors and acrylic finishes).

Structure

Sometimes a small space can actually be enlarged physically by raising the ceiling to the roof, borrowing space from an adjacent room, or burrowing into the studs to install cabinets and equipment. At other times, physical changes yield but an appearance of increased size: Moving a door or window may yield a long unbroken wall for work. When a pocket door is employed, no evidence of its opening invades the room.

Tearing down a wall between kitchen and dining or living room opens up a space whose separate functions can be demarcated by an island. Cram more in by stacking appliances in columns or what designer Clodaugh calls the "skyscraper technique. I can't go out, so I go up."

When there is no room for an island and countertops are at a premium, steal an idea from hospitals that cart their machines around on pullout tables or shelves with wheels. Picking ingredients up at the prep area, it totes them to the stove and ultimately to the dining room.

Windows

Infusing a kitchen with light simultaneously expands its volume. Maximize natural light without assuming space that could be used for storage. Create a bay, skylight, or clerestory ring below the ceiling or march windows around the backsplash. Have as many windows as possible. To prevent their coverings from overwhelming, limit them to a simple shade.

Lighting

Though lighting should be plentiful, fixtures should not be prominent. To achieve a uniform effect, pass up a chandelier and track lights for recessed cans in the ceiling. Blow up a space with hidden cove lighting or floor lights that angle up and wash a wall. Accent lights play a dramatic part in a small kitchen, adding subtle shadings of depth, shadow, and texture.

Cabinets

Since cabinets occupy such a large part of a kitchen, their bulk must be managed carefully. They appear less massive visually if finished in light woods or colors, custom-built to wrap precisely around a space they can better use every inch of, and faced with a glass toe kick to float above. Touch latches break up their flow less readily than stick-out knobs or pulls. Glass-paneled doors—or no doors—also minimize their presence.

Open cabinets not only look less voluminous than closed but extra storage can be gained from the space devoted to their doors. Removing cabinet backs also increases storage space, though it weakens the box structurally.

Cabinets without fronts or back, essentially wooden or glass shelves, can be mounted in front of a window or in other out-of-the-way places where cabinets fear to tread.

Inch for inch, frameless cabinets offer 15 percent more space for storage than framed cabinets with structural struts. Their sleek flat doors and hidden hardware also make the room seem larger.

Thinner stainless-steel cabinets up that ante with 20 percent more storage space. More storage still? Make base cabinets deeper and build wall cabinets or pantries to the ceiling.

Wise storage is the true key to a keyhole space. To achieve it means using every inch in every nook and cranny and using it well. Replace common items with those that store better or more creatively. Trade in odd pots, bowls, and trays for nesting stacks. Transfer pots or wineglasses to hanging ceiling racks, where they can be decorative as well as functional. Use toe kicks to store lids, wine bottles, shallow platters, or step stools. In other words, go up to the ceiling, down to the floor, and into the studs.

Appliances

The smaller imported European ovens provide proportionately greater interior space for their exterior dimensions. Those (or domestic models) with convection heat allow baking to occur simultaneously on multiple racks. Though not a first choice for a single oven in a large kitchen, it or, better, a multimode oven is an efficiency in a smaller one. When open, the doors of smaller ovens take up less aisle space (as does a side-by-side refrigerator when compared to a unit with a single door).

Two burners might suffice for a cooktop if an electric skillet or portable gas, electric, or induction burner stands by for times more heat is needed. When not in use, smooth tops can be covered with a cutting board, doubling as a countertop.

Trash compactors, portable dishwashers, and refrigeration can all be stored outside the kitchen. For an inside job, opt for a refrigerator that fits under the counter and a dishwasher that fits under the sink, on the counter, or in an eighteen-inch-wide slot.

Waterworks

Sinks prove flexible in small settings. Installing the faucet on a wall above a modular undermount or integral sink without a space-wasting deck makes the best of this situation. A shallow sink with a gooseneck faucet is another combo that takes care of large pots

while providing more storage in the cabinet below. Placing the drain in the back of the sink increases interior cabinet space as well.

Dining

Some relief can be brought to a small space by setting up dining facilities like a Murphy bed: when you need them, not full-time. For temporary facilities, use a wall-hung folding table, a drop-leaf table, a pullout table recessed in the wall, or a secretary cabinet with a hinged pull-down door. A custom table can be built to suit awkward or leftover space.

Double efficiency by assigning dual purposes to all tables and counters and building drawers or shelves into their bases and below their seats.

Eliminating space for walking behind or pulling out a chair, scrunch seating into the back of an island or peninsula. Or push it against the window or wall in an alcove or bay. Backless benches make the kitchen look larger, while stacking stools or chairs buy space while they're off-duty.

Decoration

Color can significantly alter the perception of space. A long narrow corridor kitchen seems wider if dark colors are painted on its short ends and light colors on its sides. Wood beams expand the direction they run in, while a trompe l'oeil panel provides far-off vistas. The kitchen looks larger when light colors or a monochromatic palette is selected for appliances, surfaces, and cabinetry. Boundaries disappear when the same colors and materials are used throughout; when cabinets, counter, and appliance panels are, for example, all laminate; when flooring is repeated from adjacent or shared rooms.

Fabric and wallpaper patterns should be small or vertical, pulling the eye up as the stripes short people sport while pretending to be stately and thin. With grout lines to telescope the room, tiles should be small (eight to twelve inches) but not too small, or they appear busy. Mount borders or moldings in areas where they underscore a ceiling's height or interesting shape.

With all this emphasis on simplicity and subtlety of form and shade, there should still be an architectural focal point to rally around.

Decoration takes on another aspect in a kitchen open to other rooms. Not only must the kitchen look good, but it must integrate with its neighbors from a design perspective, appearing attractive from their vantage points as well as its own.

HOOKUP
Plotting Electric, Gas, Plumbing, and Heating Byways

Electricity

Planning electricity for a new kitchen can be left in the capable hands of a licensed electrician, who is obligated to follow national and local codes. Yet, once again, it pays to be knowledgeable about this field and for you, the designer, and the contractor to be in constant communication with an electrician while dealing with this important subject.

Service Panel: The electric service panel and circuits should be reassessed—wattage demands totaled—once all lighting and appliances are chosen even if they seemed ample during the initial evaluation. When a new box is indicated, *it should exceed standards established by Underwriters Laboratories, Inc. (UL), handle twenty-amp circuits, and allow circuits to be added in the future.*

Most boxes today contain circuit breakers. These are triggered when the system is overloaded, shutting it down. To start the electricity running again, they are simply switched back on. Boxes were formerly protected by fuses, which had to be changed out once they were blown. Though this was a hassle, fuses were more sensitive to a problem than circuit breakers and able to respond more quickly. If you have a functional fuse box, there is no reason to replace it.

Circuits: To double-check circuits, make a list of everything that runs on electricity and determine its wattage. In addition to lighting and major appli-

ances, look at small household goods, such as a clock, electric knife, or cappuccino machine, and don't forget the prewiring necessary for an operable remote-controlled skylight.

A twenty-amp circuit handles up to two thousand watts. But, as you will see from the following list, any appliance greater than fifteen amps requires its own circuit with a fuse or circuit breaker. Each circuit in turn must have its own switch or plug to shut off the electricity in a fire or other emergency. A plug allows you to reconnect the electricity afterward; a switch may require an electrician's assistance. The house must also have a central *disconnect switch.*

Review new circuits to see if some could be eliminated by sharing power with preexisting runs and find out where junction boxes will join new wiring to old.

Each of the following appliances warrants its own circuit even if less than fifteen amps. Check the exact voltage demands of your equipment with its installation book, for it may differ depending on its size and power.

Range: **240-volt circuit**

Cooktop: **240-volt circuit**

> *Gas cooktop:* **120-volt circuit for an electric ignition, clock, and other electric controls**

Oven: **240-volt circuit**

> **Cooktop and oven or double ovens can share a circuit of 50 amps. If amperage is limited in the house, be very careful of a double oven's requirements.**

Microwave: **120-volt circuit**

> *Microwave-convection or range combo:* **240-volt circuit**

Large toaster oven: **120-volt circuit**

Refrigerator: **120-volt circuit**

> *Refrigerator/freezer combo:* **120-volt circuit**

Freezer: **120-volt circuit**

Icemaker: **120-volt circuit**

Wine cooler: **120-volt circuit**

Dishwasher: 120-volt circuit

Some codes require flexible conduit connectors.

Disposer: 120-volt circuit

Some codes allow circuit to be shared with dishwasher, but this is not recommended.

Trash compactor: 120-volt circuit

Instant hot water: 120-volt circuit

Computer: 120-volt circuit

TV: 120-volt circuit

Grounding Appliances: All appliances must be grounded so that a frayed wire, malfunctioning appliance, or voltage surge will discharge electricity into the ground rather than into a shocked bystander. To ground an appliance, plug it into either a three-hole receptacle or a two-hole receptacle with a grounding adapter. A *polarized plug* (with one wider prong) further ensures proper connections among wires.

In spite of these precautions, a shock can still occur near a water source. To interrupt the current if there is a leak, a *ground-fault circuit interrupter* must be installed within six inches of the sink. This can be portable, connected to a circuit breaker, or placed in a wall receptacle, the easiest way of checking and resetting this device. A *surge arrester* should also be installed at the main service panel where electricity enters the home.

Electric Receptacles (Outlets): When determining the location for appliance receptacles and light switches, check their installation booklets to see if an exact placement is specified. Note how much space they occupy and how far they project from the wall.

If an outlet is going into an existing wall, investigate first whether it will interfere with any plumbing housed there. Avoid a wall obscured by a swinging door or one fitted with a sliding pocket door.

To eliminate dangerous dangling extension cords, place each outlet as close to the equipment's point of use and storage as possible. The recommended height for an appliance receptacle is eight and one-half inches above the counter, but you'll also need outlets near the baseboard or floor for a lamp, computer, or electric broom.

Electrifying an island eliminates cords draping across aisles, but once this is accomplished the island is immobilized. Plugs must be sunk into an island so you don't knock against them while working.

For convenience and flexibility of kitchen operation, there almost cannot be too many outlets. Place a double outlet next to the refrigerator, on both sides of the sink and stove, in each section of an appliance garage, and at least every eighteen to twenty-four inches on a backsplash. Devote one outlet to a charging flashlight that comes through in a power outage and guides nighttime raids on herb and vegetable gardens.

Rather than cutting up a backsplash and second-guessing where you want outlets, a more practical solution lies in an *electrostrip* with a plug at any point or the *surface runways* with built-in equidistant outlets. For oversized plugs to fit, the receptacles must be oriented correctly. Attractive in a chrome finish, these are placed under wall cabinets that have a molding attached to the bottom for hiding the wiring.

Undercabinet space has to be prioritized carefully, or you end up with a traffic jam greater than the New Jersey Turnpike's. Undercabinet light panels can usually cozy up to the plug strips, but if you want to fit a pull-down message center or rack for spices, knives, or cookbooks under there as well, the wall cabinet will have to be deeper than the standard twelve inches.

Smart House: More and more, consumers are subscribing to the Smart House concept and integrating the operation of all their electric tasks on a single electronic *keypad* or *bus*. This system can be programmed to operate all electrical appliances connected to it from the clock to the intercom to the exterior irrigation system and opening and closing of living room drapes. If you incorporate one of these systems, delineate its placement carefully.

Lighting: Each light fixture must have its own junction box regardless of whether it is plugged into a receptacle, operated by a switch, or mounted on the wall or ceiling.

Switches: Individual three-way switches with dimmers for every light should be installed at all entrances to the kitchen. Turning everything on and off when you enter or exit the room, you can light areas discriminately without having to backtrack in the dark. Mount duplicate switches for task and accent lighting at their source.

When too many switches accumulate, the wall looks like a rocket ship panel. Multiple switches can be stationed in one plate, but these systems are expensive, and you may prefer dispersing switches throughout the room. *Mercury switches* flip on and off most quietly.

When several switches are ganged together, name the switch for the light used most frequently number one in the lineup. The switch for a light over the sink should, for example, be the first you touch; the switch for the disposer the second.

To avoid reaching behind an open door, house switches on the door's lock side, four feet from the floor. Install a switch for outside lighting even if you don't need it now, for the odds are you'll add fixtures for decoration, security, or alfresco cooking or dining at a future date.

Gas

The location of each gas line and its *shutoff valve* must be plotted; sufficient space allotted for its large *connectors* housed frequently in adjacent cabinets. Most points are decreed by code, for the shutoff valve must be quickly reached. In earthquake country, an *automatic shutoff valve* could prove lifesaving.

A single gas line runs from the gas meter to the range or cooktop and can be left as is if appliances aren't moved more than several feet from where they were initially. Some codes require that flexible tubing be used; others a solid line.

To simplify cleaning, have a gas stove castered and hooked up to a gas line by a *quick-disconnect* coupling that makes it easy to move out. In this case, the stove will also have to be chained to the wall with a *restraining device.*

Commercial woks, cooktops, ranges, and grills demand their own three-quarter-inch gas line. A line

is imperative, too, for generating heat in a gas-driven fireplace; a great convenience for igniting the logs in a wood-burning hearth.

Plumbing

Plumbing plans, like electrical drawings, should be done in collaboration or at least in consultation with a plumber. An agreement must be reached about the type of new pipes and the extent of their replacement. Expensive for their weight and difficult installation, cast-iron pipes remain relatively impervious to chemicals and temperature change. Copper is costly, too, and performs poorly in hard- or soft-water conditions and in freezing temperatures, where it must be insulated. Yet its longevity is commendable, and this is the material generally used. If new copper pipes are joined to old galvanized ones, a special *kielectric union* must be used. Don't, however, consider galvanized pipe for a new installation because it corrodes too quickly. Undesirable as well, plastic pipe can be destroyed by chemicals and is not approved in many municipalities.

Original pipes may be used when new sinks are located in the same spot or extended when moved no more than several inches. A sink can sometimes also be connected to lines in an adjacent bathroom. Otherwise, new supply and drain lines must be added. In plotting pathways, mount waste vent ducts five feet away and two feet higher than a skylight that will transmit its unsavory aromas and moisture inside.

If pipes run under a floor, their route cannot be mapped until the subfloor and flooring have been designated and laid out. Whatever their course, locate pipes far from outside walls and insulate them to protect against freezing. Bury those that run outside below the frost line.

Situate hot-water supply lines as close as possible to the heater to decrease the time lag while water warms up. When distances are great, a *recirculating loop* is recommended for returning water to the heater.

Equipment pipes must correspond to the diameter specified in their installation booklets. In addition to a cold-water line for faucets, one is needed for an icemaker, a cold-water dispenser, a washing machine, and a refrigerator with ice and water on the door. A hot-water dispenser utilizes a hot-water line. Depending on local codes, each dishwasher requires a vacuum breaker or *air gap* that prevents contaminated water from backing up into it when the drain clogs.

Heating

Whether new or expanded, a forced-air system presents the best heating solution and greatest placement options. Consisting of a supply and a return register (that can be placed outside the kitchen) plus ducting and on/off switches, its exact whereabouts must be pinpointed in advance, or unsightly modifications may have to be made to walls and doors. Systems based on gas or oil must also be vented.

Heating registers can be placed in baseboards, toe kicks, the wall, or a soffit. Floor locations prove practical as long as they aren't in front of a sliding door or area where people trip over them.

Have an HVAC contractor determine how many registers are needed and check out the peregrinations of their ductwork so it doesn't interfere with plumbing, electric, or ventilation lines. Unless you like watching potatoes sprout, be sure they don't run under a pantry or cabinet where food will be stored.

Since heat rises naturally by gravity, lower stations are most economical, particularly in cold climates. They will be the toastiest, too, for once the floor is warm, you can be fooled into thinking it is warm all over. Contrarily, cool air falls naturally, rendering air-conditioning more efficient when flung from a higher perch.

This contradiction poses particular complications with a commercial cooktop, range, or grill. Producing considerable heat, they make some type of cooling system desirable; read imperative.

Split the difference by installing multiple supply registers with one up high; another down low. When situating the higher system, keep it far enough away so its less-than-decorator looks don't intrude visually and orient it so it doesn't blow air directly on people below. If you elect to keep the system low down, be sure it has enough force to direct the air-conditioning skyward.

When heating/cooling are provided by individual heat pumps, they are usually placed above the baseboards, but they are free to roam anywhere an electric connection can be made.

A separate cooler can also be inserted in a kitchen wall or window when no central air-conditioning exists, but it will be noisy, and again it is not a looker. Less satisfactory than a cooling system, a ceiling fan moves air around at variable speeds to create a breeze. Supported by a crossbrace, these hang one foot below the ceiling joist and at least seven feet above anything that interferes with the movement of its blades. As anyone who has seen the fans at Bobby Flay's Mesa Grill restaurant in New York can attest, these can be quite dramatic if not very effective.

To maintain a hot-water, steam-heat, or other system, plan its placement and installation according to information collected while assessing your utilities' capabilities (page 12). Foist piping and radiator decisions on an expert HVAC contractor and coordinate them with plumbing, ventilation, and electric routings.

The thermostat for a heating/cooling system can be in or out of the kitchen as long as it is situated in a spot representing average ambient temperature. Distance it from a heater, window, fireplace, or outside wall that can skew its response and seat it at a height of forty-eight inches above the floor.

An indulgence well worth considering for children or barefoot cooks is a *radiant heating system* in the floor. Consisting of hot-water pipes or electric cables attached to the subfloor and a thin concrete layer, the system is regulated by a heat sensor. Particularly good for zoned heating in a single room when the furnace is far away, radiant heat is more even than forced air and doesn't waste valuable space with registers. It does, however, take longer to heat the room than forced air and has been estimated to be about 11 percent more expensive. Additional air-conditioning requires separate ducts.

KITCHENSPEAK:LAYOUT

Island: A freestanding table or base cabinet at least two by two feet, situated in the work space. It can constitute an entire kitchen if placed in an open space or form a two-row kitchen when situated parallel to a wall or a second island. When large enough, an island can host appliance installations.

L-Shaped Kitchen: A kitchen laid out along two perpendicular walls that intersect at right angles.

One-Row or One-Wall Kitchen: A one-wall kitchen with a minimum expanse of twelve feet containing a refrigerator, sink, and stove.

Open Kitchen: A very large kitchen that floats within the walls of a room rather than being attached to them or, more commonly, a joint space shared by the kitchen and a den, family room, or dining room.

Peninsula: Attached to a wall or cabinet on one side, a peninsula extends perpendicularly to divide the kitchen space while providing an additional work area. When large enough, appliances can be installed within it.

Soffit: The empty enclosed space between the top of a wall cabinet and the ceiling.

Eastern Soffit: A soffit that extends twenty-seven inches from the wall and is large enough to accommodate lights.

Triangle: A layout has traditionally been considered optimum when a line drawn between the center of the assigned spaces for the sink, stove, and refrigerator forms a triangle. With the number of cooks and appliances increasing in recent years, design is viewed more flexibly today; both two overlapping triangles and one triangle intersecting with other byways are viewed as acceptable layouts.

Two-Row, Corridor, or Galley Kitchen: A kitchen occupying a rectangular space that is composed of two parallel rows or a single row and a long island.

U-Shaped Kitchen: A three-sided workplace with the refrigerator, stove, and sink each usually occupying a separate side.

Universal Design: A multi- or transgenerational habitat designed so that young and old alike can work safely and comfortably regardless of agility.

PRIMARY PRINCIPLES
OF GOOD KITCHEN DESIGN

_____

With all the machinations about what goes where or this stove or that, there are higher principles paramount in a kitchen design.

The well-designed kitchen is a secure haven for all generations to work and play, one that meets prerequisites when kids are grown. Within the confines of this *universal* space, you should be able to age gracefully with decreasing visual, auditory, and muscular agility.

To provide this multi- or transgenerational habitat, municipal building codes and provisions of the Americans with Disabilities Act have recently mandated guidelines. Beyond these recommendations, there is a general caring philosophy that should be applied to each decision. Negligent, we've allowed thirty-two thousand children to be scalded each year.

Practically speaking, it is much less costly to child-proof a kitchen or anticipate its inhabitants' changing mobility when walls are down during a remodel. Retrofits are, plain and simple, more expensive, especially later in life when expenses increase and income decreases.

Safety and universality are but the cocoon for the kitchen's primary function: preparation of healthy food. Yet it is ironically, oxymoronically, in facilitating meals for a well-balanced diet where today's kitchens are most remiss.

Though we have been bombarded with a spate of confusing health advice over the last decade or so that could drive even the most disciplined of us to a juicy fat ballpark hot dog, a clear and present message has emerged for the fulfillment of a healthful diet: minimal fat, majority of nutrients from natural fruit, vegetable, and grain categories, and a variety of comestibles, whose consumption is balanced over a period of several days.

Two programs, one under the aegis of the American Institute of Wine and Food, the other directed by Oldways Preservation and Trust, have pioneered models for healthy eating that derive many of their precepts from Asia and the Mediterranean, where nutritious diets have been observed since ancient times.

To follow their prescriptions, we must be able to cook the dishes from these cultures simply and easily. But most of our kitchens are not set up for this purpose and consequently are all too seldom used for it. Ingredients abound—wonderful fruity olive oils, exotic produce, opalescent pearls of Arborio rice, mysterious Eastern sauces and condiments—but our kitchen appliances have not been designed for nourishment.

Shelves on our refrigerator doors have been enlarged to hold gallon bottles of Coke, but produce bins are too small to hold a five-day supply of fruits and vegetables. Cooktop burners aren't large enough to hold a large skillet let alone a wok, steamer, fish poacher, or couscousière, tools of healthful cooking. There has been a welcome influx of grills into the home kitchen, but most of these don't have enough heat to perform the basic tasks of this implement: sear the outside of a food-stuff and retain its juices. Even a small country like Morocco does a better job of healthy cooking with the charcoal braziers its cooks fire up on the streets.

No matter what layout is finally conceived and signed off on, it can be considered a success only if it is safe for all users and promotes the confection of healthy meals. To design a kitchen with these attributes, refer frequently to the following chart during the decision-making process. Adapting the suggestions under "A Universal Kitchen" depends on individual needs.

Refrigerator: Large fruit and vegetable bins

Sink: Large with colander and cutting board accessories

Faucet: Pullout spray hose for cleaning produce

Waste: A compost bucket, garbage disposer, and/or ample bins for fresh produce peelings

Cooktop: Burners with a large enough diameter to hold a 12-inch skillet or wok

Burners placed one behind the other so they can cradle a large steamer or fish poacher

High heat capability

Ability to maintain a low simmer

Grill: Separate high-Btu gas grill to cook foods without additional fat

Oven: Infrared broiler for proper grilling

Ventilation: Wall-mount system with powerful squirrel-cage blowers rated for your cooktop

Storage: Ample storage for bowls, knives, cutting boards, and other implements for preparing fresh foods

Large deep pullout shelves to hold oversized pots for cooking pasta and vegetables

Special appliance garages for storing oversized woks, steamers, fish poachers, and a couscousière

Large pantry for storing grains, pulses, exotic spices, and condiments that lend flavor without fat

Means of storing cutting boards for chicken and pork that can be cleaned in the dishwasher to prevent cross-contamination

Countertops: Long uninterrupted countertops between refrigerator and sink for preparing produce

Windows: Greenhouse window for growing fresh herbs (or access to outdoor herb garden)

Miscellaneous: Dehydrator for preserving fruits and vegetables

---

A SAFE KITCHEN

Refrigerator: Built-ins installed with clips so they don't tip over

Faucet: No or mandated low level of lead

Cooktop: Not placed on an island, at the end of a long cabinet run, or near a door or narrow walkway (unless separated by a divider)

Close to sink and away from traffic, creating an unobstructed passageway

Landing space on both sides so pot handles can be turned away from the aisle

Burners that glow when hot, whether off or on

Installed following fire codes

Two feet of noncombustible material installed on each side

Oven: Well insulated

Not placed above a cooktop

Oven floor installed 1 to 7 inches below a bent elbow

Not placed near a door or busy thoroughfare

Countertop next to oven to receive hot baking dishes

Range: Close to sink and away from traffic, creating an unobstructed passageway

Installed with straps or clips to prevent tipping

Baking soda, large pot lids, and a halon-filled fire extinguisher with a gauge kept between range (or cooktop) and exit of house (electric fires not extinguished with water)

Controls in front of range or side of cooktop, not in back

Microwave: Not placed above a cooktop

Shelf placed 3 inches below shoulder height

Ventilation: Consider installing a professional automatic fire extinguisher in range hood of a commercial stove or for frequent frying or grilling

Avoid switch that goes automatically to high when excess heat is registered

Motor placement orchestrated carefully (a motor on the roof can be a fire hazard, especially over a barbecue)

Cabinets: Drawer glides with stops

Locks installed for cabinets in earthquake country or other natural disaster areas

Storage: Spices and other tools not stored behind a cooktop

Knives secured in a countertop slot or drawer block, not on a magnetic strip

Space planned for everything so unbalanced items don't tumble off of shelves

Frequently used items stored within easy reach, the lower level chosen when the choice is between a toe kick and a high shelf

Sturdy step stool stored in a handy location

Surface: Tempered glass preferred for small honeycomb shapes it forms when shattered

Countertops:	Rounded beveled edges, curved contoured lines, no sharp or acute angles	**Electric:**	Enough outlets planned so appliances can operate without extension cords dangling over counters or across aisles
	Landing spaces for hot foods within easy reach, not overhead		Appliances given a permanent home so cords can be shortened
Floor:	Nonslip material		Cordless telephone
	No scatter rugs		All appliances grounded with a three-prong plug that is plugged into a three-hole receptacle or a two-hole receptacle with a grounding adapter
	Steps, raised thresholds, and two different floor heights avoided, even if transition is well marked		
	Circulation paths moved outside work areas		Polarized plugs, either a three-prong plug or a plug with one wider prong
Table:	Rounded beveled edges, curved contoured lines; no sharp or acute angles		Ground-fault circuit interrupter installed for all receptacles within 6 feet of any water source
	Chairs, not stools, for eating		
Lighting:	All floors, steps, and work areas well lit		Shutoff valves for gas and electricity placed under sink or where they will be accessible
	Low-voltage lighting to prevent shock		
Windows:	No windows behind a cooktop or within 12 inches of its sides		An automatic gas shutoff valve installed in earthquake country
	Over a walkway, a double-hung instead of a casement window		A hard-wired smoke detector installed just outside of kitchen or in ceiling light fixture
	Windows positioned low enough so they can be opened without standing on a step stool, or fitted with reciprocal hardware	**Miscellaneous:**	First-aid kit in kitchen
	Slider window large enough to fit through when the only escape route from a kitchen		

A CHILDPROOF KITCHEN (A SAFE KITCHEN PLUS THE FOLLOWING)

Refrigerator:	Antientrapment device (refrigerator can be opened from inside)	**Cabinets:**	Locks
		Storage:	Pull-down step stool installed on a cabinet door
	Lock for refrigerator		Toys, snacks, and TV placed in low base cabinet a child can reach, away from a cooking or walking aisle
Sink:	Exposed pipes covered to guard against burns		
Faucet:	Antiscald valve or temperature memory		
	Water-heater thermostat lowered to 120°F		Knives, matches, toothpicks, and other sharp objects together in a locked drawer
	Single-lever faucet with a wide band of low and medium temperatures		
	No lead		Locked liquor cabinets
Hot Water:	Lock		Locked-up cleaning supplies
Waste:	Batch-feed disposer	**Hardware:**	Oversized knobs too large to swallow
	Trash compactor that locks		Touch latches that discourage young children from opening a cabinet
Cooktop:	Either controls on top that are difficult to reach, side controls that lock, or controls hidden by a tilt-down panel; look for childproof push-turn controls	**Surface:**	No glass block
		Countertops:	Cutting board lowered to a child's height
		Floor:	Tile avoided (too cold and hard)
	Guardrail installed	**Windows:**	Window guards installed so kids don't fall out
	An induction cooktop	**Electric:**	Appliances parked in an inaccessible garage
Oven:	Well insulated		Unused sockets filled with plastic plugs that are not easily swallowable; or a childproof receptacle
Range:	No noninsulated commercial range (commercial-style ranges also get very hot, particularly with raised broilers)		
Microwave:	For children's use, placed undercounter at a height easily reached	**Gas:**	No liquid petroleum gas (leaks settle near the floor, a level hazardous for children)

Refrigeration: Side-by-side refrigerator or one with freezer on the bottom

Freezer large enough to set in a good supply of food, reducing shopping trips

Pullout shelves

Automatic icemaker and ice and water on the door; or below-counter water system

Sink: Insulated pipes and flexible plastic plumbing

For someone with a poor grip, sink with slanted bottom to slide things in and out

Shallow sink to reduce bending

Faucet: Automatic-sensor, long wrist-operated wing blades or single-lever ring handle with a wide band of low and moderate temperatures

Aerator and long retractable spray hose

Antiscald device

Pot filler faucet at the stove

Dishwasher: Elevated so bending isn't necessary

Waste: Foot pedal for opening trash door

Trash and recycling bins stored in base cabinets

Trash easily accessible and disposable

Cooktop: Cooktop lowered 7 or 8 inches

Controls in front

Big, easily readable dials

Alarm installed to indicate "on" if vision is a problem

Smooth tops and burners that don't indicate "hot" avoided

Induction burners

Oven: Wall oven rather than range

Side-opening oven

Microwave: Convenient height for each user

Cabinets: Upper and/or lower cabinets motorized to vary height

As many base cabinets as possible

Largest, heaviest items stored in base cabinets

Wall cabinets hung directly on counter or no more than 15 inches above

Open shelves, shallow shelves 6 to 12 inches deep, or pullout shelves and pullout drawers with full-extension hardware

Front and back openings to base cabinets on a peninsula

Large pantry to reduce number of shopping trips

Storage: Most frequently used items stored between shoulders and knees, usually 30 to 60 inches off floor

Small appliances stored undercounter on pullout shelves or motorized lifts

An idea from *Consumer Reports*: stable removable bowl built into a pullout undercounter shelf

Backsplash used for storage

Racks placed on doors; swing-out shelf racks in corners

Hardware: Touch latches or large C- or U-shaped handles that can be opened with hand or wrist

Surface: Matte finishes that don't increase light reflections and glare

Countertops: Countertops motorized so they can be raised or lowered

Countertop customized to fit height of each kitchen user

Work countertop 30 to 32 inches high with chair underneath

Pullout cutting boards installed in lower cabinets to employ from a seated position

Countertop edge finished in material that contrasts with countertop, marking its edge visually

Floor: Floor visually contrasted with countertop

Lighting: Natural and artificial light increased

Indirect light from recessed ceiling cans that won't be harsh

Lights in floor lamps or close to ground so bulbs can be changed without climbing a ladder

Wide switches with rocker knobs or sliders that go up and down

Windows: Casement windows with extra-long crank

Doors: Lever handles

French doors

Electric: Light switches, electric outlets, and thermostats no higher than 42 inches off floor

Electronic controls that are easy to see and use

Electrical, TV, and telephone jacks raised to 18 inches off floor

Remote controls for ventilation, cooktop, and skylight switches to an accessible height

Electric can and jar opener

Electric dumbwaiter to transport groceries

Miscellaneous: Low-maintenance, easily cleanable kitchen

Laundry in kitchen to eliminate steps

TEARING IT DOWN AND BUILDING IT UP

■

GEARING UP

"Seven months ago I could give a single command and 541,000 people would immediately obey it. Today I can't get a plumber to come to my house."

—Norman Schwarzkopf on postwar life
Newsweek, November 11, 1991

A woman goes to the gynecologist: "This is my fourth marriage, and I want to get pregnant now that I finally have a chance," she says. "My first husband was an eye doctor, and all he did was look. The second was a shrink, and all he did was listen. The third guy was even worse. He was a contractor and never showed up."

Slanderous, unkind words? An insult to the many well-mannered professional remodelers who not only show up but do an excellent, high-quality job once they get there? Perhaps. But in a field where 96 percent of all businesses fail within the first three years and 40 percent of all work has to be redone, you're wise to do some reality testing.

Remodeling proceeds more smoothly in small towns sheltering old-fashioned artisans and crafts-people; in the rural pockets of America where neighbors know each other and the unscrupulous can't go from one block to the next, defrauding the faithful. But basically, even in the best of times, construction is hell.

The day starts at 6:15 A.M. with lilting strains of "f—k you, man." Exhibiting no regard for personal property, phalanxes of invading workers seize your private nest for their construction zone. These gentle poets roll wheelbarrows into your dining room, run extension cords across your bed, drip grease on your driveway, and nick your walls with the hammers swaying from their hips—on the rare occasions they actually remember to bring their hammers.

They take your tools and break your tools . . . after destroying your favorite belongings. At the end of a day of constant drilling, your head feels like the Alaskan pipeline, and dust coats your mouth for many months afterward as you write your name in its droppings.

Workers follow you into a closed closet while you're getting dressed, unpack your crystal for lunch, and give your housekeeper their laundry to do. They bring their dogs, their children, their friends and friends of friends to see the house they're working in. And many male teams display little respect for women.

Lynne Tamor wanted moldings on the floor. "Tough shit," they responded. "It's too much work." Husband Michael Sugar reiterated her request. "We have forty-two colors," they said. "Which do you want?"

One shaky survivor, a psychiatrist, claims never to have met so many crazy people. "Remodelers belong to a separate tribe," he surmises.

I tell you all this not to send you screaming in the opposite direction (although this is definitely an option worth considering), but to impress on you the need to take care of yourself and to monitor what's going on.

Once a contract is signed and a starting date decreed, preconstruction activities include:

Obtaining a permit from the building and safety department

Removing hazardous substances

Establishing temporary eating and sleeping quarters

Holding a preconstruction meeting

Ordering all materials and equipment

Packing up the old kitchen

OBTAINING A PERMIT

As alluded to previously, a permit for the job must be obtained at the local department of building and safety office before construction starts. Each municipality has its own requirements, but generally speaking a permit is mandatory if the exterior of the

CONSTRUCTION

A kitchen goes through some pretty ugly dirty stages before becoming beautiful. *Clockwise from top left:* Here you see the walls and fireplace being framed, tiles laid, insulation blown in, and cabinet boxes installed.

home is being altered, plumbing or electricity moved, or a fireplace added. If you are caught remodeling without a permit, the job can be terminated; penalties are stiff. Whenever you are found out, your insurance will be invalidated and the path paved for a future owner to sue.

The building office monitors the renovation to be sure it conforms to stipulations in the local code. This varies somewhat from one community to the next in its protection of the environment and the health and safety of its denizens. An inspector visits each site to enforce the regulations, evaluating structural, electrical, heating, cooling, gas, and plumbing work. If he finds *any* hazardous conditions existing in the house, he may require you to fix them, regardless of their expense or relationship to the remodel.

This surveillance protects consumers from unscrupulous or inexperienced contractors who cut corners that might result in a house collapsing or going up in flames. It has nothing to do with aesthetics or cosmetic quality of workmanship. The inspector doesn't care if your kitchen looks pretty.

A permit is secured after the contractor's contract is signed but before materials are ordered or the preconstruction meeting is held. This way, any changes the office demands can be made easily. It is usually good for one year.

To obtain the permit, the contractor must present construction documents (final drawings, elevations, renderings, and the separate electric plan) along with a tax bill or legal description of your property. He is liable for fulfilling the obligations of the permit and for arranging inspections. If he balks at any of these responsibilities, find another contractor.

If the plan has already passed plan check, it will be a simple matter of paying the permit fee—easily several hundred dollars—and collecting a stamp. Otherwise, you can wait six weeks or so for the card to come back saying you've passed or adjustments are required.

When our permit was obtained, the contractor also paid an optional fire hydrant fee. We had it refunded, learning the importance of staying on top of all bills even before work actually started on the kitchen.

REMOVING HAZARDOUS SUBSTANCES

Asbestos

Before it was banned in 1979 as a potential carcinogen, asbestos was commonly used in construction materials such as drywall, insulation, ductwork, patching compounds, acoustic ceilings, furnace pads, roofing felts, and vinyl flooring (and the glue affixing it). After that date, no materials could be produced from asbestos, but any remaining inventory containing it could still be sold. The result: Most homes being remodeled today contain some asbestos. Since construction work can shake safely encapsulated asbestos fibers loose and send them flying, any asbestos must be repaired, enclosed, or removed before demolition.

Although some states allow less than a hundred square feet of asbestos materials to be handled by a contractor, you'll feel safer having its evaluation and control under the auspices of a special licensed company. You can either manage its appraisal and containment before construction starts or hire the contractor or designer to take care of it. An approved source of asbestos work can be located in the yellow pages. For counsel, contact the Consumer Products Safety Commission.

Radon

Radon, a known cause of cancer, can be found in some porous soils that contain uranium, phosphate, shale, and granite. More prevalent on the East Coast and in newer airtight homes, it invades living quarters through a basement crawl space or cracks in the foundation. It can also be a component of concrete building blocks. Test for radon's presence with charcoal or a device called an *alpha track detector*. If present, it must be dealt with before work begins. Waterborne radon will be discovered by evaluating the water supply and can be treated accordingly (page 295).

Lead Paint

If the home's paint will be considerably disturbed during the remodel, and its application predates 1978, it should be evaluated for lead content. Working with the contractor, test to see if lead is present and in what concentrations. Then review options for removing or encasing it.

SEEKING REFUGE

Sleeping

If you rent another home and move out during the remodel, extra expenses accrue, and the action is more difficult to monitor. Stay at home, and you have a ringside seat to a filthy nightmare. As bad as things got, I was comforted by sleeping in my own familiar bed. If, however, I'd had children at home, I probably would have moved my family off-site. As my editor, Ann Bramson, suggests, line up a series of friends with fabulous estates who are going on vacation. Or rent an RV and park it in your driveway. At least you'll have a clean bed with center-stage seats.

Eating

For a temporary kitchen you need a place to eat and a source of water for cleanup. This can be a basement, den, dining room, or garage. I set up a small oven in my bedroom, depending on an adjacent bathroom for water. When I got tired of washing the turkey in the bathtub before roasting it, I made reservations.

As bizarre as this may sound, I kept cooking right through the mess for the emotional nourishment it provided me. Along with chunks of plaster and broken glass, I got used to finding peas in my bed. Not because I was a princess, mind you, but because that was the only place to shell them.

To prepare meals, a slow cooker, electric frying pan, toaster oven, and/or countertop microwave or convection oven comes in handy. Use three-pronged plugs where necessary and be careful not to overload circuits in rooms not wired for gobbling current. In summer you can call on a grill and camp stove.

A source of refrigeration is imperative, while a freezer stocked beforehand with premade *construction cuisine* will be a blessing.

Regardless of how elaborately this temporary kitchen is outfitted, you will probably eat standing up and out of hand as Flo Braker did, subsisting on raw snow peas and six bananas a day. "Searching for

RTEs (ready-to-eats), you will discover new aisles in the supermarket you didn't even know existed before," promises Ken Krone. Whatever you do, set in a supply of paper plates, thousands of them.

PRECONSTRUCTION MEETING

Before construction starts, schedule a meeting to review the construction process and responsibilities among the customer, the designer, the contractor or salesperson who sold the job, and the head worker who will be on-site daily.

The contract, plans, and prior decisions should be reviewed point by point in great detail, any outstanding points resolved, and the site toured to identify electric, gas, and water shutoff valves. Add any results of this meeting you want legally binding to an addendum in your contract.

In addition to the following topics, the agenda should include a review of security, mail, dependents, rest rooms, telephone access, and disposal of debris even if they have been dealt with in your contract.

Parking: Establish a parking place for workers' cars, trucks, and delivery vehicles that won't block traffic in the neighborhood or interfere with *your* comings and goings.

Access: Decide on how workers and subs will gain entrance to the house and who will be there to introduce you to them on the first day. After that, will you let them in, give them a key, or use a *lockbox*? Where will they enter the house? Is it possible to establish an entrance that segregates the kitchen and keeps them from tromping through the entire premises?

Protection: What will be covered and closed off? Who will be responsible for maintaining the coverage? What materials will be used?

Schedule: At this meeting the contractor should present a written work schedule for your job. If not, don't make any payments until you receive it. This document should list each step with an estimate of how long it will take. A *Gantt* chart, used by some contractors, is a particularly good illustrated scheme that depicts each task and its expected time period graphically on a horizontal time line. If your contractor uses one be sure drying and curing time is built into it, and add any vacations you're planning. Once labor commences, you should be able to track it by glancing at the chart.

Set up a regular weekly meeting for reviewing this schedule with the contractor and a time at the beginning or end of each day for communicating with him either in person or by telephone.

Communication: Review expectations:

- State that you must be warned *before* electricity and water are turned off.

- Earmark what is to be saved from demolition, the condition it needs to be in, and where it should be housed.

- Confirm who will be ordering what materials. Agree on a place for them to be stored when they arrive and a staging area for work. Designate a place as well for leftover materials to be placed.

- Establish change order procedures.

Obtain contractor and designer beeper numbers and provide them with a means for instantly reaching you.

Designer: Reexamine the designer's responsibilities and role in the construction. Ascertain his availability and define the circumstances under which he should communicate with you and with the contractor as well as the route of communication. Set up a rough schedule of his site visits, securing as many as possible. To evaluate workmanship, have them correspond to the completion of a task on the payment schedule. (Frustrating as it is, designers—and suppliers—don't visit the site frequently enough to see if construction corresponds to their design.)

Subs: Have the contractor provide a continually updated list of all subcontractors and workers on your job, their telephone numbers, and any license or insurance numbers. Reconfirm that everyone is licensed, bonded, and insured under a specific policy.

ORDERING MATERIALS

Before one hammer is hoisted, purchase every material and have it on-site, regardless of whether you or someone else secures it, or a storage facility must be rented. This includes small items such as hardware and cabinet inserts as well as the cabinets themselves.

Though you can pick up some things locally, most merchandise will have to be ordered, for companies keep little on hand. Back orders take months, even if industry standards state several weeks. My kitchen sat half done and unusable for a year and a half (yes, you read that correctly) waiting for cabinets that were supposed to take three months. *Construction should start when and only when everything has arrived.*

Many contractors argue that good cabinet fit is possible only if measurements are taken in the field after walls go up. That may be true at the extreme, but even the best custom cabinets are shimmed and filled on-site to spiff up their fit. If cabinets are made as well as they should be, a slight *gap* can be dealt with during installation.

Considerable money can be saved by locating and purchasing your own appliances. Costs vary enormously from place to place, and neither a designer nor a contractor is going to shop around for the best discount. But you can secure it: Telephone-hunt with the business pages and don't be shy about calling companies you've never heard of. The one thing you do not want to acquire on your own is granite or marble, for you will be responsible for any breakage in transport.

Watch for sales and explore ads for mail-order discount sources at the back of decorating magazines. Check warehouses and contractor outlets where discounted, discontinued, rejected, and slightly damaged goods are sold. Canvass dealers, particularly of items made locally, to find show, demo, or refurbished models at a lower cost. I secured both my dishwasher and my warming drawer this way.

You may have a friend with a resale number that gets you into a wholesale showroom, and in many states it's yours just by filling out a form.

Many wholesale and contractor outlets both sell to the consumer and offer the designer or contractor price. All you have to do is ask for it. Designers or contractors may be willing to buy some things for you at their cost or at a small markup, while plumbers can often be persuaded to procure sinks or faucets from their connections.

Before ordering anything, you need to learn its unique lingo. Specifications vary from item to item, with *width* and *height* used differently. For windows, width is stated first and then height along with unit, rough opening, sash, and glass size. Wall thickness must be known as well in case *extension jambs* must be added.

Companies use different proprietary names for the same cabinets. Sometimes companies change their specs after you have placed an order, and sometimes their spec sheets are wrong to start with. When Campanile restaurant's oven arrived, its dimensions were off by six inches.

Hardware offers its own opportunity for fun and frolic. The hardest task is apparently counting the correct number of pieces. My carpenter said I was the first person he'd ever worked with who ordered the right number. (Don't ask. I have no idea how I did it.) His rule is to add up doors and drawers three times and then increase the total by two.

Generally not included, hardware screws have to be found separately. To get the right length, you need to know the thickness of the cabinet. No matter where hardware is purchased, request that its holes not be drilled until after cabinets are installed.

Real size and rounded-off nominal *stated* size differ significantly. To figure tile, you need to know its actual dimensions and the width of the grout line to be used. Then throw in another 10 percent for breakage plus 10 percent or more to match a pattern. Every piece you need—including trims and milled pieces—must be ordered at the same time to get the exact same color and pattern. This is true of all materials. "The only time you can't see different dye lots," says wallpaper hanger David Hanna, "is when you have your eyes closed."

Before ordering equipment, you must sift through, settle on, and coordinate every option with other materials and installations: How many holes in the sink deck? Will there still be enough room in the cabinet underneath to secure the sink to the countertop? Is the cast-iron sink to be mounted undercounter? If so, order it with a glazed rim. If the countertop is specified at thicker than the standard three-quarter inch, can the faucet be installed in it? Should the griddle have a thermostat or just a low, medium, and high regulator? Were the custom panels double-checked with the appliance's manufacturer for fit, and can they be raised and lowered with the appliance?

Double-check choices with installers. If they won't stand behind the installation of this item, choose something else.

Best deal is another mystery to unravel. Although one dealer may sell a dishwasher for less money, it can end up costing more than it would elsewhere when taxes, delivery, and installation are added. All else being equal, it is usually easiest and cheapest to get things from the same place and same person you can drive a deal with. But have bids broken down. You may be surprised.

Before purchasing something, find out if it can be returned. Sometimes only a dealer can get a problem fixed or accept an exchange. *Whatever is ordered and whomever it is ordered from, state that it is a rush* and you need it immediately. Arrange for delivery simultaneously.

Delivery, a seemingly innocuous subject, can be a real maimer. My contractor refused to pick up my stove regardless of what I paid him. The store I bought it from would deliver it only to the curb: "Oh, we don't have insurance to go inside." One month and *fifty phone calls later,* I finally arranged for its arrival. When the big day came, four men girdled with leather support straps unloaded the one-ton stove in my driveway. One look at the incline leading to the house, and they were off to their gym to sucker two more helpers. Together these six musclebuilders took an entire day to move the stove into my kitchen. You can guess at the cost. Hint: It was more than most stoves. Unexpected, it was not in my budget.

Regardless of who orders the material, it should be in your name and delivered to you if you pay for it. Hold a copy of the order and track its expected delivery date. Do not pay for anything until the item is in your hands and, where appropriate, you receive a proper receipt and lien release from the supplier. Never pay cash. If pressed to do so, yield only when given a complete legal receipt.

Once materials start arriving, both you and the contractor should check them off. Compare each item to its order form to be sure it is what you wanted and check for quality, color consistency, and surface scratches or blemishes. You'll want to examine tiles especially carefully to confirm you weren't shipped seconds. Be watchful.

In addition to uneven coloring and a substandard percentage of air bubbles and holes, my saltillo tiles have paw prints from animals who danced on them while they dried. My slate was not the texture I picked, a fact my contractor disputed, my designer confirmed.

Do not cut or install any material you question, for once altered, it cannot be exchanged or returned even if incorrect or faulty.

Check in all construction materials against the bid to be sure they are the quality agreed on and as a precaution against the contractor's claiming designer error when he runs out of boards after wasting them. Confirm that the contractor has all final specifications and installation instructions, along with a translation of any in a foreign language. (I'll spare you that story.)

PACKING UP

Start packing day by photographing and perhaps videotaping the old kitchen, chronicling the *before* as well as what were, hopefully, happy memories. D-Day (Demolition Day) is your last chance to eliminate the broken-down stuff you haven't been using; the same flotsam you were supposed to throw out during the "Appraise Your Current Kitchen" assignment (page 9). This time, be strict. Do it! Take the opportunity as well to move infrequently used items to a storage place outside the kitchen.

In packing everything safely away for the remodel's duration, separate things out for your makeshift kitchen. Base selections on the likelihood that this *temporary* situation will last longer than anticipated. Much longer. As for flour and other dry goods, be relentless about discarding them: they spend their hibernation reproducing disgusting black things that fly.

In addition to kitchen paraphernalia, lock up tools, valuables, and silver or deposit them in a bank vault. Remove pictures and artwork from adjoining rooms that might shake from their moorings and take down drapes throughout the house that absorb dust no matter how tightly doorways are sealed. Expect to feel a bit sad and sentimental during this sorting process, for you are definitely entering a new phase of your life.

TEARDOWN: IN THE BUFF

Before your kitchen gets beautiful, it gets ugly. Real ugly. The muscle men arrive first to do their demolition in the rough. Starting anew, they grade the site, lay a foundation, and follow up with siding, sheathing, and framing. They snake ducts, pipes, and wires through the walls, insulate them from noise and chill, and close them up with drywall or plaster. Dust storms swirl everywhere, and there is a sense of enormous activity; a Phoenix rising; the shape of a new kitchen being born.

At this point work slows to an excruciating crawl. The contractor catches what my brother, Sam Friedman, calls *remodelosis*. Since there is not enough work to occupy a crew, you may find only one person puttering at the site. Days go by when no one appears. Yet, though there may be little hint of it, this is finish work time.

Installers put in flooring, cabinets, hardware, countertops, and appliances; plumbers return to attach fixtures; electricians do lighting; decorative touches are applied. This work is not to be trivialized. It takes a great deal of finesse, and its quality will determine whether your entire job is judged slovenly or excellent.

To execute your job, the contractor might function as a jack-of-all-trades or hire someone for this role, along with a licensed plumber and electrician. Alternatively, he might turn to a different specialist for each task. Specialization can get out of control to the point where the man who delivered Susan Kane's new range refused to install it because her old one hadn't been removed as promised.

Some workers and subs appear for a single facet such as drywall; others return again and again to work their magic. (Hopefully it's not black.)

One approach you may encounter with a big firm, heavily promoted by Walter Stoeppelwerth, is that of the *lead carpenter*. In this scheme, one person appears daily after framing is completed to supervise subs and do all other work necessary to finish the job. Replacing the crew that seemingly shows up at random, this practice will probably become increasingly prevalent after more people are accredited by the NKBA's new installer program.

The pros who may sidle through your door include a stonemason, a bricklayer, a door hanger, a locksmith, a roofer or flasher (without a raincoat), a mason to pour concrete for a new foundation and fireplace, a plasterer or *rocker* to install drywall and a *spackler* to tape it, a specialist in sheathing, siding, subflooring, flooring, and skylights, a glass man for windows and mirrors, a solid surface or sheet metal fabricator, a licensed plumber, electrician, and HVAC contractor, cabinet and appliance installers, a painter and wallpaper hanger. Whirling around these specialists, a group of rough carpenters will dervishly attack framing, prefab fireplaces, cabinets, and countertops while a team of fine-trim carpenters trot in for moldings and finish work.

Outdoors you may engage a landscape architect, drainage plumber, or soil engineer.

INSPECTIONS

Inspections are scheduled throughout construction. The stages are dictated by the building department and arranged by the contractor upon reaching each specified point. Usually they occur just before a *cover-up*: a foundation is checked for waterproofing and insulation *before* concrete is poured and its condition obscured, framing is viewed preceding installation of a subfloor, and plumbing lines are traced before drywall is applied.

Inspections can get mean and ugly. Our job passed plan check and received a permit, implying that codes were met. Yet when the inspector came to look at our fireplace, he claimed the chimney wasn't in the proper position and refused to sign off on it. We had to rip out the entire structure and rebuild at our expense. The result? An eyesore that doesn't function.

We should have applied for a *variance* but didn't know about this option at the time. Our contractor didn't mention it because he wanted to get on with the job. What did he care? It didn't cost him anything. Neither did the designer, who had been instructed to design to code and who ignored this demand to do the design she wanted, knowing that if she got caught she wouldn't have to pay for it.

Inspection arbitrariness is handled differently throughout the country. In California, contractors apparently do lunch with the inspectors, perhaps mistaking them for Hollywood agents. In the East, they run pipes over property lines and tip the super. "This is New York," explains one city planner, "we work it out."

WHO'S ON FIRST? YOU ARE!

During the process your role is simply—clearly—that of monitor. Though your craft is not to hover or to convey antagonism and distrust, the outcome of the job depends on your involvement and watchful eye. Available for queries, decisions, and *before* demonstrations of where holes are to be drilled, you walk the fine line of slapping hands but not getting in anyone's face.

Before each task is performed, demand to be shown its end result. Where and how will it be installed? Plans are vague in this regard. Distances between knobs is *personal*, and you may well not share the workers' aesthetics. Amazingly, even the word *centered* is open to all kinds of interpretations.

Without understanding what was involved, I had the string pull chains for my closet lights replaced with electric switches. I got my switches all right. With them came ugly surface-mounted conduits and a savage butchering of my beautiful old moldings.

Although an element has been previously agreed on, you must review it again and again. Ask for a sample of the color that is to *match* the cement. Have tile or other seamed material laid out beforehand, or you will find it lopped off haphazardly and asymmetrically.

SUPERVISORY CHORES

Work Schedule: Begin each week with an expectation of what is to be accomplished within those five days and update the work schedule, noting reasons for any delays.

Daily Conference: Use the daily tracking conferences with the contractor to catch any problems before they proliferate. Keep the punch list updated as well, listing tasks that need to be done, the date by which they are to be accomplished, and the person responsible for completing them.

Subs: Confirm that subs have been scheduled in advance, given the lead time they need to put your job on their calendar, and informed of the date the contractor will actually be ready for them.

Before a sub begins work, double-check that the two of you are in agreement on instructions and choice of materials. When the job is finished, be sure the sub gives you any warranties and all leftover stain, paint, granite, tile, and so on.

Daily Check: After everyone has left each day, check appliances, surfaces, and cabinets with a level and tape measure. If you see lots of shims under a greenhouse window, it's a good hint that walls aren't level.

Compare the work to the original plans at night as well as during the day when the light changes, paying close attention to exact sizes, locations, and even materials. Susan King had clear doors installed instead of the sandblasted ones that were specced, wood shelves instead of glass, and a mantel that bore no resemblance to the original drawing. Her fireplace and warming drawer were also installed incorrectly.

Stay on top of cleaning as well and ensure that things remain covered and protected.

When you discover a problem or an inappropriate material, communicate it to the contractor or supervisor, not to the sub or worker who perpetrated it. In communicating your concern, stand your ground and have the courage of your convictions. If you think a table is too big, make sure you are heard. If no amelioration is forthcoming, stop the job, express the problem in writing, and proceed with its solution according to the method called out in your contract.

Diary: Be compulsive about making daily diary entrees, describing every visit, meeting, telephone call, decision, and assumption of responsibility. Write down why each decision is made, for you will forget.

Note who is on the job each day, hours spent, and length of lunch break, or you will find yourself charged for labor not done. Record the progress of each stage visually with a still or video camera. Chronicle *every* minute problem and mistake on film before it is fixed, even if resolved courteously. File records of all change orders and make and track payments in accordance with lien releases.

DOIN' IT

The following brief overview describes the construction of a new kitchen with structural and exterior modifications. The work performed in your home and its order will vary according to your specifications—which tasks you assume yourself; what is repaired instead of replaced. Regardless of your involvement, consider hosting a Demo Derby the night before starting, providing guests with hammers (and protective eyewear) to get the process rolling.

Demolition

After you move out of the kitchen, the construction crew moves in. These workers isolate the kitchen from the rest of the house by covering floors with paper, furniture and doors with plastic sheets. The sheeting should be larger than the door openings they are covering and attached to the side of the door where work is transpiring. Tape can do considerable damage, so review its appropriateness with the contractor and watch for marks or other problems. Instead of taping door sheets to the floor, weight their bottoms.

Before demolition, they will turn utilities off and cap pipes and electric wires. Heaters and vents are closed so debris doesn't blow throughout the house. Appliances to be salvaged are cleaned, taped shut with their wires and plugs attached to their backs, and stored in a clean, dry place. Equipment, plumbing fixtures, cabinets, countertops, moldings, flooring, and lights are removed—generally in that order—and then, with Humpty Dumpty forewarned, the walls come tumbling down.

Once you've reached the studs, that dreaded termite infestation may manifest itself. The floor and subfloor may also reveal water damage from a leaking sink or dishwasher. If not being replaced, they will have to be repaired.

Foundation

If the kitchen is being extended beyond the exterior of the house, the contractor may be able to lay the new foundation, install drain water pipes, and start framing before intruding on your current kitchen.

The foundation can consist of a concrete slab, concrete block masonry, or concrete with a basement or crawl space underneath. A slab sinks in soil with a high moisture content and thus is not often seen in the Northeast. A foundation not being replaced may still have to be repaired.

Fireplace

If a masonry fireplace is being added, its foundation will be poured concomitantly with the foundation for the room. A prefabricated fireplace, in contrast, is installed during framing. Whenever it is installed, a fireplace needs a damper and ducts to bring air into the system for combustion. Its chimney runs up a wall on the outside corner of the house or through the roof where its junction must be *flashed* (covered with sheet metal to prevent leaks).

Framing

All design decisions should have been made long before framing starts, but this is, admittedly, a last chance to make changes while walls are still open, so review any remaining issues that are bugging you.

Framing is the process of structuring the room with two- by four-inch vertical *studs* placed sixteen inches apart. (Two- by six-inch studs placed twenty-four inches apart are chosen when a room is to be *superinsulated*.) Horizontal *joists*, small beams less than five inches thick, are used on the ceiling and floor. To prevent the room from shaking and rattling when you walk, their numbers should exceed local code recommendations. Augmenting studs and joists are *posts*, which are large corner studs, and *beams*, big horizontal members.

Lumber should be kiln dried and number-two grade. Douglas fir, western larch, and southern yellow pine are recommended by contractors in the know. It and boards for flooring should be delivered only in dry weather and allowed at least five days to acclimate in the room before installation.

Though rooms historically have been framed with wood, steel is starting to be used instead. Less expensive, it is used primarily for floors and non-load-bearing interior walls, where its lower insulating properties are less significant.

Workers should frame with appliance specs in hand to be sure proper placement is allotted. If a sink or cooktop is to be housed in an island, the locations of its studs must be determined in tandem with the plumber or electrician.

Framing must also be specific to the exact doors, windows, and skylights you are using, for *lintels* (horizontal header boards) vary with the type utilized. You may want to install a hopper or casement window upside down or turn it ninety degrees, lowering its hardware to a point on the wall where it is easier to operate. If shelves, racks, or railing systems are going to be hung on the wall,

backing needs to be emplaced for support before walls are covered up.

Once framing is finished, doors and windows are set in and glazed. Be sure adequate turn space is left for casement window handles. After a skylight is framed, it is flashed and then *hot-mopped* (sealed with tar) by a roofer.

Check to see that apertures open and close easily. Attach stops immediately so doors don't get nicked, rout and weather-strip external doors so they don't leak. Foam-filled weather-stripping is tightest and most energy efficient. For this protection to last, nail it on.

Mechanicals

After framing is done, mechanicals—wires and pipes—for plumbing, electricity, and ventilation are snaked through the studs and/or under joists. Wires for TV antennae, stereo speakers, intercoms, telephones, security systems, outdoor irrigation, and Smart-House operations are wiggled into place now as well. To facilitate future updates of these systems, ream in extra wire and coaxial cable while walls are open and access is relatively inexpensive. Smoke alarms must be hard-wired now, too, and linked by cable to others in the home so sounding is simultaneous. For insurance against a blackout, keep one on battery backup.

Ventilation ducts and heating ducts or pipes usually go in first, followed by drains, pipes, and water supply lines for equipment to be plumbed. In addition to a house shutoff valve where the main water pipe enters the premises, each fixture requires its own closure on the line. To avoid drainage problems, the sink's waste pipe must be installed a specified distance from the vertical stack. A disposer is emplaced with its drain no higher than seventeen inches off the floor.

Rough electric work finishes mechanicals. Receptacles and switch boxes are inserted in the framing at a point where they will be flush with the backsplash and finished wall surface. Wires are run from the service panel to switches and receptacles and installed at least one and one-quarter inches from the edge of a stud or joist. To protect cables from drywall nails, they are run in a channel or wrapped in a metal sheath.

Old wiring may be preserved or moved and joined to new wiring in junction boxes. When electricity is added to an extant wall, the same person who cuts the wall should repair it. During rough electrical work, the electrician also checks placement of recessed ceiling cans. Regardless of size, their rim should fit flush with the ceiling and their bulb pulled high enough above the edge to be invisible from a distance of four feet. To review lighting placement, read its entry in "Kitchens by the Numbers" (page 365).

Insulation

Insulation is poked into the walls and around windows and skylights to maintain warmth and decrease sound transmission. *Fiberglass batts, blankets,* or *rock wool,* the most common types of insulation materials, are usually faced with foil to prevent moisture transfer and permeation. Avoid rigid insulation, which retains dampness.

Insulation is given a *sound transmission classification (STC)* that usually runs from thirty-two to thirty-six. More is desirable when the kitchen is below a highly trafficked area or next to a bathroom, or if you want to work in the room during off-hours without disturbing other occupants. Generously insulate any attic above so heat doesn't rise up and out. A three-inch clearance must be left between insulation and any light fixtures or electric motors not rated for it.

Insulation is also classified by its *heat resistance (R).* The thicker the insulation, the higher the R-value bestowed. To determine the correct R-value for your climatic conditions and the airtightness of your home, check with the local utility company. Once established, confirm that your contractor uses enough bags of insulation to achieve it. Finally, insulation should have a *flame spread index* (the speed fire moves across it) of less than twenty. In all cases, avoid polystyrene and polyurethane foams, whose smoke is quite toxic.

Additional Insulation: In addition to insulating floors, ceilings, and walls, you may want to wrap water lines and pipes, warming them in transit from the heater. Hot water comes on faster; fuel bills decrease.

When placed in the ceiling, plastic plumbing pipe must be insulated, or it will be very noisy. Think, too, of adding rigid fiberglass to a dishwasher so it runs more quietly. For increased efficiency, install foam sheets between a refrigerator and any hot appliance you've had to place next to it.

Closing Up the Walls

A *lath and plaster* wall surface, the wet wall finish traditionally applied by artisans, has pretty much given way to *drywall,* known also as *gypsum board, plasterboard,* or *Sheetrock,* its brand name. Providing a finer finish, a *skim coat* or *veneer plaster* can also be applied. Both can be smooth or textured, but the latter finish is a pain to keep clean in the kitchen. There is also a drywall system designed to absorb sound.

Available in four-foot-wide sheets, drywall is most commonly sold in eight-foot lengths, but ten- and twelve-foot sizes mean fewer seams, particularly when hung horizontally. Vertical seams are, however, less likely to show.

Sheets for the kitchen should be water resistant and at least one-half inch thick. A fire-rated board with fibers is thicker, at five-eighths inch. Peruse edges and corners for nicks and other damage.

Drywall is usually applied with nails, but screws are more secure, albeit a more expensive installation. Seams are taped and then covered with a joint compound that bears more than a passing resemblance to fluffy seven-minute frosting. Walls should receive *three* coats of spatula-applied compound, particularly if they will be covered with satin or gloss paint that reveals every seam and nail head. A curved wall requires four coats. But even then you will see fibers from any area sanded too roughly.

Once walls are up, the area covering each electric outlet and recessed light is cut out. Double-check that all openings are made. To evaluate a drywall job, look for a smooth surface with no visible dimples or blemishes and plumb (perfectly straight) walls. Walls will absorb moisture, so they must dry completely before flooring or other materials are brought in.

Finishing Walls and Ceilings

Paint: Once drywall is dry, walls and ceilings can be readied for painting with a coat of oil primer. Though new paint is bound to get banged as work proceeds, the process should be completed at this stage except for touch-up or perhaps a final coat—with this proviso: You can sing in the rain, but you don't want to paint under these conditions. After cabinets and appliances are installed, it is harder to secure an estimable paint job; impossible to cover walls behind them.

Use high-quality paint that may cost more initially but will stand up longer. With paint composition varying from locality to locality according to Air Quality Management District (AQMD) restrictions, it will pay to snoop around paint stores in your community, where you can talk to painters and salespeople, picking their brains to see what brand is flourishing and regarded as least likely to yellow.

Whatever you get, the higher its gloss, the more durable and easier to wipe off greasy dirty fingerprints. Though harder to apply, enamel (alkyd) provides a much richer, smoother long-lasting finish than latex. Slow drying, it should be indulged in a dust-free environment. At double the price of most paints, the speckled multicolored Polomyx is favored for its ability to hide imperfections; Zolatone for its flecked granitelike finish. And then there are the latest mixed colors from Martha and Ralph.

To choose a color, paint swatches of three or four *finalists* in several different places on the wall and watch their metamorphosis as the light changes. If the ceiling is in good enough condition, a glossy white will reflect its light and brighten the kitchen.

To give the kitchen some character, have a family portrait or mural painted on the wall. Or hang up a map or children's drawings and protect them with liquid plastic. Applying one of the popular glazing techniques will transform even a modest kitchen into a million-dollar baby. The following decorative techniques can also be applied to cabinets and, in some cases, to a wood floor.

Sponging: A natural sponge lays on the paint in a mottled fashion.

Rag rolling: Rags or plastic bags stamp or roll on the paint.

Scumbling: Rough-textured fabric from natural fibers rolls or blots on the paint.

Stippling: The ends of a stiff-bristled brush are tapped on the surface to apply the paint.

Strié or *hand-dragging:* A long-bristled brush pulls the paint across the wall.

Stenciling: Stencil patterns are applied to the wall.

Faux surface: The texture and appearance of stone, marble, or another material are imitated on the wall in paint.

Wallpaper: Wallpaper can also be added to the kitchen at this point for texture, depth, or intrigue. It can cover all the walls or be limited to a border or accent. Like kitchen paint, it should be readily cleanable. Center choices on paper that is *washable* with a sponge or *scrubbable* with a brush. Cover any uncoated papers with silicone or urethane for protection and use a lining paper to hide the wall's imperfections and smooth the application.

Strippable papers are easiest to remove, while *peelables* leave a thin layer of paper or paste behind to deal with. Do-it-yourself hangers are happiest with *pretrimmed, prepasted* papers.

Varying in width, most wallpaper rolls run thirty-six square feet with one-sixth of the roll blown off in waste. For every roll figured, deduct a half roll for each window, door, and fireplace.

Rules? Begin hanging paper on the most visible wall and end it in an inside corner where seams will be least visible. Avoid a horizontal pattern near a ceiling edge, where it would emphasize an uneven juncture. Use a small pattern or paint on a low ceiling so it is not overwhelming. Camouflage one that is irregular with textured paint or material.

Other Coverings: Depending on the weight a wall can withstand and whether it is bearing or nonbearing, it can be decorated with other materials. In contrast or continuation with a surface used elsewhere in the room, affix laminate, solid-surface, and ceramic, cork, vinyl, granite, or marble tiles to the wall. Applied decoratively in other areas, copper and stainless usually hold functional court behind cookers. Brick, flagstone, and adobe also climb the walls handsomely.

Wood paneling is not used in a kitchen as often as in other rooms if only because walls aren't free for it. When one is available, a rough board can make a strong design statement in a farmhouse or country mode; a fine wood panel or wainscoting in a traditional decor. Quality paneling includes hardwood boards or plywood with veneer sheets. Edges should interlock so gaps don't form as the wood expands. Though panels don't need as tough a finish, protect them with polyurethane as you would a wood floor.

Wood, either as sleek modern or rustic beams, dramatizes any high-ceilinged space. Stamped tin, another ceiling treatment, adds considerable character to rooms celebrating bygone eras. Panels discolor when touched by hands, so handle with gloves and seal with polyurethane before installation. They can also be painted.

INSTALLATION

The order in which items are installed varies somewhat according to the materials used. Orchestrate the sequence with the designer and contractor together with plans for protecting newly installed flooring and appliances while finishing the rest of the job. Get hardier materials in first, but expect the inevitable bumps, bangs, and retouches.

The competence of installers varies enormously, with *incompetent* too often the operative word. Pointing blame in their direction, Maytag's Consumer Education Department attributes many appliance calls to inadequate skills. B. Leslie Hart, *Kitchen & Bath Business* editorial director, tells of the manufacturer who responded to a consumer's complaint and found his cabinets hung upside down.

Confirm an installer's prior experience with the contractor and halt any questionable practices. Warranties are often invalidated when installation doesn't proceed according to Hoyle. If any parts are lying around afterward, find out why.

The gas company often hooks up a gas appliance knowledgeably and for no or little charge. Tom Brucker's contractor claimed this was too hard to schedule when, in truth, he just didn't want to lose his cut from the installer. Be sure flexible cable is used for appliances rather than the rigid connections that cause noisy vibrations.

Flooring

Sometimes you have to spend a fortune getting the floor ready for the floor. Old flooring, subflooring, and/or underlayments (surface above a substrate) have to be replaced if torn or worn or prepared with different substances to bond to a new layer. When a new floor is to be laid over an old vinyl covering, assess its asbestos content before sanding.

Extend both flooring and subflooring to all corners of the room to discourage dry rot and visitors in the bug, mice, and water families. Money can be saved by laying an inexpensive flooring under cabinets and appliances, but if you ever change out these items, you'll be stuck with an area that doesn't match.

When flooring is roughly textured slate or tile, a refrigerator or other appliance must have a smooth flat flooring. Some contractors stick a board under their feet, but it makes it almost impossible to move the appliance in and out over this board for cleaning.

Flooring must be installed before cabinets or appliances. If it goes in afterward, you'll never be able to move this equipment out. You can install it at a higher level to leave room for a new floor at a later date, but this will probably prove awkward.

Whatever type of flooring you use, be sure that it is not loose, squeaky, or uneven and that seams are well filled and equal in width. While it is going in, pay careful attention to threshold slope and ease of transition from one room to another. Jillian King's

CONSTRUCTION
The construction process moves along: glass fronts are added to the cabinet boxes and doors affixed, and the gaps between floor tiles filled with grout.

exterior threshold slopes backward so water floods into the kitchen when it rains. Brent Keene's is so high you need a pogo stick to cross it.

Tile: Tile layout has to be preplanned carefully to ensure the symmetry of the pattern and use of full tiles in focal areas. Starting in the center of the room, installation moves toward the periphery with tiles halved as necessary when corners are reached. *Separators* (or built-in *ears*) are employed to make sure distances are equivalent. If tiles are cut on the job rather than ordered in halves, equipment used should be capable of producing straight, even lines.

For proper techniques and materials, installers should turn to the Tile Council of America's *Handbook for Ceramic Tile Installation*. To save money, tiles are *thinset* into *mastic*, an organic adhesive that should not even be considered over concrete or wood. In fact, a stronger rigid *thickset* bonding is preferable in all kitchen situations. Set over a waterproof material, this classic wire-reinforced mortar bed *mud* method brooks no comparison.

Cement-based mortars have habitually been used to bond the tile. Sometimes *latex additives* are incorporated to augment the structure, decrease water absorption, and provide a better cure. Though it's more costly and challenging to work with, installers are increasingly excited about the improved *epoxy mortars*, whose superstrength and chemical resistance are just what the kitchen doctor ordered.

Grouts, applied between tile joints, can also be based on cement, latex, or epoxy. When joints are larger than one-sixteenth inch, sand is mixed in for strength and resistance to shrinkage. The width of the grout depends only somewhat on the design. Although it can be one-eighth inch wide or less for machine-made tiles, it doubles to one-quarter inch with handmade uneven-edged pavers.

Grouts come in different colors to match or contrast with the tile. Most advice hinges on choosing colors least likely to show dirt. Though white can be bleached, off-white is preferred because "it starts out looking dirty." The safest color is the same color as the tile. In this case any grout absorbed through

microscopic cracks on its surface won't show. Darker colors, perhaps one shade darker than the tile, are less revealing of stains. Grout can be custom-colored, but it may be hard to match when a tile needs to be replaced, and it, like any designer color, tends to become dated.

Depending on grout and tile type, one or both will have to be sealed after a period of curing. Some tiles are presealed or covered with a *grout release* that prevents staining during installation. A topical acrylic-based or penetrating *sealer* (often silicon) needs to be renewed less frequently than one composed of petroleum. Watch for loose tiles and cracked grout. Brick (three months) and concrete (one month) are also sealed after curing. When cured, terrazzo is sanded so as not to be slippery.

Wood: Sensitive to variations in moisture that cause it to expand and contract, wood floors should not be installed when plaster and paint finishes are wet. A gap must be left around the rim of the room for this movement. The slab must be pretested for dryness and a fifteen-pound flooring felt, a vapor retarder with a U.S. *perm rating* of less than one perm, placed over it.

If not prefinished (the preferable scenario), a wood floor is sanded and given a coat or two of finish before cabinets go in. At the end of the job, they are resealed and buffed. Special nailing machines are brought in for square-edge strip floors that must be *face nailed*; tongue-and-grooved boards are *blind nailed*. A well-finished hardwood floor should be smooth with no swirls, splotches, sanding marks, or embedded debris.

Resilient Flooring (Vinyl, Cork): A thin resilient floor must be installed over a perfectly smooth surface of five-sixteenths-inch particleboard or one-quarter-inch plywood and a fifteen-pound flooring felt. Otherwise, nail holes, cracks, and debris will be evident. A warranty should accompany an underlayment stating that floors won't warp, delaminate, buckle, ridge, or telegraph because of its failure.

Vinyl rolls come in six-, twelve-, and fifteen-foot widths. The widest, though harder to install, requires fewest seams. These should run no more than one-sixteenth inch unless the flooring is adjacent to another material. Less cumbersome to install than rolls, tiles loosen more readily if water gets underneath.

To prevent a checkerboard effect, the grain of each tile must face the same direction. Gluing is considered the best installation method, but sheeting is often nailed. In your evaluation, look for its *pops*. Vinyl comes with a factory finish that has to be removed and the floor recoated *in situ*.

Hood

A hood is installed after flooring but before cabinets or the cooking surface it is covering. Ducting has to be installed as specified for ventilation to work. Unless it extends to the ceiling, a backsplash should not be measured or installed until the hood is in.

Cabinets

Cabinet installers must have *as-built* drawings to work from. Before attaching the units, they measure whether floor, ceiling, and soffits are plumb and square so they know what adjustments must be made. They also mark studs where cabinets will be attached by a hanging rail or screws. Nails are considered *verboten*.

Beginning at the corner of a wall that requires no fillers, most people start with wall cabinets first so base cabinets are less likely to be damaged. This approach is reversed when a full-height backsplash is already in place or a tall utility cabinet interrupts the middle of a run.

The first cabinet installed must be level, plumb, and square, or the entire row will be crooked. To achieve this, installers depend on three- or six-inch-wide filler pieces for a cabinet with a frame; four-inch pieces for frameless. A cabinet may also come with wide stiles called *ears* used as filler pieces. When you see installers constantly leveling legs, fussing with hinges, and *scribing* panels (fillers) in odd-shaped spaces, they are compensating for a bad job.

A full-overlay door on a frameless box poses special problems. When not well hung, it rubs against appliances. To ensure proper operating clearance, a three-quarter-inch-wide panel is sandwiched between the cabinet and appliance (range, dishwasher, trash compactor, refrigerator, and/or freezer).

Cabinets will have to be moved over and fillers inserted as well when oversized hardware prevents corner doors and drawers set perpendicular to each other from opening completely.

After doors and drawers are installed, check that they line up, hang well, and open smoothly.

The sides of cabinets must be finished at the end of a run and between two base cabinets in its middle where an opening has been left for an appliance. For these latter panels, you may prefer stainless or another metal instead of the cabinet material.

Moldings: Cabinet, baseboard, window, and door moldings should be installed and finished on the job. When finished beforehand, they turn yellow where nailed. To ensure moldings are parallel to the doors, they are installed after doors are hung. Check that they are mitered properly and sanded smoothly with nail holes filled. According to contractor R. Dodge Woodson, *colonial-style* baseboards are better quality than *clam-type*. *Finger-joint* trim is less expensive than *clear*, but it has to be painted, not stained.

Hardware: Though many doors and drawers arrive predrilled, holes for hardware should not be made until cabinets are installed. Unless walls and cabinets are perfectly plumb, handles will line up cockeyed like buttons in the wrong hole.

Before installing hardware, show the carpenter where it should be placed. Jessica Koran's installer merrily mounted six handles in the center of her drawers and then handed her the six that were left over. There were supposed to be two per drawer.

A single drawer handle should be centered from side to side but not top to bottom, because it always looks off. A good guide is to place it one and one-half (shallower drawers) to one and three-quarters inches down from the top edge of the drawer to the center of the hole. Double handles and door handles should descend similarly. Place a door handle the same distance from the edge of a door.

While plotting hardware hanging, pinpoint whether rectangular pulls are to be poised vertically, horizontally, or in alternate directions. Their look changes completely with orientation. Drawers usually receive horizontal positioning and swinging doors vertical, but a well-mounted pull hiphops happily in any direction.

Countertops

Some countertops are laid over a cabinet; some joined to it. Some precede a sink; some follow. A tiled countertop, for example, goes in before a self-rimming sink and after a recessed one. Others have to be raised about one-quarter inch so that dishwashers, compactors, drawers, and cutting boards can open.

Granite, solid-surface, and stainless countertops demand a precise fit. Consequently, they should not be measured until cabinets are installed even though their fabrication can take several weeks. Prone to cracking, narrow pieces of granite are particularly problematic at the sink and should be lined with a double channel of metal struts before installation.

When countertop material separates two sinks set side by side with several inches in between, its edges should be sloped so splashing water doesn't pool or roll off the counter.

Postformed (bent) laminates come from the factory; *edge-glued* are built on site. In both cases, keep your eye open for chips and joints where delamination can occur.

Extremely brittle, marble must be handled like glass with its edges protected.

A butcher-block countertop demands room to expand and contract. As an aid, screw holes may come slotted. If not, manufacturers recommend an undersized screw centered in a *counter sink pilot hole.* Increase flexibility at its joints with a nontoxic silicone sealer considered safe for food.

A tile countertop, as a floor, needs to be laid out beforehand. Here, too, a thickset mortar bed should be used.

Substructure for a countertop is very important, particularly in front and back of the sink where, unsupported, the narrow strips express their stress with fracture lines. Though it divides the sink cabinet inconveniently, a central top-to-bottom strut is necessary for supporting a heavy countertop.

The countertop's angle and extension are particularly important at the sink, where dripping water can destroy the finish of the cabinet below. Check that all countertops are level with even, smoothly sanded, and well-filled joints. All grout, adhesive, and caulking should correspond to countertop and sink colors.

Backsplash

After countertops, backsplashes and trim go in that have not yet been installed. In some situations, they're added after appliances. Some rail storage systems go in simultaneously with the backsplash.

If a tile backsplash is abutted to a different countertop material, a silicone-based caulking is a better anticrack joiner than grout. When backsplashes are fitted with mirrors, burglar gloves must be donned, for the glass turns black if body oil comes in contact with its silver backing.

Appliances and Fixtures

Appliances are installed after the countertop so they can be taken out for repair or replacement. To move them easily, have refrigerators or stoves on casters or wheels. Installation specifications for their clearances, ventilation, trim kits, filler pieces, and door panels must be followed precisely. After mounting, they are hooked up to drains, water supplies, and electric outlets. Plug and switch covers are installed (check that they are straight) along with light fixtures, undercabinet lighting, and lightbulbs.

When a mirrored or other highly reflective surface is used, undercabinet lighting hardware may become visible. Minimize this reflection by mounting the light as close to the front of the cabinet as possible and shielding its back.

Refrigerators: The new generation of refrigerators, replete with automatic defrost systems, icemakers, and more energy-efficient compressors, is announcing its presence like any new baby: with clicks, whining, gurgling, and other irritating noises. To muffle these sounds, be sure it does not touch the wall behind unless it is a built-in model. As a further silencer, carpet the wall or cover it with acoustic ceiling tile. Insist that the refrigeration unit be level and its defrost water collection plate correctly in place.

Sinks: Sink installation is called *trimming out* or *setting the fixtures*. Most sink cutouts require *radius* corners to prevent cracking. Check that the rim of a drop-in enamel-on-cast-iron sink is not chipped. A rimless sink can be finished with a separate rim, usually stainless. Requiring a special mounting clip, stainless cannot be screwed to a solid surface. Drop-in self-rim sinks are supported with caulking; other types with clips as well.

Sinks to be fronted with tilt-outs need to be set far enough back in the counter so there is room for these trays, often a problem with an undermount. Undermount sinks cannot be attached to particleboard.

Faucet: Lay out any faucet and accessory holes to be drilled on-site in the sink deck or countertop beforehand, ensuring that spouts extend over the edge of the sink and vessels fit underneath for filling.

Once sink, faucet, and instant hot and cold dispensers are hooked up, check water pressure and drainage and keep an eye cocked for leaks. Leave the aerator off the faucet for several days, giving any debris that has accumulated in the pipes a chance to wash away.

Disposer: To minimize noise and eliminate vibration during grinding, cushion the disposer with rubber mountings.

Dishwasher: A dishwasher is quieter when plumbed independently than through a disposer. Some municipalities demand, however, that the latter approach be taken.

The dishwasher is either attached to the bottom of the counter or separated by a one-and-one-half-inch clearance. Some machines must be reset *in situ*

to decrease energy consumption. Order special door springs from the dealer for models fitted with heavy custom panels.

Cooktop: A separate cooktop, like the sink, may need radius corners so the top doesn't crack.

Adjusted initially at the factory, gas appliances may have to be revamped if you are using bottled or propane gas, which doesn't need as large an orifice as natural gas. Plates are affixed to ranges stating setting and type of gas required.

CROSSING THE FINISH LINE

Once everything is installed, dings refilled with drywall, and paint touched up and feathered out, towel bars can be hung and curtains or shades pulled up. These can be coordinated with wallpaper or other fabric and should be likewise washable if hung in the line of spatter. When designing curtains, remember the adage "It's better to use cheap fabric richly than rich fabric cheaply."

The room is now complete except for the final punch list. Make sure it contains every detail you want finessed, or the contractor will consider it warranty work to be tackled after the final payment is made. Checking off the punch list should take no more than a day or two. That, unfortunately, is too pragmatic a view. The norm is for it to stretch on for months, building enormous frustration.

Sandy Feldman needed only two more hours of work before pronouncing her job complete, yet her contractor—to whom she owed money—turned into Charlie of the MTA, the man, as the Kingston Trio sang, who never returned. Nothing out of the ordinary here. Rather than driving yourself crazy calling the contractor as Sandy did, keep the defined retention fee (page 49) holdback and hire a handyman to finish up.

A job is formally considered finished when the building department inspector signs off on it, every task on the punch list is complete, and the last payment is made to the contractor in exchange for a final lien release and warranties. Contact your insurance company at this point to reassess your home's mortgage and insurance. If you added a policy for the remodel, a refund may be forthcoming for unused coverage.

The one moment you've been waiting for—unpacking into the new kitchen—may not happen as quickly as imagined. A transition through a strange ambivalent period, it takes some time before you can call this space your own. "You've forgotten how to cook," says food professional Gwen Wayne. "You're in the habit of eating out, and you don't want to get your new kitchen dirty," observes Flo Braker. It also takes a surprisingly long time to learn to use your new equipment and take care of it; to feel comfortable with operation. Don't be discouraged. Habituation comes eventually with familiarity.

Whenever the strangeness passes and you start unpacking, remember that this is really the last call to dispose of everything that should have been thrown out when you first assessed your kitchen and then again when you packed it up. If your belongings didn't look grungy beforehand, you can count on them look-

ing like *disgustingville* in this brand-new shiny arena.

Before putting everything away, line shelves with rubber matting so their contents won't shake and vibrate when kids turn the kitchen into a ballpark. Secure a typewriter pad under a mixer or food processor as well to keep them from moving during operation. Once tools are in the drawers, organize them with dividers. To determine partition placement, arrange gadgets on a table or graph paper or just put them on the floor as they come out of the box. You have to wash them anyhow. In your enthusiasm to get settled, be careful removing seals. You don't want to cut your new refrigerator door shaving off its sticker with a razor blade.

MAINTENANCE AND UPKEEP

You've gone to a great deal of time and trouble, not to say expense, to get the very best equipment. Its performance and longevity are now in your hands. Once new equipment is in, read the use-and-care booklet, locate its water and electric shutoff valves, test it immediately, and purchase recommended cleaning materials to have on hand. Instruction books are vague, so check the many questions that arise with the manufacturer or with friends who own the same equipment. Pursue any question not answered satisfactorily. Our authorized refrigerator repairman knew neither where the compressor was located nor how frequently it should be cleaned.

When you have to call a service person, check the cost of repairs before the person comes out. Get a receipt with the date and description of any problem even if it is under warranty and there is no charge for its repair. When a serious problem arises that can't be resolved, recourse lies with the Major Appliance Consumer Action Panel (MACAP), an organization that directs your complaint to the manufacturer or confronts it in-house.

Following are a few of the recommended upkeep tasks. Add others to this list as you learn of them. To stay on top of these jobs, write the date and materials necessary to perform them in your appointment book.

ITEMS				
Cleaning Materials				
Cleaning tasks & Frequency				
Warranty				
Company Phone #				
Service Company Service Person Phone Number Address				

Hood: Keep baffles and filters clean and grease-free.

Refrigeration: Clean coils, drip pans, and vacuum compressors twice a year; quarterly if a pet frequents the room and monthly if your unit's compressor is on top. Defrost manual freezers regularly. If the warranty covers spoilage in the event of a freezer's breakdown, keep a record of what you store in it.

Check seals by inserting a piece of paper in an open door and closing the door on it. If the paper can be removed without a tug, tighten the screw on the refrigerator door or change gaskets.

Sink: Pour a pot of boiling water down drains every day (when you remember) to prevent clogging. Give stainless a mineral-oil rubdown to make it gleam.

Garbage disposer: Run a pot of hot water with one-half cup baking soda dissolved in it through the disposer each month. Grind small bones and ice on occasion to contain odors and rub deposits off tank walls.

Faucet: Clean out the screen in the faucet head regularly to free it from debris.

Dishwasher: Keep drains and filters free from debris. Patch any interior rust areas as soon as they develop with an epoxy kit obtainable from the manufacturer.

Surfaces: Reoil butcher block with mineral or vegetable oil monthly. Polish granite professionally every few years. Protect appliances with a coat of car paste wax to prevent moisture and dirt from destroying their finish and encouraging rust. Obtain paint from the manufacturer to touch up blemishes and prevent rust.

When washing tile, don't use a vinegar or acid cleaner that crazes the tile and disintegrates the grout. Change water frequently so the grout doesn't absorb dirt.

During cold and rainy seasons, keep a humidifier in a room with wood floors to minimize expansion.

Cabinets: Tune cabinets once a year, adjusting the hinges so doors line up.

Ground-Fault Circuit Interrupter: Test once a month. If it is working, the reset button will pop out. Reset after testing.

Plumbing: Drain the plumbing system if the house is closed up during the winter.

Electric: Turn all circuit breakers off and on at least once a year whether or not they have been tripped.

Heating: Clean the filter of the air conditioner or heat pump after the number of hours stated in its instruction booklet.

Gas: Be conscious of a gas flame turning yellow at the tip, alerting you to carbon monoxide in the mix. Use a gas spark igniter to light a burner in an airtight house.

KITCHENSPEAK: CONSTRUCTION

———

Asbestos: A potential carcinogen banned in 1979, asbestos was used in construction materials and must be removed or encased carefully by a licensed abatement contractor before construction begins.

Beams: Large horizontal boards used in forming the ceiling during the framing of a room. See also Framing.

Building Permit: A license sanctioning the remodel that is obtained by the contractor at the local department of building and safety before construction starts.

Drywall: A method of applying a wall surface using what is variously called *gypsum board*, *plasterboard*, or *Sheetrock* (its brand name). This approach has generally replaced lath and plaster.

Flame Spread Index: The speed fire moves across insulation; it should be less than twenty.

Flashing: A sheet metal covering at the junction of the roof and a skylight to prevent leaks.

Framing: The process of structuring a room vertically and horizontally with strong wood boards.

Gantt Chart: A bar graph utilized by many contractors that depicts each task and its expected time frame graphically on a horizontal time line.

General Contractor: The person responsible for the management and execution of the job; for hiring workers and subcontractors from various trades and organizing and monitoring their work.

Heat Resistance (R): Classification of insulation whereby the thicker it is, the higher its R-value.

Joists: Small boards less than five inches thick installed horizontally on the ceiling and floor during framing.

Lath and Plaster: A wall surface applied in a wet state after framing is completed. Requires a skilled artisan.

Lead Carpenter: Practice of keeping one worker employed at a remodel each day after framing is completed.

Lintels: Strong horizontal header boards, usually of steel or stone, installed over a door or window opening during framing to support the weight of the structure.

Lockbox: A safe way of leaving a key for people to have access to your home when you are absent.

Mechanicals: The process of installing wires and pipes through studs and/or under joists for plumbing, electricity, and ventilation after framing is completed.

Posts: Large vertical boards sunk in the corners of a room during framing.

Preconstruction Meeting: A meeting before construction starts among client, designer, contractor, foreman, and salesperson who sold the job to review the upcoming process and each individual's responsibilities.

Punch List: The continually updated checklist of major work and finishing details left to be done. The final punch list consists of tasks remaining to be done before the last payment is made.

Radon: A known carcinogen, radon is found in some porous soils containing uranium, phosphate, shale, and granite. More prevalent on the East Coast and in newer airtight homes, it invades through a basement crawl space or cracks in the foundation.

Rocker: What most of the workers on a remodel wish they were. The tradesperson who installs drywall.

Sound Transmission Classification (STC): Rating given to insulation, generally from thirty-two to thirty-six.

Spackler: The tradesperson who tapes drywall.

Studs: Two- by four-inch boards placed vertically sixteen inches apart to frame a room. Two- by six-inch boards are utilized twenty-four inches apart when a room is to be superinsulated.

Subcontractors: Workers from the building trades who are hired by the general contractor to do specific jobs on a remodel. The subcontractor reports to and is paid by the contractor.

Thickset: A strongly recommended method for installing tiles in a rigid mortar *mud* bed reinforced with wire.

Thinset: A method of installing tiles into mastic, an organic adhesive that does not bond strongly enough for kitchen situations. See also Thickset.

Variance: Formal permission from department of building and safety to proceed in a manner that varies from the code. People who want to install commercial appliances in a residence may have to apply for a variance.

CABINETS

Variation is the master key to a cabinet's visual success. Judiciously chosen organizers—narrow shelves, many shallow partitioned drawers, and base cabinets with stepped shelves for bottles—make a kitchen a fantastic, well-functioning work space. Choose hardwood cabinets that can be resanded, repainted, or restained.

ISLANDS

Islands can serve a multitude of purposes, providing extra countertop for cooking, multiple work stations, a landing surface for a stove or side-by-side refrigerator, and a snack or dining bar.

STORAGE

In well-organized cabinet storage, everything has a home designed to suit its particular needs. Drawer storage is much easier to access than a cabinet with doors and shelves. Pull-out base cabinet storage, door racks, step organizers in cabinets and drawers, and clear, see-through storage containers all make access to supplies quick and easy.

SURFACES

Surface materials—decorative high-pressure laminate, Nuvel, solid surface, ceramic tile, metal, slate, hardwood, and glass blocks—used alone or in a mix, bestow a unique personality on a kitchen. The durability of a surface material—whether counters, backsplashes, or floors—is almost more closely allied to its proper installation than to its own properties.

FLOORING

With the rigors of cooking intensified by standing, comfortable flooring is a treasure. Kitchen flooring should be smooth, safe, and nonslip even when wet, and effortless to maintain. Warmth is important too when you walk barefoot. When choice is unfettered, my preference is a traditional, medium to dark solid wood floor.

Proper lighting is indispensable in making the kitchen an effective and comfortable workplace. Whether using tracks, recessed cans, chandeliers, luminous ceiling, or task lighting, you can't have too much light in a kitchen.

LIGHTING

WINDOWS

Windows are intrinsic to a sense of well-being in the kitchen.
As long as the right type of window is used, impeccably fits in its
opening, properly glazed and well maintained, it preserves energy
and lowers heating bills.

BACKDROP

4

UP AGAINST
THE WALL

CABINETS

■

"Choosing a cabinet is even more important than choosing a spouse," says Lou Gans, the owner of California Kitchens. "The average marriage hangs together less than seven years, while decent cabinets celebrate a silver anniversary."

Don't bet on it.

My cabinets didn't make it through the first day (and they were much more difficult to select than my spouse, Mr. Gans). Cabinets are a blind, mind-bogglingly expensive acquisition, and even the most careful shopper can be hoodwinked.

A large part of my challenge initially was in identifying a look that integrated commercial equipment, a Mediterranean-style home, and a personal predilection for modern. I also had difficulty justifying putting so much money into a boring box. Finally I realized the impact of cabinets cannot be dismissed: they dictate the overall look of the kitchen. Like violins, they *are* the orchestra.

For all my personal quirks complicating cabinet selection, the real culprits were the people selling them. Slyly, many dealers told me that cabinets cost the same as a car and then asked what I drove. From what I could infer without revealing my driving preferences, Chevies get the $7,000 package; Cadillacs the $70,000. This industrywide approach is presumptuous as well as bizarre. What you spend on cabinets has no connection with what you spend on cars unless you're planning to drive both of them.

Things didn't get easier when I tried to compare quality and price. Smallbone stated unequivocally that its cabinets were "most expensive, bar none." Then, "pinning it down," the company listed them at "25 percent more costly than Poggenpohl." Poggenpohl told me it couldn't determine cost until it drew a plan, and that would cost $1,500. Adding to the confusion, another company dismissed cost, claiming it didn't guarantee excellence. "We give you better quality for less money because we don't have advertising expenses."

Get me out of here.

I thought I solved the problem when I hired a contractor and decided to have the cabinets built by his cabinetmaker, whose work I admired. The problem was that neither the contractor nor the architect listened to this cabinetmaker when he said the veneer we'd picked was too expensive and hard to work with. By the time our kitchen was torn out and we were ready for the cabinets, this man was no longer available. With our remodel now ground completely to a standstill, I was desperate.

Remembering some fine Canadian cabinetry I'd seen at the National Kitchen & Bath Association trade show, I contacted a man I'd met in the booth who had claimed to be one of the company's reps. At that time, I didn't know to be suspicious that he didn't have a showroom or to check his credentials. Given the professional venue where we'd met, and the fact he'd sounded knowledgeable, there was nothing to arouse any doubts.

Defrauding me, this dude took twenty months to spec and deliver shoddy inferior cabinets he had fabricated on the local market in cahoots with the contractor. When I caught on to their substitution during installation, he broke into my house and commandeered some pieces to hold hostage for the remaining payment. An investigation on my part revealed that I was only one of many he had misled, but there was no recourse. Mr. Slimebag skipped town, and the local company to whom he owed the money I had already paid him through the contractor slapped a lien and suit against me. All these many years later, I'm still writing checks to a lawyer to resolve this mess.

Be smarter than me. Put your money into a renowned craftsperson or showroom representing a company that is widely available and highly esteemed in your area. A few other tips: Do not pay 50 percent down if you can help it. Argue against paying even 10. Control costs by choosing standard finishes and door styles. Don't go for *different* unless you're convinced those burgundy pilasters will still look fabulous ten years hence; those teal pediments set you aquiver. Maintain your modesty unless you can afford to be extravagant. In that case, go for the very best and don't worry about cost, because you won't be able to say the figure out loud without choking.

After fleetingly considering—and dismissing—orange crates, read the following section to inform yourself about cabinetry and then go shopping. You may not be able to afford the very best quality, but you'll know what you're getting and be able to discern value within your price range. From all this Jabberwocky I learned how I should have approached this project. This hindsight revelation obviously didn't help me, but hopefully you'll benefit from my painful experience.

Should I refinish or reface my old cabinets?

Before taking another step, this is the question to ask. If you're not gutting your current kitchen or changing its layout, a cosmetic makeover may be all that's necessary. This "kitchen cabinet beautification program" can be limited to freshening the finish or extended to replacing doors, drawers, frames, end panels, interiors, and/or hardware. There comes a point, however, when you get further ahead financially and aesthetically by starting from scratch.

When considering a company to perform a facelift, visit several of its installations to evaluate workmanship. You're not going to be happy with cabinet liposuction if you can see the scar. A contract for refinishing cabinets should be as exacting as it is for new goods and a sample finish or door obtained as necessary. If your cabinets are too far gone for a nip and tuck, read on.

QUALITY CABINET COMPONENTS

Cabinet Materials

Hardwood has long stood for status in cabinetry as it has in fine furniture. In recent years, as wood has become scarce (read expensive) and laminating technology improved, other materials have invaded wood's territory while it took a momentary dip. It is climbing once again, accounting for over 75 percent of cabinet door sales reported by *Kitchen & Bath Business* in July 1995. At 8 percent, melamine (low-pressure laminate) is tied with thermo foil. A sheet of polyvinyl chloride (PVC) bonded to a substrate, it jumped from 3 percent in 1991. Negligible, the share of high-pressure laminate is 3 percent, vinyl 2, steel 1, and polyester and lacquer less than 1 percent.

Though choice usually depends on personal preference, durability is the characteristic that determines ultimate satisfaction. Hardwood is hardiest, while stainless steel dents or scratches and high-pressure laminate, melamine, vinyl, foil, wood veneer, and polyester chip without possibility of repair.

If you aren't someone who likes the inevitable lived-in look, limit your selection to hardwood cabinets that can be repainted or refinished. When ordering veneer, laminate, or melamine, request extra to have a match on hand for replacing any damaged panels.

Hardwood: Any cabinet composed primarily of natural hardwood, whether boards, veneer, or plywood, sports a label attesting to this fact from the Hardwood Institute. Streaked with minerals or resin deposits, hardwood boards vary in color and grain. Seduced more by the idea than the actual reality of a hardwood cabinet, many people don't like these inconsistencies. If you find them unappealing and still want wood, a grained laminate may make you happier.

Hardwood is used primarily on cabinet door and drawer fronts, but styles are limited because of the material's propensity for expansion, contraction, warping, and splitting. Because of these properties, it is impossible to make a door from hardwood without constructing a frame with a panel that can float and move within it or joining vertical strips of hard-

CABINET MATERIALS
To make this kitchen more interesting visually and echo the materials used elsewhere in the room, the cabinets have been fabricated from a mixture of glass, stainless steel, and hardwood. The maple doors consist of panels that float within a frame so they can expand and contract according to temperature fluctuations without warping.

wood and holding them together with a horizontal board (*batten*) on the back.

Keeping the concept of sustainable forestry in mind, red oak—and its more finely grained white cousin—have long been in the forefront of hardwood species used for cabinets. Maple is quickly gaining on them with cherry, hickory, mahogany, walnut, pecan, red alder, Swiss pear, and ash (white is esteemed) muscling in.

With subtle graining and a natural finish, birch, beech, alder, and poplar are increasingly chosen for contemporary nooks. Pine and cedar offer soft bases for a distressed look or painted finish. In search of excellence and individuality, cabinetmakers are on the prowl for wengé, padauk, paldao, and other exotics, if only to use as trim. With its beautiful even grain, *quartersawn* wood is used on finer cabinetry, the haphazardly striated *plainsawn* on rougher work.

Wood Veneers: Expensive exotic woods appear primarily as veneers in the cabinet industry. These tissue-paper layers of lacewood, satinwood, pearwood, etc.—species of trees only the rarest birds have heard of—are mounted on a substrate (see "Core Materials," page 135), creating cabinets of great beauty.

Becoming ever thinner for the sake of saving trees, they are wrought with great respect for the environment. The type of cut—*flat, quarter, rift, rotary,* or *half round*—determines their dramatic pattern and its movement. Between the unique quality of the wood and the expert labor necessary to line up (*book match*) their colors and pattern, these cabinets can become quite an expensive proposition. More common woods, of course, make for less expensive cabinets.

Most veneers come in widths of ten to fourteen inches or more. Anything narrower requires too many seams. No seams (or one at most) should be made on the front of a door or drawer, and it should be well matched. To mask the substrate, all side panels and bottoms of wall cabinets must also be covered with veneer, and door and drawer edges taped, covered, and buffed. Avoid patterns with raised textures that cannot be repaired when chipped and court round edges that are less susceptible to damage than square.

Damage is, unfortunately, an awful reality for veneer cabinets in kitchens that get lots of use; an impractical venue. Their finish must be hard, thick, and continually renewed. Once water seeps through, the veneer separates from its substrate and the marred panel will have to be replaced.

Laminates: Like wood veneer, a laminate is a sheet affixed to a substrate. Cabinets in this category can be made from high-pressure laminate, low-pressure laminate (melamine), vinyl, or thermo foil. As with wood veneers, laminate needs to cover side panels and bottoms of wall cabinets as well as edges of doors and drawers. A better-quality cabinet is laminated after fabrication so that seams hide only in its corners.

High-pressure laminate, the most durable, is also most expensive. Composed of plastic resin–impregnated papers fused under force, it is available in a multitude of colors and patterns, including faux wood and stone printed from a photographic process. Laminates used for institutional cabinets are more durable and expensive, though limited in design.

At .028 inch, high-pressure laminates used for cabinets are even thinner than those wedded to countertops. You may want to substitute the latter grade or a thicker, stronger rendition.

Low-pressure laminate papers are impregnated with *melamine* and, as their name suggests, bonded under low heat and pressure. Melamine comes in different grades with thicker, higher-quality papers more prevalent in Europe. Appearing frequently on a plain door and finished with a high sheen for a modern stance, it is not strong enough to stand up to daily abuse. Melamine is fine for the inside of a cabinet, where you don't mind as much if it gets knocked up, but don't waste your money this way unless you're looking for a here-today-gone-tomorrow cabinet. The same can be said for *vinyl,* a film affixed to a substrate with heat and adhesives.

Thermo foil, a rigid sheet of *polyvinyl chloride (PVC),* is also bonded to a substrate with heat. It can be uniquely laid over a *routed* (carved or grooved) door, forming a mock raised panel. Since it does not fade, crack, or turn yellow as paint can, and goes on smoother than a high-pressure laminate, foil has become an increasingly popular, cost-effective solution for people wanting a white cabinet. For all its advantages, it has an unfortunate propensity for scratching.

In recent years, there has been an influx of gorgeous rainbow-hued glossy cabinets that could upstage Madonna. Covering a substrate, their lush complex buffed polyester finish is sometimes incorrectly equated with a thinner pigmented lacquer. Much tougher, shinier, and richer looking than lacquer, polyester cannot be repaired once it does chip. Lacquer, on the other hand, can be fixed, but it is difficult and expensive to find someone to do so. In my book, neither is strong enough to qualify for kitchen cabinets unless you just want to gawk at them.

Stainless Steel: Ironman steel cabinets are very much at home in a high-tech kitchen or one stocked with commercial equipment. Available in plain stainless or with a baked-on enamel coating that further divides into a smooth or pebbled texture, the metal used is twenty-gauge, too soft a ranking to prevent scratching or denting under heavy impact. As anything with a baked enamel finish, colored versions can also eventually chip.

Environmentally friendly, these boxes are particularly suitable for individuals sensitive to *outgasing*, the release of fumes from formaldehyde utilized in wood cabinetry. To hush them up, some companies combine stainless-steel door and drawer fronts with other, quieter materials. With all this to recommend them, they are currently available only through a stainless fabricator. They have, however, been produced by companies in the past and, in this musical-chair kitchen world, are likely to be so again.

Core Materials

Medium-Density Fiberboard (MDF)/Particleboard: Cabinets made from compressed wood particles, medium-density fiberboard (MDF), and particleboard are called *engineered wood panels*. Smooth, dense, and dent, warp, and moisture resistant, these boards neither expand nor contract worrisomely like solid wood, making them good substrates for cabinet boxes, doors, drawers, and shelves that are to be painted, finished with lacquer or polyester, or surmounted with veneers, laminates, foil papers, and vinyls.

More expensive, MDF is the superior of the two products, particularly when a sizable board is indicated. Composed of finer fibers than particleboard, MDF is stronger, denser, and less friable, holding screws and nails more securely. It also takes a smoother coat of paint.

Plywood: Made of thin sheets of wood veneer sandwiched with the grain in alternate directions, plywood is less brittle, lighter in weight, and better at holding screws than particleboard. Possessing a strength that recommends it for shelves, drawer bottoms, or cabinet sides, it is rent with voids and valleys that render it ineffective for doors or drawer fronts. Decorative hardwood veneers tend to separate when mounted on plywood.

Plywood panels should be made from hardwood graded A on one face and B or better on the other. N grade, the best, is brought in when this material is used on the exterior and to be finished naturally. *Classic Core*, a new mix of plywood sandwiched between layers of engineered aspen flakes, is a smoother substrate.

Glues

People with a sensitivity to formaldehyde need to know the kind and composition of glue used in cabinet construction and materials. *Phenol* formaldehyde is considered less toxic than *urea*.

Cabinet Box A cabinet box can be a mix of hardwood, plywood, particleboard, MDF, and/or plastic. Most important criteria? *The box must be rigid and structurally sound and consist of complete top, bottom, side, and back panels that run full length for support.* The bottom of a wide cabinet may have to be braced further to prevent sagging. A back shuts out dry rot and wannacome visitors from the fauna family, while a top discourages dust. In a base cabinet, it also reinforces the countertop and discourages items from jamming in the drawer.

A strong case depends on square corners and good solid interlocking joints at each juncture, fine furniture joinery such as *mortise and tenon, tongue and groove, rabbet* (page 172), or dowels. Screws support these joints in better boxes, though nails and glue are sometimes used. Triangular hardwood blocks are glued at corners to strengthen joints. Steer clear of boxes that have been stapled or clipped together.

Face-Frame Versus Frameless Construction: Cabinet boxes are produced both with (*face-frame*) and without (*frameless*) a frame on their front. In the more common situation where a frame exists, doors are

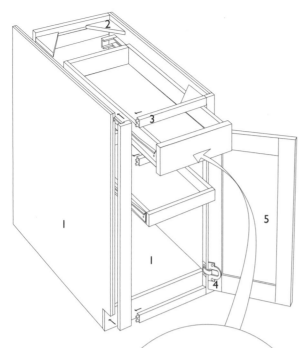

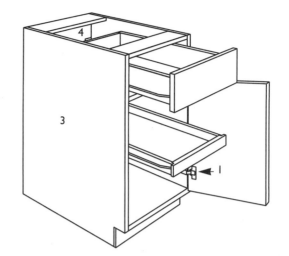

CABINET CONSTRUCTION

The durability of a cabinet depends upon the type and thickness of materials used and the method of construction. A quality cabinet will have the following characteristics.

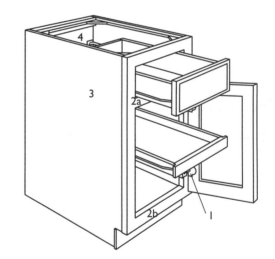

DRAWER CONSTRUCTION

1. Complete Top, Bottom, Side, and Full-Length Back Panel
2. Triangular Hardwood Corner Gussets
3. Fine Furniture Interlocking Joinery (Mortise and Tenon, Tongue and Groove, Rabbeting, or Double Dowels)
4. Strong, Self-Closing Door Hinges
5. 3/4-1 1/4-inch-thick Door

1. 1/4-3/8-inch-thick Hardwood Sides
2. 1/4-3/8-inch-thick Bottoms
3. Separate Drawer Front with Invisible Screws
4. Dovetail Construction Joinery
5. Two Full-Extension Captive Channel Self-Closing Glides with stops to support 75 to 150 pounds

FRAMELESS CONSTRUCTION

Minus a face-frame for attaching a door, these cabinets are constructed so that the door attaches to the side of the cabinet box.

1. Doors attached to box with concealed hinges
2. Holes predrilled 32 mm apart
3. Side panels 5/8-3/4 inch thick
4. Back panel 1/2 inch thick

FACE-FRAME CONSTRUCTION

The most common type of cabinet is constructed with a frame on its front or face to which doors are attached.

1. Doors attached to face-frame (above the frame, overlay [cover] the frame or inset into frame) with concealed, visible, or semivisible hinges
2. Face-frame consisting of stiles (2a) and rails (2b) that are 3/4 inch thick and 1 1/4-1 3/4 inches wide
3. Side panels 1/2-3/4 inch thick
4. Back panel 1/4-inch thick

hinged to it and typically raised above the frame or aligned flush within it. (Difficult to pull off, this latter style should be requested only from a very fine craftsperson.)

When doors completely overlay the frame, a face-frame cabinet looks just like a frameless one whose doors are attached to the side of the box. With doors and drawers very close to each other in both of these situations, measurements must be precise, or you end up playing bumper cabinets.

A face-frame occupies valuable space in a cabinet, reducing the size of its door opening and room left for storage. Interior fittings are harder to insert and manipulate than they are in a frameless box. These boxes are also harder to ship, particularly if preassembled. They are, however, easier (and less expensive) to install and more successful at hiding any lesser materials used on their sides.

A frameless box, on the other hand, is less sturdy and harder to square. For this reason, it should not be much larger than thirty-six inches wide. Most are built with a preengineered drilling system in which all holes in a panel are drilled simultaneously an equidistant thirty-two millimeters apart before pieces are fit together.

Though enthusiasm for frameless cabinets is down from their peak five years ago, these boxes still win for increasing storage space and making tools easier to retrieve. As long as the box is well joined, and you like the overlay door look, go for it.

Side panels on frameless boxes should be five-eighths to three-quarters inch thick, the back one-half inch thick. With more support, face-frame boxes can be thinner, with side panels one-half to three-quarters inch thick, the back one-quarter inch thick. The frame is joined to the cabinet box by an interlocking *dado* joint (page 172).

Face frames, often made of hardwood, have *stiles* (vertical side pieces), *mullions* (center vertical piece), and *rails* (cross pieces) at least three-quarters inch thick and one and one-quarter to one and three-quarters inches wide.

Wall cabinet bottoms in both frameless and face-frame construction should be at least one-half inch

thick so lights and plug strips can be attached to them.

Narrower cabinets are stronger, but the price adds up faster than it does with broader cases. Adjustable legs should be attached to the box so cabinets can be leveled and lined up.

Doors

Door Style: Door styles run the gamut from ornate fine furniture to sleek contemporary slabs. They can be rustic, distressed planks, or modern high-gloss, high-tech plastic panels. A tribute to the decorative arts, they can be beset with carvings, stencils, or pierced sheets of copper, brass, or tin. Representing an era or culture, shoji screens bow to an Asian decor.

Once either/or, choice of door style today is just as likely to be both or all of the above. Taste, once polarized as traditional or contemporary, has evolved as elements blend, distinctions among movements blur, and multiple types of cabinetry mix and match rather than integrate into a uniform run.

Orthodoxy is out: Contemporary laminates are edged with traditional woods; traditional raised panels are finished with contemporary shiny polyesters. With door style variations seemingly infinite, kitchens are increasingly individualized. *Door style, along with its material and finish, is the primary determinant of a cabinet's price.*

Least expensive is a minimalist doorless cabinet. Practical for cooks-on-the-grab and for displaying beautiful objects, these dust and grease collectors aren't for hoarders who cram belongings together and prefer hiding messes behind closed doors.

Breaking up a monotonous bank of identical boxes, the best compromise is to mix closed cabinets with open shelves for things used too frequently to gather dust. Or omit doors and shelves, substituting deep natural wicker baskets mounted on pullout slides. With the beautiful metal hardware and brackets available, it also makes sense to *hold* the sides, top, and bottom of a cabinet and just use wall-mounted or hanging shelves. *Niches* can also be carved into the walls.

People who want to know what's behind closed doors will also find glass doors effective, even if used only on dish, crystal, and display cabinets. Glass doors have their own set of choices: Should the glass have *mullions* (dividers)? If so, are these square, arched, or fan shaped? Is the glass clear, colored, stained, opalescent, leaded, sandblasted, etched, ribbed, seeded, beveled, or colored frosted panels in an anodized-aluminum frame?

Should it be mixed, a signature of designer Charles Morris Mount, with sandblasted glass on the bottom to hide the mess and clear on top to display treasures? Will it wow like the panel of mirror strips alternating with sandblasted glass? Shall it be treated to resist fingerprints? Regardless of what type of glass is utilized, make sure it is mitered into the door, not shoddily butt-joined.

Sliding or pocket doors are sometimes placed on cabinets when an aisle is too narrow for a door to open. Better, no doors. Otherwise, you'll be forever sliding doors back and forth with greasy hands while swearing at the cabinet in frustration.

Cabinets can be covered with fabric *curtains*, but when we're talking doors, the choice generally comes down to either a modern flat panel or one with decorative moldings. Regardless, a door should be three-quarters to one and one-quarter inches thick and sealed with a gasket or dust barrier.

A curved door can be customized or formed from laminates or tambour roll-ups. Yet beware of elaborate doors and drawers. They may prove too busy when many unusual-shaped pieces are executed. The more intricate doors are, the more dusting and cleaning they'll need. Be wary of moldings and trim that can cheapen an expensive closure, but don't shy away from unusual materials that add interest. Not shy at all, architect Brian Murphy adapts aluminum diamond plate found on the running boards of trucks.

The following door styles are among those available. If the budget is limited, stop here and get real excited about the least expensive flat panel door.

Flat contemporary

Picture frame (mitered, beveled, pegged, rounded, square, with fabric)

Cathedral with arch

Double cathedral diamond

Raised panel (radius)

Recessed panel (plain or V-grooved)

Horizontal slats

Vertical slats

Diagonal slats

Pin-striped

Recessed (top and/or bottom) channel

Glass with divided panels

Continuous pull

Hinges: Regardless of how solid their construction, doors droop and creak like the Bates Motel unless well hinged. Hinge type depends on door style and its weight, width, thickness, and material. Though hinges are conventionally side opening, a pull-up hatchback or pocket door hinge enables doors to be operated as they are in an entertainment center and moved out of the way while you work. Specialty hinges are also available for pull-down doors and diagonal, blind, and pie-shaped corner cabinets. A pneumatic telescope hinge lifts a door with a mere tap. Hinges also differ according to whether cabinets are frameless or face-frame, whose width has its own requirements.

Frameless cabinets have concealed wraparound hinges, while face-frame fasteners can be visible, semivisible, or concealed. Like cabinet hardware, visible and semivisible *knife* hinges contribute to appearance and must coordinate with door and drawer pulls. Whether brass, chrome, or forged iron, modern or traditional, hinges should be harmonious with the cabinet's style. Exposed hinges should be high enough quality to leave *au naturel*. Once painted, they chip, committing you to a never-ending process. Leave brass or copper uncoated.

A well-hung door has enough hinges to hang by with the specific number stated in the cabinet catalog. Generally, for a three-quarters-inch-thick door, the range is two hinges for a fifteen- to twenty-inch-tall

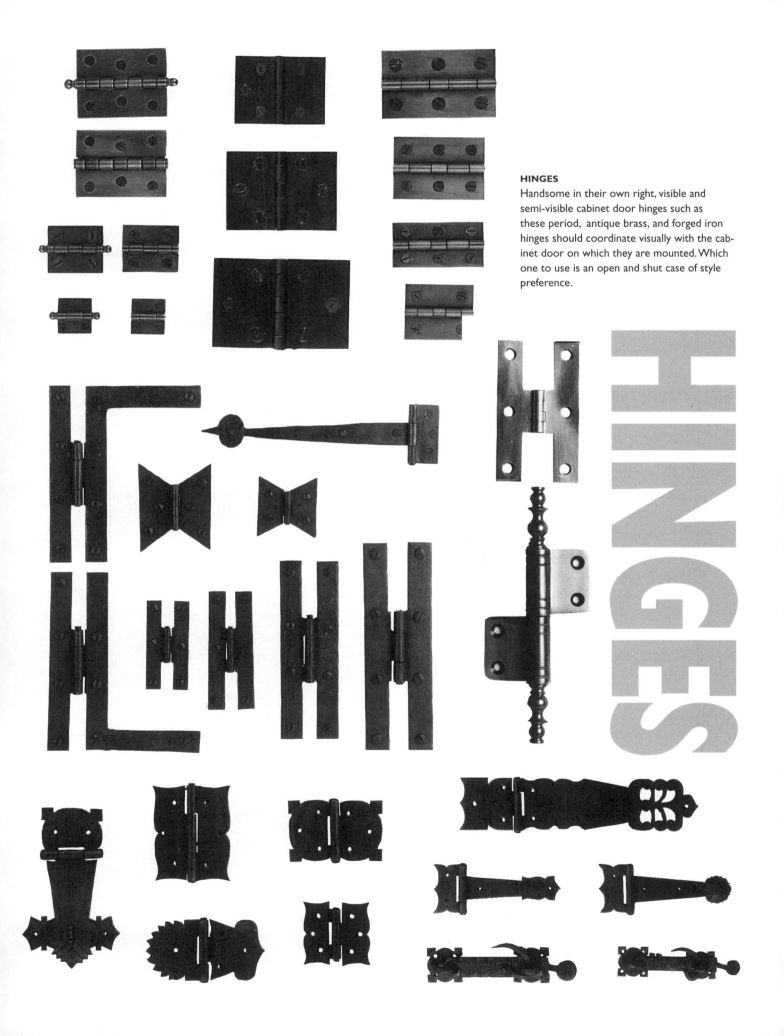

HINGES

Handsome in their own right, visible and semi-visible cabinet door hinges such as these period, antique brass, and forged iron hinges should coordinate visually with the cabinet door on which they are mounted. Which one to use is an open and shut case of style preference.

HINGES

door to five hinges for an eighty-inch door. Like all good justices, cabinet manufacturers recommend a trial (experimental hinging) before a hanging.

A good hinge adjusts in 3-D (height, width, and depth) without special glasses and is self-closing. Some snap-on, clip-on hinges can be affixed with no tools and removed without any signs of having been there. Their openings range from 95 to roughly 180 degrees, with 135 providing a generous general clearance.

Limit a 95-degree hinge to the end of a run or location where you don't want doors to bang into each other. Above 170 degrees, hinges become large, unwieldy, and expensive, so reserve them for situations where they are warranted. One such is a base cabinet with roll-out shelves behind its doors. With a wide-angled hinge, the door folds back away from the cabinet frame, allowing shelves to occupy the entire box and pull out with no need for spacers.

In addition to hinges, doors need protective *bumpers* and, sometimes, locks. These can be serious combinations when cabinet contents are dangerous or just a deterrent catch to discourage young hands or an earthquake's rumblings.

Drawers *Quality drawers are usually composed of a plywood bottom (one-quarter to three-eighths inch thick), four hardwood sides (one-half to three-quarters inch thick) and a separate drawer front.* So as not to waste space, this should be well aligned with the bottom of the drawer and attached with invisible screws. Thicker measurements need to be used with pot or appliance drawers in particular, and some bracing may be in order for a copper or cast-iron collection. Joints should be dovetailed or otherwise interlocking, not nailed, glued, or stapled; edges banded or well sanded and finished.

Drawers should occupy the full depth of the cabinet. (If this sounds like a given, come see Susan Jordan's dead space along with all the things that disappear from her drawers and fall into it.) The glass-front drawers that hold grains, flours, or pulses look appealing in a kitchen. Unfortunately, bugs think so, too.

Acceptable drawers can be made with laminated MDF (not particleboard) or molded plastic whose ends are rounded for easier cleaning. Riding the crest of high-tech European cabinets' popularity is the drawer with aluminum or less expensive steel sides doubling as glides. Available only in certain sizes, these squander a lot of space and do not accept double-tiered storage organizers. Gallery rails are available for deeper drawers with dividers for bottles, but basically you're dealing with open, nonstable sides. When hit by a pot, they dent and rust, disqualifying them as fine furniture.

If drawers are going next to doors, cushion their ends with bumpers.

Drawer Glides: Shrinking in size, glides seem to be going the way of baby vegetables. At least they're moving in the right direction, for the smaller the glide, the larger the drawer can be. The most important thing is that they do their job, *tripping quietly and smoothly without sticking or veering to the side.*

Glides are rated according to capacity with 75 to 150 pounds generally high enough to tote their load. They earn their heavyweight status on pot drawers.

A drawer needs one glide on each side with *auto-alignment* features compensating for drawers differing in width from front to back. New slick runners mount at the bottom of a drawer or underneath, doing their job out of the public eye. "A far cry," says designer Jo Davis, "from those old clunkers that look like they are wearing braces."

If you get to vote, go for *precision captive roller channel glides.* Those with ball bearings tend to be noisier and clumsier and can emit grease. White and almond epoxy-coated glides—as well as custom colors offered by some companies—are more expensive alternatives to sturdy zinc old-timers. They look handsome with light-colored drawers, but their color can chip off.

Glides can be three-quarters extension, seven-eighths, full (pulling out all the way) or overextension, traveling an inch beyond the edge of the drawer frame (a boon for pullout tables or removable trash can inserts). Regardless of extension, glides need *stops* so they don't pull out of the cabinet.

Not surprisingly, the farther glides come out, the more they cost. Pay the price unless you never want to see what's in the back of your drawers again. A seven-eighths glide provides a nice compromise between value and price for drawers storing long-handled items. Like hinges, better glides are *self-closing.*

Releasable glides can be used for cutting boards or butcher block tables you want to detach and remove for cleaning. Be sure the hardware locks to steady the boards while you work.

Drawer Hinges: In most situations, drawers operate best when pulled out on glides. One exception is the pull-down-and-out or tip-out hinge for the drawer occupying an entire base cabinet for trash, dirty laundry, and oversized bags of charcoal or dog food.

When a pullout cutting board or table inhabits a drawer space, the drawer head requires a pull-down hinge to keep it out of harm's way—and your stomach—while the board is in use. Tilt-down hinges also appear on sink drawer fronts backed with holders for sponges and brushes.

Interiors

The cabinet's interior should be finished in the same material as the shelves (or vice versa). They, in turn, should correspond color-wise with the cabinet exterior. Although a lighter interior makes it easier to find things inside, it is too jarring when the exterior finish is dark. A medium brown drawer in a white melamine box is quite ugly (she says knowingly).

When glass doors are used, shelves should be glass; the interior an exact match to the exterior door and drawer finish. If not, the look is strange. Believe me.

Fittings should also coordinate with cabinet finish and hardware: If the cabinet finish is shiny, a lazy Susan looks much better with a high-gloss coating than a matte one. *Remember, it's the details.*

Shelves: Steel shelves are thinnest and strongest. When a composite material reigns, the shelf's length

DRAWER CONSTRUCTION
A sturdy dovetail drawer is constructed with fine furniture tongue and groove joinery and a separate drawer front. Bottom-mounted glides are hidden below the drawer and leave more room for storage than side-mounted runners.

depends on its thickness. The thicker the shelf, the longer it can be without sagging; the fewer vertical supporting struts necessary. The result? More usable *gettable* storage.

Use a one-half-inch-thick shelf up to a two-foot expanse, five-eighths-inch-thick to three feet, and three-quarters-inch-thick to four feet. Above that, go to a one-inch-thick shelf. Use some discretion as well, increasing thickness when the load is heavy. MDF or plywood performs better than particleboard. For upkeep, have a washable high-pressure laminate or melamine bonded to *all* sides of the shelves. These materials will of course separate from the substrate if they get wet. Hardwood and PVC plastic are sometimes used as edge banding.

Shelves of one and one-half to three-inch depth can be hung on the back of cabinet doors to accommodate cans or spices. When perching there, interior shelves need to be narrowed and pulled back the same depth from the edge of the cabinet so the two don't bump into each other. Essentially dividing a shelf, this approach makes things much easier to find and is worth the extra cost.

Adjustable shelves are more flexible than fixed. Frameless cabinets have holes bored vertically into the side walls according to their *thirty-two-millimeter construction system*, while face-frame cabinets have metal slotted rods mounted on the surface or routed into the sides of the box. Shelves tip if holes aren't straight and supports locked into place. Stronger than plastic supports: metal clips or plastic with interior steel pins.

An exception, glass shelves should be fixed permanently, for they can't be adjusted readily. Custom-drill only necessary holes, for a rod or line of holes is unsightly through glass doors. Glass shelves, used primarily in two- to three-foot-wide cabinets, should be one-half inch thick. Above that, engineer them carefully in consultation with a glass expert.

Cabinet Finish

How well cabinets stand up to abuse and torture depends a great deal on the tenacity of their final finish. To prepare the cabinet for a finish, door and drawer edges should be smooth and splinter free; any glue exuding from joints vigorously rubbed out. Blemishes and pores must be filled and sealed; the entire cabinet well sanded: just not too-well sanded. Turn off the radio. Pacing themselves to rock music, overexuberant workers flatten edges and transform square corners into rounds.

The type of finish a cabinet receives depends on its original material. Lacquers, polyesters, laminates, and thermo foils usually require no further embellishment; veneers occasionally a stain, always a protective sealer. Wood, on the other hand, has so many possibilities its checklist looks like the queen mother's family tree. To test the feistiness of a finish, rub a hidden corner with some acetone and see if it stands up to this assault.

Whatever paint, stain, or sealer coat is chosen should include *ultraviolet protection* so it doesn't fade. A finish is applied most effectively at the factory in a controlled, hermetically sealed, properly ventilated dust-free environment that has spray booths created specifically for this task. Cabinet sides should be finished as well as the front. This may sound obvious—certainly it should be obvious—but, unfortunately, it ain't. Whatever is applied should be particularly tough where hardware is mounted and hands are likely to touch.

Paint: Hardwood and engineered-wood cabinets can be painted with semi- or high-gloss alkyds or automobile paint. Though these coverings have to be renewed, a fresh coat of paint is always a delight even if its process isn't. There is no need to wait for the cabinets to look distressed. Start out this way by painting each of several layers a different color and then sanding through.

White is to be avoided, as popular as it is, for it cracks at junctures and is tinted by underlying glues and resins seeping through. Attractive, the wire-brushed liming and whitewashing pickled finishes, prevalent just a few years ago, are pretty passé now.

Painted cabinets can be stenciled, glazed with the same antique faux techniques used on walls, or treated as a backdrop for a trompe l'oeil mural. Though we have left the realm of durable, these finishes look fantastic and are certainly *à la mode*.

Stain: Wood can also be stained. Turning darker woods milky, pastels should be reserved for lighter varieties. *Water-based* stains last longest but, harder to apply, are resisted by some finishers. Good alternatives are *pigmented oil stains* for fine-grained woods and *penetrating oil stains* for coarser-grained species with large pores. Avoid murky spirit- or alcohol-based stains that poke through the sealer.

Sealer: Light or dark, rich woods with beautiful grains can be finished without painting or staining. Either way, all wood must be protected with a sufficient sealer to prevent water damage around the sink and wear in the proximity of cabinet hardware or other well-used areas.

Danish oil, a mixture of linseed oil and turpentine, is the simplest sealer. Acquiring twenty coats and frequent updates, an oil-finished cabinet gets more rubbing than it would from a masseuse clocking overtime. Experts suggest augmenting this finish with a brown paste wax.

Strong durable premium finishes for kitchen cabinets are *catalyzed conversion varnishes* and *catalyzed lacquers*. Resistant to chemicals and moisture, the products used for these finishes need to have a large percentage of solids to be effective. When applied in a shop, two or three coats of these sealers are baked on with a good hand-rubbing and sanding in between.

Even harder, *polyurethane*, a nonpenetrating surface top coat, is considered a tough-guy cabinet finish with 50 percent solids. Clear polyesters are born again as a sealer to add high gloss. But once damaged, they can't be repaired any easier than they are as a pigmented surface.

For all of these details, this is probably not the time to worry about understanding sealer distinctions, for they are currently being modified to meet mandates of the Environmental Protection Agency. Within the next few years, the familiar finishes may well be traded for the more environmentally friendly *waterborne copolymers.*

Containing lower levels of toxic evaporating solvents, these finishes are enhanced by a greater percentage of solids that harden the finish. At this writing, they neither stand up to moisture and heat as well as the catalyzed finishes nor repair as readily. Yet the response they're garnering is much more optimistic today than at their inception in California, when the state's cabinet companies moved lock, stock, and barrel to Mexico to avoid wrestling with them.

CABINET TYPES

Cabinets can be made individually and left unfitted like a piece of fine furniture or interlocked into a continuous or interrupted run. Standard modular cabinets increase in three-inch increments, while imported European models operate on a five-millimeter measure.

The three primary types of cabinets are *wall, base,* and *pantry* or *utility* with a twelve- to eighteen-inch-high backsplash separating the first two. The descriptions that follow are for standard basic cabinets. Modifications are eminently possible.

Wall Cabinets

Starting at twelve inches and increasing to forty-eight inches, the typical wall cabinet is generally thirty inches high. Smaller units mount above a refrigerator, wall oven, sink, or cooktop, whereas larger ones attach to the ceiling or soffit for maximum storage space when Penn and Teller are in residence with their stilts.

Some companies offer insulated cabinets for installation above refrigerator and stove. In these locations, they are most convenient to use when their depth is equivalent to that of the appliance, and they are fitted with vertical slats or pullout shelves.

A range hood, microwave shelf, and drawers are sometimes inserted into a wall cabinet. When this occurs, line up the bottom of these items flush with the bottom of contiguous cabinets. Available with single or double doors and shelves, wall cabinets also float freely at different heights or as modular units. Increasingly they are doorless for a display cabinet.

Shallower than base cabinets, a wall mount typically has a depth of twelve inches so you can work comfortably at a deeper countertop underneath without banging your head. Double-check your plate size before accepting this depth. Another inch may make all the difference in what you can store here. Know, too, the kind of lights, electric strips, and accessories you want to hide under the cabinet so its door is lengthened or appropriate molding added.

Base Cabinets

Extending from nine inches (some lines) to forty-eight inches wide, base cabinets traditionally have one drawer on top and a single or double door with a half and full shelf below. Though more expensive, better use can be made of their standard twenty-four-inch-deep space by placing full-size shelves on pull-out glides. If pots are bigger than this, provide for them with deeper cabinets.

Doors or drawers? More practical than doors and shelves, drawers make it easy to find things in the cabinet's hinterlands. With heavy full-extension

FREESTANDING CABINETS
This freestanding wall and base cabinet also serves as an island, a bar, and architecturally as a room divider.

CABINET TYPES

MODULAR CABINETS

This cabinet line is composed of individual interchangeable modules.

CABINET TYPES

A standard cabinet mix (right) is composed of shallow wall cabinets, deeper base cabinets, and tall pantry or utility cabinets. These cabinets combine all three types plus the less common blind corner base cabinet, appliance garage, and sink drying cabinet in one short L-shaped run. Toe kicks line up harmoniously around the room while cabinet height is rhythmically varied for visual interest.

UNFITTED CABINETS

An unfitted style is achieved with cabinets that resemble individual pieces of furniture. With a combination of open and closed cabinets, and pillars, cornices, and other trims, this heirloom kitchen looks as if it was assembled over a number of years.

glides and strong hardware, a one-handed pull operation is much easier than a two-handed, three - step, open - the - doors - and - pull - out - the - shelves samba sequence. Drawers cost less than doors/ shelves, and they don't gouge and bang together when opening as doors do.

Though hardware and the space separating drawers are wasteful, the organization this sacrifice provides in return is the best gift a cook could receive. In my kitchen, this wonderful present is orchestrated into banks of shallow three-inch-high drawers for utensils, place mats, silverware, molds, custard cups, etc. No more sifting through messes looking for that fork while the onions are burning.

Pot storage is the one exception where I prefer doors and shelves to drawers. Though many people disagree, I find pullout shelves with very low fronts and sides the easiest way to locate and lift out heavy cookware, even if it means I have to open doors to get to them. Doors are also a better option than dummy drawers on a base cabinet under a cooktop that will have to be removed for repair.

Toe Kicks: Base cabinet height of thirty-four and one-half inches (thirty-six inches when countertop is added) includes a toe kick that is recessed at least two inches behind the bottom of the cabinet. A face-frame cabinet is integrated with the toe kick, while frameless boxes are set onto a separate pedestal or *plinth*. Toe kicks on American-made cabinets run three to four inches high; European six to nine inches. At this latter height, you don't have to bend as far to reach the cabinet bottom, and you can store lids, linens, or a stepladder in a drawer inserted in its space.

The bottom of the toe kick should be at the same level all the way around the kitchen, lining up with appliances for a harmonious horizontal line. Before deciding on its height, check appliance height and adjustability to ensure everything lines up evenly. To fight mop attacks, the toe kick can be ordered in metal or other durable material that withstands its blows.

Pantry or Utility Cabinets

These tall cabinets are desirable in spots where you want to hang your witch's broomstick or maximize storage when counter space is unnecessary. From nine to forty-eight inches wide, they grow to a height of ninety-six inches. To soften their massiveness, you may want to add molding or trim. Sometimes the utility cabinet is shortened and smaller cabinets added above. Depending on door style and cabinet material, two shorter doors can be used instead of a tall one to prevent warping.

Utility cabinet depth varies from twelve to twenty-four inches, but once they get much beyond twelve inches, some sort of expensive pullout inserts are necessary to make the space efficient. In a narrow—or not so narrow—space the cabinet door can be attached vertically to a pull-out pantry. Before ordering a pantry, assign storage space in case extra shelves must be specified.

Corner Cabinets

When base, wall, or even utility cabinets turn a corner in an L- or U-shaped kitchen, usurping Little Jack Horner's seat, some adjustment must be made so drawers and doors can be opened without crashing and usable space preserved.

The simplest, least expensive option is a three-inch filler strip on each side of the corner. Using the space, a *blind* cabinet wraps around the corner, opening on only one of its sides. Shelves attached to the door pull out when it opens. A *pie-cut* cabinet, on the other hand, has stationary shelves.

Larger, the *carousel, merry-go-round,* or *lazy Susan* cabinet provides a door—sometimes a pocket door—on each side of the corner. The unit's mechanism consumes significant space, but it also provides real usable storage. To maximize the room, use a full-round carousel whose diameter corresponds to the corner cavity.

An intriguing pivotal corner unit, the Dual Function Slide-Out sold by Häfele, is expensive and cumbersome to operate, but when it's used, *dead* is not a word that can be applied to this corner store.

Finally, corners are also treated by installing wall and base cabinets across them on the diagonal. Often an appliance garage is parked here too.

Despite all these excellent solutions for cabinets with corner locations, there is no contest for best use of space: the revolving three-trash-can recycling unit by Feeny. First runner-up is the ten-inch-wide corner base cabinet with a pocket door designed by Florence Perchuk to house a step stool. *Second* goes to a floor-to-ceiling corner pantry with pocket doors offered by some companies.

Specialty Cabinets

Noncabinet Cabinets: Mandatory in a small kitchen, numerous opportunities exist in any space for combining storage with decorative elements. Shelves can be inserted in pillars, strung across windows or doors, or recessed in the wall.

Built-ins: Cabinets designed for built-in refrigerators, ovens, or microwaves come with trim kits to hide any gaps between the appliance and cabinet. Before determining cabinet size, check appliance insulation, installation, and clearance requirements. A backless unit or one with an electric hookup within may be most appropriate for this situation.

Appliance Garage: Out of sight—but not out of mind—housing for small or ancient appliances making their last stand can be built between the countertop and wall cabinet. These *garages* are not something to plop into the middle of a counter but to weave into the overall design.

I did so brilliantly (she says, patting herself on the back). To create an appliance garage, I extended frameless wall cabinets in one section of my kitchen down to the countertop. The sides of the cabinet rest on the countertop, while its doors fall a fraction above so they can open. The cabinet bottom was removed to house my appliances. With no ledge, they drive easily in and out of the garage. Regular shelves occupy the top of the cabinet with the first shelf sixteen inches above the countertop.

The garage can be as tall or deep as you wish, its dimensions carefully determined by what it cloisters.

Make it two stories for a beverage bar with coffee machines on the bottom; mugs on top.

To accommodate a garage and still have usable work space, the countertop (base cabinet) where it sits should be at least eighteen inches deeper than the garage or have pullout cutting boards below. Sometimes just the countertop is made thirty inches deep and the base cabinets left a standard twenty-four inches. To do so, the cabinets are pulled six inches from the wall, or what is called *furred out.* To hide the resulting gap, a thirty-inch-deep panel covers the sides of the cabinet.

An appliance garage is typically closed with a pocket door or roll-up tambour door (of wood, veneer, laminate, or metal). It can have a flipper door that fits in the frame above, or regular doors that do the same disappearing act they do in a TV cabinet. Another option is to put the appliance on a pullout shelf behind a pull-down door. (And, hey, while you're at it, why not put it on remote?) The goal here, of course, is to get doors out of the way while you work. Provide electric outlets along the garage's length, installing any plug strips so doors can still close.

Sink Cabinets: Considered a specialty cabinet, sink cabinets are really just empty base cabinets with doors below a false front or two hinged pull-down drawers.

Dish-Drying Cabinet: Placed over the sink, this bottomless wall cabinet contains slotted drainboards instead of shelves so dishes can drip discreetly into the sink. When doors are closed, the drainboard is invisible.

Double-Access Cabinets: Two-faced wall or base cabinets that you can trust provide double door and drawer access in island or peninsula installations.

LINKING CABINETS

The aesthetic effect of cabinetry depends on its overall design—how units are combined and integrated and what decorative finishing details are applied.

TWO-SIDED CABINETS
The wall cabinets can be opened from both the front and back, making them easy to reach from several places in the room.

APPLIANCE GARAGE
This housing keeps appliances out of sight until it is time for them to be used, at which point they can easily be pulled out onto the countertop. Often otherwise wasted space, a corner makes an ideal parking spot.

PULLOUT POT SHELVES
Simple pullout drawer storage offers many benefits over a door-drawer combo except for pots, which are much easier to grab from a shallow pullout shelf.

CORNER CABINETS
Different types of doors and various shapes of revolving shelves have been designed to maximize the limited awkward space left in a corner cabinet. This corner cabinet has a single bifold door and pie-shaped carousels.

STORAGE RACKS
Racks have been added to the back of cabinet doors and a lazy Susan to the interior of this wall cabinet so ingredients are more accessible.

BREAKING UP A CABINET RUN
A hanging shelf, random heights, two different finishes, and a curve on one end of the island are just a few of the design elements added to vary the cabinet's appearance and break up the monotony of a repetitive run.

DECORATIVE DETAILS
A cup rack, plate rail, copper-pierced drawer panels, frieze of Christmas tree cutouts, small drawers beneath the cabinets, and a picket undercabinet valance are decorative details that distinguish these cabinets and help create a rustic country lodge theme.

VISUAL INTEREST
Stepping back the sink, incorporating a variety of drawer styles, an open plate rack, and standing the boxes on sculpted feet are ways of adding intrigue and variety to a line of cabinets.

Variation is the master key to a cabinet's visual success. This can be achieved by:

- **Combining fitted and unfitted cabinets**
- **Varying heights of wall cabinets**
- **Interrupting the rowhouse effect with an island, peninsula, or diagonal cabinet; by bumping out some cabinets and stepping others in**
- **Mixing open and closed shelves**
- **Breaking up space with an open wine cabinet or corner display shelf**
- **Alternating two different finishes such as stain and paint**
- **Integrating two materials, such as light and dark oak, laminate with wood, stainless with wood or glass**
- **Utilizing both horizontal and vertical grains**
- **Adding different unusual shapes**
- **Stepping cabinets back from the soffit**

Once the cabinet's basic structure is established, decorative details can be administered:

- **Rounded corners**
- **Serpentine curves**
- **Sculptured crown moldings**
- **Detailed fretwork**
- **Handsome chair rails**
- **Ogee edging**
- **Dentil work**
- **Fluted valences**
- **Carved routed details**
- **Cutouts**
- **Hammered copper or tin overlays**
- **Filaments**
- **Pilasters**
- **Pediments**
- **Corbels**
- **Balustrades**
- **Spindled railings**
- **Friezes**

PURCHASING CABINETS

Armed with knowledge of what constitutes a quality cabinet and the different types available, it's time to hit the stores. Before starting out, there are some issues to consider.

Should cabinets be fabricated by a factory or local cabinetmaker?

Citing the advantages of a suit sewn by a tailor over one bought off the rack, many people believe a cabinet crafted by a cabinetmaker is more finely designed and detailed than one constructed at a factory. Recalling a suit made for my husband by a tailor that would have fit someone twice his girth and half his height, I can only observe that things are not always what they seem.

After my contractor admitted his fraudulent substitution with the cabinet man, he said, "Aren't you glad we had your cabinets made nearby since they don't fit?" Though his remark reminded me of the murderer who killed his parents and then threw himself on the mercy of the court because he was an orphan, the convenience of a neighborhood shop was underscored. (Not that anyone took advantage of this proximity to fix my cabinets.)

Local craftspeople have the advantage of being close enough to recheck measurements *in situ*. A dialogue can be maintained and progress checked more cozily with them. Yet as they increasingly purchase prefabricated cabinet doors, drawers, and boxes, many so-called artisans are little more than an assembly shop.

Lacking samples, these carpenters may also present you with some nasty surprises or build only the boxes, leaving you to coordinate their finish. Though a custom cabinetmaker can match existing cabinets and fit odd-shaped sites, the many factories offering custom work can also do this. The bottom line: *Factories achieve better results more often than custom cabinetmakers.*

Dollar for dollar, there is no way a small custom cabinetmaker can produce the quality of a factory that makes the same cabinet repeatedly in a con-

AN ANGLE ON AESTHETICS
Curves and angles have been incorporated into the layout of this factory-built L-shaped cabinet run and island for aesthetic reasons and in hopes of better using every inch of space. A tall utility cabinet with a door and drawers anchors one corner. If placed in the middle of the run instead, it would interrupt the continuous countertop.

trolled environment with costly precision equipment and that, buying in volume from the same purveyors, is able to get lower prices and superior supplies. This holds true today as companies also buy more prefabricated components. In the more-likely category: Delivery and installation flow more smoothly with a factory, disputes can be resolved in a more satisfactory manner, and money can be recouped in a bankruptcy or reorganization.

Finally, if the factory cabinet line is certified by the Kitchen Cabinet Manufacturers Association (KCMA), this organization can be of help when problems arise. Though many fine cabinet companies don't belong to this group—and those that do don't have all their lines evaluated—certification guarantees that cabinets have met basic structure (ten-year) and finish (five-year) standards. To determine which cabinets have been certified, order the directory of *Certified Cabinet Manufacturers* from KCMA.

Having said all this, I still deem it worthwhile to seek out local cabinetmakers and compare their work to factory-produced cabinets. A real old-world craftsperson is a rare treasure in this mass-produced world. If you find one, grab him.

Do I want factory-built cabinets to be a stock, semicustom, or custom line?

At one time, the cabinet industry was clearly divided into stock and custom lines. Briefly, *stock* cabinets are already in stock, mass-produced in certain limited styles, materials, and modules and then stored in warehouses, ready to be ordered from a catalog. Delivery runs four to six weeks or less; installation is by homeowner or contractor. Unfinished and the much improved ready-to-assemble (RTA) boxes are least expensive.

Custom cabinets are built to exact individual specifications upon ordering with seemingly infinite configurations and options. They solve the challenge presented by a unique space or commercial appliances with unusual dimensions. They also address special circumstances. Along the Jersey shore, where flooding is commonplace, cabinets are built on tall legs with detachable doors and drawers to grab when the water rises.

Custom companies have the flexibility to respond to each unique situation while also offering standard-sized units and components. They must be ordered at least three to four months in advance or even longer, particularly if coming from Europe. Most are medium or, usually, high end. To keep it this way, one cabinet company boasts, " . . . her kitchen was so customized that she couldn't shop our price anywhere." (Gotcha.) The dealer usually installs these cabinets.

Today a *semicustom* line servicing some individual requests along with its stock and/or standard offerings has blurred distinctions. Further confusing categories, semicustom and stock lines currently have enough parts, finishes, and designs *in stock* to be mistaken for custom. SKUs (stock-keeping units or cabinet components) tripled in one company from twenty-five hundred to seventy-five hundred just between 1986 and 1992. And where cabinet companies come up short, the retrofit industry is standing by. To make choices even more difficult, stock cabinets can be elegant or shlocky.

From an economic perspective, it makes sense to start by seeing if there are stock cabinets you like. By varying their height, width, and sections that are open and closed, modifying them with decorative valences, trims, and moldings, mixing them with custom pieces or an island, and/or substituting a thicker door, you can make your kitchen state of the art, up to the moment, and as handsome as any boasting an original signature.

GOING FISHING

As previously discussed, cabinets can be obtained from a dealer who designs your entire kitchen, in which case this will not be a separate process. Alternatively, your designer may detail them completely and contract for their fabrication matter-of-factly as part of layout services. Or you may find the cabinets and have them configured in conjunction with your designer's input. Regardless, before signing off on a design, do some shopping to see what's out there in the name of quality. At a minimum, have an expert in cabinet space planning assess your drawings, even if you have to pay extra for the feedback.

At the suggestion of friends or the yellow pages, visit showrooms and/or craftspeople's studios around town. Their salespeople's first question will unfailingly be "What is your budget?" Sound familiar? Deal with this query the same way you dealt with it when posed by your designer.

If you know that you have a specific limited amount, tell the person that number minus 20 percent. If he can't help you with cabinets in this range, ask who can. More often than not, you need to go fishing. Tell the person that you can't come up with a budget until you understand the differences among cabinets—what makes one superior and what spending more money will bring. You're trading your potential business for education. If he's not interested in this deal, move on.

Evaluate the quality of the showroom's cabinets, opening and closing doors and drawers, by the criteria you've learned. If the craftsperson does not have samples, visit at least three of his installations.

Because door style affects cost more than any other element, start there. When you've identified the type you like, ask to see the least expensive example in this category. As a safeguard, find out what types cost less in case you overshot your budget. When compromises must be made for cost, be particularly careful that cabinets are strong and stable.

Visit a variety of cabinet shops until you decide on the exact door style, material, and finish you want and whether the cabinet is to be face-frame or frameless. Once you make this commitment, you'll have to do some savvy comparison sleuthing since people won't do a complete bid until your signature is on *their* dotted line.

Return to the showrooms you liked with your designer's cabinet plan. If this has not yet been done, compile an arbitrary list of components in a wall and base cabinet run of a specific size. Ask the firm what this section (or a section of your real plan) will cost based on the door style, material finish, and cabinet type you selected.

Repeat this exercise, bidding the exact same thing in each shop without sharing previous quotes.

FREESTANDING CABINETS
Adding a piece of unfitted cabinetry to a room with a formal run can break up the boxy homogeneity with an exciting visual counterpoint. As you might note, the style of these cupboards varies.

CABINET TRIMS
A classic ogee (S-shaped) crown molding caps off a cabinet handsomely. This elaborate cornice boasts a dentil inset and rests on a rosette-capped pilaster.

You will not learn the ultimate price of your cabinetry or even what it will actually look like. But by having several people price the exact same components, you will at least know where the better value lies. This exercise should also signal an alert when you've exceeded your price range.

While you're in each showroom, ascertain whether the cabinet style you've chosen is available in a commercial and residential line and which is less costly. Learn the showroom's pricing structure: Is a corner cabinet charge doubled? How are islands and peninsulas priced? Is measuring included? Hardware? Design services? Ordering? Compare warranties, delivery period, and shipping and installation costs. Can something be returned? What kind of down payment is required? Find out if there is a regional warehouse and how the company handles blemished components.

Once you've narrowed down your choice to a craftsperson's cabinets, check his references much as you did your designer's and contractor's. For factory-made cabinets, talk to the local rep and distributor. Visit many or all showrooms selling the line locally to assess the company's history and viability. Talk to installers to determine their expertise and impressions of this line. When your contractor is doing the installing, investigate his experience with it. If the company is local, so much the better. If the cabinets are shipped in, find out how they're acclimated to temperature changes.

When you purchase cabinetry, you are turning over a substantial amount of money to an unknown person you must trust to do the right thing by you. In this situation, you are paying for the character of the manufacturer as well as for the product. Problems arise without exception, and you must know how the company will deal with them.

Unlike a contractor or designer, whom you can fire and replace with someone to continue the work, the cabinet company may have all your money, and you have nothing. There are many people who will *sell* you cheap cabinets, but they may not *deliver* them. And if they do, you may wish they hadn't. To reiterate, *assess the company itself in addition to the quality of its cabinets.* See as many recent local installations of its work as possible and find out if they came in on time, on budget, and with any flaws.

After settling on someone to design your cabinets, give this person the measurements of everything you want to store in them. Include your list of appliances with their dimensions and the number of inches they can be raised or lowered. Apprise the designer of countertop material and thickness. State the hardware type you will use and whether locks, touch latches, inset or recessed finger pulls (page 00) need to be added. Inquire whether the cabinet is built in inches or metrics, for it will affect all other placements.

As in a layout, cabinet shop drawings and elevations come after a plan is agreed on. Once they are completed, double-check that a space has been provided for everything on your "must store" list. Unless you are getting a cabinet identical to one in a display, have a sample door made and finished. Though it can take a month or more, and you will have to pay for it, you will at least know what you are getting. You will have a sample to test resistance to stains and knocks and a witness if there is a discrepancy in the actual cabinets delivered. After approving the sample, you should receive a bid listing all points described in the following contract. When the bid is signed by you, the cabinet company, and the cabinet designer, and a deposit paid, it becomes your contract.

CABINET CONTRACT

You know the drill here. And you know why. The contract should state:

ASSURANCES

- That the cabinets will be built exactly like the approved elevations and the sample door.

- What will be considered substandard (e.g., warped boards, non-book-matched, or poorly laid veneers or laminates).

- All side panels, inside doors, and bottoms of wall cabinets will be the same material (or covered with the same material) as the exterior of doors and drawers.

- The date cabinets will be delivered and the date by which they will be completely installed. The penalty for late delivery and/or installation. The award for early delivery and/or installation.

- Amount and kind of extra materials such as veneer ordered for future repair.

- How cabinets will be packed and shipped.

- How they will be delivered.

- That a guarantee of origin will accompany delivery.

- The process for repairing cabinets that come in nicked, chipped, or in any way substandard.

- A warranty for structure and finish, including nonfading. (Five years is recommended for wood finishes.)

COSTS

- Total cost of cabinets.

- Any additional cost for finishing the toe kick.

- Any additional finishing cost.

- Taxes.

- Freight charges.

- Delivery charges.

- Installation charges.

- Payment schedule and means of payment. What is the percentage required for deposit? I would suggest that 30 percent be paid with a custom order, 50 percent when the cabinets are installed to satisfaction, and 20 percent when they have been completely aligned and finished and interior options added. For stock cabinets, 30 percent should be paid when the cabinets arrive or perhaps 25 percent and 5 percent with the order.

NAME, ADDRESS, AND PHONE NUMBER

- All companies or individuals producing a part of the box, including the finish, toe kick fabrication for a frameless box, and laying up of laminate or wood veneer.

- The person you are purchasing the cabinet from, his business or contractor's license number, and his relationship to each of the preceding individuals.

- The person who will be responsible for delivering the cabinets to the site.

- The address and responsible party for any interim delivery.

- Who will be responsible for uncrating cabinets.

- Who will be responsible for installing cabinets. The experience of the company stated and your contractor's relationship, if any, to the installation.

CABINET BOX

- Dimensions of each.

- That the box will be completely covered on the top, bottom, sides, and back.

- Thickness of top, bottom, sides, back, and any face frame.

- Type of joint used in each part of the box.

- Existence of corner support blocks.

- Material and finish used on each part of the box, including sides, frames, and interiors.

- Dimensions of the toe kick.

- Alignment of the toe kick around the room.

- Dimensions, type, and finish of any moldings.

- Dimensions, type, and finish of any decorative pediments, valences, etc.

DOORS

- Dimensions of doors.

- Number of doors.

- A drawing of a door.

- Accepted clearance between doors.

- That a dust strip will be inserted between doors.

- That core and overlay material will be used on *both* front and back.

- Type of edging.

- If veneer or laminate, the number of pieces used (seams on front and back).

- Thickness of veneer or laminate.

- Type, material, degree opening, adjustability, and warranty of hinges.

- Side of the door that hinges will be mounted on.

- Flush fit of the inset door.

- If glass doors, type of glass, mullions, and joint.

- If raised panel doors, that parts will be finished separately before they are joined together.

- Other descriptions and assurances as pertinent to the type of door style selected.

- Type of bumper guards.

HARDWARE

- Type, size, finish, and manufacturer.

- Who is responsible for purchase.

- Who is responsible for purchase of its screws.

- Who is paying for it.

- Where and when in the process it will be installed.

- Who will install it.

- That hardware holes will be omitted.

DRAWERS

- Dimensions of drawers including height of sides.

- That there will be a separate drawer face.

- Number of drawers.

- Drawing of drawer.

- Type of joints.

- That core and overlay material will be used on bottom and sides.

- Type of edging.

- Type of glides.

- Load capacity of glides.

- Extension of glides.

- Any pull-down hinges.

- That cabinets will have stops and be self-closing.

- That any locks planned will be installed.

- That drawers will extend the full depth of the cabinet.

SHELVES

- Dimensions of shelves.

- Number of shelves.

- Core and overlay material used on both top and bottom.

- Type of edging.

- Adjustability of shelves.

- Number and type of shelf supports and support rods.

- That shelves will extend the full depth of the cabinet.

INTERIOR

- Finish material used.

- Storage options included.

- Exact drawing or photograph of each of these with manufacturer, size, style number, and finish.

- Who is responsible for ordering and delivering any cabinet inserts not offered by the cabinet company.

- Name, manufacturer, size, style number, and finish of these additional inserts.

- Who is responsible for installing these additional inserts.

FINISH

- Description of sanding and filling.

- Description of type of finish used, where it is to be done, and by whom.

- Description of finish process.

- That all sides and parts of the cabinet will be finished, all door and drawer edges taped, covered, and buffed.

INSTALLATION

- That cabinets will be plumb and level.
- That gaps between cabinets and ceilings or walls will be less than one-quarter inch.
- That cabinet gaps will be shimmed and filled as necessary.
- That doors will be aligned.
- That toe kicks will line up around the room or as agreed on.

- That built-in microwaves, warming drawers, or other appliances will fit flush with the bottom of the cabinet or as agreed on.
- That cabinets will line up precisely with freestanding appliances, or as agreed on.
- That there will be no visible gaps between cabinets and adjacent appliances or cabinets and the soffit.
- That cabinets will be furred out, if desired, and all gaps eliminated with a full-side panel that extends to the wall.

PERSONAL PICKS: CABINETS

The truth is out. I hate the look of cabinets. Their massiveness feels oppressive, and their sameness, even with the clever visual trompe l'oeil tricks of the design trade, is boring and repetitious. This is a pretty serious accusation given that cabinets occupy about 80 percent of a kitchen. Yet their antidote, modular furniture arranged salon style, just doesn't provide enough space for organized storage.

To secure storage aids, I had to close up some of the areas that would have made my kitchen feel more spacious and less boxy. As much as I would have liked this feeling of openness, I'm not sorry. My judiciously chosen organizers—narrow shelves, many shallow partitioned drawers and base cabinets with stepped shelves for bottles—have made my kitchen a fantastic, well-functioning work space. I didn't, however, do so well in choosing a veneer cabinet type. (If only this book had served as the research for my own kitchen rather than as the result of it.)

Even when finished with a strong protective coat, thin veneer layers are not strong enough to withstand the rigors of kitchen life and its de facto aqueous environment. Veneer warps, buckles, and lifts off its substrate, and it cannot be repaired. Neither can a laminate, polyester, or lacquer cabinet, nor a melamine interior. Replacement comes at enormous cost and hassle. Once cabinets start to look shabby and worn, the entire kitchen looks terrible. My advice—at least in the sink area—is to go for a hardwood cabinet that can be resanded, repainted, or restained. Thoroughly fed up, I would take this advice one step farther and go for a rustic country kitchen with wood that has been deliberately predistressed. With a crackle finish, these cabinets would also be at home in an elegant contemporary setting. Regardless of the cabinet material, be sure that their toe kick is mop-proof.

CABINET HELPERS

■

Before I remodeled my kitchen, there were some not-so-subtle signs that the interiors of my cabinets desperately needed reorganizing. Bread dough rose before I found the bran flakes, and last year's Halloween candy surfaced while I was hunting for a flour sifter. More time was spent searching for tools and ingredients than cooking dinner. When my mother visited and refused to put dishes away, I knew things had really deteriorated. Luckily, there was help at hand.

Innumerable well-designed gizmos—boxes, shelves, bins, dividers, racks, and rails; rollouts, pullouts, pull-downs, and pull-ups—have been developed to organize groceries and kitchen equipment. Once made only for cabinet manufacturers, these burgeoning storage aids can now be picked up at the supermarket. Since most are geared for installing in existing cabinetry, it's not necessary to redo to revamp.

According to the National Kitchen & Bath Association, in 1993 the typical kitchen housed "eighteen cans of vegetables, ten casserole dishes, nine mixing bowls, twenty-three spices, six boxes of cereal and more than ninety cups and glasses," but no turtle doves. The 376 utensils, pots, pans, and dishes stored in 1948 exploded to 791, with the increase mainly in tabletop and entertaining ware, not cooking paraphernalia. To find a home for all these food waifs demands discipline.

Like Chinese pork cookery, which utilizes every part of the pig but the squeal, good cabinet organization is based on commandeering every cranny.

The backside of doors, interiors of drawers and cabinets, bottoms of wall cabinets, and backsplash are all potential spaces to exploit.

For shallow drawers, there are single- and double-tiered trays to hold silver, gadgets, cutting boards, and knives. These should be snuggled safely in slotted blocks that shield, separate, and maintain sharp edges. Of all materials, wood performs these tasks best.

Deeper drawers are accessorized by bottle dividers as well as bread and vegetable bins. Vent the latter outdoors in temperate climes to keep food fresher and dissipate those heady garlic aromas.

Fittings for cabinet interiors include lazy Susans, towel racks, full-height pullout pantries, pullout shelves and baskets for food, pull-up shelves to support small appliances, door racks for spices and cans, and vertical tray dividers. (These win more friends when they pull out on glides and their individual slats adjust to tray thickness.)

Attached to the bottom of a wall cabinet, pull-down racks play hide but not seek, while railings with optional modular accessories run across a backsplash. Long ignored, the backsplash is doing the forward stroke into the limelight as more and more companies produce shelves, containers, cubbyholes, and cabinets for this wall, some of which are built into the studs for greater depth. In a small kitchen storage capacity can be doubled just by incorporating this area. A second level steps up to stash things when you run a ledge or shelf around the backsplash.

Of all kitchen items, dried spices and herbs probably have the most storage possibilities. Since heat and light destroy their delicate flavor and fragrance, store no more than a short-term supply of anything near the stove or in direct sun. For convenience, scatter several spice holders throughout the kitchen in places where they are used.

Wine and alcohol are cool-weather friends, too. Keep them away from light and heat; from cookers and vibrating refrigerators. Restrict them to base cabinets—down low, not high, where heat rises—and impose term limits on the wine's residency, or it will soon be destroyed by temperature fluctuations.

Fit liquor cabinets with stepped shelves to hold bottles upright, racks to cradle wine horizontally. This beverage can also be stored in special temperature-controlled units (page 275).

In a category by themselves, pot racks are exemplary in adding both decorative and utilitarian ele-

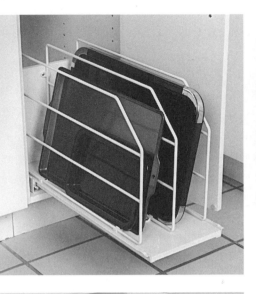

PULLOUT BASE CABINET STORAGE

In well-organized cabinet storage, everything has a home designed to suit its particular needs. When this home is mobile, you'll be on the road to perfect organization. Vertical tray dividers are designed for baking sheets and slatted wire drawers for root vegetables that need aeration to prevent spoilage. These wire racks are fitted with cross wires for bottle definition, while the shallow, chrome-plated shelves work beautifully for pots (or food).

DRAWER STORAGE

With drawer storage so much easier to access than a cabinet with doors and shelves, organizers abound for the myriad items likely to be maintained within. This stepped organizer hides spices from heat and light, but lets you see all labels at a glance. Gadget dividers come both single- and double-tiered. Combining a wooden cutting board with knife storage, this unit is installed with a drawer front that hinges down so the board doesn't have to be removed from the drawer to use.

TRAY STORAGE

Vertical slats, in this case, fixed, divide trays and baking sheets. Placed above my refrigerator, out of the main work path, this cupboard is designated for less frequently used items.

POT RACKS

These wall and ceiling mounted racks are very handsome as well as convenient when you want to reach for a pot.

TILT-DOWN SINK STORAGE

Removable trays attached to pull-down drawers hold sponges, brushes, and other cleaning supplies, freeing the sink ledge.

REMOVABLE CUTTING BOARD

I built this removable cutting board into a pullout drawer with a drop-down drawer front so that I can cut lemons and mix drinks in this bar area without banging my head on the upper wall cabinet. The bottles are stored in a base cabinet with stepped shelves while glasses reside in the cabinet.

KNIFE STORAGE

Both fingers and a finely honed edge are protected when knives are secured in a slotted block. This knife block with its protective scabbard built inside the cabinet is an example of safe, easily retrievable ergonomic storage. This stainless knife rack can be built in as well. It can also be attached to an island or the wall. It is easier to choose a knife when its protective skirt is omitted, but not as safe. Designed for the food service industry, the rack is solid and sanitary to use though, unfortunately, expensive.

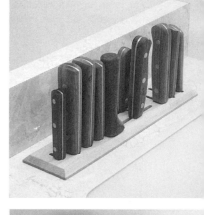

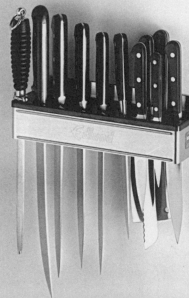

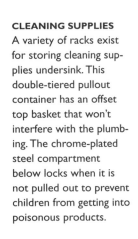

CLEANING SUPPLIES

A variety of racks exist for storing cleaning supplies undersink. This double-tiered pullout container has an offset top basket that won't interfere with the plumbing. The chrome-plated steel compartment below locks when it is not pulled out to prevent children from getting into poisonous products.

STEPPED SHELVES

This custom step organizer can be cut to fit the interior of any cabinet up to fifty inches wide and is particularly suited for shallow upper cabinets. It enables you to see all items at a glance and is ideal for spices as well as for small cans and bottles. The same idea can be adopted for storing large condiment bottles and liqueurs in a base cabinet.

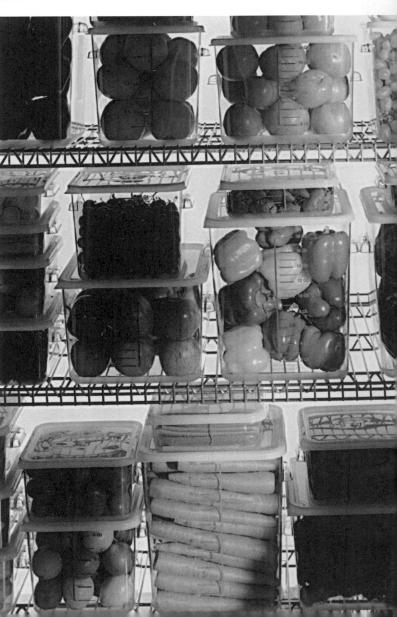

STORAGE CONTAINERS

Transferring boxed and bagged grocery dry goods to clear, see-through plastic containers eliminates the odd-shaped packages that occupy lots of room in the cupboard and are hard to retrieve, makes whatever you are seeking recognizable at a glance, and contains any unwelcome critters that are rude enough to hatch in your home. Frequently used items can be stored in this small integrated pullout unit, while everything else can be housed in these individual see-through containers. Available in all sizes, rectangular containers stack more readily and use space more efficiently than round ones.

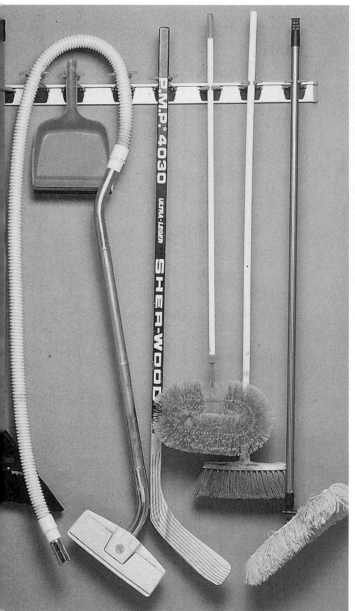

BROOM CLOSET
Railings with hooks for cleaning supplies can be placed in a broom closet or on a wall. Racks such as these, available in smaller increments, should satisfy anyone into serious cleaning.

CUSTOM PANTRY
The interior of a pantry can be fitted and divided according to the types of items you want to store in it. This custom pantry consists of swing-out shelves for individual ingredients, shallow, pullout drawers for pots and heavy canned goods, and a box on a roll-out shelf for bottle storage. In the pantry, rows of tight mesh shelves are mixed with pullout baskets.

BACK OF DOOR STORAGE
When the back of a cabinet door is used for storage, its interior shelves must be shallower and line up with the door racks in order for the doors to close. With narrower shelves, it will be easier to find things in the cabinet as well as on the door. These door racks match cabinet interiors. The back of a cabinet door is also an excellent place to affix a towel rack such as these triple plastic-coated bars.

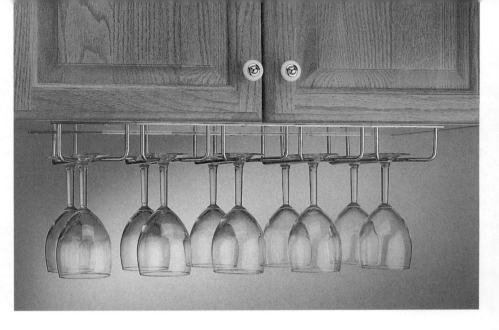

BACKSPLASH AND WALL STORAGE

Often wasted, the backsplash area and noncabinet wall surfaces can be put to good storage use. A grid system, available with a broad range of accessories, can be hung on a wall or over a sink. When paired with a worktable or fold-down prep counter, it can function as an independent work space. Designed for the food service industry, this system exemplifies how quality restaurant equipment can be integrated into the home. Railings can also be custom cut to size and fitted with unique storage modules (left center). These individual modules, minus the railing, can also be hung on a wall. An undercabinet stemware rack provides a safe haven for glasses where they won't get jostled, and frees cabinets so they can be crammed with something else. Occupying the backsplash as well, a line of pull-down organizational accessories are attached to the bottom of a wall cabinet. Choices include a spice rack, cookbook holder, office, and knife block (not pictured). When closed, they disappear completely from view if the cabinet front has been fitted with a molding.

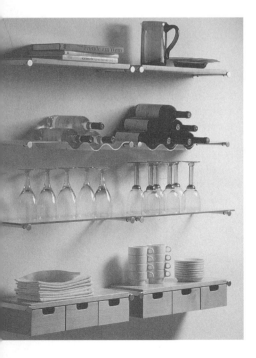

ments to the kitchen. Traditional or modern, fitted with lights or shelves, pot racks hang under a skylight, on the ceiling, or across the sink or backsplash on metal bars or rails. Their hooks can be fixed or—more flexible—movable. The only place they shouldn't be hung is where they usually are: over a stove that makes them greasy.

Charles Soriano from Artistry in Wrought Iron installs ceiling racks through joists with enough support for a 200-pound man to hang from. Go up to sumo wrestler weight when tethering copper and cast iron. To prevent collisions, pot bottoms should coincide with the height users can reach comfortably.

Playing with the plethora of organizing aids, you experience the wonderment of a child let loose in a toy store; a fantasy that ended abruptly for me when I remembered I was the adult who had to pay. Prices add up quickly. When reality testing results came in, I chose a twelve-inch-deep pantry cabinet that was shallow enough for items to be accessible without the help of special organizers. The decision was painfully simple. The elaborate shelf system I coveted with a designated compartment for each food cost $1,500 for each thirty-six-inch insert.

When purchasing cabinet storage aids, save money with do-it-yourself buying and installing. Though people seem daunted by this task, fears are unwarranted. Items have been designed specifically so even the five-thumbed can approach them. Order directly from the manufacturer by calling the telephone number on the catalog or find a local wholesaler or distributor who sells the organizer at a contractor's price.

The proliferation of cabinet storage aids has been matched by an improvement in their quality. Newer heavy-duty stainless, chrome, and gold-plated units are more solid and durable than plastic or epoxy-coated ones. If their price tag is off-putting, the latter materials will do the job as long as they are sturdy.

In addition to price, consider the amount of space the storage aid and its hardware will occupy. Talk about Miss Piggy! Nevertheless, in this case the sacrifice is worthwhile if it makes your cabinet more user-friendly.

The following are just a few of the storage possibilities that abound. Look, too, for solutions homeowners and designers have originated as you peruse magazines for ideas. They may not be for sale, but they can be copied. Some of the best I've seen for passing on:

> **Designer Clodaugh fitted shelves built on the back of a cabinet door with a coiled spring wire that keeps jars with various size "bellies."**
>
> **Architect Mike Jackson built a cookbook drawer that attaches to the bottom of a wall cabinet and pulls down at an angle. It, too, is fitted with a wire to keep cookbooks open and their bellies in place.**
>
> **Larry Koran divided the end of his pot drawer with slats spaced two inches apart to hold lids.**
>
> **An unknown magician built a frame fitted with horizontal dowels on the back of a door for tablecloths.**

In choosing among storage aids, light on ones to help you perform tasks ergonomically. For author Sam Clark, "a knife slot at the back of the counter is an example of perfect storage. . . . There is no preliminary opening of door or drawer. . . . The knives are placed at the height of the worker's hands; no stooping or stretching. The rack is fully visible and . . . prepositioned so that a hand can grasp a knife using the same grip required during use. In short, no unnecessary moves."

The quality of your storage is more important than the quantity.

CABINET STORAGE AIDS

Drawer Storage Options

> Clearing the decks, tip-out tray systems for sink fronts hold sponges, soap, and abrasive cleaning pads. One Rev-A-Shelf model includes a post to hold rings while washing dishes. Choose a system made of stainless or plastic that runs the full width of a drawer and can be removed for cleaning. Check all seams to be sure they are tight, for water will destroy your cabinet door as it drips through. Pushing the sink too far back in the countertop,

these trays cannot be used in tandem with some undermounts. (Amerock, Feeny, Rev-A-Shelf)

Single- or double-tiered trim-to-fit organizers in various configurations for cutlery and/or utensils (Feeny, Häfele, Mepla, Rev-A-Shelf, Vance)

Double-tiered organizer. The bottom holds flatware or utensils; the top is a removable lift-out routed cutting board. (Feeny—plastic)

Double-tiered knife drawer and incised wood cutting board. The drawer front pulls down. (Woodfold-Marco Manufacturing, Inc.)

Drawer dividers (Lifestyle Systems)

Knife blocks (Chef's Catalog, J. K. Adams, Lifestyle Systems, Williams-Sonoma)

Stepped spice organizer to allow you to see all bottles at a glance. Primarily for large kitchens since smaller ones do not usually have an extra drawer to allocate to spices. (Feeny, Rev-A-Shelf, Vance)

Bread drawer. Available in plastic, stainless, or tin, which can rust when scratched. (Feeny—tin or stainless; Rev-A-Shelf—polymer)

Food processor disk and blade holder (or in-cabinet storage) (Cuisinarts)

Fold-up, pullout ironing board (Feeny, Häfele, Mepla)

Cabinet Interior Storage Options

Pullout canisters for storing dry food. Mounts at the top of the shelf. (Amerock)

Dry-food storage canisters. Square take up 33 percent less space and are easier to stack than round. (Cambro, Rubbermaid, Tupperware)

Pullout towel bar with one to four prongs. Can also be used for drying homemade pasta. (Feeny, Knape & Vogt)

Pullout single- or double-row pan rack (Knape & Vogt)

Pullout cup rack (Knape & Vogt)

Pullout pot lid basket (Feeny)

Vertical tray dividers (stable and pullout) (Feeny stable; Rev-A-Shelf pullout)

Cabinet steps for jars, cans, packages, and bottles. Enables everything to be seen at a glance. (Vance)

Pullout shelf with pull-up swing mechanism for appliances, such as food processor, blender, mixer, and electric slicer. Check to see that the bracket weight rating is sufficient to support the appliance and that the shelf locks. The plug can also be placed in the cabinet, but the appliance should be plugged in only when in use. (Wood Technology)

Undersink pullout locked storage unit (Häfele)

Undersink dustpan holder (Häfele)

Built-in knife organizer (Vance)

Undersink offset pullout storage tray (Amerock, Feeny, Häfele, Knape & Vogt)

Pullout wire drawers for canned foods, potatoes, and onions (Amerock, Feeny, Häfele)

Base cabinet pullout systems (Amerock, Häfele)

Vertical pullout pantry (Häfele)

Tall pantry cabinet pullout systems (Amerock, Häfele, Rev-A-Shelf)

Complete pantries (Amerock, Feeny, Häfele)

Automated push-button movable pantry (The Kitchen Carousel, White Home Products Inc.)

Tight mesh shelving (Lee/Rowan)

Hooks for broom closet (Häfele, Hold Everything, Lee/Rowan, Rubbermaid)

Bottle storage (Häfele)

Wine racks (Feeny, J. K. Adams, Häfele, Kent Design & Manufacturing, Inc.)

Underwall Cabinet Storage Options

Pull-down cookbook rack. A wire or weight will have to be attached to keep the book open. (Amerock)

Pull-down knife rack (Amerock)

Pull-down spice rack (Amerock)

Pull-down message center (Amerock)

Stemware racks. Size varies; not all glasses will work on the same size rack (Feeny, Kent Design & Manufacturing)

Up-under spice carousel (J. K. Adams Co.)

Cutting board and rack (Hold Everything)

Knife rack (Chef's Catalog)

Back-of-Door Storage Options

Shelves (Amerock, Feeny, Häfele, Lee/Rowan)

Triple-tiered towel rack (Amerock, Feeny, Knape & Vogt)

Spice cups (Chef's Catalog, Hold Everything)

Paper towel, plastic wrap, and foil dispenser (Häfele, Polder)

Pull-down step stool (Häfele, Rev-A-Step)

Plastic bag saver (Hold Everything)

Vertical lid rack (Hold Everything)

Backsplash Storage Options

Pegboard with hooks. Julia Child stores pots and utensils this way with a line drawn around each item so it can easily be returned to its place.

Rail systems with optional shelves, holders, and racks (Ciatti, Häfele, Mepla, Becker-Zeyko)

Rack systems (Blanco, Franke, InterMetro)

Knife rack with scabbard to attach to the back-splash, wall, or butcher block table (Edlund, J. K. Adams, Professional Cutlery Direct)

Recessed backsplash or wall dispenser for paper towels, foil, and wrap (Iron-A-Way)

Miscellaneous Storage Options

Metal shelving (International Storage Systems)

Slots cut into butcher block island or counter for knives.

Yardstick on edge of shelves where baking pans are stored.

HARDWARE

■

Cabinet hardware has a profound influence on the kitchen's character. Bold and boisterous or refined and sedate, its repetition creates a dynamic rhythmic refrain in the room. When replaced by invisible touch latches, a serene tranquillity permeates in its stead.

Sculptural modern clasps transform cabinets into arty museum frames, while ponderous ornate handles bestow an air of serious gravity. Romping across the room, the many new delightful flora and fauna creations might well be cavorting after Pan. The question is, what type of hardware do you want to cavort after?

What material?

From the mundane to the magnificent, the figurative to the abstract, and the funky to the formal, possibilities mount to the millions. (All right, to the hundreds.) Minus movable parts to break down, hardware choice pretty much centers on aesthetics.

Do you want the hardware to echo the countertop material or cabinetry style? Perhaps a weighty carved wood handle on a mahogany or cherry cathedral door? Or do you seek contrast and drama, an oversized fire-engine-red siren on a shiny black background? Should it continue a theme used elsewhere in the home? And, in this day of eclecticism, who's to

say only one kind will do? Schooled in multiple-choice tests, we're adept at mix and match.

Cabinet hardware materials are as myriad as its shapes and sizes. A highly polished solid brass handle, stunning with a traditional decor, is still the classic cabinet hardware of distinction. It is not, however, the hardware of easy care. First of all, it scratches. Unprotected, it's a constant polish chore. When it's coated against encroaching deterioration, air enters even a microscopic fissure and darkens it unevenly. To clean, the sealer must be removed, a major ordeal. Take the uncoated if you're taking it. If the brass is cast, expect air bubbles and an irregular surface.

Chrome-plated brass and stainless steel are, as usual, the workhorse materials, but you don't have to stop there. Rubber, plastic, nylon, aluminum, zinc, nickel, bronze, copper, ceramic, wood, iron, marble, crystal, solid surface, and even semiprecious stones—natural, man-made, and space-age wonders—can all be affixed to your drawers.

Increasingly, two finishes—chrome and brass, metal and solid surface, rubber and bronze—are being combined as both a design statement and a means of integrating the kitchen's other materials. But by engaging a duo, you've doubled maintenance concerns.

HAPPENING HARDWARE

Cabinet hardware or jewelry comes in a variety of sizes, shapes, styles, and materials from the whimsical to the historically pure. The rule of thumb (or finger) in choosing hardware is to select a wide pull or a knob with a long shank that can be opened by looping a clean pinkie finger around it.

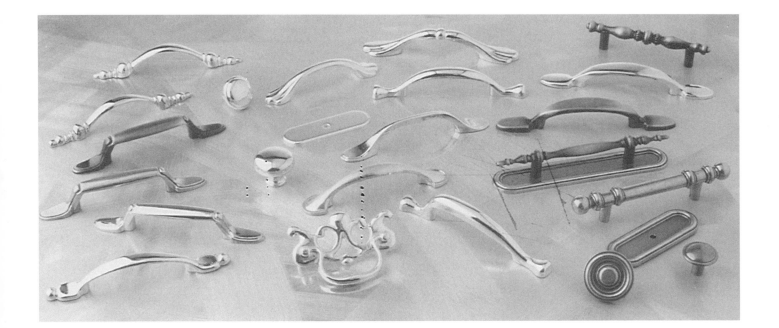

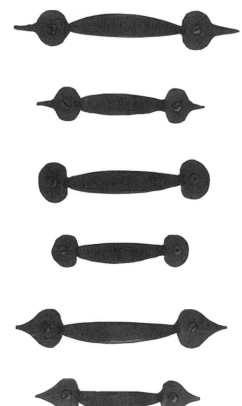

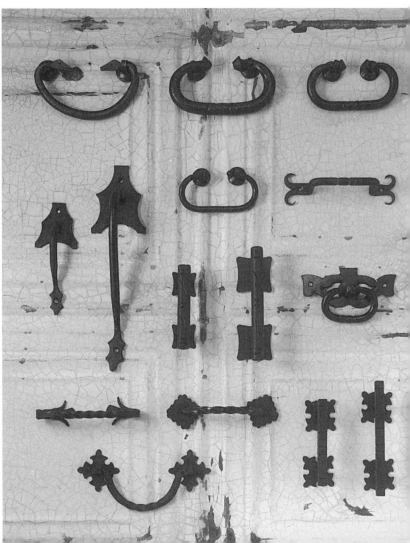

Hardware possessing the same color throughout reveals fewer chips and wear. What's hiding underneath can make a difference as well. Knobs with an interior thread are less likely to be dislodged. Reinforced with a galvanized steel core, nylon becomes stronger and more durable. If you're attracted to a particular metal or wood piece but not its finish, get it dipped, stripped, or plated after purchasing.

What type of hardware?

Look to function to be the guide in this category, for opening doors and drawers with greasy hands is not a fun thing to do. Hands-down, or hands-easy-grip, the first choice is a C- or U-shaped pull at least three inches in length that protrudes far enough to easily loop a baby finger around. A joy in any kitchen, this type of hardware is essential for arthritic cooks.

Slightly more cumbersome, concave bin pulls or thumb rings accommodate similarly. For hands to fit, the big boned or long nailed may have to rout out a cavity in the door or drawer behind the pull.

Knobs come in many more shapes, designs, and patterns than pulls and are often more suited to the style of the kitchen. Nevertheless, it can be quite vexing to try clutching one when you've just been kneading bread or carving a chicken. Given a shiny finish, they can be quite slippery, too. Single-hole square or oval knobs have a mind of their own when it comes to deciding which direction is *up*.

If you opt for a knob, go big with a protruding model that can be opened by wedging a clean part of your hand underneath.

Antique or reproduction pull-up handles, a classic choice in a traditional kitchen, require an awkward two-step operation, a jig you'll soon tire of. On the contemporary front, molded inset pulls are quite handsome, but to interact with them you need the delicate fingers of Persian carpet weavers. Their flush fit, however, is welcome in kitchens where countertops line up with the cabinetry, and protruding handles are painful to work against.

A touch latch is another choice for this scenario. It's also appropriate when a baby is underfoot or you're taking a minimalist modern stance with a flat frameless door style. Know, though, that it loses adjustment easily and the door, minus hardware, becomes a canvas for fingermarks. Magnetic latches are considered better than plastic ones.

Another subtle hardware choice is the finger-pull channel built into a door. Effective in many situations, this doesn't provide enough purchase for opening heavy drawers or doors that require a reach or have weighty shelves on their backs. Tailor the groove to the user's finger size and nail length.

A handle's size affects the opening of other doors and drawers, particularly in frameless boxes where they abut. If a pull or knob is too thick, usually one and one-eighth inches or more, doors will be hampered from opening all the way and corner drawers may not extend beyond their perpendicular neighbor's handle. Get a handle on clearance space before choosing hardware. Size also becomes a factor to balance with drawer and door dimensions.

OPEN SESAME
Hardware from the plant and animal kingdoms is increasingly crawling into our kitchens, adding a great deal of amusement. Use one or two as an accent or design statement on large utility cabinets, and pair with simpler pulls elsewhere in the room.

Incorporate flat hardware or touch latches where indicated and hitch up heavy-duty workhorse pulls on weighty drawers and doors opened frequently with dirty hands. Whatever hardware is used elsewhere is up for grabs. Just be sure you can get your hands on it.

Do I want a back or escutcheon plate?

The cabinet surface surrounding hardware can become quite stained and worn over time. Mounting the hardware on an *escutcheon* plate minimizes the wear, but you have to admire its looks and confront its additional cost.

PURCHASING

Many cabinet companies sell hardware as well, so you may want to purchase the two as a package. Wherever the hardware is purchased, choose it before ordering cabinets in case doors or drawers must be modified.

Cabinet hardware is often called *jewelry*, as much, I suspect, for the gripper's extreme cost as for its metallic sparkle. It can easily run several thousand dollars, especially when handle needs number eighty-three. To avoid disappointment, pick the hardware style and material you want and then compare prices. If you're still over budget, poke around swap meets and junk yards for real bargains in this category. Or pick a pocketbook-pleasing alternate.

I ended up with a large C-span four-inch pull in chrome-covered zinc. A die-cast pot metal, zinc occupies the lower end of the quality and economic spectrum. But if these pulls wear out, I can buy a second complete set for less than the stainless bars I'd been eyeing. And so far, they've held up beautifully, which is more than I can say about my cabinets.

KITCHENSPEAK: CABINETS

Batten: A horizontal piece of wood attached to the back of a vertical plank hardwood door to keep the door square and prevent it from expanding and contracting.

Beveled: Refers to any angle or slope except a right angle.

Butt joint: A simple flush noninterlocking joint at the point where two pieces of wood or another material meet.

Dado: An interlocking joint between two pieces of wood in which rectangular pieces of wood on one board are set into rectangular notches cut on the second board.

Dust barrier: Space between cabinet doors filled with a gasket to prevent dust from blowing in.

Face-frame: Cabinet box produced with a frame on its front that doors are hinged to.

Filler: Strips of wood inserted into a cabinet on either side of a corner so doors and drawers can open without hitting each other. Fillers are also used to buy space between abutting frameless cabinets or face-frame cabinets with overlay doors. During installation, they're employed to fill gaps and to help plumb and level ill-fitting cabinets.

Frameless: Cabinet box produced without a frame on its front. Doors are hinged to the side of the box.

Intarsia: A decorative channel cut into the top and bottom of some cabinets. The channel on top often doubles as a cabinet pull.

Level: Horizontal adjustment of cabinets during installation so they are all on the same plane. A level is also a tool used to determine whether cabinets are plumb (vertically straight) or level (horizontally aligned).

Mortise and tenon: An interlocking joint between two pieces of wood in which a plug (tenon) on one board is set into a corresponding hole (mortise) cut on the second board. Considered a form of cabinet sex.

Mullion: The central vertical strut in a face-frame cabinet or the dividers between glass panes in cabinet doors (or windows).

Plinth: The base or pedestal a frameless cabinet is set onto. It is equivalent to the toe kick in a face-frame cabinet.

Plumb: Vertical adjustment of cabinets during installation so they are equal in height.

Rabbet: A groove cut on the edge of a board that accepts a *plug* from another board to form an interlocking joint.

Rails: The crosspieces of a face-frame cabinet.

Reveal: The distance between the edge of the frame and a door in a face-frame cabinet. The word is also used to indicate the gap or distance between a soffit and the top of the wall cabinet below it. As the National Kitchen & Bath Association's technical manual so succinctly states: "how much one part of a building material sticks out from another."

Rout: To cut a channel into wood or another material. Generally this is done for design purposes.

Run: An uninterrupted row of cabinets.

Scribe: Irregular variance pieces cut to fill gaps in the cabinets. A second meaning: to mark something where it can be bent or cut.

Shim: Thin wedge-shaped piece of wood slipped into gaps between cabinets or between the wall and cabinets to help level them.

SKUs: The number of stock-keeping units or different cabinet components a company manufactures.

Soffit: A framed-out boxed-in part of the wall between the ceiling and top of wall cabinets that are hung below it. To be precise, the area is actually called a *bulkhead* with the soffit its underside. Together the soffit and bulkhead are referred to as a *furred-down ceiling.*

Stiles: The vertical side pieces of a face-frame cabinet. Any vertical piece in a cabinet frame.

Tongue and groove: An interlocking joint between two pieces of wood in which a tongue on one board is set into a corresponding groove cut on the second board.

5

SURFACE SCENERY AND COSTUME

■

Surface materials are the coverings for countertops, backsplashes, and floors. In creating almost innumerable choices (ten thousand possibilities exist within Wilsonart's Color Quest line alone), manufacturers have broken the aesthetic barrier. There is real stone, real wood, real metal, and real tile in rounds, squares, rectangles, hexagons, polyhedrons, and expansive slabs. Pass that way again and you find faux stone, faux wood, faux metal, faux tile, and flooring's answer to the tofu burger, a recycled granite wannabe made of soybeans and newsprint from Phenix Biocomposites.

Polishes are shiny, satiny, and matte; textures smooth, rough, recessed, and raised. Colors are brilliant and pale, primary and complementary with otherworldly hues. Serene monochromatic tones interweave into patterns that swirl, undulate, zigzag, and soar. A Technicolor space fantasy, the choice overwhelms us earthlings with the simple need of a surface to cut and walk on.

Bringing us swiftly back down to earth, we try cleaning these new modern materials. Despite their startling beauty, upkeep to a one is a dreadful task. With all our advanced technology, it's still a pain to wash the floor. Staining is another horrific problem. One indelible oil mark on that brand-new granite countertop, and you don't care the label said "stain resistant." Like the phrase *slightly pregnant,* this common industry euphemism is bereft of meaning. You either are or you aren't: all surface materials are (permanently stainable, that is).

Adding to this confusion, the words *nonporous* and *hard* are often incorrectly misinterpreted to mean "nonstainable" rather than "less stainable."

For protection, a material must be sealed. But know that you are trading one upkeep problem for another. Instead of being on surveillance patrol, wiping every driplet as it is dropped, your assignment is "schedule—and pay—the resealer" when the surface wears off; the time frame dictated by the paces the material is put through.

PROTECTION

Superficial top coatings such as wax or lacquer wear down quickly, entrapping dirt as they go. To be renewed, they must be completely stripped off. Penetrating sealers are preferred. Yet the harder, more penetrating the seal, the glossier and slipperier it is, the faster it wears down, and the more drastically it alters the material's natural appearance. Before putting any sealer on a countertop, be certain it is food-friendly and approved for kitchen use. Complicating all these maintenance minutiae is the difficulty of finding a sealer-savvy professional.

Until that time when manufacturers turn their

attention from creating yet one more color to producing durable goods and sealers, select whatever you like and can afford along with one of the following options:

1. Hover over it protectively, mopping up every stray greaseball.

2. Seal the hell out of it as often as necessary.

3. Leave it natural or seal it and forget about it. The more distressed and chipped it becomes, the more you can venerate its aged patina. (This approach is most harmonious with a traditional or country-style decor.)

4. Choose a material with the highest durability ratings and the best chance of remaining pristine. Though aesthetic choices are more limited, a commercial grade serves its owners most loyally. Avoid light colors that show dirt and dark tones that reveal crumbs and scratches. Trade solids for pebbled random patterns that hide transgressions and go to the matte for sheen. Shiny tells all and is fatiguing to the eyes. When more than one thickness is offered, remember that bigger stands up better.

Any guesses about which camp I'm in?

To follow point 4, the first rule is: *Utilize a material as it was intended.* The showroom showing off solid surface's versatility with a gorgeous knife rack and cutting board forgot a rather major point: Cutting directly on solid surface destroys *both* surface and knife.

Test any prospective covering to ascertain what's ahead upkeep-wise. Although some type of durability rating system has been established for most substances, performance is too individual to accept anything without further examination. If you plan to seal the item, do so beforehand. This will enable you to observe finish behavior as well as color and texture changes. When a company recommends leaving its product unsealed, test it that way.

To determine resistance to scratching, scrape a nail or drill bit across the item's surface. Set a coffee cup and water glass on it overnight to see if watermarks develop. Then soak for several days in alternative baths of oil (hold the extra-virgin for salad), red wine, vinegar, sliced beets, lemon juice, and smashed raspberries.

INSTALLATION

The durability of a surface material is almost more closely allied to its proper installation than to its own peculiar properties. Most manufacturers provide excellent detailed installation instructions with a list of recommended substrates, supports, fixatives, and adhesives. The challenge is finding an installer to follow them.

Rose Beranbaum had her cork flooring laid three times before the underlayment was pulled taut enough to become invisible. Michael Zugsmith's solid vinyl floor levitated soon after installation because the incorrect adhesive was used. Unfortunately it wasn't soon enough for the original tiles to still be available.

A material's appearance and performance also depend on having cabinets and walls that are plumb. If this is not possible, choose coverings with a random pattern and invisible seams to visually minimize this defect.

COST

The fee for materials varies according to size, shape, thickness, and rareness of color and pattern; yet these parameters have little to do with the final tag. A complex finish, trim pieces, and edge treatments drive the price of any material into the Lexus category. Everything else being equal, the least expensive item in each group is the raw material plus a simple flat edge (called a *self-edge*) that receives no further individual crafting.

Installation fees roam according to the condition of the substrate, the amount of support needed, and the intricacy of a pattern. When it came time to replace her home floor, Kathleen Fought from Eurotile found herself standing in a consumer's shocked shoes. First the contractor added 10 percent to his quote for laying out the material, then another 20 percent for cutting it on a diagonal.

Although vinyl and laminate are usually considered the least expensive materials, and granite the most, this is much too simplistic a hierarchy: The former materials have a shorter life span than the latter. Yet vinyl and laminate may be ideal, indeed, in a rental apartment, short-term living situation, household with demolition derby children, or a lean period with expectations of fat ahead.

In sum: To determine the bottom line, review the price of the material in tandem with its expected life span and fees for preparation (embellishment) and installation.

AESTHETICS

While durability, upkeep, and cost are the practical concerns in the selection of surface materials, visual factors determine ultimate satisfaction. The material must correspond to the design. A handmade tile with an uneven edge will blow a crisp, straight-lined geometric rendering. A pattern that plays well vertically may look bizarre on the horizontal: Evaluate it according to intended orientation and imagine it turning a corner or running up the backsplash. View the entire tile or slab in the real during daylight as well as under whatever lights you've chosen. Beguiling in a softly lit showroom, that one-inch square of squiggles can become a dizzying nightmare undulating across the countertops in your bright kitchen.

With countertops and flooring occupying such a large proportion of a kitchen, they dictate its personality in tandem with cabinetry. When temptation arises to forge a bold original signature, the resale specter usually channels choices down a conservative path, relegating the myriad dramatic possibilities at our fingertips to irony. "Give 'em thirty-two flavors and they opt for vanilla."

With resale in mind, as well as the fatigue factor that sets in from a strong pattern—"God, I hate those stripes"—*bold* may best be reserved for an inconspicuous corner or for readily replaceable paint or curtains. If not, remember that the same pattern will appear more subtle, if you will, on a horizontal surface than on a vertical one.

Though I've been discussing surfaces as if the choice were singular, a mixture of materials is increasingly utilized on countertops, backsplashes, and floors. Attraction to this cohabitation is inspired by the disparate muses of fashion, action, and money.

Adding a textural depth and dynamism to design, variety bonds form and function; some elements do better around fire; others around water. Wind and earth make their demands too, for materials that are recyclable and biodegradable.

With companies now coordinating their colors, you can stretch your budget by teaming a lower-cost material with a more expensive one. Reasonably priced laminate countertops can, for example, be paired with more expensive solid surface or areas demanding a tougher material with ceramic tile.

The primary choices for surface materials are decorative high-pressure laminate, Nuvel, solid surface, butcher block, ceramic tile, brick, metal, concrete, slate, granite, vinyl, linoleum, rubber, cork, hardwood, and glass block. Some of these serve countertops, floors, and backsplash; others maintain single loyalties. Additional materials are sold for these purposes, but they are not durable enough to be considered for kitchens.

Keeping all the preceding points about surface materials in mind, we'll explore each material and then compare group assets for a countertop, flooring, and backsplash.

MEET THE MATERIALS

■

DECORATIVE HIGH-PRESSURE LAMINATE

Decorative high pressure laminate is a sandwich of paper, plastic resin, and a three-quarter-inch-thick backer board fused together under heat and pressure. Used for countertops and cabinets, decorative high-pressure laminate is either rigid and *nonformable* or flexible enough to be *postformed*, or bent under heat.

Originally available only with telltale black edges, laminates are now also produced with color all the way through to the edges even when carved and cut. *Solid-core* material, as color-through laminate is called, is more costly and brittle than regular laminate, comparatively limited in size and shape, and unable to be postformed. Unless you want a carved edge, regular laminate usually proves the better choice.

Standard laminates are generally available in two- by six-, four- by eight-, and four- by ten-foot sheets, depending on the manufacturer. Thickness varies according to application. Horizontal or countertop applications require a minimum laminate grade of .050 (one-twentieth) inch; postformed .042 inch. Some companies also produce a heavy-duty, better wearing line ideal for kitchens.

NUVEL

Produced by GE and marketed by Formica since 1993, Nuvel is a mixture of a plastic resin called Valox and a mineral filler. Extruded in five different sheet sizes from 30 by 96 inches to 60 by 144 inches with color all the way through, it occupies a price and practicality niche between laminate and solid surface. Like laminate, it is affixed to a substrate, but it is thicker, less likely to crack or chip, and can be postformed into a tighter curve.

SOLID SURFACE

Solid surface, so named because it contains the same material and color throughout, is a varying blend of acrylic and polyester resins that are poured into molds and baked into sheets. The proportion of acrylic, the more flexible resin, determines the extent to which this *thermoplastic* material can be shaped by heat. The greater its polyester component, the more intense its colors can be.

To deal with its unique formula, each manufacturer trains special fabricators. For a warranty to be valid, you must use someone approved by the company. Fabricator fraud has become a problem, so be certain the person you hire is licensed by the company he claims to represent.

Depending on its properties, solid surface can be transformed into countertops, sinks, walls, backsplashes, windowsills, moldings, baseboards, cabinet hardware, and faucet handles; even light switch plates. It can also be molded into an integral sink-countertop ensemble (page 283). Settling on a solid surface company usually comes down to whether it has a color you favor and can shape the material as you wish.

Numerous companies have joined Du Pont (Corian), the first solid-surface producer. Each claims the superiority of its product over competitors', but basically this material is too new to readily compare performance. One blend reputedly expands in warm areas. If you're planning placement near a stove or window, question fabricators about this possibility and read warranties closely.

BUTCHER BLOCK

Butcher block is composed of hardwood strips—either the same or varying lengths—that are glued together and laminated under pressure. *End-grained,* the best quality, has a checkerboard of squares on its vertical edges.

Butcher block does duty as a table, portable cutting board, complete countertop, or section of another material's countertop. Eastern hard rock sugar maple builds the most durable butcher block.

Oak and beech are also commandeered, but their grain is neither as tight nor as fine.

Butcher block is treated with a nontoxic oil so that it might be cut on. Though briefly replaced by synthetic boards in recent years as food contamination increased, butcher block has been rehabilitated. A study by microbiologists at the University of Wisconsin's Food Research Institute found wood to be less—not more—hospitable to bacteria than synthetics. So much for our careful practice of food safety. Regardless, it is important that all boards (and knives) be well scrubbed after cutting any ingredient. And chicken, pork, and fish are still better prepared on a synthetic board that can go into the dishwasher.

CERAMIC TILE

Ceramic tile is formed by pressing a clay material under pressure, shaping it by hand, or extruding it through a die as in the production of dried pasta. As one company explains, "Whether tile is machine- or hand-formed will determine if . . . it is monotonously symmetrical or harmoniously unproportionate." Once shaped, tile is dried, then baked in the sun or in a kiln, where it hardens to varying degrees according to firing temperature. Beyond the brief description preceding, trying to understand tile can give you clay feet.

Some companies describe tile by the type of clay used in its composition, others by whether or not it is glazed, how many times it is fired, or its firing temperature. By themselves, these descriptors do not disclose the best type of tile for a countertop, backsplash, or floor. Luckily there are other methods for divining this information. Here is an introduction to some of the confusing nomenclature.

Monocottura tiles, the majority sold, are usually matte glazed and fired only once at a very high temperature. Thinner than other types of tiles, monocottura are at once quite durable.

Bicottura or twice-fired tiles are richly decorated with a handpainted, silkscreened, embossed, engraved, or decaled surface. Relatively fragile, they are employed primarily for walls and backsplashes. *Decorative tiles* and *decos* are other industry terms for them.

Porcelain is fired longer and hotter than other types of tile, yielding a harder, stronger, chinalike body. Often unglazed, this tile is called on for being expensive, but it counteracts this charge by being extremely durable.

The following tiles are mentioned almost exclusively in conjunction with flooring. Typically they are sold unglazed. But, like other unglazed tiles, they can be colored all the way through by adding minerals to the clay. This technique eliminates a top coat that wears down or off.

Produced from a reddish brown clay, *terra-cotta* tiles are typically extruded. *Quarry* tiles, a mixture of shale and other clays, are also extruded. *Saltillo* tiles are rough-textured squares produced in Mexico by hand or machine. Higher-quality saltillos have less *efflorescence*, holes formed by lime bubbles rising to the surface.

Unsealed, all these tiles soak up water like a tortilla. And everything else. For my money (already poorly spent on saltillos), they stain too readily and require too much resealing for a kitchen. Nevertheless, I include them here. Despite the drawbacks, buyers are seduced by their rustic rugged looks.

Tiles are formed in squares, rectangles, ovals, hexagons, triangles, oblongs, and amoebalike shapes from three-eighths to forty-eight inches and seem to be growing through-the-looking-glass-bigger as I write. Mosaics, the smallest, range from three-eighths to six inches and are sold already mounted and sometimes pregrouted. Avoid cotton, paper, and other organic backings that can disintegrate unless warrantied against dissolution. Less expensive to install, faux mosaics or large squares with painted faceted patterns are also available.

Most tiles are sized in even numbers of inches such as four by four, six by six, and, commonly, eight by eight. Odd-sized measures such as three by thirteen are available as well for fireplaces or weird cor-

SURFACES

MATERIAL GIRL

Surface materials, used alone or in a mix, bestow a unique personality to a kitchen. Granite countertops contrast with copper, brass, and stainless steel used on the countertop edges and backsplash *(top left)*. This syndecrete countertop surface is easy to care for *(center left)*. Both the countertop and integral sinks have been fabricated from solid surface material with a large overhang to pull dining stools underneath *(top right)*. Ceramic tile is used both on the countertop and floor. Though grout lines make it a bit bumpy to work on, its heatproof quality is certainly an advantage next to a cooktop *(left and above)*.

BUTCHER BLOCK
This butcher block surface does triple duty as an island, cutting board, and countertop table.

CERAMIC FLOORING
Ceramic tile provides excellent nonskid flooring.

ners. Larger tiles or *pavers*, frequently twelve by twelve, are a popular flooring. The largest tile, recently introduced in Italy, measures three by three feet. Requiring fewer seams than smaller pieces, pavers also make wonderful countertops.

Any size or shape tile is fair play as long as it is proportionate to the dimensions of the room and installation location. A small tile, for example, looks much better under a windowsill than a larger piece nipped to fit. Most companies produce a family of matching tiles that can be coordinated for floors, countertops, and walls with trim pieces for each venue. When given the option, go for a flat-back tile, which is easier to install than traditional *button backs*.

Based on standardized industry tests and observations, tile companies have been extremely responsible in rating their wares and recommending optimum installation sites. To review tests and installation procedures, ask a dealer for the *Handbook for Ceramic Tile Installation* published by the Tile Council of America. If you are uncertain about what type of seal to use, send a sample of the tile to the Ceramic Tile Institute for counsel.

The best indicator of durability is the water absorption or porosity rating. Though not a one-to-one correspondence, water-resistant tile is likely to be more stain, chip, and craze resistant as well. For kitchens, seek a vitreous tile with .5 to 3.0 percent absorption rate or, even better, an impervious tile with less than .5 percent absorption. In a cold climate, select a tile approved for freezing.

BRICK

Like ceramic tile, brick is mixed from water and a clay such as shale or sedimentary rock. It, too, is molded, pressed, or extruded through a die, then sunbaked or burned in the kiln—at temperatures up to twenty-four hundred degrees.

Rectangular in shape, brick blocks vary in size and are affixed by mortar that should be acid resistant for the kitchen. Available larger and smaller, common brick dimensions are four by four by eight,

four by four by twelve, and three by four by twelve. Some companies work with designers to create custom sizes and shapes.

Brick characteristics vary according to their intended task with some well suited for a kitchen. A firebrick made from refractory clay is ideal for a fireplace or cooktop surround. Angled bricks make curved walls or countertop corners possible, while a wedge shape defines a keystone arch for a cooking area. Larger paving bricks offer abrasion resistance. Sporting a "used" label: new bricks deliberately stressed to look old and recycled members from old buildings. Regardless of a brick's properties, protect it with a water-based acrylic sealer.

METAL

As home kitchens have adopted the laboratory look, stainless steel's influence has extended beyond the sink to the backsplash and countertop. Fabricated by a local sheet metal shop, these pieces are separate or integrated. Copper and brass are utilized in the kitchen as well, but mainly as railings, countertop edges, toe kicks, and other accent strips. Muntz metal, a brass look-alike, may be preferable for it does not tarnish.

Stainless, an alloy of carbon steel, is composed of different percentages of chromium and nickel. The exact percentage of these elements determines the quality of the stainless and its staying power. A countertop (as a sink) should contain a minimum of 8 to 10 percent nickel to maintain its luster and prevent staining, scratching, and corrosion. Chromium contributes a sparkle. In conjunction with a stainless product, this will be expressed as 18/8 or 18/10.

The gauge of the stainless, its thickness, is important as well. The lower the number, the thicker the gauge or higher-quality material it indicates. To minimize vibration and stand up to constant use, a countertop should be fourteen- (better) to eighteen-gauge (thickness). Period. Thinner twenty- and twenty-two-gauge stainless cannot do the trick. For a finish, a lustrous satin sheen, preferably hand-buffed, is appreciated more than the shiny mirror coating that scratches or brushed grain that also catches debris.

Functioning like an ice hockey safety net to catch splatter and greasepucks, a backsplash can be a thinner twenty-gauge stainless, unless, of course, you're throwing frying pans at it. Thinner than that, and it dents too readily.

CONCRETE

Acting contra-inclination once again, I include concrete in this lineup. Though its tendency is to stain and crack, it is relatively low in price and increasingly currying favor with decorators, who call its raw driveway look "high style," its blemishes "added charm."

Concrete comes in floor or countertop tiles. It can be molded directly on the countertop as well by pouring it into steel trays. Continuing upward, it can be contoured into a countertop/backsplash combo of any size, shape, or thickness. Colored pigment can be mixed into the concrete or sprinkled on top (*dust-on* or *broadcast*) for more vibrant tones. Shells or other materials can be inlaid in it. In a similar vein, terrazzo, a mixture of cement and marble chips, can function as flooring.

SLATE

Slate, a sedimentary rock split horizontally into thin uneven sheets, is at home on a countertop, floor, or backsplash. Sold in slabs at a quarry, slate is more typically purchased in random pieces or in one-quarter or one-half-inch-thick tiles set with grout. Less friable and likely to crack, the thicker tiles stand up better to heavy traffic.

Slate tiles are available as naturally *cleft* or after they are *honed* to a smooth finish that shows dirt but is easier to clean. The tiles can be *gauged* or ground so only their bottoms are smooth or *smooth-gauged*, a finer finish with no visible grinding marks. Varying in thickness, *nongauged* tile has uneven edges that don't square. It is unsuitable for the kitchen—

unless you want to ride roller-coaster countertops or floors.

Slate is embedded with a variety of minerals that determine its coloration. It can be ordered in a single color or as a mixed bag. According to Vermont Structural Slate Company, the strongest slate is cut so its longest dimension runs parallel to the grain (the direction of easiest breakage).

STONE

The word in geology circles has more marble and granite lying on American kitchen floors, backsplashes, and countertops than in Yosemite. Sliced thinner, these stones have become more affordable of late, while streamlined shipping procedures and technological strides have made them more accessible. Sort of. Prices can be curtailed further by finding trimmings or recyclables at salvage or stone yards. Author David Goldbeck suggests haunting gravestone makers. During the day, that is.

Stone comes in three finish types. A highly polished surface can show scratches, cause slipping, and require more maintenance and repolishing. A *honed* or matte surface can be high- or low-honed (more or less reflective), making for safer walking and easier cleaning. A *flamed* or *thermal* finish is textured for further slip resistance.

MARBLE

For all the properties granite and marble share, a great many differences exist between them. A metamorphic rock, marble is recrystallized from limestone or dolomite under heat or pressure. Mineral and fossil content determine its shade and veining as well as its stability. Veins, the source of a marble's beauty, are also its fracture points. The more plentiful, the more likely to shatter.

Marble is rated according to hardness. Though some patterns are harder than the most durable granite and can be used interchangeably, marble is generally a soft material, chipping and scratching readily. It is etched by acid and water marks and is

FLOORING

WOOD FLOORING

Facing page

Flat and smooth with some cushioning that makes it easy to stand on, wood makes a wonderful kitchen floor. Easy to clean, it can be refinished when it wears down. If you thought that a wood floor was a wood floor was a wood floor, look again. *Counterclockwise from top left:* Here it is shown in 5/16-inch solid oak linear strips, 1/2-inch linear strips with a beveled edge, 12- x 12-inch maple parquet tiles, with a colored diamond inset, and a wild man mix of exotic ash, wenge, and padauk in a psychedelic-mitered herringbone pattern.

OTHER FLOORING MATERIALS

Clockwise from top: One of the more durable vinyl floorings, this bold black and pearl sheeting has a wear-layer and moisture barrier. These slate tiles in variegated hues have been honed to a smooth finish. Available with a variety of finishes, these imported cork tiles have a warmth and patina that mellows with age and a mottled surface that does not reveal dirt. This 12- x 12-inch ceramic tile makes a lively and elegant floor. This 3/4-inch-thick square wood tile is composed of interwoven oak strips.

too sensitive to food stains to appear practically in the kitchen with one exception:

As the countertop or an inset for making pastry, marble has a sweet role to play in the baking center. A cold surface, it is excellent for rolling out piecrusts or pulling fondant or taffy. To facilitate these tasks, choose an A-rated hone-finished marble with no veining and seal it with a penetrating sealer compatible with food.

Instead of a slab, Steve Smith keeps large marble tiles in his freezer to pull out for making pastry and candy. A particularly good solution in a rental situation, tiles are ideal when pastry is prepared on a pull-out cart that a heavy marble top would immobilize.

GRANITE

Granite, an igneous rock found in the earth's crust, is composed of quartz, feldspar, mica, and other minerals. It can emit low levels of radon. Though this is not considered cause for alarm, you may want to have any piece you consider assessed.

Granite can be distinguished visually from marble by the spots, speckles, streaks, and fine grains that characterize its surface markings instead of veining. Obscured by these subtle patterns, stains are less likely to happen on granite for its absorption rate is lower than marble's.

Granite is not as slick, slippery or easily scratched as marble, yet it's just as cool for pastry. Avoid dark colors that cast a glare and reveal fingermarks. Otherwise you may end up like cookbook author Paula Wolfert, who works with a whisk in one hand and a spritz bottle in the other, wiping her black granite counter as she cooks.

Granite comes in slabs from four to eight feet and is also available in twelve- and twenty-four-inch tiles.

For all its Schwarzeneggerian strength, however, granite does vary in resistance and hardness. There are rumblings about inferior stone from Brazil; the greater longevity of a piece from Italy. Before purchasing, investigate your granite's properties carefully.

VINYL

Vinyl is to flooring what laminate is to countertops: an affordable everyperson's surface available in myriad patterns.

Vinyl comes in six-, nine-, and twelve-foot rolls and in eight- to twelve-inch square—and occasionally rectangular—tiles. *Solid vinyl*, pure vinyl all the way through, is available only in tile form and not widely produced. The majority of what is called vinyl material consists mainly of limestone and other resins by weight and, by the by, some vinyl. Confusingly called *vinyl tile* or *vinyl composition tile (VCT)*, it is harder, more brittle, and less shiny than solid vinyl. It is also considerably less expensive.

Two primary manufacturing methods exist for vinyl composition materials: *inlaid* and *rotogravure*. An inlaid material is composed of colored vinyl crystals or chips fused under heat and pressure. In contrast, a rotogravure material is produced in layers, consisting of a cushioned backing, a colored surface printed photographically with vinyl inks, and a protective coating or what is called a *wearlayer*.

Inlaid materials may also be protected with a wearlayer or top coat of vinyl or urethane. The latter shines on longer and provides more scuff resistance to the running shoe generation. When traffic finally gets through the urethane sheen, it can be restored somewhat with polish. A thick layer of urethane hardened with additives is called a *never wax* surface and comes with a longer warranty. Beware: Never wax does not mean never care.

In a heavily used kitchen where any top coat will be destroyed, the best choice may be a vinyl without a protective coating—the commercial approach. Unlike a sealed floor, it can be restored continually to look brand-new again, albeit with a little spit and a lot of polish.

Some companies offer only sheet or tile; others both. Some utilize both inlaid and rotogravure methods or a combination of the two techniques; others only one system or the other. Inlaid material is more expensive than rotogravure and does not have as wide a variety of patterns. Nevertheless, it is more durable, longer lasting, and a better choice for a kitchen. For longevity, look, too, at the impact resistance rating for the pattern. Finally, seek a product with a mildew or vapor barrier, avoiding a completely solid color floor with inherent shading differences.

NEW-OLD NATURALS: LINOLEUM AND CORK

Linoleum and cork are increasingly popular flooring materials for both their comfort and earth-friendliness. When Elvis was last sighted, in fact, he was standing on his mom's linoleum floor. Many of his fans have joined him, and not just for nostalgia's sake.

Today's new linoleum, a mixture of cork, linseed oil, wood dust, pine resin, clay or chalk fillers, and natural pigments, no longer contains asbestos. Backed with jute, the squares and sheets are cured and dried in an oven, making it a tough ol' hound dog. All linoleum is imported.

Cork is imported as well and is available in twelve-inch-square tiles of three-sixteenths or one-half-inch thickness. Cork is available unfinished, waxed, or polyurethane-coated in different degrees of shininess and darkness.

HARDWOOD

With its traditional strength and solidity, wood flooring is reassuring to have underfoot in the kitchen. It is occasionally used for countertops, too, but like a fine piece of furniture, it is for admiration, not abuse, and should be relegated to nonworking counters, where all it has to do is look good.

Least expensive, red and white oak are the most common hardwood flooring. While commissioned salespeople often tout the higher-priced white oak as harder and thus preferable, the two oaks perform equivalently. If you're willing to pay the price, maple, walnut, cherry—even koa, teak, rosewood, and other exotic species—make excellent kitchen flooring. Pine, fir, and other softwoods are too vulnerable to the ravages of dropped pots to be considered for this location.

Wood flooring comes in strips, planks, and twelve-inch-square parquet tiles. Varying thicknesses

are available, but three-quarters of an inch is recommended for durability. *Strips* typically run two to two and one-fourth inches wide and come in random lengths. They can be laid in straight rows or in patterns such as herringbone and basketweave. *Planks* come three to eight inches wide in random lengths and widths. To curtail warping, limit width to five inches. *Parquet,* square tiles composed of matched pieces of wood in myriad patterns, is laid out at the factory. Faux parquet is also available, and if you have nothing to do for a decade or so, you can always create your own pattern. In recent years, tiles have surfaced with nonpatterned wood strips in rainbow hues.

The best boards come *end-matched* with the *tongue* of one fitting snugly into the *groove* of the next. *Square-edged* boards butt together, a less satisfactory juncture. *Distressed* or *wire-brushed* boards accumulate too much dirt for kitchen use.

Hardwood floor boards are venerated for their solidity and naturalness. Cut first into four ninety-degree sections before being divided into boards, *quartersawn* logs are more durable than *plainsawn.* Their grain is more beautiful, too; their price less so.

In addition to hardwood boards, wood flooring comes in sandwiches of hardwood, softwood, or plywood laminated with a hardwood veneer. Set *cross-grain* or with the grain of each layer running in the opposite direction from the one below, laminated boards are more stable and less likely to warp than solid ones. Some veneers come cushioned with a foam base for comfort.

On a less positive note, laminated floors are more expensive than hardwood. Limited to several resandings, they have a shorter life span. A three-*ply* (layer) floor has more lives than a five-ply but fewer than a cat. Veneers can delaminate if soaked, and, to paraphrase Lenny Bruce, they are just not a natural act.

Both laminated and hardwood board flooring are graded. *Common* grades, with number two the most exaggerated, have more burls, streaks, knotholes, worm burrows, an occasional rat lair, and variations in tone. *Clear* grade has the fewest markings, while *select* falls in between. Though durability does not differ among grades, prices go up as knotholes go down. Your choice depends on how you feel about holes and what you want to pay for them.

Wood floors can be surface dyed with a pigmented stain, but they are easier to repair when colored with one that permeates. For a pickled or whitewashed look, a stain is preferable to a bleach, which desiccates fibers and prevents a finish from adhering. Neither is controllable color-wise.

White and light finished floors are just not good choices for the kitchen. Both the unsightly cracks that form during the floor's expansion and the permanent black marks that permeate these cracks are more visible on these lighter tones.

Floors can be stained and finished at the factory, as laminated boards usually are, or they can be purchased unfinished. Prefinished floors appeal to the instant installation set who doesn't want to go through the long *in-situ* process: "I've got a party going on this weekend, and I want a floor today."

One manufacturer's rep argues that a home finish can never be as hard as one applied at a factory. That may well be true, but a prefinished floor cannot be sanded after installation to compensate for a crooked subfloor or even the boards' expected milling differences. If boards are prefinished, spaces in between will still be unfinished, allowing water to seep underneath. Finishes, often just a wax, vary in quality and may be inadequate. No.

For wood floors to stand up to traffic, water, grease, and other kitchen substances, they must be finished properly. This is a real bugaboo. Many consumers who have wood floors hate them, claiming they don't hold up. Often these complaints derive simply from the fact that the floor lacked the correct finish or enough coats of it. It may also have been maintained improperly or not refinished soon enough.

The best finishes for wood kitchen flooring are two coats of either a *moisture cure* or *Swedish finish*. Though both have get-out-of-the-house-fast-while-this-is-going-on aromas, they are most durable. The former, a milky polyurethane type of finish with additional additives, gets harder with time and is intended specifically for areas subject to wetness.

Developed in Sweden, the latter finish is an alcohol- and acid-based sealer with acrylic and a hardener that magnifies the depth of a wood's grain. As wine writer Anthony Dias Blue observed, "This stuff can burn your house down." Flammable, indeed, it must be administered carefully. Many finishers refuse to use it because of its toxicity.

More brittle, an oil- or water-based polyurethane can be used as well. Oil-based lasts longer, but its yellow tone changes the floor's natural color; something a water-based finish won't do. An oil-based finish requires two coats, water-based three.

There are many good products on the market. There are many bad ones too. To help you avoid them, I relate the choices I hear most often from finishing experts: Glitsa for Swedish finish, ambering or nonambering Harco for moisture cure, Pacific Strong for water-based polyurethane, Zar for oil-based polyurethane.

A wood floor must be touched up with whatever finish you choose, and eventually redone completely. To delay the inevitable, a rug is often recommended in front of the sink or in heavily used areas, but my safety motto is: No throw rugs in the kitchen, ever.

GLASS BLOCK

Glass block, two pieces of molded molten glass fused with mortar or less visible silicon sealants, is a dramatic architectural element. Ever more practical is the light it admits.

Incorporated into an exterior wall, glass block functions as a window. In an interior wall, it divides the kitchen from another room. It also makes a dynamic contemporary backsplash. The faceted glass is used powerfully in an island, where it can be backlit with (1) various colored lights or (2) a mirror that reflects the cabinets and other objects in the room. Glass blocks are also used successfully as floor pavers in a less traveled area than the kitchen.

Glass block is formed in six-, eight-, and twelve-inch squares, eighteen-inch rectangles, and forty-five- and ninety-degree angled pieces for curves and corners. Available in a variety of hues, thinline blocks are three and one-eighth inches thick; stan-

GLASS BLOCK

Glass block can be utilized in many different ways in a kitchen. Here it is used as a window, bringing light into the room while maintaining privacy. It is also incorporated into the island, where the material glows when it is backlit. It also forms a partition that separates the kitchen from other working areas while welcoming natural-diffused light into the room.

dard three and seven-eighths. Once fabricated, they cannot be cut or altered to fit a space.

Blocks are designed with a variety of textures and patterns that determine their transparency and amount of light transmission. Some are assigned special tasks such as security, fire protection, and solar retention.

Blocks can be installed one at a time or in a pre-fabricated grid panel, a less expensive option.

PUTTING THEM TO WORK

■

COUNTERTOPS

Of the materials already introduced, laminate, Nuvel, solid surface, butcher block, tile, stainless, concrete, brick, slate, and granite are the most likely contenders for countertops. As with everything else in this book, there is no right answer; each has its own pitfalls and pluses.

A serviceable countertop surface is flat, firm, and comfortable to work on, easy to take care of, and able to stand up to abuse. Not only should it look attractive by itself, but food should look good on it. A standard countertop is three-quarters inch thick, but thicker granite (one and one-quarter inches) and butcher block (one and one-half inches) in particular have more endurance. They will prove a better choice as long as you can afford their higher price and their thickness doesn't make the countertop too high.

Corresponding to base cabinets below, standard countertop depth is twenty-four inches. When base cabinets are deeper, countertops are, too. Sometimes countertops are furred out to thirty inches while base cabinet depth remains two feet. In a neighborly gesture, a countertop is often pulled out to the same depth as a commercial-style stove or cooktop placed next to it. Compare materials according to the criteria that follow to see which will be the best provider for you.

Color and Pattern

Butcher block is by definition a yellowish red wood tone; stainless and concrete (unless pigmented) are gray. Adding textural interest, concrete can be raked, combed, or inlaid with *objets*; stainless quilted or carved.

Nuvel's colors pivot on variations of white; slate's hover on the dark side. Solid surface starts meekly with a limited palette of solid tones and stonelike patterns but has potential for "most original" look. Emboldened by simple inlaid bands of contrasting solid surface colors or other materials, including metal and stone, it can also be carved intricately into designs or what is called *intarsia* and filled with a liquefied solid-surface material.

Evidencing far less contrast, granite can be carved and inlaid, too. It offers myriad colors and patterns, but most are fairly muted.

At the extreme, laminate and tile know no bounds of color, pattern, and texture. Ranging from solids to complex three-dimensional images replicating stone, fabric, leather, and wood, they boast embossed, metallic, and pearlescent textures. As if this isn't enough, laminate companies give designers free rein to create original patterns, while tile artists carve bold designs with glimmering metal and gemstone insets. Inspiration lies in homey Americana scenes, a naturalist's organic themes, far-off columns of antiquity, and the magic geometrics of the Art Deco, Art Nouveau, and Arts and Crafts movements.

Color Fastness

Laminate is going through an unstable period now color-wise as dyes unfriendly to the environment are being replaced with compounds whose holding properties are as yet unknown. Jump ahead to the future with a warranty that guards against fading. *Weathering* slate changes color outdoors and in sunny locations. For the kitchen, look for one labeled *unfading*.

Grooving

Granite, solid surface, Nuvel, and stainless can all be grooved for an integrated drainboard or, as Flo

FINISHED EDGES

The squared-off finished self-edge on this solid countertop extends several inches beyond the base cabinet below so crumbs can easily be swept off, and there is no protruding hardware to work against. To decorate the countertop, a contrasting band of color has been inlaid several inches from its edge. The granite countertop below has a curve and simple rounded or beveled edge that allows diners to see each other while they converse. The ceramic tile countertop at the bottom is edged with contrasting trim pieces that are canted slightly upward to form a lip so liquids don't run off.

Braker created, a nesting place for eggs as they come to room temperature. The grooves look . . . groovy, but they're not fun to clean.

Edges

A countertop's edge is its edge on definition, individuality, and pizzazz. Depending on intricacy, it can also take a reasonably priced countertop and you to the cleaners. One of those knock-you-over hidden costs, edging options should be contrasted carefully. Regardless of the kind of edging you choose, extend the countertop one and preferably two inches beyond the cabinets below so crumbs can be collected easily, work performed at the counter without banging into hardware, and water splashed away from the cabinetry. Just avoid dangerous sharp angles likely to chip off or break. If the edge blocks the opening of drawers or appliances below, raise the countertop or install it on a thicker substrate.

A *self-edge* (page 197) is available on solid-core laminate, Nuvel, solid surface, butcher block, stainless, concrete, and granite. The edges of a post-formable laminate can be curved so the seam isn't visible or covered with an edge banding made from metal, melamine, PVC (polyvinyl chloride), or wood veneer. Straight or rounded edges can also be affixed from wood, metal, or solid surface. Slate tiles require treatment to hide their raw ends, while ceramic tiles sport their own *trim pieces*.

Nuvel, stainless, granite, solid-surface, and solid-core laminate can have a *sandwich* edge with other countertop materials as filling. They can also be routed and inlaid with accent pieces. In either case, stay clear of wood, for it requires a dust-catching gap for expansion. These edges can be sculpted into any profile: angled on a *bevel*, curved into an **S**-shaped *ogee* or *waterfall*, or rounded into a quarter- or half-inch *bullnose* (or **V**-cap). (Looking too much like a second countertop, a full bullnose is not attractive.) The lip can also be turned slightly upward for a *drip edge* to catch, well, drips.

Countertop edges are often swankily rung with brass, chrome, or copper *railings* in cabinet brochures or magazines. A *soigné* decorative finish to be sure, they are, in fact, a money guzzler and stomach puncher to work against.

Seams

Since the seams joining one tile, sheet, or slab to another are accomplished debris catchers, their numbers, extent, width, and ease of cleaning become significant on a countertop. For this reason, investigate

HOT POTATO
This stainless steel trivet can be inserted into any solid surface countertop to nestle hot pots and protect the countertop from heat damage.

the kind of seams to be used where expanses are joined and a corner is turned.

All materials but ceramic and slate tile offer an extended expanse, and even some porcelain tiles can now be butt joined. Among those that can't, remember that larger tiles mean fewer seams; inconsistent hand-shaped tiles require larger grout lines than those spewed by machine.

Materials that bend—postformed laminate, Nuvel, solid surface, stainless, and, as a matter of speaking, concrete—can be curved upward from the countertop for a *coved* seamless backsplash. With tile, a coved trim piece is usually used at this juncture. Integral or seamless connections can also be made between a stainless or solid-surface sink and countertop.

Weight

Countertop material is dependent on the amount of weight the cabinets and, in turn, the floor and subfloor can support. Brick, granite, slate, concrete, tile, and butcher block may be too heavy for some settings.

Finish

Countertop materials break down into two categories: those that come only matte (Nuvel, butcher block, concrete, slate) and those that should be ordered only with a matte or low-polished finish (solid surface, tile, stainless, and granite) that doesn't show scratches or wear. Going one step further, it is easiest to work on ceramic tile when flat and unglazed.

Cutability

Butcher block is the only surface that can be cut directly on without destroying either surface or knife. Its use does not come quietly, for revealing scratches and marks remain.

Durability

Laminates burn, stain, scratch, and chip most readily and are not repairable. With age, they can yellow and delaminate. Damage to nonsealed granite, concrete, slate, brick, and tile is also permanent. These materials crack, too, if improperly installed.

When stains and dents are caught early on Nuvel and solid surface, they can often be rubbed out with sandpaper or a Scotch-Brite pad and abrasive cleaner. Butcher block can be sanded down, too, when it gets ugly. The most resistant surface of all, stainless still scratches, dulls, and collects water spots.

Hard slate and granite are the most durable materials. Together with impervious ceramic tile and stainless, they are the only surfaces to consider putting a hot pot on. Solid surface accepts them as well *if* heat-absorbing trivets have been incorporated during its fabrication.

Noise

As the hardest surfaces, granite, tile, concrete, slate, stainless, and brick will be noisiest and the ones most likely to break something dropped on them.

Cleanability

Cleaning butcher block is most involved, for it must be rubbed and scrubbed after every use with a wire brush and lemon, ammonia, or bleach. It also needs to be reoiled frequently. Grout bogs down the cleaning of slate and ceramic tile harboring schmutz despite concerted efforts to remove it. Formed from expanding gases, pinhole bubbles entrap dirt in a glazed ceramic tile. Though a curved tile chips less readily than a knife-edged number, it collects dirt, shooting it down to the grout line. To eliminate water spots, stainless must be dried each time one hits, an obsessive, tail-chasing process. Edge details with gaps or porous seams also up the cleaning ante. In happy contrast, laminate, Nuvel, solid surface, and granite are a simple wipe-off.

Do-It-Yourself Installation

Those bold enough to undertake their own installation will find ceramic tile, laminate, and butcher block the easiest to work with from the preceding lineup.

Placement

Laminate and butcher block can warp next to the sink. Along with solid surface and Nuvel, they should

In weighing all the preceding issues, granite is the clear counterintelligence for me; everything else counterintuitive. As long as this stone has a high hardness rating and is installed with sufficient support, it will be most durable, easiest to clean, and longest enduring, amortizing its initial investment over the long haul. (And the beautiful slabs I have did not even need sealing.) To keep costs down, use a polished self-edge. One caveat: Be certain of granite's access into a building; it must enter with a crane.

In a country kitchen, I'd install a section of butcher block to cut on. With other, less compatible decorative styles, a mix of portable, pullout, and movable cutting boards that push along the countertop will suffice. Don't forget a bit of brick or slate as a cooktop surround to provide textural interest.

When solid surface is preferred and budget permits, maximize its major attributes—intricate inlays and complex edge treatments.

With tile, concrete, and laminate posing durability problems, I'd relegate them to lesser-used countertops in a cookbook corner or refrigerator landing area. For all its wonderful high-tech professional looks, I'd avoid stainless altogether; its wipe-down would give me apoplexy.

When more than one surface is going to be used for a countertop, carefully compare their heights, substrates, and edges and compensate for differences in thickness and shape. Beware of joining wood with another material, for it expands at different rates.

be separated from a commercial-style cooktop or drop-in range with a gap or another fireproof material. Stainless, granite, brick, slate, and ceramic tile, on the other hand, are excellent heatproof surfaces to place next to a cooktop, barbecue, stove, or oven.

FLOORING

From the countertop group of materials, slate, concrete, granite, and vitreous or, better, impervious ceramic tile are also contenders for floors. Joining this group that lets itself get walked all over are vinyl, cork, linoleum, brick, and hardwood.

With the rigors of cooking intensified by having to do a stand-up performance, a comfortable flooring is a treasure. For the kitchen, a good flooring material is smooth and relaxing to stand on, safe and nonslip even when wet, and effortless to maintain. Warmth is important, too, when you walk barefoot or have children playing on their bottoms. Keep these issues uppermost in mind when comparing materials according to the following parameters. Review notes under countertops, too.

Color and Pattern

Other than ceramic tile, flooring materials are fairly neutral. This is a relief, given how overwhelming a startling pattern could be. Available only in different shades of variegated honey brown, cork is the most monochromatic. Linoleum and vinyl both offer subtle color and patterning, while vinyl also has embossed textures and facsimiles of other materials in its line. Hardwood can be bordered, inlaid with patterns, and stenciled or embellished with decorative painterly techniques. On the brighter side, hardwood square tiles come in thirty-five hundred hues. To jazz up a floor, insert contrasting strips of wood, vinyl, ceramic, or granite between tiles.

Color Fastness

Vinyl, cork, and unweathered slate are most prone to fading.

PERSONAL PICKS: FLOORING

When replacing a floor in a home or apartment, find out first how much weight its foundation can bear and whether the substrate needs to be fixed or replaced. If this underlayment is in good repair, the least expensive option is to install the new floor directly over the old one. In this case, your flooring choice will be limited to one that is thin enough for doors to open and will transition smoothly to other rooms. It must also be able to bond with the original material.

Choices are greater in a complete down-to-the-studs remodel as long as the subfloor is reinforced sufficiently to support the floor's weight. When a floor is installed directly on the foundation or below grade, selection focuses on a flooring that can tolerate moisture without a suspended underlayment. All precautions possible must be taken to be sure this foundation doesn't move or crack.

When a floor can be raised, you may want to put a heater underneath. If so, check to see what will be compatible with this system. Factoring in a pet or young children should send you scurrying after a grayish abstract no-show design. Finally, you must consider how harmonious a style will be with floor coverings in adjacent rooms.

If a choice still remains after you've satisfied the preceding list—and you are able to lay the floor above a crawl space—seek a resilient material that provides the most comfort. Resilience is not relevant, however, if the floor is installed on a concrete slab. It will feel hard regardless of what it is, so you might as well get whatever you like best: at last!

When choice is unfettered, my preference for kitchen flooring is a traditional medium to dark solid wood floor. For a lighthearted modern look, I'd play with a checkerboard of colored wood tiles.

Wood flooring is still flat, smooth, and comfortable enough to stand on, even over a slab. Damp mopped, it is a breeze to clean. It holds up for several years as long as it is sealed correctly at the outset, and then it's a simple matter of resealing. Minus cushioning, which dents, it lives longer than you. When it becomes tiresome, a short visit to the floor dresser alters its color. For a monochrome look, match it to cabinets or hardwood flooring in adjacent rooms.

As much as I like granite for a countertop, its thin floor tiles seem too formal for a kitchen floor in any but a modern high-tech setting. Slate, brick, and matte pebbled tile, especially hard porcelain pavers, are all attractive, strong, and good at concealing dirt, but they have to be resealed frequently. Cork and linoleum would be appealing, too, were it not for that buffing business.

I could not put up with the care of vinyl flooring, ever more demanding, even though it is the least expensive material. Julia Child, on the other hand, embraces it. "Having endured the beauty of red tile in Provence and large squares of pure white and pure black vinyl in Cambridge, floor coverings are something I refuse to suffer about anymore," she once wrote. "Both were handsome, but every footstep showed. Now we have pebble-design airport strength vinyl in Cambridge and fleck-design vinyl in France, and nothing shows at all."

Seams

Vinyl and linoleum sheet goods are winners of fewest seams. An almost invisible joint can be achieved with wood, granite, cork, linoleum, vinyl, and some porcelain tiles. Slate, ceramic, and brick have the largest gaps for collecting crumbs and water. Rounded or beveled edges, an option with granite, wood, ceramic, and vinyl tile, collect debris and water, making the floor harder to clean.

Moldings

Moldings, finishing edges, or trim pieces ring the room's perimeter, protecting walls while the floor is being washed. Coved ceramic trim pieces eliminate the seam between the floor and wall, facilitating this cleaning. Despite these advantages, the decision to have a molding is an aesthetic one with all materials but wood. In this case, molding masks the expansion gap left between the wall and the last piece of wood. There is money to be saved eliminating moldings, but the savings may end up in the wall painter's pockets.

Resilience

A floor with some give is much less tiring to work on; less painful to fall on. Cork and cushion-clad vinyl and wood are most resilient: the comfort floors. Linoleum and hard-backed vinyl and wood have some resilience, while slate, concrete, ceramic, brick, and granite have none.

As always, there is a trade-off. Soft floors dent more readily from dropped pots and furniture stationed on them; stiletto heels wreak their own havoc. In a rather unflattering comparison, a Mannington Floors brochure claims that "an average sized woman wearing high heels exerts about 30 times more pressure (per square inch) on a floor than a full sized refrigerator"; double or triple the pressure of a full-grown elephant. Thank you.

Noise

The less resilient the floor, the noisier it will be and the more likely things that drop on it will break.

Weight

In both a remodel and new construction, brick, granite, concrete, slate, and even ceramic tile may be too heavy for some multistory apartments or for subfloors in a single-level dwelling. When the subflooring can support them, it will most likely need to be reinforced.

Height

The height (thickness) of a potential floor must be considered in relation to both the height of adjacent floors and how it affects the opening of doors to kitchen cabinets, appliances, the exterior, and other rooms in the home. Brick, concrete, and ceramic pavers tend to be most problematic, but even the thinnest vinyl tile can prevent doors from opening when applied over a preexisting flooring. For it to work, doors must be able to be cut down and any pocket doors the type that can be removed from their pocket. When completed, you still have to be able to change out that dishwasher.

To move from one room to another, provide for a graceful transition using the wood and ceramic tile pieces designed for this purpose. Flooring specialists recommend raising a wood threshold on a block so the higher floor gradually slopes down to the lower one. With tile, use a transitional tile rather than butting one bullnose piece against another; an invitation to a bullfight.

Solar Power

Absorbing heat during the day, stone, slate, brick, and some tile floors can stay nice and warm in a room with a skylight and/or many windows. In general, foam-backed floors are warmer than noncushioned.

Finish

With the National Safety Council reporting twelve million falling injuries annually, slip resistance is *de rigueur* for a kitchen floor where grease and water pose constant danger. To receive a *slip-resistant rating*, tile usually has a matte, roughened, or textured surface; stone a flamed finish.

As far as staining goes, vinyl is most susceptible while some granites, slates, and ceramic tiles are

BACKSPLASH

CERAMIC TILE BACKSPLASH

Easily wiped off and resistant to heat, ceramic tile works particularly well behind a cooktop in a backsplash area *(right)*. A vertical surface, the backsplash demands an intriguing interesting design that serves as a focal point and contrasts with tile laid horizontally on the counter-top and/or floor *(center right)*. Decorative, less durable ceramic tiles such as this rope trim are ideal for the back-splash where they can show off their good looks without being subject to the damage they would receive if they were laid on a work surface *(below)*.

resistant enough not to need protection. Most floorings will need to be sealed and resealed as the finish wears off.

Durability

Durability is crucial in choosing a flooring. Not only is a floor an expensive proposition to change out, but its replacement will disturb everything else in the kitchen and, most likely, the entire house. Softer products—cork, vinyl, and cushioned wood—are more likely to tear, dent, or be cut, while harder slate, concrete, and ceramic can crack or break. Unlike most of us, linoleum gets better—tougher and harder—as it ages and oxidizes.

As long as you purchase enough matching material initially and can convince a worker to come to the house for a small job, tiles or wood can be popped out and replaced. A torn section of sheet vinyl can be exchanged as well, but it is not generally recommended, for it weakens the flooring's structure.

Durability problems can exist even with a commercially rated well-sealed flooring that is not properly utilized. Back to those stilettos: A onetime chef at Wolfgang Puck's Spago restaurant tells of the nervous hostess who paced back and forth in her high heels until it looked as if a woodpecker lived at her hardwood floor station.

Cleanability

Slop and mop, granite and wood are easiest to clean. Grout and a textured surface make this a more difficult undertaking with tile, concrete, brick, and slate. Nevertheless, their maintenance is simple enough if they've been sealed adequately. Cork requires some fussing and rebuffing, while vinyl and linoleum are demanding children who use terrible language: buffing, stripping, and polishing.

Cleaning difficulties depend on the type of flooring; frequency on the pattern picked. Regardless of material, solid floors must be cleaned more frequently than those with random patterns. When guests come for a meal, embarrassing signs of its preparation are most obvious on a light-colored solid floor. My mother warns not to compensate by going too dark or too busy. "It's impossible to wash those floors," she says. "You can't tell what you've already cleaned."

Do-It-Yourself Installation

For die-hard do-it-yourselfers the easiest floors to install are cork, self-stick vinyl or ceramic tile, and prefinished wood. Sheet vinyl is possible, too, when it does not require an adhesive and comes with an installation kit.

BACKSPLASH

After the complexity of identifying the most practical countertop and flooring surface, it is a relief to choose a backsplash, for anything goes here. If you paint or paper this space like the rest of the kitchen walls, there won't even be a decision to make. Nor will there be one if the countertop continues up the backsplash.

Once you've decided to cover the backsplash, choose something to go behind work counters that wipes off and doesn't stain. Stainless and ceramic tile make particularly good buffers behind a stove, although the latter cannot be used in tandem with a commercial range because the materials employed in its installation are too combustible for this unit's extreme heat.

Take advantage of the backsplash's equanimity to introduce new materials with texture and design interest. Mirror works well, enlarging a small space, as does etched or sandblasted glass or colored glass tiles. This is also an excellent home for glass block. When the block is not part of an exterior wall, place a mirror behind it so it does not appear dull and flat. Showing every spatter, glass materials are nonetheless easy to clean.

Outside work areas, the backsplash happily hosts frivolous opulent materials that are too fragile to be used elsewhere: beautiful high-gloss ceramic tiles, embossed metallic laminates, and lovely French limestone.

KITCHENSPEAK: SURFACES

———

Butcher Block: **A material composed of hardwood strips of the same or varying lengths that are glued together and laminated under pressure.**

End-Grained: **The best-quality butcher block, with a checkerboard of squares on its vertical edges.**

Ceramic Tiles:

Bicottura: **Relatively fragile twice-fired tiles that are richly decorated with a handpainted, silk-screened, embossed, engraved, or decaled surface and employed primarily for walls and backsplashes.**

Monocottura: **Thin, durable, single-fired matte-glazed tile.**

Porcelain: **The longest-fired, hottest-fired tile with a hard, strong, chinalike body that is often unglazed.**

Quarry: **An extruded tile made from a mixture of shale and other clays.**

Saltillo: **Rough-textured squares produced in Mexico by hand or machine. Many develop efflorescence (holes) from lime bubbles popping on the surface.**

Trim Pieces: **Curved or other shaped tiles designed to hide a seam or aid in the transition from one level (height) to the next.**

Coved Backsplash: **A backsplash that curves upward from the countertop.**

Decorative High-Pressure Laminate: **A sandwich of paper, plastic resin, and a three-quarter-inch-thick backer board fused together under heat and pressure for use in cabinet and countertop fabrication.**

Edge-Glued: **Laminate countertops built** *in situ.*

Nonformable: **Rigid nonbendable high-pressure laminate.**

Postformed: **High-pressure laminate bent under heat.**

Solid-Core: **A decorative high-pressure laminate that has color all the way through to the edge.**

Edges:

Bevel: **An angled edge.**

Bullnose or V-cap: **A rounded edge.**

Inlaid: **An edge that is routed (grooved) and inlaid with another material.**

Ogee: **Curved S-shaped edge.**

Sandwich: **An edge built up in several layers with various materials.**

Self-Edge: **A flat edge with no additional crafting.**

Waterfall: **Another S-shaped edge.**

Flamed: **A textured finish, also called a thermal finish, given to stone to make it slip resistant.**

Glass Block: **Two pieces of molded molten glass fused with mortar or silicon sealants.**

Granite: **An igneous rock found in the earth's crust composed of quartz, feldspar, mica, and other minerals. Some types are very hard and durable, making them ideal for kitchen countertops.**

Hardwood:

Distressed: **Boards that have been wire-brushed. They accumulate too much dirt for kitchen use.**

End-Matched Boards: **Best quality with the tongue of one fitting snugly into the groove of the next. They must be blind nailed.**

Grades: Common **has the most blemishes, and** *clear* **the fewest with** *select* **falling in between.**

Laminated Boards: **Sandwiches of hardwood, softwood, or plywood laminated with a hardwood veneer that are mounted crossgrain with the grain of each layer running in the opposite direction from the one above.**

Parquet: **Square tiles composed of matched pieces of wood in myriad patterns that are laid out at the factory.**

Planks: **Boards of random lengths and widths running three to eight inches wide. To curtail warping, width should be limited to five inches.**

Quartersawn: **Logs divided into four ninety-degree sections before being cut into boards. They are more beautiful and durable than** *plainsawn* **boards.**

Square-Edged: **Boards that butt together for installation. They are face nailed, which is considered a less satisfactory juncture than blind nailed.**

Strips: Random lengths that run two to two and one-fourth inches wide and can be laid in straight rows or in patterns such as herringbone and basketweave.

Honed: A matte surface applied to stone that can be high- or low-honed (more or less reflective).

Linoleum: Squares and sheets made from a mixture of cork, linseed oil, wood dust, pine resin, clay, or chalk fillers and natural pigments that are backed with jute, then cured and dried in an oven.

Marble: A metamorphic rock with veining or fracture points that is recrystallized from limestone or dolomite under heat or pressure. Most types are too soft for kitchen use other than as a pastry surface.

Slate: A sedimentary rock split horizontally into thin uneven sheets.

> *Cleft:* Slate tiles left as they are naturally cut.
>
> *Gauged:* Tiles ground so only their bottoms are smooth.
>
> *Honed:* Smooth finished slate tiles.
>
> *Nongauged:* Tiles with uneven edges that don't square sufficiently for kitchen use.
>
> *Smooth-Gauged:* A fine finished slate with no visible grinding marks.

Slip Resistant: A rating given to some tile or stone with a matte, roughened, or textured surface.

Solid Surface: A varying blend of acrylic and polyester resins that are poured into molds and baked in sheets that contain the same material and color throughout.

Intarsia: An intricate routed (carved) design that is filled with a liquefied solid-surface material.

Solid Vinyl: Produced only in tiles, not in sheets, this pure vinyl material is not readily available.

Stainless 18/8 or 18/10: A quality stainless—an alloy of carbon steel—with a thickness or gauge of 18 and a nickel content of 8 to 10 percent for maintaining luster and preventing staining, scratching, and corrosion.

Terrazzo: A mixture of cement and marble chips used for flooring.

Thermoplastic: A material such as solid surface that can be shaped by heat.

Vinyl Tile or Vinyl Composition Tile: The majority of what is called vinyl is a composition material consisting mainly of limestone and other resins by weight and, by the by, some vinyl. Available in tiles or sheets, vinyl is produced by several different methods.

> *Inlaid Vinyl Tile:* Composed of colored vinyl crystals or chips that are fused under heat or pressure.
>
> *Never Wax:* A vinyl tile topped with a thick layer of urethane hardened with additives. Though waxing is not necessary for maintaining this vinyl, it requires considerable care.
>
> *Rotogravure:* A vinyl tile produced in layers with a cushioned backing, a colored surface printed photographically with vinyl inks, and a protective coating called a wearlayer. See also Wearlayer.
>
> *Wearlayer:* A topcoat of vinyl or urethane that serves as a protective covering for vinyl composition tile.

6
DRAMATIC LIGHTING

ILLUMINATING CHOICES

■

Wise even beyond her years, my aunt Rose Friedgut cut to the quick of lighting messages: "Lighting is so important," she observed at the celebration marking her one hundredth birthday. "Most kitchens are lit terribly." She paused. "But I guess it depends on how well you can see."

If my aunt followed the formula of one designer, who adds a hundred watts to a lighting design for every five years after age forty, when vision starts to deteriorate, there would be no room left in her kitchen for anything but lighting fixtures. But even we younger pupils need to lighten up our work and dining spaces.

We need lights, lights everywhere as well as a drop to drink (and a dimmer to tone things down when it gets too bright). We can stay in the dark about the angle of *parabolic spread*; the differences between *ballast* and *beam*. We can let someone else compute the complex physics of light. Our job is to install enough *luminaires* (the fancy word for fixtures) to extend into the far reaches of the kitchen.

Grokking lighting is just short of the mastery of rocket science, a goal most of us who just want to be able to see our way to a refrigerator heist haven't bothered to set. Starting with yours truly, the majority of the unenlightened just stick any bulb into any socket and forget about it.

That's dumb and dumber, for proper lighting enables us to function comfortably in the kitchen while transforming it into an exciting place to work. When installed effectively, lighting can convert the meanest, drabbest space into a vibrant, breathtaking environment.

Suitable kitchen lighting affords the opportunity to work safely, confident in our distinction of lamb chop from finger chop. It lets us operate serenely without visual fatigue, the only glare emanating from a child who hasn't bought the Popeye bit. Like Peter Pan, we will lose our shadow. Unlike him, it will be with pleasure. And, although you may resent this revelation, dust balls will be more obvious in a well-lit kitchen. Cleaning, may I bite my tongue, will be easier.

Don't worry if lighting technology isn't within your ken. Most designers and architects don't begin to comprehend it either. Regardless of who is helping you with design, have your lighting plans assessed at a variety of dealers and lighting labs where the personnel is knowledgeable. Consider hiring a lighting consultant as well to ensure that illumination type is correct; its intensity sufficient. Armed with the information in this chapter, you should at least be able to understand what these experts are talking about.

"Good lighting need not be expensive, just well designed," says lighting consultant Jane Grosslight (yep, that's her name). "Better light is not necessarily more lighting or brighter lighting, but helpful and pleasing. You need a place to rest your eyes and a focal point of light. People enjoy the effects of light

■ *199*

as long as they don't see the source," adds designer Ken Anderson.

An effective lighting system is flexible and diverse enough to account for a variety of kitchen activities that take place individually or simultaneously. You'll know it's right when your reaction to it is "wow!" This depends less on the type of light source and lightbulbs employed than on the creation of a special mood and ambience.

What type of light source should be used?

Light sources for the kitchen include incandescent, fluorescent, and halogen at either line (regular household) or low voltage. A touch of neon along the toe kick, under or over a cabinet, or as a bulletin board does many a kitchen proud, or at least whimsical. Mixing these sources provides lighting that is at once practical and dramatic while saving valuable energy.

An *incandescent* light source, the bulb we all know and love when it goes on above people's heads in comic books, is popular in kitchens because it can be installed easily, focused on an object, and housed in a variety of fixtures. The bottom line: It is least expensive. Its profile, however, has more minuses than pluses, and it is currently being phased out—legislated out—for its waste of energy.

An incandescent bulb's life span is short. Going downhill, its illumination decreases as it ages, and a great deal of what it does put out is not light but uncomfortable heat and glare. To compensate for its shortcomings, *cool-beam bulbs* have been issued that create less heat. The new *E-lamp* or electronic bulb can also be substituted for a standard incandescent. Based on a tiny generator, each bulb uses 25 percent less energy and lasts up to two thousand times as long. (Too bad vitamin E doesn't have a similar effect.)

Compared to a 100-watt incandescent bulb, "two . . . *fluorescent* forty-watt bulbs put out four times the light and last twenty-five times longer," one-ups consultant Gerry Zekowski. Consuming considerably less energy, fluorescents distribute light much more evenly than incandescents, without the glare, heat,

or diminished intensity that comes with age. With a wider beam, fewer fixtures are needed to handle an area, and electronic ballasts now eliminate the hum and flicker that once irritatingly announced a fluorescent's oncoming.

With the introduction of *compact* (four- to six-inch) fluorescents, these bulbs finally fit small fixtures as well as their large traditional housing and can be retrofitted into incandescent sockets.

Today's fluorescents can still be purchased with the original preheat circuit that causes a delay in starting. Much more satisfying is the *rapid-start* system that hesitates only momentarily. Starting instantly, the *slimline* system consumes much more voltage. Fixtures with lenses encircling a tube provide fewer shadows and more light than those lying flat up against their housing.

With so many factors to commend this light source, why are we even bothering to have this discussion?

Fluorescents are still more expensive to purchase and install. (Jumping ahead to replacement, plug-ins are less costly than screw-ins.) A fluorescent's beam can't focus on a spot or be channeled in a particular direction. Some types cannot be dimmed at all; others only by an expensive rapid-start dimming ballast used in tandem with proper wattage and controls. Even with compacts, this light source is larger than incandescents, an ungainly monster when compared to halogen, particularly in its low-voltage incarnation.

Halogen must be what Trekkies have in mind when yelling "Beam me up, Scottie." Intense and bright-eyed, it can be dimmed and focused in its quartz housing. Less efficient than fluorescent, halogen bests incandescent in the energy area—lasting roughly twice the time—as long as it runs undimmed for at least 20 percent of its operation. A sensitive source, halogen must literally be handled with kid gloves—or a clean towel. It can get hot enough to fade fabrics or burn a surface, so purchase only UL-approved bulbs and fixtures.

Halogen lights, like incandescents, are available in either line or *low voltage.* Proof that good things come in small packages, low voltage is unique in its bright tonality, dramatic accenting, and ability to render colors accurately, underscoring an ingredient's lushness. Its fixtures can be miniaturized to fit into a five-eighths-inch-thick shelf, and it consumes negligible electricity. Running cooler, it lights up the lettuce without wilting it. On the high end ride the cost of its bulbs and contemporary fixtures.

For a light to function at low voltage, a *transformer* lowers its standard 120 volts to anywhere from the usual 12 up to 115 volts. When the transformer and fixture are purchased separately, the system is less expensive but harder to integrate and install. Regardless, the elements must be manufactured by the same company and coordinated to work together. A magnetic transformer is less costly than an electronic one, but unless you want to sing along with the hum that comes on with its dimmer, ignore this savings. The transformer can be separated from the light fixture and remoted to another location within twenty feet. Just be sure it is sizable enough to stand up to the light's consequential drop in voltage. Install it vertically, maintaining access and ventilation space.

Lightbulbs

A comparison of all these light sources is not complete without looking at their bulbs, or *lamps* as they are confusingly called by those who've seen the light. *Watts*, the amount of electricity a bulb/lamp consumes, do not translate directly into the amount of light given off. This is called *lumens* and is stated on the bulb's packaging. When two lightbulbs have the same wattage, the one with the greatest number of lumens is the most efficient, offering more light or intensity for the money.

Another term encountered in purchasing catalogs is *foot-candles*. This is not a hot massage, but the amount of light or lumens that actually reaches an object. Lighting by the numbers, a total of fifty to seventy-five foot-candles is recommended for most kitchens.

Bulbs with higher wattages are more efficient than those with lower ratings. To wit, a hundred-watt bulb consumes less electricity than two fifty-watt bulbs, which in turn consume less than four twenty-five-watt bulbs. Bulbs come in an architect or contractor grade with higher marks going to the designer model. An *extended-life* lamp can also be purchased. With its output curtailed by 20 to 30 percent, and its extra expense, one feisty designer refers to this category as *il gipos*. Reserve long-life bulbs for hard-to-access areas or a location in constant use.

When it comes to deciding on a light source, perhaps no issue is more important than the color or part of the visible light spectrum each type reflects. Incandescent lights emit warm yellowish-reddish tones that feel good to work under, complement skin tones, and replicate the real colors of most food. Washing out blues and grays, incandescents rob green peppers of their luster and make blue curaçao look even weirder than it does naturally. Incandescent lamps filled with *xenon* gas will be whiter in color, though less white than halogen, whose bright tones come closest to natural sunlight.

Halogen can appear too cold in a kitchen whose decor emphasizes red, yellow, and orange, but it enhances a white kitchen that would be muted by an incandescent's yellowish hue. When dimmed, halogen assumes the warmer reddish highlights of an incandescent bulb. Afterward, it must run for several uninterrupted hours before its normal color returns.

At the opposite end of the spectrum, fluorescents are cool-guy colors high on blue and gray. New *soft white* and *warm white* fluorescent bulbs have been introduced to render warmer colors.

The color of each light source is expressed in temperatures or *degrees Kelvin*. Incandescent bulbs fall in the low temperature zone, under three thousand degrees Kelvin, halogen and warm fluorescents in the middle at three thousand to four thousand degrees, and cool fluorescents above four thousand degrees.

COMMON KITCHEN LAMPS

A few of the many lightbulbs available, the following types and shapes are used most commonly for kitchens. To know what they are, you have to crack their code. A listing of "100 W A-15" indicates that the bulb has a hundred watts, is an *A* type, and has a diameter of fifteen/eighths or one and seven-eighths inches (bulb sizes are measured by one-eighth inch). The spread and output of the bulb depend on its wattage, lumens, housing, width of beam spread, and distance from its subject. Wattages must not exceed the maximum stated on a fixture's housing.

When surfaces and paints are glossy, lights must be chosen carefully so as not to appear harsh. Since dark surfaces and cabinets absorb light, their rooms require more illumination than those done in white or pastel. Coordinate all light sources to avoid the excessive contrast of brightness perceived as *glare*. *Beam spreads* should be broad enough for the edges of each source to overlap, preventing gaps and dark spots that give surfaces that holey *Swiss cheese* look. Recommended beam spreads are listed in purchasing catalogs.

Fluorescent Lamps

T indicates a tube; the number following its diameter in eighths of an inch. T-17 is a fluorescent tube with a two-and-one-eighth-inch diameter (seventeen/eighths).

Fluorescent lamps come in straight tubes from six to ninety-six inches long, in *Circline tubes* from six and one-half to seventeen inches in diameter, in *U shapes*, and in *compact* twin and double-twin tubes. GE's 2D pretzel-twist compact conveys the greatest proportion of light in a fluorescent without the shadows that exist at a tube's end.

Halogen Lamps

MR 16 Lamp: A low-voltage halogen spotlight with tight beam control. In many situations, a fifty-watt MR 16 can be substituted for a 150-watt *R* or PAR lamp, at a great savings in energy, and with a better control of beam spread. These lamps have a dichroic coating, which keeps them cooler by sending heat out the back of the lamp.

PAR 36 Lamp: Low-voltage PAR lamp that has a larger beam of light than an MR 16 and can be controlled over longer distances.

T Lamp: Single- or double-ended quartz tube lamps.

Incandescent Lamps

A Lamp: This is the common general-service pear-shaped household bulb. It can be used in any type of fixture and distributes light in all directions.

PAR (Parabolic Aluminum Reflector) Lamp: These floods possess four times the light of an *A* lamp along with a more controllable beam. When a *dichroic* coating is added, different colors can be filtered out.

R Lamp: These *reflective* bulbs throw twice as much light on a subject as an *A* lamp. Housed in recessed or enclosed fixtures, their beam of light is controlled by a mirrorlike reflective surface. A clear bulb indicates a *spotlight* with a small narrow beam; frosting reveals a *flood* with a wider spread.

What type of fixtures are optimum for kitchen lighting?

In the kitchen, fixtures are needed for general illumination, the performance of specific tasks, accenting treasured objects or focal point areas, and elevating or subduing the mood. In most circumstances, each of these requirements is served by a specific fixture and light source, but, properly aligned, some may do double duty. When combining sources to utilize simultaneously, select those with similar color temperatures that work well together, such as an incandescent and soft or warm white fluorescent with a three-thousand-degree temperature.

GENERAL LIGHTING

General or overall lighting is Snoopy's "blanket of light" that illuminates the entire room sufficiently for carefree navigation. From the standpoints of energy, longevity, and ability to diffuse light, a fluorescent light source is ideal for overall lighting. Fitted with GE's highly touted SPX 35 or another warm or soft white lamp, its light falls moderately between hot and cold, rendering colors truly.

When the kitchen color scheme is blue and gray, parlay them with a cooler, higher-temperature color. In a white kitchen, a halogen PAR lamp or xenon-filled incandescent may be more satisfying. If you do opt for incandescent, take advantage of a PAR or reflector bulb's greater output.

As a guideline, the American Institute of Kitchen Designers recommends 175 to 200 watts of incandescents or 60 to 80 watts of fluorescents for every fifty square feet of floor area. These requirements can be met easily by choosing any of the following fixtures.

Chandelier

Although good kitchen lighting is light-years beyond that single bulb in the middle of the room, laudable general illumination still includes a central fixture that fits flush with the ceiling or a *chandelier* that hangs from it. Consider, too, the single or multiple *pendant* lights that swing from the ceiling on a chain or cord. Smaller than a chandelier, they come cloaked in opaque shades to mask glare.

Luminous Ceilings

Designed to diffuse an even layer of light, *luminous ceilings* make a powerful architectural statement while doing their light housework. Created with wood, metal, or plastic, a matrix or "egg carton grid" secures lights under translucent acrylic panels, stained or decorative glass, or the high-tech metallized louvers that constitute a *parabolic ceiling*. These panels can be encased and lowered to float above an island or dining table. When built to echo the shape of the area they are lighting, their effect can be sensational.

Recessed Cans

A far cry from the prominent out-there "look at me" swagger of luminous panels, the demure *recessed can* disappears up into the ceiling. For heat and glare not to be too pronounced, ceiling height should be a minimum of eight feet, with cans placed where people will not sit or stand directly beneath these *downlights*. To sink the cans so their rim is flush with the ceiling, adequate space must exist in the joists above.

Cans generally come in rounds or ellipses from four to eight inches in diameter, in squares from six to ten inches, and in rectangles six by ten inches or larger. The six- or seven-inch can is used most frequently. Much smaller than that and you need so many cans to light the room, the ceiling looks as if it has measles. Recessed lights must ventilate out the top to prevent heat buildup yet be sealed well enough so rain, debris, and bugs don't blow in.

A variety of trims exist for a recessed can light, each with an assigned function. For the "most light in the kitchen with the least amount of holes in the ceiling," Wayne Williams and other consultants recommend cans with an Alzak aluminum interior. Diffusing light evenly while maximizing its reflection and efficiency, these cans are available in black, gold, or the clear/mirror that throws out the most light.

When a narrower beam is sought than the Alzak provides, a white can will reflect more light than the ubiquitous black one. The step *baffle* or grooved interior controls glare, while a ribbed *Fresnel* lens hides the light source. These cans are less expensive than an Alzak, but more will be needed to yield the necessary amount of light. Rather than painting the edges of the can—an invitation to chip—pick a color that matches the ceiling paint or match the paint to the edge.

To be installed in a ceiling that has been insulated, a recessed can must have an *IC (insulated ceiling)* rating—a great savings in energy. Sloped or cathedral ceilings dictate specially designed cans. Though limited in size, wattage, and trim choice, those listed under "economical" may be just the ticket for your job.

Track Lights

The tracks made by *track* lighting during the last several decades are being followed somewhat less frequently today. Attached to the ceiling over a lengthy area or suspended below it, they shorten the distance to the floor, making a kitchen appear smaller. A person standing between its fixtures casts a shadow, and with all the louvers, baffles, and shutters designed for tracks, they are often not shielded adequately to prevent glare.

LIGHTING

Don't write off track lighting. It is too good-looking to dismiss and will follow you around from one locale to the next, whether attached to a junction box or juiced by a cord and plug.

Tracks, in nominal lengths of two, four, eight, and twelve feet that can be divided further, are laid in single circuits or in double runs that operate with separate controls and can be butt joined at any angle up to ninety degrees. Open tracks are most flexible, allowing lights to be coupled and uncoupled at will anywhere along their channel. Easier to clean, a closed channel cannot be changed once fixtures are inserted. Available only with an open frame, a nifty theatrical track is produced from solid steel rod and cold rolled steel tube.

Cable Lights

Slimming tracks down to two thin parallel tension cords, an electrified low-voltage *cable lighting* system can be strung across the kitchen and fitted with all manner of amusing contemporary fixtures. Requiring a multitude of spots to light a space adequately, aesthetic and economic reality relegates this delightful system to a small area.

Indirect Lighting

All the fixtures we've spoken about provide direct light from an obvious—sometimes too obvious—source. *Indirect lighting*, with the bulb hidden from sight, also offers general illumination.

Indirect lighting usually implies *cove lighting*, or a curved concave molding built above wall cabinets to mask a fixture behind it. This area can be insulated as well for sound absorption. Most effective

ALL-PURPOSE LIGHTING
General illumination fills a kitchen with a basic layer of light for navigation and activities that don't require close concentration. Different types of lighting systems can be employed to achieve this effect. Lights can be strung throughout the room on conventional white and black tracks or on hot-looking red, white, or blue channel tubes. Or a central fixture, chandelier, or pendant light can be hung from the ceiling.

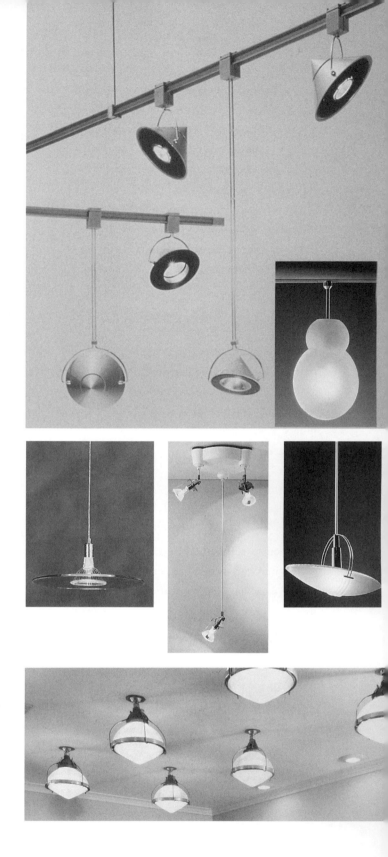

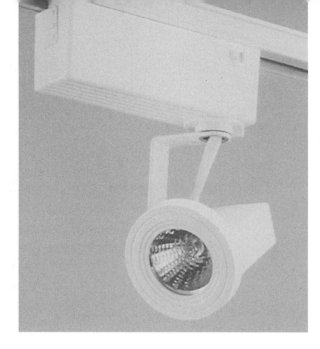

DOWNLIGHTS

When multiple lights are recessed in the ceiling, their beam spreads must be wide enough to overlap or the effect will be one of glare and shadow. Highhat cans are usually sunk so their rims fit flush with the ceiling as they are in this lighting bridge, their interiors varied according to task. An eyeball beam directs the light.

UNDERCABINET LIGHTS

These lights are mounted under cabinets to light countertops for a brighter working environment.

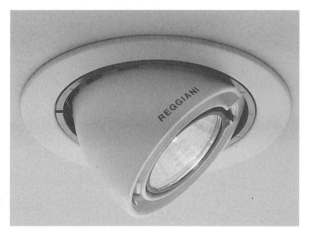

ACCENT LIGHTING

A track light or recessed can fitted with an eyeball or narrow beam spotlight will highlight whatever it is focused on.

with a cathedral ceiling, a cove should be located a minimum of twelve inches below its edge, the exact distance determining the breadth of the beam spread. For light to bounce off it, ceilings must also be reflective and painted a white or light color.

Indirect lighting can also be sequestered in a *valance* or board built specifically for this task on the wall or ceiling or above cabinets or draperies. In this case, the light can be thrown up, down, or up and down.

The black abyss a skylight and window turn into at night make their own special demands on general lighting. To combat these cavernous holes, brighten a window with a valance or recessed cans. Wake a skylight up by building indirect lighting into its light well or frame, rimming its perimeter with recessed cans, or choreographing cable lights to dance below it. To enhance these holes with a magical aura, light the windows and skylight of a home or ground-floor apartment kitchen from the exterior.

TASK LIGHTING

General lighting should be intense enough to perform kitchen tasks such as stirring at the stove, chopping at a counter, or washing dishes at the sink. Nevertheless, work is ever so much easier when its tools and precise location are lit separately.

Hang the source for *task lighting* directly over the surface you will be working at or to one side of it. When it's situated above or behind, you end up in your own shadow when bending over to work. With their controlled, concentrated beams, low-voltage halogen and incandescent spots and floods are excellent for these demanding situations.

Of the sources described, a recessed can converts to task lighting when fitted with an *eyeball* lens that directs its light toward a specific object. A track's fixture can be swiveled purposefully to focus as assigned. Pendants that can be raised or lowered also adapt beautifully.

When a ceiling fixture fulfills both general and task lighting roles, install it eighteen inches from the front of cabinets so it can light countertops as well as shelves and drawers.

The following designated areas are those most apt to receive task lighting. Specific recommendations come from the American Home Lighting Institute. Before adapting them, be certain their color rendition is appropriate for your kitchen.

Above a Counter

Some people recommend lighting a countertop by installing lights in an eastern soffit, but this can cast shadows over your work. Much more helpful are undercabinet fixtures that light up the counter directly below. As a safeguard, house lights mounted above a toaster or other hot appliance in glass, not plastic, and pull the appliance out on the counter to operate. The heat from the lights themselves can be destructive to oil, vinegar, and spices stored underneath, so plan their storage accordingly.

Fluorescent tubes or individual compact units possess an excellent beam spread for undercabinet lighting. Figured at eight watts per foot of counter length, they should cover at least two-thirds of the counter. In a rental situation, use a model with a cord and plug rather than one installed permanently.

When you want to dim down undercabinet lights for atmosphere or to hide a mess, line or low-voltage halogen surpasses fluorescent as the best choice. Whatever you desire, avoid fixtures whose lamps can't be replaced and the flimsy ribbon or seed bulbs that get knocked up or out from roving bowls and tools.

When a counter has no wall cabinets above, it can be lit with a wall-mounted fluorescent tube placed twenty-four inches or so above it. Size and wattage requirements are the same as for undercabinet lights.

Inside a Cabinet

Rigged to turn on as cabinet doors open, a small low-voltage light reveals items hidden in the far crevices of a cabinet. If a soffit exists, the light can be mounted inside it above the cabinet. Otherwise, insert lights into or below each shelf, at the front of the cabinet, or vertically on the sides, where the source won't be visible. Those with plug-in connectors pack up and move to a new house with you.

Above a Table

To light a worktable or an island, use pendant fixtures or recessed cans spaced fifteen to eighteen inches apart with seventy-five-watt reflector bulbs.

When specific lighting is desired for a dining table, a track or recessed light can be positioned so that it illuminates each place setting. Employ a chandelier or pendant(s) when the entire table is to be lit. Following guidelines, hang the fixture twenty-five

to thirty inches above the table with an additional three inches added for every foot an eight-foot ceiling is raised. Whatever chandelier is chosen should be six inches narrower than the table on each side so people don't bang their heads when getting up. Lamps should equal 120 watts of incandescence; 32 to 40 watts of fluorescence.

On the Range

Although most range hoods come with built-in lights, they are often not intense enough to see inside pots. Try to get at least forty watts of light for a thirty- or thirty-six-inch cooktop. To supplement them, hang a flexible heat-resistant fixture in the hood, clip it onto a pot rack or railing on the hood, or shoot a beam in off the side from a focused track light or recessed can with an eyeball. Sandblast the bulb to prevent glare.

Over the Sink

Most recommendations for lighting over the sink include sixty watts of fluorescent or, for more precise lighting, two seventy-five-watt incandescent floods placed fifteen to eighteen inches apart. A recessed, track, or valance fixture can be employed here.

TASK LIGHTING

Contiguous undercabinet lights illuminate the counter, making the work area safe and easy to see, and facilitating the task at hand.

On the Desk

Fitted with either a 32-watt fluorescent or a 150- to 225-watt incandescent bulb, a lamp for a kitchen desk should meet the same requirements as one installed elsewhere in the home. Choose a lamp with a shade whose bottom rim stands fifteen inches above the desk. Situate it twelve inches back from its front edge and fifteen inches from the center of writing papers. When using a computer, position the lamp so papers and keyboard get lit instead of you or the screen.

ACCENT LIGHTING

Within any of the lighting scenarios just described, there may be a particular item worthy of *accent lighting*—a beautiful vase or dish cabinet seeking recognition. If there isn't, make one up, for accenting makes lighting exciting.

To give your prized possession a riveting "focal glow" that draws people's attention, its lighting must

AREA LIGHTING

The stove is lit by a handsome halogen lamp that swivels so that it can be hung directly over the stove or to one side of it so you're not working in your own shadow. Each of the tables is surmounted by a pendant fixture hung twenty-five to thirty inches above its center to illuminate the complete surface. Each of the lights is six inches narrower than the table on every side so diners don't bang their heads getting up.

be three times as intense as that generally used. To avoid glare, position the light source high above eye level or hide it on a shelf or behind a plant.

To accent an object, fit a recessed can with an eyeball and narrow beam spotlight or low-voltage halogen. Turn to track lights fitted similarly, for they do their best work with an accent. Swiveled to a thirty-degree angle at twenty-four to thirty inches from a corner of the wall, they highlight paintings or art objects.

Installed within one foot of a wall, they *graze* a dark surface with light, emphasizing its texture. A bit farther away—three to four feet—they *wash* or flood a wall, the light blending elements while defining space and expanding it visually. PAR lights are particularly good for the latter two techniques.

When fitted with low voltage, a cove is transformed into a stunning accent fixture, highlighting the baskets, plants, or vases displayed atop cabinets. Moving to the bottom of a cabinet, a toe kick is another place to trail strips of accent lights. Lighting placed under (and around) an object makes it appear lighter in volume. As long as the floor is not highly reflective, dark cabinets will seem to float.

Task lights inside cabinets backlight a stained-glass door or add a sparkle to glasses displayed behind a clear closure. With lighting on top of the cabinet and a mirror on the bottom shelf, stemware is set aglimmer. It is also effectively lit from the bottom. In either case, place cabinet shelves at the same level as the bottom of the glass on the door so stems show in their entirety.

AMBIENT LIGHTING

Ambient lighting assumes all forms in a kitchen, creating a particular mood or tone. Whether brightened to get that lively conversation going or softened to a romantic glow for dinner *tête-à-tête*, ambient lighting is the life force of a kitchen, bathing it in pleasure, warmth, and good cheer. Controlling ambience depends not on a specific fixture or type of light source as much as on a dimmer or rheostat that can be turned up or down to suit the mood.

Dimmers

At its least expensive, a dimmer is a simple rotating knob. One disgruntled designer finds "builders' models as cheap as you can make them and still stay out of jail." Increasingly sophisticated dimmers offer a toggle switch or touch plate with a slide bar. For speakeasy dimmers, you tap once for "on," two for "dim," and three for "off" and "Joe sent me." Other than for low voltage, which has its own requirements, use only incandescent dimmer switches with special circuitry that suppresses static for radio and TV operation.

Switch plates have of late become fashion plates. Streamlined, they snap onto a base, hiding screws underneath. Aided by an illuminated rim, they become night-lights glowing in the dark. Fitted with a delay fade, they light your escape route from the room. Models filled with motion sensors light up automatically when you enter the room with your hands full of groceries.

Each dimmer controls up to a certain number of watts. For a light to function independently, it needs its own dimmer. This way, one bank of lights can be fully charged while another cashes out completely.

Set dimmers side by side like a cockpit or combine them in one neater high-tech housing. Connected to only one light switch, these multiple-dimmers-in-one can be programmed into different *preset* channels that light up with a different scene. To operate, you punch whatever appeals to you. The same switch can also control Smart House (page 98), which functions simultaneously. Like an elephant, these dimmers never forget; their settings remain even when power goes out. Don't you forget the romance button.

PERSONAL PICKS: LIGHTING

I feel the same way about lighting as I do about chocolate: You can't have too much of it. Leaving no cabinet unturned, I would install a light under every wall cabinet and in every cabinet interior with glass fronts or deep dark recesses. I would light each area of the kitchen individually, providing for different intensities with a dimmer switch, and generously illuminate the sink, stove, and other work areas with a mix of lighting types.

Though bulb choice should depend on the kitchen colors you want to emphasize, I am a moth drawn to low-voltage halogen, for its pure intense white light is so easy to work under. From an energy perspective, a compact fluorescent with a rapid-start system is most commendable. Cove lighting, hidden at the top of wall cabinets, adds a dramatic touch to kitchens without a soffit. Downlight cans do an excellent job of general lighting, but a parabolic ceiling is much more dramatic. In all cases I'd add some track or cable lighting for the amusing sophisticated sensibility these stunning fixtures bring to the design of a room. Which fixtures you choose depends primarily on individual taste, so spend time pondering catalogs and then have all potential choices reviewed by an expert to be sure you don't end up working in shadows or glare.

KITCHENSPEAK: LIGHTING

Accent Lighting: A focal point achieved by increasing the intensity of the lamp to three times that of any neighboring light.

Grazing: Accenting the texture of a wall with lights installed one foot away.

Washing: Accenting a wall by expanding the space visually with floodlights that are mounted three to four feet away.

Ambient Lighting: The number, type, and intensity of lights that are set to create a particular mood.

Cool-Beam Bulbs: A type of incandescent bulb that produces less heat than is typical for these lamps.

Cove Lighting: Indirect lighting that is hidden behind a curved concave molding built above wall cabinets that are open to the ceiling.

E-Lamp: A new energy-efficient electronic bulb that can be substituted for a standard incandescent bulb.

Fluorescent Lamp: A glass tube coated with phosphorus that glows when it is bombarded by an electric beam passing through its vaporized mercury-filled interior.

Foot-candles: The amount of light—or lumens—that actually reaches an object. See also Lumens.

Glare: An excessive contrast of brightness.

Halogen Lamp: A small intense incandescent lamp that is filled with halogen gas.

Incandescent Lamp: The standard household bulb that produces light by passing an electric current through a tungsten filament.

Kelvin: The color of each light source is expressed in temperatures or degrees Kelvin. Incandescent bulbs fall into the low temperature zone under three thousand degrees Kelvin, halogen and warm fluorescents in the middle at three thousand to four thousand degrees, and cool fluorescents above four thousand degrees.

Lamp: The common pear-shaped general-service incandescent bulb.

Low Voltage: A lighting system that operates on 12 volts after being stepped down from the normal household 120 volts by a transformer.

Lumens: The amount of actual light a bulb gives off regardless of its wattage.

Luminaires: Another word for fixtures.

Luminous Ceilings: A diffused even layer of light provided by acrylic panels, decorative glass, or metallized louvers (parabolic ceiling).

PAR (Parabolic Aluminum Reflector) Lamp: Floods that possess four times the light of an A lamp as well as a more controllable beam. When a dichroic coating is placed on these lamps, it allows different colors to be filtered out.

Parabolic Ceiling: See Luminous Ceilings.

Pendant Lights: A single—or multiple—fixture that hangs from the ceiling on a chain or cord and is cloaked in an opaque shade to mask glare.

Recessed Cans: Downlights that are mounted in the ceiling and fitted with different trims and interior linings that dictate the dispersion of light.

R Lamp: Reflective bulbs that throw a great deal of light on a subject.

Floodlight: A frosted R Lamp bulb with a wide beam.

Spotlight: A clear R Lamp bulb with a small narrow beam.

Valence: A board built over a lamp source to provide indirect lighting.

Xenon: A gas used in some incandescent lamps that provides a very white color.

WINDOWS: A NATURAL ACT

■

Choosing a window is as much about what—and whom—you want to keep out as it is about which elements you want to let in. This varies according to season, window exposure, time of day, and local climatic conditions, making the ultimate formula more than a bit tricky to balance.

Heat and light are universally welcomed through the panes in winter as long as they leave cold air in the firmament. In the summer, natural nonglaring light comforts with its caress, but heat glows *persona non grata.*

Opening the windows to chase out hot stale air blows in unwanted creatures along with fresh breezes. Screening the windows thwarts the vermin but obscures the view. If one of these parameters gets out of whack, a kitchen can seem more like a sauna or deep freeze. What's a person to do?

Windows are intrinsic to the sense of well-being a family experiences while cooking and dining. Yet,

after making the millions of decisions a kitchen remodel demands, few people have energy left to deal with them. Believing you can always flick a switch if there is not enough light, they turn window choice over to designers, who rarely concern themselves with anything beyond shape.

Unversed in the priorities of a kitchen at the time of my remodel, I was one of those consumers who delegated window solutions to my architect and contractor. Imbued with this responsibility, they replaced a small slit that kept the room mean and cold all year with a skylight and windows that made it unbearably hot. Anyone who dares to enter this room during summer meets the same fate as Icarus. Consequently, you will find me rabid about the importance of choosing windows possessing the climate-controlling parameters described here.

As with other important kitchen decisions, review your choice and intended location with several experts. Before purchasing, consult with different dealers in the neighborhood who are familiar with the inclement elements you'll be encountering.

What style window?

With all my emphasis on acquiring the right window for a particular weather condition, I'm no less concerned about window dressing. A dramatic window can transform a bland kitchen into an exciting dynamic stage where a light show dances across surfaces with streamers of transparent beams.

Window shape may well be dictated by other people if you live in an apartment, co-op building, or historic landmark, but regardless of who makes this selection, the form should be consistent with the building's other apertures, preserving the harmony of the exterior. Architecturally, windows bestow integrity on a home.

Employing any component that strikes your fancy, the most winsome windows are a combination of fixed and operable units in an original configuration, the proportion of panels that open depending on the amount of fresh air sought. With many, many standard windows to choose from, a design can be pulled off the shelf without the expense of a custom production. When you are replacing an old window with a new stock item, filler strips may, however, be necessary for a tight fit. No matter what type of window is selected, a curved arched top gathers more light.

WINDOW WALL
This glass wall runs across the back of my own kitchen, bringing the garden into the house. See-through cabinets, suspended from the soffit, are hung over part of the wall, with a slider window within a fixed frame marking the center of it.

WINDOWS ON THE KITCHEN WORLD

A combination of fixed and movable windows creates distinctive sculptural shapes that define the character of a space while infusing the room with magical light and air. These rectangular apertures, some stationary and some double hung, echo the L shape of the kitchen *(top)*. Capped with a custom arch, this beautiful window wall has two casement windows in its bottom row that open to admit air *(center left)*. The casement windows in this kitchen are crowned with a fixed elliptical arch that augments the light entering the room *(center right)*. Fixed windows come in every imaginable shape to be used by themselves or grouped into an inventive artful design *(above)*. Adding a magical glow to the dining area, these double-hung windows *(right)* are divided into panes (lights) by muntins (perpendicular wood dividers), which replicate those used in colonial America.

Fixed windows come in rounds, ellipses, ovals, octagons, hexagons, pentagons, parallelograms, triangles, and trapezoids—a plethora of sizes and shapes that should do Pythagoras proud. They can be hung either in vertical *stacks* or in horizontal *ribbons*.

Taking windows to the max for a kitchen with a view are the seamless picture window that wraps around a ninety-degree corner without an intrusive supporting strut and the linear *variant* window that can form a backsplash or entire wall, where cabinets can be affixed (with an engineer's assistance).

With fewer and less interesting forms, the most common operable windows are *casement, slider, jalousie, double-hung,* and *awning* (opens out; hinged top or bottom)/*hopper* (opens in; hinged bottom) styles. Operable windows are harder to seal than fixed, with sliders hanging loosest. Least expensive,

TILT-DOWN MAN
These double-hung windows open up from the bottom and fold down into the room for cleaning.

the latter windows are also least appealing, for their central post obscures the view, and their track is a dirt catcher. When small, they can be hard to get through, a deterrent to chubby burglars.

At the other extreme, casement and awning/hopper windows fit snuggest. Crank or hardware-operated, these two types are also the easiest to reach above a countertop. For more facile operation, choose long *easy-grip* cranks and look for hardware attachments that can be cleaned readily.

If windows open out onto a walkway where approaching visitors aren't visible, a double-hung window is safer than a casement or awning type. Though harder to get purchase on when standing in front of a countertop, they are less likely to fell a passerby. Tilt/turn models that pivot in their frames can be folded down into the room, making it no big deal to admit you do "do windows."

Another crank-operated window, jalousies have narrow horizontal glass slats that open and close simultaneously. Offering security as well as obscurity, they are often employed in restaurants hungry for the fresh air and shade they provide. With more pieces than a Waldo puzzle, these are windows you don't do—at least not happily. With many exits for heat to escape, they are not a good cold-climate choice, either. Generally produced from aluminum, a chrome or stainless frame and sandblasted glass transform plain-Jane jalousies into contemporary sculpture.

Some windows can be either fixed or operable. Providing privacy while admitting gobs of light, handsome *clerestory* windows march along the top of the wall to the roof line in the space often claimed by a soffit. When operable, they act as a natural air conditioner, dispensing heat as it rises to the ceiling.

A *bow* window curves, and a *bay* projects beyond the house with side windows angled from thirty to ninety degrees. This found space can be usurped for a dining area and fitted with a window seat that has storage below, or it can be garnered for a greenhouse (page 88).

Bows and bays, like casements, can have clear panes or be divided French style into individual square or rectangular *lights* (panes) with *muntins.*

Traditionally a grid, muntins can assume any form, adding yet one more charming aspect to a kitchen. In the days when fine craftspeople roamed the land, dividers were built permanently into the frame. Still constructed that way, they appear more commonly as a vinyl or wood grill that snaps on—or off—for cleaning and painting. Though of much lesser quality, the snap-ons are also one-third the price, a draw to those for whom the dollar is decision maker. Snap-on muntins appear more authentic when they go on both the exterior and the interior of the window and have no gaps between them.

Do you want a skylight or roof window?

While windows are housed on walls that could be used for storage, skylights and roof windows voluntarily assume a purposeless space, an asset in tight kitchens. They also provide three times the light of a wall-mounted window. The terms *skylight* and *roof window* are used interchangeably, but some distinction can be made between them. A *roof window* can be reached easily through an attic and operates as any window, although those that pivot 180 degrees don't accept screens.

Moving up eye-to-eye with Jack of beanstalk fame, a *skylight* is an aperture high in the roof. It can be closed permanently, fitted with a ventilation flap, or, for an upcharge that can run 40 percent, be operable to varying specific degrees.

One other *minor* point: To install a skylight, as both windows shall henceforth be known, you need a roof or attic directly over the kitchen. After that, the decision hinges on whether you want to incur its expense and you can curtail the excess glare, heat, chill, and drafts that ride on its light waves.

As long as other operable windows exist in the kitchen, it is probably not as important that a skylight open as that it have a retractable screen, shade, venetian blind, or awning on the exterior to halt unwelcome elements before they enter. Merrill Shindler's shade was on permanent "close," for the sun coming through his skylight was perfectly poised to rot the food in his glass-fronted refrigerator.

An insulating interior shade, treated with a protective coating on the window-facing side, can be pulled on wintry nights to prevent heat gathered during the day from escaping. You may also want to leave an opening in the frame for a storm window to be inserted in winter. In one especially clever custom design, a skylight covered with a redwood shutter operates like a sliding door.

Skylight coverings—and operable skylights—can be controlled long distance with manual or motorized extension rods or a remote-control pad. Some include a rain sensor that closes the skylight automatically when heavens burst.

The method of weather control should be decided at the same time as the type and configuration of the skylight. Retrofitting a covering will be makeshift at best, leaving no possibilities for hiding the ugly tracks and hardware in the skylight's frame or light well.

Conducting light from a pitched roof or attic to a skylight installed in a flat ceiling, a light well's shape affects the splay of light, with a flare (and white color) spreading it farthest.

A single skylight can be either a flat panel or a domed bubble. More obtrusive, the latter is somewhat self-cleaning with the help of rain and good for sloughing off snow. Single skylights can be ganged for a larger covering or fashioned into a peaked or barrel-vaulted pyramid, polygon, or rectangle with multiple sections.

Available in any dimension, a kitchen skylight is often specced at 10 percent of floor space. A more practical guideline is the intensity of light and heat received at the intended location. For easiest installation, a skylight's measurements should correspond to the distance between roof trusses or rafters.

What type of skylight is used will depend on the slope of the roof and its materials. The flatter the roof, the larger, more obtrusive the skylight's curb must be for water to run off it. Frames must all have some insulation so they don't conduct heat or cold and a gutter for collecting and holding moisture until it evaporates.

ROOF WINDOWS
These stationary, venting and vent/tilt roof windows (that can be folded down into the room for cleaning) can all be used on the ceiling. The rectangular opening, inauspicious by itself, is transformed into high drama when enlarged and ganged in multiples. The round window plays out the sculptural effect.

GLASS BLOCK
By installing glass block or another type of window in the backsplash, valuable kitchen wall space is freed for cabinets (*above*).

ART GLASS
Stained or leaded architectural glass (*above right*) brings artwork into a kitchen, emphasizing its historic antecedents.

WINDOW DRESSING
Roof windows are used once again to theatrical effect on a cantilevered wall in a dining area (*right*). Fitted with manual or remote electric-operated venetian blinds, these sunscreens are ready for any vagaries in the weather. Just be sure that any skylight, roof window—or any window—has the proper glazing to balance the heat and chill streaming through.

What type of window frame do you want?

In my mind's traditional eye, windows can be only wood, for they denote quality and character, particularly if constructed with mortise-and-tenon joinery. From the standpoint of upkeep and expense, however, there are many reasons to go to vinyl or aluminum, particularly in a high-rise building or skylight, where the windows are not all that visible from outside, or when drapes will be continually drawn over them.

Wood frames are generally joined from ponderosa pine or Douglas fir, though oak or other expensive woods can be used. Thicker frames are better quality. Available primed or raw with thermal insulating properties, they do not conduct heat or cold from outside into the home. They do, however, expand and contract, getting stuck in their frames, and must be repaired and repainted frequently. Otherwise they can split, crack, or rot. As paint layers build up, windows stick. Sanding takes down edges and corners, leaving gaps and cracks for wind to whistle through. (Did I say I liked wood windows?)

One compromise has been to protect the exterior of a wood window with an aluminum or vinyl *cladding.* Cladding colors are generally limited to the tan, white, and gray families. These windows are costly, with a heavy-gauge extruded cladding better than one that is rolled. Since you still have to deal with the wood inside the home, my sense is that it's better to commit yourself to one material or another and accept its inherent problems.

Less expensive than wood, neither aluminum nor vinyl frames require much maintenance. Thin aluminum can dent, but it neither rusts, peels, flakes, nor suffers termite invasions. Sashes don't stick, and scratches don't show because its wide range of anodized colors go all the way through.

Though their technology has improved, vinyl is not recommended for extreme cold, where frames can crack. Easy to produce, they do offer the best chance of getting a correctly sized replacement window. Better ones have fuse-welded corners without nails and thicker members in the 2.33-millimeter range.

Aluminum is superior to vinyl at reducing the amount of air filtering through the window and leaking around it when, inevitably, it cracks around the joints. Its downfall is in conducting heat and cold more readily. Inserting thermal breaks between the window's exterior and interior, many companies are able to reduce temperature transfer and prevent condensation from forming.

With all this talk about aesthetics, it's all the stranger that window hardware is so universally ugly. This is puzzling in view of the handsome drawer pulls available. Is somebody listening? For any windows beyond your reach, choose *reciprocal* hardware that can be opened with a long pole.

What type of glazing do you want?

Regardless of frame material, a window's transparent *glazing* can be either plastic or glass. Plastic scratches, discolors or distorts, expands and contracts, and is more expensive than glass. On the plus side, its lighter weight commends it for a skylight, while its impact resistance discourages burglars. Among plastic materials, acrylic has the best clarity and is less expensive than polycarbonate; the latter excels in impact resistance.

Window glass can be clear or sandblasted with designs or pictures. If you select sandblasted glass, be sure that it is truly sandblasted, not treated with an impossible-to-clean impostor. A new miracle *privacy* glass switches from clear to frosted using liquid crystal technology. Leaded, stained, or what is called *art, decorative,* or *architectural* glass can be used as well.

Cracking and shattering rather than breaking outright, *tempered* glass, the new lightweight Sentry-Glas, and *laminated* glass (glass bonded to plastic) are safest for the kitchen. (With enough layers, laminated glass can be bulletproof.) To prevent glass from breaking into shards, apply clear and tinted safety coatings.

A frame and glazing in one, glass block (page 186) is a relatively inexpensive alternative for a kitchen window. Depending on its design, it admits varying amounts of heat and light. In hot regions, a reflective coating or fiberglass insert is needed to derail the heat; in cold, protection against condensation. Mortar in the block's grid also deflects the heat while sealing the window against dust, air infiltration, and break-ins. Generally inoperable, glass block can also be obtained with screened vents.

What should glazing composition be?

With climatic conditions varying from day to day or, as it seems, minute to minute, locating a window on a wall receiving optimum exposure (page 75) is only a partial solution to regulating the amount of heat and light transmitted. For climatic comfort, consider the following factors before settling on a glazing's composition. Expensive additions, they can't be retrofitted, so weigh them wisely. Find out how a window will look with a particular fitting both during the day and at night, or you may find yourself looking up to see the beautiful stars and find a shiny blue or bronze mirror looking back down at you.

The simplest deterrent to the sun's rays and glare is tinted bronze or gray single-pane glass. But, rain or shine, your window will always be bronze or gray. More natural in appearance, lightly tinted films can be applied to the glass to block ultraviolet light that fades fabric and materials. Eventually these bubble and peel.

A more permanent solution, insulated or *thermalized* multilayered panes are the psychiatrists of windows, preventing transference of heat and light while saving on air-conditioning costs. Be sure foam, chemicals, or another method deters moisture collection and condensation.

Double-glazed windows consist of two panes sealed together with one-fourth to one-half inch of airspace in between them. Measuring three-quarters to one inch thick overall, they reduce heat passage to half that of a single-pane window. Glass block offers similar protection.

Some double-glazed windows allow one pane to be removed temporarily and a shade or blind to be secured in the middle, but the seal is not as tight. A shade collects more dust on the outside of the window, but I'd rather have it there to admire the texture of its fabric.

A *triple-glazed* window contains three panes with one-fourth to one-half inch of airspace in between and ups heat blockage to 65 percent. Rather than a costly triple-glazed window, general consensus gives the nod to a double-glazed window with a storm window added in winter. Storms (and screens) are easiest to take on and off when they are fitted to the window's interior.

Reflecting heat back toward its point of origin, a *low-E* (emissivity) coating is another way to improve the insulation of a double-pane window. The ultimate gatekeeper, it blocks out summer rays, while preventing heat from escaping during winter. A thin metal film, sprayed-on *soft coat*, is more successful than the baked-on *hard coat* in its ministerings. Almost clear, it is also less intrusive visually. A third type, *heat mirror*, a coated plastic film available in different strengths, is inserted between the panes.

To boost the protective power of a *low-E* coating by a third, the airspaces of a double- or triple-glazed window are filled with *argon* or the more efficient *krypton gas*.

Pirouetting up through the alphabet, a *low-I* window increases heat gain. Minus the iron oxides that absorb heat, these glazings allow 10 to 15 percent more of the sun's energy to pass through.

How are a window's glazings rated?

A window's properties have long been evaluated by various groups for comparing energy efficiency, but, like the five blind men, they were all rating different parts of the elephant. In 1989, the National Fenestration Rating Council was formed to establish energy standards nationwide that could be measured by independent testing laboratories. Look for their seal listing a window's U-value. When comparing other ratings, check that they were compiled by the same organization.

The *U-value* or measure of heat flow through a window describes the energy efficiency of the entire window—frame, glazing, sash, et al. It is expressed in Btus. Look for ratings here under .5, indicating lower—less—heat movement through a window.

An *R-value* measures the insulation of a window and its glazing's ability to minimize heat flow and condensation. A higher number, indicating more insulation, is desirable with this rating. Generally a single-glazed window will rate R-1, double-glazed R-2 to 2.5, and triple-glazed R-3.5; a low-E coating will rate R-4 to 4.5. Some new trademarked *Superglass* windows with multiple coatings are topping out at R-8 and R-9.

A *shading coefficient* measures the amount of heat gain through a window above the temperature reading outside. Numbers less than .7 indicate low heat gain.

UV blockage is the percentage of ultraviolet rays prevented from crossing that glazing border.

Light transmittance corresponds to the clarity of the glazing. A window that looks clear will have a visibility rating of 60 percent or more, while tinted glass checks in at 5 to 45 percent.

Essentially measuring the glazings fit in the frame, *air leakage infiltration* is the cubic feet per minute (cfm) of air that passes through the window. A tight fit runs .01 and .02; loose over .5.

Solar heat gain factor (SHGF) measures how much of the sun's energy is getting inside. Running from .8 to 1, the greater number indicates a larger percentage. Tax rebates are often available for windows with high passive solar ratings.

Resistance to condensation goes up with a higher *condensation resistance factor* (CRF) number.

Sound transmission class (STC) ratings measure a window's ability to block out street noises. If the motorcycles are rumbling, look for a rating of 32 or more. Helping to run the numbers, laminated glass and low-E coatings with heat mirror also conspire against noise transmission.

In sunny climes, you want low shading coefficients and the protection proffered by low-E coatings, perhaps with argon- or krypton-gas-filled interiors. Low-E^2 panes from Cardinal Glass are good aids in fighting heat gain, particularly in skylights and hot climates.

Higher shading coefficients, solar heat gain factors, and R-values are sought in cooler climates and in windows with a northern exposure that you might want to face from behind a Superglass. To reach a happy medium where extremes of weather conditions exist, aid whatever window you choose with a window covering in summer and insulated drapes or shutters in winter.

High visible light transmittance, high security, and resistance to condensation and ultraviolet light are desirable in all environments. Low-E coatings prevent fading. Tinted glass and films do so as well but not without decreasing visible light. To discourage break-ins, some windows now lock automatically when closed, while others can be kept locked even while providing ventilation. A pocketed sill has been developed that is harder to crack than one that is flat.

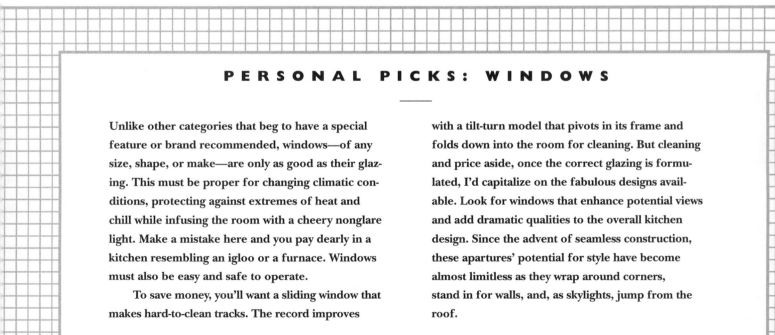

PERSONAL PICKS: WINDOWS

Unlike other categories that beg to have a special feature or brand recommended, windows—of any size, shape, or make—are only as good as their glazing. This must be proper for changing climatic conditions, protecting against extremes of heat and chill while infusing the room with a cheery nonglare light. Make a mistake here and you pay dearly in a kitchen resembling an igloo or a furnace. Windows must also be easy and safe to operate.

To save money, you'll want a sliding window that makes hard-to-clean tracks. The record improves with a tilt-turn model that pivots in its frame and folds down into the room for cleaning. But cleaning and price aside, once the correct glazing is formulated, I'd capitalize on the fabulous designs available. Look for windows that enhance potential views and add dramatic qualities to the overall kitchen design. Since the advent of seamless construction, these apertures' potential for style have become almost limitless as they wrap around corners, stand in for walls, and, as skylights, jump from the roof.

Awning: A window that is hinged on either its top or bottom and opens out.

Bay: A single window or series of windows that projects out beyond the exterior of the house with side windows angled from thirty to ninety degrees. A *sun bay* admits light through its top as well as its three sides.

Bow: A single window or series of windows that forms a curve, projecting out beyond the exterior of the house.

Casement: A window that is hinged on the side and opens inward or outward with hardware or a crank.

Cladding: An aluminum or vinyl covering that is placed over the exterior of a wood window to protect it against weather damage.

Clerestory: Windows placed in the top of the wall just below the ceiling in the space often claimed by a soffit.

Double-Glazed: Two panes sealed together with one-fourth to one-half inch of airspace in between them. A *triple-glazed* window has three panes.

Double-Hung: A window with two sashes where both the top and bottom move up and down to open. In a single-hung window only the top or bottom part opens.

Fixed Window: A window that does not open.

Glazing: The glass or plastic installed in a window frame.

Greenhouse: A bay window or sun bay for housing plants that is often fitted with electricity for fluorescent tubes or mercury-vapor grow lights.

Hopper: A window that is hinged on the bottom and opens in.

Jalousie: A window that consists of narrow individual horizontal glass slats that open and close simultaneously with a crank.

Laminated Glass: A safety glazing consisting of glass bonded to plastic.

Lights: Individual windowpanes.

Low-E (emissivity): An insulation coating on the glazing that reflects heat back to its point of origin.

Low-I (iron oxide): A glazing that increases heat gain.

Muntins: The grid that divides a window into individual panes.

Privacy Glass: A glazing that switches from a clear to a frosted coating by using liquid crystal technology.

Roof Window: Though the term *roof window* is often used interchangeably with *skylight,* this aperture differs from many skylights in that it is easily reached through an attic and operates like any window.

Safety Coating: A protective layer that can be applied to a glass glazing to prevent it from breaking into shards.

Skylight: An aperture high in the roof that is covered with a flat panel or domed bubble.

Slider: Two windows that are divided by a post and move back and forth in a track.

Tempered Glass: A protective safety glazing that is treated so it cracks and shatters rather than breaking outright.

Tilt/Turn: A window that pivots in its frame and can be folded down into the room for cleaning.

U-Value: The measure of heat flow through a window, describing the energy efficiency of the entire window—frame, glazing, sash, et al. It is expressed in Btus. Look for ratings under .5.

BASIC PROPS, TOOLS, AND APPLIANCES

7
COOKERS

COOKTOPS, OVENS, AND RANGES

■

A good stove handles like a high-performance automobile. Starting and stopping with the flick of a wrist, its cooktop shifts speedily from slow (a low simmer) to fast (an ebullient boil) and roars into steady cruise control humming. Facilely it maneuvers delicate transition roads, caramelizing onions with nary a scorch and thickening custard before the curds attack. Cooktop burners cushion different-size skillets much as car seats buttress drivers of varying shapes, regardless of whether they (pots or people) have seen better days.

Dream on. Drive on. Today's stoves are still pretty much in first gear. Unless consumers are willing to spend the price of a car—and that's neither a guarantee nor a realistic, reasonable expectation—a cook had better forget the stove and settle for a copy of *Manifold Destiny: The One! The Only! Guide to Cooking on Your Car Engine* by Chris Maynard and Bill Scheller. The market is saturated with terrible stoves seemingly designed for people who eat out, a condition not due to lack of technology.

Stoves boast transformers, transistors, thermistors, and thermostats, but cooktop burners heat up so slowly that food grows faster than it cooks. We harness electromagnetic energy while watching pots wobble on flimsy grates. A remote-control panel exists to turn a cooktop on from anyplace in the world but not burners large enough to hold a skillet sized for sautéing four chicken breasts.

We can conduct, induct, convect, radiate, and zap, but few ovens brown a cake evenly. Full or half-on ovens convection-conduction-microwave-bake-and-broil in any combination, but they are so complicated that a professor friend with a chair at Stanford hasn't figured out how to change the temperature in his wall oven without first turning it off.

And, after multiple viewings of the accompanying instruction video, he still managed to self-clean a salmon.

Several explanations account for the discrepancy between our sophisticated technology and the impractical cookers that greet us at the end of a long, exhausting day. Particularly irksome is the predominant attitude loose in stoveland: the conventional wisdom, if you will, that substantial heat is something only the *gourmet* cook (whatever or whoever that is) desires. Do you have to be a gourmet cook to want pasta water to boil quickly; to prefer a high-heat broiler that sears a steak to the typical low-heat rods that stew it? C'mon.

Other problems include the lack of coordination among the manufacturers of stoves, stove components, and cookware, the poor understanding fabricators have of cooking techniques, and their lack of communication with the consumer. Energy and safety considerations further cloud these terrains.

Burners originating in Europe are geared to cookware and culinary habits prevalent abroad. The largest burners offered in the German-made smooth-top cooktops, for example, are oval. Pots with this shape, favored *über alles* in the Rhineland, are not readily available here. Since these cooktops work only with pots that correspond to burner shape, they aren't exactly geared for our kitchens, where they sit, slick, and handsome, to be sure, but useless. And yet they are widely promoted and sold for the American dream.

Companies producing burners for stove manufacturers claim they can make their heat ports larger with higher, on-the-dime-responsive watts or British thermal units (Btus) but nobody wants them. Utility companies balk at their approval for fear they won't be insulated and fireproofed properly in the home. And while these regulators underestimate consumers' ability to assume this responsibility, they themselves are skittish about dealing with lots of heat.

Typical is the supposedly sophisticated saleswoman for one stove company who confesses to finding the high-heat burner she "once tried" in a restaurant range overwhelming. "There was too much heat in my face," she explains, "I felt I couldn't control it." With attitudes like this among people selling us stoves, it's not surprising what we're stuck with.

Feeling comfortable with a substantial amount of heat is largely a matter of experience and education. If only manufacturers could provide them. Rather than lowering the heat in a white cooktop as one brand did, limiting the capacity of the unit to solve a discoloration problem, the company should have educated its customers about this shortcoming.

Please, manufacturers, don't give us an inferior product in the name of fashion and aesthetics. Inform us. Talk to us. Tell us why white is not a viable color for a cooktop. Give us simple stoves that work at reasonable, affordable prices.

Without a doubt, many people stay out of the kitchen today because they can't stand the heat. Cooktops and, to a lesser degree, ovens are so unresponsive that they turn the sensual pleasures of cooking into a dreadful chore. Stephanie Miller finds a cooktop irrelevant because she doesn't like to cook. Yet she, of anyone, should have the best unit on the market for it can transform the task she dislikes into something less odious.

Of all the money-gobbling kitchen appliances,

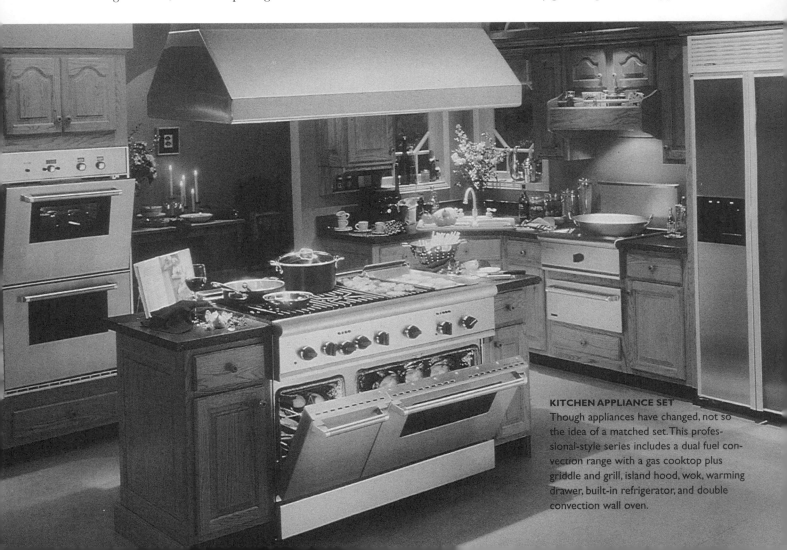

KITCHEN APPLIANCE SET
Though appliances have changed, not so the idea of a matched set. This professional-style series includes a dual fuel convection range with a gas cooktop plus griddle and grill, island hood, wok, warming drawer, built-in refrigerator, and double convection wall oven.

the cooktop is the one item worth spending as much on as you can afford, for its payback in terms of value, quality, and function can single-handedly orchestrate the ease of kitchen operation. Yet a high price doesn't automatically guarantee a great stove.

Many of the new high-end cookers have more to do with trends than with food; with slick forms, buzz-words, and bandwagons than with the high-heat, practical configuration, and quick response time that constitute a good cooktop. Where to spend your hard-earned money has to be carefully considered and based on educated comparison.

Before deciding what you want after shopping and sorting through the following information, find out if the ancient stove you have can be refurbished, for many old pieces are constructed more solidly and user-friendly than what's touted as new. Check the yellow pages, too, to see if a local company sells renovated antique ranges. New or old, reckon whether you want a unit that can be pulled out and moved with you to a new abode.

Do you want a range or separate cooktop and oven?

Once limited to "Which freestanding range?" choice among cookers today has escalated to thousands of models. The most flexible option? Separate cook-tops and ovens that allow a cook to better tailor con-figuration, number, and placement to individual needs. You can purchase a large six-burner cooktop with a small oven, two large ovens with one four-burner cooktop, or several two-burner cooktops scat-tered throughout the kitchen.

Multiple placements provide elbow room when more than one cook or cooking area exists. In a large kitchen, it may prove more practical to situate a cooktop between a sink and refrigerator; an oven elsewhere with baking gear. If the cooktop is used almost exclusively, the area below might be better reserved for pot storage than for the oven. Buttress-ing this argument, it is easier to load/unload a waist-high wall oven and to work over a cooktop when you're not blasted with oven heat from below.

Divorcing the cooktop from the oven gives you better odds at getting what you want in each piece.

This dissolution proves so practical that I advise it even when the oven must be installed directly below the cooktop in an island, a small galley kitchen, or a home where heat-producing equipment shares a ventilation system or is safely ensconced in a group far from children. Despite my glowing recommenda-tion for separating cooktop and oven, there are sev-eral compelling arguments for a two-in-one range:

The price: A range is much less expensive than a separate cooktop and oven, particularly when the costs of specialized cabinets, multiple hookup cir-cuitry, and additional ventilation are factored in.

Pollution: If you broil in the oven or roast spat-tering ducks and geese, and don't want two separate ventilation systems, the oven can be ventilated opti-mally under the cooktop, even if it is a separate unit.

The look: Stylistically, today's cookers go to two extremes, varying from oversized ranges that could be mistaken for the hulk at Universal Studios to slim, thin built-in cooktops and ovens with the svelte pro-files of the x-ray women in Tom Wolfe's *Bonfire of the Vanities.* If you want a hulk, you're not going to be sat-isfied with separates that disappear into the cabinetry.

Speaking of looks scrolls up *finish,* in addition to size and shape. Personal preference dictates the choice among stainless, glass, and porcelain (a baked-on epoxy powder *paint* currently in white, black, or almond with a few wild rides on the red, burgundy, or teal side). Porcelain chips and stains, glass scratches and stains, and stainless scratches as well as dents.

The verdict: Upkeep on all stoves is a hassle. I'd choose the more durable stainless finish, upcharge or not, for the patina it develops as it ages. Given the telltale wear and tear cookers get, it would behoove manufacturers to provide pickup and delivery and make refinishing a cinch.

Do you prefer gas or electricity as the source of cooking fuel?

Whether you're stir-frying over high heat or simmer-ing over a low setting, the cooking process is stream-lined by a responsive, efficient burner that goes instantly from low to high and on to off without main-taining residual heat. Since this is the description of gas cookery, it is clearly the fuel of preference for cooktops. And it costs half the price of electricity to run. The visible flame of a gas burner frightens many people, making electricity appear safer. Why, I don't know, for it is easier to get burned on an electric grate that doesn't glow red when it is on than on a flame you can see. A less efficient electric burner requires pots to be the same diameter and flat on the bottom. With an adjustable flame, gas burners accommodate pots of most any size or condition—even warped bent souvenirs from an early first marriage.

Influenced by trends from Europe, consumers are increasingly choosing to buy both gas and electric cooktop modules, or *hobs* as they are called across the sea, without recognizing this practice abroad as a security measure: one day the gas works, the next day electricity.

There is also a misconception that electric burners are better for simmering or long slow cooking than gas, when, in fact, this depends on a particular burner's design and the *amount* of heat, not the type of fuel. No ambivalence. Gas is the best heat for a cooktop.

Determining whether gas or electricity is preferable for an oven is less clear-out. Some bakers report that an electric oven is more uniform, particularly if it has an upper and a lower burner element. Others report the same result with a gas oven. It all depends on who is doing the reporting (and on the oven). To see what camp you fall in before purchasing, put an oven through its paces at a kitchen store or distributor's warehouse.

Repairman Scott Cox feels a gas oven heats more evenly, while an electric has hot spots alleviated by convection. Things burn more readily on the bottom shelf of an electric oven. More insulated, it also dries the food.

Fearful of burns from its minimal insulation, some states don't allow below-counter installation of a gas oven. In most cases this is an overreaction. Where it is allowed, test the gas oven beforehand to see how hot its door gets.

An oven's heat source is not as important as its insulation, configuration, heating pattern, and, most important, its broiler (page 239). A plus for gas: its flame absorbs smoke, making broiling smokeless and conductible with the oven door closed.

Responding to the conventional wisdom that the best results derive from gas cooktops and electric ovens, some companies have recently introduced *dual-fuel* units. Again, this is conventional wisdom, not necessarily reality they are responding to. When you make your selection, base it primarily on the quality of the cooktop and broiler.

Whether electricity is preferred becomes a moot issue when gas is unavailable or it becomes too costly to pipe in natural gas or obtain liquid petroleum gas in tanks or bottles. Not all gas appliances work on both types of gas, either, so check beforehand.

Electricity may also be more satisfying in an apartment or other situation that does not allow the ventilation necessary for eliminating the by-products of gas combustion. If you do end up with gas, you still need an electric line to run a gas unit with a clock or a light. Grills and griddles on gas cooktops are often fueled by electricity, too.

Responding to environmental demands, electronic ignitions have replaced standing pilots in most gas units. These break down readily, short out from spills, turn on with an annoying click, and don't work in electric blackouts. Pluses? Without continual heat, the kitchen is cooler and energy consumption cut by 30 percent.

I'm going to look first at cooktops and ovens separately and then at the two united in a range. Most of what is said about individual units is applicable to evaluating their combined force.

COOKTOPS

The cooktop has become ever more important in our quest for speed and convenience. Always in a rush, we can cook more quickly on top of the stove than we can in an oven. As the source of heat for a wok, steamer, fish poacher, and stove-top grill, the cooktop is home to the tools that enable us to prepare food in the healthiest manner. When tackling only a single dish or two, we use less energy cooking on a burner than in an almost-empty oven.

How large should the cooktop be?

When a stockpot, spaghetti cooker, eleven-inch skillet, *tagine, couscousière,* and canning kettle are added to the equipment lineup already described, the cooktop can be confused with the zoo. To host this *batterie de cuisine,* you will need as many large burners as your countertop permits.

Cooktops, constructed with or without a backsplash panel, are generally thirty or thirty-six inches wide and designed to fit into a standard twenty-four-inch-deep counter. Many run less than three inches thick. They also run thicker, shallower, deeper, narrower, shorter, and wider (forty-eight inches or so). Or you can go cooktopless and compose your own working surface out of modules in twelve-, fifteen-, and twenty-four-inch lengths. Some modules come with covers to hide them when not in use, but it is the covers that should be hidden.

The size of the cooktop is not as important as the number of its burners, their dimension, and configuration. A standard cooktop contains four burners, but five, six, and eight are also available. If you are not buying a replacement cooktop that ties you to a particular countertop cutout size, seriously entertain the idea of six burners: no more juggling three large pots simultaneously.

When more than one cook is stirring away, consider installing one four-burner and another two-burner cooktop in separate labyrinths of the kitchen, an arrangement that, unfortunately, necessitates multiple ventilation. *What makes no sense is wasting counter space with the thirty-six-inch cooktop that holds the same four burners (same size, same shape, same power) offered on a thirty-inch top.*

How are burners best arranged?

The most practical cooking arrangement is a line of single burners strung out horizontally. With space in between units, each burner is fully usable so an adequate cooktop can be formed with merely four burners. There are no hot pots to reach over, and the elongated space is large enough for two people to cook side by side. Single burners are, unfortunately,

less available than they were in the past, and few kitchens have sufficient counter space for welcoming them.

A more feasible—if less practical—arrangement is a cooktop (or module) with pairs of burners installed one behind the other. With pots sliding easily from front to back, two burners can support large pans such as roasters on the gravy train. When attached, check that these burners aren't too heavy to lift out for cleaning.

An alternate cooktop configuration is one with staggered burners. The advantage here is that you can reach each burner directly without leapfrogging over another that may be on. Flexibility disappears with this organization, however, as well as the means of lodging large pots.

When evaluating burner configuration, seek low and high heat capability in both front and back of the cooktop. A low-heat burner is helpful in front for whisking a custard and in back where meat simmers unaided. Stir-frying, deep-frying, and other high-heat cookery proceed safely in front, while sauces merrily reduce unattended on high in back. If a desired cooktop doesn't divide its burners this way, you may be able to convince the company to custom-fit them.

The relationship of burners to cooktop controls also affects performance. While some control panels are independent of the cooktop and can be installed either on the counter or below, or even remoted, the majority are intrinsic to the unit. Look for one suited to your handedness. It should be situated far enough from the burners so it doesn't heat up and clearly marked or backlit to indicate which burner is on from across the room. Controls at horizontal *off* catch dirt faster than those resting vertically. If young children are around, check to see that controls have childproof catches.

Gas Cooktops

Gas is measured in *Btus* with one unit equal to the amount of heat necessary for increasing the temperature of one pound of water by one degree Fahrenheit. Forget the water. What's important to cooks is

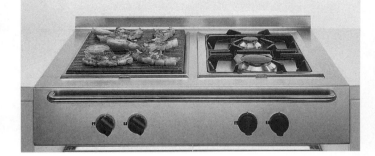

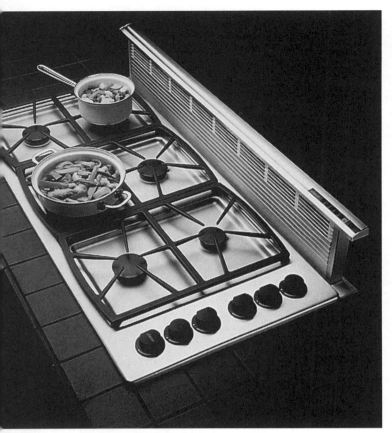

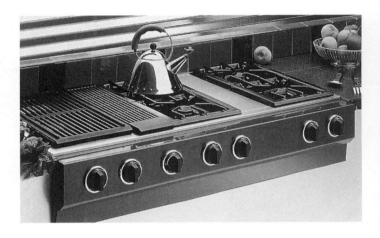

COOKTOP CONFIGURATIONS

Gas burners are most efficient when organized one behind the other to balance large pots, slide smaller ones back and forth, and make gravy in that roaster. What used to be a standard four-burner cooktop is increasingly doubling or becoming a sextuplet. Here six burners go full tilt, three at 12,500 Btus and three at 8,500 Btus *(above)*. Here is a version with four burners and a grill, two of the burners can be interchanged with a wok and griddle *(top right)*. Either two or three two-burner gas or electric modules can be chosen to slip into this brushed stainless steel cooktop frame *(center right)*. With all these choices a two-burner cooktop may still come in handy when one cook reigns in a mini kitchen, or multiple cooks share a kingdom. Though small, this twin with a zigzag grate packs a walloping 15,000 Btus in each burner *(right)*.

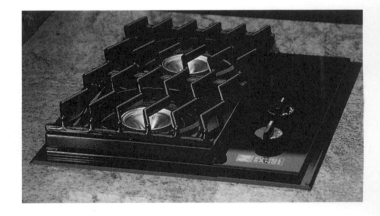

DUEL FUEL RANGE

This contemporary-crafted Duel Fuel Range with electronic controls was designed to be the best of both worlds for cooks partial to a gas cooktop and an electric oven.

Commercial in style, this handsome cooktop rotates around six 14,000 Btu burners that go down to 400 Btus to simmer. The unit is pictured with a thermostatically controlled griddle. A grill can also be ordered.

the amount of heat. Output varies depending on the distance of the flame from the burner grate and the number of ports or slots (openings) in the burner. Generally, the more Btus, the greater the heat and the faster the cooking. Effective burners deliver at least fifteen thousand Btus. More typically, two burners hover at seven thousand Btus, two in the nine thousand range.

There is, however, some play here: As I learned from David Schwartz, a friend with a passion for high-heat Chinese cooking, more power is yours simply by calling the gas company. In our experience, a *complaint* that something is awry brings a cheery repair person who opens the gas orifice to *maximum*.

Gas cooktops differ in their ability to reach and hold a gentle simmer over low heat, a capacity cherished in sauce and custard preparation. Several commercial-style burners reduce to 360 Btus or less, cycling on and off to hold a real simmer. To have this capability involves the position and configuration of the burner as well as its Btus, so check all burners you are considering by melting chocolate on them. If it seizes, a cast-iron *simmer plate* will be needed to diffuse the heat. Companies seem to be simmering along, adding a low range to their burner thermostats, so hopefully this won't be a problem for long.

Gas burners come round or square. When contiguous, the latter shape is more practical for sliding a pot back and forth. Seek solid, stable grates that don't rattle in their cages with prongs geared to cradling both large and small pots. Porcelain-coated cast-iron grates are more responsive than steel ones.

With no escaping flames and 100 percent of its gas focused on a pot, *sealed burners* are more efficient and easier to clean than ones with drip plates. Some cooktops include a *burner with a brain* to maintain a preset temperature. Mine turned out to be a slow learner, so check nimbleness before buying. When *automatic reignition* rules, flames are rekindled after being extinguished by a pot boiling over.

A *grid* fitted over cooktop burners works well for sliding pots as long as wires are close enough together to prevent them from tipping. A similar design replaces individual burners with a continuous *S-shape* or *zigzag grate* that covers the entire cooktop. Once again, this is terrific for playing sliding pots, and you don't have to worry about tipping. But gas dissipates widely in this setup, and flames may creep up around small vessels. The entire cooktop fires up, retaining heat like an electric cooktop. Food continues to cook once it is done unless immediately removed from the surface.

Electric Cooktops

Watts determine the speed and efficiency of an electric cooktop much as Btus affect a gas cooktop. *Voltage* also affects its function: An electric cooktop hooked up to a 240-voltage supply is more responsive than one working off 208 volts.

A four-burner electric cooktop usually has two six-inch burners and two eight-inch burners. A nine-inch and, on rare occasion, eleven-inch burner are sometimes available. Since a pot's diameter must correspond to that of the burner on an electric cooktop, you'll want the largest burners as well as those with greatest wattage. Unfortunately, both are generally insufficient. Look for six-inch burners with a minimum of two thousand watts, eight-inch burners with twenty-six hundred watts, nine-inch burners with thirty-two hundred watts, and eleven-inch burners with thirty-five hundred watts.

When you're limited to electricity, a commercial electric cooktop offers a way to circumvent this utility's restrictive heat. Available in two-burner modules, these units can't be built in and are deeper than a standard countertop, but at fifty-two hundred watts, they are roughly equal to twenty thousand Btus (multiply watts by four for an approximate Btu equivalent).

Electric burners lag in their response to an increase or decrease in heat unless they have *quick* temperature controls. To streamline mealtime preparation, keep one burner on high and another on low, switching pots between them as necessary. Burners retain their heat after being switched off, so food must be removed immediately once it is cooked. To avoid being burned, choose a cooktop whose indicator light stays on while it is in use, as well as in cooldown.

What type of electric burner and cooktop best suit your needs?

There are two main types of electric cooktops: those whose burners protrude above a glass, stainless, or porcelain cooktop and those whose burners hide below what is most commonly a *glass-ceramic smooth top*. Offered in proprietary patterns by most stove manufacturers, these cooktops are inset into a slim two-inch frame and sunk almost flush with the countertop. Busier patterns mask scratches and fingermarks most successfully. Location of the burners, usually two six-inch and two nine-inch elements, is stenciled on the cooktop. A larger *dual-circuit burner* exists on some smooth tops for accommodating two pans of different sizes. Some smooth-top control panels include *timers* for setting cooking schedules in advance. Others, such as Dacor's Touchtop, don't even have control panels and just need to be *tapped* on.

Electric cooktops are available with four different kinds of burners. Coils float either above or below the surface, while solid disks are installed solely above the cooktop, halogen and induction burners below. Although these burners are all fueled by electricity, considerable differences exist among them.

Electric Coils: The traditional circular *cal-rod* or *spiral resistance burner rods* with a drip plate underneath.

Solid Disks: Thick cast-iron plates that are sealed to the cooktop with a stainless or black metal rim. Some come with a silver *sensor* in the center that holds a precise temperature like an oven, while others are encircled by a ring of light that glows when hot. Without one, *on* is a mystery. An *UltraPower* burner has greater wattage.

Halogen: Burners, sequestered below a glass cooktop, are powered by vacuum-sealed quartz glass lamps filled with halogen gas. Newer models have six or ten specific power levels for maintaining a *continuous heat* instead of *infinite switches* that cycle on and off. Burners surrounded by a *resistance coil* have the most even heat distribution.

Induction: Burners are fitted with an *electromagnetic coil* that converts electricity to a higher frequency, creating a magnetic field that induces a second current directly into a pot. For this electricity to be transmitted, cookware must be composed of a magnetic material such as cast iron, enamel on cast iron, enamel on steel, or stainless with a magnetic carbon steel core. Only the pot's bottom heats up, so burners, cooktop, and kitchen remain cool. Secured below ceramic tiles or a glass cooktop, burners don't come on until a pot makes contact and go off as soon as it is removed.

Of these four types of burners, I'd plunk my money down on the old-fashioned protruding coils. Admittedly, these burners define frumpiness, and their unevenness makes it hard to level a pot. Nonetheless, they are the least expensive electric burners, the ones most tolerant of dented warped cookware. Less dense than solid disks, they heat up faster and cool down more quickly. Detractors argue that coils are harder to clean because they have drip pans, but if these are porcelain, they can go in a self-cleaning oven. Nonstick pans can also be purchased.

Solid disks require the same seasoning and finicky care as cast-iron pans, and they can stain. When heated, their silver rim turns gold and must be cleaned with silver polish. With no drip pan to vent through, pollutants often escape through a hole in the back of the cooktop, leaving a telltale spot.

Disks with a red dot in their center have a temperature sensor, or *thermal limiter*, to turn off the heat if a pot boils dry. This scarlet *letter* is also triggered when excess heat amasses under an oversized pot. Ask food writer Barbara Kafka how she felt when this burner shut down while she was demonstrating a bouillabaisse in her first cooking class. For a cooktop with solid disks, choose *UltraTemp burners* that reduce heat rather than shutting it off completely.

Halogen tubes of gas heat up more quickly than coils or disks, but they don't heat up far. Their immediate visual response—flashing red lights—can send a cook scrambling for sunglasses. This may play well in Hollywood, but it's not exactly lighting to fry by. For even cooking, pans must be a dark color.

At the opposite extreme, induction barely indicates when it is on. And, to all intents and purposes, it is not. Food cooks best by induction the closer it is to the bottom of the pan, suiting these burners for skillet cookery or small-batch simmers that don't require high heat.

On the plus side, induction burners respond quickly to changes in temperature and are 60 percent more energy efficient than other electric elements. If they become available in single or double modules as they were initially, I'd install a unit for low-heat simmering or saucemaking. Some imports are available as portable models.

Halogen and induction cooktops are expensive. Coils are more costly in smooth tops than in cooktops, where they protrude above the surface. More energy is consumed in the latter situation, too, since heat transfer is less direct through glass. Smooth-top cooktops are least tolerant of cookware with bumpy bottoms and a larger diameter than the burner, responding best to a concave stainless-steel pan with a thick bottom. As a testimony to looks over function, smooth-top sales are soaring. If experiments progress, we will soon have gas burners under glass. Better pheasant, I say.

Do you want additional cooktop modules?

The latest trend in cooktops calls for interchangeable plug-in modules. In this situation, a burner can be removed and a module such as a wok, deep fryer, griddle, grill, canning element, roasting pan, rotisserie, or kebab attachment plugged into its place. Having proper equipment for a specific task is a cook's dream, but I can't plug this approach. At all.

First of all, it is a pain. It is hard enough to pull out heavy pots, let alone unwieldy cooktop modules that must be fiddled with. Furthermore, if you have room to store these modules in your cupboards, you probably have space to install them on the countertop.

More to the point, most of these modules are neither properly constructed nor adequately juiced to perform their designated tasks. An eighteen-hundred-watt wok isn't hot enough for stir-frying any-

thing. Purchasing one is a waste of money and valuable space. These comments apply as well to the many similarly underpowered built-in units that exist.

As long as you have a cooktop with large high-heat burners, you will be able to perform most special tasks. If you do a particular type of cookery repeatedly, purchasing the specific equipment for it would be a joy. Do so, though, only if you can afford the best of its kind and can give it a permanent home. Woks, grills, and griddles, in particular, merit their own address.

Woks

Regardless of whether you gaze east or west for culinary inspiration, there is probably no piece of stovetop equipment more versatile than a wok. Blessed with a conical shape and large hot cooking surface, it enables you to stir-fry large quantities of food quickly while sealing in its juices. This tool accommodates large stacks of steamer trays and doubles as a deep fryer.

Unencumbered with a fryer's filters and gears, the wok is easier to clean and performs its job with less oil than a cylindrical pot. Performing mightily, it obviates any reason for purchasing a separate deep fryer even if you, like my significant other, make french fries nightly.

Unlike a regular burner, whose flame reaches only a wok's bottom, or the faux frame suspending a wok over a burner, a special wok stove has a deep recessed cavity, encircling the pan's circumference with a ring of fire. At 125,000 Btus, its heat is a mite higher, too. Possessing a diameter of sixteen inches up or down, a built-in or portable wok stove also accommodates large stockpots or skillets that don't fit on standard burners.

A space and money hog, a wok stove is surely a luxury for all but ardent Asian cooks for whom it is daily issue. I sure wish I had one.

Grills

In its ability to cook foods swiftly and flavorfully without additional fat, a high-Btu gas grill is ideal for

WOKS

WOK ON

As more people appreciate the fresh flavors and health benefits of wok cookery, and as more cooktops possess the higher heat it requires, more quality woks have entered the market either as a separate dedicated appliance or as a frame that locks onto a regular burner.

today's health- and convenience-oriented lifestyle. So much so, in fact, that I highly advocate the purchase of a separate dedicated grill or commercial-style cooktop with an infrared grill in its lineup.

If lack of space or budget makes this untenable, buy a ridged rectangular cast-iron pan sized to fit over one or two contiguous burners like that produced by Le Creuset. Though this may seem hard to believe, it delivers as good or better charbroiled zest than most electric or low-Btu gas grills or grill modules included on a cooktop.

Residential gas grills with electronic ignitions and Btus in the twenty thousand to thirty-six thou-

sand range are available for standard twenty-four-inch deep countertops. Excellent compromises for a home kitchen, they don't begin to have the branding power of a restaurant grill with double to triple the Btus (and a lower price).

Freestanding in a variety of sizes with lava rocks or radiant grates, commercial grills or *underfired* broilers can be set on a stand or on top of a lowered countertop. Professionals seem to prefer radiants for their more even heat and less drying quality. At upward of seven hundred degrees, lava rock models run about one hundred degrees hotter with their highest temperature in the center. Lava rocks absorb

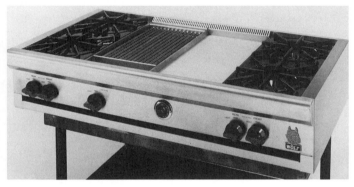

GRIDDLES

SUNDAY MORNING PANCAKES
Flapjacks can be flipped on a portable griddle that slips over two burners or on a surface given a permanent home on a cooktop. If offered the choice, choose one operated by thermostatic controls over another marked high, medium, and low.

Griddles

When I recommend a griddle, I'm often asked, "Who needs it?" "I do," I say. In my intimate family of two, I've found it a great asset for cooking several servings of sandwiches, tortillas, potatoes, onions, French toast, and pancakes—fast. With its low sides and large surface, a griddle makes flipping a cinch; sticking a nonproblem. Copying Donna Kamin, I had a cutting board made to fit over the griddle that transforms it into a work surface when not griddling.

When purchasing a commercial griddle, look for one with infrared power burners or pulse combustion, new technologies that offer even, efficient heating. Insist on a thermostatically controlled dial over one marked high, medium, and low. If you do not buy one of these griddles or have a separate unit on a restaurant-style cooktop, I'd opt for a portable designed to fit over one or two contiguous burners. Sold in housewares departments or restaurant supply houses, they are available with or without a nonstick coating. Food browns better without it. A bit of a texture, though, keeps butter from slipping and sliding all over.

When evaluating a griddle or grill, consider the ease of heat adjustment, cleaning, and grease collection. To compare power among units, divide the square inches of cooking surface by the total number of Btus.

drippings, reducing flaring, but they are harder to clean and disintegrate over time, requiring replacement.

Divided into multiple independently operating zones, commercial grills can be turned down to avoid the charred-on-the-outside, raw-within syndrome. Both heat and grates (flat or tilted) are adjustable. Juices and grease flow into a pan underneath that is removable for cleaning.

Salamanders

Unparalleled in browning surfaces, a salamander or elevated *overfired* high-heat broiler guarantees to overheat and seems like overkill in a residential kitchen, especially one stocked with an underfired broiler. One friend bought it to make crème brûlée. Costing $2,000 or more, this appears a bit frivolous unless you're heading for a prize in gratinéing. Hard to reach and hard to clean, it is mounted above a cooktop and cannot be fueled by bottled gas.

OVENS

A good oven must bake evenly as well as broil at a high temperature. To monitor its performance, purchase a reliable oven thermometer. *Consumer Reports* rated the Springfield 203 dial type the highest. If you are a serious baker, you may want to splurge on a professional probe. Those that have been recommended to me are the Pronto Digital Thermometer from Thermo Electric Instruments and the Flexible Probe from National Controls Corporation.

To preheat or not to preheat? In most ovens the set temperature is reached in five minutes or so. The recommended fifteen-minute preheating time is for stabilizing them.

How large should the oven be?

The standard twenty-four-inch oven built into a wall or installed in a cabinet is increasingly being replaced by those that are twenty-seven and thirty inches wide. Several models, at thirty-six inches, look more like the fins of a fifties Cadillac. It's the varying interior specifications, though, that are most telling in calculating how much room there is for those cookie sheets. One oven with an exterior measurement of thirty inches has an interior of twenty-two inches; another twenty-four and one-half.

In making measurements, include the dimension of the shell as well as number of racks, space between them, and size of their attachments. (These can be hefty enough to interfere with a baking tray.) In a true convection oven, count the entire cavity, for food can cook on the oven floor. For an electric oven, check, too, that top and bottom racks are far enough away from burner elements so the food doesn't incinerate while baking. Go for the largest interior cavity that space allows, for it offers the most options. When evaluating that space, don't forget the Thanksgiving turkey.

How many ovens are necessary?

Friends talk about their two wall ovens and double ovens in their range as if they were basic staples. What they are using them for is beyond me. Unless your kitchen functions as a full-scale catering operation, two ovens seems the maximum necessary. Space willing, it's also the minimum.

After living in a home with two ovens, I down-scaled to one in a new residence. The first time I entertained there, I neglected to reprogram my schedule. When I went to put in the main course, I found the hors d'oeuvres cooking. There was rather a long wait between courses that evening. Ten years later, we were still waiting between courses, for my menus somehow never worked with one oven.

In addition to two full-size ovens, you may want a microwave (page 249) and a small countertop or toaster oven to handle baked potatoes or minimeals.

Wall ovens play singles or doubles with one set of controls on top of the first oven. Some matches pair a conventional (called *thermal*) or *thermal-convection* oven with a microwave or microwave-convection oven on top. Two single ovens placed side by side are generally preferable to a double stack (or one and one-half stacks in the case of European ovens), for they allow waist-high placement.

Do you want a convection oven?

Convection, the upward movement of warm air in an oven as it is heated, occurs naturally in all ovens. When a fan is added to blow the air around, it is called a *convection oven*. Its heating coils are in the oven and food still cooks unevenly. For an oven to be *true convection*, the heating element must be placed outside the cavity with the fan wrapped around it to balance heat and air movement. Hidden behind a wall, this housing will shorten the oven's depth.

True convection ovens are heated equally throughout, eliminating hot spots. All parts of the oven can be utilized simultaneously without having to switch trays around halfway through cooking. Typically these ovens come with three racks as compared to a thermal oven's two, four when the oven floor or bottom shelf is brought into play: More food can be cooked in a smaller cavity without fear of its burning on the lower rack above the heating coil.

A convection oven defrosts or dehydrates food on a low setting. There is less spatter here, for moving air seals the outside surface of whatever is cooking while the filter covering the fan absorbs by-products that escape through vents in a conventional oven.

Convection technology, developed initially for use on submarines, has made a splash in the stove industry. Nevertheless, with all its advantages, it is being hyped excessively and sold without proper explanation, *mis*leading cooks into troubled waters.

It is appealing to think of baking cookies without having to turn them halfway to equalize the heat. Friable shortbread or biscotti, that is. If you are a moist-chocolate-chipper fan, you will find these cookies coming out too crisp from a drying convection medium. Ditto cakes, vegetables, and baked potatoes. And Thanksgiving isn't going to conclude satisfactorily with a crisp cheesecake or pumpkin pie.

On the other hand, this drying quality makes a convection oven great for pastry, phyllo dough, and poultry skin. Yet you don't need convection to obtain this crunch. To realize the same crispness, roast a chicken on a rack at four hundred seventy-five degrees for forty-five minutes or brown a piecrust slowly at 300 degrees for one-half hour. *If you have the cooking techniques, you don't need the technology.*

To obtain successful results in a convection oven, manufacturers recommend lowering the temperature of your favorite recipe by twenty-five degrees and cooking it for five minutes less. When this works, the convection oven becomes a bit of an energy saver, but you can't generalize these instructions across the board. Translation: You have to adapt or develop your own recipes. As for those ads showing one oven crammed with a turkey, baked potatoes, and cherry pie, this works only if the items you are cooking share the same optimum baking temperature.

For convection heat to do its job, food must be cooked uncovered in a shallow pan. Parchment paper or aluminum foil liners for baking sheets need to be glued down, or they blow around the oven. Convection fans operate (and cool down for several hours) at Led Zeppelin's top decibel level, and the ovens cost about 20 percent more than a conventional thermal cavity.

If you are intrigued by the latest technology, will-ing to put up with its shortcomings, and purchasing more than one oven, there is no reason not to get a convection oven. But when you're limited to only one oven, there are too many things convection doesn't cook well to depend solely on it.

Do you want a multimode oven?

Convection can also be obtained in a multimode oven, where it exists along with thermal heating and, in some cases, with a microwave. (For a discussion of microwave-convection ovens, see page 254.) In this case, you can switch from one mode to the next, making convection a more practical alternative in a single oven. Yet with burner elements in the oven that can still burn things cooked on a bottom rack, this is not a true convection situation. Marlene Sorosky's oven split the difference, roasting her turkey with a line directly through the middle. One side was golden; the other pale lemon yellow.

When a salesperson announces a multimode oven as a great deal because you get three ovens in one, think about dinner: Every time you want to cook a chicken, you must decide whether it should be baked by thermal, convection, microwave, thermal-convection, thermal-microwave, convection-microwave, or thermal-convection-microwave heat. Or would you rather convention- or convection-broil it? This is not a decision I can deal with, although you might want to if you are mechanically inclined.

Keep in mind, too, that watt for watt a microwave operates faster and more efficiently in a smaller cavity than in a regular oven, and when you want a microwave you want it now. You don't want to wait for something else to finish cooking before having access to it.

For the pleasure of making fifty decisions before starting dinner, you may pay more than twice as much as you would for two separate ovens plus a microwave. A basic single thermal oven costs about $600, whereas one that also has convection and microwave can come in at $2,300 or more. A European thermal convection combo can rise above $3,000. Running smaller than American versions, these imported multimode ovens may make sense in

WALL OVENS

Wall ovens are available as singles or doubles (sharing controls) with gas or electricity in 24-, 27-, and 30-inch widths with some behemoths at 36 inches. Convection has become very much the oven buzzword of the day. Whether it is true convection which includes a third heating element wrapped around a fan outside of the oven cavity or fan-assisted convection that is limited to a fan inside the compartment blowing air around to encourage even heating, most built-in ovens have some sort of convection system. This single oven, topped with a microwave, also boasts an atomizer which injects steam, making this model a bread baker's dream *(top left)*. This smaller 24-inch electric oven has a fan-assisted oven in the top and a separate operating thermal oven and broiler in the bottom *(top center)*. This new stainless double has a space-age insulation that permits proportionately more usable interior space *(top right)*. These two European ovens *(above)* are beautiful enough to wear to the ball. Side-hinged, the smaller one has a curved glass door that offers a panoramic view of a roast. It, like its larger sibling, is blessed with a rotisserie, infrared broiler, and pizza baking stone.

a tiny kitchen or replacement situation, where a new oven must fit into a small existing cabinet.

Broilers

To operate properly, a broiler must have high enough heat to sear the surface of whatever it is cooking and to seal in its juices. Ineffective, most broilers are underpowered, stewing and toughening whatever is placed in their charge. Resolving this problem: the infrared broiler, a ceramic shield that absorbs heat radiating from light waves. Its high temperatures—about sixteen hundred degrees—focus directly on the food, penetrating it deeply and reducing cooking time. Preheating takes less than two minutes.

If you do not like one of the ovens currently available with an infrared broiler, choose an electric oven with a broiler of at least three thousand watts or a gas oven with a broiler offering a minimum of twelve thousand Btus, but don't expect them to be equivalent to an infrared broiler in their performance. Broiler type is less relevant if you also have a high-Btu countertop grill, but browning will still be a challenge.

A broiler should have at least six *passes* (*rods*) and be ensconced in the top of the oven rather than in a separate compartment underneath as some gas broilers are. Lower broilers give you the bends and are too small either to accommodate a large pan or to distance food sufficiently from the heat source.

Some ovens now offer *half-on heat* for small quantities and/or a *variable temperature control.* Adjusting the heat instead of the pan, this is a boon for cooking fish, chicken, and thick pieces of meat that require a lower temperature.

Do you want a self-cleaning oven?

An oven with a dark interior hides dirt and radiates more heat than one with light-colored walls, while porcelain is easier to clean than steel. Better insulated, a self-cleaning oven simplifies this task even further, although it can throw the thermostat off by one hundred degrees. The higher price of this oven can supposedly be justified by adding up the cost of cleaning supplies for non-self-cleaning models. It is also considered a more environmentally friendly way to clean, although I have trouble thinking of friendly and cleaning in the same breath.

There are two types of self-cleaning ovens. The first, the *catalytic* or *continuous-clean* oven, has a catalytic material mixed into the oven liner that prevents oxidation and enables the oven to clean as it cooks. Nicknamed the "continuous dirty" oven, it is pretty much being phased out because some stains remain, and people aren't satisfied with it. I had one that worked beautifully as long as I occasionally ran it for several hours at five hundred degrees. Some current models have only a one-year warranty. If this finish wears off in spots, you'll never be able to clean the oven.

For an additional $100, you can have a *pyrolytic* oven, which has a separate high-heat cleaning cycle of seven hundred to nine hundred degrees. The oven locks during its three-hour maintenance, so check to see that it operates facilely. In a double oven, look for separate controls so one oven can be used while the other cleans.

Vital Oven Parts

Doors: Contemporary wall oven doors are increasingly stainless or glass and frameless. A solid heavy door with tight gaskets is obviously a plus for insulation, but you've still got to be able to maneuver it. Too large, and you may have to stand to the side to pull things in and out. For this reason a short person may be happier with a door hinged right or left. Removable doors facilitate cleaning. Check that handles (and doors) do not transmit heat and are easily grasped.

Windows: Having a window in an oven door is as frustrating as eavesdropping on your parents when you are a kid: You just can't get enough information to know what's going on. Either the glass is too dark or too opaque or too patterned or the oven light is positioned poorly. After straining to see what's going on, you usually end up opening the door anyway. Listen to food scientist Harold McGee, who claims that it takes an oven only one minute to return to its set temperature after a door is opened. Forget the win-

CONSERVING ENERGY

- **Plan meals that require the same piece of equipment. When using the oven, make sure it is full. Don't turn on an entire oven for two baked potatoes. When grilling meat, grill the vegetables as well.**

- **Bring food to room temperature before cooking.**

- **Cover pots when bringing water to a boil or cooking on the cooktop.**

- **After bringing liquid to a boil, reduce the heat so the mixture simmers. Cooking won't proceed any faster at a rolling boil.**

- **As cooking draws to a finish, turn off the heat on an electric cooktop and continue with residual heat left in the burner.**

- **Adjust the burner flame of a gas cooktop so it does not extend beyond the bottom of the pan.**

- **Cooktop drip/reflector bowls absorb less heat when clean.**

- **Ovens work more efficiently when clean.**

- **Clean a self-cleaning oven right after it has been used to take advantage of residual heat.**

- **Arrange oven racks before turning the oven on to preheat.**

- **When baking in glass dishes, lower the oven temperature by twenty-five degrees.**

---

dow. The door is easier to clean without it. If energy mavens get their way, it will be eliminated anyway.

Light: Once the door is open, the light becomes an asset, so confirm that it is easy to change and conveniently located in a place where it will not get hit.

Racks: Oven racks should move easily in their tracks and extend fully yet lock so they don't pull out of the oven unless you want them to. Putting them back in correctly should be easy, too.

Drawer (on Range): Ditto "Racks."

Buttons and Bells: Some ovens still have electromechanical rotary dials arranged by number and task; others require that two separate controls be set for preheating and baking. Controls are less precise than they were formerly, with a twenty-degree spread in either direction now considered *standard.*

Increasingly *à la mode,* electronic push buttons with digital clocks and temperature readouts include programs for scheduling self-cleaning, delayed onset of baking, timed bake, and automatic off or cooldown. Accompanied by audible signals, they announce when a set temperature is reached, baking or self-cleaning is complete.

A *probe* is designed specifically to turn the oven off or down when a preset internal meat temperature is reached. Its accuracy depends on how close it is to the heating element and the regularity of an oven's temperature.

A *rotisserie spit,* the caveman's culinary legacy, transforms poultry and meat into succulent roasts. As it rotates above a tray, a meat's exterior is air-dried, crisping any skin and sealing in savory juices. If your oven does not offer a rotisserie, simulate this effect by purchasing the frame for birds called a *vertical roaster* or the Amco Adjustable Rotisserie, my single favorite kitchen gadget designed originally by Wade Bentson, that has just been reintroduced into the marketplace after a hiatus of several decades. Both are available in housewares departments and at cookware stores.

RANGE

When any oven and cooktop are combined in a single unit, the sum seems greater than its parts, for the range often becomes the focal point of a kitchen.

Do you want a freestanding, slide-in, or drop-in range?

Ranges are distinguished as freestanding, slide-in, or drop-in according to the way they are installed. The *freestanding* range is the biggest seller. With finished sides and its own legs to stand on, it has the broadest placement possibilities in this group. Its lower price tag probably plays a part in its popularity as well.

Freestanding ranges are generally twenty-four inches deep and thirty inches wide, shrinking down to twenty- and twenty-four-inch-wide models and expanding up to thirty-six inches (gas), and forty inches (electric). Wider models have two ovens or an oven plus a storage cabinet below the cooktop. A pot drawer is often underneath, with those running the full width of the stove offering more space. Install an antitipping device with all ranges.

When a freestanding range is sandwiched between two cabinets, they must be straight and sized perfectly to allow a snug fit. Gaps look ugly while functioning as dirt collectors. Another drawback to this style of range is the location of its control knobs. Perched inconveniently on the stove back, they are difficult to see and potentially dangerous to reach.

A *slide-in* range rests on the floor like a freestanding model. Minus its sides, it snuggles between two base cabinets for a built-in look. When its rim extends over the seam edge, there is no visible gap. Available with or without a back, its dials are mounted on or under the cooktop so adjustments can be made without reaching across a lit burner. A *drop-in* range is similar to a slide-in except that it hangs from the countertop or rests on the toe kick.

In addition to these three basic types of ranges, there is a *bilevel* or over-under style with one oven above the cooktop and one below. Providing two ovens in only a thirty-inch-wide space, this option may appear practical for a small kitchen. It's not. The top oven protrudes over the cooktop, seriously limiting the height of pots that can be used there. Lifting hot pans in and out of the oven overhead is unsafe. Third strike? Ventilation is ineffective in this situation. Count it out.

Count in a drop-in or slide-in range or even a freestander if you are swayed by its price or in need of its finished sides. Whatever range you pick, be sure the legs are adjustable (freestanding or slide-in) and check whether the base lines up (drop-in) with the cabinet toe kick or other horizontal line you want to echo. Look for a minimum of seams and rounded corners to simplify cleaning and a prop stick to hold up the cooktop during its scrub-down.

COMMERCIAL-STYLE COOKERS

A restaurant-style range, the superman of stoves, is either loved or hated for its commercial looks and power heating. Until the last eight years or so, cooks who purchased a restaurant stove got the same high-fired gas range as their city's finest dining establishments.

These behemoths put out goodly amounts of heat and require a complex fireproof installation with clearances maintained between the stove and any adjacent combustible surface or cabinet. Some companies refuse to sell these ranges to a homeowner or to honor their warranty in a residence for fear they will be held liable for fires or accidents resulting from improper installation.

In the mid-eighties, states such as California passed energy bills disallowing standing pilots in the home. This statute made commercial ranges illegal just at the time they were becoming the latest must-have status symbol. Envisioning their market potential, restaurant range manufacturers, such as Garland, Dynasty, and Wolf, reined in their powerful stoves with a pilotless ignition and insulation that enabled them to be installed without fireproof materials or significant clearances. Following quickly in their footsteps, other companies, such as Viking, Thermador, and Five Star, upstyled residential ranges to where they were more professional in looks and capability, with controls on the front of the stove. Today this is the cooker category of greatest change.

In addition to the forty-eight- and sixty-inch ranges fabricated initially, thirty- and thirty-six-inch ranges with a depth of twenty-four inches are now produced to fit flush with base cabinetry, serving as replacements for a standard residential range. Commercial-style cooktops are in distribution as well.

Noninsulated commercial ranges with standing pilots cost several thousand dollars less than a modified range, but they waste energy and expend considerable heat. Many people deal with standing pilots by shutting them off and relighting as necessary with a spark igniter. The gas company cautions against this procedure, concerned that a control can be cocked unknowingly, inviting an explosion.

Commercial-style ranges are supposedly better insulated, minimizing the chance of a child's being burned, but this is not, in fact, the case, and this big child has scars to prove it. Basically I think you're better off with the heavier higher-Btu commercial range than with a commercial-style impostor if you have no children around or visitors who might unwittingly turn on the burner when you've shut off the pilots. Owning this type of range is a big responsibility, with a clear-cut commitment to its safe operation.

Regardless of whether you purchase a commercial range or a modified commercial range, monitor its installation to be sure the company's specifications are followed. Noncompliance can cause a fire and invalidate your insurance.

RANGES
Even traditional ranges such as this freestanding electric model are being streamlined with sleek new looks, while the commercial-style ranges with their high Btu burners and infrared grills are becoming residentialized and shallower in depth. Shrinking, they now fit flush—or almost flush—with the cabinetry.

The initial cost of these ranges is only a small part of their price. The gas line must be changed from one-half to three-quarters inch, adjacent walls and cabinets fireproofed and surfaced with noncombustible materials, and the floor reinforced to accommodate this quarter-ton leviathan. Related purchases include a major ventilation system, new heavy-duty pots, and a sink large enough to accommodate its grates. Then there is delivery: Who will bring it in, and will it fit through doors and passageways?

There are other aesthetic and cookery issues to confront before making this major purchase. Available with or without a high back with a shelf, many of these ranges are taller (a problem for short people) or deeper than countertops and uneven with cabinet toe kicks. Some ovens do not go down to a warming temperature or burners to a simmer, mandating a separate cast-iron simmer plate.

Ovens are sometimes difficult to calibrate, and service calls run at higher rates. Grates and doors are heavy to operate; niceties such as self-cleaning, clocks, timers, and probes are nonexistent. Turned on less frequently at home than they would be in a restaurant setting, these cookers don't accumulate the slick greasy surface that discourages rusting.

And, as writer Merrill Shindler observes, "You don't have a small enough oven to cook a bloody baked potato. For the $4,000 I spent, I should have gotten a Nubian slave with a fan. Instead, I had to buy

an additional countertop oven. It's the epitome of Yuppie crocks. The more you pay, the less you get."

Why am I going on and on about these commercial and commercial-style cookers when costs and problems associated with their purchase are so enormous? The answer is simple: I love the solidity and full-throttled responsiveness of my range as does everyone I know who has one.

As kitchen designer Laura Odell has remarked, "Manufacturers are selling us toys instead of tools; gadgets instead of quality." At least a commercial stove is a ticket to stability and power. I just wish these virtues were standard issue on more reasonably priced ranges. To buy one right now, you have to be crazy like me or have real deep pockets. If you're lucky, you might catch a bargain at an auction of used or new restaurant equipment that won't require you to dig quite as deeply.

HEIRLOOM RANGES

There are two other types of stoves that deserve special mention, both for their uniqueness and for the fact that we all deserve the chance to dream. Not a purchase for a temporary dwelling, they are an heirloom to pass on as part of a legacy. Just hope that you are on the receiving end.

Produced in Shropshire, England, the intensely hued cast-iron Aga scores one for the Commonwealth with four ovens and three boilerplate cooktops that each performs its own designated task from frying to yogurt making. Fueled by gas or coal and

HEIRLOOM RANGES

Hiding behind these old-fashioned porcelain doors is the most modern high-tech convection oven. The same can be said of the 30-inch electric range pictured with it. Gas and wood-burning models are available in various sizes and configurations with a water source and warming drawer. Wood cabinets complete this Norman Rockwell painting *(left)*. True heirlooms, the French and English ranges *(below)* have had a long venerable history. The purchase of one can be as emotional as choosing a pet, for these stoves soon insinuate themselves into a family, often causing great schisms as children vie over their inheritance.

HEIRLOOM RANGES

bereft of temperature controls, it is always on, working by the principle of retained heat. Darina Allen, a cooking teacher and owner of the Ballymaloe House in Ireland, attests that you can't live without an Aga if you were raised with one. "The kids come and sit on it," she explains. "It is a friend in the kitchen with a personality all of its own." Princess Diana reportedly has an Aga in royal blue. It doesn't seem to have done much for her family, but then you never know.

Moving across the channel to France, La Cornue has also wended its way into the homes of royalty and a bevy of Rothschilds. Painted in deep vitreous enamel hues or quavering flowers that could have graced Madame Pompadour's boudoir, this museum piece's Le Château, for example, has a cooktop with two 2,000-watt electric burners, two 23,900-Btu gas burners, a gas grill, and a flat top composed of a bull's-eye surrounded by two rings that gradually decrease in heat as they move out from the center. One oven is gas; the other electric. Though too few of us can own La Cornue, we can all enjoy its philosophy which is all too easily forgotten in the materialism of a remodel.

"Some companies have had as a primary motivation the lure of profit," the owner's manual reads. "But it seems that 'LA CORNUE' would rather be motivated by the appetite. A solid appetite for the pleasures of the table and for the good cheer, of good quality, in respect to the cuisine, which, in France—and we should not forget it—has become and is now one of the Fine Arts."

COOKING OVER WOOD

With time-consuming start-up and learning times, wood- or coal-fed stoves may seem an anathema in this instant, high-pressured era. But they bring comfort and pleasure to those patient enough to learn their ministerings and are a means of saving money as oil and electricity prices mount. Certainly they are welcomed in colder climes, where their radiating heat is considered a benefit.

Though the alloyed cast iron used today is not as strong as that used in days of yore, you must be very cautious when purchasing an old stove. Seek expert counsel when buying from an estate or at auction and consult the fire department before planning its installation.

When organizing a kitchen for a woodstove, include an outlet for its chimney flue and place for a wood box and any necessary tools. As with a fireplace, the chimney must frequently be cleaned and inspected for creosote buildup so it doesn't become a fire hazard.

To cook over a hearth, you must put in a wood-burning masonry fireplace, not a prefab box that can't tolerate the grease. Hearth cookery has continued to exist in America since colonial times, particularly in the Northeast. Yet its recent resurgence has, I suspect, less to do with a desire to hark back to these roots than to emulate trendy restaurants demonstrating these techniques in front of our eyes. Before cooking like a Pilgrim, listen to Phyllis Nobel. "I did a Tuscan dinner in our fireplace," she recalled, "and I couldn't walk for a week."

Wood-burning ovens are also increasingly popular in the kitchen or backyard thanks to Chez Panisse and its disciples turning out pizza, bread, and cute roasted chickens in a manner made all the more romantic, primal, and mystical by the challenge of building and controlling a fire and the removal of soot and ashes left in its wake.

Faced with brick, marble, or granite, these adobe-shaped ovens are made from high-heat refractory material that can withstand its searing seven-hundred-degree temperatures. Some offer gas as an igniter or alternative fuel. Investigate wood-burning ovens by visiting local restaurants that employ them. Follow chefs and workers responsible for their operation around and practice if they'll let you. Do you still want to build that fire?

OTHER COOKERS

Wood-fired ovens, some available as preassembled units, have been designed with the home kitchen or patio in mind. Interiors are built with refractory elements, hard ceramic tile floors, and cast-iron doors to be faced as desired. Wood- and coal-burning stoves are available as well either as antiques or as new models with a warming drawer on top. They bring comfort in the midst of all this newfangled stainless steel. It's too bad they don't also bring someone to build the fire.

WOOD and COAL

FOOD WARMERS

Some type of food warmer comes in handy for everything from storing dinners for laggers and keeping the next course warm to heating plates and assembling enough toast to make BLT sandwiches for a crowd. Carol Doran turns on her warming drawer, pops in some meringues, and goes to bed, letting them dry overnight.

As a primary warmer, the drawer is probably the most practical of all the devices, though it occupies the greatest space. Costly commercial models that stack are freestanding or built in with each drawer possessing its own temperature control; single residential entries can only be built in. These can be set "crisp" so french fries don't sog or "moist" for warming muffins, proofing yeast, or rising bread. Controls are labeled in degrees or marked high, medium, and low.

Some models come with removable inserts. Some shut off automatically. Those that don't can be a problem since the *on* light isn't visible when the drawer is closed and it's easy to forget to turn it off.

Other food-warmer options include infrared lights, an electric warming box from two to six feet long (placed above the food), or a thermal shelf placed underneath or built into the counter. Make it cozier, sandwiching the food between two units: one above and one below.

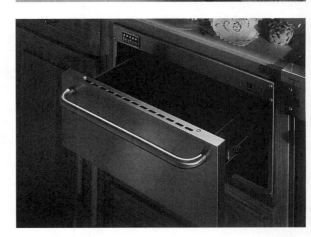

WARMING DRAWERS

Warming drawers switch from a moist to a crisp setting and are available in 24- or 27-inch models. Designed to match the styling of the other appliances in a company's line, they come in a variety of finishes, and can be placed either near a cooking or serving area. Different shaped dishes and racks are available to make their interior space more flexible.

PERSONAL PICKS: COOKERS

This category has the dubious distinction of being the most important with the fewest good options. And the best of its show is extremely expensive. Yet you'll want to spend the money if you can manage it, for the power, quality, and control delivered in exchange will enable you to bid farewell to the era of scorched pans and slow-cooked dinners.

Starting at the beginning: If you can bring a gas line into the house, do so to have a gas cooktop. In a gas cooktop, go for the highest Btus you can get from fifteen thousand on up. I would forgo the commercial-style cooktops (or cooktop on a range) for the real commercial six-burner restaurant cooktop made by companies such as Wolf, Garland, Jade, South Bend, etc. This costs about half the price and packs considerably more power than the commercial-style offerings currently cashing in on this trend by lowering the quality of all the things that made commercial cooktops and stoves better cookers in the first place.

Commercial cookers are supposedly less insulated than commercial style and in need of more careful fireproof installation and handling to guard against burns, but the latter in-group still gets hot enough to brand a mean welt.

The one piece of commercial equipment you'll want to avoid is a range with a raised broiler. With a fat lip, nothing but a shallow pan will fit underneath for gratinéing, and if you pull out the shoddy jury-rigged rack to check doneness of a steak, its juices will flood your floor.

You'll also have to be careful that commercial cooktop controls are not inadvertently cooked if you turn off their pilots, a move ill advised by the gas company. Afraid of liability, many commercial companies will resist selling you one of their stoves or cooktops for the home. To get its installation approved, you will probably have to apply for a variance from the department of building and safety.

If all this seems like too much of a hassle, get one of the commercial-style cooktops (or ranges) such as that made by Wolf, Five Star, Dynasty, Garland, or Viking, with the choice depending on general quality as well as local availability and service. I'm happy with my six-burner locally built Wolf, but this market is changing so rapidly that you're better off comparing options when you're ready to buy. Just be sure that the burners are able to maintain a low simmer. For a commercial-style cooktop with a zigzag top, look at Thermador and Russell Range.

If gas is not a possibility, consider freestanding single or double electric modules from food service suppliers such as Wells or Star that possess a higher wattage than residential electric cooktops. Combine these units with induction burners whose heat is more controllable than that of coils or solid disks. As of this writing, General Electric makes a four-burner induction grouping. Fasar offers individual burners, but a single turns out to be almost as expensive as a four-

some. Portable induction burners can often be found in cookware stores or electronic outlets and should prove useful in any kitchen as an extra cooktop burner.

Whether you want this cooktop as part of a range or as a separate piece of equipment depends, as always, on multiple factors. I bought a Wolf range because the heft and hulk I detest in cabinets looks gorgeous to me in commercial equipment. (Strange eyes in this beholder.) You will, however, have a better chance of getting the best of both worlds if you buy a separate cooktop and oven, and money can be saved by mixing a simple residential oven with a commercial cooktop, the one piece of equipment that offers a major difference in performance.

Neither a commercial nor a residential oven is tall enough to hold a deep pot without first removing one of its racks, but a residential model offers self-cleaning and preprogramming options not available in commercial equipment. An electric oven does not appear necessarily better to me than one with gas, but the existence of an infrared broiler such as that offered by Amana would be mandatory if I didn't have a separate grill. As a bread baker, I still covet Frigidaire's Euroflair oven with an automatic steam injector. Gaggenau's thirty-six-inch-wide oven is so beautiful I pant deeply every time I see it. It's functional, too, with a pizza stone and rotisserie. You already know how I feel about convection, but if you succumb to a salesperson's pitch, at least buy true convection with the fan wrapped around the heat source outside the oven cavity. If space permits, take advantage of a separate oven's flexibility and go for singles installed at waist level.

My general philosophy about the superiority of commercial high-Btu equipment over commercial-style or residential offerings generalizes to grills and woks, and there is no piece of equipment I like better than my twenty-four-inch commercial Wolf grill. Since these are not the primary pieces of equipment in a kitchen, most jurisdictions do not require special permits for them. A residential warming oven, first offered by Thermador, is, on the other hand, perfectly adequate.

KITCHENSPEAK: STOVES

Automatic Reignition: Gas burners that rekindle immediately after their flames are extinguished by a pot boiling over.

Commercial Style: See Restaurant Style.

Convection: An oven whose heating element is outside its main cavity and wrapped with a fan to blow hot air evenly throughout.

Dual Fuel: Ranges that consist of a gas cooktop and an electric oven.

Electric Coils: The traditional circular cal-rod or spiral resistance burner rods with a drip plate underneath.

Glass-Ceramic Smooth Top: A flat electric cooktop whose burners are hidden below its surface.

Halogen: Electric burners, sequestered below a glass-ceramic cooktop, that are powered by vacuum-sealed quartz glass lamps filled with halogen gas.

Hob: The British name for a cooktop.

Induction: Electric burners fitted with an electromagnetic coil that converts electricity to a higher frequency while creating a magnetic field, which induces a second current directly into a pot.

Infrared Broiler: A ceramic shield that absorbs heat radiating from light waves, enabling it to focus temperatures of roughly sixteen hundred degrees directly on the food being broiled.

Multimode Oven: An oven that offers convection or microwave heating in addition to conventional thermal heating.

Plug-In Modules: Interchangeable modular elements such as a wok, deep fryer, griddle, grill, canning element, roasting pan, rotisserie, or kebab attachment that can be exchanged with an electric cooktop burner and plugged into its place.

Probe: An instrument that is inserted into a roast before cooking and turns the oven off or down once the meat reaches its preset temperature.

Range: A *freestanding* range has finished sides and stands on its own legs. A *slide-in* rests on the floor like a freestanding model, but, minus sides, it appears built-in. A *drop-in* resembles a slide-in except that it hangs from the countertop or rests on the toe kick. Considered unsafe, a *bilevel* or over-under style offers one oven above the cooktop and one below.

Restaurant Style: Appliances with the heft and looks of commercial equipment that have been modified for residential installation with reduced power, increased insulation, and the addition of pilotless ignition. *Restaurant* equipment is unaltered from that used in a commercial setting.

Self-Cleaning Oven: A *catalytic* oven cleans continuously while it cooks, whereas a *pyrolytic* oven has a separate high-heat cleaning cycle.

Solid Disks: Thick cast-iron electric burners that are sealed to the cooktop with a stainless or black metal rim.

Thermal Limiter: A temperature sensor in some electric disks that automatically turns off the heat if a pot boils dry. An UltraTemp burner reduces the heat rather than shutting it off completely.

Zigzag Grate: A single continuous **S**-shaped grid that covers the burners on a gas cooktop.

MICROWAVE OVENS

■

Chocolate blesses us with baptisms in bittersweet baths. A temptress, it beckons with hedonism and sensuality. Manifesting itself as a stain on Percy I. Spencer's pants, it also brought us the microwave.

Whether the chocolate was actually in Mr. Spencer's pocket (as some report) or in the radar vacuum tube he was testing at Raytheon (as others recount), the sight of the microwave-melted sweet stimulated this engineer to develop the radar range—and, probably, some guilt over having bought a candy bar.

Since that apocalyptic day in 1945 at least one microwave oven has found its way into over 80 percent of American homes. One prominent publisher starts each week with a refrigerator full of Chinese take-out food to zap after work. Children in Nikes nuke Kids Cuisine and Kids Kitchen. Merging the old world with the new, Patricia Wells, a food and travel writer living in France, microwaves her frozen baguettes that have been baked traditionally over a wood fire. More fundamentally, "Microwaves have changed our perception of time," says Mona Doyle, president of Consumer Network Inc. "It has made even fast-food restaurants not seem fast because at home you don't have to wait in line."

Microwaves, a member of the *electromagnetic* wave family, make waves fast. Shorter (micro) and higher in frequency than radio and TV counterparts, they beam heat instead of *The Lone Ranger* and Oprah. To produce microwaves, an electronic vacuum tube called the *magnetron* converts household electricity into high-energy waves that bounce off the oven's impenetrable metal walls like unruly children. Although most machines have a fan or "stirrer" to distribute the waves, they strike in what one Spanish teacher calls "*mas o menos*" (more or less) fashion. Limited in number, they must be shared, so it takes a lot longer to get two hot potatoes than one.

Vibrating at 2.45 billion cycles per second, microwaves are absorbed by the water molecules in food. Agitated, they create friction and heat.

Microwaves bombard all sides of a food simultaneously, penetrating several inches. After this point, *conduction* kicks in, moving heat progressively inward. To finish cooking, food needs to sit after being removed from the oven.

This siege—plus the fact that foods cook unevenly at different rates according to liquid content—explains the seemingly bizarre practice of heating a hot fudge sundae in a microwave oven; the warm reheated pasta whose zucchini is still ice cold. For safety's sake, these idiosyncrasies mandate a check that pork and poultry are cooked all the way through.

Most experts agree that microwave cooking works best with seafood, vegetables, and other foods that either contain a high percentage of moisture or crave an aqueous steaming, poaching, or braising environment. Microwaves—like the best of us—are attracted to fat and sugar, but they are less successful at browning, roasting, grilling, and baking.

"You wouldn't boil an egg in a toaster, so why try to bake in a microwave?" asks Robert Schiffmann, a microwave consultant. Barbara Kafka, author of two groundbreaking microwave cookbooks, says, "One modestly sized piece of equipment cannot be asked to do the work of an entire kitchen." And yet that is often exactly what is expected.

"Moist and Creamy Omelets in a Fraction of the Normal Cooking Time," a newspaper headline promises. This miracle recipe takes the same amount of time as an omelet prepared stove-top, requires the cook to pull it in and out of the microwave to stir, and calls for a "colorful sauce . . . to hide the . . . pale exterior." And how long does it take to make this unnecessary colorful sauce?

More to the point when the subject is dinner: "It will do it," says cookbook author Marion Cunningham, "but can you eat it?"

Not very well, according to Takayuki Shibamoto and Helen C. H. Yeo, two chemists at UC Davis who found off flavors in the microwaved foods they tested.

From a cook's perspective, this cold steel box restricts a sensual exchange with ingredients, inhibiting the lusty aromas of food asimmer on the back burner. With it zapping away, no one comes home after work or school and says, "Boy, does it smell good in here."

I have used the microwave for cooking broccoli, corn, potatoes, and bacon, for popping corn (there were lots of unpopped old maids), and for reheating leftover rice, pasta, couscous, pizza, etc., tasks it is venerated for. While this eliminated muss and fuss and, when quantities were small, could compete with the Batmobile for speed, taste was not a word I would apply to the results. Taste, however, is not necessarily relevant for children needing a quick fix or for hungry, tired family members who come home after everyone else has eaten. And I never heard Jane Kane's cat complain after her food was heated up in it.

Providing an additional pair of hands, the microwave reheats mashed potatoes or dishes that would otherwise have to be stirred on top of the stove. For Joan Shymkio, manager of Friedmans' microwave store, this oven is for things she used "to burn stove-top."

The microwave is also touted as a defroster, a role it plays to mixed reviews. It works fine with soups, stocks, and sauces—though the buzzer goes off every ten seconds for you to adjust their stance—but meats and poultry start cooking on the outside before their interiors thaw. It can also be drying.

Perhaps the microwave's greatest asset is as a *sous-chef* for *mise en place*, getting things ready to cook. In many restaurant kitchens, it is given a post of honor for presoaking beans, caramelizing sugar, opening chestnuts and oysters, and reheating a beurre blanc without breaking it down.

It readily melts chocolate, butter, and jelly (for glazes). Heating herbs and chilies in a liquid, it extracts their essence. Most serendipitous was the discovery of how well it renders chicken fat. At half the saturation of butter, it is, gulp, a healthier delicious ingredient for a piecrust. Supporting a nutritious diet, the microwave also cooks ingredients without oil, butter, or additional fat.

The microwave plays a felicitous role as *dishwasher*. Minimizing cleanup, the same pan can be used for preparation, cooking, serving, and storing leftovers; freezing and reheating. Many foods can be cooked on paper towels or in plastic wrap, and take-out rewarmed directly in its container. Michelle Schmidt became a convert after washing ten pots used for heating one meal's leftover Chinese food.

Requiring a simple wipedown, the microwave stays clean since only food heats up, and spatters don't bake on oven walls. Pushing the domino effect, this means the kitchen also stays cool.

There is definitely a learning curve in operating a microwave, with each oven possessing its own unique rhythm. No standardization or consistency exists from one model to another, even within the same brand.

Microwave recipe directions cannot be applied generally. A dish cooked on full power comes out differently in a five hundred- and seven hundred-watt oven and in two different brands of seven hundred-watt ovens. Precise timing becomes an astrological art when dishes must stand after being removed from the oven to cook through. If your desired degree of doneness differs from the machine's, you will have to rework recipes in the instruction manual or preprogrammed memory.

Microwaved food overcooks in a microsecond with nary a clue. If dishes aren't checked repeatedly, cooks will share Marty Olsen's experience of vaporizing a chicken liver, with only the smell and a black blob left on its plate. (This may be desirable if you also want the microwave to act as a garbage disposer.)

Metal reflects microwaves, causing arcing, so stainless, copper, cast iron, aluminum, etc. are prohibited. Options are limited to ceramic, glass, paper (not recycled), and some plastic. Which plastic not to use is discovered after the container melts with your dinner in it. According to the *Nutrition Action Healthletter*, chemicals from "plastic 'cling' wraps" and "heat-susceptor packaging" can " 'migrate' . . . into your pizza, popcorn, or waffles."

MODERN MICROWAVE
This boldly designed stainless microwave with a ribbon of black glass strikes a handsome pose in today's professional-style kitchens. The 800-watt countertop or undercabinet unit has a 1.2 cubic foot capacity and is shown here with an optional built-in trim kit. Another model is available with Sensor Cook.

Equipment size, shape, and composition affect results more in a microwave than in a conventional oven. Square pans are jettisoned for round because microwaves meet and overcook *corner* food. You may need to purchase special cookware along with your microwave—and find a place to house it.

Operating a microwave safely is intrinsic to preventing hard-cooked eggs or plastic baby bottle liners from exploding because of steam buildup. Unsuspecting consumers can be burned by baby bottles, coffee, soup, and jelly doughnuts that feel disarmingly warm to the touch on the outside while boiling within. Steam from popcorn can cause corneal burn and eye damage.

Both the magnetic computer codes and heat-susceptor pads on food packages can cause a fire in the oven. So can grease accumulating in the microwave dispersion housing. Although microwaves must meet the U.S. Bureau of Radiological Health Emission standards and can easily be tested, there are still some Thomases doubting, worrying about leakage.

There seem to be three entirely different groups of microwave users: The "technozaps" more interested in technology than gastronomy, the "quick-ettes" preoccupied solely with convenience, and the "practocats" who sign the microwave up only for what it does best: simplifying tasks that don't compromise taste. If after reading this you still belong to the dwindling fourth group of "nonmicrowavers," remember that chocolate also melts seductively in a water bath on top of the stove.

What type of microwave do you want?

Once you decide to get a microwave oven, you need to know where it will be harbored before determining what type to get.

FREESTANDING

The freestanding category offers flexibility in placement as well as the greatest number of models to choose from if you can afford to give up a counter or shelf or even a wall to build in an oven with a trim kit.

UNDERCABINET

Undercabinet microwaves occupy otherwise unused space. Long and narrow, their shape is limited by the cabinet's twelve-inch depth, so they won't hold anything larger than a ten-and-one-half-inch dinner plate. A freestanding unit can go under a deeper wall cabinet.

BUILT-IN

Built-in microwave wall ovens can be purchased in tandem with a lower conventional oven with which it may or may not share a control panel. Chances of both the microwave and the conventional oven being the best in their category are slim, so one or the other will be a compromise.

Combining a microwave and conventional oven bestows a streamlined look on the kitchen, but this pairing is almost guaranteed to present problems down the road. With a shorter life span, a microwave will need to be replaced sooner than the regular oven, at which point it may be difficult to find a similarly sized unit to fit its space. If the ovens share a control panel, both units may have to be replaced.

When placing the microwave above a self-cleaning oven, inquire first whether this is recommended. If it is a go, order an additional vent to protect it from the heat.

MICROWAVE/RANGE HOOD COMBO

Microwaves are also available above a cooktop in tandem with a range or range hood. Though it is argued that this arrangement is a good solution for a small kitchen, both situations are must-misses. Too high to reach safely, this location courts disaster above a hot burner. The cooktop's continuous bombardment of heat will probably also hasten the microwave's demise, and it is insufficient as a ventilator (see page 260).

What do you want it to look like?

Microwaves vary in appearance from wood-grain-veneer stalwarts to sleek high-tech boxes colored more costly in black, white, and stainless, the most durable coating which will outlast the machine. Painted acrylic or ceramic chips. Some microwaves have an interior light. Less than convenient, it may have to go back to the shop to be replaced.

What size microwave do you want?

Microwaves, which have changed a bit since Raytheon introduced its six-foot 750-pound behemoth in 1948, are roughly classified according to their interior capacity as subcompacts (0.5 or less cubic feet), compacts (0.6 to 0.7 cubic feet), midsize (0.8 to 1.0 cubic feet), and full size (1.0 cubic feet or more). Since exterior and interior dimensions are not necessarily related, usable space is the most important criterion.

The midsize microwave is considered adequate for most tasks, but it does not keep options open as well as a full-size machine. Larger models are only slightly more expensive, offering welcome space and flexibility regardless of a machine's purpose. Unconvinced by a salesperson's similar argument, I watched one woman spend $200 on a compact number she wanted only to reheat coffee. Since a machine this small can do little else, the unsolved mystery is why she didn't just buy a thermos instead.

Microwaves have as great a variety of body types as people. Whether you are attracted to the long skinny ones or the short fat ones depends on your pots and space allotment. A machine long enough to hold two plates side by side may not be high enough for a soup tureen.

Neither capacity nor dimensions, however, are as important as the wattage they imply. A large machine needs more power to do the same job in its more capacious cavity than a small one.

In 1990, the U.S. Department of Energy set new standards for measuring microwave power. Adopting an internationally recognized testing procedure, it changed the wattage rating so that an old microwave with 650 watts would be equivalent to an 800-watt machine today. An old microwave is not less powerful, just rated differently. In either case, ratings are not always accurate. As a rough guide, most people are happiest with a full-size machine with a minimum of 800 to 1000 watts.

An energy saver, a microwave consumes the same amount of electricity as a six-inch cooktop element but operates at different *power levels*. Some machines are marked high, medium-high, medium, medium-low, and low, while others have up to ten varying levels (five are probably sufficient). High is always equivalent to 100 percent, but anything under that can vary; medium-high can be 50 or 70 percent power. Power level rotates according to local electric consumption, decreasing during peak usage. The particular level chosen may or may not be displayed in the digital readout.

What kind of bells and whistles do you want it to have?

The first question to ask about any of these items is whether you have the patience and time to learn how to ring all the bells and blow all the whistles. *Automatic defrost* and *sensor controls*, particularly for reheating, are universally appealing. A *clock* that operates as a *timer*, even when the oven is on, eliminates one more gadget from the countertop.

Technozaps, of course, will want additional buttons to push. Coming up? A microwave they can talk to. Programmed to open and shut its door on voice command, it will have an electronic screen that displays recipes and a picture of the finished dish.

At its best, a microwave is a convenience tool. When you ask it to do things that have nothing to do with convenience, you will probably be better off with another tool. Many features offer marginal benefits at best and are just one more thing that can break down.

All *keypads* should be logical, comfortable, clearly labeled, and easy to use, a definition met best by electronic controls. Your choice is between the *sequential pattern*, where the cooking time is punched in a number at a time, and the *count-up*. In this case, the second button is pressed down until your number comes up.

Sensors: The latest generation of microwaves is governed by sensors that determine *doneness* of certain foods by the amount of humidity or steam they emit. Determining power levels and cooking times automatically as well, they eliminate the need to check cooking directions. For these sniffers to work, food must be covered. They are least successful with liquids, breads, and large cuts of meat, but the microwave doesn't do a good job with the latter two items anyway.

Microwaves that come with a *probe* to register meat temperature don't, however, know that. Once the probe reaches a designated preset number, the oven turns off or reduces power to a *keep-warm* level, making the microwave a hurry-up-and-wait machine. Though this makes no sense for a microwave per se, it does if you want it to double as a warming drawer. A probe's accuracy is affected by its point of insertion and is awkward to read, particularly when a turntable halts it at the back of the oven.

Similar to the probe in function, without the worry of where to stick it, *weight cook* simplifies preparation of large cuts of meat and is somewhat more accurate and easier to use. You merely punch in the item and its weight, and the oven automatically adjusts power levels and determines cooking time.

Automatic defrost works essentially like weight cook. You enter the item and its weight, and the oven adjusts power levels with built-in rest periods for more even defrosting. Machines without an automatic setting use 30 percent power to defrost.

Preprogrammed Recipes: The sensor's comparative ease has outdated preprogrammed recipes. Requiring slavish adherence, they are thrown off by two tablespoons more or less of something.

Programmed Cooking: Two to four different commands or sequential cooking stages (power levels) can be programmed into the oven, which will automatically switch from one stage to the next. Since even defrosting food needs to be checked, two stages are ample and probably two stages too many. The *standing time* feature adds extra nonheat time.

Programs that prompt with a *digital readout* are homework free. All are getting friendlier. One cues with cooking and reheating hints—in English, Spanish, or French, with metric or standard measure. Another lets you program in multiple items by touching the keypad three times (for three potatoes). The machine then computes appropriate cooking time.

Automatic short-cook, minute-plus, and other similar signals for programming brief spurts of full-power cooking time duplicate the keypad.

Delayed start seems as inappropriate as *keep-warm* in a machine that convenience seekers want to be faster than a speeding bullet.

Carousel: Also called a turntable, an intrinsic component for some machines and an on/off option for others, this is intended to compensate for the unevenness of microwave cookery. Diminishing usable interior space, its effect, according to *Consumer Reports,* is to make "the unevenness more predictable." Food still has to be stirred.

Rack: A rack divides an oven so that it can cook several dishes concurrently. Of dubious advantage, it cooks the dishes at different rates, and the more there are of them, the longer they take. Two-level "doneness" can be predicted as confidently as when E.T. will phone home.

Browning Trays, Built-In Quartz Heaters: Rather than accumulating additional paraphernalia, finish foods that need to be browned under a broiler or relegate them to a conventional oven.

Do you want a microwave-convection combo oven?

As the microwave market becomes saturated, new combination ovens are being introduced to stimulate sales. Microwave-toasters and microwave-broilers are too slow to be serious, but microwave-convection ovens are appearing on more and more countertops. The question is: What are they doing there?

Advertised as combining the speed of a microwave with the browning ability of a convection oven, they switch back and forth between their dual cooking modes, blowing confusion in their wake. Jill Amand, the person I know who is fondest of this combo, is a technowizard willing to sacrifice flavor for the convenience of throwing in a chicken she for-got to defrost. Comments made about convection in a full-size radiant or multimode oven (page 237) apply to these smaller units as well.

Demanding and complicated to operate, a microwave with convection is roughly twice as expensive as one with a singular sway. Food bakes onto its surface during the hot convection phase, transforming the machine into a cleaning monster. While you're scrubbing, say good-bye to a cool kitchen, for the exhaust is not equipped to handle fat. If the convection phase is turned on first, the microwave won't kick in until the oven cools down. Paper and plastic can no longer serve as cooking vessels without going into meltdown. Meanwhile, too many of these ovens reportedly go into breakdown.

The microwave's petite size makes it suitable for doubling as a second oven when small amounts of food are cooked; a potato baked, pizza slices reheated. But not everyone likes the microwave's handling of these tasks. Too drying, the convection oven doesn't do a much better job. For the universal good (and sake of that single baked potato), pair a microwave with a radiant instead of convection oven.

PERSONAL PICKS: MICROWAVE OVENS

As someone who finds that food loses its vital essence when cooked or reheated in a microwave, I am not the person to recommend one brand over another. Yet I can certainly see why a family with hungry children and limited time would put this appliance on their shopping list.

My Sharp microwave has a large cavity and high wattage and fits under an extra-deep wall cabinet. I chose this machine because of these three attributes. Of course there was also an attractive deal sweetened by some scratches on the box. For a microwave, this seems just fine except during defrosting, when its knock-out button rings in ten-second rounds to announce the need for repositioning. Along with Sharp, Panasonic, Quasar, General Electric, and Amana have been considered leaders in the field. Since food doesn't come out well from any of them, you might also want to consider the KitchenAid, which comes in a spiffier stainless-steel box.

KITCHENSPEAK: MICROWAVE OVENS

Interior Size:

   Subcompact: **0.5 cubic feet or less.**

   Compact: **0.6 to 0.7 cubic feet.**

   Midsize: **0.8 to 1.0 cubic feet.**

   Full Size: **1.0 cubic feet or more.**

Magnetron: **An electronic vacuum tube that produces microwaves by converting household electricity into high-energy waves that bounce off the oven's impenetrable metal walls.**

Microwave: **A short electromagnetic high-frequency wave.**

Power Levels: **Varying from one machine to the next, the microwave's heat intensity is indicated either by percentages or the words** *high,* *medium,* **and** *low.*

Sensors: **Machines with sensors determine the** *doneness* **of certain foods by the amount of humidity or steam they emit.**

Stirrer: **A fan that distributes the waves in a microwave box.**

VENTILATION

■

We fret about smog, decry toxic chemicals, and rail against ozone depletion, remaining oblivious to the pollution in our own kitchens. "A family of four produces one-half to one gallon of grease a year," says Vent-A-Hood's Ed Gober. Left to its own devices, the slick gloms onto walls, cabinets, and countertops, luring insects with its pungent rancidity. Nitrogen dioxide, carbon dioxide, carbon monoxide, and water vapor—its lethal by-products—leave mold, mildew, fungus, and destruction: Our kitchens are disgusting.

My preremodeled kitchen qualified for first prize in this category. Touching something in this sooty space was like walking in quicksand. Always miserably hot, it could have been mistaken for a desert campfire, a condition I thought preferable to dealing with the noise from my rickety ventilation system.

A ventilation system sounds like a motorcycle marathon, costs more than you could imagine in your worst nightmare, and can be an eyesore if you're not into its looks. I can think of many other things—millions of other things—I'd rather spend my money on. Even paper towels are more interesting, and they don't make noise at you. But the alternative—to go without one—is worse.

Most often, ventilation is an afterthought. The stove and cabinets are already installed; the budget depleted. One Saturday morning you mosey down to pick up a unit, only to learn that the hood requires thirty-seven and one-quarter inches of space, not the thirty-seven and one-eighth the contractor allotted. Then you find out the price. "Forget it," you say, choosing a cute little fan number that doesn't do ventilation: massacre the bad guys.

My attitude toward ventilation changed when I purchased a commercial grill. I knew I had to get serious about this subject or live with the threat of a potential fire. Such a choice. Somehow the former seemed wiser. In the crossover, I found ventilation religion and became a fanatic. For health, cleanliness, and safety reasons, it's now right up there on the equipment priority list right after the cooktop. As infuriating as it is to spend money this way, my advice is to go for broke as long as it doesn't break you.

It was clear my architect knew nothing about ventilation. She found three-day-old food odors appetizing. The unit she drew—supposedly in conjunction with a restaurant designer—violated every tenet of good ventilation. My contractor was equally uninformed. After checking with a commercial fabricator, he returned with a bid of $12,000 and the assurance that the company would equip my home with the same system it had installed at the mall. Huh?

Flash. My friend Donna Kamin had the same stove I was buying. She'd know, I thought.

Donna's hood, with its imported tile facing, was magnificent. Its interior, however, gave new meaning to Stephen Hawking's discovery of the black hole. Inside there was nothing. No exhaust system. No ductwork. No ventilation!

Donna has a ventilation system now. So do I. So should you. This includes a hood to collect the air, an exhaust system for removing noxious cooking byproducts, ducts to carry the cleansed air outside, and a pressure-activated backdraft damper that closes when the fan is off, preventing cold air from flowing back into the house. Having these elements is half the battle. You've also got to turn them on. To create a curtain that draws the air, start the system several minutes before cooking begins.

HOOD

A holding area, the hood functions most efficiently above the cooktop or grill, where it captures heat rising naturally. Air expands eighteen hundred times as it is heated, obliging the hood to be a generous canopy rather than a thin box, telescope, or slimline silhouette. Alluring visually, these minimalists are among the reputed 90 percent of hoods performing at barely 10 percent efficiency. "Looks good" and "works good" are not necessarily related in this category.

According to research by the University of Minnesota, a hood's gathering power is augmented by twelve-inch-wide side baffles extending down from the hood to the cooktop. Though I've not yet seen these screens utilized commercially, they could easily be incorporated into a custom system. For temporary employ, set them up to pull down from the hood much like a window shade. I've tested this concept informally by hanging aluminum foil from the side of my hood and found it to be a great aid in removing smoke from duck and ribs that were living it up on the grill.

A hood should be three inches longer than the cooktop on each side (six inches, if possible, for a commercial-style cooktop or grill) and wide enough to extend beyond the edge of the front burners. The closer the hood to the cooktop, the better it behaves. Experts suggest a distance of twenty-one to thirty inches (*maximum*) between the top of the work surface and the bottom of the hood.

A narrower hood is usually hung closer to the work surface, while a wider one can be farther away. Many people fear they will bang their head at this low height when in fact the opposite occurs: A hood and your head are safest within your line of sight.

Adhere to recommendations. Hanging a hood just one inch above this point diminishes its drawing power by 5 to 10 percent. The loss escalates exponentially until six inches, where you might as well forget it altogether. Motorized hoods are available that move up or down, a rare instance where the additional expense of flexibility does not seem justifiable. When you need a hood, you need it where it does its job best.

A hood placed above an island must be configured even more carefully than one mounted against a wall, for air currents move crosswise in this location, scattering contaminants throughout the room. In this situation, extend the hood three—better six—inches beyond the cooktop on all sides.

Attaching to the wall, soffit, or ceiling, hoods vary in style, from an unassuming invisible tilt-out to the massive, showstopper statement. Available in a variety of shapes, they are finished in brass, copper, plaster, glass, baked enamel, ceramic tile, solid surface, or stainless. In the last case, utilize a thick fourteen- (better) or sixteen-gauge stainless that won't buckle. A hood can also be faced with a real or

HOODS

phony trompe l'oeil cabinet front. Or purchase just the shell and enrobe as desired.

Substantial hoods boast smooth welded edges with invisible seams and a gutter for catching grease as it vaporizes. To increase capacity, eliminate mitered edges in any hood shallower than the depth of the cooktop. All canopies above a commercial-style cooktop must be lined in metal.

Plate racks, shelves, and pot hooks decorate some hoods; spice racks others. In exchange for their aesthetic contribution, spices will be short-lived in this hot box; plates and pots grease-spattered. Limit shelves to a depth of eight inches or less so as not to interfere with the ventilator's travail.

Rig the hood with vaporproof lights, sandblasted to reduce their glare. Those with variable intensities can be turned up to work under or down for a night-light. Build fire-extinguishing equipment into the hood as it is in restaurants. A heat-sensing device that releases its goods automatically, a *water sprinkler,* or *wet or dry* (hardest to clean up) *chemical system* comes to the rescue.

EXHAUST SYSTEM

Two primary types of exhaust systems exist. Both extract the grease before channeling the heated,

CANOPIES

In order for a ventilation system to be effective, its hood must be a substantial canopy. A wall-hung hood should be long enough to extend three inches beyond each side of the cooktop and wide enough to completely cover its front burners. A ceiling mounted hood above an island should extend three—better six —inches beyond each side of the cooktop. In all cases, the distance between the top of the cooktop burners and the bottom of the hood should range only from twenty-one to thirty inches.

expanded air into ducts. Far superior is the *rotary pressurized blower* in what is called a *squirrel-cage system.* Operating by centrifugal force, it cools and removes grease instantly before sending the air on through in a swift, smooth, relatively quiet manner.

The second kind of exhaust depends on a *propeller-* or *axial-driven fan.* Mounted in a tube, the latter type vibrates less and is quieter. Comparatively ineffective, this method (henceforth called *fan*) continues to be a player, for it is less costly than a squirrel-cage system.

A fan spins air, moving it more slowly and unevenly through the ducts than a centrifugal blower. It creates more turbulence, drag, and static, or backpressure. Noise is considerable. In the worst scenario, a ticking sound emits as blades hit duct walls.

Some centrifugal pressure blowers *squeeze* grease out into a *collection cup,* but most of these systems and those that are fan-driven depend on *filters* to absorb the grease. Prominent in the restaurant industry, *baffle filters* are preferred to *wire mesh,* for they are quieter and less prone to clogging and catching ignitable lint.

To work well, a mesh filter must be thick and cleansed regularly. Eventually it self-destructs.

Where should the exhaust system be mounted?

An exhaust system can be installed completely inside the hood or divided, with filters in the hood and blower or fan motors remoted to the roof. A remote installation is usually more expensive as well as more difficult to access and maintain. In a New York apartment, it can cost $500 per story. Many homeowners are not fond of having "this big ugly thing on the outside," either. When it's placed next to their bedroom window, neighbors will be even less enthusiastic.

A ventilation system's noise source is twofold, assaulting you from the exhaust motor as well as from movement of air. When a motor is installed inside a hood, both sounds are audible. Displacing the motor to the roof eliminates one racket as long as its outlet is far from the kitchen and angled away from the hood. When the motor caps a straight duct run of only six or seven feet, air whooshes back into the kitchen like *Apollo* landing. Complicating the picture, these remote blowers can spread a fire, drawing flames from cooktop to roof.

A motor of any capacity can be placed on the roof, chalking up an advantage for a remote installation when a hood is too small to pack in a high-powered system. A larger motor runs more slowly and thus more silently.

When blowers or fans are installed inside a hood, their number depends on cooktop burners and components. Mount them directly over the burners they are servicing and a separate griddle or grill. Anchoring one between units is insufficient.

Each blower or fan should have its own speed control that switches from low to high according to whether cooking is light or heavy. Moving up, some systems have electronic controls with infinite speed, a timer delay that operates the system for five minutes before shutting it off, a light that comes on when filters need cleaning, a memory that returns the system to a previous setting, or a switch that automatically increases the exhaust to high when a certain temperature is reached. At best these automatic functions seem frivolous, and they could be dangerous. By switching to high when a fire starts on a burner, a blower or fan feeds the flames.

DUCTS

Ducts conduct exhausted air, moving it from blower or fan through walls, soffit, or ceiling to a screened capped outlet in an exterior wall or roof. When the exhaust system has been remoted to the roof, ducts convey the air from the hood to this system.

DUCTS

AIR MOVEMENT
Ducts conduct air through walls, the soffit, or ceiling to the exterior of a home. The length and shape of the path it travels is dictated by the system's manufacturer and must be followed precisely for the ventilation to work.

All ducting must end outdoors and any cabinet or combustible material it crosses insulated with fireproofing. If the duct for an island installation can't be threaded through the ceiling, it can be attached to it and then covered with a false beam. Just keep it away from an operable skylight where it can pump its pollutants back into the room.

The shorter and straighter the ductwork path, the better the ventilation system works. Turbulent backpressure builds to resist air flow in even a short shot. The longer the run and the more turns it makes, the less efficient the best ventilation system becomes. An adjustable elbow or one at forty-five degrees foments fewer eddies than one at ninety, for air turns round corners only, not square ones. When do-si-doing its corners frequently, the system is noisy.

Once again, manufacturer's recommendations for duct sizes and materials must be observed precisely. Joints must be tight and well sealed to avoid leakage or pressure drop; flexible ducting avoided. How well the system works depends on how well it is installed. Despite precautions, a cold front sometimes moves in around the hood.

How much noise do you have to put up with?

As you might have guessed by now, noise pollution is going to be an issue no matter which ventilation system is purchased. Between the whir of the motor and the movement of air through filters and ducts, the cacophony can be deafening. To bring some order to this chaos, ventilation systems carry a *sone* rating, or measurement of sound. This number is of only minimal value, for it is arrived at in many a fashion. All things being equal, choose the system with the lowest sone rating. The Home Ventilating Institute has established nine sones as maximum for a five-hundred-CFM blower. A non-MTV ventilation system should run about seven. As a point of reference, a quiet refrigerator is rated at one sone.

When is a ductless ventilation system indicated?

"I've never been in a house where I couldn't run a duct to the outside," claims Bob Bergstrom from VAH Marketing. That may be the case, but in some high-rise buildings a duct path can be too expensive and, no matter how bad it is, a ductless system the only realistic choice.

In this arrangement, the air passes through an aluminum charcoal filter that absorbs some of its odors before circulating it back into the kitchen. The thicker the block, the longer it takes to activate but the more noxious aromas it absorbs. This method ignores both heat and smoke and requires frequent maintenance and replacement. Ventilation is negligible at best. If you are limited to this option, buy the least expensive unit you can find.

Do you want a downdraft ventilation system?

The hoodless or downdraft ventilation system is increasingly popular, particularly on islands, among folks who don't like the heft of a hood. Operating at 40 to 50 percent efficiency, it gets a lot of praise—not because it is good, mind you, but because so many overhead installation systems are useless or installed in a manner that renders them that way. In practice, a downdraft has about the same effect on grease as a glass of water on a forest fire. In case you can't tell, I don't think this system does the job.

Minus a hood, the downdraft consists of a vent in the countertop—either behind or next to the cooktop or between cooktop modules—and an exhaust below. Fighting physics—pulling down what wants to go up—the downdraft creates a low-pressure zone above the burners that pushes air into a filter and then ducts its degreased molecules outside through a basement or crawl space.

Longer than the duct run through a wall or ceiling, this system is consequently less efficient. It may well not be feasible if you reside in a home built on a slab or in an apartment with no path for ducts.

Some downdrafts are integral parts of the cooktop; others are purchased separately. Better performers rise six to nine inches, but even these are minimally effective, and only in tandem with low-heat, shallow pans of three inches depth or less, and cooking methods that don't call for spattering fat. Get those french fries at McDonald's.

Higher-powered downdrafts may, ironically,

extinguish a gas flame or divert heat from whatever is being cooked. In many instances, a large pot won't fit on the burner adjacent to an operating downdraft. Some cooktops with a downdraft produce so little heat that they obviate the need for ventilation. In this case, you get both an inferior cooktop and an inferior ventilation system. Its noise is nasty and light insufficient unless installed in the ceiling overhead. Great.

After saying all this, I recognize that many people may still prefer a downdraft, particularly when their cooking revolves around skillet fare. If this is your preference, evaluate the system's ease of cleaning and the amount of space it occupies in the cabinet and confirm that it has a damper for closing out cold air.

How powerful a ventilation system do you need?

Power is the key to a ventilation system's prowess. It does little good to collect the air in a huge hood if the system isn't powerful enough to exhaust it. Power is rated in CFM or the number of cubic feet of air a blower or fan can move per minute. To check a system's CFM rating, look at the label attached to the hood.

The type of cooking you do influences the amount of power needed. People who grill, stir-fry, deep-fry, or engage in other high-heat cookery need more power than those who occasionally put up a pot of tea. The National Kitchen & Bath Association's technical manual suggests fifty to seventy CFM per square foot for a hood installed against a wall (three hundred CFM minimum) and one hundred CFM per square foot for one over an island (six hundred CFM minimum). A high-heat commercial cooktop requires roughly twelve hundred CFM for six burners. Figure on eighteen hundred when adding a grill to this lineup.

Commercial or commercial-style cooktop owners may be more comfortable with formulas used for commercial installations. For a cooktop against a wall, the formula is A (area) × 100. If the hood is 3 by 2 feet or an area of 6 feet, multiplying it by 100 yields 600 CFM. If a grill is added, the formula becomes A × 150. Over an island, the numbers increase to A × 200 for burners and A × 300 with a grill. Though this power may not always need to be switched on high, it is there when needed.

Though both of these formulas suffice, the truest reading is the amount of CFM left at the point where air exits from the house, a measurement that takes into account the loss of efficiency over a long or winding duct run. To determine it, have your contractor or HVAC consultant compute the length of ducting you will have and the number of its turns. Figure .1 inch of static pressure for every ten feet of duct; .2 inch for every ninety-degree elbow. Then call the manufacturer of the ventilation system you are considering and ask for the CFM rating necessary at your static pressure.

Do you need makeup air?

The ventilation system is the only example I can think of where too much of a good thing may be too much. While you need enough power to remove heat, moisture, and pollutants from the kitchen, you don't want to remove more air than is entering, or you may find yourself dangling from the ceiling, sucked up by the negative pressure that rushes in to fill the void.

Negative pressure, or *backdrafting* as it is called, can also drive by-products of furnace or water-heater combustion—or any radon present in the soil—back into the house. Telltale signs? Look for walls that feel cold to the touch, pilots that blow out, and doors that slam shut and resist opening. Gaseous odors and frequent headaches are further indicators.

Negative pressure situations have increasingly materialized as tighter, energy-efficient homes have been built over the last decades, eliminating the cracks where fresh air once entered to replace the exhausted supply. A window across from the hood or adjacent to it should provide enough air to maintain a delicate balance. If this is still a concern, explore a *supply fan* or *heat recovery ventilator.*

An *exhaust fan* helps cool the kitchen down during summer and recirculates warm air that rises from the stove during winter. Mounted on a ceiling or wall adjacent to the cooktop that vents directly outside, it does not remove contaminants or in any way substitute for a ventilation system. To determine the CFM an exhaust fan needs, multiply the square footage of the kitchen by two.

PERSONAL PICKS: VENTILATION

To qualify as a ventilation system, whatever you purchase must include a hood, an exhaust system, and ducts. The minimalist thin flat hoods and downdraft systems just don't remove pollutants adequately. Neither does the combo microwave/hood nor any unit with minsky two hundred CFM. And if you can possibly afford to get around it in a high-rise, avoid a ductless system. Many of my picks have been superficially based on looks, so I can't exactly fault someone else for behaving similarly, but I urge hood haters to choose a system that is adequate for removing contaminants.

There seem to be two basic approaches to consider here. One is for a thirty- or thirty-six-inch residential-type cooktop that is installed against a wall or on an island. In this case I'd go for a squirrel-cage system with a grease collection cup or baffle filters and a minimum of three hundred CFMs for a wall installation; six hundred for an island. A more powerful system is required for a commercial-type cooktop (twelve hundred CFM minimum) plus a grill (eighteen hundred CFM minimum). This could be remoted to the roof as long as it is not over the hood in a short duct run, or you will soon be on the run from the noise. If you are a major fryer or are considering a commercial grill, I'd suggest having pull-down baffles added to the sides of the hood.

I have been speaking primarily about ventilation for a cooktop or range, but if you are going to be doing some heavy-duty broiling in a wall oven or roasting lots of splattering ducks, a ventilation system above an oven will be welcome as well.

After speaking to a variety of fabricators and not understanding one word of what they were saying, I finally settled on a Vent-A-Hood. My hood is not particularly nice looking, and its price, though less than many other quotes I had, was ghastly. What won me over was the ability of Bob Bergstrom, the company's local representative, to explain what I needed and why in a logical manner that instilled confidence. The people I've spoken to at the headquarters for Abbaka and Russell Range also seem quite knowledgeable. This is not a system to be romanced into buying. Talk to as many people as necessary until you feel comfortable that you've made the right choice for your situation. Brand seems less important in this category than having a unit with the correct dimensions, a sizable hood, a squirrel-cage exhaust system, and sufficient CFM. Above all, follow the experts' recommendations for size and installation. And be sure they are as *expert* as they claim.

KITCHENSPEAK: VENTILATION

Backdraft Damper: Pressure-activated flap that closes when the ventilation fan is off, preventing cold air from coming back into the house.

CFM: The *cubic feet per minute* or power a blower or fan possesses to move air.

Collection Cup: Gathers the grease extracted from the air in some squirrel-cage exhaust systems. See also Squirrel-Cage.

Downdraft Ventilation System: Minus a hood, a down-draft consists of a flat or raised vent in the countertop that pulls the air down into a filter, where it is degreased and then ducted outside through a base-ment or crawl space.

Ductless System: An inadequate ventilation system that passes the air through a charcoal filter to remove some of its odors and then recirculates it back into the kitchen instead of removing it from the house.

Ducts: Once air has been cleansed in the exhaust sys-tem, it is carried outside through a series of ducts.

Exhaust System: Removes noxious cooking by-products before moving air to the ducts. See also Squirrel Cage.

Filters: Installed in an exhaust system to absorb grease. Baffle filters are more effective than wire mesh.

Hood: Collects the contaminated air that needs to be expelled.

Makeup Air: If more air is removed from a kitchen than enters it, creating negative pressure, the balance must be restored with makeup air.

Remote Exhaust System: An exhaust system installed outside the house on the roof.

Sone: The unit of measurement for expressing the amount of noise generated by a ventilation system. Seek a measurement in the range of seven.

Squirrel Cage: The most efficient type of exhaust sys-tem with a rotary pressurized blower that removes grease by centrifugal force.

8

CHILLERS

REFRIGERATORS* AND FREEZERS

■

The refrigerator is a heat mover much as Los Angeles's Beverly Center mall is a people mover. While the mall moves people from one floor to the next—depositing their money along the way—the refrigerator pushes the heat that causes food to deteriorate out into the atmosphere, leaving cooled air in its wake. To complete this cyclical process, the refrigerator has typically expended at least 20 percent of the total energy used in the home, an excess that has targeted it for modification.

Prodded not so gently by the U.S. Department of Energy and the Environmental Protection Agency's mandates for minimal energy efficiency standards, refrigerator manufacturers have been revamping their systems, with numbers to prove their great strides forward. Energy consumption (annual kilowatt usage) has dropped by over 50 percent since 1972, while energy efficiency, mode of operation, has increased by over 150 percent for a refrigerator with an automatic-defrost freezer above and by over 130 percent for side-by-side and bottom-mounted units.

In the period during which greater energy efficiency has been sought, the very same chlorofluorocarbons (CFCs) that could facilitate this achievement have been banned, hampering this quest. Both *CFC 11*, a component of foam insulation, and *CFC 12*, an element of the coolant freon, have rendered the refrigerator more efficient in recent years—at the expense of the environment. Believed to deplete the ozone layer that protects us from harmful ultraviolet radiation, this price can no longer be paid.

In a new collaborative approach to addressing industry challenges, the *Super Efficient Refrigerator Pro-*

gram (SERP) was born in 1992. Banding together, a group of public and private utility companies offered a reward of $30 million to the company that designed the winning "super-efficient, nontoxic refrigerator" without CFCs that bested EPA standards. Frigidaire and Whirlpool were this contest's cofinalists, with the award ultimately going to the latter company. Whirlpool, KitchenAid, Sears, GE, and U-Line all have CFC-free refrigerators on the market as of this writing, but this is only the tip of the iceberg storer. Stay tuned.

Alterations made to increase energy efficiency thus far are so low on the attention-grabbing scale as to not be noticeable. When you go to purchase a new refrigerator, it will probably look similar to your previous one, but it will possess at least some of the following innovations:

■ *Separate refrigeration systems for refrigerator and freezer in combo models.* Separate refrigeration systems allow both refrigerator and freezer to run at optimum temperatures without the extra energy expenditure of cooling down the refrigerator to reach a desired freezer temperature. When one door is opened, cool air need be replenished in only that unit. In addition to more accurate temperature con-

---

*Unless specified separately, the word *refrigerator* means a refrigerator-freezer combination in this chapter.

trol, a dual system reportedly keeps foods fresher and prevents transfer of odors between refrigerator and freezer.

- *Top-mounted refrigeration system.* As heat rises, it moves away from the unit more naturally when the refrigeration system is mounted on top rather than in back as was the norm. Permitting a larger interior space, top mounting also simplifies maintenance. The unit no longer needs to be pulled out for cleaning and repair: Both compressor and condenser are optimally accessed from the front.

- *Smaller motors and compressors*

- *Improved insulation*

- *Energy-saver switches.* Heaters prevent sweating and condensation that form when warm moist air hits a cold surface during humid weather. Switching heaters off during dry stretches saves electricity.

- *Improved door seals*

- *Heavier hinges.* Heavy plate steel or die-cast hinges keep doors aligned so they don't sag. Some companies cover the top hinge to match the refrigerator cabinet.

- *Improved automatic defrosting. Frost-free* freezers have fewer, shorter defrost cycles. This baby is now being defrosted automatically on demand rather than on a preset schedule.

The *manual-defrost* freezer, the most energy efficient of all—as well as the least expensive—is, ironically, hard to find. I would make some hefty concessions to get my old one back. Unlike a fluctuating frost-free unit, its temperature never wavered. It was quieter, too, for its compressor ran less. Food lasted longer with no fan to dry it out, and peas that went in fresh did not come out freeze-dried.

Between manual and frost-free in efficiency, *cycle defrost* proceeds automatically once activated by the consumer.

- *Through-the-door shelves.* Reaching a shelf *through* the door utilizes less energy than opening the door in its entirety. (This savings does not extend to on-the-door water and ice delivery, which belongs in the heavy-energy-use category.)

ENERGY-EFFICIENCY FACTORS

When shopping for a refrigerator, you can determine its energy efficiency—*energy-efficient factor (EEF)*—by checking its yellow *energy guide* label. To figure the appliance's estimated annual energy cost, divide its cubic feet by the number of kilowatt-hours it consumes. *Your* actual cost varies according to how you employ the unit, the percentage of cubic feet available for food storage, and the precise local energy rate, which is averaging about 8.25 cents per kilowatt-hour. The lower the refrigerator costs to operate, the higher the EEF, or the more efficient it is.

To find the lifetime cost of each refrigerator you are considering, multiply the estimated cost of annual operation as stated on the Guide by twenty (the average life of a refrigerator). Then add its purchase price to this number. When comparing units, the one with the lowest number costs less overall.

The number of years it takes to make up the extra expenditure for a model that is more expensive initially but more energy efficient and thus less expensive over the long haul can be figured as well. To do so, subtract the lower purchase price from the higher; the lower lifetime operating cost from the higher. Then divide the subtracted purchase price by the subtracted operating price. To assess these costs precisely, substitute the local fee per kilowatt-hour as stated on your monthly electric bill.

While we're speaking of costs, *if you're trying to save money, the refrigerator is the perfect place to begin.* Starting at $1,600 to $1,800 and traveling straight up, many of the sleek new models are quite seductive. Yet you don't need sleek here; just a box to keep food cold. The refrigerator doesn't even have to do that very well if you shop frequently and look to its freezer only for short-term storage. In this case, base purchase totally on price and put the savings into a better cooktop, oven, ventilation, and even dishwasher, tools that throttle a kitchen full-tilt.

Unlike many illustrious citizens who have difficulty *chilling out*, refrigerators handle this feat quite admirably—regardless of price. Yes, consumers carp about the configuration of the box they've purchased (without adequate forethought), but only one friend bemoans a lemon, and what other appliance can you say this about? As a representative of the now-defunct Defiance company told her, "You had the misfortune to purchase the last refrigerator that came off the line, and the men just didn't care very much."

What kind of refrigeration do you want?

A refrigerator only?

A freezer only?

Both a separate refrigerator and separate freezer?

A combined unit with a freezer placed above, below, or to the refrigerator's side?

A second refrigerator for the kitchen or in an outlying area such as a bar or patio?

A second freezer for the kitchen or in an outlying area such as a garage or utility room?

Multiple undercounter compact refrigerators and freezers scattered throughout the kitchen? Single units? Combined units? A refrigerator combined with only an icemaker for a bar?

A separate icemaker (page 276)?

A wine cooler or beer tap (page 275)?

If budget and space are generous, a separate refrigerator and freezer are preferable. Tailored specifically to individual needs, the size and shape of each unit can differ accordingly while offering eye-level storage and several shelves that can be reached without stooping. When placed outside the primary work area, the freezer frees a venue for more frequently tapped equipment.

In a small kitchen or one where considerable freezer space is desired, a more pragmatic scenario is to have a refrigerator with a top- or bottom-mounted freezer for frequently used items in the kitchen and a second larger freezer in a garage or utility room.

These vaults offer comfort and convenience to gatherers and hunters of all ilk: to vegetable gardeners, do-ahead cooks, Lean Cuisine zappers, Häagen-Dazs stockholders, country folk down the road a far piece from the store, and bread bakers whose

recipes read "divide into eight balls." In my freezer, a voyeur would be rewarded with duck fat to render for cooking potatoes and duck and lamb bones (which you can't buy) for making stock. Taking the freezer about as far as it will go, Julie Murphy has usurped her smaller unit to store angora sweaters where they won't shed.

With today's kitchens used by more cooks, divided into separate work zones for baking, microwaving, and bartending, and called on to perform a variety of high-wire acts such as pasta cutting, pizza twirling, bread baking, and canning, they may be better served with several smaller undercounter refrigerators, freezers, and/or icemakers distributed throughout the room than by the single traditional hulk.

Reduced to the size of small fry, these compact units see eye to eye with children, who find them a cinch for going in and out of, while adults complain they cause a case of the bends. The one drawback to multiple units (and styles with pull-out drawers instead of doors) is remembering what you put where.

Compact units can be stacked, left freestanding, and, front-vented, built into a base cabinet with space remaining for upper cabinets or windows. Available from fifteen to twenty-four inches wide, single units can be housed side by side, mixing refrigerators, freezers, wine coolers, and icemakers in one cool area.

How large should your unit(s) be?

When purchasing an appliance, I go for flexibility above all, buying the biggest affordable model that fits into a designated space. The refrigerator is my single exception to this rule. Too important to ignore, energy conservation forbids indulgence in a bigger-than-necessary unit.

The refrigerator runs sweetest two-thirds full, neither under- nor overstocked. If your estimate is incorrect or needs change, you may find yourself in the same predicament as my mother. Baking less frequently these days, she keeps her freezer filled with toilet paper ballast instead of cookies. (I've not had the nerve to ask what frozen paper feels like.)

Refrigerators run the gamut from under-two-cubic-foot countertop squatters to thirty-some-thing-cubic-foot side-by-side behemoths. General guidelines suggest eight to twelve cubic feet of refrigerator space for a two-person household plus two cubic feet for each additional person. From what I've observed, however, there seems to be as much correlation between the quintessential refrigerator and the number of people it services as there is between a bag of marshmallows and the number of sticks for s'mores.

For starters, a manufacturer's assessment of *cubic feet* may be misguided. Depending on the compressor's location and configuration, some interior space may be wasted. More telling are the box's culinary tenants and landlord.

Phyllis Nobel regards the refrigerator as a "museum of memorable meals," while Barbara Picheny is a devotee of refrigerator-as-mausoleum. "You're not so old," her birthday card read, "I got stuff in my fridge that's older than you." She wasn't kidding. Some years ago, she unearthed a tinfoil-embalmed packet marked July 10, 1977. The date was December 3, 1992. If you resemble one of these women and like to stuff your refrigerator to the gills, lay claim to the largest box you can find.

Some people use the freezer to hide food they feel guilty about throwing out or, believe it or not, for refuse. If you opened the refrigerator of my husband's prior boss, you found nothing but bags of garbage waiting for collection day. Since there was nothing in the refrigerator to cook, it was hard to tell where all this garbage came from. But, then again, this boss didn't last very long.

Catering to only two adults, my 17.9-cubic-foot refrigerator is crammed. My neighbor, who feeds two active children, two large dogs, and a husband with a voracious appetite, has a minsky 10.3-cubic-foot box that looks like an advertisement for a vacancy.

Shopping daily as she did when living in Europe, Elke Solomon maintains a refrigerator that is too empty to run efficiently during the week and too full to hold platters for her weekend antipasti and dessert buffets. Aiko Lee needs a box just for the gallons of milk and apple juice sons Jeremy, Zack, and Timmy John down. Yet when the last son goes to college, it will be as empty as her nest.

Prescribing the correct refrigerator size is a lot harder than answering Brillat-Savarin's query, "Tell me what you eat and I shall tell you what you are."

The best way to determine ideal refrigerator size is to evaluate current capacity while anticipating lifestyle changes. If groceries reside comfortably in your current refrigerator and no additions or subtractions are anticipated in family constellation, buy another box with the same capacity. If not, go up or down according to whether it is too small or too large and the types of things, if any, it doesn't hold.

Do you need wider shelves on the door or more height between them for taller containers? A separate refrigerated drawer for cheese and cold cuts? Larger crispers for fruits and vegetables? *Address overall dimensions, available space, and the size of the doorway it must fit through as well as the proportion of storage to be relegated to refrigerator and freezer.*

Do you want a built-in refrigerator?

Historically this was not a choice. Running roughly twenty-seven to thirty inches deep, the refrigerator protruded awkwardly beyond the standard twenty-four-inch base cabinet unless it was recessed into a wall or adjacent cabinets were pulled out. Today the norm *is* a built-in refrigerator, a built-in look (a refrigerator that slides into a twenty-four-inch-deep space and is fitted with a perimeter trim kit), or a boxed-in refrigerator (a unit set into a frame of equal depth). Door handles, custom panels, and venting space requirements extend some built-in look styles, so cabinets may still need to come out for a flush fit.

Perhaps the ultimate built-in no-see is the European refrigerator squirreled away behind a cabinet door. Designed for a populace that shops daily, these units tend to be too small and run too warm to suit most American lifestyles.

Unlike machines given a built-in look, true built-ins consume more energy and accept custom panels on their ends as well as on their front. Freezers generally fall to the side or below the refrigerator. Price-wise, they're up there in stratosphere land, but they eliminate dust-ball-harboring crevices and the pain of pulling out the unit for cleaning.

It's easy to find food on these refrigerators' shallower shelves, but you won't find a sizable turkey, ham, or even a cake or baking sheet for a large oven, for they're too shallow to hold these items. And, with many companies now offering refrigerator shelves that pull out—a brilliant innovation—it's now possible (with luck) to locate edibles in a deeper box.

As classy as built-ins are, you'll receive much better overall service by jimmying cabinet and counter size for the look than by reducing—and sacrificing—the depth of a refrigerator (and all the flexibility this implies) to twenty-four inches. Another bonus is the handy thirty-inch-deep counter this organization will yield.

In a refrigerator-freezer combo, where is the freezer optimally located?

Roughly 70 percent of refrigerators have freezers on top, providing more models to choose from in this category. Nonetheless, reasons abound for placing them on the bottom or side as well. Whether the freezer is more convenient above or below the refrigerator depends on user height and popularity of refrigerator and freezer.

If you are at least average height or taller and crave refrigerator foods more than frozen ones, a *bottom-mount* freezer shortens the reach to the crisper and raises most frequently sought foods to eye level. With a pullout bin, it's easier to retrieve food from a bottom-mount freezer than one on high. For this privilege, you have to forgo the luxury of ice and water on the door, not currently offered in this position.

A bottom-mount freezer is more expensive than a *top-mount* and less energy efficient. Close to the motor, it runs hard, whereas the top-mount minimizes exertion by blowing the freezer's cold air down into the refrigerator. Most expensive and reportedly more likely to break down, *side-by-side* units earn the label "least energy efficient" every time their full-length door is ajar.

Offering more shelf space within the ultimate easy-reach zone between twenty-two and fifty-six inches off the floor, side-by-side refrigeration provides more items at the front of the box and eye-level storage regardless of height. Everybody—whether seated or standing—can reach food in both refrigerator and freezer, an option not otherwise available to children and wheelchair occupants.

Side-by-sides usurp the greatest expanse on a wall, but, possessing narrower doors, they don't need as large a walkway to open into. Rarely proffering a choice of hinge side, doors open from the middle with no convenient landing area to the side.

Side-by-side models possess more freezer space proportionately. Some models have a second, separate energy-saving freezer door for the ice compartment, and an ice and chilled-water dispenser may hold court on the door. But both refrigerator and freezer in a side-by-side are constricted, making it awkward to move food in and out of their confines. Once again, that mother of a hen turkey and oven-ready cookie sheet or roasting pan are homeless. The increasing number of larger forty-eight-inch-wide units addresses this issue somewhat, but not many kitchens can accommodate them.

Similar to a side-by-side, the seldom-seen two-door *French-style* box consists of two refrigerator sections that open from the middle with a freezer that runs the fall length below both parts.

The one freezer location to avoid is the top of a single-door refrigerator. Partitioned from the refrigerator by a flimsy door, these *freezer sections* or *freezer compartments* run too warm unless you like ice cream soup. To keep food in a frozen state, you need a full *food freezer* or *frozen food storage compartment*, completely separated from the refrigerator by its own door. For *optimum* preservation of food, keep the freezer set at zero degrees or below.

Of all configurations, a refrigerator with a pull-out bottom-mounted freezer is most workable. A top-mounted freezer gets my second vote, followed—except in special circumstances—by a side-by-side.

CHILLERS

REFRIGERATORS AND FREEZERS

Refrigeration comes in all sizes and configurations. The best relationship as well as the most luxurious—in terms of storage space—is a separate refrigerator and freezer as exemplified by these two large units *(top left)*. When these coolers are combined, a refrigerator with a bottom-mounted freezer puts more fresh food at eye level than a top-mounted box and is easier for most people to use, especially when the freezer consists of a pullout drawer *(top center)*. A side-by-side refrigerator and freezer also puts fresh and frozen food at any eye level, but once you've seen it, it's harder to retrieve. Of the side-by-sides, the largest 48-inch-wide boxes prove most practical for baking trays and that Thanksgiving turkey *(top right)*. Many of these models are available with custom panels and an ice and water dispenser on the door *(bottom left)*. As kitchens host more cooks and more work areas, we are increasingly seeing smaller undercounter refrigeration of various dimensions throughout the room. Consisting of two pullout drawers, this revolutionary doorless model can be had as a refrigerator or freezer *(bottom center)*. Energy has been addressed as well in this efficient refrigerator which uses roughly 60 percent fewer kilowatts per day than similarly sized units *(bottom right)*.

Should a separate freezer be an upright or a chest model?

Narrower and more attractive, an upright freezer is the looker's choice for kitchen placement. Making it easier to find things and move food in and out, it is also the user's choice. No contest. But when you mention the word *price,* all of a sudden that chest model starts to look attractive. Costing less to purchase and to run, it also takes longer to build up frost. With freezer coils in the door, cold air flows downward, preventing loss when it opens.

Temperature fluctuates more in an upright model, so food doesn't last as long in these boxes. Move items in there for the long haul to the back. Uprights are harder to defrost, especially when shelves contain coils; chest models occupy considerably more floor space. Both require a heavy-duty floor that stands up to their packed-full touchdown weight, equivalent to that of four or five football heroes.

Possible accessories for both types of freezers include a door lock, interior light, manual-defrost drain, and safety signal light (announces electric power loss). Glide-out baskets and bulk package guards enhance the entrance to an upright. The ice cream maker offered with some models is only as good as the machine itself. Before choosing it over an independent model, taste the ice cream it produces at a demonstration of the model or call the distributor to arrange a lick.

To preserve foods for a long time with the least amount of deterioration, freezing must occur instantly. A freezer with *quick-freeze* coils in its shelves helps achieve this state. *Fast-cool* and *fast-freeze* modes, available in some models, lower temperatures to their coldest point for a set period, a boon for people who add a boodle of unchilled foods all at once. Unless the freezer has a digital readout, keep your pulse continually on the temperature with a good freezer thermometer such as one made by Taylor Instruments.

What is the ideal interior configuration?

A well-designed interior enables consumers to store food without performing a balancing act: opening the door with one hand while restraining foods from falling out with the other. This translates best as open, unobstructed, undelineated space. We all eat too weirdly for someone else to compartmentalize a refrigerator that works for our groceries.

At twenty-five to thirty-one degrees, a meat storage drawer preserves its charges longer and better than a regular refrigerator shelf, run optimally at thirty-six or thirty-seven degrees. The same could be said of a dairy drawer operating between thirty-two and thirty-five degrees. Yet, if you don't eat much meat or dairy, separate cold lockers are a waste of valuable refrigerator space. Even if you do, who is to know that what you want to put in them will correspond to their size?

Unless your inventory meshes with a specific interior, you're better off storing things for slightly shorter periods than going for a box divided for someone else. With the plethora of sturdy plastic containers on the market, necessary resources exist for organizing food storage according to what you actually eat and drink.

Glass Shelves Versus Wire Grids

People applaud tempered-glass shelves fitted with spill guards as being simpler to clean than wire, and for not sieving food spilled on high throughout the refrigerator. Always the iconoclast, I prefer wire with close struts and a central supporting bar of rustproof stainless (not plated chrome, which corrodes). Glass breaks, obscures light (unless clear), is harder to move up and down, inhibits air circulation, and needs to be wiped more frequently since it shows every ring. It is also more expensive.

Check whatever shelf is chosen to see that it is securely attached to the wall and tightly fit into rubber gaskets that prevent wobbling and rattling.

Drawers

Drawers are starting to replace crispers and shelves for storage. One new undercounter line offers only pull-out drawers. Though this is very convenient for retrieving crisper items with recognizable forms, it may prove somewhat frustrating when you try to pick out a less readily identifiable bottle or food while looking down at it. Like cabinet drawers, these should slide smoothly and easily without veering to the side; on rollers, not plastic glides.

Effective Storage Aids

- *Adjustable shelves.* With adjustable shelves, the interior of a box can be divided to store short or tall food in response to your household's dietary predilections.

- *Additional shelf.* Regardless of configuration, I recommend ordering an extra shelf for the refrigerator and, if it fits, for the freezer. Stowed at the top of my units or added temporarily, they rev into gear for storing a decorated platter or dessert bump-free and for parking a pie, baking sheet, or roasting pan before cooking.

- *Deep door shelves.* Large bottles of juice, gallons of milk, and other frequent drinks or eats are most easily obtained from deep door shelves. Some sort of restrainer makes these doors suitable for small items as well. More flexible shelves adjust height-wise and come off for cleaning. When door shelves are deep, interior shelves are, consequently, shallow and, like a similarly organized cabinet, simpler to sort through.

- *Large crispers.* With the consumption of vast amounts of fresh fruits and vegetables intrinsic to our good health, crispers will, hopefully, become ever larger. Some are available with *moisture controls.* Closed to provide leafy vegetables with humidity, they remain open for fruits whose spoilage hastens in a wet environment. Once again, you have to question if the produce you purchase divides equally along these lines. A heavy durable polycarbonate or ABS (acrylonitrile butadiene styrene) plastic maintains the greatest resistance to overstuffing.

- *Automatic icemaker.* Though this costs extra, increases plumbing fees, occupies space, has a propensity to break down, and must be disconnected before vacation, it sure beats those sloshing ice cube trays. By a long shot. To inform, not discourage: Cubes can come faster or slower than consumption and develop an off flavor if they sit too long. Cube size and shape vary, so you may want to check them out before adding this machine to your purchase list.

- *Well-positioned interior lights*

- *Lit controls*

- *Leveling legs and casters.* Adjustable legs to level the unit capped with rollers to move it facilely during installation and cleaning.

Sometimes-Effective Storage Aids

- *Butter compartment.* Some butter compartments are kept warmer than the rest of the refrigerator to maintain spreading consistency. If you're on the stick regularly, this will be a nice perk. If not, you'll find your butter turning rancid more quickly. More to the point, the compartment should be well sealed so butter does not absorb flavors and aromas from other foods. It's helpful, too, when its door is hinged to stay open while you remove the container. The generic non-temperature-controlled dairy compartment is another instance of someone else controlling your space.

- *Meat and cheese drawer.* As long as it can be kept colder with a separate temperature control or by drawing air from the freezer, this drawer can be a boon if you consume goodly amounts of cheese, cold cuts, bacon, or sausage or wish to store meat or fish briefly before cooking. Caveats expressed earlier still stand.

- *On-the-door ice and chilled-water dispenser.* One way to keep the refrigerator from opening constantly is to have a unit with ice (cubes or crushed) and a chilled-water dispenser mounted outside the refrigerator, whose retrieval is easier when the nook is lit. Some new models shelter a built-in water filter. If not, the water supply can always be hooked up to an external filter. Invaluable in a thirsty family, this luxury also feeds purchasing, plumbing, and repair costs, and tubes do apparently like to break. Before opting for this big chill, consider whether your family would prefer a freestanding automatic icemaker plus a cold-water tap at the sink.

REFRIGERATOR INTERIORS

Modifications are being made to refrigerator interiors as well as exteriors. A filter has been added to some models with ice and water on the door to reduce impurities in the water that could contribute an off-flavor. The utility bin on this refrigerator door moves left or right to make room for large bottles stored below. A shallow drawer in this built-in refrigerator protects prepared dishes from jostling, poking, and theft.

- *On-the-door shelf.* Mounted on the refrigerator door, this drop-down door opens a direct passageway to food stored on the refrigerator shelf behind it, another convenience and energy saver in a family of refrigerator robbers.

Less-Than-Effective Storage Aids

- *Vertical dividers.* Occupying usable storage space, they may interfere with your organization.

- *Half-width shelves.* Adjustable half-width shelves seemingly cater to more individual items than full-length shelves, but food teeters precariously near their edges, begging to fall. Unstable, they offer less total storage space, rejecting large platters. Stocking them requires careful handling and a patience people like me don't have for this task.

- *Wine caddy.* The refrigerator is too cold to store wine, other than just prior to serving. During this brief interlude, wines can rest safely on their side. A permanent one- or two-bottle caddy diverts valuable space without going far enough when you're hosting a vertical tasting of Corton-Charlemagne.

- *Egg containers.* Eggs should be stored in a covered container or the box they come in so as not to absorb aromas from other foods. Place them on a shelf, not the door, where they will be jostled and exposed to temperature fluctuation.

- *Microwave holding tank.* A compartment with plastic containers for storing leftovers to be microwaved does not make much sense unless (1) you can be counted among the 80 percent that own this machine and (2) you can predict the size of the container necessary for holding the exact amount of rice left over from Sunday's dinner. If you are otherwise eager for a model that has this drawer, see if it can be ordered without it.

- *Chilled-beverage compartment.* Once again, the refrigerator manufacturer would have to be more clairvoyant than Nancy Reagan's seer to know how many beverages you need chilled. Forget it. Ditto juice-can racks on freezer door—unless you drink canned juice and the number of indentations corresponds to your purchases.

What type of finish do you want?

Today's refrigerators, available primarily in white, black, or almond, have a neutrality that should give them a little more longevity than the harvest gold of yore. (Not that they can't be given a coat of psychedelic paint to shock them into a design statement.)

Making the invitation to slip in custom door panels more appealing, exterior surfaces are increasingly textured in an attempt to hide fingermarks. This finish rusts readily and is hard to clean while looking tacky. Besides, what child makes fingermarks you can hide?

When fronting a refrigerator with a decorative wood panel, choose one that is similar to the door style of specified cabinets. If a hardwood cathedral door has been summoned, for example, order a similar panel, not a one-quarter-inch-thick flat veneer sheet that will look odd by contrast.

Stainless (inside and out) is starting to take over mid- and upscale lines. Like all other stainless, you want to check its gauge for durability. Magnets don't adhere to quality stainless, so consider yourself forewarned if the refrigerator door serves as your children's art gallery. When pictures are the priority, follow Alice Medrich's advice and order a magnetized stainless-steel (series 400) through a sheet-metal shop.

Glass doors (without shelves) are available in a limited number of boxes, reducing this appliance's bulky appearance. Unless you are a food stylist, the refrigerator is apt to look messy, revealing any secret food fetishes. With Diet Coke stacked from floor to ceiling, the door of one addict looks like a 7-Eleven.

As for interior and door bins, stainless, a high-impact polystyrene (HIPS) or ABS plastic stands up better (in that order) than paint or porcelain on steel, which chips.

Handles

Once an intrinsic part of the package, refrigerator handles are still primarily either a separate piece supplied by the manufacturer or a long channel for a finger pull. Making inroads, one line now accepts a customer's handles.

CONSERVING ENERGY

As responsible energy consumers, we can both choose units that are more efficient and utilize them carefully by observing the following tenets:

- Shun true built-in units that consume almost double the amount of energy.

- Purchase freezers that can be defrosted manually.

- Reduce the number of times a long door is opened by choosing module units or a refrigerator with a pull-down-through-the-door shelf. In a side-by-side unit, opt for a freezer with two doors.

- Keep open doors ajar as briefly as possible.

- Anticipate what you need and take everything out.

- Add food to the freezer in small batches.

- Keep refrigerator and freezer two-thirds full. Beyond that, cold air can't circulate. Occupy any extra free space with water bottles.

- Cool hot food to room temperature before storing in the refrigerator; chill cool food down further in the refrigerator before adding it to the freezer.

- Cover containers of liquids to keep in the humidity.

- Level the unit to keep the doors well sealed.

- Check the door seals periodically for any leakage.

- Keep condenser coils clean so they work efficiently.

- As a matter of food safety, defrost foods in the refrigerator rather than at room temperature.

PERSONAL PICKS: COOLERS

I am in love with my twin Traulsen refrigerator and freezer. When I bought them, there was no need to look further if you were insane enough to spring for their prices and liked their looks, which fans of more demure appliances found intrusive. They didn't offer ice and water on the door, but you got something in exchange for those dollars: a large stainless-steel interior, strong racks, good open space to configure, and a quality cooling system. Like all good things, they have changed. Noncompliant with the energy codes, they are not allowed to pursue the residential market. Current Traulsens have no shelves on their doors and no icemaker. They are deeper (thirty-two or thirty-four-plus inches) or shallower at twenty-four. They are not family-friendly.

I've also long been impressed with Northland refrigeration, which, sadly, has curtailed its line and is currently making only twenty-four-inch-deep boxes. I just don't understand this mania for built-in refrigeration since its shallowness leaves a large turkey and baking sheet out in the cold, and its look can be duplicated so easily without spending the extra money these units demand.

Northland is the only side-by-side I would consider unless there was landing space across the way, for each of the doors hinges in the middle, permitting a landing counter for both the refrigerator and freezer. The freezer in any unit under forty-eight inches wide is so narrow that only a skinny chicken will fit into it. But, Catch-22, the only side-by-sides that are currently forty-eight inches are only twenty-four inches deep, which brings us full circle to that skinny chicken.

While I'm griping, I'd like to lament the passing of the matching all refrigerator and all freezer models, now only made by Traulsen, Northland, and Sub-Zero. This is the best, most organized, easiest retrieval storage for all family members in every situation but a small kitchen.

There is something to be said as well for multiple undercounter units in a large kitchen or one with several cooks, but you'll end up having to duplicate ingredients, and the space might be put to better use.

Refrigeration is one area where you can save money and still have good function as long as you stick to a simple box with no ice and water on the door. For the ten years preceding my remodel, I depended on a secondhand White-Westinghouse that was probably one hundred years old when I bought it for $135. It never disappointed. Are my Traulsens nicer than the White-Westinghouse? Yes. Were they worth five hundred times the price? I think I won't answer that, for any honest response is a resounding "no."

Whirlpool deserves support for its innovations in creating the best superefficient refrigerator, as does Frigidaire, the runner-up in the SERP contest. General electric and Sears, which offers a bottom-mount freezer, have always satisfied.

Unless a family consumes a lot of ice, an icemaker in the freezer is preferable to a unit because it takes up less room and produces a much harder cube. But if I were purchasing an icemaker, I'd go for the Whirlpool, which also has a water spigot.

KITCHENSPEAK: COOLERS

Bottom-Mount: A unit with a refrigerator on the top and freezer on the bottom.

Built-in: Appliances that are sized so that they will line up flush with twenty-four-inch-deep cabinets. True built-in appliances do not have finished sides and are generally more expensive than freestanding equipment. By pulling out the cabinets, making them deeper, or creating a frame, you can make freestanding refrigerators look built-in.

CFC: Chlorofluorocarbons that have made the refrigerator more energy efficient are being phased out for their reported depletion of the ozone layer.

Cooling System: A refrigeration system consists of the following components:

Compressor: Exerts pressure on the refrigerant, moving it into the condenser.

Condenser: A tubular grid system where the refrigerant flows under high pressure and converts back into a liquid, releasing the heat it has carried from the evaporator and compressor out into the room.

Evaporator: The pipe where the refrigerant expands into a gas, sucking heat out of the box and cooling its contents.

Refrigerant: A gas that vaporizes and liquefies as it moves throughout the cooling system.

Cycle Defrost: A freezer that defrosts automatically once it is activated by the consumer.

Energy-Efficient Factor (EEF): A refrigerator's annual energy consumption cost, noted on its yellow "*Energy Guide*" label, is determined by dividing its cubic feet by the number of kilowatt hours it consumes. The less the refrigerator costs to operate, the higher the EEF or the more efficient it is.

Energy Saver: A switch activated during dry weather to turn off the heater that prevents sweating and condensation from forming when warm humid air hits the refrigerator box's cold surface.

Fast Cool and Fast Freeze: Modes, available in some freezers, that lower temperatures to their coldest point for a set period.

Freezer Section: A compartment at the top of a refrigerator that freezes inadequately due to its lack of a separate sealed door.

French-Style: Similar to a side-by-side unit, this seldom-seen box consists of two refrigerator sections that open from the middle with a freezer underneath.

Frost-Free: A freezer that defrosts automatically as necessary.

Ice and Chilled Water Dispenser: A unit mounted on the outside of the refrigerator for easy beverage retrieval without opening the door.

Manual Defrost: A freezer that must be defrosted by hand.

Moisture Controls: A humidity regulator available on some produce crispers.

On-the-Door Shelf: A drop-down shelf mounted on the exterior of the refrigerator door for accessing food stored on the shelf behind it.

Quick Freeze: Freezer shelves that contain coolant-filled coils to help hasten the freezing process.

Side-by-Side: A single unit with a full-length refrigerator and freezer that are usually hinged on the sides with each door opening from the middle.

Top-Mount: A combination unit with a freezer on the top and a refrigerator below.

WINE COOLERS

■

Running much warmer than the refrigerator it resembles physically, a temperature-controlled unit for storing wine in the kitchen is more aptly referred to as a *wine cooler*. Whatever you call it, this is one extraordinarily expensive way of coddling a wine collection, particularly if a dark, cool, energy-efficient closet or cellar exists elsewhere for stashing it without jostling.

Unless the kitchen is large, the space devoted to a wine cooler might well be put to better use. Yet when nothing else is crying for its spot, why not keep trophies by your side? Reserve the cooler for wines destined to be consumed imminently; kitchen conditions are too variable for long-term storage.

The purpose of a wine cooler is not to chill wine down for drinking but to embrace it with a temperature that promotes its maturation more gently and gracefully than a noncooled cupboard or wine rack. When you are ready to drink a bottle of sparkling or white wine, move it to the refrigerator for only the two to three hours it takes to cool down, or to an ice bucket for 15 to 20 minutes. Though sweet wines can handle a bigger chill than dry, too low a temperature masks a wine's subtle bouquet and flavor.

For drinking, a temperature of forty-five degrees is considered ideal for white wine; forty-two degrees for sparkling wine. Red wine, on the other hand, is toasted at an ambient temperature of sixty-five to sixty-eight degrees. An exception, young fruity Beaujolais-type bottlings are refreshing served slightly chilled.

Designed to maintain wine in ideal conditions, some wine coolers operate at a temperature of fifty-five or so degrees, while others divide the unit into zones: forty-five degrees for sparkling wines, fifty to fifty-five for whites, and sixty for reds. Obviously there will be some spill when all three zones are in the same box. Larger units separate them completely.

Wine coolers enclose anywhere from thirty-two bottles in a fifteen-inch-wide undercounter box on up to 320 bottles in a full-height forty-eight-inch-wide double tower. One rebel shoots to eighteen inches wide and eighty-four inches tall. Some coolers have special racks for larger magnum bottles; others have pull-out shelves. Vented from the front, they can be freestanding or built in.

Doors are glass, stainless, vinyl, and baked acrylic enamel, with the first two most durable. Seamless rounded interiors are easiest to clean. Like regular refrigerator doors, some wine-cooler doors accept custom panels; others have reversible hinges and a lock for protecting your investment from interlopers (and teenagers).

To do its job, a wine cooler needs:

- **A consistent humidity of 50 to 70 percent to prevent corks from drying out.**

- **Sturdy heavy-duty wooden shelves or chrome-plated racks that cant wines downward, keeping their liquid in perpetual connection with the cork.**

- **A vibration-free interior, aided by heavy insulation and leveling legs.**

- **A tight door seal.**

- **A heavy dark door that says "no trespassing" to damaging UV rays and light. Though a solid door fulfills this obligation most completely, glass tempts those wanting to show off their wares. As a minimum precaution, be sure the glass is tinted and double- or triple-paned.**

- **Interior lights for reading labels, if you are using glass doors. These are most convenient when flipped on without opening the door. Resist the temptation to use them for illuminating your display. Light is wine's enemy.**

Which unit? This depends first on the space available and the number of wines to be stored. After ascertaining that it has all the qualifications to do the job, look at finish, configuration, sturdiness of shelves, and, regrettably, price.

BEER ON TAP

Monday Night Football viewers may prefer to have beer on tap rather than opening their precious wines. A half-keg portable beer cooler with a draft arm dispenser either snuggles against the wall or rolls to the game on casters. Handling a quarter-keg, a smaller unit can be built in. Any beer not guzzled during a play-off will remain fresh for six weeks.

ICEMAKERS

■

When your home is constantly filled with merrymakers, it may be time for the iceman to cometh to this party in the form of a separate icemaker. Welcome in the kitchen, bar, or pantry, this guest is sought most eagerly when an inhospitable freezer refuses to accept an automatic icemaker.

Before signing up for a caseload of these thirst-quenching devices, know that the ice made in a portable or undercounter unit (built in flush with the cabinetry) differs dramatically from cubes produced in a freezer, either with an automatic ice-maker or an ice cube tray. Ice machines are first and foremost designed for commercial use. Ice size, shape, and surface area, often curved or circular, have been deliberately created to fill a glass attractively to convince the consumer that his $8 martini is mostly alcohol. Wink. Wink.

Smaller, these ice cubes melt faster, diluting a drink while prompting a phrase a bartender loves to hear: "I'll have another." And when flaked ice

CHILL OUT
Wine refrigerators are increasingly finding their way into kitchens where proud collectors can show off their wares while controlling storage conditions. Beverage refrigerators with an ice source earn their keep in a bar area or under a counter that is far away from the main work center. Icemakers come in self-contained units as well as in this 18-inch-wide machine that can be built-in flush with the cabinetry. They're great as long as you really use lots of ice and understand that its cubes aren't hard enough to use in an ice cream maker.

replaces cubed, one-third to one-half more is needed to chill down the same beverage.

Hastening its liquefaction, machine ice starts out softer and wetter than that hardened in a home freezer. Borderline cold, the ice from Karen Berk's machine never gets firm enough to set up the mixture in her ice cream maker.

As ice is formed and cut on a grid, it is sent careening into an insulated bin (noisy), intended for immediate consumption. Undisturbed, it can probably last a few days in the nonrefrigerated receptacle, but cubes will stick together as they begin to melt.

If the amount of ice consumed varies daily, the machine will have to be turned on and off or a timer rigged up by a refrigeration specialist.

Approximate first how much ice your family consumes; excess translates into wasted plumbing and electric bills. As a guideline, restaurants allot one and a half to one and three-quarters pounds per person to cool water at the table, two and a half to three pounds for drinks in the bar. Soft drinks are roughly one-quarter to one-third ice. Twenty-five pounds of ice consists of eleven hundred (plus or minus) three-quarter-inch cubes.

In your computations, beware that figures in ice-machine literature bear interpretation. Yield refers to the maximum amount of ice that can be pro-duced in a twenty-four-hour period, yet volume stored at one time may be considerably less. And production figures are valid only under certain conditions, usually from fifty-degree water in a seventy-degree room.

In the summer, when ice is mainlined, the machine turns stingy. For this reason, residents of hot-weather climes are advised to order a machine with greater capacity than their numbers indicate. Machines with a water-cooled condenser heat the kitchen up less than an air-cooled one, but they are illegal in many states.

In the process of producing ice, minerals and impurities are removed from the water, making the ice-machine cube clearer than that produced in a residential freezer whose water is not filtered. A filter can be added to some of these machines as well, extending their warranty as well as their life span.

Ice machines sized for the home run eighteen and twenty-four inches wide. Most have a hopper door that accepts a decorative panel and spew forth three-quarters-inch square cubes. Built either manual or self-defrost, some require a drain. Bins, usually polypropylene, are easier to clean with rounded corners; service more practical from the front. The same machine generally costs less at a commercial outlet than from an appliance dealer.

9
WATERWORKS

SINKS

■

Pulling cleanup duty, the sink has been on KP since its humble origins as a trough. Never more. With equipment switching roles faster than characters in a Noh drama, cleaning is now only one of the many parts it plays.

Loftily called "water appliance," "kitchen systems," "food preparation systems," and "the new kitchen appliance" in marketing newspeak, the plain old sink has disappeared. Outfitted regally, most contemporary numbers come with a colander, basket, cutting board, and dish drainer; some have removable inserts for trash and composting. With an ice-cold and/or 190-degree hot-water dispenser, the sink undertakes tasks relegated to refrigerator and range while a hand-lotion dispenser moves it into the realm of personal groomer. Faucets and water-filtering devices complete these waterworks.

For this cleaning/prepping/recycling/cooling/heating/beautifying/washing/drinking fountain to go with the flow, components should be chosen together. They should be appropriate—no knife-defying solid-surface cutting boards—and sizable enough to do the job. Many cutting boards, baskets, and trash holes (page 309) aren't large enough to hold anything but a carrot. While large versions of these tools could be a tremendous aid, these miniatures are helpful only to a rabbit.

The 60 to 70 percent of time spent in front of the kitchen sink is bound to increase since recent formation of the Sinkies, members of the International Association of People Who Dine over the Sink. (Interested parties may purchase *The Official Sinkies Don't Cook Book* with *heirloom* recipes for "Mush in a Rush," "Cakeless Frosting," and "Celery with Anything.")

Combining magnificent form with excellent function, modern basins are produced in practical sizes with sensual sculptural lines. Long just a boring rectangle, sinks have metamorphosed into circles, squares, hexagons, ellipses, kidney shapes, and other whimsical forms. Not forgetting its roots, the old-fashioned trough, a rectangular *apron* sink with a rim, is very much the wash barrel of the moment. Avoid that sinking feeling: Don't give sink selection short shrift; a mistake cannot be easily changed.

How big?

Though sinks may be becoming as dear as gemstones, the best do not come in small packages. *Au contraire.* If there is any information that should sink in about sinks, it's size. *Big is not just better but best.*

Each individual sink basin should have the maximum length, width, and depth the countertop permits. Eventually you may reach the compromise point where space must be left for performing other tasks, but don't shorten the sink before then.

This advice is intended for everyone with a roasting pan, a cookie sheet, and an oven rack; for singles as well as extended families; and for primary as well as secondary installations.

Known as a bar or vegetable sink, those puny

pools commonly used as a second sink are virtually useless. The real minis—ten to twelve inches—come minus a pop-up drain and are unable to accept a disposer. For very little extra money, you can have a large flexible basin to execute whatever you ask of it.

A small sink may be justifiable in a bar far from any other work area, but pass up all those space-wasting compartments intended for five maraschino cherries and three pickled onions. Your manhattan drinker may gobble up a peck of those red-dye fruits.

Not too long ago, sink dimensions could be recited as automatically as the alphabet: A single sink measured twenty-five inches long by twenty-two inches wide; a double, most common, thirty-three by twenty-two. A triple was something you got only from Yogi Berra or the Good Humor man.

Today a single sink can be as small as seven inches long; a double up to forty-three inches. Recently introduced, triple-basin sluggers hit sixty-three inches, the height of the average woman. When purchasing one of these conglomerates, the demarcation between basins should be lower than the rim and slanted so water doesn't splash.

Though sizes have shifted, the real evolution in sinkdom is the introduction of individual modules to combine as desired. One company offers thirteen different basins for mixing and matching into four hundred possible configurations. With half-basins, three-quarters basins, whole basins, and basins-and-a-half, there are more sink choices than cappuccinos. *Standard* is no longer a word to apply to the sink unless you are replacing an elderly double.

To change out an old twenty-two- by thirty-three-inch sink without altering its cutout or moving pipes, options are two thirteen-and-one-half- by sixteen-inch sinks, one larger sink with a half sink or disposer basin, and one large single sink. With an eye on *big*, I'd deep-six the hump and go for the largest single sink.

In models with drains in back or to the side, there is more room in the cabinet below, and a single sink can function like a double, separating debris from dishes being cleaned. Two tasks proceed easily at once —say, draining salad greens and stacking dirty dishes.

A half-sink or minidisposer basin is a clever concept . . . intellectually. In reality these compartments are best suited for airlifting missiles of flying food. Channeling waste down these drains, particularly when centered under a faucet, is like feeding a baby: Food goes everywhere except its mouth.

Growing from the typical five, six, and seven inches to eight, nine, and ten, sink depths are also on the move. Take the plunge to lower depths with a twelve-inch laundry sink. Deeper, like longer and wider, hold more, cushion the larger pasta pots we're using, hide dirty dishes we're putting off washing, and diminish the chances of our getting splashed when we do.

The vertically challenged—very tall and very short people—find working at the bottom of a deep sink a stretch. If you fall into one of these categories, plumb different depths for comfort, trying on a bilevel sink with one shallower basin. Shallow basins are also indicated when more space is needed in the sink cabinet, a dishwasher is installed underneath the sink, the sink is a retrofit, or you want to add a disposer without changing drainpipes.

Whatever the depth, basin corners should be rounded gently. Square are too hard to clean; big

DRAINS
Sink drains now come in a host of colors and metals to match the sink. This line is fabricated from the same non-chippable, color-all-the-way-through plastic used for football helmets.

curves wasteful of work space. Some cylindrical models, gracious at the top, funnel down to negligible footage on the cleaning floor. Sinks fitted with shelves for draining fruit are fine for that apple, but not when you need their ledge for doing dishes. Intrusive, they are always there.

How many?

There are two questions here: How many basins and how many locations? Two modules or one large double basin seems adequate for any situation as well as for multiple locations. More than that and you're doing drama, not dishes. If space allows, a second location can prevent migraines, particularly when there are numerous cooks, guest chefs, or diners who inevitably choose to wash their hands just when you want to drain the Brussels sprouts.

In a small kitchen, greater sink access can be achieved in one location just by doing a Prince Charles and Lady Di: *Uncoupling* a double sink and installing two single basins—each with its own faucet—about six inches apart.

Should it have an integrated drainboard?

No. Gorgeous they are. Nevertheless, sinks with integrated drainboards occupy considerable counter space, are a pain to clean, and may have no correlation in size or shape to items needing to be drained. Many are too thick for dishwashers to be installed below.

What material?

Choosing a sink material is like camp color war: people are on one team or another. Fine metal sinks of chrome, brass, copper, and even gold are fabricated for kitchen use, but unless you have a polishing lackey it is prudent to ally yourself with one of the materials described next. If your fealty is based on durability, stainless, soapstone, and an impervious granite are the guys of the hour, followed by the composite group. On the wild side, slate, softer granites, and Syndecrete will be great for that lived-in villa look.

STAINLESS STEEL

Tough and nonchipping, stainless is the most durable sink. The best quality is eighteen-gauge and labeled 18/10 or 18/8 (page 180). Twenty- and twenty-two-gauge sinks dent and scratch too readily and are noisy. With its modern high-tech looks, stainless never fades or becomes last year's color. Yet it is just this coldness that some object to.

Lightweight, stainless is easy to install. Hot pots can be placed on its surface. Easy to keep up, it does water-spot. "It is never clean, but never dirty," says designer Jo Davis.

Developing a beautiful patina as it ages, the sink's texture should be smooth, not rough, or it entraps dirt and dulls. For the finish on a stainless countertop, a lustrous hand-buffed satin sheen is preferred to a brushed grain or shiny mirror coating. Finally, a good-quality stainless is cushioned with fiber pads or a spray-on coating to prevent condensation and deaden sound and vibration.

ENAMEL ON CAST IRON

Colored in glorious rainbow hues with names like sunshine, these sinks bring great cheer and beauty to a kitchen. Many consumers admire their intense vibrant colors before choosing white. This is probably good thinking, for pronounced colors fade, in hue as well as in popularity. If water has a high mineral content, dark tones like black and blue require constant cleaning, bruising the cook. As one wag says, "Everyone has had a dark car . . . once."

These sinks' high-gloss glaze and weightiness bespeak a solidity that age and use can, unfortunately, chip away at. Once revealed, the black cast iron underneath can rust, and it's not repairable. I would be devastated if my new sink chipped, but the many, many people I know who have this material haven't had a problem and are, to a one, completely pleased with their choice.

For color, consumers are turning to lighter-weight composite sinks that do a disappearing act and offer a more forgiving surface to dishes and glassware. I report this trend with sadness, for there is no handsomer, richer-looking sink than enamel on cast iron.

ENAMEL ON STEEL

Beautifully colored when new, these sinks are fired at an even lower temperature than enamel on cast iron and chip too readily—revealing the steel below—to stand up to constant, rigorous kitchen use.

FIRECLAY

Long produced in Europe, high-fired ceramic sinks are appearing in greater numbers in these parts. Made from a glazed nonvitreous high-impact fireclay, these sinks have the sparkle of enamel on cast iron. A higher firing temperature makes them harder and more durable than this more familiar material, while a better bonding leaves their finish less rippled and dimpled.

Fireclay sinks do not yet come in the variety of practical sizes, shapes, or colors of other materials. Unacquainted with their characteristics, contractors tend to chip edges on installation. And these sinks have not been available here long enough for consumers to know whether they will endure.

COMPOSITE

Made from varying composites of minerals and man-made materials, this burgeoning sink category reflects the high-technology era in which it is produced. The lightweight synthetic look says space age to some, imitation to others.

Solid-surface sinks, a blend of acrylic and polyester, are brought to you by the same people offering solid-surface countertops (page 176). Some of these sinks are premade as individual units, but most are fabricated on demand, customizing the sink package.

Other composites, varying proportions of quartz (a hard silica) and fiberglass or resins (acrylic or polyester), are made by increasing numbers of firms who've added them to their stainless line, not to be caught short in these days of the colored sink. The greater the percentage of quartz, the harder the sink.

Manufactured in England, the Asterite blend is used by companies such as Spring Ram, Acriform International, and Kindred Industries. Most brands, however, have created their own unique mix of elements or at least one on which they bestow a proprietary name. Composite sinks can be ordered shiny or matte and in solid colors or pebbly faux-stone patterns. Thicker three-quarters-inch-thick materials stand up better, keeping water hotter in their basins.

Composite sinks are usually treated chemically to resist acids and stains. Stubborn marks, chips, or scratches can be sanded *in situ* or cleaned with abrasive and a Scotch-Brite pad. They do scratch, are less durable than stainless, and generally can't tolerate hot pots directly on their surface. Many blends are still too new to determine longevity, color fastness, or resistance to cracking.

SYNDECRETE

Syndecrete is the proprietary name of a lightweight precast concrete material mixed with minerals and recyclables including brass tacks, old pencils, and pieces of strawberry baskets. Custom shapes and sizes can be fabricated with or without integrated drainboards and countertops. The standard bowl is large enough to bathe owner David Hertz's new baby.

Available in a polished or matte finish, this is an exciting textural material. Any chips can be filled in and repaired, but it can stain if oil or other food is left on it. Hot pots are unwelcome on its surface. Save it for a second, less-used sink installation.

SOAPSTONE

Neither widely known nor distributed, soapstone sinks have been formed by the Vermont Soapstone Company since 1850. Available only in a soft rich whitish gray with a lighter quartz marbling, these substantial sinks are composed of 55 percent steatite (talc) that renders a soapy feel. As the sink ages and talc permeates the stone, it becomes more stain resistant.

An excellent heat retainer, and accepting of hot pots, soapstone sinks were used as bathtubs in colonial America (one bowlful *did* an entire family). Today they meld with a modern decor as splendidly as a traditional one. They're easy to clean, and any acquired scratches or dents can be sanded out.

A maximum size of thirty by forty-eight inches, soapstone sinks can be custom designed, edged, and ordered with an integrated backsplash and/or drainboard. Finished on all sides, they are installed freestanding on a countertop or low cabinet. Like all apron sinks, they diminish storage space in the cabinet below and don't accept tip-out tray systems.

SLATE

Staining if soft or sealed improperly, slate is more difficult to keep up than soapstone and hard on dropped dishes. Manifested in reddish, blackish, and purplish tones by Vermont Structural Slate Company, no other sink possesses the texture and organic beauty of this fine-grained metamorphic rock. All sinks and countertops are made to order according to drawings supplied by an architect or kitchen designer.

MARBLE AND GRANITE

Both marble and granite are surfacing in custom sink installations. They're fabulous looking, so their prevalence is no surprise. Generally too soft, marble, as you already know, is not recommended (page 181). Granite (page 184) is probably better off in a second, seldom-used sink unless it is a very hard slab that doesn't require sealing and won't succumb to staining and etching. Test the material carefully.

Should the sink ledge (deck) be mini or maxi?

Other than modular sinks that are ledgeless or models intended for undermounting (page 286), sinks are decked out with mini- or maxiledges to be used for accessories. Some encircle the sink; others vary in width, often widening in the expanse between two basins. What is an optimal-size ledge depends on the objects it is hosting. Larger than necessary, a ledge becomes a space waster, occupying the counter without contributing to work room in the sink.

Most sink ledges arrive with three or four predrilled holes for mounting a faucet and other accessories. A single-lever (single-hole) faucet or European metric model may not correspond to these punchings, and given all the toys available for the sink today, a need for additional holes is likely.

Address these issues by custom ordering holes where you want them. Have the sink company lay them out in a drawing you then sign off on. In organizing, leave room between handles for operation. Keep a water dispenser off a disposer sink, where it plays bumper cars, and away from a far edge that feeds it onto the countertop. Holes cost more when added during installation, and can't be moved once drilled. A hole in the wrong place can sometimes be hidden by mounting the faucet on a cover or *escutcheon plate*, but the look will be layered.

The number of holes necessary depends on what you choose from the following list:

One to three for a faucet

One for separate spray hose

One to two for chilled-water and/or hot-water dispenser

One for filtered-water dispenser

One for a drinking fountain for Little Leaguers

One for pop-up drain

One or two (two dishwashers) for an air gap

One for soap dispenser

One for hand-lotion dispenser

One for garbage disposer air switch

The first five items are essentially different kinds of faucets, the first four of which will be discussed in the faucet (page 288) and water treatment (page 294) sections.

Long overdue, an automatic *pop-up drain* button operates the drain from the sink ledge, eliminating the need to scrounge about in scummy water. In addition to chrome and stainless, sink drains are now fabricated from Celcon, a nonchippable, color-all-the-way-through engineered plastic used for football helmets. Sporting the latest designer colors, they've been given some durability backup lacking in epoxy-colored drains.

A soap dispenser eliminates goopy soap and soap goop and, along with a hand-lotion dispenser, bottles lying about the sink. In the past, dispensers were ordered from the same company as the faucet to ensure a match. Today, since longer dispensers have been introduced with three-and-one-half-inch spouts that fit better over the sink ledge, it makes more sense to go for size. As with drains, chrome and stainless are most durable. If you insist on color, go for one from the same material as the nonchippable drains.

Packing all the items listed onto a sink ledge is somewhat like arranging four elephants in a Volkswagen. To ensure that the sink deck accommodates what you want, it is, once again, necessary to choose a sink, faucet, and accessories at the same time. Remember that trade-off. Rather than one of those soap dispensers, you may want to consider a handsome stainless container that mounts on the wall. My deck is so crowded it looks like Rube Goldberg run amok, and my plumber still suffers suffocation nightmares from trying to fit everything underneath the sink.

Accessories for a ledgeless sink are mounted on the countertop during installation. Be sure the installer is good at drilling holes . . . in the right place.

Should the sink be integrated with the countertop?

Possible with stainless, solid surface, soapstone, granite, slate, or Syndecrete, a sink can be affixed to a countertop of the same material. Include the back-splash and the seemingly seamless piece makes a striking modern statement: an individualized dude-smooth look that is stunning. And hip. Deflating this bubble: If either sink, countertop, or backsplash is damaged, all three pieces may have to be replaced.

When the choice is solid surface, expect some sink colors not to be available in countertops. When the *same* color is used without decorative banding in between, use a recessed-undermount installation for the sink. Flush mounting reveals any color variation in sheet goods.

As previously stated, a stainless countertop may take too much upkeep unless you enjoy water polka dots or wiping.

What type of installation?

Sinks may be sunk in the following ways with different visual and practical results. In some cases, installation type depends on the specific sink, in others on aesthetics. Many sinks can be ordered with the rim you prefer.

SELF-RIM

Sinks fabricated with rolled edges perch above the countertop in such a way that *overmount* or *top mount* would be a more descriptive name for their drop-into-a-cutout-hole installation. While enabling a sink to be retrofitted without movement of countertop or pipes—great for chippable enamel on cast iron or inexpensive sinks you hope to replace when money is more plentiful—this guarantees a lifetime of cleaning gunk at sink seams and sweeping water from the counter back up over the edge into the basin. This mounting also makes the sink appear more prominent.

RIMMED

Flat-rimmed sinks or those with a flat rim added to their perimeter can be installed with edges flat against the countertop or seamed slightly below. This seam is easier to maintain, and water can easily be swept into the sink.

SINKS

facing page

APRON SINKS

Sinks come in myriad sizes, shapes, and materials with single or multiple basins. The old-fashioned apron-fronted troughs which rest on the sink cabinet are undergoing a revival in these times of the farmhouse/villa look. The examples here are made of enamel-on-cast iron, fireclay, and soapstone, which has been produced since 1860, but has a timeless patina that seems strangely contemporary today. A custom fabrication up to 30 by 48 inches, it can be integrated with a backsplash, countertop, and/or drainboard.

INSTALLATION POSSIBILITIES

Some sinks can be mounted in several different ways; others can be ordered for different mountings; a few stay true to a lone method. The following four sinks illustrate these different options. Self-rim sinks have rolled edges that perch above the countertop. Rimmed sinks have a flat rim—either intrinsic or added—that allow them to be installed with edges flat down against the countertop or slightly below it. Flush mount sinks have a square edge that lines up evenly or flush with the countertop edge. Undermount sinks are set below the countertop so that their edge and that of the countertop line up precisely, or they may protrude slightly beyond the countertop edge or pull back from it. The sink deck can be left in an undermount situation or eliminated as it is when modules are employed, in which case the faucet is mounted directly in the countertop.

STAINLESS STEEL

Though there are much bigger and more utilitarian shaped sinks with square or softly curved corners, this high-quality 18-gauge satin-finished stainless brings some whimsy to washing. It can also be uncoupled and ordered as separate oval and kidney basins to undermount without the countertop occupying ledge.

this page

SOLID SURFACE

Solid surface, a man-made blend of acrylic and polyester, is usually designed and fabricated to order for sinks. The bowls shown here (*top*) are integrated with the countertop and backsplash to form a single unit.

SINGLE SINKS

When room does not exist for a large double sink or two large single modules or when a double sink is being replaced in a standard 33- by 22-inch cutout, a large single sink such as this handsome enamel-on-cast-iron octagon with a 9-inch deep basin may prove much more practical than two smaller basins.

PUSHING THE CUTOUT

This cleverly designed double bilevel sink makes the best of limited space. It fits the standard 33- by 22-inch sink cutout in the countertop, while curving out beyond it on top, usurping more work room in the sink.

FLUSH MOUNT

A sink with a square edge can be set even or flush with the countertop edge. This installation works well in tandem with ceramic tile countertops as long as materials are able to bond together.

UNDERMOUNT

Even more discreet than a flush mounting, an undermounted installation has become increasingly popular as more modular sinks are employed minus the rim required for other settings. This application works on models with a flat rim as well, disqualifying a rolled edge. Its spatial demands may prevent a tip-out sponge tray from being installed on the sink's face. Check all measurements to see what fits and how.

Undermount limitations lie more with countertop than sink type. Stainless, tile, granite, and solid surface allow this bonding; laminate and butcher block do not. Yet the latter two water-damage-prone materials should not be used near the sink anyway. When they are, self-rimming is preferable.

With undermounting, bowls of different shapes can be employed or one angled vertically and another horizontally. Faucet and accessory placement is more flexible and parsimonious with valuable counter space.

In this installation, the sink can be *flush* with the countertop's cutout edge, *recessed* back from it, or *extended* beyond it. The first method works best when both materials are the same, and a seam won't be as unsightly. In a *tiled-in* undermounting, trim tiles are inset at the junction of a tile countertop and sink.

UP AGAINST THE WALL

In the spirit of the old-fashioned wash tub, the sink is mounted on or against a wall, eliminating the backsplash.

PERSONAL PICKS: SINKS

I am enamored of two entirely different types of sinks. My favorite, the custom Vermont Soapstone sink, has an old-world sensibility and an ageless patina that blends in beautifully with any style of kitchen. A freestanding trough with an apron front, it rests directly on a cabinet. The one drawback to this design is that it doesn't permit tilt-down sponge drawers. Neither do many of the rimless modular sinks of which I am also quite fond for their parsimonious use of counter space. In this category I'd choose two of the largest modules I had space for—say nineteen inches square each—or a larger one if I had a larger skillet, and I would undermount them.

For an 18/10 stainless, Kohler, with almost square corners, is practically constructed so that its entire space is usable. Franke and Elkay also offer large single modules. American Standard and Kohler come to the fore with enamel on cast iron. It might be fun to mix these materials and shapes as well. If I were using only one set of sinks, I'd provide each with its own faucet.

I don't have either of the sink styles described here, for I bought my sinks before I knew about soapstone or individual modules were readily available. Bowing to my bent for function first, I chose stainless for its durability, but looks prevailed when it was a choice between a more attractive sink and a basin sizable enough for my skillets. A mistake. Big mistake.

KITCHENSPEAK: SINKS

Apron: A rectangular old-fashioned trough-shaped sink that is finished on all sides and sits on top of a cabinet rather than being installed within it.

Composite: A sink made from solid surface or from varying mixes of minerals and man-made materials.

Installation:

Flat-Rimmed: Sinks that are installed with their edges flat against the countertop or seamed slightly below.

Flush-Mount: A sink with a square edge that can be set even or flush with the countertop edge.

Self-Rim: Sinks fabricated with rolled edges that perch above the countertop.

Undermount: Rimless modular sinks or sinks with a flat or flush rim set below the level of the counter-top. The sink can be flush with the countertop's cutout edge, recessed back from it, or extended beyond it.

Integrated: A sink that is joined with a countertop, backsplash, and/or drainboard to form one single unit. These combo units are formed either from a single piece of material or from several that are seamed subtly.

Pop-up Drain: A button that operates the drain from the sink ledge, eliminating the need to scrounge about in scummy water.

Soapstone: Sinks composed of a quartz marbling and 55 percent steatite (talc) that gives it a soapy feel.

Standard Cutout: Space for a traditional-sized sink that measures twenty-two by thirty-three inches.

FAUCETS

■

The relation of the sink to the faucet is similar to that between Pinocchio and his nose. As sinks have gotten bigger, so spouts have grown longer or taller and more swively. While sinks have become more sculptural and painterly in their vibrant hues, faucets have exploded with color and the sinuous curves of a Henry Moore.

Unlike a sink, a faucet's real beauty lies below the surface, where inner mechanisms mastermind its water flow. Possessing a heft and density, the handles and spout of top-quality faucets are fabricated from solid die-cast brass parts. Valves are washerless nonleaking ceramic disks that go from full off to full on in a mere quarter-turn flick of the wrist.

With the aim of saving water, all faucets benefit from a built-in aerator or water-flow restrictor that can be preset. Mixing air with water, an aerator promotes a forceful flow while reducing water consumption by up to 50 percent. Some municipalities mandate this savings. When not available with the faucet, an inexpensive device from the hardware store can be fitted to its head (unless the faucet is to be connected to a portable dishwasher).

An additional restrictor, available in some models, works as an antiscald control. Locking in a maximum temperature, it prevents accidental burns. Other safe choices, particularly when children are afoot, is a faucet with a *temperature memory* or a single-lever faucet with a wide band of low and moderate temperatures. Under $10, ScaldSafe attaches to a faucet to shut water off before it hits 120 degrees.

Another safety issue is lead. As its hazards become better understood, the amount that can be leached from a faucet's brass fittings is ever more important. Requiring compliance by October 1994, Section 9 of National Sanitation Foundation (NSF) Standard 61 addressed this issue. The California current standard of five parts per billion is most stringent. Nonetheless, before purchasing a faucet, you may want to check with the Environmental Protection Agency (EPA) or the Environmental Qual-

ity Institute at the University of North Carolina to see how different faucets fare in their comparison studies.

Lead is leached more quickly from hot water than cold; from a faucet that hasn't been turned on for six hours or so. To be safe, draw only cold water for cooking, fill the "good morning" coffeepot before going to bed, and run the faucet until the water turns cold before using. Indicating that a fresh supply from underground pipes has reached the house, this will take from fifteen seconds to several minutes. Save runoff water for the garden or house plants.

Where do you want to mount the faucet?

When choosing a faucet, decide first whether priority is placement, practicality, or appearance. Once this hierarchy is established, it is easier to narrow options. Sort of.

As indicated, faucets can be mounted on the ledge (or deck) of the sink—if it has a ledge—or in the countertop if it does not. It can also be mounted on the wall behind the sink—if there is a wall. It's sort of like, "If you have ham, you can have ham and eggs, if you have eggs."

As long as the spout is sizable enough to reach all corners of the sink, the choice here is one of space availability and aesthetics.

What type of faucet do you want?

People's opinions vary as to which faucets operate easily, so practice on any you are considering, pushing all buttons and pulling all cords.

As sinks have grown to human proportions, a faucet with a generous ten- or eleven-inch spout and 180-degree swinging radius may not be sufficient for cleaning their far reaches even when partnered with a pullout spray hose. Practice cleaning with any sink and faucet combo you are considering even if you have to rig up a dummy model. In extreme cases, two faucets may be necessary.

The height and curvature of a faucet's spout determine the ease of cleaning large pots or filling pitchers under it. This push becomes shove at a bar sink or under the spout of a two-handled faucet. Without a *gooseneck* or spray hose, you can't scrub anything sizable.

SINGLE-HANDLED FAUCETS

The most practical faucet? Simple: a single-handled faucet with one top-mounted U-shaped loop, lever, or long bar that can be operated by the arm, wrist, or elbow as well as by the hand. This handle is an easy grabber for the elderly, the almost elderly, the arthritic, and the doughy, dirty, greasy palmed. Moving from cold to hot in one fell swoop, it mixes temperatures internally without the fuss and fiddle a two-handled number demands. Once you get to know the faucet, you hit the temperature you seek almost automatically.

A single handle mounts on the side as well as on the top of some faucets. Perhaps a bit less convenient to use this way, this design allows the spout to have a greater curve.

Swinging to and fro, single-handled faucets work readily in a sink with multiple basins of different sizes. Occupying only one hole on the sink ledge, this minimalist cedes space to other accessories.

TWO-HANDLED FAUCETS

Less generous than a single-handled faucet, these two handles, plus the spout or high arc (gooseneck) they flank, triple the number of deck holes filled. Their spouts may neither be long enough nor swivel far enough to work in a double or triple bowl, particularly if basins differ in size. To mix hot and cold water to a desired temperature requires manipulation.

Don't, however, consider these negatives a dismissal, for a much more individualized look can be obtained with two-handled faucets. Available in almost innumerable styles, different-shaped spouts can be mixed and matched with handles of myriad

materials: ceramic, wood, metal, marble, onyx, crystal, and solid surface—even precious gems.

Though the looks of two-handled faucets are paramount, their purchase doesn't necessarily eliminate practicality. *Wing-tip* (aka elbow, hospital, or wrist blade) handles also operate with an arm or elbow. Easier to turn on than lever, cross, round, oval, or T-shaped designs, they are far more desirable for kitchen operation. If you're sold on one of the latter styles, at least choose one with textured bands or ridges that respond to the fast-draw dirty-hand grip. Wyatt Earp, take notice.

FAUCETS FOR FILTERED WATER

When first introduced into the kitchen, water treatment systems were hooked up to a separate dedicated faucet on the sink ledge. Recently companies have started adding a third spigot to their regular faucet for drawing *filtered* water along with *cold* and *hot*. Because the system yields very little water in a twenty-four-hour period, the filtered water should be reserved for drinking and, perhaps, cooking. As discussed (page 297), these faucets are worth considering only if their filter is capable of removing elements from your water that you want removed.

Do you want a spray hose?

Once available only as a separate tool on the sink ledge, today's pullout spray hoses are also sleekly integrated into the head of a single-handled faucet. In some models, this feature locks on. A sometime irritation, debris can get into the seam between button and head, interrupting flow. Check the gap to see how likely this will be.

On call, a spray hose can be pulled out to clean the crevices of a large sink, fill a bucket on the floor, swish water around a pitcher, give vegetables (or the dog) a bath, water plants outside the window, or play squirt gun. Yet for all the hose's helpfulness, some people actually prefer the nozzle aerator attachment sold at the hardware store to the hose that must be stuffed back into a hole.

Regardless of spout material, some spray heads

HOT AND CHILLED WATER DISPENSER
The dispenser offers hot and chilled water instantly from the sink ledge with a simple flip of a lever. The hot spigot heats up to sixty cups of water per hour to almost 200 degrees for tea, plumping raisins, or peeling tomatoes, while the cold tap can be connected to a chiller and/or filter unit. A hot-only dispenser is also available.

FAUCETS

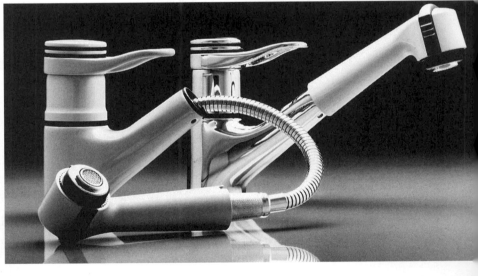

AERATOR
An inexpensive aerator can be attached to any faucet unless a portable dishwasher is to be hooked up to it. Its role is to minimize water consumption by converting a hard stream to a misty spray.

SINGLE LEVER FAUCETS
The most popular faucet type today for its sleek good looks, cinch cleanup, and ease of operation—even with sticky fingers and bread dough hands—is the top-mounted single lever that can be operated with a wrist, elbow, or arm. Each of the examples here has an integrated pullout hose to streamline its wash-down action, and can be aimed to fill a pitcher or wash the dog.

OLD-FASHIONED SINGLE LEVER FAUCET

The single lever (along with a ceramic disc valve and modern workings) is also being utilized on faucets with an old-fashioned exterior housing designed to go with an historic, country, or farmhouse kitchen. One model shown here has a long swivel spout, the other a large gooseneck, which will reach into the far corners of a large sink. In both cases, the pullout hose is given its own hole on the sink deck.

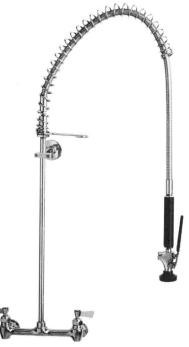

DOUBLE-HANDED FAUCET

When a two-handed faucet is preferred for its design, choose one with a large swivel spout and wing tip handles that can also be operated with a wrist, elbow, or arm. Though not as easy to grip as the wing tip, these four-pronged handles can be prodded on or off with less than a full hand.

RESTAURANT FAUCET

Mounted on the wall or backsplash, this restaurant-style pre-rinse faucet has wing tip handles and a pull-down swivel spout fitted with a spray hose. A swing-spout faucet from 6 to 16 inches can be added to the mix. This style may, admittedly, splash a bit more than a typical residential faucet, but it's so much fun to use, you might even get the kids to do the dishes.

are fabricated from plastic on the grounds that it stays cooler than metal when water courses through. Metal is, however, not a problem, and the issue here is more one of cutting costs.

The hose, a flexible plastic tube ranging from thirty-six to sixty inches, snakes through a flexible stainless or chrome-plated sheath, interlinked so it doesn't pull out like a Slinky.

At the opposite extreme visually from the integrated hose is the huge arcing, restaurant-swivel or spring-style hose, called *prerinse unit*. Attached to a two-handled wing-tip faucet, it literally makes a big splash and is a bit unwieldy, but it adds a tremendous sense of fun. And, as we all know, washing dishes needs all the fun it can get.

Lacking a vacuum breaker to interrupt backflow, spray hoses are not approved in some communities. If negative pressure develops while the hose is lying in a filled sink, dirty water could move back through the system, contaminating the supply throughout the house. Most companies are adding devices to bring their faucets into compliance with codes. But before setting your heart on a particular style, confirm its viability with your plumber.

Do you want a faucet that turns on and off automatically?

A "Look, Ma, no hands" faucet is a marvelous asset for a cook with greasy, sticky hands or for someone who has difficulty turning handles. One option is an automatic faucet with an infrared light sensor that starts water flowing when a hand or object crosses its path. There is a slight time lag, as anyone knows who has waited for these devices to click on in public rest rooms, and you still have to adjust the temperature or continuous-flow knob. For hands-free operation, a better choice may be the faucet with foot or knee pedals like those used in laboratories or doctors' offices.

What type of finish do you want?

Faucets are finished in almost every metal, including a glittery gold, and can be polished up to a shine or down to a satin. Colored finishes are in full bloom, particularly in tandem with metal. Hard to clean, these duos are better for singing than for faucets.

Once again, if you make decisions practically, the clear—and usually least expensive—finish choice is an easily cleaned double-coated chrome. Matte and polished chrome are equally durable, a brushed finish less so.

While pewter and nickel don't tarnish easily, brass and copper faucets darken every time an air molecule blows by and are hard to keep up. A baked-on epoxy powder coating is more durable than a sprayed-on liquid lacquer that is heat-cured. If you don't want to play musical chair faucets, purchase one that has not been coated and shine it on demand.

Faucets plated with twenty-four-carat gold are available as well to tempt status seekers. To have any longevity, the nontarnishing plating should be *heavy*, with a thickness of thirteen to fifty millionths of an inch. Cleanable only with a damp cloth, a satin finish hides marks better than a polished one.

Color finishes are probably least durable of all unless, like the aforementioned soap dispensers (page 283) and strainer baskets, they are fabricated from an engineered plastic. Although a baked epoxy powder coat is stauncher than an enameled one, color still chips, and it fades from cleanser and sun.

Whether applied over color or metal, a good finish "lies flat." Perfectly smooth, it lacks the bumps called "*orange peel*" in the industry.

Do you want a separate faucet at the stove for filling pots?

As someone who has sloshed water from the sink to the stove while filling my stockpot enough times to set an Olympic record, I craved a pot filler mounted at the stove. Ready to go, it has never disappointed. Pasta and soup cooks will welcome this spout as well.

Pot fillers come with either a double-jointed pullout spout to mount above the stove or a hose to hang to its side or on a railing at the hood. The latter style is more viable for a high-backed stove, particularly if a vent runs through it. Otherwise the filler must be hung so high it splashes the stove instead of filling a pot. Pot fillers last longer if they can be shut off at the wall as well as at the spout. Only cold water is needed at this locale since hot leaches lead too quickly to be used for cooking.

Do you want a hot and/or chilled-water dispenser on the sink ledge?

No more waiting for water to reach a desired temperature. Preheated and/or prechilled water awaits at the sink, obtained from a dispenser connected to a tank in the cabinet below. Cold water can also be remoted or run off the refrigerator for a deeper chill and the supply connected to a water treatment filter. Lead-free byways are being developed for these units.

Hot and cold-water dispensers can be purchased individually or in a single shared dwelling. A combo makes more sense when both services are desired, for it occupies less space (only one hole on the sink deck) and is lower in cost than a twosome.

Like faucets, dispensers are available in chrome or color (with the same kudos and caveats) and are designed as goosenecks with levers or spouts with push buttons or twist tops. Spouts appear more substantial, but goosenecks better accommodate large or odd-shaped containers. Similar to a wing-tip faucet handle, a lever is much easier to operate with sticky hands than a twist top.

Hot-water tanks hold one-third to two-thirds gallons and heat forty to sixty cups of water from 140 to 200 degrees each hour, depending on their wattage—a great convenience when you want a quick cup of tea or cocoa. Innumerable other uses: to slip off tomato skins, plump raisins, reconstitute dried mushrooms, and boost the heat of cooking water for eggs or rice. One rather perverse acquaintance prefers an electric teakettle with an automatic shutoff to a hot-water dispenser. If not overfilled, this does consume less energy.

A deflector plate prevents lime buildup in a hot water dispenser. Though you can just turn the unit off while you're away, a plug simplifies draining. Operating at scalding temperatures, it calls for a locking or childproof catch when children are around.

Chilled water can be a boon when the Boy Scouts invade after a hike, but at forty to sixty degrees this water is just cold, not ice-cold. An ice-maker or ice and water combo on the refrigerator door may be a better way to salute the troops. Should it spring a leak, however, it will drain on the floor in this location instead of safely running down the sink.

PERSONAL PICKS: FAUCETS

———

Choosing a faucet was my easiest decision, for it was a case of love at first sight, and I have never wavered from this emotional response despite all the beautiful temptress faucets available. Luckily, my infatuation was a case of practicality as well. My chrome Hansa faucet, a sculptural beauty, has a top-mounted lever and a retractable integrated hose that cleans all crevices of the sink and fills a container of any size.

As long as a faucet has a ceramic disk and can be operated with a wrist, arm, or elbow when hands are dirty, any style you like will be satisfying. Harrington Brass has an extensive old-fashioned collection, Gemini a contemporary one.

In addition to the faucet, it would probably have been useful to put foot pedals at the sink, for I often have my hands filled with bread dough. Happily I did mount the Fisher pot filler faucet above my cooktop for what has turned out to be one of the most helpful tools in my kitchen. When filtered water is added to your mix, Franke's Triflow Water Filtration System Faucet is ideal with three spigots. This company's sleek newly designed Little Butler for hot and cold water at the sink permits wrist and elbow operation. I, of course, have the previous less sleek model.

KITCHENSPEAK: FAUCETS

Aerator: A flow restrictor that mixes air with water to curtail water consumption.

Antiscald Control: A restrictor that locks in maximum water temperatures to prevent accidental burns.

Automatic Faucet: A faucet with an infrared light sensor that starts water flowing when a hand or an object crosses its path.

Escutcheon Plate: A metal bar or plate for mounting a faucet before it is attached to the sink ledge or countertop. Hardware is also often mounted on an escutcheon plate, which gives both it and the faucet a layered look.

Hot and/or Chilled-Water Dispenser: Faucets mounted on the sink ledge for dispensing preheated and prechilled water from a tank in the cabinet below.

Orange Peel: A poorly applied bumpy finish that doesn't lie flat on the faucet.

Pot Filler: A cold water faucet installed at the stove for filling pots.

Vacuum Breaker: A device inserted in a spray hose to prevent backflow when negative pressure develops while a hose is lying in dirty water.

Wing Tip: Two-handled faucets with large blades that can be operated by the wrist, arm, or elbow.

WATER TREATMENT SYSTEMS
STILL WATER PROBLEMS RUN DEEP

THE PICTURE

There may be nothing to fear but fear itself, but when it comes down to the safety of the water supply, there are mysterious microbes with multisyllabic names waiting to get us just for quenching our thirst or lubricating our wrinkles. In some areas, we are only just realizing the clear and present danger poisoning our wells, landfills, groundwater, and septic tanks.

Soberingly, the EPA and Centers for Disease Control and Prevention warn that boiling our water is the surest way of eliminating organisms. Contaminating our nightmares, a parade of horrific images: raw sewage, agricultural pesticides, industrial pollutants, hazardous wastes, and microbiological entities.

Frivolous in comparison, objectionable tastes and aromas of chlorine, algae, iron, and sulfates, simple cosmetic and aesthetic issues, further shame the water flowing through our taps. "Yuck, that water is disgusting." Our water may also be too hard, staining the sink, liming the pipes, and spotting glassware and dishes.

To complicate this frightening picture, unscrupulous salespeople of water treatment systems prey on our anxiety while restaurateurs charge $12 for a few glasses of bottled water, hyping minerals into a fad. Carrying chicness to the max, a Beverly Hills worker was spotted pouring Crystal Geyser into a cement mixer. Trendiness aside, the most disconcerting report reveals employees of municipal water and power departments turning to the bottle over their local supply.

The water supply is generally assumed safe in large urban areas, where it is processed and monitored carefully to protect the consumer. The reality lies slightly short of this point, for water conditions vary from day to day and can be affected after departing from the plant.

The chlorine added for protection can mix with decayed organic material into what is believed to be cancer-causing *trihalomethane* (*THM*). Lead, so damaging to children neurologically, can be currently leached from brass faucets as well as from pipes and solder that joined copper to water mains before 1986.

Trying to sort through all these mixed messages, separating true from false, could drive anyone to drink. And I don't mean water. Though not in Rome, I propose that we all do what the Romans did when their cisterns turned brackish: Pop open a bottle of wine.

REALITY TESTING

Back to the real world: If any concern exists about the safety of the cooking and drinking water in your kitchen, or if you just don't like the way it tastes or smells, there are positive actions to take. Start by requesting an annual water quality report from the local department of water and power. When the water source is a well, contact the public health department. Query its administrators about the frequency and method of testing employed and any problems observed locally. Apartment dwellers can interview landlords to see what lies behind their walls.

For peace of mind or when an alarm sounds, have your water tested, an exam worth repeating on an annual basis. Check first with the local public health office, which may test for bacteria or other contaminants without charge. To find a neutral laboratory approved by the state or EPA consult the yellow pages under "Laboratories" or have the test performed through mail order. When results reveal a problem, have the test repeated by another lab to allow for a margin of error.

POSSIBLE SOLUTIONS

When your tap water is diagnosed with a problem, or you just want the worry to go away, there are two options. Purchase bottled water to use for cooking and drinking or install a special system to treat the identified problem.

The fact that we have come to this point is enormously sad, for neither choice is appealing: Both are extremely expensive and expansive in their encroachment on valuable kitchen storage space. Both consume much too much time and fussy attention, not to mention social and political implications.

Bottled water requires schlepping containers back and forth for recycling or arranging for deliveries of jugs in a timely enough manner not to run out. And next time you're feeling warm and fuzzy drinking those bottled bubbles, conjure up an image of that benzene one make recently was reported to contain. Bottled water is unregulated and untested. Many brands have had their fluoride filtered out, important for preventing tooth decay. If nothing else, check out the source. One water bottled in Los Angeles is based on drainage from Forest Lawn Cemetery.

If you elect to purchase a water treatment device, you must keep pace with its output—less than a pasta pot full at one time. With its protective chlorine removed during treatment, the water can become contaminated if stored at room temperature for any period. It must be cleaned and maintained constantly and rigorously. Filters or cartridges must be changed as soon as they are clogged or depleted, or, once again, contamination can occur. Unrelenting in their upkeep demands, water systems don't suffer a "No dear, I'm too tired tonight" routine.

Many systems require a plumber for installation and service. And you're going to have to crystal-ball it to be sure the company will be around to provide replacement filters and cartridges. Increase the odds by choosing a unit previously installed in numerous restaurants and large corporations.

Certain water treatment systems can be screwed into a faucet head or set up on the countertop, but water doesn't stay in these minimodules long enough for them to modify anything but odor and taste, and they clog swiftly.

For identified problems and long-term use, install a high-volume system anywhere in the kitchen where water is drawn. Generally housed under the sink and hooked up to a dedicated faucet for easy

This faucet uniquely offers filtered as well as hot and cold water from a single spigot.

WATER CENTER
Recognizing the increasing presence of water in our life, several companies are making freestanding or built-in water bars for the kitchen. This system purifies water before dispensing it chilled or steaming hot. Another model also routes soda, juice, and carbonation for beverages.

FILTERED WATER
Whether you are choosing filtration for aesthetic or contamination purposes, the system generally consists of a cartridge or housing for the water treatment system stored in the cabinet under the sink, and a faucet mounted on its deck for dispensing the cleansed water. This water will run cold if a chill tank is also hooked up to the filter. Many different styles of interchangeable faucets exist for a water treatment system. This stainless lead-free model has an extra-long 6-inch spout which is good for filling large pitchers and for installations set back from the sink ledge.

transfer, the system is attached to the cold-water line, for high temperatures are damaging. To purify secondary water sources, lodge a water treatment system near the coffeemaker and/or icemaker.

Though most water problems are treated directly in the kitchen, some must be detoured before they get there. Hard water is treated where it enters the house by an *ion exchange:* Calcium, manganese, and iron, the minerals that make the water hard, are traded for sodium compounds. Radon problems are also addressed at the unwelcome mat and filters secured to waylay sediment before it hits a water heater or dishwasher.

As a bridge over these troubled waters, several companies are shoring up their businesses with freestanding or built-in *water bars* offering a varying water menu of hot, chilled, or carbonated water and ice cubes treated by an in-bar filter system. Costing $1,500 to $4,000, this space-occupying appliance goes on the luxury wish list, but only if its system can fix your particular water problem.

Which type of water treatment program?

Where to put the water treatment device can be a challenging question even in a large kitchen. *But if it is not designed to treat the water problem you've had diagnosed, don't bother putting it anyplace at all.* Based on different techniques, each system is designed to treat a particular condition. Prozac isn't going to cure your cold, and you don't wear jeans to the prom (at least you didn't use to). Whatever the motivating force behind the purchase of a water treatment system, *taste the water from the device you are considering and be sure you like it.*

To find the optimum system, obtain a copy of the National Sanitation Foundation (NSF) listings after analyzing your water. An independent nonprofit source, the NSF has established standards for drinking water treatment units. To determine compliance, the organization tests and rates systems submitted for appraisal.

Though companies must pay for this evaluation, thereby eliminating those who cannot afford certifi-

WATER TREATMENTS OF CHOICE

Carbon Absorption/Filtration: radon, industrial pesticides and pollutants, volatile organic chemicals, chlorine, chloroform, and algae

Reverse Osmosis: nitrates, particulate lead, uranium, radium, pesticides, bacteria, sodium, and minerals

Distillation: nitrates, chlorine, lead, and minerals

Ultraviolet Disinfection: bacteria

Mechanical Filtration: cysts, uranium, radium, radon, iron, asbestos, bacteria, rust, and sediment

Ion Exchange: nitrates, fine lead, hard water

---

cation or who chose not to apply for it, the approved list provides consumers with the names of units that treat a particular problem. NSF approval extends only to the particular model or system part carrying its seal. As further insurance, New York and California residents can drink easier knowing that it is against the law in their states for health pronouncements to be made about a product unless they can be substantiated.

Carbon filtration and reverse osmosis are the main water treatment systems found in a kitchen. Some problems, chlorinated organics for example, will need a hit from both systems. Distillation, mechanical filtration, and UV disinfection also have water problems to solve.

Activated charcoal carbon filtration systems come in blocks, granules, and powder, in descending order of durability. The carbon block is most absorbing, corralling all water to pass through it. With looser granular and powder forms, the water eventually cuts a channel through the carbon as it ages. Before hitting the carbon, heavily sedimented water must be filtered.

Some carbon systems announce filter-changing time by shutting down after a certain amount of water passes through; others beg for constant surveillance. This system is employed primarily for aesthetic and aromatic purposes.

Reverse osmosis (RO) systems are the hogs and turtles of the water treatment world. The water, forced slowly through semipermeable membranes under pressure, lose healthful minerals and salts (considered good riddance by some) along with the bad stuff, leaving a fairly flat-tasting beverage. All waste five, six, seven—and up from there—gallons of water for every gallon of filtered water produced; some continue to waste water even when the reservoir is full and filtration has ceased.

The water's chlorine and pH level determine the type of membrane necessary; each has its own filter and maintenance requirements. Sold without containers for collecting the purified water, some countertop models must be guarded closely so they don't overflow.

Distillation, another method of separating out intruders, involves boiling the water until it turns to steam and passes through a series of tubes and baffles, where it deposits impurities before recondensing. Like the RO method, this dance is done in slow motion, leaving pretty tasteless water when its music stops. Wasteful of electricity, it also runs hot and noisy. Some of these chemistry sets corrode readily; others cannot be plumbed into a separate faucet.

Ultraviolet disinfection works by decimating water enemies with a germicidal lamp that operates in tandem with activated carbon. A prefilter may be necessary to eliminate sediment that decreases the lamp's efficiency.

Mechanical filtration offers a series of filters with pores in the fraction-of-a-micron level, sized according to what they are being entrusted to remove. Fine screens sieve bacteria, while *depth filters* above ten microns wipe out the big guys.

DISHWASHERS

■

In this age of convenience first, it is hard to fathom why dishwashers are part of the life cycle in roughly only half our homes. Off-loading dirty dishes into this labor-saving wonder machine equals a "two-week vacation yearly away from the kitchen sink," reports *Appliance Letter.* It would seem that the only benefactors of the dishwasher's less-than-lustrous popularity are rubber glove salespeople.

This machine may, admittedly, not adapt to areas where water is scarce; a supply fed by cisterns and wells imposing modified washing methods. Correctable, poor water quality can also impede its functioning. Other than these limitations, the only drawback I can think of is that a dishwasher doesn't come with someone to load it.

Dishwashers have been used for everything from cooking salmon to washing baseball caps in a *Ball-Cap Buddy,* but they more than earn their keep as a clean machine and hideout, secreting dirty dishes out of sight until a load accumulates. Accommodating more tableware than a drying rack, they free up valuable counters. (In exchange, of course, they do occupy floor space.) Not to be underestimated, a dishwasher also saves money spent on manicures.

I have been indebted to a dishwasher since purchasing a portable in the olden days. Living on a student's meager stipend, I knew where my priorities lay. Though this machine took all the color out of my new wedding china, and dishes came out of one machine in its waning years dirtier than they went in, I have been ever grateful for its loyal aid.

One salesman reports that people spend less time choosing a dishwasher than any other piece of equipment and complain most about how badly it works. Yet there's no longer a need to dish the dirt on dishwashers, for these machines have cleaned up their act.

During the last decade or so we've seen the quality construction and high performance of European and Australian machines adapted by American man-ufacturers while the saner price points established nationally have braked our mentors' out-of-control costs.

Possessing an edge on sleek modern looks, most peregrinating machines from the continent perform their jobs more proficiently, but American-made models are quickly moving up behind them. Certainly they've evolved from pre–Civil War days when the ancestral wooden tub was hand-cranked on both sides of the Mason-Dixon line.

Choosing a good dishwasher is one of the simpler kitchen chores. This ballot box is stuffed in your favor regardless of whether your vote hinges on a replacement model that must fit into an existing space or a machine for a new cabinet that can be anything you want.

A super-duper dishwasher still costs $700 to $900; a less awesome figure when lowered water and electric bills are factored in. When price drives the decision, a simpler machine from a quality producer delivers more than meaningless extras from a lesser brand. The trade-off: Fewer cycles, mechanical controls, and decreased insulation for a machine that cleans well and consumes a minimum of water without making much noise about it.

THE NEW SUPER-DUPERS

Sh-h-h-h!

Marveling at my dishwasher's serene silence, a repairman said, "I leave my house just to get away from the noise of my dishwasher. The reason I talk so loud is that I am continually shouting over it. Your machine is running, and here we are whispering."

Insulated with foam, fiberglass and asphalt felts and foils, dishwashers have quieted down in recent years to the point where you don't even know they're on. Acoustic dampening materials muffle vibrations when applied to both inner and outer walls as well as to doors, access, and toe panels. To increase sound-proofing, water impellers have been altered; pumps slowed, housed in rubber and mounted to the base pan instead of to the tank.

Other benefits accrue from this wrapping: less heat escapes into the kitchen, and water stays hotter, consuming minimal energy. Though ratings are neither consistently nor accurately enough measured to be gospel, a machine taking the oath of silence runs in the forty- to fifty-something-decibel range.

Lower Water Consumption

With the exception of Aiko Lee, who works faster and more ecologically than any machine, dishwashers use 5.8 fewer gallons per load than "personwashers," a 1988 study by Ohio State University revealed. Reducing energy consumption by 45 percent in just a decade, many of today's machines far exceed this figure with the current benchmark hovering roughly around 5.3 gallons total.

Manufacturers are meeting standards for greater energy efficiency by forcing recirculated water through smaller holes under greater pressure. Shrinking the size of the water reservoir, the most successful companies have gone to a two-pump system—one for filling, the other for emptying.

To participate in raising the energy consciousness of a dishwasher, compare operating costs stated on the energy guide labels before purchasing. Run the machine on a short cycle with cold rinses and no drying cycle. If electric rates go down during off-peak usage hours in your municipality, turn it on then and only when completely full.

Cleanliness Moves Right Up There

With one advantage feeding another, less water available for washing means cleaner water sieved continually before recirculating. Depending on a triple filtration system, new machines remove debris formerly deposited on dishes. They just say "no" to Maytag's query: "Do you wash your dishes before you wash your dishes?"

Dishes going into new dishwashers require only a mere scraping. The complete cleaning my mother subjects her dishes to removes the particles soap depend on for activation. Any large pieces of food are pulverized in the machine's grinder or collected in a cup. Some sieves are then self-cleaned by a backwash; others must be removed from the machine for flushing.

Staying Out of Hot Water

Since 80 percent of a dishwasher's operating cost is spent heating water, reducing it will be a financial boon as well as a further energy saver. New machines have rallied to this demand as well.

Available with a booster heater whose additional cost soon pays for itself, dishwashers heat water internally to the 140 degrees necessary to dissolve soap. As a consequence, the home water heater is lowered to the 120 degrees adequate for other activities, saving 10 to 15 percent of annual heating costs. With an in-machine heater, there is no worry about depleting the hot-water supply when running several loads successively.

The one antiheater message is that *successive* now means *long*. A heater raises the temperature one and one-half degrees per minute according to Maytag's estimate, clocking almost two hours for a complete load. Heaters with thermostats are most precise, but the main concern is that a machine not start operating before it reaches 140 degrees.

For best results with a dishwasher lacking an internal heater, push its start button only after water runs very hot at the tap, and when it is not commandeered for showers, laundry, or other depleting tasks.

DISHWASHER DILEMMAS

Is water quality appropriate for a dishwasher?

Pressure

Before purchasing a machine, check its brochure to determine if your household pressure is sufficient for a dishwasher to fill properly. Varying from one machine to another, KitchenAid, for example, demands a pressure of 20 to 120 psi; Asko 18 to 176. Some machines fill by timers; others by a volume-sensitive flotation valve. If pressure is low, the safer choice is a machine that measures level by volume. A booster pump should also be added.

Hardness

Hard water can interfere with a dishwasher's functioning. In areas where the water supply is higher than seven grains on the hardness scale—some dealers say as low as three to five grains—dishes will streak unless a water softener is installed or a model selected with an internal softener. Water that contains significant amounts of sulfur, iron, manganese, turbidity or has an excessively high or low pH may require intervention from a water treatment company.

Do you want a portable or built-in dishwasher?

I have not asked the question "Do you want a dishwasher?" for unless you are Aiko Lee, or limited by one of the conditions just described, the most practical answer is a confident yes.

Built-in dishwashers are designed to fit undercounter and hook up permanently to water and electricity. Finished only on the front, they are loaded from this position as well. When installed at the end of a cabinet line, matching side panels can be added.

Portables can loiter anyplace in or out of the kitchen. When it is their turn, they are pulled up to the sink, plugged in, and connected to the faucet. Some have a water-release button to access water during their operation. Fitted with a chopping-block top, they contribute an extra work surface.

A portable can be loaded from the front like a built-in or top-loaded with a rack attached to the lid. This latter method supposedly allows larger items to fit in the bottom, but it's a real drag, and this machine can't be built in. To convert a front-loader, remove its sides, casters, and top.

Portables are ideal for apartment dwellers with insufficient undercounter space, renters who want to take their investment with them, and situations where alterations necessary to accommodate them aren't feasible. Portables are relatively more expensive than built-ins, but you save on installation fees. Lacking a cabinet for cushioning, they are noisier when they run.

What size?

Most dishwashers are twenty-four inches wide and constructed to fit into a standard cabinet thirty-six inches high and twenty-four inches deep. With trim kits, deviants also fit snugly. Some models, particularly European, have adjustable legs and toe kicks that make them ideal for slipping in as a replacement when a floor isn't being removed.

Smaller, eighteen-inch-wide models also exist for a bar area, boat, or small kitchens and households. Handling about half the number of place settings of a standard machine, a new compact gnome line can be built in or left freestanding on a countertop. With a tiny kitchen in mind, one company produces a dishwasher combination that sits under a sink. Miniaturization is certainly an asset in a small space, but after a point it may be easier to wash a few dishes by hand than to bother with a doll's dishwasher.

Do you want a commercial dishwasher or "dish machine"?

Although I've always fantasized about having a speedy restaurant dish machine that cleans twenty-five plates or forty-five glasses in two and one-half minutes, its multiple racks require too much storage space for most kitchens. I suspect its $2,500 price tag may also work as a deterrent.

DIAGRAM OF A DISHWASHER

Cycles

To maintain a spotless reputation, a dishwasher requires two complete wash cycles, each with fresh or recirculated water and detergent. From this basic figure, advertisers have managed to mix and match over twenty cycles whose options only a Kentucky Derby pari-mutuel bettor could compute.

The following cycles are those that machines most frequently tout. Button pushers beware: Although the name may be the same, a particular cycle is put through its paces quite differently from one machine to the next. A pots and pans cycle, for example, can vary in length, water temperature, and number of washes and rinses.

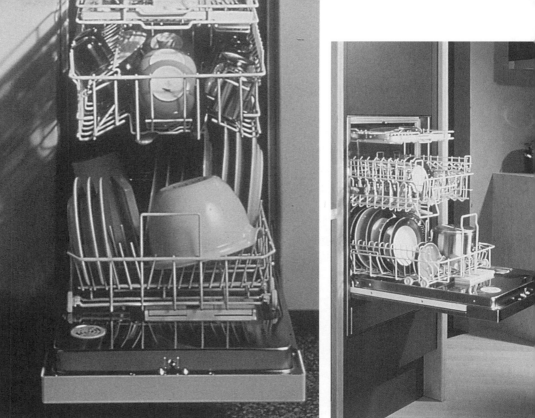

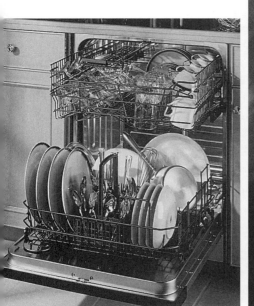

IMPORTED DISHWASHERS

European dishwashers have established a standard for cleanability, quiet durable stainless-steel interiors, and restrained use of water. This model *(top left)* has recently been reconfigured with wider prongs for stoneware dishes, an increased-capacity lower rack, taller upper rack, and slide-out basket for large cutlery. It can be covered with a custom panel and completely integrated so that both its control panel and door line up with adjacent cabinets. The company will paint the control panel to match a customer's color sample.

SMALL SPACE

Most dishwashers are twenty-four inches wide. An exception, this seventeen and one-half-inch model *(top center)* maintains the same high quality of its line's full-sized machines, possessing a well-designed interior that handles eight place settings. Two of these units might be helpful in a kosher household where a separate machine is required for dairy and meat dishes.

RAISED DISHWASHER

By raising the dishwasher and installing it twelve to eighteen inches off the ground *(top right),* loading and unloading can be accomplished without a bend.

This dishwasher does the thinking for you, adjusting—and readjusting—the optimum water temperature and type of cycle throughout the cleaning process according to the state of your load.

If the new GE Profile or Maytag Intellisense machines are any indication, cycles may soon be a thing of the past. Fitted with microprocessor *sensors*, dubbed "Fuzzy Logic" technology, these machines test the waters to see how dirty they are and then automatically compute the most effective temperature, cycle, time, and detergent measure.

Rinse and Hold: People who live alone or who don't cook very much can prerinse dishes that must wait several days for a load to gather.

Light/Delicate Wash: With a reduced speed and temperature, this cycle is designed for crystal and china. Nevertheless, it is not the force of the water that damages these fine wares as much as the composition of the soap. Not to worry, this run's 110 to 130 degrees is not hot enough to dissolve the soap—or to clean the dishes. Before subjecting Great Aunt Gertrude's heirloom crockery to possible abuse, check with its manufacturer. If it can go in the dishwasher, use a regular cycle and titrate soap amounts carefully.

In some systems, water pressure has been adjusted to spray a finer mist over dishes in the top rack. This is an asset only if you want to reserve this rack for crystal, not if you want the freedom to load pots, dishes, and glasses wherever they fit best. So as not to be limited, be sure any pressure knob is adjustable.

Short Cycle: With fewer washes and rinses, this cycle guzzles less water, an energy saver when dishes aren't very dirty.

Heavy/Pots and Pans/Soak and Scrub Cycle: A third wash, hotter water, and/or longer cycle can be called on to tackle the aftermath of a barbecue or sauté spree. Many people argue that it's foolish to waste a dishwasher's valuable space on pots, but as long as they aren't cast iron (or have a cast-iron core), there is nothing I'd rather delegate to the dishwasher. "Steam" is a buzzword used to flex an appliance's cleaning muscle: It is hype!

Sani-Cycle: Ranging from 150 to 174 degrees, the higher temperatures offered by this cycle supposedly sanitize as they halt the spread of disease. The dish-washer is not a doctor. Nonetheless, higher temperatures do cut grease and get dishes cleaner, and that's nothing to sneeze at.

Plate Warmer: The heating cycle turns on to warm plates.

Cancel Button: After this is pushed, the machine finishes its wash or rinse cycle and drains to be reset.

Dryer: To compensate for the new energy-saving no-heat switch, some high-end models have added a blower to spread the machine's residual hot air. There is, however, no need to seek any help in drying the dishes. Just open up the door, pull out the racks to dissipate moisture, and let the dishes dry themselves.

Exterior

Door Panel: Dishwashers are available in stainless and in black, white, or almond lacquer or acrylic enamel. Some accept a decorator panel, running one-eighth inch thick for a European machine; one-quarter inch for an American. As with a refrigerator, be sure the panel corresponds stylistically with the cabinetry.

Integrated dishwashers allow a cabinet front to be attached, further muting its sound. Trim kits come in different colors or wood. Unifying the dishwasher with the kitchen, its doors are increasingly designed so control panels line up with a cabinet drawer; doors with a toe kick. One company now hides controls in the dishwasher's interior; eliminating all clues to its existence. Others are sure to follow suit.

Door Springs: Springs must be heavy-duty when sporting a panel, or it falls off when the door opens. Maintaining the door in any open position, heavier *compression springs* are less likely to have to be replaced than lighter *expansion coils*.

Controls: Moving up the line, the dishwasher's mechanical action is activated by dials, more streamlined push buttons, and, ultimately, electronic controls. Once guaranteed to go on the fritz, these solid-state touch pads, carrying a surcharge of about $100, are much more rugged today.

A *delayed-start* button allows the machine to be programmed for future operation (up to nine hours hence) while its *memory* recalls the previous setting in the absence of a power outage. Some have a *pause* button for inserting dirty dishes, a *rinse agent indicator*, and a readout of the temperature and point reached in the cycle. Those with an *all-done* light are great in families with shrewd children who get out of emptying the dishwasher by claiming they did not know it was done. When a problem does arise, it helps with a diagnosis. To discourage children, one control you do want is a *lock*.

Interior

Dishwasher interiors come in three flavors: stainless, plastic-coated steel, and porcelain enamel on steel. Surgical-grade eighteen-gauge stainless is considered the most seaworthy. Easy to clean, it does not chip or rust, creating pockets for debris to lodge. Retaining heat, it aids in drying the dishes, contributing to that energy saving. In better machines, this stainless will also be found on the tank, pipes, filters, inner casing, and spray arms. Nonrustproof, a lower-grade stainless is sometimes employed: If a magnet sticks to its surface, reject it.

Surprisingly noisier than stainless, plastic-coated steel is second hardiest. It can be cut, but neither rusts nor chips. Porcelain both chips and cracks, beginning an unfortunate rusting process that starts before some machines even come off the line.

Rinse Agent: Dispensers for liquid rinse agents are included to prevent water spots. A major problem when water is hard, these break down the water's surface tension, encouraging it to sheet off.

Lights: Guiding lights are beginning to be added to the interiors of some machines.

Spray Arms: Machines with rotating wash arms in the top, bottom, and middle of the machine bathe dishes more thoroughly than those splashing on only one or two levels. As any sixties hot tub freak can tell you, a good water massage depends on the number, pressure, and direction of high-speed jets. Newer models have eliminated the water tower that climbs through the center of the machine, leaving more space for dishes.

Racks: With most dishwashers able to do a creditable washing job, rack design and configuration become even more important in distinguishing among them. The distance between some racks is too small to allow the loading of anything but gremlin feeders, while others are divided into barely usable space by wash arms and silverware baskets. These are least intrusive in the bottom rack's front row center seats or on the door, where, unfortunately, their contents often don't get cleaned well.

Racks should be sturdy and well balanced, gliding easily even when full. Most are composed of plastic-coated steel wire or rubber, but these materials are happily being replaced by a more resilient nylon or tougher graphite nylon that doesn't craze. Look for a double or triple coating and cushioned tips that guard against rust.

To increase flexibility, some racks can be tilted, moved up and down, or fitted with removable inserts that require storage space. Intellectually this sounds great, but in reality who wants to futz with them?

For the most manageable solution, pick the rack design that gives you the largest interior space and is configured for *your* belongings, including odd-shaped pieces. European china is generally thinner than American—pottery thicker—and does not include cereal bowls. To be sure dishes will fit, evaluate the width between prongs as well as overall size.

Increasingly specialized, some racks are designed for stemware and silver, but by the time you painstakingly—painfully—arrange each piece, you could wash and dry them by hand and put them away. The silver rack that can be transferred directly from the dishwasher to the drawer is another seemingly logical idea. Yet unless all your silverware is washed each time, it lacks a practical application. In contrast, the covered basket is handy for measuring spoons, pastry tubes, baby bottle caps, and other small items. If basket holes are too large, line them with muslin or cheesecloth.

Rack one up for the dishwasher.

PERSONAL PICKS: DISHWASHERS

One less-than-helpful dealer told me that since most people buy dishwashers according to the class of machine they had before, he could help me only if I told him what I had had. Pity meeting him head-on if you'd never had a dishwasher—and even if you had!

Choosing a dishwasher is actually one of the simpler kitchen decisions. Your choices are excellent regardless of whether you are buying a replacement model that must fit into an existing space or a machine that will go into a new cabinet run and can have any characteristics you want.

The first choice to make is between a European and an American machine. It is to the European models that I say take my money and run, with some frustration that these sprinters take a lot more of my money than their American counterparts. These machines also may not fit into a standard American cabinet. Coming from abroad, they may be difficult to install and service; their replacement parts nonobtainable. Unaware of the Asko's internal power switch, installers who don't bother to read their manuals often erroneously report this machine as defective.

My allegiance goes to the Europeans for their production of a machine that actually cleans unrinsed dishes and their innovations in dishwasher design. For these visionaries it was not sufficient to have a door that accepted a custom panel that matched the cabinets; their dishwasher door had to be fully integrated with (attached to) a cabinet door. These solutions still left the dials visible, but this too has been resolved in the latest Gaggenau, which banishes them to the machine's interior.

I have been pleased with an early Asko, which has recently been reconfigured with more space and wider prongs to accept pottery dishes and fashioned in the latest colors of plum, teal, deep rose, and slate blue. When I purchased my Swedish machine, it seemed to offer the best value among the Europeans, and I was swayed by its first place in a cleanability test, though slightly suspicious of its sponsor, the National Swedish Board for Consumer Policy. Considerably more expensive, the Miele offers the largest interior, hosting oversize platters and glassware. It also offers a third level where silverware can be laid out as if it were being put to eternal rest, but I think loading this would require the care and agility involved in playing pickup sticks. Intended for the computer generation, the Miele can be reprogrammed from a laptop.

On the domestic front, KitchenAid has always been the frontrunner, and unlike many machines with heaters, it warms its water before beginning a wash, so hot water exists throughout the cycle. General Electric Profile and Maytag Intellisense, fitted with microprocessor sensors, are giving KitchenAid some techno-competition. Oblivious, Whirlpool and Sears just hang in there doing a solid job.

KITCHENSPEAK: DISHWASHERS

Booster Heater: This mechanism heats the water in the dishwasher to 140 degrees, the temperature necessary to dissolve soap. By doing this, the home water heater can be lowered to the 120 degrees adequate for other activities while saving 10 to 15 percent of annual heating costs.

Built-in Dishwashers: These dishwashers are designed to fit under a counter and be permanently hooked up to water and electricity. Finished only on the front, they are loaded from this position as well.

Compression Springs: These heavy springs keep the dishwasher door open in any position and are less likely to have to be replaced than lighter expansion coils.

Hard Water: In areas where the water supply is higher than seven grains on the hardness scale—some dealers say as low as three to five grains—dishes will streak unless a water softener is installed or a model selected with an internal softener.

Integrated: Dishwashers that accept the attachment of a cabinet front, further muting their noise.

Portable Dishwasher: A freestanding dishwasher that is finished on all sides and moves around the room on casters. Some have a release button to access water during operation; others are front loaders, leaving them with an option to be built in.

Rinse Agent: Dispensers for liquid rinse agents that prevent water spots by breaking down the water's surface tension and encouraging it to sheet off.

Sensors: Microprocessors now being used in some machines with fuzzy logic technology that test the dirtiness of the water and then automatically compute the most effective temperature, cycle, and duration as well as the amount of detergent necessary.

Spray Arms: Machines with rotating wash arms in the top, bottom, and middle of the machine bathe dishes more thoroughly than those splashing on only one or two levels.

Water Pressure: Each dishwasher requires a particular pressure for optimal operation. If pressure is low, the safest choice is a machine that measures level by volume rather than by a timer. A booster pump may also have to be added.

10

TAKING OUT
THE TRASH

Each of us, according to Newsweek, generates at least thirty-five hundred pounds of refuse per year or "enough to fill a bumper-to-bumper convoy of garbage trucks halfway to the moon." (In the Bay Area, the per-person average is reportedly six thousand pounds, but those northern Californians always did have more of everything.)

With environmental concerns ever more serious, and solid waste management mandatory, we are recognizing the importance of recycling refuse. Methods for collecting trash are changing, with states such as Wisconsin requiring dispensables to be divided into seven different categories. Now that garbage is going to the dwarfs, it's no longer feasible to toss everything down one hole after Alice.

To sort discards according to local jurisdiction, most citizens of this "recycling decade" are going to need more than one outlet for kitchen debris. This, in turn, will depend on the kind of trash generated. People preparing primarily fresh foods have different requirements from those utilizing a preponderance of canned and paper goods.

Start by trashing all preconceived notions and keep these questions in mind while perusing options suggested in this chapter:

- **What is going to be recycled, and how is it going to be sorted? Are glass, plastic, tin cans, newspapers, and food trimmings to be disposed of separately?**

- **Is everything to go into a receptacle, or are food trimmings to be dispensed to a compost bucket and/or disposer? Will a trash compactor flex its *ram* to help out?**

- **How much of each item above do you generate? How large does each receptacle need to be?**

- **Can some items such as newspapers or bottles be collected outside the kitchen?**

- **Is it possible to remove trash from the kitchen daily, or do you want to do this once a week when the *sanitation engineers* pick up?**

- **Do you want all trash bins banished out of sight?**

GARBAGE DISPOSERS

■

Some states require garbage disposers; others forbid them, making the question "Do you want a garbage disposer?" not necessarily yours to answer. If one is allowed, it certainly seems worthwhile.

Reportedly consuming less water per day than

one flush of a low-flush toilet and less electricity than a night-light, it is respectful of our resources. Broken down faster than they would be in a landfill, food scraps are carried to the municipal sewer system by pipes, where they are processed into sludge for compost or soil treatment. When transferred to a septic tank, they are reduced to gases and liquids.

Whether a disposer can be used in conjunction with a septic system has been a point of debate. General consensus now supports the union as long as the tank and its absorption field are increased by 50 percent or cleaned out twice as frequently. If a dishwasher and washing machine were previously hooked up to it, capacity should be sizable enough already.

A garbage disposer eliminates a great deal of garbage quickly before its unpleasant odors mount, attracting bugs and vermin. Instantly sweeping away trimmings of food prepped in the sink, it cleans up after you.

Do you want a batch-feed or continuous-feed disposer?

Acting as its switch, the cover of a batch-feed disposer must be engaged before it operates, whereas an uncovered continuous-feed disposer works ceaselessly once its wall or sink deck switch is activated. Roughly 25 percent more expensive, a batch-feed is safer in a home with young children and easier to install in an island sink.

Receiving food while running, a continuous-feed is much more responsive to the cook who doesn't want to be bothered turning a disposer on and off for each scrap. Its installation price mounts when a switch, not yet in place, must be added. Both systems rely on cold water to harden and flush out grease. When hot water is utilized, grease is deposited on pipes, clogging them.

When purchasing a disposer, there is no rationale for saving money that will ultimately end up in a plumber's pocket. Relatively inexpensive, this is one category to go top-of-the-line: for a model with one horsepower that handles harder waste quicker. (Not every company offers a batch-feed at this echelon.)

A heavy-duty disposer has a permanent magnet motor, automatic reversing action for antijamming, and sound deadening baffling for quieter operation. To prevent corrosion, the shredder, grinding ring, grinding chamber, and swivel impellers that push food against the graters should all be stainless or other corrosionproof metal. The sink flange should also be stainless or, if you wish color, from an engineered plastic, not metal with a baked-on color coat that chips.

Always on the lookout for a place to save money, I reused my old disposer without knowing that this wasn't recommended with a model three to four years old. Disposers at this age reportedly refuse to work when returned to the sink after lying fallow during a remodeling period, an experience I was thankfully deprived of. If you do reuse a disposer in a new sink, replace its old beat-up flange so everything looks sparkling new.

TRASH COMPACTORS

■

Available since 1978, the trash compactor was the last piece of equipment to take its place in the kitchen pantheon. Transforming electric energy into mechanical force, a trash compactor ram exerts approximately twenty-three hundred to five thousand pounds of pressure on a bag-lined bin, compressing garbage to roughly one-quarter of its volume in anywhere from twenty-seven to sixty seconds. The major complaints it garners—food rots, bugs visit, and the compactor stinks—are due to misuse: Bottles should be washed, and no food, wet sewage, or putrescibles should be placed in one. Previously compressed newspapers or magazines are not accepted.

Saving three out of four trips to the trash bin, a compactor beats carrying out bags and bags of garbage every day. That is if there is someone strong enough to lift the compacted disposables—which weigh in at thirty to fifty pounds. (If there isn't, factor chiropractor bills into the choice.) Having a compactor also simplifies trash disposal in areas where no collection service is provided and lowers costs when collection fees are based on the number of receptacles.

The compactor's potential was sharply eroded when recycling—sorting trash—was enforced and a concern expressed that mixed compacted materials break down less readily in landfills. The machine can still be an asset in large families utilizing considerable nonfood trash in one recycling category or in a kitchen with multiple waste bins, where each bag of recyclables is crushed after it is filled.

Built-in or freestanding?

A freestanding compactor provides flexibility in placement. It can be moved to a hallway, laundry room, or garage or stored next to a counter in the kitchen, freeing more base cabinet space. It is also easier to repair. When topped with butcher block, it becomes an additional work surface. A built-in compactor gives a more streamlined look to a kitchen.

What width?

Compactors come in twelve-, fifteen-, and eighteen-inch widths. (Built-ins are designed to fit into twenty-four-inch-deep cabinets.) Twelve-inch models are better limited to situations where space is tight, for garbage must be aimed at their narrow containers without getting it on the floor. Lacking a foot petal, the eighteen-inch behemoths become increasingly heavy and awkward to open as they fill. Their *mail slot* tops, though, are receptive to single entries. To paraphrase Goldilocks, the midsize—fifteen-inch compactor *with a foot pedal*—is just right.

A compactor's most valuable asset is an ease in dispensing trash—removing crushed bags and inserting new ones. Possible features include storage for refill bags, a deodorizer and fan, safety lock and key, and sound-deadening insulation. Like other appliances, they are available in black, white, and sometimes almond and occasionally accept custom door panels.

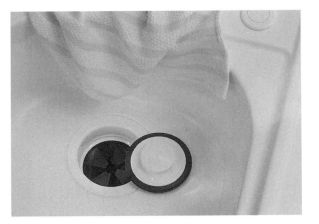

WASTE DISPOSER
This one-horsepower continuous-feed disposer is available with a flange and stopper in white, almond, or black to match its colored sinks. The button on the sink deck is an air-activated control switch for operating the disposer, a handy location when the sink is placed under a window, and no walls exist nearby for mounting the switch.

COMPACTOR
The 15-inch-wide trash compactor has a toe-bar drawer opener, a charcoal filter for absorbing off-aromas, solid-pack option for increased bag capacity, and the ability to be fitted with a matching cabinet panel. A freestanding convertible model is also available.

TRASH HOLES

■

With more people saving biodegradable food scraps for composting, some sinks now include trash holes that shoot down into a bucket below. While the idea is superb, the holes are so small it is difficult to coax trash into them, and buckets must compete for room under the sink. Uncovered, the bucket's *aromas* can be pretty heavy, even when emptied frequently.

Inserted into a hole cut in the countertop, a covered bucket with handle and plastic lining eliminate the odor problem. Although convenient to empty, it's too small with a diameter of six to nine inches for bull's-eye trash disposal. If space allows, carve a larger hole and have a custom bucket fabricated.

Composting collection is a messy task any way you look at it; at least this method contains it.

Much more hassle than a drop in the bucket, a canister with a handle and snug-fitting lid of stainless or other noncorrosive non-odor-absorbing material also works for composting.

Unlike wet trash, dry trash or recycling bins can be stored uncovered in a cabinet under a hole cut in the countertop that is fitted with a plug or lid made of the same material. This method works beautifully for a *quick in*—as long as the bucket underneath also can make a *quick out*. For a fast, easy getaway, Jeff Zinsmeyer keeps his thirty-five-gallon undercounter can on rollers.

WASTE AND RECYCLING BINS

■

Capitalizing on the idea that different self-contained work areas make for a well-functioning kitchen, multiple refuse bins are at the ready throughout the room, particularly near sinks, cutting boards, and work areas. On the other hand, one bin is usually adequate for each item being recycled, no matter whether all recyclables are grouped in one location or dispersed throughout the kitchen—or outside of it.

To contain aromas and discourage guests, a lid is necessary on any can designated to receive wet trash or food wrappings. Some lids open automatically when the can is pulled out; others have push-down tops. One design works like a mail slot, staying open until all trash is deposited.

To determine the size and style of bins you need, review:

- **How much each should hold.**
- **How convenient it is to move trash in and out of. Is it easy to line and lift out for emptying?**
- **Whether the receptacle opens automatically with a foot pedal or will accept one added separately.**

- **Whether it has a lid and, if so, if it automatically pops off for adding trash to the can.**
- **Whether you can close it with an elbow or knee.**
- **How easy it is to clean.**

Not to miss an opportunity to put a fashion spin on the gravest issue, trends are emerging in waste bins with their quality and design debated as hotly as whose turn it is to take out the trash. As mentioned under cabinets, my favorite is the triple-basket recycler that fits a thirty-six-inch corner base cabinet and rotates like a lazy Susan.

Rising to the occasion, many cabinet companies include trash storage options, so check these out when choosing your boxes. If their styles don't suit, many other bins are available to choose from.

A small bin is always useful under the sink with an automatic lift-off lid that opens with a foot pedal. Larger bins can be placed in a base cabinet. Attached to the back of the cabinet door (ideal), these either swing out or pull straight out with the opening door. In a less convenient arrangement,

RECYCLERS

Recycling baskets come in every combination from single to double, triple, and even quadruple bins—sometimes with a shelf for storing newspapers. They are much easier to pull out when attached to the cabinet door, especially when a loop handle is used instead of a knob. Available in different widths, they can be adapted to any cabinet size. A cover is appreciated when wet trash is stored.

AMOEBA BIN

Attaching to the inside of the sink cabinet, this flexible bin compresses where necessary when closing the door pushes it against plumbing paraphernalia. An ideal retrofit basket, it assumes its natural shape once the door is reopened.

SPINNING BINS

You'll no longer have to worry about using a corner cabinet efficiently when this three-basket recycler is installed in that space.

LOOK MA, NO HANDS

By attaching a foot plate to the bottom of a cabinet, the door can be opened with the tap of a shoe, enabling trash to be easily disposed of when hands are dirty or full. This free hands device is particularly helpful at a sink cabinet door.

PERSONAL PICKS: TRASH

DISPOSERS

Any of the disposers with a one-horsepower motor will crunch up waste fast and furiously, but Sinkmaster's Bone Crusher wins my vote for its name, catalog with a he-man cover, and lifetime guarantee. By the time you get to this place in the purchasing process, you probably won't care what this does, but it is worth some savings in money to compare warranties, local price wars, and plumbers' opinions.

TRASH COMPACTOR

Trash compactors seem best suited for big families who discard a large volume of cans, bottles, plastic, and paper goods. Since this is not a niche I occupy, I don't have a trash compactor, but I would if I did. With a width of fifteen inches, an easily removable bag, foot pedal that enables a handless opening, and the choice of a built-in or freestanding model, both Whirlpool and KitchenAid are good contenders in this category. The latter also has a charcoal filter for absorbing untoward odors. The rumor is that Whirlpool builds both, but KitchenAid is usually more expensive because its label carries more cachet. If room exists for only a 12-inch compactor, the General Electric with a foot pedal is a good choice.

they can also be pulled out—like pull-out shelves—after the door is opened.

Bins come halved for sharing or as singles, doubles, triples, or quadruples. Some bins fit directly on the track; others into a frame. Some share the platform with a rack holding cleaning supplies and, on occasion, a deodorizer bar. To manipulate easily, all require heavy-duty full-extension or overextension glides.

In a once-popular approach, a base cabinet is lined with a basket or plastic bag and hinged so it tilts down. Hard to manipulate, this method is best replaced with one of the new options created for this recycling heyday.

With all the devices for concealing trash bins, it is often more convenient to stash strong, handsome commercial-style wastebaskets next to a counter or in out-of-the-way spots.

Though newspapers can go on a shelf or in a bin, they are usually collected temporarily in the kitchen and then moved to a container in the garage or utility room. The most practical consist of a frame with a hook for holding a spool of twine that is unwound under the papers. When recycling time comes, papers are tied up and removed and another piece of twine positioned for the next batch.

CASTING CALL

11

SHOPPING AND INFORMATION SOURCES

SELECTION CHECKLISTS

■

You've read the book, learned about different materials and equipment that go into the kitchen; now it's time to go shopping and select the products that resonate best with your needs and pocketbook.

This chapter, a list of sources, checklists, and informational materials corresponding to each category, has been conceived as a helpmate to provide background material and to keep you company during your spree. Though it is repetitious and as interesting to read as any shopping list (it isn't), it will hopefully compensate for its dullness by helping you remember pertinent points and focus on value and quality as you pick among the plethora of choices assaulting you.

If you haven't already done so, request *full-line* catalogs of the items you need to purchase from the companies listed in this chapter. This list is intended as a get-you-going mover, not an end-all, be-all list. It names products that offer unique attributes as well as general items within a category that are widely esteemed. Don't get attached to any manufacturer or a particular model, just to what's important in its functioning. Models and companies change very quickly. Things went into and out of production just during the course of writing this book. If you know what to look for, it won't matter if a particular brand

or serial number is available the day you want to buy something.

Familiarize yourself with the catalogs. Browse through them, underscoring features of interest while winnowing down choices. Learn whether standards have been established for this commodity, what they are, and who regulates them. If at all possible, plan on seeing everything in person that you are considering, even if it means tracking down a distributor or finding someone who owns the item. Many reputable brands that appeal in pictures turn out to be less than sensational when viewed firsthand.

Before embarking on a scouting expedition, reread the relevant chapters. You might also want to review the sections "Select Appliances and Materials" (page 16), "Ordering Materials" (page 111), and "Money-Saving Tips" (page 23). Use the following blank chart for your peregrinations to record cost, features, accessories, and impressions of items for future comparison. Note retailer and date to help you track.

To make shopping easier, familiarize yourself

SHOPPING FINDS

CATEGORY				
	ITEM I	ITEM II	ITEM III	ITEM IV
Manufacturer				
Model				
Material				
Color				
Features				
Accessories				
Cost				
Delivery Fee				
Installation Fee				
Availability				
Dealer				
Date of Visit				
Impressions				

KITCHEN APPLIANCE SELECTIONS

ITEMS				
Name				
Brand				
Number				
Dimensions (length x height x width)				
Color/Finish				
Fuel Type				
Optional Features				
Installation Requirements: (Clearances, Trim Kit, etc.)				
Price with taxes				
Delivery (Company name, address, phone number, and price)				
Delivery Date				
Installer (Name, company, address, phone number, and price)				
Installation Fee				

with the checklist of primary characteristics to follow in comparing different models and brands.

While you're out, gather brochures with separate spec sheets listing dimensions and installation instructions, plus use and care manuals. That nifty cooktop may seem less attractive once you know how complicated its upkeep is. Play with it, moving doors, drawers, and shelves.

After shopping is finished, shut off further stimuli. Find a quiet nook to write down priorities for a particular item, then make a list of models exhibiting these criteria. Don't ignore appearance. You won't enjoy something whose looks you don't love, yet function and quality should remain paramount. Every time I try to place a skillet in my beautiful designer sink, I still rue its choice over the less comely behemoth that would have held the pan flat.

Draw up a secondary list of bennies and discard models that don't make the cut. At this point, you should be down to several choices. Enumerate the pros and cons of each model and see which stacks up best with your priorities. I was able to talk myself out of a trash compactor this way. Moving in the other direction, Alice Medrich went for an undermounted sink even though it cost extra. Her justification? "I've got to be able to shove stuff directly into the basin in one movement."

Be steered by trade-off and compromise. Florence Quinn paid for the pantry she wanted with savings acquired by substituting Formica for more expensive Corian. At each crossroads, remember the words of George Nelson as quoted in *Julia's Kitchen . . . A Design Anatomy* and choose the quality *tool* that enriches existence rather than the *possession* that merely enhances status.

Run any plumbing fixtures—disposer, dishwasher, hot- and cold-water dispensers—by the plumber before making a commitment. He knows how easy it is to install and obtain parts, what brands he is called back to fix most frequently, and what these replacements and repairs cost. He also has more knowledge of inner workings not immediately visible to you—which ceramic disk valves are ground too coarsely.

Don't be romanced into buying anything. Talk to as many people as necessary until you feel comfortable that you've made the right choice for your situation. Trust your instincts and look for someone who can explain what you need and why, in a logical manner that instills confidence. Above all, follow experts' recommendations for size and installation.

All other things being equal, give a locally produced item the nod. Freight is usually less expensive, and a local person is on board should problems arise.

Live with finalists until a clear winner emerges based on price, availability, functionality, or pure wanton unbridled passion.

As you make each selection, enter it on a chart, such as the one on page 314, to reference throughout the layout and remodeling process. Note name, brand, number, dimensions, finish, optional components, and type of fuel, if applicable.

Record installation fee (if available) and requirements, including clearances, ventilation spaces, and trim kits. (These are essential both for augmenting fit and for providing proper air circulation.) Although it is the designer's and contractor's job to confirm these numbers, you can monitor construction more carefully if you know what they are.

EVALUATING PURCHASES

Universally applicable, the following questions should constitute part of your comparison of every item along with the points on each checklist.

- Do you have a large enough pathway and door or window to bring it into your kitchen?

- Do you have a gas hookup or large enough electric service board to run it properly? Does it have a UL (Underwriters Laboratories), AGA (American Gas Association), or AHAM (Association of Home Appliance Manufacturers) Seal of Approval that assures compliance with safety standards?

- Does it fit the principles of safety, health, and universal design discussed under "Primary Principles of Good Kitchen Design" (page 102)?

- Is it easy to clean and maintain, internally and externally? Look for seamless construction, rounded corners where dirt can't lodge, and an ability to be installed flush, eliminating crumb-accumulating gaps.

- Is it durable? Will it scratch, chip, or mar easily?

- Will it save time? Is it convenient to use, simplifying kitchen tasks?

- Is it respectful of energy and natural resources?

- How quiet is it to operate?

- Does it offer features you will actually use? Do you really need the top of the line? Or do the extras just make it needlessly complicated?

- Does it fit in with the style you have chosen?

- Does it come in the color or finish you want, and will it coordinate with other kitchen choices? Most enduring are timeless classics: traditional woods; black, white, or stainless.

- Do you want an appliance that accepts custom front panels? If so, find out the panel's exact dimensions and any special fabrication or installation requirements. (Designer Morton Block warns that many panels are being ordered incorrectly due to lack of necessary information.) Does it line up with the toe kick?

- Is the appliance's design flexible enough to suit your needs, or does every nook and cranny speak to a specific purpose that may not be yours? Refrigerators offend worse in this regard.

- Do you want to spring for a solid-state electronic keypad? Though more costly than electromechanical controls and prone to break down, they are more precise and easier to clean and operate. Possessing microprocessors, they program sequential behavior, diagnose problems, and communicate information in their digital displays.

- How easy are the machine's parts to access for service? Is service readily available? For foreign-made machines? Who will repair it? What is their experience? Where will parts come from? Are they stocked locally? Is there a local dealer?

- What kind of warranty does it have? Is it for a particular period (most common) or for a specific amount of use? What parts are covered and for how long? Is it *limited* to certain aspects or *full*, covering even consequential damage such as a floor that becomes warped from a leaking dishwasher? Does it offer replacement or refund when repair is not possible?

- Warranties are important in comparing items, yet they require a certain wry perspective. The lifetime replacement my disposer offered was invalidated two years later when the company went belly up. Faucets often come with terrific warranties because manufacturers assume you'll throw them away when they break down rather than hassle with a plumber. But when you see a one-year, two-year warranty on something, realize that that may well be its death knoll. Extended warranties available for purchase do not prove worthy of their price.

SOURCES AND INFORMATION

■

The following section presents sources to contact along with decisions that must be made and points of comparison. It is divided by chapter, corresponding to the text in the preceding part of the book. Chapters 1 and 2 contain addresses of organizations, while Chapter 3 focuses on specific needs. Chapters 4–10 are dedicated to individual categories.

CHAPTER 1 Setting the Stage

American Society of Home
  Inspectors
P.O. Box 95588
Palatine, Illinois 60095
(800) 743-2744; (847) 290-1959

Association of Home Appliance
  Manufacturers
Major Appliance Consumer Action
  Panel (MACAP)
20 North Wacker Drive
Chicago, Illinois 60606
(312) 984-5816
(Free bulletins and consumer
  complaints about appliances)

Building Research Council
University of Illinois
One East St. Mary's Road
Champaign, Illinois 61820
(800) 336-0616
(Remodeling videos and brochures)

Consumer Information Center
P.O. Box 100
Pueblo, Colorado 81002
(Consumer information handbook
  and catalogs)

Federal Housing Administration
(800) 733-HOME
(Title I Financing)

National Appropriate Technology
  Assistance
(800) 428-2525
(Home energy conservation)

National Association of Home
  Inspectors
4248 Park Glen Road
Minneapolis, Minnesota 55416
(800) 448-3942

Shop-at-Home
P.O. Box 221050
Denver, Colorado 80222
(Wholesale catalogs)
(800) 315-1995

Thomas Regional Directory Co. Inc.
Five Penn Plaza
New York, New York 10001
(212) 629-2100
(Resource directory)

CHAPTER 2 Choosing the Players

American Institute of Architects
  (AIA)
1735 New York Avenue, N.W.
Washington, DC 20006
(202) 626-7300

American Society of Interior
  Designers (ASID)
608 Massachusetts Avenue, N.E.
Washington, D.C. 20002
(202) 546-3480

Home Owners Warranty
  Corporation
P.O. Box 152087
Irving, Texas 75015
(800) 433-7657
(Warranty for contractors)

Kasmar Publications, Inc.
41-905 Boardwalk, Suite L
Palm Desert, California 92211
(800) 253-9992; (619) 773-2874
(Professional kitchen and bath
  design books)

National Association of Home
  Builders (NAHB)
1201 15th Street, N.W.
Washington, D.C. 20005
(202) 822-0216

National Association of the
  Remodeling Industry (NARI)
4900 Seminary Road
Suite 320
Alexandria, Virginia 22311
(800) 966-7601

National Kitchen & Bath Association
  (NKBA)
687 Willow Grove Street
Hackettstown, New Jersey 07840
(800) 367-6522; (908) 852-0033

Residential Space Planners
  International (RSPI)
20 Ardmore Drive
Minneapolis, Minnesota 55422
(800) 548-0945

Rockport Publishers
146 Granite Street
Rockport, Massachusetts 01966
(800) 284-8232
(Designer source)

To Start Shopping

Layout Aids

Design-Aid
P.O. Box 32
Glen Cove, New York 11542
(516) 759-9642
(Kitchen design and layout)

Design Works
Department TH
11 Hitching Post Road
Amherst, Massachusetts 01002
(Home and remodeling kit)
(413) 549-4763

Floor-Plan Plus 3D by
    ComputerEasy
    International
IMSI
1895 Francisco Boulevard East
San Rafael, California 94901
(800) 522-3279

Hammacher Schlemmer
9180 Le Saint Drive
Fairfield, Ohio 45014
(800) 233-4800
(Kitchen planning system)

Job Cost Estimating

Craftsmen Book Company
P.O. Box 6500
Carlsbad, California 92018-9974
(800) 829-8123

HomeTech Information Systems
5161 River Road
Bethesda, Maryland 20816
(800) 638-8292

R. S. Means Company, Inc.
100 Construction Plaza
P.O. Box 800
Kingston, Massachusetts 02364
(800) 334-3509

Islands/Worktables/Carts

Ciatti a Tavola
See, Ltd.
920 Broadway
New York, New York 10010
(212) 228-3600

Haute House
1428 Danby Road
Ithaca, New York 14850
(607) 273-9348

John Boos & Company
P.O. Box 609
Effingham, Illinois 62401
(217) 347-7701

Suzanne Table Co.
17270 Apache Court
Penn Valley, California 95946
(916) 432-4163

Entertainment/ Communications

Undercabinet Mounts:
General Electric
Appliance Park 6, Room 129
Louisville, Kentucky 40225
(800) 626-2000
(Steam/grease-resistant radio,
    cassette player, TV)

Sony Electronics Inc.
12451 Gateway Boulevard
Fort Myers, Florida 33913
(800) 222-7669
(Radio, TV)

Small Wall Fax:
Sharp Electronics Corporation
Sharp Plaza, P.O. Box 650
Mahwah, New Jersey 07430-2135
(800) BE SHARP

Pet Doors

America's Pet Door Outlet, Patio
    Pacific
Department ZZ
1931 North Gaffey Street, Suite C
San Pedro, California 90731-1256
(800) 826-2871

PET DOORS U.S.A.
Department NW-96
4523 30th Street West
Bradenton, Florida 34207
(800) 749-9609

Dumbwaiters

Flinchbaugh
390 Eberts Lane
York, Pennsylvania 17403
(800) 326-2418; (717) 854-7720

Silent Servant
Miller Manufacturing, Inc.
165 Cascade Court
Rohnert Park, California 94928
(800) 232-2177

Heaters

Embassy Industries, Inc.
300 Smith Street
Farmingdale, New York 11735
(516) 694-1800
(Heating units that fit beneath
    cabinets)

Small Kitchens

Becker-Zeyko, SBK Pacific, Inc.
1030 Marina Village Parkway
Alameda, California 94501
(510) 865-1616

Dwyer Products Corporation
418 North Calumet Avenue
Michigan City, Indiana 46360
(800) 348-8508; (219) 874-5236

Acme Kitchenettes
Route 9
P.O. Box 348
Hudson, New York 12534
(800) 322-4191; (518) 828-4191

Modular Units

Ciatti a Tavola

General Electric
(Dishwasher that fits under a sink)

SPACE-SAVING APPLIANCES

Though these all save space, they bring crumbs with their shrink wrap. Double-check that they won't be too hot for a laminate finish on counter-top or cabinet. The toasters may not be wide enough for fat breads. Check your local telephone book or yellow pages for a local source.

Undercabinet Appliances:

Black & Decker Spacemaker (Toast-R-Oven Broiler, toaster, coffeemaker, can opener)

General Electric (electric knife, drip coffeemaker, can opener)

Hamilton Beach (can opener, coffeemaker)

Norelco (can opener, coffeemaker)

Oster (can opener)

Presto (can opener)

Rival (can opener)

Robeson (coffeemaker)

Sanyo (can opener)

Sunbeam (can opener, coffeemaker)

Toastmaster (toaster)

Toshiba (coffeemaker)

Waring (blender–can opener combo)

Built-in Appliances:
Brumatic (undersink coffeepot)

Wall-Recessed Built-in:

Iron-A-Way Inc. (toaster, can opener, ironing center, and paper towel and food wrap dispenser)
220 West Jackson Street
Morton, Illinois 61550
(309) 266-7232

VINYLIZED FABRIC LAMINATION

Custom Laminations
932 Market Street
Paterson, New Jersey 07509-2066
(201) 279-9174

ENVIRONMENTAL PRODUCTS

AFM Enterprises, Inc.
350 West Ash Street
Suite 700
San Diego, California 92101
(800) 239-0321; (619) 239-0321
(Low-toxin home renovation products, paint, etc.)

HARDWARE FOR ADJUSTING COUNTERTOP AND SINK HEIGHTS

Häfele America Co.
3901 Cheyenne Drive
P.O. Box 4000
Archdale, North Carolina 27263
(800) 423-3531

ADDITIONAL SOURCES AND INFORMATION

Center for Universal Design
The Accessible Housing Design File by Ron Mace
North Carolina State University
Box 8613
Raleigh, North Carolina 27695-8613
(919) 515-3082

Consumer Products Safety Commission
(800)-638-2772

Department of Housing and Urban Development
Adaptable Housing: A Technical Manual for Implementing Adaptable Dwelling Unit Specifications
(800) 245-2691

Dimension Express
(702) 833-3633 (information)
(702) 833-4748 (fax request to receive installation dimensions on products you are considering)

Environmental Protection Agency
(800) 368-5888
(Asbestos abatement)

National Association of Home Builders Research Center
A Comprehensive Approach to Retrofitting Homes for a Lifetime and *Directory of Accessible Building Products*
400 Prince George Boulevard
Upper Marlboro, Maryland 20774-8731
(800) 638-8556
(301) 249-4000

Perfectly Safe
7835 Freedom Avenue, North West
North Canton, Ohio 44720-6907
(800) 837-KIDS
(Catalog)

Radon Hotline
(800) SOS-RADO

Lighthouse
3620 Northern Boulevard
Long Island City, New York 11101
(800) 829-0500

CABINETS

This checklist is designed to evaluate factory-produced cabinets. Apply the same standards when evaluating cabinets fabricated by a craftsperson. Most cabinets look at least adequate in a showroom. Your task is to identify those that will still look good a decade hence. Once you've chosen a finish and door style, it pays to get a sample laid up. Do not choose an inset door in a face-frame cabinet without first seeing the company's skill at producing this style.

   Before you shop, remind yourself of low-, middle-, and high-end cabinet features by referring to the chart on page 20.

Homework: Order a *Directory of Certified Cabinet Manufacturers* along with *Construction Standards for Kitchen and Vanity Cabinets* from KCMA.

Supplies: Take project dimensions and any layouts already drawn to showrooms so you can estimate size and number of cabinets you'll need. Bring your list of items you will be storing in these cabinets along with the measurements of any unusual-sized objects. Pack a 30-pound weight.

Tests: Use the weight to test how smoothly drawers open with it inside. After the sample door is made, take it to a lighting lab to evaluate under the lights you've specced to be sure they will enhance it.

Decisions:

Door style?

Material?

Face-frame or frameless?

If face-frame, do you want the door overlaid, flush, or inset?

Painted or stained finish for wood cabinets?

Matte or high-gloss finish?

Appliance garage?

Type of cabinets for corners?

Will wall cabinets have lights, pull-downs, or electric strips mounted underneath? If so, order an extra-long door or special molding to hide them.

EVALUATION

Material: Decide whether you want the cabinet to be made out of hardwood, wood veneer, high-pressure laminate, thermo foil, or steel.

HARDWOOD

- Choose type of wood.
- If finish grade, confirm that it is made from finer quartersawn wood with an even grain.

- Check variation in grain and color that will exist from one door, drawer, and face-frame to the next.
- In raised panel doors, confirm that parts are finished separately before being joined together.

WOOD VENEER

- Remembering that square edges and raised patterns damage more easily, choose type of wood and whether it is to be sliced flat, quarter, rift, rotary, or half-round.
- Confirm that door and drawer veneers are applied to a medium-density fiberboard (first choice) or particleboard (second choice) substrate. MDF should meet ANSI standard A208.2, while particleboard should possess ANSI A208 and be of industrial grades 1-M-2 and grades 1-M-3 (45-pound commercial grade).
- Check that veneer is well affixed to its substrate and doesn't appear as if it will peel off.
- Confirm that there will be no seams on the front of a door or drawer unless the veneer is narrower than the piece. In that case, confirm that there will be no more than one seam.
- Confirm that pieces (seams) will be book matched.
- Confirm that all side panels, inside doors, and bottoms of wall cabinets will be covered with the same veneer as doors and drawers.
- Is veneer 0.7 or 0.8 ($^1/_{32}$ inch) thick?
- What guarantee is given against the veneer's fading?

HIGH-PRESSURE LAMINATE

- Confirm that all side panels, inside doors, and bottoms of wall cabinets will be covered with the same laminate as doors and drawers.
- Confirm that the cabinet was laminated after fabrication so seams hide only in its corners.
- Be sure laminate is a high-pressure material, not the less-durable vinyl or melamine.
- Confirm laminate has at least the standard thickness of .028 inch. Determine what a thicker laminate would cost or one used for institutional cabinets that is more durable. If the cost is manageable, see if there is a pattern you like.
- Confirm that door and drawer laminates are applied to a medium-density fiberboard (first choice) or particleboard (second choice) substrate. MDF should meet ANSI standard A208.2, while particleboard should possess ANSI A208 and be of industrial grades 1-M-2 and grades 1-M-3 (45-pound commercial grade).
- Check that laminate is well affixed to its substrate and doesn't appear as if it will peel off.

- If you choose stainless as your material, you have a choice of the much more durable plain finish or a baked-on enamel that can chip. If you choose the latter, the choice is between a smooth and a pebbled texture.

STRUCTURE:

- If cabinets are factory-made, have they received the seal of approval from the NKCA? If not, why? Did they apply for this certification?

- If you are sensitive to formaldehyde, confirm that any glues are made of phenol formaldehyde, which is considered less toxic than urea.

- Is the box square?

- Check that boxes are rigid and structurally sound with a complete top, bottom, side, and back panel that runs full length for support.

- Check that cabinet sides are made of medium-density fiberboard or plywood, not particleboard, which won't hold shelves as solidly.

- If the cabinet is to be wide or hold heavy cast-iron pots, check that the bottom can be braced.

- Check that there are no warped boards.

- Confirm that box joints are double-doweled or constructed with a mortise and tenon, tongue and groove, rabbeting, or other interlocking joint. Screws should support these joints in better boxes, though nails and glue are sometimes used, never staples or clips.

- Confirm that triangular hardwood blocks are glued at the corners to further strengthen joints.

- Confirm that side panels of a face-frame cabinet are $1/2$ to $3/4$ inch thick and its back at least $1/4$ inch thick.

- Confirm that the stiles, mullions, and rails of a face-frame cabinet are at least $3/4$ inch thick and $1 1/4$ to $1 3/4$ inches wide.

- Confirm that side panels of a frameless box are $5/8$ to $3/4$ inch thick and its back at least $1/2$ inch thick.

- Confirm that the bottoms of wall cabinets are at least $1/2$ inch thick.

- Check that doors and drawers aren't too close together to open and close properly.

- Do base cabinets have adjustable legs that enable them to be installed without a shim?

Doors:

- Confirm that doors are $3/4$ to $1 1/4$ inches thick.

- Does a 24-inch-wide cabinet have two doors for support?

- Double doors should have no more than $1/4$ inch of space between them.

- There should be a gasket or dust barrier between the doors.

- Confirm that doors have bumper guards.

- Confirm that doors are self-closing.

- If you want locks, check to see how they will be added.

- If doors have glass panels, be sure they are mitered, not butt joined. Decide the shape of the glass insert, whether it will have mullions (dividers), and the type of glass used. Indicate whether you want the glass to receive the printproof treatment that prevents fingermarks. Decide if you want lights in the cabinet. If so, the shelves must be designed to accommodate them.

- Do you need childproof or earthquakeproof locks or safety guards?

Hinges:

- Confirm that the number of hinges is correct for the size and style of door. On a $3/4$-inch-thick door, they generally range from two hinges for a 15- to 20-inch-tall door to five hinges for an 80-inch door.

- Are hinges adjustable in height, width, and depth, allowing doors to be well aligned? Check to see that doors open and close easily.

- Do hinges allow the door to open sufficiently? Generally 135 degrees is ample for pulling out a shelf. Indicate anywhere you need special types of hinges or ones that open to a different degree.

- Frameless cabinets should have concealed wraparound hinges, while face-frame can sport visible, semivisible, or concealed hinges. If visible, they should be coordinated with door and drawer pulls.

- Choose hinges that are nice enough to leave unpainted so you don't have to deal with chipping. Confirm that copper or brass can be left uncoated.

Drawers:

- Are drawers strong, or is the bottom able to separate from the sides when you push down on it?

- Confirm that drawers have four full-height sides joined by mortise and tenon or other interlocking joint. In addition, they should have a separate drawer face.

- Drawer sides should be $1/2$ to $3/4$ inch thick and made of hardwood.

- Drawer bottom should be $1/4$ to $3/8$ inch thick and made of plywood (first choice), particleboard, or molded plastic. MDF is excellent, too, but heavy.

- Drawers should extend full length of cabinet.

- Confirm that drawers are self-closing.

- Confirm that drawers have stops so they aren't pulled out too far.

- Confirm that drawers have bumper guards.

Glides:

- Check that drawers open and close smoothly without sticking or angling.

- Confirm that glides have auto-alignment feature.

- The best glides are precision captive-roller channel glides.

- Confirm that all glides are full extension.

- Confirm that overextension glides are used where needed.

- Confirm that the load capacity of glides is sufficient for your belongings.

- Confirm the size of glide you want and whether you want to mount it on the sides of the drawer or underneath.

- Confirm the finish you want the glide to have, remembering that colored finishes will chip.

Shelves:

- Are shelves the proper length and thickness? A $1/2$-inch-thick shelf for up to a 2-foot expanse, $5/8$ inch thick to 3 feet, and $3/4$ inch thick to four feet, etc. Do you have lots of heavy pots that require thicker shelves? Do the shelves sag?

- Confirm that shelves have the proper number of supporting struts.

- Confirm that cabinet shelves are full depth.

- Shelves should be made of MDF or plywood and bonded on *all* sides with high-pressure laminate or melamine.

- Edge banding should be hardwood or PVC plastic.

- Shelves should be adjustable with holes or spacers for shelf clips installed straight.

- Shelf clips should be metal, or plastic with a metal pin in them.

- Glass shelves should be used behind glass doors. A 2- to 3-foot length should be $1/2$ inch thick. They should be permanently fixed with holes drilled just where you want to attach them and shelf clips installed so they are not visible.

Interior:

- Check that cabinet interior and shelves are the same color as the exterior.

- Confirm that the cabinet interior is divided for maximum efficiency.

- Check that a larger-than-necessary stile hasn't been used in the middle to accommodate stock doors.

- Confirm what storage systems are available with the cabinet. Check that fittings coordinate with cabinet finish and hardware—a shiny lazy Susan used with a high-gloss finish.

Finish:

- Check that box edges and doors are smooth and well sanded with the grain and that no slivers remain.

- Confirm that doors have not been overly sanded so they've lost their straight lines and square edge.

- Check that any nail holes or blemishes have been filled and that there are no chips or nicks.

- Check that all edges are banded or filled, sanded, buffed, and well finished.

- Check that finish is smooth without scratches, blisters, residue, or dust embedded in it.

- Check that finish is consistent in all areas and that front edges match the sides.

- Confirm that the toe kick is finished to match the cabinets or as specified.

- Confirm that any stain is water based, if allowed by the EPA. If not, is a pigmented oil stain used on a fine-grain wood; a penetrating oil stain for coarser-grained species with large pores? The stain should be hand-rubbed between applications.

- Confirm that any sealer other than a natural oil is a double or triple coat of a catalyzed conversion varnish, catalyzed lacquer, or polyurethane with 50 percent solids applied at the factory. Finishes may differ according to local EPA rulings.

- Confirm that UV protection has been included in the finish so it doesn't fade.

UNIQUE ATTRIBUTES

*Modified Cabinets
for Universal Design:*
LesCare Kitchens, Inc.
1 LesCare Drive
Waterbury, Connecticut 06705
(800) 811-9390; (203) 755-1100

Merillat Industries
P.O. Box 1946
Adrian, Michigan 49221
(800) 624-1250; (517) 263-0771
(Horizon and Nouveau lines)

*Suspension System
for Ceiling-Hung Shelves:*
Häfele America Co. (page 319)

CABINETS

Companies Fabricating Stock,
Semicustom, and Custom Cabinets:
LesCare Kitchens, Inc. (page 322)
Merillat Industries (page 322)

Millbrook Custom Kitchens
3581 Route 20
Nassau, New York 12123
(518) 766-3033
(Laminates)

Schrock Cabinet Company
6000 Perimeter Drive
Dublin, Ohio 43017
(800) 223-6548; (614) 792-4100

StarMark, Inc.
600 East 48th Street North
Sioux Falls, South Dakota 57104
((800) 755-7789; 605) 335-8600

UltraCraft
6163 Old 421 Road
P.O. Box 1249
Liberty, North Carolina 27298
(800) 262-4046; (910) 622-4281

Stock Cabinets:
Aristokraft, Inc.
P.O. Box 420
One Aristokraft Square
Jasper, Indiana 47546-0420
(812) 482-2527
(Also semicustom Decora)
(812) 634-2288

Semicustom Cabinets:
Jay Rambo Co.
8401 East 41st
Tulsa, Oklahoma 74145
(800) 647-2626; (918) 627-6222

Custom Cabinets:
Becker-Zeyko, SBK Pacific, Inc.
   (page 318)

Crystal Cabinet Works
1100 Crystal Drive
Princeton, Minnesota 55371
(800) 347-5045; (612) 389-4187

Fieldstone Cabinetry, Inc.
P.O. Box 109
Highway 105 East
Northwood, Iowa 50459
(515) 324-2114
(Also semicustom)

Heritage Custom Kitchens, Inc.
215 Diller Avenue
New Holland, Pennsylvania 17557
(717) 354-4011

IEA International, Inc.
5 Hunter Drive
Armonk, New York 10504
(914) 273-4142
(Rational, Neff)

Kennebec Company
One Front Street
Bath, Maine 04530
(207) 443-2131

Poggenpohl, U.S., Inc.
Wayne Plaza 1
145 Route 46 West, Suite 200
Wayne, New Jersey 07470
(800) 987-0553; (201) 812-8900

Rutt Custom Cabinetry
P.O. Box 129
1564 Main Street
Goodville, Pennsylvania 17528
(800) 706-7888; (717) 445-6751

SieMatic Corporation
2 Greenwood Square,
3331 Street Road, Suite 450
Ben Salem, Pennsylvania 19020
(800) 765-5266; (215) 244-6800

Snaidero International USA
201 West 132nd Street
Los Angeles, California 90061
(310) 516-8499

Wellcraft Custom Cabinetry
Division of Wellborn Cabinet Inc.
P.O. Box 1210
Ashland, Alabama 36251
(800) 336-8040; (205) 354-7151
(Traditional wood)

Wood-Mode, Inc.
1 Second Street
Kreamer, Pennsylvania 17833
(717) 374-2711
(Also semicustom)

Steel Cabinets:
Bulthaup USA
153 South Robertson Boulevard
Los Angeles, California 90048
(310) 288-3875

Ready-to-Assemble (RTA):
Mill's Pride
423 Hopewell Road
Waverly, Ohio 45690
(800) 441-0337; (614) 947-7535

Metal Door Panels:
The October Company
51 Ferry Street
Box 71
Easthampton, Massachusetts
   01027-0071
(800) 628-9346

Cabinet Locks:
Lamp Sugatsune America, Inc.
221 East Selandia Lane
Carson, California 90746
(800) 562-LAMP
(Also catches and latches)

Rev-A-Shelf (Rev-A-Lock)
P.O. Box 99585
Jeffersontown, Kentucky 40269
(800) 626-1126

Simplex Access Controls
P.O. Box 4114
Winston Salem, North Carolina
   27105-4114
(910) 725-1331

Pullout Table:
Häfele America Co. (page 319)

Step Stool:
Häfele America Co. (page 319)
(Fits in toe kick)

Rev-A-Shelf
(Pull-down that attaches to cabinet
   door)

ADDITIONAL SOURCES AND
INFORMATION

The Finishing School
120 Woodbine Avenue
Northport, New York 11768
(516) 262-0058

Hardwood Manufacturers
   Association
400 Penn Center Boulevard
Suite 530
Pittsburgh, Pennsylvania 15235
(412) 829-0770

Hardwood Plywood & Veneer
Association
P.O. Box 2789
Reston, Virginia 20195-0789
(703) 435-2900

Kitchen Cabinet Manufacturers
Association (KCMA)
1899 Preston White Drive
Reston, Virginia 22091
(703) 264-1690

National Particleboard/Medium
Density Fiberboard Institute
18928 Premiere Court
Gaithersburg, Maryland 20879
(301) 670-0604

CABINET HELPERS

TO START SHOPPING

Primary Manufacturers:
Amerock Corporation
P.O. Box 7018
4000 Auburn Street
Rockford, Illinois 61125-7018
(815) 963-9631

Feeny Manufacturing Company
P.O. Box 191
Muncie, Indiana 47308
(800) 899-6535; (317) 288-8730

Häfele America Co. (page 319)

Knape & Vogt Manufacturing Co.
2700 Oak Industrial Drive,
North East
Grand Rapids, Michigan 49505
(800) 253-1561

Lee/Rowan
900 South Highway Drive
Fenton, Missouri 63026
(800) 325-6150
(Bins, racks, and pullouts)

Mepla, Inc.
909 West Market Center Drive
High Point, North Carolina
27260-1469
(800) 456-3752

Rev-A-Shelf (page 323)

Pot Racks:
Commercial Aluminum Company
(Calphalon)
591 J Street
Perrysburg, Ohio 43551
(800) 809-PANS

Independent Inc.
191 Coney Island Drive
Sparks, Nevada 89431
(800) 763-8232

Lavi Industries
27810 Avenue Hopkins
Valencia, California 91355-9900
(800) 624-6225
(Stemware hanging rack)

Backsplash Racking Systems:
Becker-Zeyko, SBK Pacific, Inc.
(page 318)

Ciatti a Tavola (page 318)

Franke, Inc.
Kitchen Systems Division
212 Church Road
North Wales, Pennsylvania 19454
(800) 626-5771

Häfele America Co. (page 319)

InterMetro Industries Corporation
651 North Washington Street
Wilkes-Barre, Pennsylvania 18705
(800) 433-2232
("Metro Smart Wall" racking
systems and wire shelves)

Mepla, Inc.

Storage Containers:
Cambro Manufacturing Company
7601 Clay Avenue
Huntington Beach, California
92647-2000
(800) 854-7631

Rubbermaid Commercial Products
Inc.
3124 Valley Avenue
Winchester, Virginia 22601
(800) 347-9800; (540) 667-8700

Tupperware Home Parties
(800) 858-7221

Special Aids:
Cuisinarts, Inc.
150 Milford Road
East Windsor, New Jersey 08520
(800) 726-0190
(Blade storage)

Edlund
159 Industrial Parkway
Burlington, Vermont 05401
(802) 862-9661
(Knife storage)

International Storage Systems
11230 Harland Drive,
North East
Covington, Georgia 30209
(800) 874-0375
(Wire shelves)

Iron-A-Way Inc. (page 319)

J. K. Adams Company
Route 30
Dorset, Vermont 05251
(800) 451-6118
(Knife blocks, spice carousels)

Kent Design & Manufacturing,
Inc.
3522 Lousma Drive, South East
Grand Rapids, Michigan 49548
(800) 373-4627
(Stemware racks)

Lifestyle Systems
P.O. Box 5031
Huntington Beach, California 92615
(800) 955-3383; (714) 964-3383
(Plastic drawer dividers, knife
blocks)

Polder, Inc.
8 Slater Street
Port Chester, New York 10573
(800) 431-2133
(Dispenser for foil, plastic wrap,
wax paper, and paper towels)

Professional Cutlery Direct
170 Boston Post Road,
Suite 135
Madison, Connecticut 06443
(800) 859-6994
(Knife racks)

Vance Industries, Inc.
7401 West Wilson Avenue
Chicago, Illinois 60656
(708) 867-6000
(Cutting boards, utensil trays,
knife racks, cabinet steps)

White Home Products
2204 Morris Avenue, Suite 203
Union, New Jersey 07083
(800) 200-9272
(Automated kitchen carousel)

Woodfold-Marco Mfg., Inc.
Box 346
Forest Grove, Oregon 97116
(503) 357-7181
(Knife drawer, cutting boards)

Wood Technology, Inc.
225 Elf Way
Box 1301
Pittsboro, North Carolina 27312
(800) 231-9522
(Appliance lifts)

Nonrefrigerated Wine Storage:
Häfele America Co. (page 319)

J. K. Adams (page 324)

Kent Design (page 324)

Mail-Order Catalogs:
Chef's Catalog
3215 Commercial Avenue
Northbrook, Illinois
   60062-1900
(800) 338-3232

Hold Everything
P.O. Box 7456
San Francisco, California
   94120-7456
(800) 421-2264

International Wine Accessories (IWA)
11020 Audelia Road, Suite B-113
Dallas, Texas 75243
(800) 527-4072

Williams-Sonoma
P.O. Box 7456
San Francisco, California
   94120-7456
(800) 541-2233

The Wine Enthusiast
P.O. Box 39
Pleasantville, New York 10570
(800) 356-8466

HARDWARE

Tests: Measure hardware depth to be sure it is shallow enough to open perpendicular corner cabinets beyond it and that it won't interfere with the full opening of cabinet doors. Check that the hardware or channel fits your hand size and fingernail length and that you will be able to grip it easily even when hands are greasy and sticky. If not, will you be able to rout out a radius behind the pull to make more room for your fingers? Check how it looks with any cabinet hinges that will be visible.

Decisions:

Type of hardware? Multiple types?

If you want a rectangular pull, do you prefer a single piece with round, square, or offset edges or a bar with two supporting members?

What size?

Custom to match solid-surface sinks or wallpaper?

What material? Uncoated polished solid brass? Chrome? Black chrome? Stainless? Copper? Nickel? Zinc? Forged iron? Aluminum? Ceramic? Porcelain? Wood? Marble? Crystal? Nylon? Plastic? Solid surface? Semiprecious stones? A mixture of materials?

Back or escutcheon plate?

EVALUATION

Knob: Does it have an interior thread for strength?

Cast Brass: Is the surface smooth and nonpitted?

Nylon: Galvanized steel core?

Colored Finish: Does color go all the way through? Do pieces come with screws? Are they the proper length for your drawer and door thickness?

UNIQUE ATTRIBUTES

Discount Hardware:
Knobs, Knockers & Butts
P.O. Box 8355
Greenville, North Carolina 27834
(800) 527-5662

Custom Knobs:
The Worthy Works Inc.
1220 Rock Street
Rockford, Illinois 61101-1437
(800) 373-5662
(Accepts wallpaper, laminates, etc.)

Stained-Glass Inlays on Brass:
Simon's Hardware Inc.
421 Third Avenue
New York, New York 10016
(800) 291-0984; (212) 532-9220

Antique Hardware Match:
Liz's Antique Hardware
453 South La Brea
Los Angeles, California 90036
(213) 939-4403

HARDWARE

Food, Nature, and Animal Motifs:
Michael Aram, Inc.
c/o Details
8625 1/2 Melrose Avenue
West Hollywood, California 90069
(310) 659-1550
or through Lewis Dolin, Inc.
    (914) 232-7465

Beemak
1156 West 135th Street
Gardena, California 90247
(310) 324-9302

Chris Collicott
1151 1/2 North La Brea
Los Angeles, California 90038
(213) 876-5112

Gem an Eye Arts
23-10 45th Avenue
Long Island City, New York 11101
(718) 729-2363

Hemisphere
450 Harrison Avenue
Suite 226
Boston, Massachusetts 02118
(617) 292-5160

Laure Dillon Designs
1760 South Beretania Street
#10C
Honolulu, Hawaii 96826
(808) 949-0551

Liz's Antique Hardware (page 325)

Wonderpull Creations by Doreen
Doreen J. Spychala
HC4, Box 58
Payson, Arizona 85541
(520) 474-8701

Mixed Styles and Materials:
Avanté Hardware
TFI Corporation
2812 Hegan Lane
Chico, California 95928
(800) 752-2037

Belwith-Keeler
4300 Gerald R. Ford Freeway
P.O. Box 127
Grandville, Michigan 49468-0127
(800) 453-3537

Berenson Hardware
2495 Main Street
Suite 222
Buffalo, New York 14214-2152
(716) 874-9025

Colonial Bronze
P.O. Box 207
Torrington, Connecticut 06790-0207
(860) 489-9233

Dec Har
520 Homestead Avenue
Mount Vernon, New York
    10550-3004
(914) 699-5550

Häfele America Co. (page 319)

Lamp Sugatsune America, Inc.
    (page 323)

Wood Technology, Inc. (page 325)

Traditional and Reproduction:
Period Brass
117 Foote Avenue
P.O. Box 520
Jamestown, New York 14702
(800) 332-6677
(Oriental collection)

Crown City Hardware Company
1047 North Allen Avenue
Department J93
Pasadena, California 91104
(800) 950-1047; (818) 794-1188

Horton Brasses
Nooks Hill Road
P.O. Box 95
Cromwell, Connecticut 06416
(800) 754-9127; (860) 635-4400

Liz's Antique Hardware (page 325)

Paxton Hardware Ltd.
P.O. Box 256
Upper Falls, Maryland 21156
(800) 241-9741; (410) 592-8505

Forged Iron:
Acorn
P.O. Box 31
Mansfield, Massachusetts 02048
(800) 835-0121

Dimestore Cowboys
407 2nd Street South West
Albuquerque, New Mexico 87102
(505) 244-1493

Southwest Door Company
9280 East Old Vail Road
Tucson, Arizona 85747
(520) 574-7374

Nylon:
Hardware Concepts
3728 North West 43rd Street
Miami, Florida 33142
(305) 638-5922

Hewi Inc.
2851 Old Tree Drive
Lancaster, Pennsylvania 17603
(717) 293-1313

Laminate and Solid Surface:
Rock Solid Inc.
3220 Commercial Avenue
Madison, Wisconsin 53714
(608) 249-6988

Semiprecious Stones:
Pinecrest
2118 Blaisdell Avenue
Minneapolis, Minnesota 55404-2490
(800) 443-5337; (612) 871-7071

With myriad patterns to choose from, selecting surface materials can become overwhelming. Defuse the situation by going from store to store until you find a salesperson who is not only knowledgeable but also able to help you make decisions quickly. In all categories, look at materials recommended for commercial installation first, for they will be strongest and most resistant to stain. Find out if the material has to be sealed. If so, what is used, what does the sealing process involve, and how often will it have to be repeated?

Before you shop, remind yourself of low-, middle-, and high-end surface materials by referring back to the chart on page 20.

Homework: Request results of all standards and tests administered on materials you are considering. Compare products according to these tests, looking closely at impact and durability ratings. Tile results are reported in the Ceramic Tile Council of America's handbook. From this organization, also order *How to Decorate with Ceramic Tile* and *How to Install Ceramic Tile*.

Supplies: Take along project dimensions or the completed layout to help estimate amounts.

Tests: Get a sample piece of all materials you are considering. If the material is to be sealed, seal it before conducting tests. Drag a nail or drill bit across to see if it resists scratches. Set a coffee cup and water glass on it overnight and immerse in alternate baths of oil, vinegar, lemon juice, red wine, beets, and raspberries to evaluate stain resistance.

If the material has a repeat pattern, check how it will look where it is seamed and turns corners. Figure how much extra money a patterned piece costs with waste inherent in matching seams. Check to see that color and pattern are consistent from slab to slab and tile to tile.

To be sure you will like the material once it is installed, examine it:

- **Under natural daylight.**
- **Under lights specced for the room.**
- **Along with other materials chosen for the room.**
- **Along with materials in adjacent rooms.**
- **Vertically or horizontally, according to the orientation of its installation. If it is to be used both horizontally on the countertop and vertically on edges and up the backsplash, evaluate it from both directions.**

Decisions:

Which material? Materials?

Color and pattern?

Texture? Matte is most durable and least revealing of accidents. It is important to compare sheens, interpreted differently by each manufacturer, rather than going by the word *matte*.

Edges, moldings, and trim pieces?

Custom sizes or shapes?

EVALUATION

Countertops:

- **Check that food looks appetizing on the surface, particularly if using it as a backdrop for buffets.**
- **Check that sealers are approved for food service.**
- **Ascertain the fire rating.**
- **Determine additional fabrication costs.**

Laminate:

- **A postformable laminate that can be bent should have a thickness of .042 inch; if not bent, a thickness of at least .050 ($1/20$) inch.**
- **Find out how long colors are guaranteed against fading.**
- **Look for extra-heavy-duty rating.**

SOLID SURFACE

- **Choose the company that produces the color you like best.**
- **If you desire any of the following options, check with the fabricator to see if the company can do them and in the color you want:**

  Integrated sink

  Integrated backsplash

  Special shape

  Liquid inlay or intarsia work

  Trivet inlay to accept hot pots

- **Thickness should be at least $1/2$ inch.**
- **If placing it near a stove or window, inquire whether it expands with heat.**
- **Confirm that the fabricator uses the same color seam as the solid-surface material.**

BUTCHER BLOCK

- **Choose an eastern hard rock sugar maple block.**
- **Check that it has a checkerboard end grain, indicating proper lamination.**
- **A $1^1/2$-inch-thick board performs better than the standard $3/4$-inch-thick piece.**

CERAMIC TILE

- **Choose a vitreous tile with a water absorption rate from .5 to 3.0 or, better, an impervious tile with less than .5 percent.**
- **Compare breaking strengths. How far is the tile above the industry standard of 250 pounds?**
- **Compare abrasion resistance. How far is the tile above the industry standard of 50?**

- Does the tile rate at least a 6 or 7 out of 10 on the hardness scale scratch test, which measures resistance to abrasion from various minerals?

- Does a floor tile have a slip resistance or COF (static coefficient of friction) of at least .5 or .6?

- If tile is being placed near the stove, be sure it has shown no expansion and contraction defects in tests.

- If its intended location is subject to freezing temperatures, be sure tile is approved for this situation.

- Choose a tile rated for heavy or light commercial use.

- Choose a straight- or knife-edged tile that is easier to clean than one with a curved or beveled edge.

- Check that the glaze has a negligible number of bubbles or pinholes.

- Confirm that trim shapes are available for the tile you've selected. A mitered piece with a 45-degree angle enables corner edges to fit flush.

- If tiles come backed on cotton or paper, be sure the backing is covered under warranty.

- When given the option, choose an easier-to-install flat back tile over one with a button back.

- If you choose saltillo tile, be sure it is kiln-fired and pocked with a negligible number of efflorescence holes.

- Buy tile from a store that lets you choose each piece.

Brick

- Confirm that brick is acid and abrasion resistant.

Stainless

- Use only an 18-gauge or thicker (lower number) stainless with an 18/8 or 18/10 rating.

- Choose a satin finish.

- Test a fabricator's panel with a magnet before okaying it. Don't accept it if it sticks.

Slate

- Compare hardness, water absorption, acid resistance, and rupture tests.

- Confirm that the slate is unfading.

- Confirm that the slate has been cut to its strength with its longest dimension running parallel to the grain (the direction of easiest breakage).

- Check that the slate's edges are even and square.

- Check that the slate is free of blemishes or cracks.

- Choose a honed or smooth-gauged slate.

- Determine whether you want single or multiple colors.

Granite

- It is difficult to compare granite, for many companies do not know its source, its ratings, or its name other than a proprietary designation. Test the stone carefully for resistance to abrasion, acids, and chemicals.

- Inquire if the slab has been tested for radon. If not, consider doing so.

- Reject slabs with mud veining or mineral intrusions that will be susceptible to water damage.

- Consider a 1¼-inch-thick slab for a countertop instead of the standard ¾ inch.

Vinyl

- Choose a pattern that has been inlaid rather than produced by rotogravure.

- Compare impact resistant ratings.

- Review upkeep methods carefully to determine which material you'll be comfortable dealing with. Go for a urethane top coat over a vinyl one.

- Seek a product with a mildew or vapor barrier.

Wood

- Choose a hard, not a soft, wood.

- Choose which grade you want and then compare woods to find one with a beautiful grain.

- If going for a planked floor, do not use pieces wider than 5 inches, which can warp.

- Choose end-matched boards with tongue-and-groove.

- If using veneer boards, purchase a three-ply floor, which can be refinished more times than a five-ply.

- Do not consider wood with a vinyl-impregnated coating, which is no longer really a hardwood floor.

UNIQUE ATTRIBUTES

Custom Stainless Applications:
Elkay Manufacturing Company
2222 Camden Court
Oak Brook, Illinois 60521
(630) 574-8484

Custom Brick:
Acme Brick
P.O. Box 425
Fort Worth, Texas 76101
(800) 932-2263

Slip-Resistant Sealer for Concrete, Ceramic, Slate, and Stone Floors:
Aegis Floorsystems
14286 Gillis Road
Dallas, Texas 75224
(800) 544-1443; (214) 788-2233

Sundek Safety Floor Systems
6320 Clara Street
Bell Gardens, California 90201
(310) 806-3757

Coordinated Finishes:
American Olean Sizzle strips with plumbing fixtures from Kohler and American Standard; Bruce hardwood floors and cabinets; Wilsonart's decorative laminates, Florida Tile's Natura Shannon series

Laminate:

Abet Laminati
60 West Sheffield Avenue
Englewood, New Jersey 07631
(800) 228-ABET

Formica Corporation
10155 Reading Road
Cincinnati, Ohio 45241-5729
(800) FORMICA

Nevamar
8339 Telegraph Road
Odenton, Maryland 21113-1397
(800) 638-4380; (410) 551-5000

Pionite Decorative Laminates
Pioneer Plastics Corporation
One Pionite Road
Auburn, Maine 04210
(800) 746-6483 (P10-NITE);
(207) 784-9111

Wilsonart International
2400 Wilson Place
P.O. Box 6110
Temple, Texas 76503-6110
(800) 433-3222
(Custom laminates)

Solid-Core Laminate:
Colorcore (Formica)

MelCor II (Pioneer Plastics
   Corporation)

Wilsonart Colorthrough Laminate

Laminate Edge Banding:
Pionite

Laminate Flooring:
Formica Corporation

Wilsonart International

Solid Surface:
Avonite
1945 Highway 304
Belen, New Mexico 87002
(800) 4-AVONITE

Du Pont Corian
Chestnut Run Plaza
Building 702
P.O. Box 80–702
Wilmington, Delaware 19880-0702
(800) 4-CORIAN

Fountainhead (Nevamar)

Gibralter (Wilsonart International)

Surell (Formica)

Solid-Surface Accessories:
Poly-Tech
Teak Isle Manufacturing Inc.
401 Capitol Court
Ocoee, Florida 34761
(800) 393-8885
(Custom countertops and sink
   cutting boards)

Rock Solid Inc. (page 326)

Surface Technology Corporation
270 Tosca Drive
Stoughton, Massachusetts 02072
(800) 287-2036; (617) 341-2036
(Stainless steel rods for solid
   surface trivets)

TFI Corporation
2812 Hegan Lane
Chico, California 95928
(916) 891-6390
(Prefab Corian cornice moldings
   and trim)

Butcher Block:
Block Tops Inc.
4770 East Wesley Drive
Anaheim, California 92807
(714) 779-0475

John Boos & Company (page 318)

Michigan Maple Block Company
P.O. Box 245
Petoskey, Michigan 49770-0245
(800) 678-8459

*Sliding Wood Work-Top Cutting
Board:*
Bulthaup USA (page 323)

Ceramic Tile:
American Olean
1000 Cannon Avenue
P.O. Box 271
Lansdale, Pennsylvania 19446
(800) 933-TILE; (215) 855-1111

Crossville Ceramics
P.O. Box 1168
Crossville, Tennessee 38557
(615) 484-2110

Dal-Tile Corporation
7834 Hawn Freeway
Dallas, Texas 75217
(800) 933-TILE; (214) 398-1411

Florida Tile Industries, Inc.
P.O. Box 447
Lakeland, Florida 33802
(800) FLA-TILE

Hastings Tile/Il Bagno Collection
230 Park Avenue South
New York, New York 10003
(212) 674-9700

Latco Products
13536 Saticoy
Van Nuys, California 91402
(818) 902-5424

Laufen International Ceramic Tile
P.O. Box 6600
4942 East 66th Street North
Tulsa, Oklahoma 74156-0600
(800) 758-TILE; (918) 428-3851

Marazzi Tile
359 Clay Road
Sunnyvale, Texas 75182-9710
(214) 226-0110

Porcelanosa
Ceramic Floor Tiles
1301 South State College Boulevard
Suite E
Anaheim, California 92806
(714) 772-3183
(Minimal joint seams)

Summitville Tiles Inc.
P.O. Box 73
Summitville, Ohio 43962
(330) 223-1511

Handcrafted Ceramic Tile:
Cosmos Tile, Stones & More
438 8th Street
San Francisco, California 94103
(415) 558-TILE

Quarry Tile Company
6328 East Utah
Spokane, Washington 99212
(800) 423-2608; (509) 536-2812

Shel Neymark Architectural
Ceramics
P.O. Box 25
Embudo, New Mexico 87531
(505) 579-4432

Trikeenan Tileworks
9 Forest Road
Hancock, New Hampshire 03449
(603) 525-4245

Reproduction Ceramic Tile:
Richard Thomas Keit Studios
206 Cañada Street
Ojai, California 93023
(805) 640-9360

Glass Tile:
Bisazza
8032 North West 66th Street
Miami, Florida 33166
(800) 398-8071

Glass Block:
Glass Blocks Unlimited, Inc.
126 East 16th Street
Costa Mesa, California 92627
(800) 992-9938; (714) 548-8531

Pittsburgh Corning
800 Presque Isle Drive
Pittsburgh, Pennsylvania 15239-2799
(800) 624-2120; (412) 327-6100

Marble and Granite:
Granit Design
P.O. Box 130
Watertown, South Dakota 57201
(800) 843-3305; South Dakota
(800) 658-3503

Intertile Distributors
1230 Trade Zone Boulevard
San Jose, California 95131
(800) 339-1494; (408) 263-2300

Slate:
American Slate
515 Independent Road
Oakland, California 94621
(800) 553-5611; (510) 430-1237

Vermont Structural Slate Company
P.O. Box 98
Fair Haven, Vermont 05743
(800) 343-1900

Wood Moldings:
Artistic Woodworking
R.R. 2, Box 40B
Imperial, Nebraska 69033
(800) 621-3992; (308) 882-4873

Bendix Mouldings, Inc.
37 Ramland Road South
Orangeburg, New York 10962
(800) 526-0240

Tin Ceilings:
Chelsea Decorative Metal Company
9603 Moonlight Drive
Houston, Texas 77096
(713) 721-9200

Shanker Industries, Inc.
3435 Lawson Boulevard
Oceanside, New York 11572
(516) 766-4477

Tambour:
Global Specialty Products Ltd.
123 Columbia Court North, #201
Chaska, Minnesota 55318
(612) 448-6566

Railings:
Lavi Industries (page 324)

Premier Brass
483 Armour Circle
Atlanta, Georgia 30324-4014
(800) 251-5800

Hardwood Floors:
Anderson Hardwood Floors
P.O. Box 1155
Clinton, South Carolina 29325
(864) 833-6250

Bruce Hardwood Floors
16803 Dallas Parkway
Dallas, Texas 75248
(800) 722-4647; (214) 931-3100

Harris-Tarkett
P.O. Box 300
Johnson City, Tennessee 37605-0300
(800) 842-7816

Kährs International, Inc.
951 Mariner's Island Boulevard,
  Suite 630
San Mateo, California 94404
(800) 800-5247; (415) 341-8400

Kentucky Wood Floors
P.O. Box 33276
Louisville, Kentucky 40232
(800) 235-5235; (502) 451-6024

Lükken Color Corporation
19 Rockwood Lane
Greenwich, Connecticut 06830
(203) 869-4679
(Custom-colored wood floor tiles)

*Hardwood Grills for Floor Heating
Registers:*
Grill Works, Inc.
P.O. Box 175
Marshall, Minnesota 56258
(800) 347-4745

Vinyl:
Armstrong World Industries, Inc.
P.O. Box 3001
Lancaster, Pennsylvania 17604
(800) 233-3823; (717) 397-0611

Congoleum Corporation
3705 Quakerbridge Road
P.O. Box 3127
Mercerville, New Jersey 08619
(800) 274-3266

Mannington Resilient Floors
P.O. Box 30
Salem, New Jersey 08079
(800) FLOOR-US

Cork:
Dodge-Regupol Inc.
P.O. Box 989
Lancaster, Pennsylvania 17608
(800) 322-1923

Hendricksen Natürlich
P.O. Box 1677
Sebastopol, California 95473
(707) 824-0914

Linoleum:
Forbo Industries, Inc.
Humboldt Industrial Park
P.O. Box 667
Hazleton, Pennsylvania 18201
(800) 842-7839

Gerbert Ltd. Linoleum
P.O. Box 4944
Lancaster, Pennsylvania 17604
(800) 828-9461; (717) 299-5035

Hendricksen Natürlich (page 330)

Ceramic Tile Institute of America
12061 Jefferson Boulevard
Culver City, California 90230
(310) 574-7800

Glitsa American
327 South Kenyon Street
Seattle, Washington 98108
(800) 527-8111

Hardwood Manufacturers
    Association
Department HI
400 Penn Center Boulevard
Suite 530
Pittsburgh, Pennsylvania 15235
(800) 373-9663

Italian Tile Center
499 Park Avenue
New York, New York 10022
(212) 980-1500

Oak Flooring Institute
22 North Front Street
Suite 660, Falls Building
Memphis, Tennessee 38103
(901) 526-5016

Tile Council of America
P.O. Box 1787
Clemson, South Carolina 29633
(864) 646-TILE

Tile Heritage Foundation
P.O. Box 1850
Healdsburg, California 95448
(707) 431-8453

Select lights with similar colors that work well together such as an incandescent and soft or warm white fluorescent with a Kelvin temperature of 3,000 degrees. If you want to take fixtures with you to a new home, get them with plug-in connectors instead of building them in.

Before you shop, remind yourself of low-, middle-, and high-end lighting possibilities by referring to the chart on page 21.

Decisions:

Incandescent, fluorescent or halogen (line or low voltage)?

A touch of neon?

Cool-beam or E-lamp incandescents?

Compact fluorescents?

Remote transformer for halogen?

What color or degrees Kelvin to emphasize?

Type of lamp?

Type of fixtures?

Location of fixtures?

Tracks: Single or double? Open or closed? Separate controls?

Type of dimmer? Programmable multiple dimmers-in-one?

Type of switch plate?

EVALUATION

Fluorescent:

- Confirm that it has an electronic ballast that eliminates hum and flicker.
- Confirm that it is a rapid-start or slimline system that goes on instantly.
- Look for a fixture that encircles the tube, providing fewer shadows and more light than one lying flat up against it.
- To dim a fluorescent, it will have to have a rapid-start dimming ballast.

Halogen:

- Confirm that bulb and fixture are both UL-approved.
- Purchase an electronic, not a magnetic, transformer.

Light bulbs:

- For a given wattage, choose the bulb with the greatest number of lumens.

- Purchase *architect*-grade, not *contractor*-grade bulbs.
- Reserve long-life bulbs for hard-to-access areas or locations in constant use.

Recessed Can Lights:

- Use an Alzak interior. When a narrower beam is sought, choose a white interior that is more reflecting than a black one.
- A step or grooved baffle cuts glare.
- To hide the light source, go for a ribbed Fresnel lens.
- Pick a trim color that matches the ceiling color (or vice versa).
- Check that lights ventilate out the top to prevent heat buildup, yet are sealed well enough to prevent rain, debris, and bugs from blowing in.
- If installed in an insulated ceiling, be sure it has an IC (insulated ceiling) rating.
- To accent an object, fit the can with an eyeball and narrow beam spotlight or low-voltage halogen.

Track Lights:

- Choose open, not closed, tracks when you want to be able to add lights to the system.
- Use PAR lights for washing or grazing.

Undercabinet Lights:

- Avoid a fixture with nonreplaceable lamps and flimsy ribbon or seed bulbs.
- If you want to be able to dim undercabinet lights, choose low-voltage halogen lights, not fluorescent.

Dimmers:

- Use only incandescent dimmer switches with special circuitry for suppressing static for radio and TV operation.
- If desired, check that the dimmer offers programmable switching, delay fade, and a screwless plate.

UNIQUE ATTRIBUTES

Fluorescent Dimmer:
Lutron Electronics Company Inc.
7200 Suter Road
Coopersburg, Pennsylvania
18036-1299
(800) 523-9466
(Hi-lume)

LIGHTING

Recessed Cans:

Conservation Technology
(Con-Tech)
3865 Commercial Avenue
Northbrook, Illinois 60062
(800) 728-0312; (847) 559-5500

Juno Lighting, Inc.
2001 South Mount Prospect Road
P.O. Box 5065
Des Plaines, Illinois 60017-5065
(800) 323-5068; (847) 827-9880

Lightolier
631 Airport Road
Fall River, Massachusetts 02720
(800) 215-1068; (508) 679-8131

Troy Lighting
14625 East Clark Avenue
City of Industry, California 91745
(800) 533-8769; (818) 336-4511

Track:

Artemide Litech
1980 New Highway
Farmingdale, New York 11735
(516) 694-9292

Capri Lighting
6430 East Slauson Avenue
Los Angeles, California 90040
(213) 726-1800

Con-Tech

Flos USA
200 McKay Road
Huntington Station, New York
    11746
(800) 939-3567; (516) 549-2745

Juno

Reggiani USA
108 South Water Street
Newburgh, New York 12550
(914) 565-8500

Tech Lighting
1718 West Fullerton
Chicago, Illinois 60614
(800) 522-5315; (773) 883-6110
(Also theater track)

Parabolic Louver Ceilings:

A.L.P. Lighting & Ceiling
    Products, Inc.
6333 Gross Point Road
Niles, Illinois 60714
(800) 633-7732; (773) 774-9550

American Louver Company
7700 North Austin Avenue
Skokie, Illinois 60077
(800) 323-4250;
    Illinois (847) 470-3300

Cove:

Celestial Products
14009 Dinard Avenue
Santa Fe Springs, California 90670
(800) 233-3563

Cable:

Ingo Maurer Ya Ya Ho
c/o Diva
8801 Beverly Boulevard
Los Angeles, California 90048
(310) 278-3191

Tech Lighting

Undercabinet:

Con-Tech

Danalite
16200 Commerce Way
Cerritos, California 90703-3130
(800) 446-3262; (310) 802-7525

Litelab Corporation
251 Elm Street
Buffalo, New York 14203-1675
(800) 238-4120; (716) 856-4300

Starfire Lighting (Xenflex)
317 Saint Pauls Avenue
Jersey City, New Jersey 07306
(800) 443-8823
(Low voltage)

Tivoli Industries
1513 East Saint Gertrude Place
Santa Ana, California 92705
(800) 854-3288; (714) 957-6101

In-Cabinet Spots:

Häfele America Co. (page 319)

Hera Lighting Inc.
6659 Peachtree Industrial Boulevard
Suite M
Norcross, Georgia 30092
(800) 336-4372

Hettich America
6225 Shiloh Road
Alpharetta, Georgia 30202
(770) 887-3733

L. I. Laminates
35 Engineers Road
Hauppauge, New York 11788
(800) 221-5454; (516) 234-6969

Dimmers and Switches:

Carlon
Lamson Home Products
25701 Science Park Drive
Beachwood, Ohio 44101
(800) 327-8864
(Motion sensor)

Leviton Manufacturing
    Company, Inc.
59-25 Little Neck Parkway
Little Neck, New York 11362
(800) 323-8920

Lutron Electronics Company Inc.
    (page 332)

ADDITIONAL SOURCES AND INFORMATION

American Lighting Association
P.O. Box 420288
Dallas, Texas 75342
(800) 274-4484

Homework: Review the intended location of windows, type of glazing, and glazing protection that has been specified with neighborhood window dealers who know what safeguards are necessary for combating local climatic conditions.

Tests: Bang a sample of any aluminum frame you are considering on different surfaces to see how easily it dents. Check any protective coating you are considering to see how it looks both during the day and night, and if its color is attractive.

Decisions:

Style of window?

Size of window?

Shape of window? A window with a curved arched top gathers more light than a straight one.

Fixed or operable?

Clerestory, bow, or bay? What angle from 30 to 90 degrees do you want the side windows of the bay to be?

French-style window with divided panes?

Greenhouse window?

Glass or plastic glazing?

If glass, clear, sandblasted, leaded, stained, or decorative?

If plastic, acrylic (best clarity, less expensive) or polycarbonate (impact resistant)?

Privacy glass that switches from clear to frosted?

Skylight? If so, skylight or roof window? Remote control opener?

Type of frame? Color of cladding and aluminum or vinyl window? Type of finish for wood frame?

Type of glazing protection?

Single, double, or triple pane?

Inner shade between panes?

Low-E? With argon or krypton? Low I? What U, R, and other ratings?

Track for storm window?

EVALUATION

Window Type:

CASEMENT

- Choose whether you want the window to open in or out.

- Evaluate slider attachments to see how easy the window will be to clean. One whose arm is 4 inches or so in from the corner will be easiest.

- Do you want regular hardware or a longer crank that is easier to grip?

- If window is French style with divided panes, and built-in muntins are not affordable, choose those that snap

on to *both* interior and exterior of window with no visible gaps between them.

DOUBLE-HUNG

- Decide if you want a tilt/turn model that pivots in the sash and folds down into the room to be cleaned.

- For easier cleaning, the sash should be removable.

SLIDER

- Check to see that it has a roller system and moves easily in its track.

- Look for a slanted track where water and dirt won't pool.

- Look for a track that can be removed easily for cleaning.

HOPPER/AWNING

- Check to see that it opens far and easily enough to clean.

Window Frames:

WOOD

- Compare thicknesses of wood frames. A thicker frame is better quality.

- Survey the frame carefully to be sure there are no cracks or blemishes and that it is knot-free—less likely to warp.

- Check that the frame has been treated with a preservative to reject water and retard warping.

- Look for durable mortise and tenon joinery.

- If the window is being purchased prepainted, check what kind of paint was used and the length of its warranty. If not, decide whether you want it primed or raw.

CLADDING

- Cladding should be heavy extruded, not rolled.

- Avoid nailed joints and look for those that are fuse welded together.

- Do you want standard tan, white, or gray cladding or a custom color?

ALUMINUM

- A powder coat is the most durable finish.

- Check that aluminum is thick enough so that it will not dent easily.

- Confirm that windows have thermal breaks between the exterior and interior to reduce temperature transfer and prevent condensation from forming. Get a low gloss spacer rather than a shiny metal, which can be glaring.

VINYL

- Check that it has fuse-welded corners.

- Confirm that it is 2.33 millimeters thick or thicker.

Skylight:

- Decide on method of weather control at the same time as type and configuration of skylight. Retrofitting a covering will be makeshift at best, leaving no possibilities for hiding the ugly tracks and hardware. Check that hardware for skylight coverings can be hidden.

- Do you want a flat or domed skylight?

- If you choose a roof window, do you want one that can be screened?

- In snow country, check that the skylight will stand up to the weight of snow.

- Do you want the skylight to open? If so, how far?

- If you choose an electronic opener, do you want it to have a rain sensor?

- Confirm that the skylight has a channel for collecting moisture and condensation.

- Do the skylight dimensions correspond to the 16 or 24 inches commonly found between a roof's trusses or rafters, or will expensive installation/ roof work be necessary?

- Double-check that the skylight's curb is the correct size for the slope of the roof.

- Confer with experts to choose the right flashing for the type and angle of your roof.

- Confirm that the skylight price includes flashing in it.

Glass Block:

- Does it need a reflective coating or protection against condensation?

- Do you want it to have screened vents?

Glazing:

- Review types of glazing protection on page 218, request a copy of a window's test results, and confirm that the glazing is appropriate for the type of protection needed.

- Double-check that it is possible to put the recommended glazing into the window shape you've planned.

- For all but single-pane windows, check the spec sheet and a cross section to confirm that the window has multiple chambers. Be sure a track exists for a storm if you want to add it during the winter.

- Confirm that a double-pane window is ¾ to 1 inch thick.

- Confirm that windows are insulated so they don't conduct heat or cold.

- Be sure insulated or thermalized multilayered panes have a foam, chemical, or other method for deterring moisture collection and condensation.

- Look for the National Fenestration Rating Council's seal listing a window's U-value (energy efficiency).

Purchasing:

- To avoid a custom situation, see first if you can buy windows ready-made.

- Confirm that the window is consistent with others in the house from the standpoint of shape, style, and frame material.

- Windows should have weather-stripping that seals the window tightly and completely with no gaps when closed. Foam-filled weather-stripping is tightest and most energy efficient.

- Check the window's security system. Does it lock automatically when closed? Can it be locked while open for ventilation? Does it have a pocket sill that is harder than a flat sill to slip a crowbar under? For extra security, choose tempered glass, SentryGlas, laminated glass, or a safety coating that prevents glass from breaking into shards.

- For windows to be hung at a level above easy reach, choose reciprocal hardware that can be opened with a long pole.

- Find out if the company has the window you want in inventory. If not, how long will you have to wait for it to be produced and delivered?

- Since components are priced separately, be sure the price you are given includes each part of the window as well as its installation.

- Be sure the window you sign a contract for is the one you want. Both misunderstandings and deliberate obfuscations are common.

UNIQUE ATTRIBUTES

Customized Cladding Colors:
Pella Corporation
102 Main Street
Pella, Iowa 50219
(800) 847-3552

Reflective Pipe:
Brings light from the roof to a dome in the ceiling that diffuses only the light, not heat, at much less money than a skylight. Looks like R2D2 is sitting on your roof.

The SunPipe Company
P.O. Box 2223
Northbrook, Illinois 60065
(800) 844-4786

Windows and Skylights:
Andersen Windows, Inc.
P.O. Box 203070
Austin, Texas 78720-9623
(800) 426-4261

Marvin Windows & Doors
P.O. Box 100
Warroad, Minnesota 56763
(800) 346-5128

Pella Corporation (page 335)

Peachtree Doors
P.O. Box 5700
Norcross, Georgia 30091-5700
(888) 888-3814
(No skylights)

Velux-America, Inc.
450 Old Brickyard Road
P.O. Box 5001
Greenwood, South Carolina
    29648-5001
(800) 283-2831

Weather Shield Manufacturing, Inc.
P.O. Box 309
Medford, Wisconsin 54451-0309
(800) 222-2995

Glass Block

Architectural Glass:
Arthur Stern Studios
1075 Jackson Street
Benicia, California 94110
(707) 745-8480

Motorized or Hand-Cranked
Clerestory or Skylight Extension
Poles:
Velux

ADDITIONAL SOURCES AND
INFORMATION

National Fenestration Rating
    Council
1300 Spring Street
Suite 120
Silver Spring, Maryland 20910
(301) 589-6372

COOKTOPS, OVENS, AND RANGES

Before you shop, remind yourself of low-, middle-, and high-end features in these appliances by referring to the chart on page 21.

Supplies: A tape measure and favorite cookie sheet, broiling pan, and/or turkey roaster for the oven; stockpot, wok, and largest skillet for a cooktop.

Tests: Measure oven and broiler interiors, the size of the cooktop burners, and the space in between them. See how well pots fit on top of the burners, in the oven, and under the broiler. Move pots from one burner to the next and see how easily they slide. Determine how well burner grates support pots.

If possible, cook on the equipment to evaluate its functioning. If nothing else, make a delicate sauce on the cooktop to determine how well it holds a simmer, and bake a cake or cookies in the oven to check performance and evenness of browning. Move the oven racks and drawer to see how easily they slide. Play with the controls to see how they operate and whether they heat up. Check doors and handles as well for heat conduction.

If considering a solid-disk cooktop with a sensor in the center of the burner to hold the temperature, try it out first.

Decisions:

A range or separate cooktop and oven?

Porcelain, glass, or stainless (most durable) finish? If porcelain, white, almond, black, or a custom color?

RANGE

Gas, electric, or dual fuel?

If gas, LP or regular?

Freestanding, slide-in, or drop-in?

Commercial-style? Low or high back?

An heirloom or wood-burning range?

What size?

COOKTOP

Gas, electric, or both?

If gas, LP or regular?

If electric, coil, disk, halogen, or induction?

Commercial style?

How many cooktops?

Single top or individual modules?

Extra modules?

A continuous top (smooth top on electric, zigzag on gas)?

How many burners?

Separate griddle or grill?

Separate food warmer?

OVEN

Gas or electric?

If gas, LP or regular?

How wide? 24-, 27-, 30-, or 36-inch oven?

How many?

For two ovens, do you want two singles or a double with one mounted on top of the other with shared controls?

Convection?

Self-cleaning?

Bells and whistles?

Wood-burning?

Commercial?

Oven, shelf, or lights?

How many?

EVALUATION

Cooktop, Oven, and Range:

- Confirm that the unit can be vented internally if external venting is not possible.

- When children are around, check that control knobs are lockable or childproof (push in before turning).

- Imperative for an electric cooktop, confirm that an indicator light glows both when the unit is on and while it cools down after it has been turned off.

- Check to see if the color or finish you want is available for the model you are considering.

COOKTOP

- Confirm that there are high- and low-heat burners on both the front and back of the cooktop.

- Confirm that burner size is large (and small) enough for your pots. Is there at least a 10-inch or, even better, an 11-inch burner to hold a large skillet?

- Do you want four (30-inch cooktop), five or six (36-inch cooktop), or more burners? Four burners on a 36-inch cooktop are a waste of space.

- Confirm that controls are easy to read and operate. Are they clearly marked so you know which burner each operates? Are they in the front of the cooktop, off to the side, or below, where they are easiest to reach and remain cool? Do they correspond to your handedness?

- Do you have the option to remote controls, or lock them, if you so desire?

- Are controls vertical or horizontal (catch dust more readily)?

- If you want a timer for presetting a cooking schedule, is this available?

Gas Cooktop

- If you want individual burners rather than a zigzag grid top, they are most practical square and paired one behind the other.

- If burners are covered with a grid, wires should be close enough together so pots don't fall through.

- At least one burner should be 12,000 Btus or higher.

- At least one burner should go down to 350 Btus or be configured to hold a steady simmer low enough for a custard or delicate sauce.

- Does the cooktop have automatic reignition to relight the burners if the flame goes out?

- Confirm that grates are sturdy and stable and their prongs able to cradle both small and large pots.

- Grates should be porcelain coated, with porcelain-coated cast iron most solid.

- Check that grates aren't too heavy to lift for cleaning.

- Sealed burners make cleanup easier and focus flame more directly on the pot, but often will not accept a wok.

Electric Cooktop

- What is the wattage? Does a 6-inch burner have at least 2,000 watts, an 8-inch burner 2,600 watts, a 9-inch burner 3,200 watts, an 11-inch burner 3,500 watts, and a commercial electric burner 5,200 watts?

- If it is a solid element, does it have the greater wattage provided by an UltraPower burner?

- How well does it simmer?

Solid Disk:

- If it has a thermal limiter, burners should be Ultra-Temp, reducing but not shutting heat off when it becomes excessive.

- Do you want the rim to be stainless or black metal?

- Confirm that burners are encircled by a ring of light that glows when they are hot.

- Do you want a silver sensor in the center of the burner that holds a precise temperature?

Halogen:

- Confirm that burners have specific power levels for maintaining a continuous heat rather than infinite switches that cycle on and off.

- Confirm that burners are surrounded by a resistance coil to ensure even heat distribution.

Smooth Tops:

- Is the unit's pattern busy enough to mask scratches and fingermarks?

- Confirm that elements correspond to the size of your pots.

Special Modules

Wok:

- With the ideal being 125,000 Btus, it should have a minimum of 23,000 Btus.

Grill:

- This should offer a minimum of 20,000 Btus.

- A commercial grill is more practical with radiant grids than lava rocks. Four burners of either style will yield about 58,000 Btus. Grill heat should be able to be lowered for fish, chicken, and other delicate items.

Griddle:

- A thermostatically controlled dial is more accurate than one labeled low, medium, and high.

- Check to see that grease is collected efficiently and that its pan is easy to remove and clean.

Oven

- What are the interior dimensions?

- If the oven is convection (recommended only if you have two ovens or a convection-radiant combination oven), confirm that it is true convection with the fan and heating element outside the oven cavity.

- How many racks does it have? Check that they are full extension, easy to move in and out, and lock in place. Their attachments should not be so large as to interfere with baking sheets. Check that they can be removed to clean the entire oven. Confirm that there is sufficient space between racks for a large pot and that the top and bottom racks of an electric oven are far enough away from burner elements so food baked on them won't burn.

- Check to see that oven door and handles don't get hot, particularly when children are around. Is the handle easy to grip? Flush enough for a kitchen with a built-in look?

- Check to see if the oven door lifts off for cleaning, making the task easier.

- Look at the interior. Dark is easier to clean than light; porcelain easier than steel.

- Are interior lights easy to change but not in the way, where they can block a pot or get hit?

- If you choose a pyrolytic self-cleaning oven, check that its locking device is simple to use and easy to grip. In a double oven, confirm that you can bake in one oven while the other cleans.

- Does it have any bells and whistles you want? One button only for preheat and on? Controls for scheduling delayed onset? Timed bake? Automatic off or cooldown? An audible signal when setting is reached? A meat probe or rotisserie? A clock? Is it digital? Are these helpers easy to read and operate?

- Check that any oven drawer (or warming drawer) moves smoothly in and out.

BROILER:

- Confirm that the broiler is in the main cavity of the oven, not in a small separate compartment in the bottom of the oven.

- Confirm that the broiler has variable heat or that it can be raised and lowered. Can you heat only half of it if desired?

- An infrared broiler is highly recommended. If another broiler is purchased, it should have at least 3,000 watts or 12,000 Btus.

- Check the width of the broiler and the number of rods (passes) it has. It should be well covered with six rods.

RANGE

- Check that the range has an antitipping device or that one can be added.

- Check that the controls are easy to reach and visible even with pots on the cooktop.

- Confirm that the legs are adjustable and that the bottom of the range lines up with the cabinet toe kicks or other horizontal lines in the kitchen.

- The pot drawer should run full width and glide easily in and out.

- Is there a prop stick or some way of holding up the cooktop while cleaning?

UNIQUE ATTRIBUTES

Steam-Injected Oven: Great for bread.

Euroflair (imported by Frigidaire
    Company)
6000 Perimeter Drive
Dublin, Ohio 43017
(800) 451-7007; (614) 792-2153

Russell Range, Inc.
229 Ryan Way
South San Francisco, California 94080
(800) 878-7877

Three-Foot Oven:
Gaggenau
425 University Avenue
Norwood, Massachusetts 02062
(800) 828-9165; (617) 255-1766
(With pizza stone)

Viking
P.O. Drawer 956
Greenwood, Mississippi 38930
(800) 467-2665; (601) 455-1200

Autoset Program: Cooks automatically without setting temperature or time.

KitchenAid
2303 Pipestone Road
Benton Harbor, Michigan 49022
(800) 422-1230

Old-Fashioned Look:
Elmira Stove Works
595 Colby Drive
Waterloo, Ontario
Canada N2V 1A2
(519) 725-5500

Heartland Appliances Inc.
5 Hoffman Street
Kitchener, Ontario
Canada N2M 3M5
(800) 361-1517; (519) 743-8111

Colors:
Jenn-Air Co.
240 Edwards Street South East
Cleveland, Tennessee 37311
(800) JENN-AIR; (423) 478-3333
(Tinted stainless)

Viking
(Greatest number of colors;
    brass handles, too)

Horizontal or Vertical Installation:
General Electric Monogram
    (page 318)

Side-Hinged Oven:
Frigidaire

Gaggenau

Gas Cooktops:
Dacor
950 South Raymond Avenue
Pasadena, California 91109
(800) 793-0093; (818) 799-1000

Jenn-Air Co. (page 339)

Regency VSA Appliances, Ltd.
P.O. Box 3341
Tustin, California 92781-3341
(714) 544-3530

Gas Zigzag Cooktops:
Russell Range, Inc.
(page 339)

Viking (page 339)

Cast-Iron Simmer Plates:
Chef's Catalog (page 325)

Electric Cooktops:
Jenn-Air Co. (page 339)

Commercial Electric Cooktops:
Cecilware
43-05 20th Avenue
Long Island City, New York 11105
(800) 935-2211; (718) 932-1414

Star Manufacturing
   International, Inc.
P.O. Box 430129
St. Louis, Missouri 63143
(800) 844-5058; (314) 781-2777

Wells
P.O. Box 280
Verdi, Nevada 89439
(800) 777-0450

Electric Induction Cooktops:
Electronic Cooking Systems
P.O. Box 4678
Sunland, California 91041
(818) 365-6757

General Electric (page 318)

Jenn-Air Co.(page 339)

Portable Induction Cooktop:
Iwatani International Corporation
   of America
1025 West 190th Street
Suite 225
Gardena, California 90248-4302
(800) 331-4627; (310) 324-9174

Miele Appliances, Inc.
22D Worlds Fair Drive
Somerset, New Jersey 08873
(800) 843-7231

Individual Cooktop Units:
Star Manufacturing International, Inc.

Wells
(2,600-watt 10-inch burner)

Wolf Range Company
19600 South Alameda Street
Compton, California 90221
(800) 366-9653
(20,000 Btus)

Module Cooktops:
Gaggenau (page 339)

General Electric (page 318)

KitchenAid (page 339)

Miele

Russell Range, Inc. (page 339)

Ovens with Infrared Broiler:
Amana Home Appliances
P.O. Box 8901
2800 220th Trail
Amana, Iowa 52204-0001
(800) 843-0304

Caloric (see Amana Home
   Appliances)

Dynasty Range Corporation
7355 East Slauson Avenue
Commerce, California 90040
(213) 728-5700

Five Star
P.O. Box 2490
Cleveland, Tennessee 37320
(800) 553-7704; (423) 476-6544

Viking (page 339)

Wolf Range Company

24-Inch Ovens:
Caloric (see Amana Home
   Appliances)

Euroflair (22$^1/8$) (page 339)

Gaggenau (page 339)

General Electric (page 318)

Miele

Dual-Fuel Ranges: Gas cooktops
with electric ovens.
Dacor

Five Star

Frigidaire (page 339)

Jenn-Air Co. (page 339)

Thermador
5119 District Boulevard
Los Angeles, California 90040
(800) 735-4328; (213) 562-8100

Viking (page 339)

Commercial-Style Gas Cookers:
Dynasty

Five Star

Garland Commercial Industries
185 East South Street
Freeland, Pennsylvania 18224
(800) 25-RANGE; (800) 424-2411

Russell Range, Inc. (page 339)
(Cooktop only)

Thermador

Viking (page 339)

Wolf Range Company

Heirlooms:
Aga Cookers, Inc.
17 Towne Farm Lane
Stowe, Vermont 05672
(800) 633-9200

La Cornue
Purcell-Murray Company
113 Park Lane
Brisbane, California 94005
(800) 892-4040

Rotisserie:
Amco Adjustable Rotisserie
Williams-Sonoma (page 325)

Oven Thermometers:
National Controls Corporation
1725 Western Drive
West Chicago, Illinois 60185
(800) 323-2593
(Probes)

Thermo Electric Instruments
109 North Fifth Street
Saddle Brook, New Jersey 07663
(800) 766-4020; (201) 843-5800
(Digital oven thermometer)

Wok Stoves: Check yellow and business pages as well for restaurant supply houses and Chinese cookware stores.

Doubarn Sheet Metal, Inc.
12919 South Figueroa Street
Building 515
Los Angeles, California 90061
(310) 532-1193

Robert Yick Company, Inc.
261 Bayshore Boulevard
San Francisco, California 94124
(415) 282-9707

Seidman Brothers, Inc.
25 Sixth Street
Chelsea, Massachusetts 02150
(800) 437-7770; (617) 884-8110

Thermador (page 340)

Individual Residential Grills:
Russell Range, Inc. (page 339)

Thermador (page 340)
(Rotisserie attachment)

Warming Drawers:
Dacor (page 340)

Frigidaire (page 339)

Hatco
635 South 28th Street
P.O. Box 340500
Milwaukee, Wisconsin 53234
(800) 558-0607
(Commercial)

Merco/Savory, Inc.
725 Vassar Avenue
Lakewood, New Jersey 08701
(800) 547-2513
(Commercial)

Thermador (page 340)

Wells (page 340)

Range with Warming Drawer:
Frigidaire (page 339)

Heartland (page 339)

Food Warmers:
Merco/Savory, Inc.

Mouli
1 Montgomery Street
Belleville, New Jersey 07109
(800) 789-8285; (201) 751-6900

Wood-burning Ovens:
Earthstone Wood-Fire Ovens
1233 North Highland Avenue
Los Angeles, California 90038
(800) 840-4915; (213) 962-5878

Renato Specialty Products, Inc.
2775 West Kingsley
Garland, Texas 75041
(972) 864-8800

Wood-burning Ranges:
Heartland Appliances (page 339)

Portland Stove Company
P.O. Box 37
Fickett Road
North Pownal, Maine 04069
(207) 688-2254

Brick Oven Construction:
Alan Scott
Ovencrafters
5600 Marshall Petaluma Road
Petaluma, California 94952
(415) 663-9010

Simmer Grates:
Colonial Garden Kitchens
Hanover, Pennsylvania 17333
(800) 245-3399

MICROWAVE OVENS

It is easier to choose a microwave than many other appliances since a prospective choice can readily be tested at a friend's home or in a microwave store, where they are often live. Some stores even allow a model to go home for tryouts.

Supplies: To be sure pots or plates will fit, take along samples of anything you want to be able to use in the microwave.

Tests: Operate the keypad and all bells and whistles to see how easy they are to use. Is the keypad arranged logically so that directions can be entered with ease? Do "start" and "stop" buttons stand out from others so that the eye goes right to them?

How is cooking time punched in? Some people prefer the sequential pattern where 40 seconds would be entered by pressing in each number. Others vote for count-up, which involves holding or pressing the 10-second button until 40 comes up.

How easy are directions to enter? How many buttons do you have to push to program a task? Can you, for example, stop and restart the oven without resetting it?

Check for hot and cold spots and evenness of cooking since microwave distribution patterns vary greatly.

Decisions:

How many?

Microwave-convection combo?

Freestanding, undercabinet, built-in?

Wattage?

What size interior?

Bells and whistles?

Exterior glass, wood grain, stainless?

- Looking for maximum interior capacity relative to exterior size, check to see that dimensions of the machine fit your allotted space.

- What is the wattage of the machine? If space allows, purchase a large machine with 800 to 1,000 watts, which cooks food most quickly.

- How many cooking power levels does it have? Five are adequate as long as one of the levels is 10 percent of full power or less for gentle cooking tasks.

- Does it have bells and whistles you want? Sensors? Weight cook? Automatic defrost?

- Programmed cooking? If you choose this option, check that step-by-step programming instructions are printed out in the digital display, for this is easier than consulting the manual.

- How easy is the digital printout to read? Machines using a dark gray liquid crystal display on a gray background are more difficult to see than those with a diode that prints out in green, blue, or red.

- Microwaves open to the left almost universally, so check to see if you have enough clearance for the door to swing properly or if you need a model with a pull-down door.

- Does the door open smoothly and close tightly? With dirty hands? A handle is easier to grasp; a button more obliging when hands are full. Can you lock out the kids if desired?

- Check to see that it is easy to see through the door. Glass is easier to see through, but plastic is being used increasingly to cut expense.

- Does the interior light provide good visibility? Can you change the bulb yourself, or must a repairperson service it?

- How does the timer operate? If you want to use it as a general kitchen timer as well, you'll want to know whether it operates even when the microwave is on and if it works independently of the machine's blower and light.

- If purchasing a microwave to build in over a self-cleaning oven, check that it can survive this location.

- Check noises. If the machine beeps a confirmation once a task is entered, do you find this annoying? Are *done* signals readily or too readily heard? How noisy is the oven fan?

- To determine cleaning ease, check the bottom to see if a lip prevents spills from running out. In machines where microwaves enter from the top, check the housing to see if there are perforated screens or wands to accumulate grease. Any glass tray should be removable.

- Is there a good instruction manual and cookbook—important aids in a category where uniformity does not exist among machines?

- Does the store you are buying your machine from give free introductory cooking classes?

- Check the warranty for the expensive magnetron and touch-pad controls. Will you have to bring the machine in for repair, or will a serviceperson come to your home?

- If you are buying a microwave primarily to reheat frozen food, does it allow you to reheat the food in its aluminum tray?

UNIQUE ATTRIBUTES

Drop-Down Door:
General Electric Monogram or
   General Electric Profile (see
   General Electric, page 318)

Sharp Electronics Corporation
   (page 318)

Stainless Exterior:
KitchenAid (page 339)

Browning Capability:
KitchenAid Krisp (page 339)

TO START SHOPPING

MICROWAVE OVENS

General Electric (page 318)

KitchenAid (page 339)

Panasonic
Matsushita Consumer Electronics
   Company
One Panasonic Way, 2F-3
Secaucus, New Jersey 07094
(800) 222-4213; (201) 348-9090

Sharp Electronics Corporation
   (page 318)

VENTILATION

If you install a fire extinguisher in your hood, coordinate its purchase and design with the ventilation system.

Tests: Compute the duct run and number of elbows necessary before going shopping (page 258) so you know how much static pressure will develop in your system and the amount of power that will be necessary to compensate for it.

Listen to any ventilation system you are considering to get an approximate idea of what it sounds like. Good news. If anything, it will be slightly quieter once it is hooked up.

Decisions:

How large?

What style?

Custom or premade?

What finish? Brass, copper, plaster, glass, baked enamel, ceramic tile, solid surface, or stainless (14- or 16-gauge)?

What number CFM?

How many blowers or fans?

Remote exhaust system?

Fire-extinguishing equipment built into hood?

EVALUATION

- Does the system have a hood, exhaust, ducts, and back-draft damper?

HOODS

- If the hood is going against the wall, is it 3 inches longer than the cooktop on each side (6 inches for a commercial cooktop or grill) and deep enough to cover the edge of the front burners?

- If the hood is going over an island, is it 3 (or 6 inches) longer than the cooktop on all sides?

- Will you be able to hang it at the height recommended by the manufacturer (usually from 21 to 30 inches maximum above the cooktop)? If not, will you be able to expand its length and depth proportionately?

- If your ceiling is above eight feet or angled, does it have a telescopic flue or an adapter?

- Does the hood have a large canopy to capture the air?

- Check that edges are mitered and welded with invisible seams and no hardware. Forgo corner-cutting mitered edges if the hood borders on being too shallow.

- Confirm that the hood has a gutter to collect grease as it liquefies.

- If you are designing a custom hood, consider 12-inch side baffles that pull down from the hood, extending to the cooktop.

- Lights should be vaporproof and operate separately from the exhaust. Do you want them sandblasted to cut glare and to switch from high for working to low for a night-light?

EXHAUST SYSTEMS

- Following the National Kitchen & Bath Association Standards of 50 to 70 CFM per square foot of a hood against a wall (300 CFM minimum) and 100 CFM per square foot of one over an island (600 CFM minimum), how many CFM do you need? Allow roughly 1,200 CFM for a six-burner commercial-style cooktop and 1,800 if you add a grill to your lineup.

- If you can afford a more powerful system and follow commercial standards, how many CFM do you need (100 per square foot against a wall for a cooktop; 150 per square foot against a wall for a grill or commercial cooktop; 200 per square foot in an island for a cooktop; 300 per square foot in an island for a grill or commercial cooktop)?

- Will you need additional CFM to compensate for static pressure in your system?

- Does the hood have room for the number of blowers or fans you will need, or will it be better to remote the unit on the roof, where it won't be noisy?

- Is the exhaust system a squirrel cage with a rotary pressurized blower that operates by centrifugal force?

- If you must settle for a fan-operated system, does it have an axial fan rather than a propeller, which vibrates more?

- Does it have baffle filters? If it has the less effective mesh filters, are they at least 1 inch thick and made from a noncorrosive material such as brass, bronze, or stainless? Can filters be detached easily for cleaning?

- Is the system's sone level in the 7-or-below range? Have it put in writing. Do not go above 9.

- Confirm that each blower or fan has an independent control and can be switched between high and low speed. Switches should be easy to reach.

- If you have to buy a ductless system, look for the least expensive unit.

- If you elect a downdraft, get one that rises at least 6 to 9 inches.

- How easy are exhaust components to clean? Can they go in the dishwasher?

- Do you also need a supply fan for makeup air?

- Do you want an exhaust fan? Is it rated correctly for the size of your kitchen?

UNIQUE ATTRIBUTES

Extends to 9-Foot Ceiling:

Abbaka
1500-A Burke Avenue
San Francisco, California 94124
(800) 548-3932; (415) 648-7210

Fire Barriers:

Vent-A-Hood
1000 North Greenville Avenue
Richardson, Texas 75083
(214) 235-5201

Channel for Inserting Wallpaper, Fabric, or Trim:

Russell Range, Inc. (page 339)

Remote On/Off Switch:

Broan Manufacturing Company, Inc.
"Chuck Wagon"
P.O. Box 140
926 West State Street
Hartford, Wisconsin 53027
(800) 558-1711; (414) 673-4340

Russell Range, Inc. (page 339)

TO START SHOPPING

VENTILATION

Most of these systems are completely or partially custom, and many can also be remoted to the roof. Check the yellow and business pages as well for names of HVAC consultants and companies that make ventilation systems for restaurants.

Abbaka

Artisan Metalworks
232 Madison Avenue
Wyckoff, New Jersey 07481
(201) 891-0102

Greitzer, Inc.
P.O. Box 40
Elizabeth City, North Carolina
    27907
(919) 338-4000

Independent Inc. (page 324)

Modern-Aire
7319 Lankershim Boulevard
North Hollywood, California 91605
(818) 765-9870

Russell Range, Inc. (page 339)

Vent-A-Hood

ADDITIONAL SOURCES AND INFORMATION

Home Ventilating Institute

The Air Movement and Control Association
30 West University Drive
Arlington Heights, Illinois
    60004-1893
(847) 392-6009

REFRIGERATORS AND FREEZERS

When investigating a new refrigerator, order the *Consumer Selection Guide for Refrigerators and Freezers* from the Association of Home Appliance Manufacturers (AHAM). Though not all refrigerators are included, there is good information about size, style, and energy efficiency for those that are.

To narrow your search, figure out whether most of your food is stored in the refrigerator or freezer and the best relationship of these units for your optimum retrieval. You should also know where you are going to install the unit. Some doors require a greater amount of clearance for bins and drawers to be pulled out. Larger ones demand a wider aisle to open into. *Before you shop, remind yourself of low-, middle-, and high-end refrigerator features by referring to the chart on page 22.*

Supplies: Take along a ruler to measure interior space and an extension cord to test operating noise level. Check to see that its noise is tolerable. Otherwise you will have to remote the machine—an expensive proposition.

Make a list of food you typically store in the refrigerator and freezer on weekends as well as on weekdays. If you won't be able to imagine how well these groceries will fit, take them along, too.

Tests: Compare energy consumption ratings. Look at the size and shape of cubes produced by an automatic icemaker. Test any ice and water dispensers on the door to see that their contents don't splay all over. If you are getting this luxury for its crushed ice, check its consistency. Practice using any ice cream maker that's included in the purchase package (and bring along some hot fudge to taste the results). Check drawers to see that they move smoothly in and out. If there is any question, fill with food to test the smoothness of their operation when full.

Decisions:

Refrigerator only? Freezer only? Upright or chest? Manual, cycle, or self-defrost? Separate refrigerator and separate freezer? Combined unit with a freezer placed above, below, or to side of refrigerator? Multiple undercounter compact units? Separate icemaker? Wine cooler/beer tap?

Built in? True or built-in look?

What size?

Shelves or drawers?

Glass shelves or wire grids?

Interior organizers?

Ice and water on the door?

Through-the-door shelf?

Automatic icemaker?

Electronic flashers and alarms announcing temperature, "door open," "clean coils," and breakdowns, etc.?

Ice cream maker?

EVALUATION

Size:

- **Does it have maximum interior capacity relative to exterior size?**

- **Does the unit have enough refrigerator capacity for the kind of food you eat?**

- **Enough freezer space?**

- **Does it fit your allotted space?**

- **Does it have adjustable leveling legs to line up with the toe kick or fit in the space? How high can they go? How easy are they to adjust? If legs adjust only from the front, the unit must be installed on a flat floor. Do they lock?**

- **Do door panels or handles of machine with a built-in look extend beyond 24-inch base cabinets? Does it come with a trim kit? Does it need additional room for venting in back?**

- **Is the upper grill or refrigeration unit adjustable to line up with cabinets?**

Construction:

- **How well is the refrigerator built? Can the word *solid* be applied to its hinges, handles, trim, shelves, drawers, storage aids, and glides? Are hinges die-cast or heavy plate steel to keep doors aligned? Are hinges covered to match the refrigerator cabinet?**

- **Do the refrigerator and freezer both have a separate compressor and controls to run at optimum temperatures without extra energy expenditure?**

- **Where are condenser coils mounted? How easy are they to reach for repair and cleaning? Top front-mounted coils are easiest. Back-mounted coils don't get as dirty as bottom-mounted, but they are more difficult to clean, and the refrigerator must be pulled out to reach them.**

- **How accessible is the drip pan under the refrigerator that collects water during automatic defrost? If not cleaned routinely, it becomes a medium for a moldy message.**

- **Does it have an energy-saver switch?**

- **Can the door be ordered so it hinges on the side you want, or are hinges reversible?**

- **Does the door have steel or magnetic gaskets that seal well?**

- **Are the doors easy to open and self-closing with stops?**

- Does the freezer have its own door, and is it a separate completely enclosed unit?
- If you choose an on-the-door ice and chilled water dispenser, check that pitchers and glasses fit under it. Does it have a light?
- Does it come in the exterior finish you want? Stainless? Colored steel? Textured/nontextured? Does it accept a trim kit and custom door panels? If you choose a true built-in, do you want panels on sides as well as on the front?
- Is the interior a durable stainless, high-impact polystyrene, or ABS plastic?
- Are seams smooth and clean with no rough, sharp edges?

Temperature:

- If relevant for your climatic conditions, find out how well the unit performs when the temperature falls below 60 degrees or above 90 degrees.
- Are temperature controls near the front or outside of the box, where they are accessible?
- Does the refrigerator have a fast-cool mode? This is particularly important if you tend to stock it with a lot of uncooled food at once.

Interiors:

- Is enough space left undivided to organize it according to your comestibles?
- Are shelves adjustable and attachments firm and stable?
- Are shelves whole, which are better than half shelves for organizing? If you choose half shelves, do they fit together when placed side by side, or will there be a large gap?
- Are glass shelves tempered and clear? Are wire grids set close enough so small items don't fall through? Nonrusting? Check that shelves come with spill guards and extend to the edge of the box so nothing slips through.
- Is it possible to order an extra shelf for the refrigerator and freezer to have on hand for baking?
- Does it have the particular storage aids (page 270) you want?
- Are door shelves deep enough to hold a six-pack or gallon container? Do they have retainers to keep small items from falling out? Check that they are adjustable and removable for cleaning.
- Is any butter compartment well sealed? Does its door stay up automatically?
- Are crispers large, transparent, and well sealed? Do you want them to have separate humidity controls? Are they made of a heavy durable polycarbonate or ABS plastic, which will stand up best to abuse?

- If you want a meat/deli drawer, check that it is well sealed and has a separate temperature control.
- Do bins glide in and out smoothly on steel runners?
- Do bins and drawers have stops?
- Are interior lights well shielded and positioned conveniently so as not to interfere with storage? Ditto controls? Are controls lit? Are bulbs easy to reach and change?

Freezer: See questions under other categories as well.

- If frost-free, does it have electronic sensors to defrost only when necessary rather than at preset times?
- Does it have a quick-freeze or fast-freeze compartment or shelf?
- Does it have a fast-freeze mode?
- Is the temperature control up front or outside the box, where it is convenient to reach?
- Are shelves (shelf) adjustable?
- Do shelves extend the full width of the box?
- Does it have bins or baskets, making storage easier? Do these pull out easily.
- Are door shelves deep enough? Do they have retainers to keep small items from falling through?
- Are ice cube trays configured with a lip and a bowl that is deep enough to fill easily?

Separate Freezers: See questions under other categories as well.

- Does it have a door lock?
- Does it have an *on* indicator interior light and another light that alerts you to electric power loss?
- Is there an inventory list or convenient place for securing one?
- Does a chest model have a counterbalanced lid that locks easily when opened?
- Does a chest model come with an adequate water drain and hose assembly to aid in manual defrosting?
- Does a chest model come with storage organizers that correspond to your needs?
- Does the warranty provide for food loss with a power outage or breakdown? What amount? Under what conditions?

Automatic Icemaker:

- If you choose not to get an automatic icemaker, will you have the opportunity to retrofit one if you desire?
- Is it included, or does it cost extra?
- How long does it take to make ice? How much does it make in a day?
- Are the icemaker and bucket easily removable when you need extra space?

Oak Furniture Casing:
Northern Refrigerator
21149 Northland
Paris, Michigan 49338
(616) 796-8007

Old-Fashioned Casing:
Heartland Appliances Inc.
(page 339)

Tall, Narrow Refrigeration:
Northland Kitchen Appliance
701 Ranney Drive
P.O. Box 400
Greenville, Michigan 48838-0400
(800) 223-3900
(18 inches wide; up to 84 inches tall)

24-Inch-Deep Refrigerator:
Amana Home Appliances (page 340)
(True built-in)

General Electric (page 318)
(Ice and water on door)

General Electric Monogram
(page 318)

KitchenAid (page 339)

Northland Corporation
(True built-in)

Sub-Zero Freezer Company, Inc.
P.O. Box 44130
Madison, Wisconsin 53744-4130
(800) 222-7820
(Freezer available on bottom)

Traulsen & Company, Inc.
P.O. Box 560169
College Point, New York 11356-0169
(800) 937-0013; (800) 825-8220

*Side-by-Side Refrigerator with
Reversible Hinges:* Side-by-side
doors hinge in the middle so food
can easily be moved to a landing
space on either side of the refrigerator or freezer. Possesses freezer
shelf that converts to a refrigerator shelf when extra space is
desired in that area.

Northland Corporation

Custom Handles:
General Electric Monogram
(page 318)

Built-in Ice and Water Filter:
Frigidaire (page 339)

Power Interruption Switch: Shuts
off power to refrigerator without
going to the fuse box.

KitchenAid (page 339)

Reduced Energy Consumption:
Uses 60 to 90 percent less energy
than standard models. Can be
powered with three 50-watt photo-
voltaic modules.

Sun Frost
P.O. Box 1101
Arcata, California 95518-1101
(707) 822-9095

LP Gas Refrigerator:
Teeco Products, Inc.
16881 Armstrong Avenue
Irvine, California 92606
(800) 426-9456; (714) 261-6295

TO START SHOPPING

REFRIGERATORS AND FREEZERS

General Refrigeration:
Amana Refrigeration, Inc.
(page 340)
(Freezer available on bottom)

Frigidaire (page 339)

General Electric Appliances
(page 318)

KitchenAid (page 339)

Northland Corporation

Sears Kenmore
Highways 35 and 66
Ocean, New Jersey 07712
(800) 359-2000; (800) 948-8800
(Freezer available on bottom)

Traulsen & Company, Inc.

Whirlpool Corporation
Mail Drop 0120
2000 M-63 North
Benton Harbor, Michigan 49022
(800) 253-1301

Compact:
Marvel Industries
P.O. Box 997
Richmond, Indiana 47375-0997
(800) 428-6644

Sub-Zero Freezer Company, Inc.
(Integrated built-in units with
drawers, not doors)

Traulsen & Company, Inc.

U-Line Corporation
8900 North 55th Street
P.O. Box 23220
Milwaukee, Wisconsin 53223
(800) 779-2547; (414) 354-0300

Refrigerator/Icemaker Combo:
General Electric "Spacemaker"
(page 318)

Marvel

U-Line

ADDITIONAL SOURCES AND
INFORMATION

American Council for an Energy-
Efficient Economy (ACEEE)
*The Most Energy-Efficient
Appliances*
1001 Connecticut Avenue,
N.W., Suite 801
Washington, D.C. 20036
(202) 429-8873

Association of Home Appliance
Manufacturers (page 317)
*Annual Directory of Certified
Refrigerators and Freezers*

Energy Conservation and Services
Department
Pacific Gas and Electric Company
(800) 933-9555

Wisconsin Energy Bureau Fact
Sheets
Wisconsin Energy Bureau
P.O. Box 7868
Madison, Wisconsin 53707
(608) 266-8234

WINE COOLERS

Decisions:

What size?

How many bottles to store?

What size bottles to store? Magnums?

Single or multiple temperature zones in the same unit?

Finish?

Configuration?

Lock?

EVALUATION

- Check that it maintains a consistent humidity of 50 to 70 percent.

- Be sure shelves are sturdy and slanted to cant wines downward.

- Check that there are leveling legs and good insulation to guard against vibration.

- Check that the door seal is tight.

- Check that the door is either solid or a tinted double- or triple-glass pane to prevent passage of damaging UV rays and light.

- Is there an interior light to read labels by that turns on without opening the door?

TO START SHOPPING

WINE COOLERS

KitchenAid (page 339)

Marvel Industries (page 347)

Northland Corporation (page 347)

Traulsen & Company, Inc.
(page 347)

U-Line Corporation (page 347)

Catalogs:
International Wine Accessories
(IWA) (page 325)

The Wine Enthusiast (page 325)

BEER ON TAP

Marvel Industries (page 347)

ICEMAKERS

Check to see if prices are lower at stores selling commercial equipment.

Decisions:

18 or 24 inches wide?

Add filter to the machine?

What finish? Custom panel?

Manual or self-defrost?

Evaluation

- Are ice size and shape acceptable?

- Does the machine's capacity correspond to your needs once climatic conditions affecting production are factored in?

- If your state allows it, consider a machine with a water-cooled condenser that heats up the kitchen less than an air-cooled one.

- Does it require a drain?

- Is it serviceable from the front?

UNIQUE ATTRIBUTES

Icemaker with Chilled Water:
Whirlpool Corporation (page 347)

TO START SHOPPING

ICEMAKERS

Crystal Tips Ice System
2007 Royal Lane
Dallas, Texas 75229
(800) 527-7422

Marvel Industries (page 347)

Scotsman Ice Systems
775 Corporate Woods Parkway
Vernon Hills, Illinois 60061
(800) 533-6006; (847) 215-4550

Sub-Zero Freezer Company, Inc.
(page 347)

Whirlpool Corporation (page 347)

Before you shop, remind yourself of low-, middle-, and high-range features in these fixtures and appliances by referring to the chart on page 22.

SINKS

Supplies: Large skillet, cookie sheet, and, if you want to wash an oven rack easily in the sink, take that, too. Bring a ruler, for many catalogs indicate only external dimensions when it is the internal ones that count.

Tests: See how well the skillet, cookie sheet, and oven rack fit into the sink. Check corners on the floor of the sink carefully, for many large sinks have such wide curves on their floors that they cannot handle large skillets.

Decisions:

How many installations?

How many basins?

Single, double, or triple bowl?

Linear or diagonal for a corner placement?

How long and wide?

How deep? Bilevel?

What shape?

Individual modules or a basin with a ledge?

Attached drainboard?

What material?

If solid surface, do you want it prefabricated or custom?

What style? Apron sink?

None, mini, or maxi sink ledge?

Accessories?

Soap dispenser?

Deck mounted pop-up drain?

Integrated countertop and backsplash?

EVALUATION

Size and Shape:

- Is each basin as long and wide as the countertop can accommodate?

- Is each sink as deep as possible when your height and undersink space are considered?

- Is each basin big enough to be utilitarian?

- Is at least one basin large enough to handle large pots? More precisely, your pots? Your oven rack?

- Is each basin configured practically?

- Is the sink designed with a drop lip to prevent water from overflowing onto the counter? Is the divider between two basins lower than the rim so water won't overflow? (If the sink is to be undermounted, this is not an issue.)

Material:

STAINLESS

- Is it 18-gauge?

- Does it have an 18/10 or 18/8 (chromium/nickel) rating?

- Does it have a smooth texture?

- Does it have a satin finish?

- Does it have an undercoat to dampen sound and vibration?

ENAMEL ON CAST IRON

- Has it received two coats of enamel and a double firing?

- Is the enamel applied smoothly (not bumpy)?

- Is the color light enough to clean easily and not show mineral deposits?

COMPOSITE

- Is it solid surface (color goes all the way through)? If uncertain, ask to see a chip showing a cross section.

- Does it offer the color or pattern you want?

- If there is a choice of finish, do you want it matte, semigloss, or high gloss? If sheen is important, choose a company that makes what you want.

- If the sink is custom, has it been made by an approved fabricator? If not, the warranty will be invalidated.

- Does the material have a thickness of $3/4$ inch, which has good durability?

- If it contains silica, is the percentage roughly about 60 percent? (As the percentage goes up, staining increases while impact resistance and toughness decrease. Much lower, and scratching increases while heat resistance decreases.)

- What is its heat resistance? (How hot a pot can you put on the surface?)

- Do you want a textured bottom? Though nonslip, it will show repairs.

Mounting:

- Does this sink mount the way you want?

- Do you want the sink to integrate with the countertop? Will this one do so?

- If it is a replacement sink, can it be installed easily? If it is a temporary sink or one that is not very durable, will it be easy to remove?

- Do you want to install the sink yourself? If so, solid surface is not an option.

Drain:

- If you have designated a basin for a disposer, does it have the right size drain hole (usually $3^{1}/_{2}$ inches)?

- In a single basin, is the drain positioned to the back or side of the sink, creating a cleaning and catchment area? This placement puts plumbing in the rear of the sink cabinet underneath, leaving more room for storage.

- Does the drain seal well?

- Do you want a standard chrome or stainless strainer basket or one with a special finish or color? To avoid chipping, choose one made out of plastic whose color is intrinsic to the material.

- Does the sink come with a deck-mounted drain control so you don't have to fish around for it in scrungy water?

Accessories:

- Is the deck large enough to accommodate your chosen faucet and accessories? How many holes do you need drilled (page 282)?

- Is a soap dispenser spout at least $3^{1}/_{2}$ inches, long enough to extend over the deck and put a pot underneath it? Chrome or nonchippable plastic?

- Do you want a strainer, colander, crockery basket, drainboard, defrost tray, or cutting board tailored to fit your sink?

- Are available accessories (especially cutting boards) big enough to be serviceable? If not, a large fitted board can be ordered from another company. Are accessories made of material that can be cut on?

- Do you have room to store these accessories?

- What do prices include? Drain? Pipes? Accessories? Custom holes?

Liquid Soap and
Hand Lotion Dispensers:

- How easy are they to fill?

- Will they handle thick lotion without getting clogged?

- Do they have at least a $3^{1}/_{2}$-inch spout or one that extends over the ledge and is easy to put your hands under?

- Do you want a chrome or color finish (see notes under "Finish," page 292)?

UNIQUE ATTRIBUTES

Prefabricated Solid Surface:
The Swan Corporation
One City Centre, Suite 2300
St. Louis, Missouri 63101
(800) 325-7008; (314) 231-8148

Tray Sink: Measuring 21 by 16 by 2 inches, this sink is designed for school projects, cleaning produce, decorating cookies, and washing the baking sheet. Too shallow for general tasks, it offers possibilities in a kitchen housing multiple sinks.

Kohler Company
444 Highland Drive
Kohler, Wisconsin 53044
(800) 4-KOHLER

CHAPTER 9 *TO START SHOPPING*

SINKS

Stainless:
Blanco America, Inc.
1001 Lower Landing Road,
   Suite 607
Blackwood, New Jersey 08012
(800) 451-5782

Elkay Manufacturing Company
   (page 328)

Franke, Inc. (page 324)

Kindred Industries
1000 Kindred Road
Midland, Ontario
L4R 4K9 Canada
(800) 465-5586

Kohler Company

Vance Industries, Inc. (page 324)
(Unusual shapes)

Enamel on Cast Iron:
American Standard
P.O. Box 6820
Piscataway, New Jersey 08855-6820
(800) 524-9797; New Jersey
   (908) 980-3000

Eljer Industries
P.O. Box 879002
Dallas, Texas 75287-9002
(800) 4-ELJER-2; (800) 423-5537

Kohler Company

Composite:
American Standard

Astracast, Inc.
2761 Golfview Drive
Naperville, Illinois 60563
(800) 276-7726

Blanco America, Inc.

Franke, Inc. (page 324)

Kindred Industries

Syndesis
2908 Colorado Avenue
Santa Monica, California
   90404-3616
(310) 829-9932
(Syndecrete)

Solid Surface:
Avonite (page 329)

Du Pont Corian (page 329)

Formica (page 329)

The Swan Corporation

Wilsonart International (page 329)

Fireclay:
Kallista, Inc.
2701 Merced Street
San Leandro, California 94577
(510) 895-6400; (888) 452-5547

Kohler Company (page 350)

Soapstone:
Vermont Soapstone Company
P.O. Box 168
Stoughton Pond Road
Perkinsville, Vermont 05151
(800) 284-5404

Slate:
Vermont Structural Slate Company
    (page 330)

Copper:
Verdigris Copperworks
810 Camelia
Berkeley, California 94710
(510) 525-1922

Waterworks
29 Park Avenue
Danbury, Connecticut 06810
(800) 899-6757

Apron Sink:
Kohler Company (page 350)

Vermont Soapstone Company

Waterworks

Sinks to Work At Seated:
Elkay Manufacturing Company
    (page 328)
("ADAR 3321" with off-center drain
    and 5³/₈-inch-deep bowl)

Kohler Company (page 350)
("Assure" with concave apron)

Remote-Control Drains:
Franke, Inc. (page 324)

Kohler Company (page 350)
("Duostrainer" dry cable drain
    system for one or two drains)

Colored Drains:
Opella Inc.
4062 Kingston Court
Marietta, Georgia 30067
(800) 969-0339
(From color-through nonchippable
    engineered plastic)

Cutting Boards for Sinks:
Ribbonwood Products
HC2 Box 136A
Harrison, Idaho 83833
(800) 255-4691; (208) 667-1105

Soap Dispenser:
Bobrick Washroom Equipment, Inc.
11611 Hart Street
North Hollywood, California
    91605-5882
(818) 982-9600

Rohl Corporation/KWC Faucets
1559 Sunland
Costa Mesa, California 92626
(800) 777-WSMC

Wall-Hung Soap Dispensers:
Continental Manufacturing
    Company
13330 Lakefront Drive
Earth City, Missouri 63045
(800) 325-1051; Missouri
    (314) 770-9949

Kroin Inc.
180 Fawcett Street
Cambridge, Massachusetts 02138
(800) 655-9646; (617) 492-4000

ADDITIONAL SOURCES AND
INFORMATION

Sinkie World Headquarters/
    N.H. Associates
1579 Farmers Lane
No. 252
Santa Rosa, California 95405
(707) 577-0470

FAUCETS

Select the style and finish of a faucet first, and then compare price and warranty, particularly when considering the less hardy brass and colored brands. Bad water or plumbing can destroy the best faucet in no time, and since there is no agreement about who makes the best, it may prove wisest to choose the faucet with the most comprehensive warranty.

Some ceramic disk valves go through a very stiff period if they have not been ground finely enough. Consult with a plumber before deciding, to see which ones have been troublesome.

If you want an integrated hose in the faucet head, check to see whether your local code requires a vacuum breaker or antibacksiphoning device.

Supplies: Large deep pots and pitchers.

Tests: Place pots and pitchers under the faucet to see how they fit and fill. Turn the faucet and any spray hose on and off and switch back and forth between spray and stream to determine ease of operation. Request a cutaway showing a cross section of faucet to ascertain its construction.

Test your final selection with the sink you have chosen to be sure the reach is adequate.

Decisions:

How many? If more than one, should they be the same or
    different?

Where to mount?

How long a spout?

What degree swinging radius?

Single lever or two handles?

If lever, what shape and on top or to the side?

If two handles, what material?

Pullout spray hose? Separate or integrated?

Hot, cold, and/or filtered water?

Floor pedals?

Automatic on/off faucet with infrared sensor?

Finish?

Metal: shiny or matte?

Pot filler?

Hot and/or chilled water dispenser? If both, one combined unit or two separate ones?

Liquid soap or hand-lotion dispenser?

EVALUATION

- Is the faucet large enough for its sink? Is the spout about 11 inches or long enough so water will reach all parts of the sink without splashing? Will it swivel far enough to reach crevices?

- Does it have a gooseneck or spray hose for filling large pots?

- How does the faucet feel in your hand? Is it heavy and substantial? Examine a cross section. Is it fabricated from solid die-cast brass parts without zinc or pot metal?

- Is it lead-free? Are tests available to indicate the amount of lead it leaches? Is it below national requirements or the more stringent standards demanded by California Proposition 65?

- Is the valve a washerless nonleaking ceramic disk?

- Does it have a built-in aerator or water flow restrictor, or will you need to purchase one to attach to it?

- Does it have an antiscald device or a temperature memory to protect children and the elderly?

- When considering a European import, see if the plumbing attachments are geared for American dimensions or if an adaptor kit is necessary. A company that refits a faucet will have a greater investment in servicing the market here.

- Does price include handles, spout, an escutcheon plate, integrated hose, and plumbing/installation supplies?

- If you have a portable dishwasher, will you be able to hook it up to this faucet?

- If there is a spigot for filtered water, does the filter remove the elements you want removed?

Handles:

- Can handles be operated with the wrist, elbow, or arm? If they must be gripped with the hand, do they have raised ridges or bands? Are they easy to hold and turn? Will you be able to operate the faucet with dirty, greasy, or weak hands?

- If you choose a lever mounted on the side, it should correspond to your handedness. As you face the faucet, the lever should be on the right for a right-handed person.

Finish:

- Choose double-plated chrome for the most durable finish. A polished or matte chrome is more durable than brushed.

- For brass or copper, choose one that has not been coated. If it has, look for a smooth surface that "lies flat" without "orange peel" and has been applied electrostatically.

- For a colored finish, choose an engineered plastic or polyester where color goes all the way through or, second, a baked epoxy powder coat that will chip. Sprayed-on enamel is too fragile.

- If the faucet is a mixture of color and metal, can you clean one part without getting its cleaning solution on the other?

- A gold faucet should have a plating with a thickness of 13 to 50 millionths of an inch. A satin finish hides marks better than a polished one.

Spray:

- Is the spray nice, broad, and controlled, or does it splash all over?

- Is the hose at least 59 inches or long enough to reach all over the sink?

- Is the hose a heavy solid stainless or chrome? Is it interlinked and double wound, or is it spiral like a Slinky and prone to coming apart?

- If you want an integrated hose and a vacuum breaker or an antibacksiphoning device is required locally, check to see that the faucet has it. If so, is it built into the faucet, or do you have to mount it separately on the wall or counter?

- Can you change its stream from fine to wide or jet? Is there a lock to hold down the water pattern you choose?

- Is there a large seam between the diverting button and housing on the top cap, where debris can fall through?

Pot Filler:

- Has the plumbing been installed for it at the stove, or are you able to add it easily?

- Do you have a place to mount it properly where it won't be too high or too close to the pilot light, where it could get burned? Will it extend far enough from the wall to reach your pots?

- If it is a pullout model, can it be turned off at the wall as well as at the nozzle, increasing its longevity?

Hot- and Chilled-Water Dispensers:

- Do you have room under the sink for their tanks?

- Do you want them hooked up to a water filter?

- Do you want a spout or a gooseneck shape? Will pots and containers fit under it?

- Are they lead-free?

- Do you want a chrome or color finish (see "Finish," page 292)?

- Are handles lever style or push-down buttons that are easier to operate with dirty hands than a twist-on faucet?

- Does it heat the amount of water you want (40 to 60 cups per hour)?

- Does it have a deflector plate to prevent lime buildup?

- Does it have a drainpipe to empty when you're out of town?

- Does it lock?

- Is the tank protected from overheating by a replaceable thermal fuse?

UNIQUE ATTRIBUTES

Interchangeable Spray Heads: This hose is available with one regular and three specialty heads: a brush for crystal, a scraper for pots, and a water filter.

Grohe America "Ladylux"
241 Covington Drive
Bloomingdale, Illinois 60108
(630) 582-7711

TO START SHOPPING

FAUCETS

Contemporary:
Franke, Inc. (page 324)

Gemini Bath & Kitchen Products
3790 East 44th Street, Suite 228
Tucson, Arizona 85713
(800) 262-6252; (520) 750-8433

Grohe America

Hansa America
1432 West 21st Street
Chicago, Illinois 60608
(800) 343-4431

Kroin Inc. (page 351)

Rohl Corporation/KWC Faucets
　　(page 351)

Old Fashioned:
The Chicago Faucet Company
2100 South Clearwater Drive
Des Plaines, Illinois 60018-5999
(847) 803-5000

Harrington Brass Works Ltd., Inc.
7 Pearl Court
Allendale, New Jersey 07401
(201) 818-1300

Waterworks (page 351)

Commercial Style:
The Chicago Faucet Company

Fisher Manufacturing Company
P.O. Box 60
Tulare, California 93275-0060
(800) 421-6162

Grohe America

Pot Fillers:
The Chicago Faucet Company

Fisher Manufacturing Company

Foot Pedals:
The Chicago Faucet Company

Fisher Manufacturing Company

Physically Challenged:
Gemini Bath & Kitchen Products
(Arwa "Clinic")

Rohl Corporation/
　　KWC Faucets "Vita"
　　(page 351)

Automatic Infrared:
Speakman "Sensorflo"
P.O. Box 191
Wilmington, Delaware 19899-0191
(800) 537-2107; (302) 764-9100

Faucet with Filter Spigot:
Franke, Inc. (page 324)

General Ecology, Inc.
"Seagull IV X-2KM"
151 Sheree Boulevard
Exton, Pennsylvania 19341
(800) 441-8166

Faucet/Drinking Fountain Combo:
Kohler Company "Finesse"
　　(page 350)

Drinking Fountain: To mount on sink ledge
Elkay Manufacturing Company
　　(page 328)

Aerator:
Spradius Kitchen Aerator
Real Goods
555 Leslie Street
Ukiah, California 95482-5507
(800) 762-7325

Antiscald Device:
ScaldSafe
Resources Conservation Inc.
P.O. Box 71
Greenwich, Connecticut 06836
(800) 243-2862

Hot- and/or Cold-Water Dispensers:
Broan Manufacturing Company, Inc.
　　(page 344)

Elkay Manufacturing Company
　　(page 328)

Franke, Inc. (page 324)

In-Sink-Erator (ISE)
4700 21st Street
Racine, Wisconsin 53406-5093
(800) 558-5712

Water, Inc.
321 Coral Circle
El Segundo, California 90245
(800) 322-9283; (310) 416-9854

Obtain a copy of the National Sanitation Foundation (NSF) listings. Once your water is tested, look at models it recommends to treat your specific problem.

Tests: Have your water analyzed and see if adjustments other than cosmetic should be made. If a problem is identified, have it retested by another company. Taste the filtered water of any system you are considering to see if you like it. Operate the filtration system to see how easy it is to use, to replace its cartridges. Read instructions for any unit you are considering to see if there are any contraindications for employing it with your water.

Decisions:

Bottled water or water treatment system?

How many systems? A separate one for coffeemaker or icemaker?

Where to keep it?

What type of system?

EVALUATION

- Is it the type of system or systems you need to treat your water?

- Has it been approved by NSF?

- Has the company been in business for a long time? Does it appear solid? You don't want to get caught with a system for which replacement filters aren't available.

- What does it filter out? Does it leave in healthful minerals?

- How much does it produce at once? How much does it hold? Is it enough for your needs?

- How long can the filtered water be stored safely in the tank at room temperature?

- Will it fit under your sink? Do you have room for it?

- Can it be plumbed to icemakers, chillers, and hot-water dispensers if you want?

- Is a plumber required for installation and upkeep? Does the company have its own installer?

- How does the system alert you to the need for a new filter?

- Look for a filter rated to process at least 2,000 gallons before requiring replacement. What is the replacement cost? Are filters available locally?

- Is there a shutoff valve on either side so replacement is not difficult?

- Does an activated charcoal system have a block, which is more absorbing than looser granular or powder forms?

- Does carbon accept a replaceable cartridge? If it is a sealed block, you will have to replace the whole unit.

- An RO system should come with a container for collecting the purified water, or it will have to be guarded too closely against overflow.

- What is the faucet for the system like?

- How easy is it to fill pitchers or glasses underneath?

- How easy is it to follow the manufacturer's directions for maintenance?

Water System:

- Does it include ice?

- What is its finish? Does it accept a custom panel?

- What is the temperature of its chilled water?

Water Softener:

- How easy is it to refill the salt? How frequently will this be necessary?

- What are the servicing fees?

- Can you set the controls to your pattern of water consumption?

- Does it have a backup battery in case of power outage?

- Do you want a dual-tank model with separate resin and salt tanks, which take up more floor space, or a single-tank model, which takes up less room while holding less salt?

- Do you have a space for storing the salt?

- Does it have a clock so you can set it for a convenient time and a switch so you can start it manually?

- Does it require a special faucet?

UNIQUE ATTRIBUTES

Bottled Water Pump: Stored anywhere, this pump enables bottled water to be dispensed via the refrigerator's on-the-door ice and water dispenser or through an accessory faucet at the sink.

KitchenAid (page 339)

Water-Testing Laboratories:
National Testing Laboratories
6555 Wilson Mills Road, Suite 102
Cleveland, Ohio 44143
(800) 458-3330

Suburban Water Testing
   Laboratories
4600 Kutztown Road
Temple, Pennsylvania 19560
(800) 433-6595

Filtration Systems: For a list of
NSF-certified filtration systems,
check the current NSF booklet for
the companies offering the units
best suited to your particular
water problem.

Faucets for Water Filtration Systems: Standard, long reach, and
lead free are available.

Lead Free Faucets
16725 West Park Circle Drive
Chagrin Falls, Ohio 44023
(216) 543-1660

Touch-Flo Manufacturing Company
59 East Orange Grove Avenue
Burbank, California 91502-1882
(800) 223-0490; (818) 843-8117

Water Systems:
Northland Corporation (page 347)

Water Center
2375 South West Temple
Salt Lake City, Utah 84115
(800) 888-3776

Additional Sources and Information

Environmental Protection Agency
Office of Drinking Water
401 M Street S.W.
Washington, D.C. 20460
Safe Drinking Water Hotline:
(800) 426-4791

National Ground Water Association
601 Dempsey Road
Westerville, Ohio 43081
(800) 551-7379

National Sanitation Foundation
   (NSF)
3475 Plymouth Road
Ann Arbor, Michigan 48105
(800) 673-6275; (313) 769-8010

Water Quality Association (WQA)
4151 Naperville Road
Lisle, Illinois 60532
(800) 749-0234; (630) 505-0160

DISHWASHERS

Dishwashers require different amounts of water pressure. Before shopping for one, find out how much pressure exists in the house. This way you can assess whether a given machine requires more pressure to fill properly than you have available and if you'll have to add a booster. If pressure is low, choose a machine that measures level by volume, not time.

Water hardness is another area to assess. If hardness is higher than seven grains—three to five grains according to some experts—a water softener will need to be added to the home or a model chosen with an interior softener. The water will also have to be treated (page 295) if a significant level of sulfur, iron, manganese, or turbidity exists, or there is an excessively high or low pH.

If you are shopping for a replacement model, measure the size of the cabinet it must fit. If the floor went in after the cabinet, subtract its height.

Supplies: Take a sample plate, oversized dishes, or pots that you like to put in the dishwasher, and enough items for a typical load.

Tests: Determine whether the distance between the rack grips is adequate for the thickness of your plates. Load and unload dishwashers with the typical load you've brought to compare the ease of the task and the space available from one machine to the next. If the model you are considering is not on the floor, ask to see the manual that pictures sample loads.

Decisions:

18 or 24 inches wide?

Bells and whistles?

Finish? Color? Custom door panels?

Portable or permanent?

Commercial dish machine?

Evaluation

- Do you have enough water pressure in your home's water supply to handle the machine's stated requirements?

- A switch for varying water pressure in the machine is useful only if your loads vary in the amount of pressure they require. Some machines reduce pressure on the upper rack, which is relevant only if this rack is always reserved for glasses and other delicate items.

- If needed, does the machine have an internal water softener?

- Does it have a childproof lock?

Environment:

- How efficient is the dishwasher on the energy guide labels? How much water does it consume per load? The current benchmark hovers roughly around 5.3 gallons total.

- Does it have a two-pump system—one for filling, the other for emptying—which results in greater energy savings?

- Does it have an internal heater that boosts water to 140 degrees, allowing you to lower your house water heater to 120 degrees? Does it heat the water before beginning the cycle so you are using hot water all the way through?

- Although a machine's sound level will vary according to its setting, check the decibel rating and its frequency band if noise is an important issue. Forty to 50 decibels are considered low-range.

- What kind of insulation does it have? Is there insulation on the door and service panels as well as on the tub? Are the motor and pump housing separated from the dishwasher chamber? Remember, too, that you can further insulate your dishwasher before installation.

- Does it have at least a $1/2$-horsepower motor, which operates more efficiently than a lower power?

- What is the wattage? The higher the wattage, the larger the heating element, the quicker the water gets hot, and the better the dryer.

- Does it have a fan to facilitate no-heat drying?

Cycles:

- Does the regular wash include two complete wash cycles, each with fresh water and detergent? If not, does another cycle, such as the one for pots and pans, allow you to wash dishes in this fashion?

- Are the cycles appropriate for the types of dishes you wash?

- What cycles do you want? Rinse and hold, light/delicate, short, heavy pots and pans? A cancel button or plate warmer?

- Does it have a high-heat wash of 150 degrees or above for washing very greasy dishes?

- How many washer arms does it have? Are they on at least two, and preferably three, levels? How many outlets does each arm have for water? What directions are they pointed in? Will the water reach everything in the dishwasher?

- How long does each cycle take?

- Does it have a soft food disposer (easiest) or collection cup (must be taken out and washed) and a triple-filter system that recirculates only clean, filtered water back over the dishes so they don't have to be rinsed before

loading? Are the filters self-cleaning by backwash, or do they need to be removed and cleaned outside the machine? How easy are they to clean?

Bells and Whistles:

- A delayed start? If so, how long in advance should it be preprogrammable?

- A memory for a previous setting?

- A pause for inserting dirty dishes?

- An all-done light?

- A rinse agent indicator?

- A readout of the temperature and the point the load has reached in the cycle?

- A diagnosis of any problems?

- A microprocessor sensor that automatically computes temperature, cycle, time, and amount of detergent for you?

Fit and Fittest: Aesthetics:

- If this is a replacement model, will it fit into your pre-existing cabinets?

- Can its height and width be adjusted with a trim kit so that it fits a preexisting spot? Does its control panel line up with your cabinet drawers; its toe kick with your cabinet toe kicks?

- Does it accept a $1/8$-inch-thick decorator panel (European machine) or a $1/4$-inch-thick one (American)?

- Is it an *integrated* dishwasher, allowing a cabinet front to be attached, further muting its sounds?

- What color or material is the trim kit?

- Is the interior (in descending order of preference) stainless, plastic-coated steel, or porcelain enamel-on-steel? Better machines will have tank, pipes, filter, inner casing, and sprayer arms of stainless as well. If a magnet sticks to the stainless, avoid it.

- Is there an interior light?

- Are the doors easy to open and close, or will they ruin a manicure?

- Are the door springs heavy-duty?

Interior Configuration and Racks:

- How practical is it?

- Do the washer arms and water pipes cut through the center of the racks, making loading difficult?

- What is the distance between the two racks?

- How large an item can you wash on each shelf?

- Will you be able to wash oversized items in the machine?

- Are the racks designed to hold stemware safely?

- A machine with permanently placed racks will be less fussy to use than ones that are adjustable. If they are adjustable, how easy are they to adjust and lock into place?

- If the racks have inserts to modify the configuration, how easy are they to get in and out? Will you have a place to store them?

- Are the racks heavy and solid? Do they move smoothly in and out, even when they are full? Do they fit tightly into the glides so they will stay on track?

- Are the racks and prongs made from several coatings of plastic so they won't rust or, even better, from a more flexible graphite nylon? Are the tips double- or triple-coated and cushioned to guard against rust?

- Are the prongs well placed so that glasses or large pots can be secured without bending them? Can dishes be loaded on an angle so they drain readily?

- Are the prong tips shaped to cushion glasses?

- Does the dishwasher have a long narrow silverware basket or one that doesn't cut up rack space awkwardly? Does it have a handle for easy carrying and a covered section to hold pastry bag tips, baby bottle nipples, and other small items? Or a separate basket to hold small things?

Portables:

- Are you able to get water from the sink while it is running?

- Is it easy to push around? Do the wheels move smoothly? Is the handle comfortable to grasp?

- Does it have a hose storage compartment? Is it easy to get the cord and hoses in and out of their hideaway?

- Is it simple to hook up to the kitchen sink?

- If you choose a cutting-board top, is it made out of a good thick hardwood?

- Consider only a machine that can be loaded from the front.

- Check that it can be converted to a built-in.

UNIQUE ATTRIBUTES

18-Inch-Wide Dishwashers:
Miele "Slimline" (page 340; can be turned on from a laptop computer)

Sears Kenmore (page 347)

Portable/Convertible Dishwashers:
General Electric (page 318)

Maytag
240 Edwards Street
Cleveland, Tennessee 37311
(800) 688-9900

Sears Kenmore (page 347)

Whirlpool Corporation (page 347)

Fuzzy Logic Sensor Technology:
General Electric "Profile" (page 318)

Maytag "Intellisense"

Integrated Doors:
ASKO, Inc.
1161 Executive Drive West
Richardson, Texas 75081
(800) 367-2444

Robert Bosch Corporation
2800 South 25th Avenue
Broadview, Illinois 60153
(800) 944-2904

Gaggenau (page 339)

Miele (page 340)

TO START SHOPPING

DISHWASHERS

ASKO, Inc.

Robert Bosch

Gaggenau (page 339)

General Electric (page 318)

KitchenAid (page 339)

Maytag

Miele (page 340)

Regency VSA Appliances, Ltd. (page 340)
(Can handle a large stockpot)

Sears Kenmore (page 347)

Whirlpool Corporation (page 347)

Commercial Dish Machine:
Champion Industries, Inc.
P.O. Box 4183
Winston-Salem, North Carolina 27115
(800) 228-8350; (910) 661-1992

Garbage Disposers

Before you shop, remind yourself of low-, middle-, and high-end disposer features by referring to the chart on page 22.

Decisions:

How many?

Batch feed or continuous?

EVALUATION

- Does it have a heavy-duty 1-horsepower motor that handles food better than smaller motors?

- Is it the more efficient capacitor start or permanent magnet type of motor?

- What is its motor speed? (Higher-RPM motors dispose of food faster, reportedly conserving energy.)

- Will it fit into and under your sink?

- Are grinding and shredding mechanisms and sink flange composed of stainless steel?

- Is the drain chamber fiberglass or another noncorrosive material?

- Does it have an antijam mechanism, overload, or automatic reversing switch and swivel impellers to prevent stalls?

- Are fiberglass, polyurethane, or other strong durable materials used for sound insulation? On what parts? Does it have rubber or other cushioned mountings to muffle vibration? A well-insulated disposer is particularly important in a noisier stainless sink.

- Does it have a shield to prevent damage from caustic dishwasher detergent?

- Does it have a dishwasher drain connection and guard to prevent its contents from backing up into the dishwasher?

- Does it have a water seal to guard the motor from moisture damage?

- If it is continuous feed, does it have a splash guard?

UNIQUE ATTRIBUTES

Lifetime Warranty:
Sinkmaster
4240 East La Palma Avenue
Anaheim, California 92807
(800) 854-3229

Waste King
4240 East La Palma Avebue
Anaheim, California 92807
(800) 854-3229

TO START SHOPPING

GARBAGE DISPOSERS

Franke, Inc. (page 324)

In-Sink-Erator (ISE) (page 353)

KitchenAid (page 339)

Sinkmaster

Waste King

Garbage Disposer Air-Activated Control Switch: For mounting on sink ledge or counter. Can also be purchased from a plumbing supplier.

Franke, Inc. (page 324)

In-Sink-Erator (ISE) (page 353)

TRASH COMPACTORS

Tests: Practice opening, closing, and filling a chock-full compactor with no free hands and see how easy it is to dispense with trash. Remove the compacted bag to see how heavy it is to lift and put in a clean bag to review the change-out process.

Decisions:

Built-in or freestanding?

12-, 15-, or 18-inch width?

Finish? Custom door panel?

EVALUATION

- Will it fit into your allotted space?

- Do you want a freestanding unit to have a butcher block top?

- How does it open for disposing the trash?

- If it has a pull out chute, is it wide enough to throw garbage in without getting it all over the floor?

- If it has a sliding drawer, does it move in and out easily?

- Does it have a foot pedal for opening when hands are full?

- Does it utilize special or regular trash bags? Are they available in the supermarket, or must you go to a special store to purchase them? How expensive are they? How easy are they to put on and take off?

- How easy is it to pull out the crushed bag of trash for disposal? Does it have a bag caddy with handles for lifting out the crushed trash?

- Does it provide storage for refill bags?

- How much horsepower does it have?

- Does it have a deodorizer compartment and fan?

- Does it have an antijam device?

- Does it have reversible or interchangeable door panels? Can a custom cabinet front be used on it?

- Does it have a safety lock to prevent children from seeing what it will do to baby brother or the cat?

- Does it have a sound-dampening system? (Since compactors run for such a short time, this is not as important as it is on a dishwasher.)

- Does the unit start compacting as soon as trash is placed in it, or must it first reach a certain level? (Compaction is greater when it starts immediately.)

- How difficult is it to service? If it is built in, does it have to come out, or can it be repaired from the front?

To Start Shopping

Trash Compactors

General Electric (page 318)
12- and 15-inch widths

KitchenAid (page 339)
15- and 18-inch widths

Whirlpool Corporation (page 347)
15-inch width

Trash Bins and Holes

Decisions:

Trash hole? Holes?

How many bins?

Separate or together?

What size?

Mixed trash or separated for recycling?

Covered or uncovered?

In a cabinet, back of door, pullout, pull-down, or through a plug in the countertop?

Concealed or in the aisle?

Newspaper recycling?

Evaluation

Holes:

- Are holes large enough that scraps can easily be funneled into them?

- Is there a cover to discourage permeation of smells?

- Are they lined with a bucket that has a handle for removal and easy emptying?

Bins:

- Do lids come off automatically when the can is pulled out?

- Can you close it automatically with an elbow or knee?

Unique Attributes

Furniture-Quality Recycling Island and Cabinetry:
Haute House (page 318)

Corner Cabinet Rotary Recycling Bins:
Feeny Manufacturing Company (page 324)

Moldable Free-form Trash Can: For the back of the sink cabinet door.
Feeny (page 324)

To Start Shopping

Waste Bins

Continental Manufacturing Company (page 351)

Häfele America Co. (page 319)

Hold Everything (page 325)

Rev-A-Shelf, Inc. (page 323)

Rubbermaid Commercial Products, Inc. (page 324)

Automatic Door Opener: Foot pedal operation.
Häfele America Co. (page 319)

Trash Hole (Bucket):
Franke, Inc. (page 324)

Häfele America Co. (page 319)

Compost Bucket:
Smith & Hawken
P.O. Box 6900
Florence, Kentucky 41022
(800) 776-3336

12
KITCHENS BY THE NUMBERS

Specific spatial allowances must be maintained in laying out a kitchen for cooks to function efficiently in the room. Though the numbers here are the *standard pared-down bare minimums* necessary, a lean mean skeleton that would do Jenny Craig proud, you still may have to shortchange some of these dimensions when space is at a premium. If you do so, orchestrate how you will function in the compromised areas. If you can't, rethink your layout.

This chart is intended as a quick reference for laying out your kitchen and double-checking final plans and purchases. Numbers utilized here are the *standards employed for the proverbial average.* At five feet minus, many are not for me. They may not be for you, either. Some of the recommendations that follow echo the new standards developed by the University of Minnesota in 1992 for the National Kitchen & Bath Association. Others have been adapted from additional sources or reflect my personal observations and hands-on experience.

The greatest difference of opinion exists about individual work areas and landing spaces—the size a countertop should be when it is placed next to an appliance for receiving food or cookware handled in that vicinity. Many references, for example, cite only three inches as the amount of space to be left next to a secondary sink. Somehow this doesn't seem sub-stantial enough when you are standing there with a dripping pot.

Without argument, ideal is always the longest uninterrupted expanse, but when space is realistically limited, what works best for you? Look at the size of your equipment and how you work, then revamp these figures accordingly. Once again, *they are only guidelines to be modified according to your personal style.*

The appliance dimensions included here are guidelines, too, common standard measurements employed by many manufacturers. These numbers change frequently and too many exceptions exist for them to be treated as gospel. **Before designing a space for a particular appliance, check its requirements with the manufacturer.** Once you think you have it worked out, fractions will work havoc with your measurements.

Work Triangle

Total triangle: 12–26 feet connecting the centers of the stove, sink, and refrigerator

Individual legs: 4–9 feet

    Refrigerator to sink: 5–7 feet

    Sink to range: 5–6 feet

    Cooktop to refrigerator: 5–9 feet

Adequate Working Kitchen:

12 square feet

One-Wall Kitchen

Length: 12–16 feet

Galley Kitchen

Width between parallel walls: 8 feet (to open cabinet doors simultaneously)

U-Shaped Kitchen

Base: 8 feet

Arms: 4–5 feet

Islands

Dimensions: 2 × 2 feet minimum

Island with a sink: 3 feet minimum

Width: 48 inches maximum

Height:

    Standard: 36 inches (30½-inch cabinet plus 4-inch toe kick plus 1½-inch countertop)

    Custom: Varies according to individual's optimum height for working or eating

Installation in:

    U-*shaped kitchen:* 12 feet between legs of **U**

    Galley kitchen: 12 feet between parallel walls

Aisles

One-person passageway (nonworking part of kitchen): 36 inches

One-person work aisle or aisle between island and opposite counter: 36–42 inches if no traffic; 48–60 inches if passageway, or cabinets open on both sides of aisle

Bending area: 36–38 inches

Two-person work area: 48–60 inches

Doors

Entrance to kitchen: 32 inches wide

Distance from inward opened door to cabinet: Enough space for cabinet to open more than 90 degrees; usually 16 inches is sufficient for a 12-inch-wide cabinet door

Windows

Area: 10 percent of square footage or local code

Bay window: 12 inches from outside wall

Distance between skylight and sink vent duct: 5 horizontal feet; duct must be 2 feet above skylight; may vary according to local code

Overhang to protect southern windows from summer heat: 16 inches above top of window; 30 inches deep

Trim: 3 inches

Rods: 1–3 inches

Cabinets
(see cabinet section in Chapter 4 for dimensions of quality cabinets)

Adequate Storage:

    Wall cabinets: 144 running inches of cabinets that are 30 inches high and 12 inches deep

    Base cabinets: 156 running inches of standard base cabinets (see below)

Standard Measure: 3-inch increments

Wall:

Height: 12–48 inches (30–33 standard; 36 and 42 popular)

    Above refrigerator: 12–15 inches

    Above stove: 12–15 inches

Width: 9–48 inches

    Single-door: 9–24 inches

    Double-door: 24–48 inches

Depth (without door): 12–15 inches (needs to be shallower than base cabinets to work comfortably in front of; 15 inches offers more storage and holds dinner-size plates, which don't fit in framed 12-inch cabinets, but items are harder to reach)

Installation:

    Maximum use of backsplash and counter: 15–18 inches above counter (15 inches preferred by shorter people; 18 inches allows large appliances to be stored at back of counter)

    On counter: Possible with counters at least 30 inches deep, or when heavy pullout cutting boards are located below counter, or when wall cabinet is used as an appliance garage

Over cooktop: 30 inches above for combustible cabinets; 25 inches for noncombustible

Base:

Height: 36 inches (31½-inch cabinet plus 4-inch toe kick plus 1½-inch countertop)

Vanity height: 30½ inches

For additional height: Add shallow or deep drawer to top or bottom of 30½-inch base cabinet (appliances can be installed at higher level in taller base cabinets)

Toe kick (recessed lip at bottom of cabinet):

Height: 3–9 inches

Depth: Recessed 2–3 inches

Width:

Single-door: 9–48 inches; except for 9-inch doors, most include one drawer

Double-door: 24–48 inches

Depth:

Standard (without door): 24 inches

Extra-deep: 30 inches to accommodate an appliance garage, wall cabinet mounted on counter, or to line up with a deep appliance

Installation:

Standard: On floor

Wall-hung: Any convenient height

Corner Cabinet:

Lazy Susan: 33–39 inches wall space

Blind cabinet: 42–48 inches wall space

Pie-cut cabinet: 36 inches wall space

Utility:

Height: 66–96 inches (standard ceiling height)

Width: 18, 24, and 36 inches

Depth:

Standard: 12 and 24 inches

To match wall or base cabinet: Vary

Wall Oven Units:

Height: 84 inches

Width: 30 inches

Depth: 24 inches

Storage

Reach: 5'3"–5'7" person can easily reach 66–68 inches; extend to 80 inches maximum

Over 25-inch counter: 69 inches

Side to side: 48 inches

Most comfortable accessible storage: Between hip and shoulder level; generally 24 (30 for elderly) to 54 inches off floor

Eye level: 4'11" for 5'4" person

Vacuum cleaner:

Upright height: About 4 feet

Width: 24–29 inches

Pot racks:

Height: Bottom of pot at level user can reach

Installation: Wall installation when ceilings less than 8 feet

Countertop

Usable counter space: 11 feet total length throughout kitchen

Overhang: 2 inches to get bowls under counter lip

Minimum continuous countertop:

Per-person preparation space between refrigerator and sink or sink and cooktop: 30–36 inches; 48 inches when two

tasks performed at same countertop

Per-person work space in baking area: 36–42 inches

Two-person work space: 72 inches (facing each other)

Serving counter: 12 inches for pot plus 12 inches for each plate

Minimum landing space:

Cooktop or range: 18 inches of heatproof noncombustible countertop to left and right; longer if pans longer

Cooktop or range on island: 6 inches behind cooktop in addition to left and right

Oven: 18 inches of heatproof countertop next to oven that opens from bottom; opposite hinged side or on shelf below oven that opens to the side; on island or counter across from oven if not passageway; pullout board between double ovens, longer if pans longer

Microwave: 18 inches adjacent to microwave opposite hinge side; on counter below undercabinet microwave or above one installed in a base cabinet; on pullout board below microwave installed on countertop

Refrigerator with top or bottom freezer: 18 inches next to handle side (opposite hinge side)

Side-by-side refrigerator: 18 inches on each side or, preferably, on island or counter no more than 4 feet across from opening of side-by-side

Primary sink: 24–36 inches on dishwasher side, 18–36 inches on other side, right-handed should leave more space to right of sink, left-handed to left

Secondary sink: 18 inches on each side

Height of countertop:

Standard: 36 inches from floor to work surface

Ideal: 3 inches below bent elbow for most tasks

Baking: 28 inches or 6–7 inches below elbows of extended arms for rolling or kneading dough

Depth of countertop:

Standard: 24 inches (varies according to depth of adjacent appliances)

Minimum: 19 inches

With appliance garage or upper cabinet sitting on countertop: 30 inches

Baking: 18–24-inch peninsula (three-sided access)

Island: 42 inches wide if two people working together

Backsplash

Standard: 4 inches on premanufactured countertops

Countertop to bottom of wall cabinets: 15–18 inches

Custom: Taller if storing tall appliances

Cooktop

Gas:

Width: 12–48 inches

1-burner: 12–15 inches

2-burner: 15–22 inches

4-burner: 30–36 inches

5-burner: 30–36 inches

6-burner: 42–48 inches

Height: 2–17 inches

Electric:

Width: 12–47 inches

1-burner: 11–15 inches

2-burner: 11–23 inches

4-burner: 30–36 inches

5-burner: 36 inches

6-burner: 45–47 inches

Height: 2–19 inches

Installation:

Standard: 36 inches from floor

Comfortable: 30–32 inches from floor or custom height; allows view of tall pots

Clearance:

2-foot clearance between cooking surface and non-combustible surface above (may vary according to local code)

2½-foot clearance between cooking surface and combustible surface above

2-foot clearance between cooking surface and non-combustible material on each side; no wood, plastic, or curtains

Additional clearances as recommended by manufacturer and codes

Range

Height: 36 inches (floor to cooking surface)

Backsplash: 5 inches with control panel

Width: 30–36 inches (commercial style to 60)

Depth: 24 inches (commercial style 28–32)

Access space: 36 inches for door opening and bending clearance plus 26 inches for traffic

Gas outlet: 26 inches from floor

Clearances: Same as cooktop and as recommended by manufacturer and local codes

Built-in Wall Oven

(Single electric, single gas with separate broiler, microwave oven and regular oven combo, and double oven)

Height: 10–57 inches

Width: 22–36 inches

Depth: 22–25 inches

Installation: Oven floor should be 1–3 inches below bent-elbow height; when stacked double ovens are used, upper oven should be at this height or frame between the two ovens at 36 inches off floor

Controls: At eye level

Clearances: As recommended by manufacturer and local codes

Full-Size Microwave

Height: 11–17 inches

Width: 18½–30 inches

Depth: 14–19 inches

Installation:

Standard: 42–44 inches off the floor; bottom of shelf below eye level

Safest: 3 inches below top of shoulder in general; 6 inches below shoulder for the elderly; below counter for children

Clearances: As recommended by manufacturer

Distance from radio and television: 60 inches

Ventilation Hood

Minimum capacity: 300 CFM; 600 for barbecue (to compute precisely, see page 260)

Loudness: Less than 9 sones, preferably 7

Height: Depends on whether hung from wall, ceiling, or soffit

Length: 3 inches longer than the cooktop on each side (6 inches for commercial, grill, or island installation)

Depth: Deep enough from front to back to cover burners completely; add 3 inches depth for grill or island installation

Installation: Bottom of hood 21–30 inches above cooking surface

Duct turns: Should not equal more than 180 degrees; none greater than 45 degrees

Ceiling Fan

Installation: 1 foot below ceiling joist; 7 feet above anything that interferes with blade movement

Sink

Length:

   Single: 7–24 inches (minimum 15 inches for garbage disposer)

   Double: 33–43 inches

   Triple: 43–63 inches

Width:

   Standard: 22 inches including faucet ledge

Depth: 5–12 inches

Installation:

   Front access: 20 inches

   Side access: 18 inches from edge of sink to counter at right angle

   Height: May want to raise countertop 2 inches if sink is deep

   Plumbing moved: No more than 4 feet

   Maximum distance between trap and vent: 30 inches for fixture using 1/4-inch pipe, 6 feet maximum for 3-inch pipe, 10 feet for 4-inch pipe, etc.

   Waste removal: Slope 1/4 inch for every horizontal foot

Disposer

Drain height from floor to waste disposer: 17–19 inches

Dishwasher

Portable:

Height: 36 inches

Width: 25–28 inches

Depth: 27 inches

Built-ins:

Height: 32 1/2–35 1/2 inches; adjustable

Width: 18 and 24 inches

Depth: 24 inches; some protrude to 26 1/4 inches

Installation: To fit under countertop 34–36 inches high; 24 inches deep

   Distance from sink: No further than 30 inches or according to manufacturer and codes

   Off floor: Line up with toe kick

   Raised dishwasher: 18 inches between edge of sink and raised dishwasher; 14–24 inches above floor

   Door opening: 24–25 inches plus 22 inches for standing in front

   Loading space: 21 inches between edge of open dishwasher door and counter at right angle

Trash Compactor

Height: 21–35 inches

Width: 12, 15, or 18 inches

Depth: 18–24 inches

Installation: 24–30 inches in front to pull out trash compactor receptacle

Refrigerator

Most usable space: 22–56 inches above floor

Cubic feet: Divided differently between refrigerator and freezer

Refrigerator or refrigerator/freezer combo installation:

   Top and side clearances: As recommended by manufacturers

Side clearance for lock: 2 1/4 inches

Door opening clearance: 90 degrees or more

Door opening space: 36 inches for opening; side-by-side requires 1 foot less clearance

Convenient: Elevate refrigerator with no freezer 34 inches off floor

All Refrigerator:

   Height: 84 inches

   Width: 18–48 inches

   Depth: 24–35

   Cubic feet: 10–31.6

Top-Mount:

   Height: 57–72 inches

   Width: 18–36 inches

   Depth: 24–34 inches

   Cubic feet: 10–26

Bottom-Mount:

   Height: 66–84 inches

   Width: 24–36 inches

   Depth: 24–34 inches

   Cubic feet: 10–25

Side-by-Side:

   Height: 66–84 inches

   Width: 30–48 inches

Depth: 24–34 inches

Cubic feet: 17–30

Compact Top-Mount:

    Height: 18–35 inches

    Width: 19–30 inches

    Depth: 20–27 inches

    Cubic feet: 2–8

Compact Side-by-Side:

    Height: 34 inches

    Width: 36 inches

    Depth: 24 inches

    Cubic feet: 5

Compact All Refrigerator:

    Height: 25–35 inches

    Width: 15–24 inches

    Depth: 21–25 inches

    Cubic feet: 3–6

Compact All Freezer:

    Height: 25–35 inches

    Width: 15–24 inches

    Depth: 23–32 inches

    Cubic feet: 4–5

Freezer

Upright:

    Height: 51–84 inches

    Width: 18–36 inches

    Depth: 24–35 inches

    Cubic feet: 11–25

Chest:

    Height: 35–37 inches

    Height with lid open:
    55–63 inches

    Width: 23–72 inches

    Depth: 23–31 inches

    Cubic feet: 6–28

Wine Refrigerators

    Height: 28–81 inches

    Width: 20–25 inches

    Depth: 18–48 inches

    Capacity: 24–192 bottles

Icemaker

    Height: 14–29 inches

    Width: 18–35 inches

    Depth: 21–35 inches

    Capacity: 20–35 pounds

Lighting

Fluorescent: 60–80 watts of illumination per 50 square feet of floor surface (per American Institute of Kitchen Designers)

Incandescent: 175–200 watts of illumination per 50 square feet of floor surface (per American Institute of Kitchen Designers)

Foot-candles: 50–75 recommended for most kitchens

Ceiling fixture: When providing both general and task lighting, install 18 inches from front of cabinets

Cove: Minimum of 12 inches below ceiling

Accent lighting: three times intensity of general lighting

    Accent track lights: 24–30 inches from corner of wall, swiveled to 30 degree angle

    Wall grazing: Installed within 1 foot of wall

    Wall washing: Installed 3–4 feet from wall

Undercabinet lighting: 8 watts per foot of counter length to cover at least two-thirds of counter

Counter: Hang fixture 24 inches above; wattage same as under cabinet

Worktable or island: Space pendant fixtures or recessed cans

15–18 inches apart with 75-watt reflector bulbs

Dining table: Hang fixture 25–30 inches above with 3 additional inches every foot ceiling is above 8 feet

    Chandelier: 6 inches narrower than table

    Chandelier lamps: 120 watts of incandescence or 32–40 watts of fluorescence

Range hood: 40 watts for 30–36-inch cooktop

Above the sink: 60 watts of fluorescent lighting or two 75-watt incandescent floods placed 15–18 inches apart

Kitchen desk: Lamp shade bottom rim stands 15 inches above desk, 12 inches back from front edge, and 15 inches from center of writing papers; uses 32-watt fluorescent or 150–225-watt incandescent bulb

Low voltage transformer: Remoted up to 20 feet

Light switches: 48 inches from floor

Dining

Total space for table, chairs, and people: 12–15 square feet per person (49 square feet for 4)

Table or counter space: 24–26 inches per person

Round table for 4: 3-foot diameter

Round table for 6: 4-foot diameter

Rectangular table for 6: 3 × 5 feet

Table space with armchairs: 2 inches plus width of chair

Table depth: 15 inches per person; 30 inches with two people eating across from each other at a table; 21 inches when dining area is behind cooktop on an island

Countertop dining depth: Countertop width plus 8 inches for overhang

To pull out chair and rise from table: 32–36 inches

Space to walk behind chair: 3 feet

Chair space with no walkway behind: 24 inches

Space to serve behind table: 44 inches

Banquettes:

> **Height:** 18 inches
>
> **Front edges:** Extend 3–4 inches under table surface

Height:

> **Table:** 28–32 inches (29–30 inches for children) 18-inch chairs and 20 inches leg room
>
> **Countertop:** 36 inches 24- 25-inch stools and 15 inches leg room
>
> **Bar:** 42–48 inches 30- 33-inch stools with 12 inches leg room and footrests or rails 18–20 inches below seat

Office

Desk:

> **Height:** 30 inches
>
> **Depth:** 54 inches (24-inch desk plus 30 inches to pull out chair)

Typewriter/computer:

> **Height:** 26–30 inches off floor; custom measure
>
> **Monitor:** 6 inches above keyboard

Electrical Outlets

General height: 48⅝ inches below 8-foot ceiling covered with ⅝-inch-thick drywall; 40 inches from seated position

Countertop height: 8½ inches above countertop every 4 feet of countertop

Heating Thermostat:

48 inches above floor

Laundry:

Washing machine:

> **Height:** 60 inches (stacking)
>
> **Width:** 24–30 inches

Built-in Ironing Board: 18-inch-wide drawer

GUIDELINES FOR WHEELCHAIR OPERATION

Kitchen Shape: U or L preferred shape

Doorways: 32 inches wide

Aisles: 5 × 5-foot space in center of kitchen for unobstructed U-shape turning radius; 4-foot-wide unobstructed passageways

Countertop:

> **Height:** 29–32 inches
>
> **Length:** Continuous so items can easily be moved along
>
> **Depth:** 27–30 inches so wheelchair can roll underneath
>
> **Overhang:** 12 inches to accommodate 12-inch-deep footrest, or recess toe kick 10–12 inches or angle counter 130–160 degrees

Refrigerator: Side-by-side or compact under-counter refrigeration with a height of 29 inches

Sink:

> **Sink countertop height:** 29–32 inches
>
> **Sink countertop width:** 27–30 inches for sliding wheelchair underneath
>
> **Sink depth:** 5 inches
>
> **Sink drain:** Rear placement

> **Installation:** Faucet holes on right (or left) rather than in back
>
> Insulation around plumbing so no burns

Dishwasher: Raise 1½–2½ feet

Cooktop:

> **Height:** 29–32 inches
>
> **Width:** 27–30 inches for sliding wheelchair underneath
>
> **Control panels:** On front
>
> **Installation:** Mirror over cooktop to see back of pans

Oven:

> **Door opening:** Side
>
> **Control panels:** On front

Microwave: Below counter

Cabinet:

> **Base cabinets:** Use primarily; if standard height, install pullout cutting boards at 30 inches: cut hole in center of board to accommodate and stabilize a bowl
>
> **Doors:** Narrow with piano hinges, bifold pockets, or flipper doors
>
> **Shelves:** Open or pullout
>
> **Depth:** 6 inches

Hardware: Touch latches near top of base cabinets

Floor: Commercial linoleum that won't groove; with tile, use a thin grout line so tiles are close together

Dining Table: 29–32 inches high

Lighting: Switches that slide up and down and can be operated with cane or stick

Electrical outlets and switches: 40 inches off floor and up to 16 inches from edge of countertop

13
REMODELING CONTRACTS

These remodeling contracts, drawn up by the firm of Anker & Hymes, are meant to be sample contracts for you to incorporate into your remodeling contract and are in no way meant to constitute legal advice. Your contracts will vary according to local codes and laws. Before deciding what you want your contract to include, reread pages 43–53.

Some wise words from Jonathan L. Rosenbloom, the lawyer who drew up these contracts: "The best and most important step that a homeowner can take is establishing a good relationship with contractors and designers with good reputations. The best contract in the world is not necessarily one that favors the homeowner overwhelmingly over the contractor/designer; rather, it is the contract that is fair to both sides and promotes a cooperative relationship between the parties. The best contract will not turn a bad contractor into a good one; the bad contractor will simply breach. A homeowner will go much further by establishing a cooperative relationship with the contractor/designer and keeping in mind (within reason, of course) that people's children do get sick, suppliers will misread $5/8$ inch for $3/8$ inch, and workers might not always wipe their feet at the door.

"If you play football, you should expect to be bumped and tripped; if you remodel your house, something is bound to be late or not quite right. I certainly do not advocate throwing your hands in the air and letting the chips fall where they may; however, the best combination is a comprehensive, clear contract that is secondary to an owner/contractor/designer relationship based upon fairness, loyalty, and trust."

CONTRACTOR'S CONTRACT FOR KITCHEN REMODELING BY ANKER & HYMES

A Law Corporation
Encino, California

CONTRACTOR'S KITCHEN IMPROVEMENT CONTRACT

This Contract is made by and between_____("Owner") and
_____doing business as_____
("Contractor").

Contractor is a duly licensed Contractor, whose State License Number is_____. The names, addresses, telephone, fax, and pager numbers of the parties to this Agreement, any subcontractors that Contractor utilizes on this project and any other parties involved with this project are set forth on Addendum "A," which is incorporated herein by this reference.

Contractor will construct, on behalf of Owner, a project as described in Paragraph 1 below. The project is located at_____, in the City of_____, County of_____, State of_____.

I. *Scope of the Work:* Contractor will furnish all labor, equipment, materials, scaffolding, building permits, trash removal, sales taxes, hoisting, transportation, supervision, coordination, communication, shop drawings, and storage to complete in a first-class and workmanlike manner the following work, in conformity with all applicable building codes and regulations:_____

_____

_____

2. *Exclusions:* Owner understands and agrees that the following items and services are excluded from the Contract price of the project and will be billed separately. The parties understand and agree that items not listed below shall be deemed included:_____

_____

_____

3. *Work and Materials by Owner:* The parties understand and agree that Owner shall provide the following materials and services, no later than the respective dates set forth below, for which Contractor will neither charge nor be responsible:_____

_____

_____

4. *Warranties:* Contractor shall retain and transmit to Owner all warranties covering the materials and equipment installed on the project. Contractor additionally warrants his work against defects in materials and workmanship unconditionally for a period of one year after completion of the project.

5. *Contract, Drawings and Specifications:* The project will be constructed according to drawings and specifications which the parties have reviewed and initialed and which are hereby made a part of this Contract. The Contract, drawings, and specifications are intended to supplement each other. In case of conflict, however, the specifications shall control the drawings, and the provisions of the Contract control both.

6. *Subcontractors:* The choice of Subcontractors, including cabinetmakers, shall remain within Contractor's sole discretion. Owner's availability permitting, Contractor shall personally introduce Owner to all Subcontractors hired to work on the project. Owner, Contractor, and Subcontractor shall review together the work that Subcontractor is to perform and shall formulate the parties' respective responsibilities for production, delivery, and installation, as applicable.

7. *Time for Completion of Work:* Within____calendar days after the execution of this Contract, materials will be ordered no later than____, and Contractor will be notified of both the order date and the delivery date. _____will be responsible for the ordering of the materials, and_____will be responsible for the delivery of the materials. No later than____days after the arrival of materials and cabinets, Owner will have the job site ready for commencement of construction. Demolition shall commence____days after. Contractor shall commence work within____calendar days thereafter and shall complete the work within____calendar days after commencement, subject to delays approved by Owner. Contractor understands and agrees that this Contract will be null and void if work does not commence by _____ and continue, without stoppage, to completion. The parties understand and agree that a "work-week" is five days long; that a "work-day" is____hours long, and that work shall commence each day at_____A.M. This schedule may be altered only in writing and with the consent of Contractor and Owner.

8. *Preparation:* Owner will arrange for the packing and storage of all personal property affected by the project. Owner and Contractor will arrange to ensure the safety of Owner's pets and children and the continued delivery of Owner's mail.

9. *Building Permits, Charges, and Exactions:* Contractor will provide and pay for all necessary building permits. The parties anticipate that the permits listed below will be necessary to complete the project in accordance with all applicable laws, and Owner will reimburse Contractor for the cost of securing such permits:

_____

_____

10. *Labor and Material:* Contractor shall pay all verified charges for labor and material that Contractor incurs and that are used in the construction of the project.

All materials used must comply with industry standards of excellence and must correspond to those listed on the bid. Time and Owner's availability permitting, Contractor shall allow Owner to inspect and approve all materials. Unused materials shall be returned to vendors where possible or given to the Owner. The Owner shall set forth below any materials that are to be saved during demolition and used in the project: _____

_____

_____

11. *Payment:* For all services that Contractor performs, Owner will pay Contractor the Contract price of $_____. Contractor may receive a down payment of _____ from Owner only if Contractor has submitted a work payment schedule to Owner. Contractor will submit to Owner, on or before the last day of each week, an application for payment showing the percentage of completion of the various portions of the work as outlined in the work and payment schedule. On or before Wednesday of the next week, Owner will pay Contractor 90% of the value of the work completed. Owner will not be liable for any additional charges other than mutually agreed-upon change orders. If Contractor does not receive payment when due, he can seek all remedies available to him under applicable mechanic's lien laws.

12. *Final Payment:* Fifty percent (50%) of the final payment will be due when the punch list is completed, subject to inspection and approval by Owner. The remaining fifty percent (50%) will be due thirty (30) days later. If corrective or repair work remains to be accomplished on the punch list by Contractor after the project is ready for occupancy or utilization, Contractor will perform such work within 30 days or forfeit final retention payment. Owner may then hire someone else to complete this work.

13. *Reduction of, and Payment of, Retention:* Owner will promptly sign and record a Notice of Completion when the project is complete. The retention will be paid to Contractor 35 calendar days after the Notice of Completion is recorded.

14. *Extra Work:* Should Owner, construction lender, or any public agency or inspector direct any deletion from, or modification of, or addition to, the work covered by this Contract, the cost shall be added to or deducted from the Contract price. Any such changes must be in writing. In the case of extra work, Contractor will be paid____for its overhead and ____% for profit. Payments for extra work will be made as extra work progresses, concurrently with progress payments. Orders for extra work should be made in writing, with the price agreed to in advance.

15. *Change Orders:* Change orders must be approved in writing by Owner and Contractor. The work and ensuing changes must be fully described in writing, along with a breakdown of the price, at what point it is to be paid, and the person responsible for making the changes. Scheduling adjustments arising from the change order must also be in writing and approved by Owner.

16. *Allowances:* If the Contract price includes allowances, and the cost of performing the work covered by an allowance is either greater or less than the allowance, then the Contract price shall be increased or decreased accordingly. Unless Owner otherwise requests in writing, Contractor shall use its judgment in accomplishing work covered by an allowance. If Owner requests that work covered by an allowance be accomplished in such a way that the cost will exceed the allowance, Contractor will comply with Owner's request, provided that Owner provides for the additional cost in advance.

17. *Insurance by Owner:* Contractor will produce, at its own expense and before the commencement of work hereunder, a copy of a valid policy of "all risk" insurance with course of construction, theft, vandalism, and malicious mischief endorsements attached, in a sum at least equal to the Contract price. The insurance will name the Owner and all Subcontractors as additional insureds and will be written to protect Owner, Contractor, and Subcontractors as their interests may appear. Should Contractor fail to procure such insurance, Owner may do so at the expense of Owner, but is not required to do so. If the project is destroyed or damaged by accident, disaster, or calamity, such as fire, storm, flood, landslide, subsidence, or earthquake, Owner shall pay for work performed by Contractor in rebuilding or restoring the project as extra work. If Contractor is directly or indirectly responsible for destruction of the project, Contractor shall reconstruct the same at his own expense.

18. *Contractor's Insurance:* Contractor and its Subcontractors of every tier will provide Owner the following insurance policies, along with Certificates of Insurance:

    a. Comprehensive general liability insurance, in standard form, with limits of $500,000 for bodily injury for each occurrence and in the aggregate, and limits of $500,000 for property damage for each occurrence and in the aggregate;

    b. Automobile liability insurance in comprehensive form, including coverage for owned, hired, and nonowned automobiles, with limits of $500,000 for each occurrence and in the aggregate;

    c. Workers' compensation insurance in statutory form.

19. *Communication:* Owner, Contractor and Designer (if any) agree to make themselves available for meetings no less than once a week, from the date of demolition to the date of completion of the proj-ect. These meetings shall be either by telephone or in person, subject to the availability of the parties. At these meetings, Contractor will apprise Designer and Owner of progress and upcoming inspections, as applicable. Subject to scheduling conflicts, these meetings shall take place on_____of each week at_____A.M./P.M. Contractor will also be in telephone contact with Owner daily.

The parties understand and agree that Contractor shall communicate with Owner directly and with Designer, if any.

Contractor (and Owners who work away from the site) shall wear and respond as quickly as possible to a pager, the numbers of which are set forth on Addendum "A."

Contractor shall spend no less than____hours per day at the project site and, in any event, shall be at the project at the following time and day: _____ When Contractor is not present, _____ will be in charge of the work site.

20. *Notices:* All notices called for herein shall be in writing, sent by first-class mail or facsimile transmission, to the parties' address set forth on Addendum "A" of this Agreement.

21. *Default:* If Owner defaults on any of its obligations under this Contract, Contractor may recover, as damages, either the reasonable value of the work performed by Contractor, or the balance of the Contract price, plus any other damages sustained as a result of Owner's default.

22. *Delay:* Contractor shall be excused for delay in completion of the Contract caused by acts of God, inclement weather, extra work, failure of the Owner to make progress payments promptly, or other contingencies unforeseen by Contractor and beyond the reasonable control of Contractor.

Contractor realizes that Owner will suffer damages as a result of Contractor's delay. Determining the amount of such damages would be difficult and impractical. Accordingly, the parties agree that, if such a delay occurs, Contractor will pay Owner $_____per day as liquidated damages.

If Contractor does not maintain the work pace set forth herein Contractor shall, upon receipt of written notice from Owner, immediately increase its working force and speed of delivery of materials necessary to maintain progress satisfactory to Owner. The parties agree that time is of the essence with respect to this Contract. If, within one week after receipt of written notice from Owner, Contractor has failed to institute remedial action to maintain progress satisfactory to Owner or to correct any defects, failures, or complaints with respect to labor and/or materials furnished, Owner shall have the right to:

a. Terminate Contractor's right to proceed with any of the work and let the work to another contractor or contractors and charge any increase in the cost of completion to Contractor;

b. Terminate this entire Contract and pay to Contractor only the reasonable value of the work in place, providing that the quality of work is satisfactory, and providing that Contractor has paid all of its bills and discharged all of its obligations in connection with the work.

Owner may choose any, some, or all of the foregoing remedies and conditions.

23. *Bonus:* As an incentive to finish early, Owner shall pay Contractor $_____for each day before the projected completion date that the proj-ect is complete.

24. *Concealed Conditions and Defects:* If Contractor or Subcontractor should encounter concealed conditions that they did not reasonably anticipate, such as rock, concrete or structures, they will call such conditions to the attention of Owner immediately, and the Contract price will be accordingly adjusted for such extra work. The same applies to design errors and product defects. Contractor or Subcontractors must inform Owner of the condition or defect before work begins on the task in question, and Owner must indicate in writing his/her willingness to proceed. Contractor is liable for rectifying design errors and product defects not disclosed to Owner.

25. *Cleanup:* At all times during the progress of the work, and upon completion of the work, Contractor will clean up the job site and remove debris and surplus material. The job site will be kept in a neat and broom-clean condition. Contractor will use best efforts to keep dirt, dust, and debris away from portions of Owner's home not affected by the project. Contractor will dispose of debris and broom-clean the area of the project at the end of each workday. Contractor will comply with all applicable hazardous waste removal laws.

26. *Security:* Contractor will lock up and secure the worksite at the end of each workday. Contractor will use best efforts to prevent injury on or from the project. Contractor will use best efforts to ensure that fixtures, materials, and tools are not stolen from the worksite. Work-related equipment and materials, shall be stored in the following areas :_____

_____

_____

27. *Accommodations at Worksite:* Contractor shall provide, at Contractor's expense, portable toilet facilities. Owner shall provide, at Owner's expense, a telephone line for Contractor and his/her workers. This line shall be supervised by Contractor's foreman, who shall maintain a log of long-distance and toll calls, for which Owner shall be reimbursed if they are non–work related.

28. *Attorney's Fees:* If either party becomes involved in litigation arising out of this Contract or the performance thereof, the prevailing party, as determined by the court, shall be entitled to attorney's fees and costs.

29. *Assignment:* Neither party may assign this Contract, or the proceeds thereof, without written consent of the other party.

30. *Binding on Successors:* All of the provisions of this Contract will be binding on the assignees, successors, parent companies, and subsidiary companies of both parties. If either party is acquired by a corporation through purchase, merger, or consolidation, the provisions of this Contract will be binding on the successor or surviving corporation.

Dated:_____

"Owner"

By_____

"Contractor"

By_____

ADDENDUM "A"
TELEPHONE NUMBERS AND ADDRESSES OF PARTIES AND OTHERS WORKING ON PROJECT

Owner_____	**Contractor**_____
Address_____	**Address**_____
_____	_____
Phone_____	**Phone**_____
Facsimile_____	**Facsimile**_____
Pager_____	**Pager**_____
	Subcontractor_____
	Address_____
	_____

Subcontractor_____   **Subcontractor**_____

Address_____   **Address**_____

_____   _____

Phone_____   **Phone**_____

Facsimile_____   **Facsimile**_____

Pager_____   **Pager**_____

DESIGNER'S (ARCHITECT'S) CONTRACT FOR KITCHEN REMODELING BY ANKER & HYMES

A Law Corporation
Encino, California

DESIGNER'S KITCHEN IMPROVEMENT CONTRACT

This Contract is made and entered into this _____ day of _____ 19_____ by and between_____ ("Owner") and_____ doing business as _____ ("Designer").

In consideration of the mutual covenants and agreements herein contained to be well and faithfully performed by the Parties, the Parties agree as follows:

1. *Project:* Owner does hereby employ and engage Designer under the terms and conditions in this Contract to perform for Owner all professional services incident to the preparation of plans and the design of a kitchen remodeling project, referred to as "the Project."

2. *Owner's Obligations:* Owner further agrees as follows:

    a. To give Designer the approximate cost limitations of the Project.

    b. To furnish information concerning the general dimensions of the Project, together with all available information concerning existing water and gas lines, electric and telephone services, ductwork, and other pertinent information.

    c. To give thorough consideration to all sketches, estimates, working drawings, specifications, proposals, and other documents that Designer submits, and to inform the Designer of Owner's decisions within the work schedule provided by the Designer so as not to interrupt or delay the work of the Designer.

3. *Designer's Obligations:* Designer agrees to perform all necessary professional services in connection with the design of the Project. Specifically, but without limitation, Designer agrees to perform the following services, in accordance with the deadlines set forth on Addendum "A" of this Agreement:

    a. To take exact specific measurements of the site.

    b. To prepare schematic drawings incorporating the aesthetic and functional requirements that Owner or Contractor furnishes until such drawings meet with Owner's approval and authorization.

    c. To establish a schedule for completing the design process once Owner signs off on schematic drawings.

    d. To prepare preliminary plans in accordance with the approved schematic drawings, including floor plans, sections, prospective outline specifications, detailed cost estimates and other drawings that Owner may require to indicate fully the probable cost and the general nature, arrangement and appearance of the Project.

e. To submit these preliminary plans and specifications to Owner and Contractor engaged at this point for their review and to make the changes that they request. If the detailed cost estimates indicate that the Project may exceed by more than 10% the cost limitations that Owner provided, Designer agrees to make any corrections or revisions to the preliminary plans and outline specifications as necessary to bring the estimated project cost within such cost limitations. There shall be no extra compensation for such corrections or revisions.

f. To prepare working drawings, elevations, perspective renderings, an electric and lighting plan, and complete specifications in such detail as may be required to obtain competitive bidding, said drawings and specifications to be an amplification of the preliminary drawings and outline specifications that Owner approved. These drawings and specifications shall be full and complete so as to enable Owner to enter into a contract with a Contractor. All plans and specifications are to be in full compliance with applicable building codes, ordinances, or other lawful regulatory authority.

g. Designer agrees to submit the final working drawings and specifications in their entirety to Owner for final review and corrective suggestions.

h. Designer shall manage the bidding process by furnishing all necessary copies of plans and specifications for bidders and contractors and five copies for Owner during the process of bidding and construction and shall, before receiving final payment from the Owner, deliver to Owner all tracings of working drawings and details.

i. Designer must incorporate suggestions into the Plan that are made by contractors bidding on the job and desired by the Owner, and any demands made by the office of building and safety. No further compensation will be made to the Designer for any of these alterations in the plans.

j. Designer shall participate in interviews with the bidders if so desired by Owner.

k. Designer shall, during the conduct of this work, at all times permit Owner or proper persons designated by Owner to view the plans under preparation.

l. To assign in perpetuity all proprietary rights to all of the plans described in this section to the Owner.

4. *Designer's Supervision:* Designer shall thereafter supervise the construction through the completion with thoroughness and fidelity. Designer shall visit the site at least once a week during construction to evaluate quality and compliance with plans, and participate in all meetings and conferences with Owner and the Contractor at which either Owner or Contractor requests the Designer's participation. If a construction problem arises because of an error in the Designer's Plan, the Designer must rework the plan to eliminate the error with no further compensation.

5. *Remuneration:* Owner shall pay Designer a total fee of $_____ for Designer's Services. Designer shall provide Owner with a monthly statement detailing Designer's professional services rendered. With the completion of each step set forth on Addendum "A," Owner shall pay Designer the corresponding percentage of the fee charged.

Retention Fee: The Owner holds 10% of the fee out from each agreed payment period to be paid in full when items on the Contractor's punch list total less than 1% of the construction fee.

If Owner or Designer wants to terminate the contract after several tries at schematic drawings, Owner must pay Designer 3 percent of the contract instead of the 5 percent allotted for schematic drawings.

In addition, Owner agrees to pay Designer a_____% markup on all materials and fixtures that the

Designer purchases. Designer shall first obtain the Owner's approval for any purchase in excess of $_____. Designer shall then provide Owner with an invoice showing Designer's cost for each item.

Construction Supervision: Payment of this fee is pegged incrementally to completed phases of the Contractor's work schedule.

6. *Termination:* Either Owner or Designer can terminate this contract after the Schematic Drawings are made or when either party is two weeks beyond a deadline on the Designer's Work Schedule.

7. *Attorney's Fees:* If either party becomes involved in litigation arising out of this Contract or the performance thereof, the prevailing party, as determined by the court, shall be entitled to attorney's fees and costs.

8. *Assignment:* Neither party may assign this Contract, or the proceeds thereof, without written consent of the other party.

9. *Binding on Successors:* All of the provisions of this Contract will be binding on the assignees, successors, parent companies, and subsidiary companies of both parties. If either party is acquired by a corporation through purchase, merger, or consolidation, the provisions of this Contract will be binding on the successor or surviving corporation.

Dated:_____

"Owner"

By_____

"Designer"

By_____

ADDENDUM "A"
DESIGNER'S SCHEDULE

TASK	DEADLINE	PERCENTAGE PAID
1. Submission of schematic drawings		5
2. Submission of design development drawings		25
3. Submission of construction drawings, elevations, and perspective renderings to owner, and submission of plans		50
4. Specifications to bidders and conduction of bidding process		20

PAYMENT DUE DATE

    1. After owner approval

    2. After owner approval

    3. After feedback incorporated into plans from plan check and bidding and owner approval secured.

    4. After owner approval.

SELECTED BIBLIOGRAPHY

BOOKS

■

Advanced Design Notes. Wood-Mode, Inc.

Bianchina, Paul. *Illustrated Dictionary of Building Materials and Techniques*. New York: John Wiley & Sons, Inc., 1993.

Cheever, Ellen. *Kitchen Equipment and Materials, Kitchen Industry Technical Manual, Volume 3*. Hackettstown, NJ: National Kitchen & Bath Association and University of Illinois Small Homes Council–Building Research Council, 1992.

Clark, Sam. *The Motion-Minded Kitchen*. Boston: Houghton Mifflin Company, 1983.

Conran, Terence. *The Kitchen Book*. New York: Crown Publishers Inc., 1977.

Consumer Reports Books: Guide to Kitchen Equipment. Mount Vernon, NY: Consumers Union of United States, 1986.

Cowan, Thomas. *Beyond the Kitchen: A Dreamer's Guide*. Philadelphia: Running Press, 1985.

Davidson, Alan, ed. *The Cook's Room*. New York: HarperCollins, 1991.

Davis, Jo, and Ann Otto. *Kitchen Decisions*. Los Angeles: unpublished, 1982.

Editors of Consumer Guide. *Whole Kitchen Catalog*. New York: Simon & Schuster, 1978.

Effron, Edward. *Planning & Designing Lighting*. New York: Little, Brown, 1986.

Fox, Jill, ed. *Designing and Remodeling Kitchens*. San Francisco: Ortho Books, 1990.

Goldbeck, David. *The Smart Kitchen*. Woodstock, NY: Ceres Press, 1989.

Grey, Johnny. *The Art of Kitchen Design*. London: Cassell, 1994.

Hamilton, Gene and Katie. *How to Be Your Own Contractor*. New York: Collier Books, 1991.

Harland, Edward. *Eco-Renovation*. Post Mills, VA.: Chelsea Green Publishing Company, 1993.

How to Design & Remodel Kitchens. Anne Coolman, project editor; Jenepher Walker, writer. San Ramon, CA: Ortho Books, 1982.

Jernigan, Anna Katherine, and Lynne Nannen Ross. *Food Service Equipment*. 3rd ed. Ames, IA: Iowa State University Press, 1989.

Kafka, Barbara. *Microwave Gourmet*. New York: William Morrow, 1987.

Kidder, Tracy. *House*. New York: Avon Books, 1985.

Kitchens by Professional Kitchen Designers, Volumes I, II, III, and IV. Palm Springs, CA: Kasmar Publications, Inc., 1990–1993.

Knott, Mary Fisher, consultant. *Creative Ideas for Your Home Kitchens*. Los Angeles: The Knapp Press, 1984.

Knox. Gerald M., ed. *Better Homes and Gardens: Your Kitchen*. Des Moines: Meredith Corporation, 1983.

Krasner, Deborah. *Kitchens for Cooks*. New York: Viking Studio Books, 1994.

Macaulay, David. *The Way Things Work*. Boston: Houghton Mifflin Company, 1988.

McDonald, Marylee, Nicholas Geragi, and Ellen Cheever. *Building Materials, Construction and Estimating for the Kitchen and Bathroom, Kitchen*

Industry Technical Manual, Volume 1. Hackettstown, NJ: National Kitchen & Bath Association and University of Illinois Small Homes Council–Building Research Council, 1992.

———. *Kitchen Mechanical Systems, Kitchen Industry Technical Manual, Volume 2.* Hackettstown, NJ: National Kitchen & Bath Association and University of Illinois Small Homes Council–Building Research Council, 1992.

Madden, Chris Casson. *Kitchens.* New York: Clarkson Potter Publishers, 1993.

Modlin, Robert A., ed. *Commercial Kitchens.* 7th ed. Arlington, VA: American Gas Association, 1989.

Murrell, Robin. *Small Kitchens: Making Every Inch Count.* New York: Simon & Schuster, 1986.

Niles, Bo, and Juta Ristso. *Planning the Perfect Kitchen.* New York: Simon & Schuster, 1989.

Niles, Bo. *The Country Living Book of Country Kitchens.* New York: The Hearst Corporation, 1985.

Philbin, Tom. *How to Hire a Home Improvement Contractor Without Getting Chiseled.* New York: St. Martin's Press, 1991.

Pickett, Mary S., Mildred G. Arnold, and Linda E. Ketterer. *Household Equipment in Residential Design.* 9th ed. New York: John Wiley & Sons, 1986.

Rand, Ellen, Florence Perchuk, and the Editors of Consumer Reports Books. *Complete Book of Kitchen Design.* Yonkers, NY: Consumer Reports Books, 1991.

Rogers, Dorothy. *My Favorite Things: A Personal Guide to Decorating & Entertaining.* New York: Atheneum, 1964.

Shapiro, Cecile. *Better Kitchens.* Upper Saddle River, NJ: Creative Homeowner Press, 1980.

Silvers, Donald E. *Kitchen Design with Cooking in Mind.* Tarzana: NMI Publishers, 1994.

Steinman, David. "How to Choose Safe Foods for You and Your Family." In *Diet for a Poisoned Planet.* New York: Harmony, 1990.

Vandervort, Don. *Home Magazine's How Your House Works.* New York: Ballantine Books, 1995.

Wise, Herbert H. *Kitchen Detail.* New York: Quick Fox, 1980.

Woodson, R. Dodge. *Remodeling Kitchens & Baths.* New York: Sterling Publishing Co., Inc., 1994.

ARTICLES

■

"A Sound Alternative to Hardwood," *Furniture Design & Manufacturing* (September 1994): 66–68.

Abdulazid, Sam K. "Building a Case for Trained Arbitrators," *Reeves Journal* (October 1993): 8.

Adams, Muriel. "Plastic Laminate: A Surface for the Whole House," *Home* (October 1992): 68–70.

Andrews, John. "Fridge Makers Design for the Future," *Custom Builder* (November/December 1992): 98–100.

Arnold, Don. "Things You Should Know About Upscale Products," *Plumbing & Mechanical* (March 1991): 28–34.

Arnott, Ann. "Finding the Right Place for Your Microwave," *Home* (September 1985): 38.

Averill, William R. "Putting a Priority on Slip-Resistant Tile," *Sun Coast* (February 1991): W-3.

Barnhart, Roy. "Building Inspector Blues." *Remodeling* (July 1994): 62–65.

Bellamy, Gail. "Lighting Niceties & Necessities," *Restaurant Hospitality* (August 1993): 144–148.

Benton, Janice. "Designing to Create Space," *Sun Coast* (June 1989): W-37.

Best, Don. "Building by the Book," *Home* (October 1995): 120–124.

———. "A Contract for Success," *Home* (October 1993): 50–56.

———. "Creating Homes to Last a Lifetime," *Home* (February 1993): 48–54.

Bittman, Mark. "Microwaves on Trial," *Cook's* (June 1989): 36.

Blaun, Randi. "Maximizing the Small-Space Kitchen," *The Cook's Magazine* (May/June 1988): 22–24.

Block, Morton M. "How to Build-In a Refrigerator," *Kitchen & Bath Design News* (January 1993): 34.

———. "Designing with Undermount Sinks," *Kitchen & Bath Design News* (December 1992): 15.

———. "Using Solid Surface Materials in Countertops," *Kitchen & Bath Design News* (February 1989): 20–21.

————. "Specifying Cabinet Hardware," *Cabinet Manufacturing & Fabrication* (May 1989): 20–21.

————. "Placing Doors Windows and Skylights," *Kitchen & Bath Design News* (July 1989), 28–29.

Brown, Patricia Leigh. "Linoleum: Can You Believe It's Coming Back?" *The New York Times* (March 10, 1988): C1, C6.

Brozda, Michael. "Porcelain Tiles," *Home* (September 1992): 74–76.

"Building On-Site: When All Else Fails," *Kitchen & Bath Design News* (November 1990): 46–47.

"Built-in Refrigerators," *Consumer Reports* (November 1988): 716–719.

Bukovinsky, Janet. "Ten Great Uses for the Microwave Oven," *Food & Wine* (April 1984): 14.

Burke, Veronica. "Pure & Simple Water Filters Sport New Designs," *Entrée* (January 1988): 35.

"Buying an Electric Range," *Consumer Reports* (July 1995): 475–479.

"California's New Window Labeling Procedures May Go Nationwide," *Sun Coast* (April 1992): C-4.

Caruso, Valerie. "Molding to the Rescue," *Kitchen & Bath Business* (February 1996): 32–36.

Castronova, John. "Cabinet Doors: A Business of Its Own," *Kitchen & Bath Design News* (March 1990): 96.

————. "Building Cabinets to Customer Specs," *Kitchen & Bath Design News* (November 1990): 54.

————. "Today's Cabinet Shop," *Kitchen & Bath Design News* (July 1990): 86.

————. "Steps to Ensure Hassle-Free Material Storage," *Kitchen & Bath Design News* (September 1989): 100–101.

————. "Choosing the Best Joining Method," *Kitchen & Bath Design News* (November 1989): 76.

Cheever, Ellen, "On the Floor," *Home* (December 1986): 26–28.

"Compact Microwave Ovens," *Consumer Reports* (November 1986): 708.

Costa, Janice Anne. "Necessities, Not Accessories," *Kitchen & Bath Design News* (August 1994): 30–31.

Culota, Nancy J. "Home Water Treatment: What's the Use of Point-of-Use?" *Health & Environment Digest* (July 1989, Volume 3, No. 6).

Daly, Peter. "Contractors Prevent Clashes," *Remodeling* (January 1996): 77–79.

Dean, Jacqueline. "Board Products Surviving Unscathed," *Cabinet Manufacturing & Fabrication* (April 1989): 50–53.

Deffenbaugh, Paul. "Getting the Lead Out," *Remodeling* (March 1993): 72–73.

————. "Heat at Your Feet," *Remodeling* (October 1992): 96–97.

————. "The Rating Game," *Remodeling* (January 1996): 92–96.

Dermansky, Ann. "Kitchens: Dollars & Sense Guide," *Kitchen & Bath Business* (October 1995): Special Section.

"Dishwashers," *Consumer Reports* (August 1995): 533–537.

"Dishwasher Update," *Consumer Reports* (October 1995): 669–671.

Donlin, Gina E. "Getting a Handle on Kitchen Design Trends," *Furniture Design & Manufacturing* (October 1995): 30–40.

————. "What to Expect from Waterbased Finishes," *CabinetMaker* (January/February 1994): 38–47.

"Do You Know Your Hardwoods?" *Furniture Design & Manufacturing* (December 1995): 80–87.

Fields, Margaret. "Upgrades Help Sell Sinks and Faucets," *Kitchen & Bath Design News* (January 1993): 41–43.

————. "New Techniques Widen Uses for Solid Surfaces," *Kitchen & Bath Design News* (January 1990): 74–77.

————. "Shops Moving Toward Increased Purchases of Cabinet Components," *Kitchen & Bath Design News* (May 1989): 87–89.

————. "Quality, Diversity Gaining Ground in Tile Flooring," *Kitchen & Bath Design News* (July 1989): 52–55.

————. "Skylights," *Kitchen & Bath Design News* (December 1988): 68–70.

"Finding and Keeping a Good Remodeler," *Kitchen and Bath Ideas* (Winter 1982/83): 18–20.

Finlayson, Gail. "Creating the Illusion of Space," *Southern California House & Garden* (Holiday 1988): 86–88.

"Floor Show," *Decorating Remodeling* (May 1990): 46.

Frantz, John Parris. "A Closer Look at Track Lighting," *Home* (January 1991): 70–71.

Giegerich, Andy. "Semi-Serious Builders, Remodelers, and Designers Are Becoming Accustomed to Semi-Custom Cabinetry." *Kitchen & Bath Business* (March 1991): 13–14.

Gilligan, Kathy. "Decorative Hardware Now 'Individualized.' " *Wood Digest* (January 1996): 40–44.

————. "Under the (European) Influence," *Wood Digest* (March 1994): 19–22.

————. "Is Finishing Finished? Options to Explore," *Cabinet Manufacturing & Fabrication* (July 1990): 83.

Giovannini, Joseph. "Tight Spaces: Eight Successful Small Kitchens," *The New York Times* (January 9, 1986): 15–17.

Goldner, Diane. "Microwave: Revolution that Never Happened," *The New York Times* (May 31, 1995): C1, C6.

"Granite: Real Thing and Fool-the-Eye," *Sunset* (November 1987): 40–46.

Greenguard, Sam. "Putting on the Tile," *Home* (April 1994): 58–64.

Hagerman, Dave. "Hearths in the Heart of the Home," *Kitchen & Bath Business* (December 1994): 20–22.

Harbatkin, Lisa. "Appliances Take Central Stage," *Kitchen & Bath Design News* (October 1995): 58–61.

————. "Options on the Floor," *Kitchen & Bath Design News* (August 1995): 26–29.

————. "No Longer Lonely at the Top," *Kitchen & Bath Design News* (July 1995): 40–44.

————. "Hardware Continues to Evolve with Cabinetry," *Kitchen & Bath Design News* (May 1995): 38–39.

————. "The Latest Appliances Go from Functional to Furniture," *Cabinet Manufacturing & Fabrication* (October 1994): 62–65.

————. "Hardware Enhancing Cabinet Function, Features," *Kitchen & Bath Design News* (May 1994): 30–32.

————. "Cabinet Components: Parts That Add Up," *Cabinet Manufacturing & Fabrication* (September 1993): 14–16..

————. "Kitchen Cabinets," *Kitchen & Bath Design News* (June 1992): 44–52.

————. "Diverse Styles, Sizes, Spur Ceramic Tile Sales," *Kitchen & Bath Design News* (November 1990): 39–41.

————. "New Applications Expand Solid Surface Market," *Kitchen & Bath Design News* (February 1989): 66–69.

————. "Sales Seem Solid for Solid Surfaces," *Kitchen & Bath Design News* (August 1989): 38–41.

————. "Sales Continue to Grow, While Acquisitions Slow," *Kitchen & Bath Design News* (December 1988): 46–50.

Harper, Roseanne. "Convenience Is Key for Interior Cabinet Fittings," *Kitchen & Bath Design News* (July 1990): 75.

————. "Cabinet Accessories: Convenience Is Key," *Cabinet Manufacturing & Fabrication* (July 1990): 86–89.

Hart, B. Leslie. "Mixed Messages," *Kitchen & Bath Business* (April 1994):118–121.

Herbers, Jill. "Taking Panes with Glass Block," *Home* (March 1994): 68–70.

Hinds, Michael de Courcy. "Concern Over Water Safety Is Growing," *The New York Times* (March 25, 1989): 14.

Holmes, Kendall. "Step by Step," *Remodeling* (July 1994): 45–51.

Howard, Hugh. "Remodeling Special," *House Beautiful* (September 1987): 125–139.

"How to Choose the Best Estimating System," *Furniture Design & Manufacturing* (August 1993): 53–60.

Hunter, Linda Mason. "A Fear-Free Asbestos Primer," *Home* (October 1995): 40–50.

————. "Recirculating Facts About Range Hoods," *Home* (October 1994): 66–70.

International Association of Stone Restoration and Conservation. "Tips on Specifying Natural Stone," *Sun Coast* (April 1992): 23.

Kanner, Bernice. "Microwave-Oven Market Is Hot," *New York* (July 1985): 22.

Kaufman, Mervyn. "Windows of Time," *Home* (November 1994): 44–50.

"Keep Homes in the Temperate Zone," *Kitchen & Bath Business* (July 1994): 34–38.

Kelleran, Bruce. "Should Clients See the Schedule?" *Cabinet Manufacturing & Fabrication* (December 1992): 20.

Kelsey, Leo. "Running Your Jobs," *Kitchen & Bath Business* (April 1990): 110–113.

Keough, James G. "Today's Windows: The Bright New Outlook," *Home* (June 1985): 52–57.

————. "The Easy Care Option: VINYL," *Home* (November 1983): 40.

"Kitchen Cabinets: A Buyer's Guide," *Home* (September 1985): 83.

"Kitchens Drift Toward Traditional," *Furniture Design & Manufacturing* (October 1992): 60–66.

Krengel, Jim. "Getting in Sink with Undermounts," *Kitchen & Bath Business* (August 1992): 28–29.

Kuehn, Thomas, Wanda Olson, James Ramsey, Hwataik Han, Mark Perkovich, and Sadek Youssef. "Performance of Kitchen Range Exhaust Hoods," Minnesota Cold Climate Building Research Center, University of Minnesota (1989).

———. "Performance of Downdraft Kitchen Range Exhaust Systems," Minnesota Cold Climate Building Research Center, University of Minnesota (1989).

Jennings, Lynette. "Shopping for a Kitchen," *Home* (September 1989): 30.

Johnson, Glenn M. "Lighting by Design," *Custom Builder* (March/April 1993): 33–37.

"Laminate Suppliers Seek an Edge," *Cabinet Manufacturing & Fabrication* (June 1990): 32–35.

Lavenberg, George N. "Ceramic Tile: How to Use It in Remodeling and Renovation," *Sun Coast* (February 1989): W8–W9.

"Learning How To Lighten Up," *Kitchen & Bath Business* (October 1994): 42–46.

Lefferts, Lisa Y. & Stephen Schmidt. "Microwaves: The Heat Is On," *Nutrition Action Health Letter* (January/February 1990): 1.

Lemme, Charles. "The Physics of Stovetop Cooking," IACP, *The Research Report* (May 1988, Volume 4, No. 1).

Libman, Gary. "Some Real Turn-Ons," *Los Angeles Times* (June 1994).

Lomuscio, James. "Building Blocks," *Home* (November 1993): 32–33.

"Making Every Inch Count," *Home* (June 1989): 70–77.

Margosian, Rich. "Which Way Wood?" *Wood Digest* (January 1994): 42.

Mays, Vernon, "Marble and Stone Agglomerates: Luxury Without the Cost," *Home* (February 1991): 104.

McIlvin, Jess. "Selecting and Specifying Ceramic Tile," *Sun Coast* (February 1990): 14–16.

"Microwave/Convection Ovens," *Consumer Reports* (September 1989): 580.

"Microwave Ovens," *Consumer Reports* (August 1995): 514–517.

"Microwave Ovens," *Consumer Reports* (March 1989): 145.

"Microwave Ovens," *Consumer Reports* (January 1988): 8.

Miley, Judith. " 'Greater Later' Kitchens & Baths Help Clients Age in Place," *Kitchen & Bath Design News* (February 1994): 44–46.

Moore, Alison. "Tricks of the Trade," *The New York Times Magazine* (October 14, 1990): 10–16.

Moriarty, Ann Marie. "Light Touch," *Remodeling* (January 1996): 85–91.

———. "Design-Build," *Remodeling* (June 1991): 59–61.

"The New Wave in Microwave Ovens," *Consumer Reports* (November 1985): 644.

Olson, Wanda, Thomas Kuehn, James Ramsey, Hwataik Han, and Mark Perkovich, "Residential Kitchen Ventilation," Minnesota Cold Climate Building Research Center, University of Minnesota (1989).

Orbach, David M., Esq. "A Survival Guide to a Client's Home Construction Project" (unpublished): 1–5.

Orton, Charles Wesley. "From Haphazard to Hip," *Reeves Journal* (January 1996): 40–84.

Oxley, Robert. "Using Custom Design Applications for Stock Cabinetry," *Kitchen & Bath Design News* (October 1994): 34–35.

Partsch, Bill. "Super Bowls," *Kitchen & Bath Business* (October 1994): 62–69.

———. "What's on Tap," *Kitchen & Bath Business* (August 1994): 44–47.

———. "What's Cooking," *Kitchen & Bath Business* (February 1994): 34–37.

———. "New Ice Age," *Kitchen & Bath Business* (March 1993): 46–47.

———. "Sinks & Faucets," *Kitchen & Bath Business* (October 1993): 84–89.

———. "The Dirt on Water-Saving Dishwashers," *Kitchen & Bath Business* (February 1993): 46–47.

Pell, Ed. "Cabinet Industry Report," *Kitchen & Bath Business* (July 1992): 37–101.

Petrowski, Elaine Martin. "Choosing a Kitchen Sink," *Home* (April 1995): 88–93.

———. "Refrigerators Turn a New Leaf," *Home* (April 1994): 70–74.

———. "Solid as a Rock," *Home* (April 1993): 40–43.

———. "Dollars and Dreams," *Custom Planner* (Spring 1992): 10–11.

Phillips, Dr. Karen. "What to Do If You Remodel and Find Asbestos," *Los Angeles Times* (March 4, 1990).

"Plaster and Drywall: New Materials & Applications," *Sun Coast* (April 1992): 33–35.

Process, Mark. "Inside the Smart House," *Home* (February 1989): 38–42.

Reagan, Mardee Haidin. "Microwaves: Good Vibrations," *Food & Wine* (June 1988): 83.

———. "State-of-the-Art Kitchen," *Food & Wine* (January 1988): 64.

———. "Here Comes the Mini-Microwave," *Food & Wine* (August 1985): 50.

"Refrigerators," *Consumer Reports* (March 1988): 148–154.

"Refrigerators," *Consumer Reports* (January 1987): 34–41.

"Refrigerators," *Consumer Reports* (July 1985): 432–437.

Richie, Elizabeth. "Choosing a General Contractor Wisely," *Home* (April 1994): 76.

Ringwald, Elizabeth Schmidt. "On the Eve of Universal Design," *Home* (October 1988): 95–104.

Ritzer-Ross, Julie. "Built-Ins Stand Out," *Kitchen & Bath Business* (April 1996): 38–41.

Rothschild, Ilene. "Hot Topic," *Decorating Remodeling* (April 1992).

Ryon, Ruth. "The Open House," *Los Angeles Times* (May 31, 1992).

Sause, Barbara. "About Ovens," *The Cook's Magazine* (March/April 1985).

Sefrin, Eliot. "A New Emphasis on Quality," *Kitchen & Bath Design News* (August 1995): 24–26.

———. "1989 Kitchen Cabinet Style & Design Guide," *Kitchen & Bath Design News* (September 1989): 73–87.

Sherman, Beth. "Cooking the Old-Fashioned Way," *Home* (April 1996): 40–48.

"Spotlight on Integrated Systems," *Custom Builder* (March/April 1993): 66–74.

"The State of the Cabinet Industry," *Kitchen & Bath Design News* (December 1988): 46.

Steed, Wendy. "Choosing the Right Laminate," *Furniture Design & Manufacturing* (October 1995): 88–90.

Steingarten, Jeffrey. "Fish Without Fire," *HG* (March 1988): 176.

Stumpf, Bill. "Julia's Kitchen: A Design Anatomy," *Design Quarterly 104*, Walker Art Center (1977).

"Surfacing Materials," *Kitchen & Bath Concepts* (November 1989): 49–55.

Tarver, Joe A. "Ceramic Tile: Selecting the Proper Products & Substrates," *Sun Coast* (February 1991): 9–13.

Thorne, John. "Cuisine Mécanique," *The Journal of Gastronomy* (Vol. 5, No. 4, Spring 1990): 66.

Tile Council of America. "The Industry to Benefit from Market Trends," *Sun Coast* (February 1989): 8.

Treece, James B. "The Great Refrigerator Race," *Business Week* (July 5, 1993): 78–81.

Vandervort, Don. "Getting into Hot Water," *Home* (October 1993): 153–154.

———. "Skylights: The Sky's the Limit," *Home* (March 1993): 109–111.

———. "Inside Kitchen Cabinets," *Home* (October 1992): 119–122.

Vogel, Carol. "Improving Kitchens and Baths," *The New York Times Magazine* (April 10, 1988): 51–53.

Walker, Jan. "In the Right Light," *Better Homes & Gardens Kitchen Planning Guide* (1993): 85–90.

Walsh, Michael. "Trend Alert," *Custom Planner* (Spring 1992): 12–15.

Wasik, John. "Chilling Report: The CFC Factor," *Home* (October 1992): 54–56.

"Water-Based Finish Helps Cabinetmaker Survive," *Furniture Design & Manufacturing* (September 1994): 31–38.

"Why Wood Windows?" *Sunset* (August 1987): 70–77.

Wicks, Harry. "Window Performance," *Remodeling* (June 1990): 108.

Williams, Linda Payne. "Remodeling Perils," *Practical Homeowner* (November 1989): 40–51.

Williams, Wayne. "Little Lamps Make for Big Bright Spot," *Kitchen & Bath Business*: 32–34.

———. "Indirect Lighting for the Kitchen and Bath." Unpublished.

———. "Freshen Kitchen Air with Proper Venting," *Kitchen & Bath Business* (October 1993): 50–53.

Wilson, Alex. "Energy-Efficient Windows: A Clear Advantage," *Home* (January 1991): 67–69.

Zekowski, Gerry. "Comment," *Kitchen & Bath Concepts* (March 1989): 8–12.

PHOTOGRAPH CREDITS

Page

ii   Tim Street-Porter
63   Tim Street-Porter
72   Lilliput (top left), Dwyer
     Heritage (top right)
     Starmark (bottom)
73   Keith Scott Morton (top)
     Heritage (bottom)
76   SieMatic
82   Keith Scott Morton (bottom)
83   Miele (top left)
     Flo Braker (center left)
     Tim Street-Porter (bottom left)
     Kohler (right)
86   Merillat (top)
     Scotsman (bottom left)
     Rubbermaid (bottom right)
87   General Electric (top)
     Tim Street-Porter (left)
     Triangle Pacific (right), Bruce
       Hardwood Floors
94   Rutt
107   Mike Fink
120   Mike Fink
125   Gem-An-Eye
133   Heritage
136   Merillat
139   Horton (top, center left)
     Paxton (center right)
     Dimestore Cowboy (bottom)
141   Wood-Mode
144   Keith Scott Morton
145   Becker-Zeyko (top left)
     Decora (top right)
     Rutt (bottom)
148   Latco (top)
     Aristokraft (bottom)
149   StarMark
150   Corian (top)
     Crystal (bottom)
152   StarMark
154   Shel Neymark (top left)
     Wood-Mode (top right, bottom
       left)
     Merillat (bottom right)
160   Feeny (top)
     Häfele (center)
     StarMark (bottom left)
     Aristokraft (bottom right)
161   Tim Street-Porter (top left, top
       right)
     Calphalon (bottom left)
     Aristokraft (upper center right)
     Vance (lower center right)
     Edlund (bottom right)
162   Vance (top left)
     Feeny (top right)
     Häfele (center right)
     Amerock (bottom left)
     Rubbermaid (bottom right)
163   Häfele (top left)
     Lee/Rowan (top center)
     Becker-Zeyco (top right)
     Aristokraft (bottom left)
     Feeny (bottom center)
164   Metro Smart Wall (top left),
       InterMetro
     Lavi Industries (top right)
     Amerock (lower right)
     Becker-Zeyco (lower left)
168   Gem Hardware (top)
     Horton (center and bottom)
169   Avanté (top)
     Paxton (center right)
     Dimestore Cowboy (bottom right)
     Avanté (bottom left)
     Horton (center left)
170   Chris Collicott
178   Heritage (top left)
     Formica (top right)
     © Bulthaup 1992 (center right)

179   Latco (bottom left)
     Bransky Kitchen (center left)
     Brookhaven Cabinetry (top)
     Laufen (bottom)
182   Bruce (top left, bottom right)
     Kentucky Wood Floors (top right)
     Anderson (bottom left)
183   Mannington (top)
     American Slate (center right)
     Dodge-Regupol (bottom right)
     Florida Tile (bottom center)
     Kentucky Wood Floors (bottom
       left)
187   Pittsburgh Corning
189   Avonite (top, center)
     StarMark (bottom)
190   Surface Technology
195   Heritage (top)
     Florida Tile (center)
     Latco (bottom)
204   Mikado (top), Artemide
     Tech Lighting (center left)
     FLOS Inc. (center, center top
       right, center right)
     Keith Scott Morton (bottom)
205   L.I. Laminates (top left)
     Con-Tech (top right, center right)
     Reggiani (bottom right)
     Ron Sherman (center left)
207   Tech Lighting
208   Greitzer (top left)
     Keith Scott Morton (top right)
     SieMatic (bottom right)
     Pella (bottom left)
212   Tim Street-Porter
213   Peachtree (top)
     StarMark (center right)
     Marvin (bottom right)
     Andersen (bottom left and center
       left)
214   Andersen
216   Andersen
217   Decora (top left), Aristokraft
     Andersen (top right)
     Velux-America (bottom)
226   Thermador
230   Dacor (top left)
     Greitzer (top right)
     Blue Creek (upper center right),
       Jenn-Air
     Russell (lower center right)
     Five Star (bottom right)
     Dacor (bottom left)
234   Thermador (top)
     Russell (lower left)
235   Five Star (top left)
     Wolf (center left)
238   Euroflair (top left)
     Regency (top center)
     Dacor (top right)
     Gaggenau (bottom left)
     Duplikat (bottom right)
242   (left)
     Dynasty (center)
     Viking (right)
243   Heartland Appliances (center left)
     William B. John & Partners Ltd.
       (bottom right), Aga
     La Cornue (bottom left)
245   Earthstone (top)
     Queen Atlantic (bottom right),
       Portland Stove
     Earthstone (bottom left)
246   Thermador (top right)
     Five Star (center right)
251   KitchenAid (top left)
257   Vent-a-Hood (top left, top center)
     Abbaka (top right)
258   Hammer & Nail (bottom right),
       Greitzer
     Best Canopy (bottom center)

268   Sub-Zero (top left)
     Amana (top center)
     Wood-Mode (top right)
     Sunfrost (bottom right), Real Goods
     Sub-Zero (bottom center)
     General Electric (bottom left)
271   Frigidaire (top left)
     Whirlpool (top right)
     Amana (center left)
276   Combo (center right), U-Line
     Monogram by GE (bottom right)
     KitchenAid (bottom left)
279   Opella
284   Kohler (top left, center left)
     Vermont Soapstone (top right)
     American Standard (center,
       center right)
     Vance (bottom)
285   Wilsonart (top)
     Eljer (center)
     American Standard (bottom)
290   Franke (top left)
     Grohe (top right, center right)
     Rohl/KWC Vita-Uno (bottom right)
     Colonise Garden (bottom left)
291   Harrington (top left)
     Opella (top right)
     Fisher (bottom right)
     WaterWorks (bottom left)
296   Water Center (top left)
     Touch-Flo Design (top center)
     Corinthian (top right), Franke
301   ASKO (top left)
     Miele (top center, top right)
     Maytag (bottom)
     KitchenAid (center left)
308   KitchenAid (bottom left)
     Franke (bottom right)
310   Aristokraft (top left)
     Feeny (top center)
     SieMatic (top right)
     Tim Street-Porter (bottom right)
     Feeny (bottom center)
     Plus Partners (bottom left), Feeny
     Blanco Recycling (center left)

COLOR INSERT

1   Nancy Hill
2   Wood-Mode
3   Smallbone (top left)
     Nancy Hill (top right)
     Tim Street-Porter (bottom right)
     Heritage (bottom left)
4   Keith Scott Morton (top)
     Heritage (bottom)
5   Keith Scott Morton (top)
     Nancy Hill (bottom)
6   Tim Street-Porter (top)
     Keith Scott Morton (bottom right)
     SieMatic (bottom left)
     Smallbone (center)
7   Boffi (top)
     Becker-Zeyko (bottom right)
     Smallbone (bottom left)
8   Keith Scott Morton (top)
     Nancy Hill (bottom)
9   Nancy Hill (top left)
     Florida Tile (top right, bottom)
10   Keith Scott Morton (top left)
     Nancy Hill (top right, bottom)
11   Nancy Hill
12   Keith Scott Morton (top)
     Nancy Hill (bottom)
13   Keith Scott Morton
14   La Cornue
15   Keith Scott Morton (top)
     Tim Street-Porter (bottom)
16   Nancy Hill

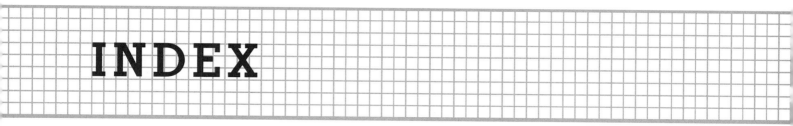

INDEX

Page numbers in *italics* refer to illustrations.

A

accent lighting, *205*, 207–209
  coves as, 209
  recessed cans as, 209
  toe kicks and, 209
activated charcoal, in carbon filtration systems, 297
activity areas, 78–84
  baking, 80, *83*, 184
  cleanup, 81–84, *83*, 95, 214
  cooking, 80–81
  eating, 81, *82*, 365
  food preparation, 79–80
  serving, 81
  storage, *see* storage
aerators, faucet, 288, *290*
Aga ranges, 243
air gaps, 100
Air Quality Management District (AQMD), 118
alpha track detectors, 108
aluminum window frames, 218
  evaluation of, 334
ambient lighting, 209
American Gas Association (AGA), Seal of Approval of, 316
American Home Lighting Institute, 206
American Institute of Kitchen Designers (AIKD), 203
American Institute of Wine and Food, 102

American Society of Home Inspectors, Inc., 9
Americans with Disabilities Act, 102
Anderson, Ken, 199–200
Anker & Hymes, contracts by, 367–375
appliance garages, *148*
  dimensions of, 147
Appliance Letter, 298
appliances:
  checklist of, 314
  in cooking area, 80
  costs of, 18–19, 21, 22, 26
  custom front panels for, 316
  dimensions of, 64, 360–366
  in eating areas, 81
  electrical demands of, 97
  flexibility in, 94
  in food preparation area, 79
  gas demands of, 99
  grounding of, 98
  heights of, 93–94, *94*
  installation of, 119, 123–124
  keypad controls on, 302–303, 316
  in kitchen islands, 74–75
  placement of, 88–90
  plumbing demands of, 100
  purchasing of, 111
  saving money on, 26
  selection of, 16–18
  servicing of, 316
  shopping for, 19, 313–315
  siting of, 77
  in small kitchens, 96

  space-saving, 319
  storage of, 79, 83
  warranties on, 316
  see also specific appliances
architects, 33
architectural glass windows, *217*
architectural symbols in drawings, *62*
asbestos, removal of, 108
Association of Home Appliance Manufacturers (AHAM), Seal of Approval of, 316
automatic faucets, 292
auxiliary areas, in multiple-cook kitchens, 78
awning windows, 214
  evaluation of, 334

B

backdrafting, 260
back-of-door storage options, 166–167
back (escutcheon) plates, 171
backsplashes, 196
  ceramic tile, 177, *195*, 196
  concrete, 181
  dimensions of, 363
  glass block, 186, 196, *217*
  installation of, 123
  mirror, 196
  slate, 181
  stainless steel, 181, 196
  stone, 181
  storage and, *164*, 167

baking area, *83*
    marble countertops in, 80, 184
    pullout carts in, 80
Ballymaloe House, 244
bars, 84, *86*
base cabinets, 143–146, *145*
    dimensions of, 143
    doors in, 146
    drawers in, 143–146
    storage aids for, *160*
batch-feed garbage disposer, 307
bay windows, 214
    in small kitchens, 95
beams, 116, 127
beam spreads, 202
Beard, James, 69
beer coolers, 276
    shopping for, 348
Bergstrom, Bob, 259, 261
Bicottura tiles, 177
bidding process, bids:
    comparison of contractors in, 69
    contractors and, 66–69
    cost considerations and, 69
    design-build and, 66
    designers and, 66
    high, 69
    low, 69
    negotiations and, 69
    scope of, 69
    spreadsheet estimating and, 67
    unit cost and, 67
bilevel ranges, 241
blind corner cabinets, 146
blueprints, *see* construction documents
book specs, 66, 68
bottle storage, 159, *160*
bottom mount freezers, 267
bow windows, 214
boxes, cabinet, 135–137, *136*
Braker, Flo, 80, 109, 125
brass, as surface material, 180
brick:
    evaluation of, 328
    flooring, 192, 194, 196
    as surface material, 180
Brillat-Savarin, Anthelme, 266
broilers, 239
    evaluation of, 339
    infrared, 239
broom closets, 84–85, *86*
    racks for, *163*
Btus (British thermal units), burners and, 229–231
budgets:
    designers and, 56
    remodeling and, 5–6
    see also costs; money-saving tips

building inspectors, 108
building permits, 106–108
    construction documents and, 108
    contractors and, 108
built-in:
    cabinets, 147
    dishwashers, 300
    refrigerators, 266–267
    trash compactors, 308
burners, cooktop, 229
    configurations of, 229, *230,* 231
    electric, 231, 232
    evaluation of, 338
    gas, Btus and, 229–231
    gas vs. electric, 228
    sealed, 231
butcher block, 176–177
    countertops, 123, 176, *179*
    evaluation of, 327
butter compartment, refrigerator, 270

C

cabinet boxes, 135–137, *136*
cabinet contracts:
    assurances in, 156
    cabinet features in, 156–157
    costs in, 156
    installation circumstances in, 158
    responsible parties in, 156
    see also contracts
cabinet doors, 146, 321
    glass, 138
    styles of, 137–138
cabinet drawers, *141,* 321
    in base cabinets, 143–146
    construction of, *136*
    glides on, 140–141, 322
    hinges on, 141
cabinet finishes, 322
    paint, 142
    polyurethane, 143
    sealers, 142–143
    stains, 142–143
    waterborne copolymers, 143
cabinet hardware, 167–171, *168, 169*
    evaluation of, 325
    finishes on, 167–170
    materials used in, 167
    purchasing of, 171, 326
    shopping for, 326
    styles of, 167
    types of, 170–171
cabinet hinges, *139*
    evaluation of, 321
    openings of, 139

specialty, 138
types of, 138
cabinet interiors, 141–142
    fittings for, 159–167
    storage options for, 166
cabinet materials, 132–137
    evaluation of, 320–321
    hardwood, *see* hardwood cabinets
    high-pressure laminates, 134–135, 320
    stainless steel, 135, 321
    wood veneer, 134, 320
cabinets, 20, 30
    appliance garage, 147, *148*
    base, *see* base cabinets
    boxes, 135–137, *136*
    built-in, 147
    for childproof kitchen, 103, 104
    comparison shopping for, 153–155
    construction of, 135–137, *136*
    contracts, 156–158
    core materials of, 135
    corner, 146–147, *149*
    custom, 152–153
    dealers, 33–34
    decorative details of, *150,* 151
    dish, 81
    dish-drying, 147
    doorless, 137
    doors of, 137–138, 146, 321
    double-access, 147
    drawers of, 140–141, *141,* 143–146, 321, 322
    evaluation of, 320–322
    factory-built, 151–153
    finishes on, 142–143, 322
    frameless, 95, 135–137, *136,* 141–142
    fraudulent dealers of, 131–132
    freestanding, *144, 154*
    glossary, 172
    glues used in, 135
    hardware, 167–171, *168, 169,* 325, 326
    hardwood, *see* hardwood cabinets
    heights of, 94
    hinges on, 138, 139, *139,* 321
    installation of, *120,* 122
    interiors of, 141–142, 159–167
    lazy susan, 146
    lighting in, 206, 209
    linking of, 147–151
    maintenance of, 126
    materials, 132–137, 320–321

modular, 143, *145*
noncabinet, 147
open, 95
pantry (utility), *145*, 146
peninsulas and, 75
purchasing of, 151–153
recycling bins in, 309–311, *310*
refinishing of, 132
RTA, 152
for safe kitchens, 103
saving money on, 24–25
shelves of, 141–142, *149, 162*, 322
shopping for, 323–325
sink, 92, 147
in small kitchens, 95–96, 147
specialty, 147, *148–149*
stainless steel, 132, 135, 321
storage aids for, 159–168, *160–164*
trims, *154*
two-sided, *148*
types of, 143–147
unfitted, *145*
for universal kitchen, 105
variations in, *150*, 151
and window placement, 77
cabinet shelves, 322
adjustable, 141–142
glass, 142
pullout pot, *149*
stepped, *162*
cabinet storage aids, 159–168, *160–164*
cost of, 165
purchasing of, 165
see also specific storage aids
cable lights, 204
canopies of ventilation system, *257*
see also hoods of ventilation systems
casement windows, 116, 214
evaluation of, 334
catalogs, full-line, 313
catalytic ovens, 239
catalyzed conversion varnishes, 143
catalyzed lacquers, 143
ceiling fans, dimensions of, 364
ceilings, treatments for, 119
cement-based mortars, 121
Centers for Disease Control, 294
ceramic tile:
on backsplashes, 177, *195*, 196
on countertops, 123, 177, *178*, 180
durability of, 180
evaluation of, 327–328

for flooring, 177, *178, 179*, 192–196
installation of, 121
shapes of, 177
sizes of, 111, 177–180
as surface material, 177–180
types of, 177
Ceramic Tile Council of America, 121, 327
Certified Cabinet Manufacturers, 152, 320
certified kitchen designer (CKD), 33, 34
chandeliers, 203
for table lighting, 206–207
change orders, 50
checking accounts, remodeling and, *109*
checklists:
appliance selections, 314
evaluation of cabinets, 320–322
evaluation of purchases, 316
shopping finds, 314
chest model freezers, 269
Child, Julia, 71, 78, 193
childproofing of kitchens, 102, 103, 104
chillers, 263–277
evaluation of, 345–346
recommendations for, 273
shopping for, 347
testing of, 345
see also beer coolers; freezers; icemakers, automatic; refrigerators
chlorofluorocarbons (CFCs), 263
circuit breakers, 97
circuits, 97
cladding of window exteriors, 218
evaluation of, 334
Claiborne, Craig, 18
cleaning supplies, storage of, 84, *162*
cleanup areas, 81–84, *83*
dishwashers in, 81
sinks in, 81
in small kitchens, 95, 214
traffic patterns in, 84
coal-fed stoves, 244, *245*
Color Association of the United States, 57
colors:
flooring, 192
in kitchen design, 57–58
in small kitchens, 96
of walls, 118
commercial-style ranges, *242*
dimensions of, 241
drawbacks of, 242–243
recommendations for, 246–247

"communing" kitchens, 71
compact refrigerator units, 265
composite sinks, 281
evaluation of, 349
compost buckets, 84
shopping for, 359
compost collection, trash holes for, 309, 359
concrete, as surface material, 181
construction, 31
glossary, 127
inspections during, 113–114
preparing for, *see* preconstruction activities
saving money on, 24
steps in, 115–119
construction documents, 66, 68
building permits and, 108
construction drawings, 30–31, 66
Construction Standards for Kitchen and Vanity Cabinets, 320
consumer education, remodeling and, 4–5
Consumer Education Department, Maytag, 119
Consumer Products Safety Commission, 108
Consumer Reports, 236, 253
continuous-clean ovens, 239
continuous-feed garbage disposer, 307
contractors, 5, 29
bidding process and, 66–69
building permits and, 108
checking credentials of, 42–43
contracts and, 44–52, 368–372
daily conferences with, 114
disputes with, 51
hiring of, 34–35
interviewing of, 40–41
preconstruction meeting with, 110
remodeling financing and, 7
"remodelosis" and, 113
subcontractors and, 113
warranties and, 50–51
contracts, 43–53
arbitration and, 51
cancellation of, 51–52
change orders and, 50
contractors and, 44–52, 368–372
designers and, 52–53, 373–375
exclusions of, 45
formalized communication and, 45–46
good, attributes of, 44
home work site and, 46–47
liens and, 49–50

contracts (*continued*)
    payment penalties and, 49
    payment schedules and, 48–49
    sample, 367–375
    scheduling in, 45
contracts, cabinet:
    assurances in, 156
    cabinet features in, 156–157
    costs in, 156
    installation circumstances in, 158
    responsible parties in, 156
    see also contracts
convection ovens, 236–237
    drying quality of, 237
    and microwave oven combo, 254
    true, 236
convertible dishwashers, 92
cookbook drawers, *164*, 165
cookers:
    evaluation of, 337–339
    inferior quality of, 225–227
    recommendations for, 246–247
    shopping for, 339–341, 342
    testing of, 337
    see also cooktops; ovens; ranges; stoves
cooking, healthful, 102
cooking areas, 80–81
    cooktops in, 80
    pots and pans in, 80
    small appliances in, 80
cooktops, *21*, 228–235
    burners of, *see* burners, cooktop
    for childproof kitchens, 103, 104
    commercial restaurant, 246–247
    in cooking area, 80
    evaluation of, 337–338
    for healthy kitchens, 103
    installation of, 124
    modules, 233
    placement of, 89
    for safe kitchens, 103
    separate ovens and, 227
    size of, 229
    for universal kitchens, 105
    see also cookers
cooktops, electric, 231–233
    burners on, 232–233
    commercial, 231
    configuration of, 231
    evaluation of, 338
cooktops, gas, 229–231
    burners on, 231
    evaluation of, 338
    simmer capability of, 229
cool-beam bulbs, 200

coolers, *see* chillers
cooling racks, 80–81
copper, as surface material, 180
cork flooring, 121–122, 185, 192–196
corner cabinets, *149*
    best, 147
    blind, 146
    lazy susan, 146
    pie-cut, 146
corridor kitchens, 71–74, *72*, 101
cost-plus fees, 36
costs:
    bids and, 69
    of cabinets, 156
    estimation of, 65, 67–68
    of surface materials, 174–175
    see also money-saving tips
countertops, *20*
    for baking area, 80
    brick, 180, 188
    butcher-block, 123, 176, *179*, 327
    ceramic tile, 123, 177, *178*, 180
    for childproof kitchens, 104
    cleaning of, 191
    color fastness of, 188
    colors of, 188
    concrete, 181
    cutability of, 191
    dimensions of, 188, 362–363
    do-it-yourself installation of, 191
    durability of, 191
    edges of, *189*, 190
    evaluation of, 327
    finishes of, 191
    granite, *178, 189*, 192
    grooves in, 188–190
    for healthy kitchens, 103
    heights of, 93
    of high-pressure laminate, 175, 176, 327
    installation of, 123, 191
    integration of sink and, 283
    lighting over, 206
    marble, 80, 184
    noise and, 191
    patterns of, 188
    placement of, 191–192
    recommendations for, 192
    for safe kitchens, 104
    saving money on, 25
    seams of, 190–191
    slate, 181
    solid surface, 175, 176, 327
    stainless steel, 123
    as tables, 93
    for universal kitchens, 105
    weight of, 191
    window placement and, 77

cove lighting, 204–205
    for accenting, 209
cover-ups, 114
crank-operated windows, 214
credentials of contractors, 42–43
crispers, large, 270
cubic feet per minute (CFM), ventilation systems and, 260
Cunningham, Marion, 249
custom:
    cabinetmakers, factories vs., 151, 152
    cabinets, 152–153
    door panels, refrigerator, 272
cutting boards, removable, *161*

D

decks (ledges), sink accessories on, 282–283
dehydrators, 103
delivery of materials, 112
Demolition Day, 112–113
design, 60–65, 68
    consultants and, 60
    coordination of decisions and, 61
    current kitchen use and, 61
    drawings and, 60, 61–64
    elements of, 65
    focal point and, 57, 65
    lighting labs and, 60
    plans and, 61–62
design-build, 34, 35, 68
    bidding and, 66
designers, kitchen, 5, 29, 33
    bidding process and, 66
    budgets and, 56
    certification of, 33, 34
    contracts and, 52–53, 373–375
    design schedules and, 60, 68
    first meeting with, 55–56
    interviewing of, 40
    layout work of, 54
    preconstruction meeting with, 110
design schedules, designers and, 60, 68
Diana, Doug, 7
diets, healthful, 102
dimmers, 209
    evaluation of, 332
dish-draining cabinets, 84
dish-drying cabinets, 147
dishwasher cycles:
    cancel button, 302
    dryer, 302
    evaluation of, 356

heavy/pots and pans/soak and scrub, 302
light/delicate wash, 302
plate warmer, 302
rinse and hold, 302
sani-cycle, 302
short, 302
dishwashers, 22, 298–305
aesthetics of, 356
built-in, 300
in cleanup area, 81
control panel of, 302–303
convertible, 92
cycles of, *see* dishwasher cycles
debris removal by, 299
door panels of, 302
energy efficiency of, 299, 356
evaluation of, 355–357
exteriors of, 302–303
glossary, 305
hard water and, 300
imported, *301*
in-machine heaters of, 299
installation of, 124
integrated, 302
interiors of, 303
maintenance of, 126
placement of, 92
portable, 96, 300
quiet, 298–299
racks, 303, 357
raised, *301*
recommendations for, 304
shopping for, 357
sizes of, 300
for small spaces, *301*
spray arms of, 303
testing of, 355
for universal kitchens, 105
water pressure and, 299–300
disputes, contractor/ homeowner, 51
distillation of water, 297
dividers:
gadget, 159, *160*
vertical tray, *160*
do-it-yourselfers:
countertop installation and, 191
floor installation and, 196
remodeling by, 32
doorless cabinets, 137
doors:
handles, placement of, 122
traffic patterns and, 75
for universal kitchens, 105
doors, cabinet, 146, 321
glass, 138
styles of, 137–138
double-access cabinets, 147

double-glazed windows, 219
double-hung windows, 214, *214*
evaluation of, 334
downdraft ventilation system, 259–260
downlights, 203, *205*
drainboards, 84
sinks integrated with, 280
drains, sink, *279*, 283
evaluation of, 350
drawer hinges, 141
drawers:
cookbook, *164*, 165
glides, *see* glides, drawer
handles on, 122–123
refrigerator, 269–270, *268*
storage options and, 165–166
warming, 246, *246*
drawers, cabinet, *141*, 321
in base cabinets, 143–146
construction of, *136*
glides on, 140–141, 322
hinges on, 141
drawings:
construction, 30–31, 66
design development and, 60, 61–64
elevations, 62–64, *63*, 66, 68
perspective, 64, 68
schematic, 54, 58–60, *59*, 68
universal symbols in, *62*
drop-in ranges, 241
drywall, 117
ducts:
installation of, 116
of ventilation systems, 258–259, *258*

E

Eastern soffits, 62, 101
eating areas, *82*
dimensions of, 81, 365
small appliances in, 81
edges, countertop, 190
education, consumer, remodeling and, 10–11
egg containers, 271
E-lamps, 200
electric coil burners, 232, 233
rough electric work and, 116–117
electricians, licensed, 97
electricity:
assessment of, 12–13, 28
for childproof kitchens, 104
demands, of appliances, 97
gas vs., 227–228
glossary, 15
maintenance of, 126

receptacles (outlets) for, 98
for safe kitchens, 104
service panels for, 97
for universal kitchens, 105
see also specific electrical terms
electrostrips, 98
elevations, 62–64, *63*, 66, 68
enamel on cast-iron sinks, 281
evaluation of, 349
enamel on steel sinks, 281
energy conservation:
cooking and, 240
dishwashers and, 299, 356
refrigerators and, 263–264, 272
Energy Department, U.S., 252, 263
energy-efficient factor (EEF) of refrigerators, 264
engineered wood panels, 135
Environmental Protection Agency, 143, 263
Environmental Quality Institute of North Carolina University, 288
epoxy mortars, 121
escutcheon (back) plates, 171
exhaust fans, 260
exhaust system of ventilation systems, 257–258
evaluation of, 343
installation of, 258
propeller-driven fan of, 258
rotary pressurized blower and, 258
extended-life lamp, 201

F

face-frame cabinets:
frameless vs. cabinet construction and, 135–137, *136*
hinges on, 138
shelves of, 142
toe kicks and, 146
factories, custom cabinetmakers vs., 151, 152
factory-built cabinets:
custom, 152–153
quality of, 151–152
semicustom, 153
stock, 152
fans, ceiling, dimensions of, 364
faucets, 288–294
aerators, 288, *290*
automatic, 292
for childproof kitchens, 103, 104, 288
evaluation of, 352–353

faucets (*continued*)
  for filtered water, 289, *296*
  finishes on, 292, 352
  glossary, 294
  handles of, 289, *290, 291,* 352
  for healthy kitchens, 103
  installation of, 124
  lead leaching from, 288, 295
  maintenance of, 126
  mountings of, 288, 349
  placement of, 92
  pot-filler, 292–293, 352
  pre-rinse, *291,* 292
  recommendations for, 293
  for safe kitchens, 103
  saving money on, 26
  shopping for, 353
  for small kitchens, 96
  testing of, 351
  types of, 288–289
  for universal kitchens, 105
faux surface, 118
fees, professional, 35–37
  cost-plus, 36
  flat, 36
  percentage of construction
    cost, 36–37
files, organization of, remodeling
  and, 8
final plan, review of, 64–65
financing of remodels, 6–8
finishes:
  of countertops, 191
  of faucets, 292, 352
  of flooring, 194–196
  on hardware, 167–170
  for hardwood flooring, 186
  of ranges, 227
  of refrigerators, 272
finishes, cabinet, 322
  paint, 142
  polyurethane, 143
  sealers, 142–143
  stains, 142–143
  waterborne copolymers, 143
finish schedules, 66
fireclay sinks, 281
fireplaces:
  gas, 91
  laying foundations of, 115
  in open kitchens, 91
  placement of, 91
  wood-burning, 91
first-aid kits, 104
fixed windows, 212, *213*
  types of, 214
fixtures, *see* sinks
flame spread index, of insulation,
  117
flashing, 116, 127

flat fees, 36
flooring, 20, *182,* 192–196
  brick, 192, 194, 196
  for childproof kitchens, 104
  cleanability of, 196
  color fastness of, 192
  color of, 192
  concrete, 181
  cork, 121–122, 185, 192–196
  durability of, 196
  hardwood, *see* hardwood
    flooring
  heat-absorption by, 194
  height of, 194
  installation of, 119–122, *120,*
    196
  linoleum, 185, 192–196
  noisiness of, 194
  parquet, 185
  patterns of, 192
  replacement of, 193
  resilience of, 121–122, 194
  for safe kitchens, 104
  saving money on, 26
  seams of, 194
  slate, 181, *183,* 192–196
  tile, 121, 171, *178, 179*
  for universal kitchens, 105
  vinyl, *see* vinyl flooring
  weight of, 194
floor plans, *see* plans
fluorescent:
  fixtures, evaluation of, 332
  lightbulbs (lamps), 202, 206
  light sources, 200
flush mount sinks, 286
focal points, design and, 57, 65
food preparation area, 79–80
  food storage equipment in,
    79
  small appliances in, 79
  utensils in, 79, 80
food warmers, 246
  placement of, 90
forced-air systems, 100
foundations, laying of, 115
frameless cabinets, 95
  construction, face-frame
    cabinet construction vs.,
    135–137, *136*
  hinges on, 138
  shelves of, 141–142
frames, framing:
  of doors, 116
  of kitchen, 116
  window, 218
freestanding:
  cabinets, *144, 154*
  ranges, 240–241, *242*
  trash compactors, 308

freezers:
  bottom-mount, 267
  chest model of, 269
  evaluation of, 345–346
  in refrigerator combo, 267
  and separate refrigerators,
    265, *268*
  top-mount, 267
  upright, 269
full-line catalogs, 313
fuse boxes, 97

G

gadget dividers, 159, *160*
galley kitchens, 71–74, *72,* 101
Gantt charts, 110, 127
garbage cans, 84
garbage disposers, 22, 306–307,
  308
  batch-feed, 307
  evaluation of, 358
  installation of, 124
  maintenance of, 126
  noise reduction and, 124
  placement of, 93
  recommendations for, 311
  septic tanks and, 307
  shopping for, 358
  siting switches for, 93
  types of, 307
gas, 13, 15–16, 28
  appliances' demands for,
    99
  in childproof kitchens, 104
  cooktops, 229–231
  electricity vs., 227–228
  maintenance of, 126
  see also specific terms
general contractors, *see*
  contractors
general lighting, 202–206, *204*
glass, as backsplash material,
  196
glass block:
  as backsplash, 186, 196, *217*
  evaluation of, 335
  installation of, 188
  in islands, 186, *187*
  as room partition, 186, *187*
  sizes of, 186–188
  window glazing and, 218–219
  for windows, 186, *187*
glass doors, refrigerator, 272
glass shelves, wire grids vs., in
  refrigerators, 269
glazing technology for walls,
  118
glides, drawer, 140–141, 322
  placement of, 122–123

gooseneck faucets, 96
granite, 184
    for countertops, 123, 192
    evaluation of, 328
    flooring, 192–196
    sinks, 282
greenhouses, 88
griddles, 235, 338
grills, 233–235
    commercial, 234–235
    gas, residential, 234
    for healthy kitchens, 103
    placement of, 90
ground-fault circuit interrupters,
    98, 126
grouts, 121
"gut jobs," 9

H

halogen:
    burners, 232
    fixtures, evaluation of, 332
    lightbulbs (lamps), 202
    lights, 200–201
Hamill & McKinney Architects
    and Engineers, 78
*Handbook for Ceramic Tile
    Installation,* 121
hand dragging (*strié*), 118
handles:
    on doors, 122
    on drawers, 122–123
    on faucets, 289, *290, 291,* 352
    pull-up, 170
    size of, 170
hardware:
    for childproof kitchens, 104
    hanging of, 122–123
    ordering of, 111
    for universal kitchens, 105
hardware, cabinet, 167–171, *168,
    169*
    evaluation of, 325
    finishes on, 167–170
    materials used in, 167
    purchasing of, 171, 326
    shopping for, 326
    styles of, 167
    types of, 170–171
hard water, dishwashers and, 300
hardwood, evaluation of, 328
hardwood cabinets:
    durability of, 132
    finishes of, 142–143
    properties of, 133
hardwood flooring, *183,* 192–
    196
    colors of, 186, 192
    durability of, 185

finishes of, 186
grades of, 185–186
installation of, 121
as recommended choice, 193
types of, 185
Hardwood Institute, 133
hazardous substances, removal of,
    108–109
hearth cooking, 244
heating/cooling systems, 14, 16,
    28
    maintenance of, 126
    needs of kitchens for, 100
    see also specific terms
heating registers, placement of, 100
heirloom ranges, 243–244
high-pressure laminates:
    cabinets of, 134, 320
    countertops of, 175, 176
hinges, cabinet, *139*
    evaluation of, 321
    openings of, 139
    specialty, 138
    types of, 138
hinges, drawer, 141
homeowners, supervisory chores
    of, 114–115
Home Owners Warranty (HOW)
    Corporation, 50
HomeTech, 5, 36
Home Ventilating Institute, 259
hoods of ventilation systems:
    decoration of, 257
    evaluation of, 343
    installation of, 122
    maintenance of, 126
    specifications of, 256
    styles of, 256–257
hopper windows, 214
    evaluation of, 334
horseshoe kitchens, *73,* 74
hoses, spray, 289–292, *291*
House (Kidder), 43
How to Decorate with Ceramic Tile,
    327
*How to Hire a Home Improvement
    Contractor Without Getting
    Chiseled* (Philbin), 41
How to Install Ceramic Tile, 327
Huxtable, Ada Louise, xiv

I

ice and chilled-water dispenser,
    on-the-door, 270
icemakers, automatic, 270,
    276–277
    evaluation of, 346, 348
    placement of, 89
    shopping for, 348

incandescent:
    lightbulbs (lamps), 202
    light sources, 200
independent designers, 33, 40
indirect lighting, 204–206
    skylights and, 206
induction burners, 232, 233
infrared broilers, 239
inspections, inspectors:
    building, 108
    during construction, 113–114
installers, installation:
    of appliances, 119, 123–124
    of backsplashes, 123
    of cabinets, *120,* 122–123
    of cooktops, 124
    of countertops, 123, 191
    of dishwashers, 124
    experience of, 119
    of faucets, 124
    of flooring, 119–122, *120,* 196
    of garbage disposers, 124
    of hardware, 122–123
    of hoods, 122
    of moldings, 122
    of sinks, 124, 283–286
    of skylights, 215
    of tiles, 121
insulation:
    heat resistance (R) of, 117
    STC of, 117, 220
    types of, 117
insurance policies, remodeling
    and, 109
interior designers, 34
interviewing of remodeling
    professionals, 37–41
islands, *73, 74–75,* 101
    appliances in, 74–75
    electrifying of, 98
    glass block in, 186, *187*
    sizes of, 74

J

jalousie windows, 214
"jewelry," *see* hardware, cabinet
joists, 116, *127*

K

Kafka, Barbara, 232, 249
key pads, on appliances, 316
Kidder, Tracy, 43
kielectric union, 99
Kitchen & Bath Business, 33–34,
    119, 132
Kitchen Cabinet Manufacturers
    Association (KCMA), 152,
    320

kitchens:
　activity areas of, 78–84
　arranging of new, 125
　auxiliary areas in multiple-cook, 78
　childproofing of, 102, 104
　colors in, 57–58
　cookbook storage in, 85
　demolition of old, 115
　designers of, *see* designers, kitchen
　design ideas for universal, 105
　dimensions of, 71, 360–366
　dream, 58
　electrical needs of, 97–99
　equipment heights of, 93–94
　fireplaces in, 91, 115
　framing of, 116
　gas needs of, 99
　glossary, 274
　healthy, 103
　heating/cooling needs of, *see* heating/cooling systems
　installation of, 31; *see also* installers, installation
　layouts of, *see* layouts
　maintenance of new, 125–126
　natural lighting in, 75–77
　offices in, 85, *87*, 366
　old, packing up of, 112–113
　packing up old, 112–113
　plumbing needs of, 99–100
　as reflection of personal style, 56–58
　safety in, 103–104
　satellites, 84–88
　seating in, 93
　small, *see* small kitchens
　televisions in, 85
　triangle, 77–78, *78*
　see also remodeling
kitchens, configurations of, 70–75
　islands, *73*, 74–75, 101
　L-shaped, *72*, 74, 101
　one-row (one-wall), 71, *72*, 101
　open, 71, 101
　peninsulas, *73*, 74–75, 101
　two-row, 71–74, *72*, 101
　U-shaped, *73*, 74, 101
knife storage, *161*
knobs, cabinet, 170

L

La Cornue ranges, 244
laminates:
　for cabinets, 132, 134
　for countertops, 175, 176
　durability of, 132

high-pressure, 134–135, 320
solid-core (color through), 176
for surface materials, 176
types of, 134
lamps, *see* light, lighting; lightbulbs
laundries, 85
　as satellites, 85
　of universal kitchens, 105
layouts, 69–105
　activity areas in, 78–84
　appliances in, 77, 88–91, 92
　glossary, 101
　of island kitchens, *73*, 74–75
　lifestyles and, 70
　of L-shaped kitchens, *72*, 74
　"motion-minded," 61–62, 64
　for multiple cooks, 78, 79
　of one-row kitchens, 71, *72*
　reaching zones and, 79
　satellite siting in, 84–88
　of small kitchens, 94–97
　traffic patterns and, 75
　triangle in, 77–78
　of two-row kitchens, 71–74, *72*
　of U-shaped kitchens, *73*, 74
　utility hookups and, 97–100
　windows and skylights in, 75–77
lazy susan cabinets, 146
lead:
　leaching of, faucets and, 288, 295
　paint, removal of, 108–109
lead carpenters, 113, *127*
ledges (decks), sink accessories on, 282–283
legal terms, definition of, 55
lien release, 124
liens, contracts and, 49–50
lifestyles, remodeling and, 4, 6, 28
　kitchen layouts and, 69–70
　refrigerator size and, 266
light, lighting, 21, 199–211
　accent, *205*, 207–209
　AIKD recommendations on, 203
　ambient, 209
　in cabinets, 206, *209*
　decisions, 332
　dimensions, 365
　dimmer controls and, 209
　general, 202–206, *204*
　glossary, 210–211
　indirect, 204–206
　pendant, 203, *208*
　recommended choices for, 210
　for safe kitchens, 104

shopping for, 332–333
in small kitchens, 95
task, 206–207
for universal kitchens, 105
see also specific sources and types of lighting
lightbulbs, 201
　beam spread of, 202
　cool-beam, 200
　E-lamp, 200
　evaluation of, 332
　fluorescent, 200, 202, 206
　halogen, 200–201, 202
　incandescent, 200, 202
　spectra emitted by, 201
lighting labs, 60
light switches, placement of, 99
linoleum flooring, 185, 192–196
liquor cabinets, 159
loans, remodeling and, 6–8
lockboxes, 110, 127
low-E window coating, 219, 220
low-pressure laminates, 132, 134
L-shaped kitchens, *72*, 74, 101
luminous ceilings, 203

M

maintenance, of new kitchens, 125–126
Major Appliance Consumer Action Panel (MACAP), 125
marble, 181–184
　countertops, 184
　sinks, 282
materials:
　checking of, 112
　costs of, 18–20, 21, 22
　delivery of, 112
　noise-reducing, 61
　ordering of, 111–112
　see also specific materials
materials, cabinet, 132–137
　evaluation of, 320–321
　hardwood, *see* hardwood cabinets
　high-pressure laminates, 134–135, 320
　stainless steel, 135, 321
　wood veneer, 134, 320
meat and cheese drawer of refrigerator, 270
mechanical filtration, as water treatment system, 297
mechanicals, 116–117
medium-density fiberboard (MDF)/Particleboard, 135
melamine, as cabinet material, 132, 134

microwave ovens, 236, 249–255, *251*
  appearance of, 252
  built-in, 251–252
  for childproof kitchens, 103, 104
  controls of, 253
  and convection combo, 254
  culinary limits of, 249–250
  evaluation of, 342
  features of, 252–254
  freestanding, 251
  glossary, 255
  placement of, 90–91
  power levels of, 252, 253
  and range hood combination, 252
  recommendations for, 254
  for safe kitchens, 103
  safe operation of, 251
  sensors of, 253
  shopping for, 342
  sizes of, 252
  testing of, 341
  undercabinet, 251
  for universal kitchens, 105
mirror, as backsplash material, 196
modular cabinets, 143, *145*
modules, cooktop, 233
moldings:
  floor, 194
  installation of, 122
money-saving tips, 23–26
  on appliances, 26
  on cabinets, 24–25
  on construction, 24
  on faucets, 26
  on flooring, 26
  general principles of, 23
  for purchasing, 23–24
  on scaling down jobs, 23
  on sinks, 26
  on storage, 25
  on ventilation, 26
  on windows, 26
Monocottura tiles, 177
"motion-minded" layouts, 61–62
"mulling time," remodeling and, 4–5
mullions, 137, 138
multimode ovens, 237–239
multiple cooks, layouts for, 78, 79
muntins, 214–215
Murphy, Brian Allen, 60, 138

N

National Association of Home Builders, 68
National Association of State Contractors, 42
National Fenestration Rating Council, 219
National Kitchen and Bath Association, 33, 131, 159
  kitchen triangle guidelines of, 7
  ventilation recommendations by, 260
National Safety Council, 194
National Sanitation Foundation (NSF), 288
  on water treatment units, 296–297
natural lighting, 75–77
negative pressure, ventilation system and, 260
negotiated bids, 67, 68
niches, 137
noise reduction:
  dishwashers and, 298–299
  garbage disposers and, 124
  materials for, 61
  refrigerators and, 124
noncabinet cabinets, 147
Nutrition Action Healthletter, 250
Nuvel, 176
  colors of, 188

O

offices, kitchen, 85, *87,* 366
  computers in, 85
Oldways Preservation and Trust, 102
one-row (one-wall) kitchens, 71, *72,* 101
open cabinets, 95
open kitchens, 70, 101
  fireplaces in, 91
operable windows, 212, *213*
  types of, 214
outlets (electric receptacles), 98
  dimensions of, 366
ovens, 21, 235–240
  for childproof kitchen, 103, 104
  convection, 236–237
  conventional, 236, 237
  and cooktops, separate, 227
  doors of, 239
  evaluation of, 338
  gas vs. electric, 228
  for healthy kitchens, 103
  lights, 240
  multimode, 237–239
  number of, 236
  placement of, *83,* 90
  probes, 240
  racks, 240, 308
  for safe kitchens, 103
  self-cleaning, 239
  size of, 236
  for small kitchens, 96
  stacking of, 90
  thermal, 236, 237
  thermometers, 236
  for universal kitchens, 105
  wall, 236, *238*
  windows of, 239–240
  wood-burning, 244, *245*
  see also cookers
overfired broilers, *see* salamanders

P

painting of walls, 118
pantries, *86*
  storage aids for, *163*
  temperature of, 84
  walk-in, 84
pantry (utility) cabinets, *145,* 146
  dimensions of, 146
parquet, 185
pavers, 180
payment schedules, contracts and, 48–49
pendant lights, 203, *208*
peninsulas, 74–75, 101
  cabinets and, 75
percentage of construction costs, fees, 35–37
Perfection Salad (Shapiro), 71
permits, building, 106–108
  construction documents and, 108
  contractors and, 108
perspective drawings, 64, 68
pie-cut cabinets, 146
pipes:
  installation of, 116
  insulation of, 117
  types of, 99
plan checks, 66, 68, 108
plans, 60, 68
  "motion-minded," 61–62
  scaled, 61–62
plant ledges, *87*
plumbers, as shopping advisors, 315
plumbing, 14, 16, 28–29, 99–100
  maintenance of, 126
  see also specific terms
plywood, 135
polarized plugs, 98
polyester, as cabinet material, 132, 134
polyurethane, as cabinet finish, 143
Popcorn, Faith, 93

pop-up drains, 283
porcelain tiles, 177
portable dishwashers, 300, 357
posts, 116, 127
pot-filler faucets, 292–293, 352
pot racks, 159–165, *161*
pots and pans:
    in cooking areas, 80
    dishwasher cycle for, 302
precision captive roller channel
    glides, 140
preconstruction activities, 106–
    113
    finding temporary living
        quarters, 109–110
    hazardous substance removal,
        108–109
    meeting, 110
    obtaining permits, 106–108
    ordering materials, 111–112
    packing up old kitchen,
        112–113
pre-rinse faucets, *291,* 292
professionals, remodeling, 32–43
    fees of, 35–37
    interviewing of, 37–41
    references of, 41–42
    referrals to, 37
    see also specific professions
pullman kitchens, 71–74, *72*
pullout carts, in baking area, 80, *83*
pullout pot shelves, *149*
pulls, 170, *170*
pull-up handles, 170
punch lists, 124
purchases, evaluation of, 316
Purdue University, Motion and
    Time Study Laboratory at,
    74
pyrolytic ovens, 239

Q

quality, remodeling and, 11–12
quarry tiles, 177
quick-disconnect couplings, 99

R

racks:
    for broom closets, *163*
    cooling, 80–81
    dishwasher, 303, 357
    oven, 240, 338
    pot, 159–165, *161*
radiant heating systems, 100
Radiological Health Emission
    Bureau, U.S., 251
radon, 108
rag rolling, 118

ranges, 26, 240–244
    bilevel, 241
    for childproof kitchens, 103,
        104
    commercial-style, *see*
        commercial-style ranges
    drop-in, 241
    evaluation of, 339
    finishes of, 227
    freestanding, 240–241, *242*
    heirloom, 243–244
    lighting for, 207, *208*
    placement of, 89
    for safe kitchens, 103
    slide-in, 241
    two-in-one, 227
    see also cookers; stoves
reaching zones, storage areas and,
    79
ready-to-assemble (RTA) cabinets,
    152
"real" size, "stated" size vs., 111
recessed cans, 117, 203, *205*
    accent lighting and, 209
    evaluation of, 332
    trims of, 203
    see also light, lighting
recycling, 306
    of newspapers, 311
recycling bins, 309–311, *310*
    evaluation of, 359
    placement of, 84, 92–93
    shopping for, 359
    size of, 309, 311
    styles of, 309
refacing of cabinets, 132
references of professionals, 41–
    42
referrals to professionals, 37
refinishing of cabinets, 132
refrigerator drawers, 269–270,
    268
refrigerators, 22, 263–274
    built-in, 266–267
    butter compartments in, 270
    for childproof kitchens, 103,
        104
    compact, 265
    cost of, 264
    custom-door panels on, 272
    doors of, 88–90, 272
    EEF of, 264
    egg containers in, 271
    energy conservation and,
        263–264, 272
    evaluation of, 345–346
    finishes, 272
    in freezer combo, 267
    and freezers, separate, 265,
        268

    handles on, 272
    for healthy kitchens, 103
    installation of, 123–124
    interior of, 269, *271,* 346
    maintenance of, 126
    meat and cheese drawers of,
        270
    noise reduction and, 124
    on-the-door ice and chilled-
        water dispenser of, 270
    options, 265
    placement of, 88, 89
    recommendations for, 273
    for safe kitchens, 103
    shelves of, 269, 270, 271
    sizes of, 265–266
    in small kitchens, 96
    storage aids, 270–271
    temperature of, 346
    for universal kitchens, 105
    wine caddies in, 271
remodeling:
    analyzing of current kitchen by,
        9–10
    appraising of utility capabilities
        by, 12–16
    bidding process and, 66–69
    budgeting of, 5–6
    checking account for, 109
    computer programs for, 61
    consumer education and, 4–5
    disruptions caused by, xiii–xiv,
        26–27
    do-it-yourselfers and, 32
    estimating costs of, 67–68
    everyday living during, 109–
        110
    financing of, 6–8
    homeowner's daily check of,
        114–115
    identifying quality and, 11–12
    insurance policies and, 109
    kits for, 61
    lifestyles and, 4, 6, 28, 69–70
    money-saving tips and, 23–26
    "mulling time" and, 4–5
    negotiations with, 109
    organization of files and, 8
    preliminary research and,
        10–11
    professionals and, 32–43
    quality and, 11–12
    resale value and, 6
    scheduling of, 26–28
    scope of, 9
    steps in, 28–31
    taxes and, 6
    see also contractors
"remodelosis," contractors and,
    113

renderings, 64, 66, 68
resale value, remodeling and, 6
research, preliminary, remodeling and, 10–11
resilient flooring, 121–122
reverse osmosis water treatment system, 297
R. H. Bruskin Market Research Associates, 4
rimmed sinks, 283
rolling carts, in cleanup areas, 81
roof windows, 215, *216, 217*
Rosenbloom, Jonathan L., 367
rotisserie spits, 240
R-value, of windows, 219–220

S

salamanders, 235
saltillo tiles, 177
satellites, 84–88
    bars, 84
    broom closets, 84–85
    greenhouses, 88
    laundries as, 85
    mixed media center, 85
    offices, 85
    pantries, 84
    pethouses, 88
schedules, remodeling, 26–28
schematic drawings, 54, 58–60, *59,* 68
scumbling, 118
sealed burners, 231
sealers:
    for cabinets, 142–143
    for flooring, 121
seams, countertop, 190–191
seating, in kitchens, 93
self-cleaning ovens, 239
self-rim sinks, 283
semicustom cabinets, 153
service panels, electric, 97
servicing, of appliances, 316
serving areas, 81
shapes of kitchens, *see* kitchens, configurations of
Sheetrock, 117
sheet specs, 66, 68
shelves:
    pullout pot, *149*
    refrigerator, 269, 270, 271
    stepped, *162*
shelves, cabinet, 322
    adjustable, 141–142
    glass, 142
    pullout pot, *149*
    stepped, *162*

shopping:
    for appliances, 313–315
    for beer coolers, 348
    for cabinets, 323–325
    checklists, 314
    for chillers, 347
    for cookers, 339–341, 342
    for dishwashers, 357
    for faucets, 353
    for garbage disposers, 358
    for lighting, 332–333
    for microwave ovens, 342
    for recycling bins, 359
    for sinks, 350–351
    for surface materials, 328–331
    for ventilation system, 344
    for water treatment systems, 355
    for windows, 335, 336
    for wine coolers, 348
shutoff valves, 99
side-by-side freezer/ refrigerators, 267
single-handled faucets, 289, *290, 291*
sink accessories, evaluation of, 350
sink materials, 280–282
    composite, 281
    enamel on cast iron, 280–281
    enamel on steel, 281
    fireclay, 281
    granite, 282
    marble, 282
    slate, 282
    soapstone, 281–282
    stainless steel, 280, *285*
    syndecrete, 281
sinks, 22, 278–287
    apron, *285*
    bilevel, 279, *285*
    cabinets, 92, 147
    for childproof kitchens, 103, 104
    in cleanup areas, 81
    depths of, 92, 279
    drains, *279,* 283, 350
    evaluation of, 349–350
    flush mount, 286
    glossary, 287
    for healthy kitchens, 103
    installation of, 124, 283–286
    integration of, with countertops, 283
    integration of, with drainboards, 280
    ledges (decks), 282–283
    lighting for, 207
    maintenance, *126*

modules, 279
    in multiple-cook kitchens, 78
    numbers of, 280
    placement of, 91–92
    recommendations for, 286
    rimmed, 283
    saving money on, 26
    self-rim, 283
    shopping for, 350–351
    single, 285
    size of, 278–280
    for small kitchens, 96
    solid surface, 281, *285*
    stainless steel, 280, 285, 349
    storage, 161
    testing of, 349
    undermount, 286
    for universal kitchens, 105
    wall-mounted, 286
skylights, 21
    coverings for, 215
    direction of, 76
    evaluation of, 335
    framing and, 116
    indirect lighting and, 206
    installation of, 215
    roof windows vs., 215
    saving money on, 26
    shapes of, 215
    sizes of, 215
    in small kitchens, 95
    views from, 77
slate, 181, *183*
    evaluation of, 328
    flooring, 181, *183,* 192–196
    sinks, 282
slide-in ranges, 241
slider windows, 214, 334
small kitchens, 94–97
    appearance of size in, 95
    appliances in, 96
    cabinets in, 95–96
    colors in, 96
    decoration of, 96–97
    dining facilities in, 96
    lighting in, 95
    sinks for, 96
    "skyscraper" technique in, 95
    storage in, 96
    structure of, 95
    windows in, 95
    workstations in, 75
Smart House, 98, 209
smoke alarms, hard-wiring of, 116
soap dispensers, 283
    evaluation of, 350
soapstone sinks, 281–282
soffits, 62–64, 101
solid disk burners, 232

solid surface:
  countertops, 175, 176, 327
  sinks, 281, *285*
sound transmission classification
    (STC), of insulation, 117,
    220
space-saving appliances, 319
specialty cabinets, 147, 148–
    149
spice holders, 159, *160*
  back of door, *163*
sponging, 118
spray arms, dishwasher, 303
spray hoses, 289–292
  evaluation of, 289–292, *291*
spreadsheet estimating, bidding
    process and, 67
staging areas, 81
stained glass windows, *217*
stainless steel:
  backsplashes, 181, 196
  cabinets, 132, 135, 321
  countertops, 123
  evaluation of, 328
  refrigerator doors, 272
  sinks, 280, 285, 349
  surface materials, 180–181
  trivets, *190*
stamped tin, 119
stemware racks, undercabinet,
    164
stenciling, 118
stepped shelves, *162*
stippling, 118
stock cabinets, 152
Stoeppelwerth, Walter, 5, 36, 67,
    113
stone, as surface material, 181
storage, 78–79, 159, *160–164,*
    165–167
  back of door, *163,* 166–167
  backsplashes and, *164,* 167
  for cabinet interiors, 159, 166
  for childproof kitchens, 103,
    104
  of cleaning supplies, 84, *162*
  containers, *162*
  dimensions, 362
  for drawers, 165–166
  for healthy kitchens, 103
  knife, *161*
  in liquor cabinets, 159, *160*
  reaching zones and, 79
  for safe kitchens, 103
  saving money on, 25
  in small kitchens, 96
  tray, *161*
  for underside of cabinets, 166
  for universal kitchen, 105
  wall, *164*

storage aids, cabinet, 159–168,
    160–164
  cost of, 165
  purchasing of, 165
  see also specific storage aids
storage racks, *149*
stoves:
  coal-fed, 244, *245*
  glossary, 248
  wood-fed, 244, *245*
  see also cookers; ranges
strié (hand-dragging), 118
studs, 116
style, personal, 56–58
subcontractors, 113
  homeowners and, 114
  see also contractors
sun bays, 88
Super Efficient Refrigerator
    Program (SERP), 263
surface materials, *178*
  aesthetics of, 175
  brass, 180
  brick, 180
  butcher block of, 176–177
  ceramic tile as, 177–180
  concrete, 181
  copper, 180
  cork, 185
  cost of, 174
  durability of, 174
  evaluation of, 327–328
  glass block, 186–188
  glossary, 197–198
  granite, 184
  hardwood, 185–186
  installation of, 174
  laminates, 132, 134, 175, 176
  linoleum, 185
  maintenance of, 173
  marble, 181–184
  Nuvel, 175, 176
  protection of, 173–174
  shopping for, 328–331
  slate, 181
  solid surface, 175, 176
  stainless steel, 180–181
  stone, 181
  testing of, 327
  vinyl, 184–185
surfaces:
  for childproof kitchens, 103,
    104
  maintenance of, 126
  for safe kitchens, 103
  for universal kitchens, 105
surge arresters, 98
switches, light, placement of, 99
switch plates, 209
syndecrete sinks, 281

T

tables:
  dimensions of, 365
  lighting of, 206–207, *208*
  placement of, 93
  for safe kitchens, 104
task lighting, 206–207
  inside cabinets, 206
  over countertops, *205,* 206,
    207
  for desks, 207
  over ranges, 207, *208*
  over sinks, 207
  above tables, 206–207, *208*
taxes, remodeling costs and, 6
televisions, 85
tempered glass, 103
terra-cotta tiles, 177
thermal ovens, 236
  in multimode oven, 237
thermofoil, 132, 134
thermometers, oven, 236
thermostats, 100
thickset, 121, 127
thinset, 121, 127
threshold slope, 121
tile, ceramic, *see* ceramic tile
tin, stamped, 119
toaster ovens, 236
toe kicks, 146
  accent lights and, 209
top-mount freezers, 267
touch latches, 105, 170
towel hooks, 125
track lights, 203–204
  evaluation of, 332
traffic patterns:
  in cleanup areas, 84
  layouts and, 75
transformers, 201
trapezoid, kitchen, 77–78
trash bins, *see* recycling bins
trash compactors, 84, 307–308,
    308
  evaluation of, 358–359
  placement of, 92–93
  recommended, 311
  shopping for, 359
  for small kitchens, 96
  testing of, 358
  types of, 308
  widths of, 308
trash holes for compost
    collection, 309
  evaluation of, 359
tray storage, *161*
triangle, kitchen, 77–78, *78,* 101
trims, cabinet, *154*
triple-glazed windows, 219

trivets, stainless steel, *190*
two-handled faucets, 289, *291*
two-in-one range, advantages of, 227
two-row kitchens, 71–74, *72*, 101
two-sided cabinets, *148*

U

ultraviolet disinfection as water treatment system, 297
undercabinet lights, *205*
    evaluation of, 332
underfired broilers (commercial grills), 234–235
undermount sinks, 286
underwall cabinet storage options, 166
Underwriters Laboratories Inc. (UL), 97
    Seal of Approval of, 316
unfitted cabinets, *145*
unit cost, bidding process and, 67
universal design, 101, 102
upkeep, of new kitchens, 125–126
upright freezers, 269
U-shaped kitchens, *73*, 74, 101
utilities, 30
    appraising of, 12–16
    layouts and hookups of, 97–100
    see also specific utilities
utility (pantry) cabinets, *145*
    dimensions of, 146
U-value, of windows, 219

V

variances, 114
ventilation systems, 21
    canopy of, *257*
    components of, 256
    downdraft, 259–260
    ductless, 259
    ducts of, 258–259, *258*
    evaluation of, 343
    exhaust system of, *see* exhaust system of ventilation systems
    glossary, 262
    for healthy kitchens, 103
    hoodless, 259–260
    hood of, 256–257
    negative pressure and, 260
    noise of, 258
    planning of, 60
    power of, 260
    recommended, 261
    for safe kitchens, 103

saving money on, 26
shopping for, 344
sone rating of, 259
testing of, 343
Vermont Soapstone Company, 281
Vermont Structural Slate Company, 181, 282
vertical tray dividers, *160*
vinyl composition tiles (VCT), 184
vinyl flooring, *183*, 184–185, 192–196
    evaluation of, 328
    installation of, 121–122
    types of, 184
vinyl window frames, 218
    evaluation of, 334

W

walk-in pantries, 84
wall cabinets, *145*
    dimensions of, 143
    uses for, 143
wall coverings, 118–119
wall-mounted sinks, 286
wall ovens, 236, *238*
wallpapers, 118
walls:
    colors of, 118
    glazing techniques for, 118
    installing of, 117–118
    painting of, 118
    storage on, *164*
warming drawers, 246, *246*
warranties:
    on appliances, 316
    contractors and, 50–51
waste disposal:
    for childproof kitchens, 104
    for healthy kitchens, 103
    for universal kitchens, 105
    see also compost buckets; garbage disposers
water:
    bottled, 295
    hard, 296, 300
    supply, safety of, 294–295
    testing of, 295
water bars, 296, *296*
    evaluation of, 354
waterborne copolymers, as cabinet finishes, 143
water dispensers, hot and chilled, *290*, 293
    evaluation of, 353
    shopping for, 353
water-flow restrictions, 288
water quality reports, 295

water treatment systems, 294–297
    activated charcoal, 297
    distillation, 297
    evaluation of, 354
    high-volume, 295–296
    mechanical filtration, 297
    reverse osmosis (RO), 297
    shopping for, 355
    testing of, 354
    ultraviolet disinfection, 297
wheelchair operation, guidelines for, 366
window frames:
    aluminum, 218
    cladding of, 218
    evaluation of, 334
    vinyl, 218
    wood, *see* wood window frames
window glazing, 218–220
    composition of, 219
    evaluation of, 335
    glass, 218
    glass block and, 218–219
    plastic, 218
    ratings of, 219–220
windows, 21, 211–221
    architectural glass, *217*
    art glass, *217*
    awning, 214, 334
    bay, 95, 214
    bow, 214
    and cabinet placement, 77
    casement, 116, 214
    for childproof kitchens, 104
    clerestory, 95
    countertop placement and, 77
    crank-operated, 214
    dimensions of, 75
    double-glazed, 219
    double-hung, 214, *214*, 334
    evaluation of, 334–335
    exposures and, 75–76, *76*
    fixed, 212, *213*, 214
    frames, *see* window frames
    framing and, 116
    glass block, 186, *187*
    glazings of, 218–220
    glossary, 221
    for healthy kitchens, *103*
    hopper, 116
    muntins and, 214–215
    operable, 212, *213*, 214
    purchasing of, 335
    ratings of, 219–220
    recommendations for, 220
    roof, 215
    for safe kitchens, 104

windows (*continued*)
  saving money on, 26
  shopping for, 335–336
  slider, 214, 334
  in small kitchens, 95
  stained glass, *217*
  STC ratings and, 220
  stock, 212
  styles of, 212–215
  traffic patterns and, 75
  for universal kitchens, 105
window walls, *212, 213*
wine caddies, refrigerator, 271
wine coolers, *276*
  capacity of, 275

  evaluation of, 348
  placement of, 89
  shopping for, 348
  specifications of, 275
Wisconsin, University of, Food
  Research Institute at,
  177
woks, 233, *234,* 338
wok stoves, 233, *234*
Wolfert, Paula, 184
wood-burning ovens, 244,
  245
wood-fed stoves, 244, *245*
wood flooring, *see* hardwood
  flooring

wood paneling, 119
wood veneer cabinets:
  durability of, 132
  impermanence of, 158
  properties of, 134
wood window frames, 218
  evaluation of, 218
working drawings, *30–31,*
  66
work space, ideal, 77
work spaces, dimensions of,
  360–366
workstations, in small kitchens,
  75